D1388529

Minimalist Syntax
Exploring the Structure of English

Andrew Radford's latest textbook, *Minimalist Syntax: Exploring the Structure of English*, provides a clear and accessible introduction to current work in syntactic theory, drawing on the key concepts of Chomsky's Minimalist Program. Assuming little or no prior knowledge of syntactic theory, Radford takes students through a diverse range of topics in English syntax – such as categories and features, merger, null constituents, movement, case, split projections and phases – and shows how the 'computational component' works within the minimalist framework. Beginning at an elementary level, the book introduces grammatical concepts and sets out the theoretical foundations of Principles and Parameters and Universal Grammar, before progressing in stages towards more complex phenomena. Each chapter contains a workbook section, in which students are encouraged to make their own analyses of English phrases and sentences through exercises, model answers and 'helpful hints'. There is also an extensive glossary of terms.

Although designed primarily for courses on syntactic theory or English syntax, this book also provides an up-to-date, clear and straightforward introduction to the field.

ANDREW RADFORD is Professor of Linguistics at the University of Essex. He has published six books on syntax with Cambridge University Press: *Italian Syntax* (1977); *Transformational Syntax* (1981); *Transformational Grammar* (1988); *Syntactic Theory and the Structure of English* (1997); *Syntax: a Minimalist Introduction* (1997) and *Linguistics: an Introduction* (co-authored with a group of his Essex colleagues, 1999). He has also published a book on *Syntactic Theory and the Acquisition of English Syntax* (Blackwell, Oxford, 1990) and numerous articles on syntax and the acquisition of syntax.

CAMBRIDGE TEXTBOOKS IN LINGUISTICS

General editors: S. R. ANDERSON, J. BRESNAN, B. COMRIE, W. DRESSLER,
C. EWEN, R. HUDDLESTON, R. LASS, D. LIGHTFOOT, J. LYONS,
P. H. MATTHEWS, R. POSNER, S. ROMAINE, N. V. SMITH, N. VINCENT

Minimalist Syntax: Exploring the Structure of English

Minimalist Syntax
Exploring the Structure of English

ANDREW RADFORD

University of Essex

CAMBRIDGE
UNIVERSITY PRESS

CAMBRIDGE UNIVERSITY PRESS
Cambridge, New York, Melbourne, Madrid, Cape Town, Singapore, São Paulo, Delhi

Cambridge University Press
The Edinburgh Building, Cambridge CB2 8RU, UK

Published in the United States of America by Cambridge University Press, New York

www.cambridge.org
Information on this title: www.cambridge.org/9780521542746

First published 2004
Fourth printing 2008

Printed in the United Kingdom at the University Press, Cambridge

A catalogue record for this publication is available from the British Library

Library of Congress Cataloguing in Publication data
Radford, Andrew.
Minimalist syntax: exploring the structure of English / Andrew Radford.
    p.   cm. – (Cambridge textbooks in linguistics)
Includes bibliographical references and index.
ISBN 0 521 83497 X (hardback) – ISBN 0 521 54274 X (paperback)
1. English language – Syntax.   2. Grammar, Comparative and general – Syntax.   I. Title.
II. Series.
PE1361.R335   2004
425 – dc22   2003055385

ISBN 978-0-521-83497-1 hardback
ISBN 978-0-521-54274-6 paperback

Contents

Preface

Aims

This book has two main aims, reflected in its title and subtitle. The first is to provide an intensive introduction to recent work in syntactic theory (more particularly to how the *computational component* operates within the model of grammar assumed in recent work within the framework of Chomsky's *Minimalist Program*). The second is to provide a description of a range of phenomena in English syntax, making use of minimalist concepts and assumptions wherever possible. The book can be seen as a successor to (or updated version of) my (1997a) book *Syntactic Theory and the Structure of English*. There is quite a lot of duplication of material between the earlier book and this one (particularly in the first few chapters), though the present book also contains substantial new material (e.g. on agreement, case, split projections and phases), and the analysis of many phenomena presented in this book differs from that in its predecessor (agreement being handled in terms of a *feature-matching* rather than a *feature-checking* framework, for example).

Key features

The book is intended to be suitable both for people with only minimal grammatical knowledge, and for people who have already done quite a bit of syntax but want to know something (more) about Minimalism. It is not historicist or comparative in orientation, and hence does not presuppose knowledge of earlier or alternative models of grammar. It is written in an approachable style, avoiding unnecessary complexity. I've taught earlier versions of the book to more than 200 students over the past three years, and greatly benefited from their mutterings and mystification, as well as their assignments (which told me a lot about what they didn't understand, and about what I needed to explain more carefully). I've worked through (and refined) the exercise material with the students, and the *helpful hints* which the exercises contain have been developed in order to try and eliminate some of the commonest errors students make. The book is intensive and progressive in nature, which means that it starts at an elementary level but gets progressively harder as you get further into it. A group of students I taught an earlier version of the book to gave the following mean degree-of-difficulty score to each chapter on a five-point scale ranging from $1 = $ *very easy* to $5 = $ *very hard*: chapter $1 = 1.6$; chapter $2 = 1.8$; chapter $3 = 2.2$; chapter $4 = 2.7$; chapter $5 = 2.9$; chapter $6 = 3.2$; chapter $7 = 3.4$; chapter $8 = 3.7$; chapter $9 = 4.2$; chapter $10 = 4.4$. Successive chapters become cumulatively more complex, in that each chapter presupposes material covered in previous chapters as well as introducing new material: hence it is helpful to go back and read material from earlier chapters every so often. In some cases, analyses presented in earlier chapters are subsequently refined or revised in the light of new assumptions made in later chapters.

Organisation

Each of the ten chapters in the book contains a detailed text discussion of a particular topic (divided into sections to facilitate reading), together with an integral *workbook section* at the end of the chapter, containing exercise material (to be done as classwork or homework) with *model answers* and *helpful hints* provided. Although the book contains numerous references to (often highly technical) primary research works, the exercises are designed in such a way that they can be tackled on the basis of the coursebook material alone. The book also includes an extensive *glossary* which provides simple illustrations of how key technical terms are used (both theory-specific terms like **EPP** and traditional terms like **subject**): technical terms are written in **bold** print in the main text (*italics* being used for highlighting particular expressions – e.g. a key word appearing in an example sentence). The glossary contains entries for key technical terms in syntax which are used in a number of different places in the text (though not for terms which appear in only one part of the main text, and which are glossed in the text where they appear). The glossary also includes an integrated list of *abbreviations*.

Companion volume

This book is being published in parallel with an abridged version entitled *English Syntax: an Introduction*. In this longer version of the text, the main text (particularly in the later chapters) is generally 30–50 per cent longer than the main text in the abridged version. This longer version is aimed primarily at students with (near-) native command of English who are taking syntax as a major rather than a minor course. The two books have an essentially parallel organisation into chapters and sections (though additional sections and technical discussion have been added in this longer version), and contain much the same exercise material (though with exercise material based on additional sections of text included in the longer version). In keeping the two books parallel in structure and organisation as far as possible, I am mindful of the comment made in a review of two earlier books which I produced in parallel longer and shorter versions (Radford 1997a,b) that some readers may wish to read the short version of a given chapter first, and then look at the longer version afterwards, and that this 'is not facilitated by an annoyingly large number of non-correspondences' (Ten Hacken 2001, p. 2). Accordingly, I have tried to maximise correspondence between the 'long' and 'short' versions of these two new books.

Acknowledgments

Particular thanks are due to three brave Musketeers (Hajime Hattori, Cris Lozano and Peter Evans) for shooting down some of the more inane parts of an earlier draft of the book when they had it inflicted on them as students. I'd also like to thank Cambridge University Press's series editor (Neil Smith) for patiently wading through and commenting on two drafts of the longer version and one of the shorter one, and managing to make his comments challenging and good-humoured at the same time. Thanks also go to Bob Borsley and Martin Atkinson for helpful thoughts on particular issues. And above all to my wife Khadija, for putting up with extended periods of authorial autism during the gestation period for the book.

Dedication

This book (like my 1981 *Transformational Syntax* book) is dedicated to Joe Cremona, who sadly died shortly before it went to press. Joe was my tutor at Cambridge for three of my undergraduate courses (History of Italian, History of Romanian, Vulgar Latin and Romance Philology). As I wrote in the preface to my 1981 book, Joe 'did more than anyone to awaken my interest in language, and to persuade me that just maybe linguistic theory wasn't quite as pointless as it seemed at the time' (when linguistics seemed to most students to be designed solely to inflict taxonomic torture on them). Thanks for everything, Joe – you will be sorely missed by the many people you helped go on to successful academic careers.

1   Grammar

1.1   Overview

In broad terms, this book is concerned with aspects of grammar. Grammar is traditionally subdivided into two different but interrelated areas of study – **morphology** and **syntax**. Morphology is the study of how words are formed out of smaller units (called **morphemes**), and so addresses questions such as 'What are the component morphemes of a word like *antidisestablishmentarianism*, and what is the nature of the morphological operations by which they are combined together to form the overall word?' Syntax is the study of the way in which phrases and sentences are structured out of words, and so addresses questions like 'What is the structure of a sentence like *What's the president doing?* and what is the nature of the grammatical operations by which its component words are combined together to form the overall sentence structure?' In this chapter, we begin (in §1.2) by taking a brief look at the approach to the study of syntax taken in **traditional grammar**: this also provides an opportunity to introduce some useful grammatical terminology. In the remainder of the chapter, we look at the approach to syntax adopted within the theory of **Universal Grammar** developed by Chomsky.

1.2   Traditional grammar

Within traditional grammar, the syntax of a language is described in terms of a **taxonomy** (i.e. classificatory list) of the range of different types of syntactic structures found in the language. The central assumption underpinning syntactic analysis in traditional grammar is that phrases and sentences are built up of a series of **constituents** (i.e. syntactic units), each of which belongs to a specific **grammatical category** and serves a specific **grammatical function**. Given this assumption, the task of the linguist analysing the syntactic structure of any given type of sentence is to identify each of the constituents in the sentence, and (for each constituent) to say what category it belongs to and what function it serves. For example, in relation to the syntax of a simple sentence like:

(1)   Students protested

it would traditionally be said that the sentence consists of two constituents (the word *students* and the word *protested*), that each of these constituents belongs to a specific grammatical category (*students* being a plural **noun** and *protested* a past-tense **verb**) and that each serves a specific grammatical function (*students* being the **subject** of the sentence, and *protested* being its **predicate**). The overall sentence *Students protested* has the categorial status of a **clause** which is **finite** in nature (by virtue of denoting an event taking place at a specific time), and has the semantic function of expressing a **proposition** which is **declarative** in force (in that it is used to make a statement rather than, for example, ask a question). Accordingly, a traditional grammar of English would tell us that the simplest type of finite declarative clause found in English is a sentence like (1) in which a nominal subject is followed by a verbal predicate. Let's briefly look at some of the terminology used here.

In traditional grammar, words are assigned to grammatical categories (called **parts of speech**) on the basis of their **semantic** properties (i.e. meaning), **morphological** properties (i.e. the range of different forms they have), and **syntactic** properties (i.e. word-order properties relating to the positions they can occupy within sentences): a set of words which belong to the same category thus have a number of semantic, morphological and syntactic properties in common. For example, **nouns** are traditionally said to have the semantic property that they denote entities: so, *bottle* is a noun (since it denotes a type of object used to contain liquids), *horse* is a noun (since it denotes a type of animal), and *John* is a noun (since it denotes a specific person). Typical nouns (more specifically, **count nouns**) have the morphological property that they have two different forms: a **singular** form (like *horse* in *one horse*) used to denote a single entity, and a **plural** form (like *horses* in *two horses*) used to denote two or more entities. Nouns have the syntactic property that only (an appropriate kind of) noun can be used to end a four-word sentence such as *They have no . . .* In place of the dots here we could insert a singular noun like *car* or a plural noun like *friends*, but not other types of word (e.g. not *see*, or *slowly* or *up*, since these are not nouns).

In contrast to nouns, **verbs** are traditionally said to have the semantic property that they denote actions or events: so, *eat, sing, pull* and *resign* are all (action-denoting) verbs. From a syntactic point of view, verbs have the property that only an appropriate kind of verb (in its uninflected form) can be used to complete a three-word sentence such as *They/It can . . .* So, words like *stay, leave, hide, die, starve* and *cry* are all verbs and hence can be used in place of the dots here (but words like *apple, under, pink* and *if* aren't). From a morphological point of view, regular verbs like *cry* (in English) have the property that they have four distinct forms: e.g. alongside the dictionary **citation form** *cry* we find the **present-tense** form *cries*, the **past-tense/perfect participle/passive participle** form *cried* and the **progressive participle** form *crying*. Since chapter 2 is devoted to a discussion of grammatical categories, we shall have no more to say about them for the time being. Instead, we turn to look at some of the terminology used in traditional grammar to describe the different **grammatical functions** that constituents fulfil.

Let's begin by looking at the following set of sentences:

(2) (a)   *John* smokes
   (b)   *The president* smokes
   (c)   *The president of Utopia* smokes
   (d)   *The former president of the island paradise of Utopia* smokes

Sentence (2a) comprises the noun *John* which serves the function of being the **subject** of the sentence (and denotes the person performing the act of smoking), and the verb *smokes* which serves the function of being the **predicate** of the sentence (and describes the act being performed). In (2a), the subject is the single noun *John*; but as the examples in (2b–d) show, the subject of a sentence can also be an (italicised) phrase like *the president*, or *the president of Utopia* or *the former president of the island paradise of Utopia*.

Now consider the following set of sentences:

(3) (a)   John smokes *cigars*
   (b)   John smokes *Cuban cigars*
   (c)   John smokes *Cuban cigars imported from Havana*
   (d)   John smokes *a specific brand of Cuban cigars imported by a friend of his from Havana*

Sentence (3a) comprises the **subject** *John*, the **predicate** *smokes* and the **complement** (or **direct object**) *cigars*. (The complement *cigars* describes the entity on which the act of smoking is being performed; as this example illustrates, subjects normally precede the verb with which they are associated in English, whereas complements typically follow the verb.) The complement in (3a) is the single noun *cigars*; but a complement can also be a **phrase**: in (3b), the complement of *smokes* is the phrase *Cuban cigars*; in (3c) the complement is the phrase *Cuban cigars imported from Havana*; and in (3d) the complement is the phrase *a specific brand of Cuban cigars imported by a friend of his from Havana*. A verb which has a noun or pronoun expression as its direct-object complement is traditionally said to be **transitive**.

From a semantic perspective, subjects and complements share in common the fact that they generally represent entities directly involved in the particular action or event described by the predicate: to use the relevant semantic terminology, we can say that subjects and complements are **arguments** of the predicate with which they are associated. Predicates may have one or more arguments, as we see from sentences such as (4) below, where each of the bracketed nouns is a different argument of the italicised predicate:

(4) (a)   [John] *resigned*
   (b)   [John] *felt* [remorse]
   (c)   [John] *sent* [Mary] [flowers]

A predicate like *resign* in (4a) which has a single argument is said to function as a **one-place predicate** (in the relevant use); one like *feel* in (4b) which has two arguments is a **two-place predicate**; and one like *send* in (4c) which has three arguments is a **three-place predicate**.

In addition to predicates and arguments, sentences can also contain **adjuncts**, as we can illustrate in relation to (5) below:

(5) (a)   The president smokes a cigar *after dinner*
   (b)   The president smokes a cigar *in his office*

In both sentences in (5), *smokes* functions as a two-place predicate whose two arguments are its subject *the president* and its complement *a cigar*. But what is the function of the phrase *after dinner* which also occurs in (5a)? Since *after dinner* isn't one of the entities directly involved in the act of smoking (i.e. it isn't consuming or being consumed), it isn't an argument of the predicate *smoke*. On the contrary, *after dinner* simply serves to provide additional information about the time when the smoking activity takes place. In much the same way, the italicised expression *in his office* in (5b) provides additional information about the location of the smoking activity. An expression which serves to provide (optional) additional information about the time or place (or manner, or purpose etc.) of an activity or event is said to serve as an **adjunct**. So, *after dinner* and *in his office* in (5a,b) are both **adjuncts**.

So far, all the sentences we have looked at in (1)–(5) have been **simple sentences** which contain a single **clause**. However, alongside these we also find **complex sentences** which contain more than one clause, like (6) below:

(6)   Mary knows John smokes

If we take the traditional definition of a clause as a predication structure (more precisely, a structure containing a predicate which has a subject, and which may or may not also contain one or more complements and adjuncts), it follows that since there are two predicates (*knows* and *smokes*) in (6), there are correspondingly two clauses – the *smokes* clause on the one hand, and the *knows* clause on the other. The *smokes* clause comprises the subject *John* and the predicate *smokes*; the *knows* clause comprises the subject *Mary*, the predicate *knows* and the complement *John smokes*. So, the complement of *knows* here is itself a clause – namely the clause *John smokes*. More precisely, the *smokes* clause is a **complement clause** (because it serves as the complement of *knows*), while the *knows* clause is the **main clause** (or **principal clause** or **independent clause** or **root clause**). The overall sentence (6) *Mary knows John smokes* is a **complex sentence** because it contains more than one clause. In much the same way, (7) below is also a complex sentence:

(7)   The press clearly think the president deliberately lied to Congress

Once again, it comprises two clauses – one containing the predicate *think*, the other containing the predicate *lie*. The main clause comprises the subject *the press*, the adjunct *clearly*, the predicate *think* and the complement clause *the president deliberately lied to Congress*. The complement clause in turn comprises the subject *the president*, the adjunct *deliberately*, the predicate *lied*, and the complement *to Congress*.

As was implicit in our earlier classification of (1) as a **finite** clause, traditional grammars draw a distinction between **finite clauses** (which describe events taking place at a particular time) and **non-finite clauses** (which describe hypothetical or projected future events). In this connection, consider the contrast between the italicised clauses below (all three of which function as the complement of *remember*):

(8) (a)   John couldn't remember *what pills he is taking*
   (b)   John couldn't remember *what pills he took*
   (c)   John couldn't remember *what pills to take*

In (8a), the clause *what pills he is taking* is finite by virtue of containing present-tense *is*: likewise, the clause *what pills he took* in (8b) is finite by virtue of containing past-tense *took*. However, the clause *what pills to take* in (8c) is non-finite by virtue of containing no tense specification – *take* here is an infinitive form which is not inflected for tense, as we see from the fact that it could not be replaced by the past-tense form *took* here (cf. *'John couldn't remember what pills to *took*' – the **star** indicating ungrammaticality).

Whether or not a clause is finite in turn determines the kind of subject it can have, in that finite clauses can have a **nominative** pronoun like *he* as their subject, but non-finite clauses cannot (as we see from the ungrammaticality of *'John couldn't remember what pills *he* to take'). Accordingly, one way of telling whether a particular clause is finite or not is to see whether it can have a nominative pronoun (like *I/we/he/she/they*) as its subject. In this connection, consider whether the italicised clauses in (9a,b) below are finite or non-finite:

(9) (a)   I didn't know *students have problems with syntax*
   (b)   I have never known *students have problems with syntax*

The fact that *students* in (9a) can be replaced by the nominative pronoun *they* (as in 'I didn't know *they* have problems with syntax') suggests that the italicised clause in (9a) is finite – as does the fact that the present-tense verb *have* can be replaced by its past-tense counterpart *had* in (9a). Conversely, the fact that *students* in (9b) can be replaced by the **accusative** pronoun *them* (as in 'I have never known *them* have problems with syntax') suggests that the italicised clause in (9b) is non-finite – as does the fact that we can optionally use the infinitive particle *to* in (9b) (as in 'I have never known students *to* have problems with syntax'), and the fact that we can replace the *have* expression by one containing the infinitive form *be* (as in 'I have never known students *be* worried about syntax').

In addition to being finite or non-finite, each clause within a sentence has a specific **force**. In this connection, consider the following simple (single-clause) sentences:

(10) (a) He went home   (b) Are you feeling OK?
     (c) You be quiet!   (d) What a great idea that is!

A sentence like (10a) is traditionally said to be **declarative** in force, in that it is used to make a statement. (10b) is **interrogative** in force in that it is used to ask a question. (10c) is **imperative** in force, by virtue of being used to issue an order or command. (10d) is **exclamative** in force, in that it is used to exclaim surprise or delight. In complex sentences, each clause has its own force, as we can see in relation to (11) below:

(11) (a) He asked where she had gone
     (b) Did you know that he has retired?
     (c) Tell her what a great time we had!

In (11a), the main (*asked*) clause is declarative, whereas the complement (*gone*) clause is interrogative; in (11b) the main (*know*) clause is interrogative, whereas the complement (*retired*) clause is declarative; and in (11c), the main (*tell*) clause is imperative, whereas the complement (*had*) clause is exclamative.

We can summarise this section as follows. From the perspective of traditional grammar, the syntax of a language is described in terms of a **taxonomy** (i.e. a classificatory list) of the range of different phrase-, clause- and sentence-types found in the language. So, for example, a typical traditional grammar of (say) English will include chapters on the syntax of negatives, interrogatives, exclamatives, imperatives and so on. The chapter on interrogatives will note (e.g.) that in main-clause questions in English like 'Is he winning?' the present-tense **auxiliary** *is* **inverts** with (i.e. moves in front of) the subject *he*, but not in complement-clause questions like the *if*-clause in 'I wonder if he *is* winning', and will typically not be concerned with trying to explain *why* **auxiliary inversion** applies in main clauses but not complement clauses: this reflects the fact that the primary goal of traditional grammar is *description* rather than *explanation*.

1.3   Universal Grammar

In contrast to the **taxonomic** approach adopted in traditional grammar, Chomsky takes a **cognitive** approach to the study of grammar. For Chomsky, the goal of the linguist is to determine what it is that native speakers *know* about their native language which enables them to speak and understand the language: hence, the study of language is part of the wider study of **cognition** (i.e. what human beings know). In a fairly obvious sense, any native speaker of a language can be said to *know* the grammar of his or her native language. For example, any native speaker of English can tell you that the negative counterpart of *I like syntax* is *I don't like syntax*, and not e.g. **I no like syntax*: in other words, native speakers know how to combine words together to **form** expressions (e.g. negative sentences) in their language. Likewise, any native speaker of English can tell you that a sentence like *She loves me more than you* is ambiguous and has two

interpretations which can be paraphrased as 'She loves me more than she loves you' and 'She loves me more than you love me': in other words, native speakers also know how to **interpret** (i.e. assign meaning to) expressions in their language. However, it is important to emphasise that this grammatical knowledge of how to form and interpret expressions in your native language is **tacit** (i.e. subconscious) rather than **explicit** (i.e. conscious): so, it's no good asking a native speaker of English a question such as 'How do you form negative sentences in English?', since human beings have no conscious awareness of the processes involved in speaking and understanding their native language. To introduce a technical term devised by Chomsky, we can say that native speakers have grammatical **competence** in their native language: by this, we mean that they have tacit knowledge of the grammar of their language – i.e. of how to form and interpret words, phrases and sentences in the language.

In work dating back to the 1960s, Chomsky has drawn a distinction between **competence** (the native speaker's tacit knowledge of his or her language) and **performance** (what people actually say or understand by what someone else says on a given occasion). Competence is 'the speaker–hearer's knowledge of his language', while performance is 'the actual use of language in concrete situations' (Chomsky 1965, p. 4). Very often, performance is an imperfect reflection of competence: we all make occasional slips of the tongue, or occasionally misinterpret something which someone else says to us. However, this doesn't mean that we don't know our native language or that we don't have *competence* in it. Misproductions and misinterpretations are **performance errors**, attributable to a variety of performance factors like tiredness, boredom, drunkenness, drugs, external distractions and so forth. A grammar of a language tells you what you need to know in order to have native-like competence in the language (i.e. to be able to speak the language like a fluent native speaker): hence, it is clear that grammar is concerned with competence rather than performance. This is not to deny the interest of performance as a field of study, but merely to assert that performance is more properly studied within the different – though related – discipline of psycholinguistics, which studies the psychological processes underlying speech production and comprehension.

In the terminology adopted by Chomsky (1986a, pp. 19–56), when we study the grammatical competence of a native speaker of a language like English we're studying a cognitive system **internalised** within the brain/mind of native speakers of English; our ultimate goal in studying competence is to characterise the nature of the internalised linguistic system (or **I-language**, as Chomsky terms it) which makes native speakers proficient in English. Such a cognitive approach has obvious implications for the descriptive linguist who is concerned to develop a grammar of a particular language like English. According to Chomsky (1986a, p. 22) a grammar of a language is 'a theory of the I-language . . . under investigation'. This means that in devising a grammar of English, we are attempting to uncover the internalised linguistic system (= I-language) possessed by native speakers of English – i.e. we are attempting to characterise a mental state (a state of competence, and thus linguistic knowledge). See Smith (1999) for more extensive discussion of the notion of I-language.

Chomsky's ultimate goal is to devise a theory of **Universal Grammar/UG** which generalises from the grammars of particular I-languages to the grammars of all possible natural (i.e. human) I-languages. He defines UG (1986a, p. 23) as 'the theory of human I-languages . . . that identifies the I-languages that are humanly accessible under normal conditions'. (The expression 'are humanly accessible' means 'can be acquired by human beings'.) In other words, UG is a theory about the nature of possible grammars of human languages: hence, a theory of UG answers the question: 'What are the defining characteristics of the grammars of human I-languages?'

There are a number of **criteria of adequacy** which a theory of Universal Grammar must satisfy. One such criterion (which is implicit in the use of the term *Universal Grammar*) is **universality**, in the sense that a theory of UG must supply us with the tools needed to provide a **descriptively adequate** grammar for any and every human I-language (i.e. a grammar which correctly describes how to form and interpret expressions in the relevant language). After all, a theory of UG would be of little interest if it enabled us to describe the grammar of English and French, but not that of Swahili or Chinese.

However, since the ultimate goal of any theory is explanation, it is not enough for a theory of Universal Grammar simply to list sets of universal properties of natural language grammars; on the contrary, a theory of UG must seek to explain the relevant properties. So, a key question for any adequate theory of UG to answer is: 'Why do grammars of human I-languages have the properties they do?' The requirement that a theory should explain why grammars have the properties they do is conventionally referred to as the criterion of **explanatory adequacy**.

Since the theory of Universal Grammar is concerned with characterising the properties of natural (i.e. human) I-language grammars, an important question which we want our theory of UG to answer is: 'What are the defining characteristics of human I-languages which differentiate them from, for example, artificial languages like those used in mathematics and computing (e.g. Java, Prolog, C etc.), or from animal communication systems (e.g. the tail-wagging dance performed by bees to communicate the location of a food source to other bees)?' It therefore follows that the descriptive apparatus which our theory of UG allows us to make use of in devising natural language grammars must not be so powerful that it can be used to describe not only natural languages, but also computer languages or animal communication systems (since any such excessively powerful theory wouldn't be able to pinpoint the criterial properties of natural languages which differentiate them from other types of communication system). In other words, a third condition which we have to impose on our theory of language is that it be maximally **constrained**: that is, we want our theory to provide us with technical devices which are so constrained (i.e. limited) in their expressive power that they can only be used to describe natural languages, and are not appropriate for the description of other communication systems. A theory which is constrained in appropriate ways should enable us to provide a principled explanation for why certain types of syntactic structure and syntactic operation simply aren't found in natural languages. One way of constraining grammars is to suppose that grammatical operations obey certain linguistic principles, and that any operation which violates the relevant principles leads to ungrammaticality: see the discussion below in §1.5 for a concrete example.

A related requirement is that linguistic theory should provide grammars which make use of the minimal theoretical apparatus required: in other words, grammars should be as simple as possible. Much earlier work in syntax involved the postulation of complex structures and principles: as a reaction to the excessive complexity of this kind of work, Chomsky in work over the past ten years or so has made the requirement to minimise the theoretical and descriptive apparatus used to describe language the cornerstone of the **Minimalist Program for Linguistic Theory** which he has been developing (in work dating back to Chomsky 1993, 1995). In more recent work, Chomsky (1998, 1999, 2001, 2002) has suggested that language is a **perfect** system with an **optimal design** in the sense that natural language grammars create structures which are designed to **interface** perfectly with other components of the mind – more specifically with speech and thought systems. (For discussion of the idea that language is a perfect system of optimal design, see Lappin, Levine and Johnson 2000a,b, 2001; Holmberg 2000; Piattelli-Palmarini 2000; Reuland 2000, 2001b; Roberts 2000, 2001a; Uriagereka 2000, 2001; Freidin and Vergnaud 2001; and Atkinson 2003.)

To make this discussion rather more concrete, let's suppose that a grammar of a language is organised as follows. One component of a grammar is a **Lexicon** (= dictionary = list of all the **lexical items/**words in the language and their linguistic properties), and in forming a given sentence out of a set of words, we first have to take the relevant words out of the Lexicon. Our chosen words are then combined together by a series of syntactic computations in the **syntax** (i.e. in the **syntactic/computational component** of the grammar), thereby forming a **syntactic structure**. This syntactic structure serves as input into two other components of the grammar. One is the **semantic component** which **maps** (i.e. 'converts') the syntactic structure into a corresponding **semantic representation** (i.e. to a representation of linguistic aspects of its meaning); the other is a **PF component,** so called because it maps the syntactic structure into a **PF representation** (i.e. a representation of its **Phonetic Form,** telling us how it is pronounced). The semantic representation interfaces with systems of thought, and the PF representation with systems of speech – as shown in diagrammatic form below:

(12)

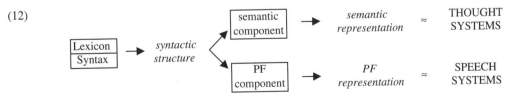

In terms of the model in (12), an important constraint is that the (semantic and PF) representations which are 'handed over' to the (thought and speech) interface systems should contain only elements which are **legible** by the appropriate interface system – so that the semantic representations handed over to thought systems contain only elements contributing to meaning, and the PF representations handed over to speech systems contain only elements which contribute to phonetic form (i.e. to determining how the sentence is pronounced).

The neurophysiological mechanisms which underlie linguistic competence make it possible for young children to acquire language in a remarkably short period of time. Accordingly, a fourth condition which any adequate linguistic theory must meet is that of **learnability**: it must provide grammars which are learnable by young children in a short period of time. The desire to maximise the **learnability** of natural language grammars provides an additional argument for minimising the theoretical apparatus used to describe languages, in the sense that the simpler grammars are, the simpler it is for children to acquire them.

1.4   The Language Faculty

Mention of learnability leads us to consider the related goal of developing a **theory of language acquisition**. An acquisition theory is concerned with the question of how children acquire grammars of their native languages. Children generally produce their first recognisable word (e.g. *Mama* or *Dada*) by the age of twelve months. For the next six months or so, there is little apparent evidence of grammatical development in their speech production, although the child's productive vocabulary typically increases by about five words a month until it reaches around thirty words at age eighteen months. Throughout this single-word stage, children's utterances comprise single words spoken in isolation: e.g. a child may say *Apple* when reaching for an apple, or *Up* when wanting to climb up onto her mother's knee. During the single-word stage, it is difficult to find any clear evidence of the acquisition of grammar, in that children do not make productive use of inflections (e.g. they don't add the plural -*s* ending to nouns, or the past-tense -*d* ending to verbs), and don't productively combine words together to form two- and three-word utterances.

At around the age of eighteen months (though with considerable variation from one child to another), we find the first visible signs of the acquisition of grammar: children start to make productive use of inflections (e.g. using plural nouns like *doggies* alongside the singular form *doggy*, and inflected verb forms like *going/gone* alongside the uninflected verb form *go*), and similarly start to produce elementary two- and three-word utterances such as *Want Teddy, Eating cookie, Daddy gone office* etc. From this point on, there is a rapid expansion in their grammatical development, until by the age of around thirty months they have typically acquired most of the inflections and core grammatical constructions used in English, and are able to produce adult-like sentences such as *Where's Mummy gone? What's Daddy doing? Can we go to the zoo, Daddy?* etc. (though occasional morphological and syntactic errors persist until the age of four years or so – e.g. *We goed there with Daddy, What we can do?* etc.).

So, the central phenomenon which any theory of language acquisition must seek to explain is this: how is it that after a long drawn-out period of many months in which there is no obvious sign of grammatical development, at around the age of eighteen months there is a sudden spurt as multiword speech starts to emerge, and a phenomenal growth in grammatical development then takes place over the next twelve months? This **uniformity** and (once the spurt has started) **rapidity** in the pattern of children's linguistic development are the central facts which a theory of language acquisition must seek to explain. But how?

Chomsky maintains that the most plausible explanation for the uniformity and rapidity of first language acquisition is to posit that the course of acquisition is determined by a biologically endowed innate **Language Faculty** (or language acquisition program, to borrow a computer software metaphor) within the brain, which provides children with a genetically transmitted algorithm (i.e. set of pro-cedures) for developing a grammar, on the basis of their linguistic **experience** (i.e. on the basis of the speech input they receive). The way in which Chomsky visualises the acquisition process can be represented schematically as in (13) below (where L is the language being acquired):

(13)

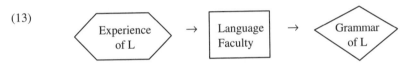

Children acquiring a language will observe people around them using the lan-guage, and the set of expressions in the language which a child hears (and the contexts in which they are used) in the course of acquiring the language consti-tute the child's linguistic **experience** of the language. This experience serves as input to the child's language faculty, which provides the child with a procedure for (subconsciously) analysing the experience and devising a grammar of the language being acquired. Thus, the input to the language faculty is the child's experience, and the output of the language faculty is a grammar of the language being acquired.

The hypothesis that the course of language acquisition is determined by an innate language faculty is known popularly as the **innateness hypothesis**. Chom-sky maintains that the ability to speak and acquire languages is unique to human beings, and that natural languages incorporate principles which are also unique to humans and which reflect the nature of the human mind:

> Whatever evidence we do have seems to me to support the view that the ability to acquire and use language is a species-specific human capacity, that there are very deep and restrictive principles that determine the nature of human language and are rooted in the specific character of the human mind.   (Chomsky 1972, p. 102)

Moreover, he notes, language acquisition is an ability which all humans possess, entirely independently of their general intelligence:

> Even at low levels of intelligence, at pathological levels, we find a command of language that is totally unattainable by an ape that may, in other respects, surpass a human imbecile in problem-solving activity and other adaptive behaviour.   (Chomsky 1972, p. 10)

In addition, the apparent uniformity in the types of grammars developed by different speakers of the same language suggests that children have genetic guidance in the task of constructing a grammar of their native language:

> We know that the grammars that are in fact constructed vary only slightly among speakers of the same language, despite wide variations not only in intelligence but also in the conditions under which language is acquired. (Chomsky 1972, p. 79)

Furthermore, the rapidity of acquisition (once the grammar spurt has started) also points to genetic guidance in grammar construction:

> Otherwise it is impossible to explain how children come to construct grammars . . . under the given conditions of time and access to data. (Chomsky 1972, p. 113)

(The sequence 'under . . . data' means simply 'in so short a time, and on the basis of such limited linguistic experience.') What makes the uniformity and rapidity of acquisition even more remarkable is the fact that the child's linguistic experience is often **degenerate** (i.e. imperfect), since it is based on the linguistic performance of adult speakers, and this may be a poor reflection of their competence:

> A good deal of normal speech consists of false starts, disconnected phrases, and other deviations from idealised competence.   (Chomsky 1972, p. 158)

If much of the speech input which children receive is degenerate (because of performance errors), how is it that they can use this degenerate experience to develop a (competence) grammar which specifies how to form grammatical sentences? Chomsky's answer is to draw the following analogy:

> Descartes asks: how is it when we see a sort of irregular figure drawn in front of us we see it as a triangle? He observes, quite correctly, that there's a disparity between the data presented to us and the percept that we construct. And he argues, I think quite plausibly, that we see the figure as a triangle because there's something about the nature of our minds which makes the image of a triangle easily constructible by the mind.   (Chomsky 1968, p. 687)

The obvious implication is that in much the same way as we are genetically predisposed to analyse shapes (however irregular) as having specific geometrical properties, so too we are genetically predisposed to analyse sentences (however ungrammatical) as having specific grammatical properties. (For evaluation of this kind of **degenerate input** argument, see Pullum and Scholz 2002; Thomas 2002; Sampson 2002; Fodor and Crowther 2002; Lasnik and Uriagereka 2002; Legate and Yang 2002; Crain and Pietroski 2002; and Scholz and Pullum 2002.)

A further argument Chomsky uses in support of the innateness hypothesis relates to the fact that language acquisition is an entirely subconscious and involuntary activity (in the sense that you can't consciously choose whether or not to acquire your native language – though you can choose whether or not you wish to learn chess); it is also an activity which is largely unguided (in the sense that parents don't teach children to talk):

> Children acquire . . . languages quite successfully even though no special care is taken to teach them and no special attention is given to their progress.   (Chomsky 1965, pp. 200–1)

The implication is that we don't learn to have a native language, any more than we learn to have arms or legs; the ability to acquire a native language is part of our genetic endowment – just like the ability to learn to walk.

Studies of language acquisition lend empirical support for the innateness hypothesis. Research has suggested that there is a **critical period** for the acquisition of syntax, in the sense that children who learn a given language before puberty generally achieve native competence in it, whereas those who acquire a (first or second) language after the age of nine or ten years rarely manage to achieve native-like syntactic competence: see Lenneberg (1967), Hurford (1991) and Smith (1998, 1999) for discussion. A particularly poignant example of this is a child called Genie (see Curtiss 1977; Rymer 1993), who was deprived of speech input and kept locked up on her own in a room until age thirteen. When eventually taken into care and exposed to intensive language input, her vocabulary grew enormously, but her syntax never developed. This suggests that the acquisition of syntax is determined by an innate 'language acquisition programme' which is in effect switched off at the onset of puberty. (For further discussion of the innateness hypothesis, see Antony and Hornstein 2002.)

1.5   Principles of Universal Grammar

If (as Chomsky claims) human beings are biologically endowed with an innate language faculty, an obvious question to ask is what is the nature of the language faculty. An important point to note in this regard is that children can in principle acquire *any* natural language as their native language (e.g. Afghan orphans brought up by English-speaking foster parents in an English-speaking community acquire English as their first language). It therefore follows that the language faculty must incorporate a theory of **Universal Grammar/UG** which enables the child to develop a grammar of *any* natural language on the basis of suitable linguistic experience of the language (i.e. sufficient speech input).

Experience of a particular language L (examples of words, phrases and sentences in L which the child hears produced by native speakers of L in particular contexts) serves as input to the child's language faculty which incorporates a theory of Universal Grammar providing the child with a procedure for developing a grammar of L.

If the acquisition of grammatical competence is indeed controlled by a genetically endowed language faculty incorporating a theory of UG, then it follows that certain aspects of child (and adult) competence are known without experience, and hence must be part of the genetic information about language with which we are biologically endowed at birth. Such aspects of language would not have to be learned, precisely because they form part of the child's genetic inheritance. If we make the (plausible) assumption that the language faculty does not vary significantly from one (normal) human being to another, those aspects of language which are innately determined will also be universal. Thus, in seeking to determine the nature of the language faculty, we are in effect looking for **UG principles** (i.e. principles of Universal Grammar) which determine the very nature of language.

But how can we uncover such principles? The answer is that since the relevant principles are posited to be universal, it follows that they will affect the application of every relevant type of grammatical operation in every language. Thus, detailed analysis of one grammatical construction in one language could reveal evidence of the operation of principles of Universal Grammar. By way of illustration, let's look at question-formation in English. In this connection, consider the following dialogue:

(14)   SPEAKER A: He had said someone would do something
         SPEAKER B: He had said who would do what?

In (14), speaker B largely echoes what speaker A says, except for replacing *someone* by *who* and *something* by *what*. For obvious reasons, the type of question produced by speaker B in (14) is called an **echo question**. However, speaker B could alternatively have replied with a **non-echo question** like that in (15) below:

(15)   Who had he said would do what?

If we compare the echo question *He had said who would do what?* in (14) with the corresponding non-echo question *Who had he said would do what?* in (15), we find that (15) involves two movement operations which are not found in (14). One is an **auxiliary inversion** operation by which the past-tense **auxiliary** *had* is moved in front of its subject *he*. (As we shall see in chapter 2, an *auxiliary* is a word like *had/would* in (15) which carries grammatical properties such as **tense/aspect/mood/modality**.) The other is a **wh-movement** operation by which the **wh-word** *who* is moved to the front of the overall sentence, and positioned in front of *had*. (A wh-word is a word like *who/what/where/when* etc. beginning with *wh*.)

A closer look at questions like (15) provides evidence that there are UG principles which constrain the way in which movement operations may apply. An interesting property of the questions in (14) and (15) is that they contain two auxiliaries (*had* and *would*) and two wh-expressions (*who* and *what*). Now, if we compare (15) with the corresponding echo question in (14), we find that the *first* of the two auxiliaries (*had*) and the *first* of the wh-words (*who*) are moved to the front of the sentence in (15). If we try inverting the second auxiliary (*would*) and fronting the second wh-word (*what*), we end up with ungrammatical sentences, as we see from (16c–e) below (the preposed items are italicised, and the corresponding echo question is given in parentheses; (16a) is repeated from the echo question in (14B), and (16b) from (15)):

(16) (a) He **had** said *who* **would** do *what*? (= echo question)
  (b) *Who* **had** he said would do what? (cf. He **had** said *who* would do what?)
  (c) **Who* **would** he had said do what? (cf. He had said *who* **would** do what?)
  (d) **What* **had** he said who would do? (cf. He **had** said who would do *what*?)
  (e) **What* **would** he had said who do? (cf. He had said who **would** do *what*?)

If we compare (16b) with its echo-question counterpart (16a) *He had said who would do what?* we see that (16b) involves preposing the first wh-word *who* and the first auxiliary *had*, and that this results in a grammatical sentence. By contrast, (16c) involves preposing the first wh-word *who* and the second auxiliary *would*; (16d) involves preposing the second wh-word *what* and the first auxiliary *had*; and (16e) involves preposing the second wh-word *what* and the second auxiliary *would*. The generalisation which emerges from the data in (16) is that auxiliary inversion preposes the *closest* auxiliary *had* (i.e. the one nearest the beginning of the sentence) and likewise wh-fronting preposes the *closest* wh-expression *who*. The fact that two, quite distinct, different movement operations (auxiliary inversion and wh-movement) are subject to the same locality condition (which requires preposing of the *most local* – i.e. closest – expression of the relevant type) suggests that one of the principles of Universal Grammar incorporated into the language faculty is a **Locality Principle** which can be outlined informally as:

(17)   **Locality Principle**
    Grammatical operations are local

In consequence of (17), auxiliary inversion preposes the closest auxiliary, and wh-movement preposes the closest wh-expression. It seems reasonable to suppose that (17) is a principle of Universal Grammar (rather than an idiosyncratic property of question-formation in English). In fact, the strongest possible hypothesis we could put forward is that (17) holds of all grammatical operations in all natural languages, not just of movement operations; and indeed we shall see in later chapters that other types of grammatical operation (including **agreement** and **case assignment**) are subject to a similar locality condition. If so, and if we assume that abstract grammatical principles which are universal are part of our biological endowment, then the natural conclusion to reach is that (17) is a principle which is biologically wired into the language faculty, and which thus forms part of our genetic make-up.

A theory of grammar which posits that grammatical operations are constrained by innate principles of UG offers the important advantage that it minimises the burden of grammatical learning imposed on the child (in the sense that children do not have to learn, for example, that auxiliary inversion affects the first auxiliary in a sentence, or that wh-movement likewise affects the first wh-expression). This is an important consideration, since we saw earlier that learnability is a criterion of adequacy for any theory of grammar – i.e. any adequate theory of grammar must be able to explain how children come to learn the grammar of their native language(s) in such a rapid and uniform fashion. The UG theory developed by Chomsky provides a straightforward account of the rapidity of the child's grammatical development, since it posits that there are a universal set of innately endowed grammatical principles which determine how grammatical operations apply in natural language grammars. Since UG principles which are innately endowed are wired into the language faculty and so do not have to be learned by the child, this minimises the learning load placed on the child, and thereby maximises the learnability of natural language grammars.

1.6   Parameters

Thus far, we have argued that the language faculty incorporates a set of universal principles which guide the child in acquiring a grammar. However, it clearly cannot be the case that all aspects of the grammar of languages are universal; if this were so, all natural language grammars would be the same and there would be no **grammatical learning** involved in language acquisition (i.e. no need for children to learn anything about the grammar of sentences in the language they are acquiring), only **lexical learning** (viz. learning the lexical items/words in the language and their idiosyncratic linguistic properties, e.g. whether a given item has an irregular plural or past-tense form). But although there are universal principles which determine the broad outlines of the grammar of natural languages, there also seem to be language-particular aspects of grammar which children have to learn as part of the task of acquiring their native language. Thus, language acquisition involves not only lexical learning but also some grammatical learning. Let's take a closer look at the grammatical learning involved, and what it tells us about the language acquisition process.

Clearly, grammatical learning is not going to involve learning those aspects of grammar which are determined by universal (hence innate) grammatical operations and principles. Rather, grammatical learning will be limited to those **parameters** (i.e. dimensions or aspects) of grammar which are subject to language-particular variation (and hence vary from one language to another). In other words, grammatical learning will be limited to parametrised aspects of grammar (i.e. those aspects of grammar which are subject to parametric variation from one language to another). The obvious way to determine just what aspects of the grammar of their native language children have to learn is to examine the range of **parametric variation** found in the grammars of different (adult) natural languages.

We can illustrate one type of parametric variation across languages in terms of the following contrast between the Italian examples in (18a,b) below, and their English counterparts in (18c,d):

(18) (a)   Maria parla francese   (b) Parla francese
     (c)   Maria speaks French   (d) *Speaks French

As (18a) and (18c) illustrate, the Italian verb *parlare* and its English counterpart *speak* (as used here) are two-place predicates which require both a subject argument like *Maria* and an object argument like *francese/French*: in both cases, the verb is finite (more specifically it is a present-tense form) and agrees with its subject *Maria* (and hence is a third-person-singular form). But what are we to make of Italian sentences like (18b) *Parla francese* (= 'Speaks French') in which the verb *parla* 'speaks' has the overt complement *francese* 'French' but has no overt subject? The answer suggested in work over the past few decades is that the verb in such cases has a **null subject** which can be thought of as a silent or invisible counterpart of the pronouns *he/she* which appear in the corresponding English translation '*He/She* speaks French'. This null subject is conventionally designated as **pro**, so that (18b) has the structure *pro parla francese* 'pro speaks French', where *pro* is a null-subject pronoun.

There are two reasons for thinking that the verb *parla* 'speaks' has a null subject in (18b). Firstly, *parlare* 'speak' (in the relevant use) is a two-place predicate which requires both a subject argument and an object argument: under the null-subject analysis, its subject argument is *pro* (a null pronoun). Secondly, finite verbs agree with their subjects in Italian: hence, in order to account for the fact that the verb *parla* is in the third-person-singular form in (18b), we need to posit that it has a third-person-singular subject; under the null-subject analysis, we can say that *parla* 'speaks' has a null pronoun (*pro*) as its subject, and that *pro* (if used to refer to *Maria*) is a third-person-feminine-singular pronoun.

The more general conclusion to be drawn from our discussion is that in languages like Italian, finite verbs (i.e. verbs which carry present/past etc. tense) can have either an overt subject like *Maria* or a null *pro* subject. But things are very different in English. Although a finite verb like *speaks* can have an overt subject like *Maria* in English, it cannot normally have a null *pro* subject – hence the ungrammaticality of (18d) *Speaks French*. So, finite verbs in a language like Italian can have either overt or null subjects, but in a language like English, finite verbs can generally have only overt subjects, not null subjects. We can describe the differences between the two types of language by saying that Italian is a **null-subject language**, whereas English is a **non-null-subject language**. More generally, there appears to be parametric variation between languages as to whether or not they allow finite verbs to have null subjects. The relevant parameter (termed the **Null-Subject Parameter**) would appear to be a binary one, with only two possible settings for any given language L, viz. *L either does or doesn't allow finite verbs to have null subjects*. There appears to be no language which allows the subjects of some finite verbs to be null, but not others – e.g. no language in which it is OK to say *Drinks wine* (meaning 'He/she drinks wine') but not OK to say *Eats pasta* (meaning 'He/she eats pasta'). The range of grammatical variation found across languages appears to be strictly limited to just two possibilities – languages either do or don't systematically allow finite verbs to have null subjects. (A complication glossed over here is posed by languages in which only some finite verb forms can have null subjects: see Vainikka and Levy 1999 and the collection of papers in Jaeggli and Safir 1989 for illustration and discussion.)

A more familiar aspect of grammar which appears to be parametrised relates to word order, in that different types of language have different word orders in specific types of construction. One type of word-order variation can be illustrated in relation to the following contrast between English and Chinese questions:

(19) (a)   What do you think he will say?
     (b)   Ni   xiangxin ta hui shuo shenme
            You think   he will say what?

In simple wh-questions in English (i.e. questions containing a single word beginning with *wh-* like *what/where/when/why*) the wh-expression is moved to the beginning of the sentence, as is the case with *what* in (19a). By contrast, in Chinese, the wh-word does not move to the front of the sentence, but rather remains **in situ** (i.e. in the same place as would be occupied by a corresponding non-interrogative expression), so that *shenme* 'what' is positioned after the verb *shuo* 'say' because it is the (direct object) complement of the verb, and complements of the relevant type are normally positioned after their verbs in Chinese. Thus, another parameter of variation between languages is the **wh-parameter** – a parameter which determines whether wh-expressions can be fronted (i.e. moved to the front of the overall interrogative structure containing them) or not. Significantly, this parameter again appears to be one which is binary in nature, in that it allows for only two possibilities – viz. a language either does or doesn't allow **wh-movement** (i.e. movement of wh-expressions to the front of the sentence). Many other possibilities for wh-movement just don't seem to occur in natural language: for example, there is no language in which the counterpart of *who* undergoes wh-fronting but not the counterpart of *what* (e.g. no language in which it is OK to say *Who did you see?* but not *What did you see?*). Likewise, there is no language in which wh-complements of some verbs can undergo fronting, but not wh-complements of other verbs (e.g. no language in which it is OK to say *What did he drink?* but not *What did he eat?*). It would seem that the range of parametric variation found with respect to wh-fronting is limited to just two possibilities: viz. a language either does or doesn't allow wh-expressions to be systematically fronted. (However, it should be noted that a number of complications are overlooked here in the interest of simplifying exposition: e.g.

some languages like English allow only one wh-expression to be fronted in this way, whereas others allow more than one wh-expression to be fronted; see Bošković 2002a for a recent account. An additional complication is posed by the fact that wh-movement appears to be optional in some languages, either in main clauses, or in main and complement clauses alike: see Denham 2000; Cheng and Rooryck 2000.)

Let's now turn to look at a rather different type of word-order variation, concerning the relative position of **heads** and **complements** within phrases. It is a general (indeed, universal) property of phrases that every phrase has a head word which determines the nature of the overall phrase. For example, an expression such as *students of philosophy* is a plural noun phrase because its head word (i.e. the key word in the phrase whose nature determines the properties of the overall phrase) is the plural noun *students*: the noun *students* (and not the noun *philosophy*) is the head word because the phrase *students of philosophy* denotes kinds of student, not kinds of philosophy. The following expression *of philosophy* which combines with the head noun *students* to form the noun phrase *students of philosophy* functions as the **complement** of the noun *students*. In much the same way, an expression such as *in the kitchen* is a prepositional phrase which comprises the head preposition *in* and its complement *the kitchen*. Likewise, an expression such as *stay with me* is a verb phrase which comprises the head verb *stay* and its complement *with me*. And similarly, an expression such as *fond of fast food* is an adjectival phrase formed by combining the head adjective *fond* with its complement *of fast food*.

In English all heads (whether nouns, verbs, prepositions, or adjectives etc.) normally precede their complements; however, there are also languages like Korean in which all heads normally follow their complements. In informal terms, we can say that English is a **head-first language**, whereas Korean is a **head-last language**. The differences between the two languages can be illustrated by comparing the English examples in (20) below with their Korean counterparts in (21):

(20) (a) Close the door   (b) desire for change

(21) (a) Muneul dadara   (b) byunhwa-edaehan galmang
          Door   close   change-for   desire

In the English verb phrase *close the door* in (20a), the head verb *close* precedes its complement *the door*; if we suppose that *the door* is a determiner phrase, then the head of the phrase (= the determiner *the*) precedes its complement (= the noun *door*). Likewise, in the English noun phrase *desire for change* in (20b), the head noun *desire* precedes its complement *for change*; the complement *for change* is in turn a prepositional phrase in which the head preposition *for* likewise precedes its complement *change*. Since English consistently positions heads before complements, it is a head-first language. By contrast, we find precisely the opposite ordering in Korean. In the verb phrase *muneul dadara* (literally 'door close') in (21a), the head verb *dadara* 'close' follows its complement *muneul* 'door'; likewise, in the noun phrase *byunhwa-edaehan galmang* (literally 'change-for desire') in (21b) the head noun *galmang* 'desire' follows its complement *byunhwa-edaehan* 'change-for'; the expression *byunhwa-edaehan* 'change-for' is in turn a prepositional phrase whose head preposition *edaehan* 'for/about' follows its complement *byunhwa* 'change' (so that *edaehan* might more appropriately be called a **postposition**; prepositions and postpositions are differents kinds of **adposition**). Since Korean consistently positions heads after their complements, it is a head-last language. Given that English is head-first and Korean head-last, it is clear that the relative positioning of heads with respect to their complements is one word-order parameter along which languages differ; the relevant parameter is termed the **Head-Position Parameter**.

It should be noted, however, that word-order variation in respect of the relative positioning of heads and complements falls within narrowly circumscribed limits. There are many logically possible types of word-order variation which just don't seem to occur in natural languages. For example, we might imagine that in a given language some verbs would precede and others follow their complements, so that (e.g.) if two new hypothetical verbs like *scrunge* and *plurg* were coined in English, then *scrunge* might take a following complement, and *plurg* a preceding complement. And yet, this doesn't ever seem to happen: rather all verbs typically occupy the same position in a given language with respect to a given type of complement. (A complication overlooked here in the interest of expository simplicity is that some languages position some types of head before their complements, and other types of head after their complements: German is one such language, as you will see from exercise 1.2.)

What this suggests is that there are universal **constraints** (i.e. restrictions) on the range of parametric variation found across languages in respect of the relative ordering of heads and complements. It would seem as if there are only two different possibilities which the theory of Universal Grammar allows for: a given type of structure in a given language must either be **head-first** (with the relevant heads positioned before their complements), or **head-last** (with the relevant heads positioned after their complements). Many other logically possible orderings of heads with respect to complements appear not to be found in natural language grammars. The obvious question to ask is why this should be. The answer given by the theory of parameters is that the language faculty imposes genetic constraints on the range of parametric variation permitted in natural language grammars. In the case of the **Head-Position Parameter** (i.e. the parameter which determines the relative positioning of heads with respect to their complements), the language faculty allows only a binary set of possibilities – namely that a given kind of structure in a given language is either consistently head-first or consistently head-last.

We can generalise our discussion in this section in the following terms. If the **Head-Position Parameter** reduces to a simple binary choice, and if the **Wh-Parameter** and the **Null-Subject Parameter** also involve binary choices, it seems implausible that **binarity** could be an accidental property of these particular parameters. Rather, it seems much more likely that it is an inherent property of parameters that they constrain the range of structural variation between languages, and limit it to a simple binary choice. Generalising still further, it seems possible that all grammatical variation between languages can be characterised in terms of a set of parameters, and that for each parameter, the language faculty specifies a binary choice of possible values for the parameter.

1.7   Parameter-setting

The theory of parameters outlined in the previous section has impor-tant implications for a theory of language acquisition. If all grammatical variation can be characterised in terms of a series of parameters with binary settings, it fol-lows that the only grammatical learning which children have to undertake in relation to the syntactic properties of the relevant class of constructions is to determine (on the basis of their linguistic experience) which of the two alter-native settings for each parameter is the appropriate one for the language being acquired. So, for example, children have to learn whether the native language they are acquiring is a null-subject language or not, whether it is a wh-movement language or not, and whether it is a head-first language or not . . . and so on for all the other parameters along which languages vary. Of course, children also face the formidable task of **lexical learning** – i.e. building up their vocabulary in the relevant language, learning what words mean and what range of forms they have (e.g. whether they are regular or irregular in respect of their morphology), what kinds of structures they can be used in and so on. On this view, the acquisition of grammar involves the twin tasks of **lexical learning** and **parameter-setting**.

This leads us to the following view of the language acquisition process. The central task which the child faces in acquiring a language is to construct a grammar of the language. The innate Language Faculty incorporates (i) a set of universal grammatical principles, and (ii) a set of grammatical parameters which impose severe constraints on the range of grammatical variation permitted in natural languages (perhaps limiting variation to binary choices). Since universal prin-ciples don't have to be learned, the child's syntactic learning task is limited to that of **parameter-setting** (i.e. determining an appropriate setting for each of the relevant grammatical parameters). For obvious reasons, the theory outlined here (developed by Chomsky at the beginning of the 1980s and articulated in Chomsky 1981) is known as **Principles-and-Parameters Theory/PPT**.

The PPT model clearly has important implications for the nature of the language acquisition process, since it vastly reduces the complexity of the acquisition task which children face. PPT hypothesises that grammatical properties which are universal will not have to be learned by the child, since they are wired into the language faculty and hence part of the child's genetic endowment: on the contrary, all the child has to learn are those grammatical properties which are subject to parametric variation across languages. Moreover, the child's learning task will be further simplified if it turns out (as research since 1980 has suggested) that the values which a parameter can have fall within a narrowly specified range, perhaps characterisable in terms of a series of binary choices. This simplified **parameter-setting model** of the acquisition of grammar has given rise to a metaphorical acquisition model in which the child is visualised as having to set a series of switches in one of two positions (*up*/*down*) – each such switch representing a different parameter. In the case of the **Head-Position Parameter**, we can imagine that if the switch is set in the *up* position (for particular types of head), the language will show head-first word order in relevant kinds of structure, whereas if it is set in the *down* position, the order will be head-last. Of course, an obvious implication of the switch metaphor is that the switch must be set in either one position or the other, and cannot be set in both positions. (This would preclude, for example, the possibility of a language having both head-first and head-last word order in a given type of structure.)

The assumption that acquiring the grammar of a language involves the relatively simple task of setting a number of grammatical parameters provides a natural way of accounting for the fact that the acquisition of specific parameters appears to be a remarkably rapid and error-free process in young children. For example, young children acquiring English as their native language seem to set the Head-Position Parameter at its appropriate head-first setting from the very earliest multiword utterances they produce (at around eighteen months of age), and seem to know (tacitly, not explicitly, of course) that English is a head-first language. Accordingly, the earliest verb phrases and prepositional phrases produced by young children acquiring English consistently show verbs and prepositions positioned before their complements, as structures such as the following indicate (produced by a young boy called Jem/James at age twenty months; head verbs are italicised in (22a) and head prepositions in (22b), and their complements are in non-italic print):

(22) (a)   *Touch* heads. *Cuddle* book. *Want* crayons. *Want* malteser. *Open* door. *Want* biscuit. *Bang* bottom. *See* cats. *Sit* down

    (b)   *On* Mummy. *To* lady. *Without* shoe. *With* potty. *In* keyhole. *In* school. *On* carpet. *On* box. *With* crayons. *To* Mummy

The obvious conclusion to be drawn from structures like (22) is that children like Jem consistently position heads before their complements from the very earliest multiword utterances they produce. They do not use different orders for different words of the same type (e.g. they don't position the verb *see* after its complement but the verb *want* before its complement), or for different types of words (e.g. they don't position verbs before and prepositions after their complements).

A natural question to ask at this point is how we can provide a principled explanation for the fact that from the very onset of multiword speech we find English children correctly positioning heads before their complements. The **Principles-and-Parameters** model enables us to provide an explanation for why children manage to learn the relative ordering of heads and complements in such a rapid and error-free fashion. The answer provided by the model is that learning this aspect of word order involves the comparatively simple task of setting a binary parameter at its appropriate value. This task will be a relatively straightforward one if the language faculty tells the child that the only possible choice is for a given type of structure in a given language to be uniformly head-first or uniformly head-last. Given such an assumption, the child could set the parameter correctly on the basis of minimal linguistic experience. For example, once the child is able to **parse** (i.e. grammatically analyse) an adult utterance such as *Help Daddy* and knows that it contains a verb phrase comprising the head verb *help* and its complement *Daddy*, then (on the assumption that the language faculty specifies that all heads of a given type behave uniformly with regard to whether they are positioned before or after their complements), the child will automatically know that all verbs in English are canonically (i.e. normally) positioned before their complements.

1.8   Evidence used to set parameters

One of the questions posed by the parameter-setting model of acqui-sition outlined here is just how children come to arrive at the appropriate setting for a given parameter, and what kind(s) of evidence they make use of in set-ting parameters. As Chomsky notes (1981, pp. 8–9), there are two types of evi-dence which we might expect to be available to the language learner in principle, namely **positive evidence** and **negative evidence**. Positive evidence comprises a set of observed expressions illustrating a particular phenomenon: for example, if children's speech input is made up of structures in which heads precede their complements, this provides them with positive evidence which enables them to set the Head-Position Parameter appropriately. Negative evidence might be of two kinds – **direct** or **indirect**. Direct negative evidence might come from the correc-tion of children's errors by other speakers of the language. However, (contrary to what is often imagined) correction plays a fairly insignificant role in language acquisition, for two reasons. Firstly, correction is relatively infrequent: adults simply don't correct all the errors children make (if they did, children would soon become inhibited and discouraged from speaking). Secondly, children are notoriously unresponsive to correction, as the following dialogue (from McNeill 1966, p. 69) illustrates:

(23)   CHILD: Nobody don't like me
            ADULT: No, say: 'Nobody likes me'
            CHILD: Nobody don't like me
            (8 repetitions of this dialogue)
            ADULT: No, now listen carefully. Say 'Nobody likes me'
            CHILD: Oh, nobody don't likes me

As Hyams (1986, p. 91) notes: 'Negative evidence in the form of parental disapproval or overt corrections has no discernible effect on the child's developing syntactic ability.' (For further evidence in support of this conclusion, see McNeill 1966; Brown, Cazden and Bellugi 1968; Brown and Hanlon 1970; Braine 1971; Bowerman 1988; Morgan and Travis 1989; and Marcus 1993.)

Direct negative evidence might also take the form of self-correction by other speakers. Such self-corrections tend to have a characteristic intonation and rhythm of their own, and may be signalled by a variety of fillers (such as those italicised in (24) below):

(24) (a)   The picture was hanged . . . *or rather* hung . . . in the Tate Gallery
   (b)   The picture was hanged . . . *sorry* hung . . . in the Tate Gallery
   (c)   The picture was hanged . . . *I mean* hung . . . in the Tate Gallery

However, self-correction is arguably too infrequent a phenomenon to play a major role in the acquisition process.

Rather than say that children rely on direct negative evidence, we might instead imagine that they learn from **indirect negative evidence** (i.e. evidence relating to the non-occurrence of certain types of structure). Suppose that a child's experience includes no examples of structures in which heads follow their complements (e.g. no prepositional phrases like *dinner after* in which the head preposition *after* follows its complement *dinner*, and no verb phrases such as *cake eat* in which the head verb *eat* follows its complement *cake*). On the basis of such indirect negative evidence (i.e. evidence based on the non-occurrence of head-last structures), the child might infer that English is not a head-last language.

Although it might seem natural to suppose that indirect negative evidence plays some role in the acquisition process, there are potential **learnability** problems posed by any such claim. After all, the fact that a given construction does not occur in a given chunk of the child's experience does not provide conclusive evidence that the structure is ungrammatical, since it may well be that the non-occurrence of the relevant structure in the relevant chunk of experience is an accidental (rather than a systematic) gap. Thus, the child would need to process a very large (in principle, infinite) chunk of experience in order to be sure that non-occurrence reflects ungrammaticality. It seems implausible to suppose that children store massive chunks of experience in this way and search through it for negative evidence about the non-occurrence of certain types of structure. In any case, given the assumption that parameters are binary and single-valued, negative evidence becomes entirely unnecessary: after all, once the child hears a prepositional phrase like *with Daddy* in which the head preposition *with* precedes its complement *Daddy*, the child will have positive evidence that English allows head-first order in prepositional phrases; and given the assumptions that the Head-Position Parameter is a binary one and that each parameter allows only a single setting, then it follows (as a matter of logical necessity) that if English allows head-first prepositional phrases, it will not allow head-last prepositional phrases. Thus, in order for the child to know that English doesn't allow head-last prepositional phrases, the child does not need negative evidence from the non-occurrence of such structures, but rather can rely on positive evidence from the occurrence of the converse order in head-first structures (on the assumption that if a given structure is head-first, UG specifies that it cannot be head-last). And, as we have already noted, a minimal amount of positive evidence is required in order to identify English as a uniformly head-first language (i.e. a language in which *all* heads precede their complements). Learnability considerations such as these have led Chomsky (1986a, p. 55) to conclude that 'There is good reason to believe that children learn language from positive evidence only.' The claim that children do not make use of negative evidence in setting parameters is known as the **No-Negative-Evidence Hypothesis**; it is a hypothesis which is widely assumed in current acquisition research. (See Guasti 2002 for a technical account of language acquisition within the framework used here.)

1.9   Summary

We began this chapter in §1.2 with a brief look at traditional grammar, noting that this is a **taxonomic** (i.e. classificatory) system in which the syntax of a language is essentially described in terms of a list of phrase, clause and sentence types found in the language. We noted that Chomsky adopts a very different **cognitive** approach to the study of language in which a grammar of a language is a model of the internalised grammatical **competence** (or **I-language**) of a native speaker of the language. We saw that Chomsky's ultimate goal is to develop a theory of **Universal Grammar/UG** which characterises the defining properties of the grammars of natural languages – a theory which is universal, explanatory and constrained, and which provides descriptively adequate grammars which are minimally complex and hence learnable. In §1.4, we went on to look at the nature of language acquisition, and argued that the most fundamental question for a theory of language acquisition to answer is why it should be that after a period of a year and a half during which there is little evidence of grammatical development visible in the child's speech output, most of the grammar of the language is acquired by children during the course of the following year. We outlined the **innateness hypothesis** put forward by Chomsky, under which the course of language acquisition is genetically predetermined by an innate **language faculty**. In §1.5, we noted Chomsky's claim that the language faculty incorporates a theory of **Universal Grammar/UG** which embodies a set of universal grammatical principles that determine the ways in which grammatical operations work; and we saw that the syntax of questions in English provides evidence for postulating that syntactic operations are constrained by a universal **Locality Principle**. In §1.6, we went on to argue that the grammars of natural languages vary along a number of **parameters**. We looked at three such parameters – the **Wh-Parameter**, the **Null-Subject Parameter**, and the **Head-Position Parameter**, arguing that each of these parameters is binary in nature by virtue of having two alternative settings. In §1.7, we argued that the syntactic learning task which children face involves **parameter-setting** – i.e. determining which of two possible settings is the appropriate one for each parameter in the language being acquired. We further argued that if parameters have binary settings (e.g. so that a given kind of structure in a given language is either head-first or head-last), we should expect to find evidence that children correctly set parameters from the very onset of multiword speech: and we presented evidence to suggest that from their very earliest multiword utterances, children acquiring English as their mother tongue correctly set the Head-Position Parameter at the head-first value appropriate for English. We concluded that the acquisition of grammar involves the twin tasks of lexical learning (i.e. acquiring a **lexicon**/vocabulary) and parameter-setting. In §1.8, we asked what kind of evidence children use in setting parameters, and concluded that they use **positive evidence** from their experience of the occurrence of specific types of structure (e.g. head-first structures, or null-subject structures, or wh-movement structures).

Workbook section

Exercise 1.1

Below are examples of utterances produced by a girl called Lucy at age twenty-four months. Comment on whether Lucy has correctly set the three parameters discussed in the text (the Head-Position Parameter, the Wh-Parameter and the Null-Subject Parameter). Discuss the significance of the relevant examples for the parameter-setting model of acquisition.

	Child sentence	**Adult counterpart**
1	What doing?	'What are you doing?'
2	Want bye-byes	'I want to go to sleep'
3	Mummy go shops	'Mummy went to the shops'; this was in reply to 'Where did Mummy go?'
4	Me have yoghurt?	'Can I have a yoghurt?'
5	Daddy doing?	'What's Daddy doing?'
6	Think Teddy sleeping	'I think Teddy's sleeping'; this was in reply to 'What d'you think Teddy's doing?'
7	What me having?	'What am I having?'; this followed her mother saying 'Mummy's having fish for dinner'
8	No me have fish	'I'm not going to have fish'
9	Where Daddy gone?	'Where's Daddy gone?'
10	Gone office	'He's gone to his office'
11	Want bickies	'She wants some biscuits'; this was her reply to 'What does Dolly want?'
12	What Teddy have?	'What can Teddy have?'
13	Where going?	'Where are you going?'
14	Me go shops	'I want to go to the shops'
15	Daddy drinking coffee	'Daddy's drinking coffee'
16	What Nana eating?	'What's Grandma eating?'
17	Want choc'ate	'He wants some chocolate'; this was her reply to 'Teddy wants some meat, does he?'

18	Dolly gone?	'Where's Dolly gone?'
19	Watch te'vision	'I'm going to watch television'
20	Me have more	'I want to have some more'
21	In kitchen	'In the kitchen' (reply to 'Where's Mummy?')
22	Me play with Daddy	'I want to play with Daddy'
23	Open door	'(Please) open the door!'

Helpful hints

If Lucy has correctly set the Wh-Parameter, we should expect to find that she systematically preposes wh-expressions and positions them sentence-initially. If she has correctly set the Head-Position Parameter, we should expect to find (e.g.) that she correctly positions the complement of a verb after the verb, and the complement of a preposition after the preposition; however, where the complement is a wh-expression, we expect to find that the complement is moved into sentence-initial position in order to satisfy the requirements of the Wh-Parameter (if the Wh-Parameter in some sense overrides the Head-Position Parameter). If Lucy has correctly set the Null-Subject Parameter, we should expect to find that she does not use null subjects in finite clauses: however, it seems clear that many of the sentences produced by two-year-old English children like Lucy do indeed have null subjects – and this led Nina Hyams in influential research (1986, 1992) to conclude that English children go through a **null-subject stage** in which they use Italian-style null finite (*pro*) subjects. If Hyams is right, this implies that children may sometimes start out with incorrect settings for a given parameter, and then later have to *re-set* the parameter – a conclusion which (if true) would provide an obvious challenge to the simple parameter-setting model of acquisition outlined in the main text.

However, the picture relating to the use of null subjects is complicated by the fact that in addition to **finite null subjects** (i.e. the *pro* subject found in finite clauses in languages like Italian but not English), there are three other types of null subject which occur in adult English (and other languages). One are **imperative null subjects**, found in imperatives such as *Shut up!* and *Don't say anything!* (Imperatives are sentences used to issue orders; they are the kind of sentences you can put *please* in front of – as in *Please don't say anything!*) Another are **non-finite null subjects** which are found in a range of non-finite clauses in English (i.e. clauses containing a verb which is not marked for tense and agreement), including main clauses like *Why worry?* and complement clauses like those bracketed in *I want [to go home]* and *I like [playing tennis]*: the kind of null subject found in non-finite clauses in English is usually designated as *PRO* and called 'big PRO' (whereas the kind of null subject found in a finite clause in a null-subject language like Italian is designated as *pro* and called 'little pro'. The terms *big* and *little* here simply reflect the fact that PRO is written in 'big' capital letters, and *pro* in 'small' lower-case letters). A third type of null subject found in English are **truncated null subjects** – so called because English has a process of **truncation** which allows one or more words at the beginning of a sentence to be truncated (i.e. omitted) in certain types of style (e.g. diary styles of written English and informal styles of spoken English). Hence in colloquial English, a question like *Are you doing anything tonight?* can be reduced (by truncation) to *You doing anything tonight?* and further reduced (again by truncation) to *Doing anything tonight?* Truncation is also found in abbreviated written styles of English: for example, a diary entry might read *Went to a party. Had a great time. Got totally smashed* (with the subject *I* being truncated in each of the three sentences). An important constraint on truncation is that it can only affect words at the beginning of a sentence, not, for example, words in the middle of a sentence: hence, although we can truncate *are* and *you* in *Are you doing anything tonight?* we can't truncate them in *What are you doing tonight?* (as we see from the ungrammaticality of **What doing tonight?*) since here *are* and *you* are preceded by *what* and hence occur in the middle of the sentence.

What all of this means is that in determining whether Lucy has mis-set the Null-Subject Parameter and has misanalysed English as a null-subject language (i.e. a language which allows finite null 'little *pro*' subjects), you have to bear in mind the alternative possibility that the null subjects used by Lucy may represent one or more of the three kinds of null subject permitted in adult English (viz. imperative null subjects, truncated null subjects and non-finite null subjects).

Since truncation occurs only sentence-initially (at the beginning of a sentence), but finite null (little *pro*) subjects in a genuine null-subject language like Italian can occur in any subject position in a sentence, one way of telling the difference between a finite null subject and a truncated null subject is to see whether children omit subjects only when they are the first word in a sentence (which could be the result of *truncation*), or whether they also omit subjects in the middle of sentences (as is the case in a genuine null-subject language like Italian). Another way of differentiating the two is that in null-subject languages we find that overt pronoun subjects are only used for emphasis, so that in an Italian sentence like *L'ho fatto io* (literally 'It have done I') the subject pronoun *io* 'I' has a contrastive interpretation, and the relevant sentence is paraphraseable in English as '*I* was the one who did it' (where italics indicate contrastive stress); by contrast, in a non-null-subject language like English, subject pronouns are not intrinsically emphatic – e.g. *he* doesn't necessarily have a contrastive interpretation in an English diary-style sentence such as *Went to see Jim. Thought he might help.* A third way of telling whether truncation is operative in Lucy's grammar or not is to see whether expressions other than subjects can be truncated, as can happen in adult English (e.g. *What time is it?* can be reduced to *Time is it?* via truncation in rapid spoken English).

At first sight, it might seem unlikely that (some of) Lucy's null subjects could be non-finite ('big PRO') subjects, since all the clauses she produces in the data given above occur in finite contexts (i.e. in contexts where adults would use a finite clause). Note, however, that two-year-old children typically go through a stage which Wexler (1994) calls the **Optional Infinitives/OI** stage during which (in finite contexts) they sometimes produce finite clauses, and sometimes non-finite clauses (the relevant non-finite clauses typically containing an infinitive form like *go* or a participle like *going/gone*). Hence, an additional possibility to bear in mind is that some of Lucy's clauses may be non-finite and have non-finite ('big PRO') null subjects.

In relation to the sentences in 1–23, make the following assumptions. In 1 *doing* is a verb which has a null subject and the complement *what*; in 2 *want* is a verb which has a null subject and the complement *bye-byes*; in 3 *go* is a verb which has the subject *Mummy* and the complement *shops*; in 4 *have* is a verb which has the subject *me* and the complement *yoghurt*; in 5 *doing* is a verb which has the subject *Daddy*, and its complement is a null counterpart of *what*; in 6 *think* is a verb with a null subject and its complement is *Teddy sleeping* (with *Teddy* serving as the subject of the verb *sleeping*); in 7, *having* is a verb which has the subject *me* and the complement *what*; in 8 *no* is a negative particle which has the complement *me have fish* (assume that *no* is the kind of word which doesn't have a subject), and *have* is a verb which has the subject *me* and the complement *fish*; in 9 *gone* is a verb which has the subject *Daddy* and the complement *where*; in 10 *gone* is a verb which has a null subject and the complement *office*; in 11 *want* is a verb which has a null subject and the complement *bickies*; in 12 *have* is a verb which has the subject *Teddy* and the complement *what*; in 13 *going* is a verb which has a null subject and the complement *where*; in 14 *go* is a verb which has the subject *me* and the complement *shops*; in 15 *drinking* is a verb which has the subject *Daddy* and the complement *coffee*; in 16 *eating* is a verb which has the subject *Nana* and the complement *what*; in 17 *want* is a verb which has a null subject and the complement *choc'ate*; in 18 *gone* is a verb which has the subject *Dolly* and its complement is a null counterpart of *where*; in 19 *watch* is a verb which has a null subject and the complement *te'vision*; in 20 *have* is a verb which has the subject *me* and the complement *more*; 21 is a prepositional phrase in which the preposition *in* has the complement *kitchen* (assume that phrases don't have subjects); in 22 *play* is a verb which has the subject *me* and the complement *with Daddy* (and in turn *Daddy* is the complement of the preposition *with*); and in 23 *open* is a verb whose subject is null and whose complement is *door*.

Model answer for sentence 1

In *What doing?* the two-place predicate *doing* has an overt object *what* and a null subject of some kind. Since the object *what* does not occupy the normal postverbal position associated with objects in English (cf. the position of the object *something* in *Do something!*), *what* has clearly undergone wh-movement: this suggests that Lucy has correctly set the wh-parameter at the 'requires wh-movement' value appropriate for English. Because the object complement *what* has undergone wh-movement, we cannot tell (from this sentence) whether Lucy generally positions (unmoved) complements after their heads: in other words, this particular sentence provides us with no evidence of whether Lucy has correctly set the Head-Position Parameter or not (though other examples in the exercise do). Much more difficult to answer is the question of whether Lucy has correctly set the Null-Subject Parameter at the value appropriate to English, and hence (tacitly) 'knows' that finite clauses do not allow a null finite *pro* subject in English. At first sight, it might seem as if Lucy has wrongly analysed English as a null-subject language (and hence mis-set the Null-Subject Parameter), since *What doing?* has a null subject of some kind. But the crucial question here is: what kind of null subject does the verb *doing* have? It clearly cannot be an imperative null subject, since the sentence is interrogative in force, not imperative. Nor can it be a truncated null subject, since truncated subjects only occur in sentence-initial position (i.e. as the first word in a sentence), and *what* is the first word in the sentence in *What doing?* (since preposed wh-words occupy sentence-initial position in questions). This leaves two other possibilities. One is that the null subject in *What doing?* is the 'little *pro*' subject found in finite clauses in genuine null-subject languages like Italian: since the verb *doing* is non-finite, this would entail positing that the sentence *What doing?* contains a null (i.e. 'silent' or 'invisible') finite auxiliary (raising questions about why the auxiliary is null rather than overt); this in turn would mean that Lucy has indeed mis-set the Null-Subject Parameter (raising questions about how she comes to do so, and why she doesn't mis-set the other two parameters we are concerned with here). However, an alternative possibility is that the structure *What doing?* is a non-finite clause (like adult questions such as *Why worry?*) and has the kind of non-finite ('big PRO') null subject found in non-finite clauses in many languages (English included). If so (i.e. if *What doing* is a non-finite clause which has the structure *What PRO doing?*), there would be no evidence that Lucy has mis-set the Null-Subject Parameter – i.e. no evidence that she ever produces finite clauses with a 'little *pro*' subject. This in turn would mean that we can maintain the hypothesis put forward in the main text that children correctly set parameters at their appropriate value from the very earliest stages of the acquisition of syntax. The error Lucy makes in producing sentences like *What doing?* would be in not knowing that main clauses generally have to be finite in English, and that main clause questions generally have to contain a finite auxiliary.

Exercise 1.2

In the text, we noted that the Head-Position Parameter has a uniform head-first setting (in the sense that all heads precede their complements) in English, and a uniform head-last setting (in the sense that all heads follow their complements) in Korean. However, we also noted that there are languages in which *some* heads precede their complements (giving rise to head-first structures), and *others* follow them (giving rise to head-last structures). German is argued by some to be a language of this latter type, in which (e.g.) prepositions, determiners and complementisers canonically precede their complements, but (auxiliary and main) verbs canonically follow their complements. Discuss the extent to which German sentences like those in 1–5 below (kindly provided for me by Harald Clahsen) bear out this claim, and say which examples prove problematic and why.

1   Hans muss stolz auf seine Mutter sein
      Hans must proud of his   mother be
      'Hans must be proud of his mother'

2   Hans muss auf seine Mutter stolz sein
      Hans must of his   mother proud be
      'Hans must be proud of his mother'

3   Hans geht den Fluss entlang
      Hans goes the river along
      'Hans goes along the river'

4   Hans muss die Aufgaben lösen
      Hans must the exercises do
      'Hans must do the exercises'

5   Ich glaube dass Hans die Aufgaben lösen muss
      I   think   that Hans the exercises do   must
      'I think that Hans must do the exercises'

Likewise, in the text we claimed that the Wh-parameter has a uniform setting in that languages either do or don't systematically prepose wh-expressions. Discuss the potential problems posed for this claim by colloquial French interrogative structures such as those below:

6   Où   tu   vas?
      Where you go?
      'Where are you going?'

7   Tu   vas où?
      You go where?
      'Where are you going?'

8   Dis-moi où   tu vas
      Tell-me where you go
      'Tell me where you are going'

9   *Dis-moi tu   vas où
      Tell-me you go where
      (intended as synonymous with 8)

Helpful hints

In relation to the German sentences 1–5, make the following assumptions about their structure. In 1 and 2 *muss* is a finite (modal) verb, *Hans* is its subject and *stolz auf seine Mutter sein* is its complement; *sein* is an infinitive verb form and *stolz auf seine Mutter* is its complement; *stolz* is an adjective, and *auf seine Mutter* is its complement; *auf* is a preposition and *seine Mutter* is its complement; *seine* is a determiner, and *Mutter* is its complement. In 3 *geht* is a verb, *Hans* is its subject and *den Fluss entlang* is its complement; *entlang* is a preposition (or, more precisely, a **postposition**) and *den Fluss* is its complement; *den* is a determiner and *Fluss* is its complement. In 4 *muss* is a finite verb, *Hans* is its subject and *die Aufgaben lösen* is its complement; *lösen* is a non-finite verb in the infinitive form, and *die Aufgaben* is its complement; *die* is a determiner and *Aufgaben* is its complement. In 5 *glaube* is a finite verb, *ich* is its subject and *dass Hans die Aufgaben lösen muss* is its complement; *dass* is a complementiser (i.e. a complement-clause-introducing particle or conjunction) and *Hans die Aufgaben lösen muss* is its complement; *muss* is a finite verb, *Hans* is its subject, and *die Aufgaben lösen* is its complement; *lösen* is a non-finite verb in the infinitive form and *die Aufgaben* is its complement; *die* is a determiner and *Aufgaben* is its complement.

In relation to the examples in 1–5, identify all the prepositions, complementisers and determiners you can find in the sentences, and say whether (as claimed above) these precede their complements. Likewise, identify all the (auxiliary and main) verbs found in the sentences and say whether they do (or do not) follow their complements, as claimed above. Pay particular attention to heads which are exceptions to the relevant generalisations about head position. Assume that exceptional word order can be accounted for either in lexical terms (e.g. that the lexical entry for a particular preposition may say that it does not occupy the canonical head-first position found in typical prepositional phrases), or in structural terms (in that a particular kind of head may undergo a movement operation which moves it out of its canonical position). In relation to possible structural factors which mask the underlying word order in German, bear in mind that German is traditionally claimed to be a **verb-second/V2** language – i.e. a language in which a finite verb (= V) in a main clause is moved out of its canonical position into second position in the clause, e.g. into a position where it immediately follows a subject expression like *Hans* or *ich* 'I'. In addition, comment on the problems posed by determining the canonical setting of the Head-Position Parameter for adjectival phrases in German.

In relation to the French sentences 6–9, bear in mind that *Où tu vas* and *Tu vas où* are main clauses in 6 and 7 and complement clauses in 8 and 9 (in that they serve as the complement of the imperative verb *dis* 'tell' in 8 and 9). Is there an asymmetry between how wh-movement works in main clauses and in complement clauses? Does this suggest that it may be too simplistic to posit a Wh-Parameter under which wh-expressions either are or aren't systematically preposed? Why?

Model answer for sentence 1

In 1, the determiner *seine* 'his' precedes its complement *Mutter* 'mother', and the preposition *auf* 'of' precedes its complement *seine Mutter* 'his mother', in accordance with the suggested generalisation that determiners and prepositions in German show canonical head-first order and hence are typically positioned before their complements. The adjective *stolz* 'proud' also precedes its complement *auf seine Mutter* 'of his mother' in 1. By contrast, the verb *sein* 'be' follows its complement *stolz auf seine Mutter* 'proud of his mother'. One possible generalisation which this might suggest is the following:

(i)   In German, verbs are canonically positioned after their complements, but
             other heads are canonically positioned before their complements

However, an apparent exception to the claim made in (i) is posed by the fact that the finite verb
muss 'must' in the main clause precedes its own complement *stolz auf seine Mutter sein* 'proud of
his mother be'. This apparently exceptional word order is arguably attributable to the status of
German as a so-called **verb-second** language – i.e. a language which has a verb-fronting
operation which moves a finite verb in a main clause out of the canonical clause-final position
occupied by verbs (including by the verb *muss* in 5) into second position within the clause: as a
result of this movement operation, the verb *muss* comes to follow the main clause subject *Hans*.
(For a discussion of the structure of verb-second clauses in German, see Radford et al. 1999,
pp. 349–54 – though some of the material there may not be clear to you until you have read the
first six chapters in this book.)

2 Words

2.1 Overview

In this chapter, we look at the grammatical properties of words. We begin by looking at the categorial properties of words and at how we determine what grammatical category a given word belongs to (in a given use): in the course of our discussion we introduce some new categories which will not be familiar from traditional grammar. We go on to show that categorial information alone is not sufficient to describe the grammatical properties of words, ultimately concluding that the grammatical properties of words must be characterised in terms of sets of **grammatical features**.

2.2 Grammatical categories

In §1.2, we noted that words are assigned to grammatical categories in traditional grammar on the basis of their shared semantic, morphological and syntactic properties. The kind of semantic criteria (sometimes called 'notional' criteria) used to categorise words in traditional grammar are illustrated in much-simplified form below:

(1) (i) Verbs denote actions (*go, destroy, buy, eat* etc.)
  (ii) Nouns denote entities (*car, cat, hill, John* etc.)
  (iii) Adjectives denote states (*ill, happy, rich* etc.)
  (iv) Adverbs denote manner (*badly, slowly, painfully, cynically* etc.)
  (v) Prepositions denote location (*under, over, outside, in, on* etc.)

However, semantically based criteria for identifying categories must be used with care: for example, *assassination* denotes an action but is a noun, not a verb; *illness* denotes a state but is a noun, not an adjective; in *fast food*, the word *fast* denotes the manner in which the food is prepared but is an adjective, not an adverb; and *Cambridge* denotes a location but is a noun, not a preposition.

The **morphological** criteria for categorising words concern their **inflectional** and **derivational** properties. Inflectional properties relate to different forms of the same word (e.g. the plural form of a noun like *cat* is formed by adding the plural inflection -s to give the form *cats*); derivational properties relate to the processes by which a word can be used to form a different kind of word by the addition of an **affix** of some kind (e.g. by adding the suffix -*ness* to the adjective *sad* we can form the noun *sadness*). Although English has a highly impoverished system of inflectional morphology, there are nonetheless two major categories of word which have distinctive inflectional properties – namely **nouns** and **verbs**. We can identify the class of nouns in terms of the fact that they generally inflect for **number**, and thus have distinct **singular** and **plural** forms – cf. pairs such as *dog/dogs, man/men, ox/oxen* etc. Accordingly, we can differentiate a noun like *fool* from an adjective like *foolish* by virtue of the fact that only (regular, countable) nouns like *fool* – not adjectives like *foolish* – can carry the noun plural inflection -*s*:

(2)   They are *fools* [noun]/**foolishes* [adjective]

There are several complications which should be pointed out, however. One is the existence of irregular nouns like *sheep* which are invariable and hence have a common singular/plural form (cf. *one sheep, two sheep*). A second is that some nouns are intrinsically singular (and so have no plural form) by virtue of their meaning: only those nouns (called **count/countable nouns**) which denote entities which can be counted have a plural form (e.g. *chair* – cf. *one chair, two chairs*); some nouns denote an uncountable mass and for this reason are called **mass/uncountable/non-count nouns**, and so cannot be pluralised (e.g. *furniture* – hence the ungrammaticality of **one furniture,* *two furnitures). A third is that some nouns (like *scissors* and *trousers*) have a plural form but no countable singular form. A fourth complication is posed by noun expressions which contain more than one noun; only the **head** noun in such expressions can be pluralised, not any preceding noun used as a **modifier** of the head noun: thus, in expressions such as *car doors, policy decisions, skate boards, horse boxes, trouser presses, coat hangers* etc. the second noun is the head and can be pluralised, whereas the first noun is a modifier and so cannot be pluralised.

In much the same way, we can identify **verbs** by their inflectional morphology in English. In addition to their uninflected **base** form (= the citation form under which they are listed in dictionaries), verbs typically have up to four different inflected forms, formed by adding one of four inflections to the appropriate stem form: the relevant inflections are the perfect/passive participle suffix -*n*, the past-tense suffix -*d*, the third-person-singular present-tense suffix -*s*, and the progressive participle/gerund suffix -*ing*. Like most morphological criteria, however, this one is complicated by the irregular and impoverished nature of English inflectional morphology; for example, many verbs have irregular past or perfect forms, and in some cases either or both of these forms may not in fact be distinct from the (uninflected) base form, so that a single form may serve two or three functions (thereby **neutralising** or **syncretising** the relevant distinctions), as the table (3) below illustrates:

(3) **Table of verb forms**

Base	Perfect	Past	Present	Progressive
show	shown	showed	shows	showing
go	gone	went	goes	going
speak	spoken	spoke	speaks	speaking
see	seen	saw	sees	seeing
come		came	comes	coming
wait	waited		waits	waiting
meet	met		meets	meeting
cut			cuts	cutting

(The largest class of verbs in English are regular verbs which have the morpho-logical characteristics of *wait*, and so have past, perfect and passive forms ending in the suffix *-d*.) The picture becomes even more complicated if we take into account the verb *be*, which has eight distinct forms (viz. the base form *be*, the perfect form *been*, the progressive form *being*, the past forms *was/were*, and the present forms *am/are/is*). The most regular verb suffix in English is *-ing*, which can be attached to the base form of almost any verb (though a handful of defective verbs like *beware* are exceptions).

The obvious implication of our discussion of nouns and verbs here is that it would not be possible to provide a systematic account of English inflectional mor-phology unless we were to posit that words belong to grammatical categories, and that a specific type of inflection attaches only to a specific category of word. The same is also true if we wish to provide an adequate account of **derivational morphology** in English (i.e. the processes by which words are derived from other words): this is because particular derivational affixes can only be attached to words belonging to particular categories. For example, the negative prefixes *un-* and *in-* can be attached to adjectives to form a corresponding negative adjective (as in pairs such as *happy/unhappy* and *flexible/inflexible*) but not to nouns (so that a noun like *fear* has no negative counterpart **unfear*), nor to prepositions (so that a preposition like *inside* has no negative antonym **uninside*). Similarly, the adverbialising (i.e. adverb-forming) suffix *-ly* in English can be attached only to adjectives (giving rise to adjective/adverb pairs such as *sad/sadly*) and cannot be attached to a noun like *computer*, or to a verb like *accept*, or to a preposi-tion like *with*. Likewise, the nominalising (i.e. noun-forming) suffix *-ness* can be attached only to adjective stems (so giving rise to adjective/noun pairs such as *coarse/coarseness*), not to nouns, verbs or prepositions. (Hence we don't find *-ness* derivatives for a noun like *boy*, or a verb like *resemble*, or a preposition like *down*.) In much the same way, the comparative suffix *-er* can be attached to adjectives (e.g. *tall/taller*) and some adverbs (e.g. *soon/sooner*) but not to other types of word (e.g. *woman/*womanner*); and the superlative suffix *-est* can attach to adjectives (e.g. *tall/tallest*) but not other types of word (e.g. *down/*downest*; *donkey/*donkiest*, *enjoy/*enjoyest*). There is no point in multiplying examples here: it is clear that derivational affixes have categorial properties, and any account of derivational morphology will clearly have to recognise this fact (see e.g. Aronoff 1976 and Fabb 1988).

As we noted earlier, there is also *syntactic* evidence for assigning words to categories: this essentially relates to the fact that different categories of words have different **distributions** (i.e. occupy a different range of positions within phrases or sentences). For example, if we want to complete the four-word sentence in (4) below by inserting a single word at the end of the sentence in the — position:

(4)   They have no —

we can use an (appropriate kind of) noun, but not a verb, preposition, adjective, or adverb, as we see from:

(5) (a)   They have no *car/conscience/friends/ideas* [nouns]
    (b)   *They have no *went* [verb]/*for* [preposition]/*older* [adjective]/*conscientiously* [adverb]

So, using the relevant syntactic criterion, we can define the class of nouns as the set of words which can terminate a sentence in the position marked — in (4).

Using the same type of syntactic evidence, we could argue that only a verb (in its infinitive/base form) can occur in the position marked — in (6) below to form a complete (non-elliptical) sentence:

(6)   They/it can —

Support for this claim comes from the contrasts in (7) below:

(7) (a)   They can *stay/leave/hide/die/starve/cry* [verb]
    (b)   *They can *gorgeous* [adjective]/*happily* [adverb]/*down* [preposition]/*door* [noun]

And the only category of word which can occur after *very* (in the sense of *extremely*) is an adjective or adverb, as we see from (8) below:

(8) (a)   He is *very* **slow** [*very*+**adjective**]
    (b)   He walks *very* **slowly** [*very*+**adverb**]
    (c)   *Very **fools** waste time [*very*+**noun**]
    (d)   *He *very* **adores** her [*very*+**verb**]
    (e)   *It happened *very* **after** the party [*very*+**preposition**]

(But note that *very* can only be used to modify adjectives/adverbs which by virtue of their meaning are **gradable** and so can be qualified by words like *very/rather/somewhat* etc; adjectives/adverbs which denote an absolute state are **ungradable** by virtue of their meaning, and so cannot be qualified in the same way – hence the oddity of *!Fifteen students were very present, and five were very absent*, where ! marks semantic anomaly.)

Moreover, we can differentiate adjectives from adverbs in syntactic terms. For example, only adverbs can be used to end sentences such as *He treats her —, She behaved —, He worded the statement —*:

(9) (a)   He treats her *badly* [adverb]/*kind* [adjective]/*shame* [noun]/*under* [preposition]
   (b)   She behaved *abominably* [adverb]/*appalling* [adjective]/*disgrace* [noun]/*down* [preposition]
   (c)   He worded the statement *carefully* [adverb]/*good* [adjective]/*tact* [noun]/*in* [preposition]

And since adjectives (but not adverbs) can serve as the complement of the verb *be* (i.e. can be used after *be*), we can delimit the class of (gradable) adjectives uniquely by saying that only adjectives can be used to complete a four-word sentence of the form *They are very —*:

(10) (a)   They are very *tall/pretty/kind/nice* [adjective]
   (b)   *They are very *slowly* [adverb]/*gentlemen* [noun]/*astonish* [verb]/*outside* [preposition]

Another way of differentiating between an adjective like *real* and an adverb like *really* is that adjectives are used to modify nouns, whereas adverbs are used to modify other types of expression:

(11) (a)   There is a *real* **crisis** [*real*+**noun**]
   (b)   He is *really* **nice** [*really*+**adjective**]
   (c)   He walks *really* **slowly** [*really*+**adverb**]
   (d)   He is *really* **down** [*really*+**preposition**]
   (e)   He must *really* **squirm** [*really*+**verb**]

Adjectives used to modify a following noun (like *real* in *There is a real crisis*) are traditionally said to be **attributive** in function, whereas those which do not modify a following noun (like *real* in *The crisis is real*) are said to be **predicative** in function.

As for the syntactic properties of prepositions, they alone can be intensified by *right* in the sense of 'completely', or by *straight* in the sense of 'directly':

(12) (a)   Go *right* **up** the ladder
   (b)   He went *right* **inside**
   (c)   He walked *straight* **into** a wall
   (d)   He fell *straight* **down**

By contrast, other categories cannot be intensified by *right/straight* (in Standard English):

(13) (a)   *He *right/straight* **despaired** [*right/straight*+**verb**]
   (b)   *She is *right/straight* **pretty** [*right/straight*+**adjective**]
   (c)   *She looked at him *right/straight* **strangely** [*right/straight*+**adverb**]
   (d)   *They are *right/straight* **fools** [*right/straight*+**noun**]

It should be noted, however, that since *right/straight* serve to intensify the meaning of a preposition, they can only be combined with those (uses of) prepositions which express the kind of meaning which can be intensified in the appropriate way (so that *He made right/straight for the exit* is OK, but *He bought a present right/straight for Mary* is not).

A further syntactic property of some prepositions (namely those which take a following noun or pronoun expression as their complement – traditionally called **transitive** prepositions) which they share in common with (transitive) verbs is the fact that they permit an immediately following **accusative** pronoun as their complement (i.e. a pronoun in its accusative form, like *me/us/him/them*):

(14) (a) She was *against* **him** [*transitive preposition*+**accusative pronoun**]
  (b) She was *watching* **him** [*transitive verb*+**accusative pronoun**]
  (c) *She is *fond* **him** [*adjective*+**accusative pronoun**]
  (d) *She works *independently* **him** [*adverb*+**accusative pronoun**]
  (e) *She showed me a *photo* **him** [*noun*+**accusative pronoun**]

Even though a preposition like *with* does not express the kind of meaning which allows it to be intensified by *right* or *straight*, we know it is a (transitive) preposition because it is invariable (so not e.g. a verb) and permits an accusative pronoun as its complement, e.g. in sentences such as *He argued with me/us/him/them*. (For obvious reasons, this test can't be applied to prepositions used intransitively without any complement, like those in 12b,d above.)

2.3   Categorising words

Given that different categories have different morphological and syntactic properties, it follows that we can use the morphological and syntactic properties of a word to determine its categorisation (i.e. what category it belongs to). The morphological properties of a given word provide an initial rough guide to its categorial status: in order to determine the categorial status of an individual word, we can ask whether it has the inflectional and derivational properties of a particular category of word. For example, we can tell that *happy* is an adjective by virtue of the fact that it has the derivational properties of typical adjectives: it can take the negative prefix *un-* (giving rise to the negative adjective *unhappy*), the comparative/superlative suffixes *-er/-est* (giving rise to the forms *happier/happiest*), the adverbialising suffix *-ly* (giving rise to the adverb *happily*) and the nominalising suffix *-ness* (giving rise to the noun *happiness*).

However, we cannot always rely entirely on morphological clues, owing to the fact that morphology is sometimes irregular, sometimes subject to idiosyncratic restrictions and sometimes of limited productivity. For example, although regular adverbs (like *quickly, slowly, painfully* etc.) generally end in the derivational suffix *-ly*, this is not true of irregular adverbs like *fast* (e.g. in *He walks fast*); moreover, when they have the comparative suffix *-er* added to them, regular adverbs lose their *-ly* suffix because English is a monosuffixal language (in the sense of Aronoff and Fuhrhop 2002), so that the comparative form of the adverb *quickly* is *quicker* not **quicklier*. What all of this means is that a word belonging to a given class may have only *some* of the relevant morphological properties, or even (in the case of a completely irregular item) *none* of them.

For example, although the adjective *fat* has comparative/superlative forms in
-*er*/-*est* (cf. *fat*/*fatter*/*fattest*), it has no negative *un*- counterpart (cf. **unfat*) and
no adverb counterpart in -*ly* (cf. **fatly*). Even more exceptional is the adjective
little, which has no negative *un*- derivative (cf. **unlittle*), no adverb -*ly* derivative (cf. **littlely*/**littly*), no noun derivative in -*ness* (at least in my variety of
English – though *littleness* does appear in the *Oxford English Dictionary*), and no
-*er*/-*est* derivatives (the forms **littler*/**littlest* are likewise not grammatical in my
variety).

What makes morphological evidence even more problematic is the fact that
many morphemes may have more than one use. For example, -*n*/-*d* and -*ing* are
inflections which attach to verbs to give perfect or progressive forms (traditionally referred to as **participles**). However, certain -*n*/-*d* and -*ing* forms seem to
function as adjectives, suggesting that -*ing* and -*n*/-*d* can also serve as adjec-
tivalising (i.e. adjective-forming) morphemes. So, although a word like *interesting* can function as a verb (in sentences like *Her charismatic teacher was
gradually interesting her in syntax*), it can also function as an adjective (used
attributively in structures like *This is an interesting book*, and predicatively in
structures like *This book is very interesting*). In its use as an adjective, the word
interesting has the negative derivative *uninteresting* (as in *It was a rather uninteresting play*) and the -*ly* adverb derivative *interestingly* (though, like many other
adjectives, it has no noun derivative in -*ness*, and no comparative or superlative
derivatives in -*er*/-*est*). Similarly, although -*n*/-*d* can serve as a perfect participle inflection (in structures like *We hadn't known/expected that he would quit*),
it should be noted that many words ending in -*n*/-*d* can also function as adjectives. For example, the word *known* in an expression such as *a known criminal*
seems to function as an (attributive) adjective, and in this adjectival use it has a
negative *un*- counterpart (as in expressions like *the tomb of the unknown war-
rior*). Similarly, the form *expected* functions as a perfect participle verb form
in structures like *We hadn't expected him to complain*, but seems to function
as an (attributive) adjective in structures such as *He gave the expected reply*;
in its adjectival (though not in its verbal) use, it has a negative *un*- derivative,
and the resultant negative adjective *unexpected* in turn has the noun derivative
unexpectedness.

So, given the potential problems which arise with morphological criteria, it
is unwise to rely solely on morphological evidence in determining categorial
status: rather, we should use morphological criteria in conjunction with syntactic
criteria (i.e. criteria relating to the range of positions that words can occupy within
phrases and sentences). One syntactic test which can be used to determine the
category that a particular word belongs to is that of **substitution** – i.e. seeing
whether (in a given sentence) the word in question can be substituted by a regular
noun, verb, preposition, adjective, or adverb etc. We can use the substitution
technique to differentiate between comparative adjectives and adverbs ending
in -*er*, since they have identical forms. For example, in the case of sentences
like:

(15) (a)   He is *better* at French than you

   (b)   He speaks French *better* than you

we find that *better* can be replaced by a *more+adjective* expression like *more fluent* in (15a) but not (15b), and conversely that *better* can be replaced by a *more+adverb* expression like *more fluently* in (15b) but not in (15a):

(16) (a)   He is *more fluent/*more fluently* at French than you

   (b)   He speaks French *more fluently/*more fluent* than you

Thus, the substitution test provides us with syntactic evidence that *better* is an adjective in (15a), but an adverb in (15b).

   The overall conclusion to be drawn from our discussion is that morphological evidence may sometimes be inconclusive, and has to be checked against syntactic evidence. A useful syntactic test which can be employed is that of **substitution**: for example, if a morphologically indeterminate word can be substituted by a regular noun wherever it occurs, then the relevant word has the same categorial status as the substitute word which can replace it, and so is a noun.

2.4   Functional categories

   Thus far, we have looked at the five major grammatical categories of English (i.e. the five categories with the largest membership), viz. **noun, verb, preposition, adjective** and **adverb**. For typographical convenience, it is standard practice to use capital-letter abbreviations for categories, thus N for noun, V for verb, P for preposition, A for adjective and ADV for adverb. The words which belong to these five categories are traditionally said to be **contentives** (or **content words**), in that they have substantive descriptive content. However, in addition to content words languages also contain **functors** (or **function words**) – i.e. words which serve primarily to carry information about the grammatical function of particular types of expression within the sentence (e.g. information about grammatical properties such as **person, number, gender, case** etc.). The differences between contentives and functors can be illustrated by comparing a (contentive) noun like *car* with a (functional) pronoun like *they*. A noun like *car* has obvious descriptive content in that it denotes an object which typically has four wheels and an engine, and it would be easy enough to draw a picture of a typical *car*; by contrast, a pronoun such as *they* has no descriptive content (e.g. you can't draw a picture of *they*), but rather is a functor which (as we shall see shortly) simply encodes a set of grammatical (more specifically, person, number and case) properties in that it is a third-person-plural nominative pronoun.

   One test of whether words have descriptive content is to see whether they have **antonyms** (i.e. opposites): if a word has an antonym, it is a contentive (though if it has no antonym, you can't be sure whether it is a functor or a contentive). For example, a noun/N such as *loss* has the antonym *gain*; a verb/V such as *rise* has the antonym *fall*; an adjective/A such as *tall* has the antonym *short*; an adverb/ADV such as *early* (as in *He arrived early*) has the antonym *late*; and a preposition/P such as *inside* has the antonym *outside*. This reflects the fact that nouns, verbs, adjectives, adverbs and prepositions typically have substantive descriptive content, and so are contentives. By contrast, a particle like infinitival *to*, or an auxiliary like *do* (e.g. '*Do* you want *to* smoke?'), or a determiner like *the*, or a pronoun like *they*, or a complementiser (i.e. complement-clause-introducing particle) like *that* (as used in a sentence like 'I said *that* I was tired') have no obvious antonyms, and thus can be said to lack descriptive content, and so to be functors. Using rather different (but equivalent) terminology, we can say that contentives have substantive lexical content (i.e. idiosyncratic descriptive content which varies from one lexical item/word to another), whereas functors have functional content. We can then conclude that nouns, verbs, adjectives, adverbs and prepositions are **lexical** or **substantive categories** (because the words belonging to these categories have substantive lexical/descriptive content) whereas particles, auxiliaries, determiners, pronouns and complementisers are **functional categories** (because words belonging to these categories have an essentially grammatical function). In the sections that follow, we take a closer look at the main functional categories found in English.

2.5   Determiners and quantifiers

The first type of functional category which we shall deal with is the category of determiner (abbreviated to D, or sometimes DET). Items such as those bold-printed in (17) below (as used there) are traditionally said to be (referential) determiners (because they determine the referential properties of the italicised noun expression which follows them):

(17) (a)   **The** *village store* is closed
  (b)   **This** *appalling behaviour* has got to stop
  (c)   **That** *dog of yours* is crazy

Referential determiners are used to introduce referring expressions: an expression like *the car* in a sentence such as *Shall we take the car?* is a referring expression in the sense that it is typically used to refer to a specific car which is assumed to be familiar to the hearer/addressee.

A related class of words are those which belong to the category **quantifier** (abbreviated to Q), and this is traditionally said to include items like those bold-printed below:

(18) (a)   **Most** *good comedians* tell **some** *bad jokes*
  (b)   **Many** *students* have **no** *money*
  (c)   **Every** *true Scotsman* hates **all** *Englishmen*
  (d)   **Each** *exercise* contains **several** *examples*

Such items are termed quantifiers because they serve to quantify the italicised noun expression which follows them. Since determiners and quantifiers are positioned in front of nouns (cf. *the boys* and *many boys*), and adjectives can similarly be positioned in front of nouns (cf. *tall boys*), an obvious question to ask at this point is why we couldn't just say that the determiners/quantifiers in (17) and (18) have the categorial status of adjectives. The answer is that any attempt to analyse determiners or quantifiers as adjectives in English runs up against a number of serious descriptive problems. Let's see why.

One reason for not subsuming determiners/quantifiers within the category of adjectives is that they are syntactically distinct from adjectives in a variety of ways. For example, adjectives can be iteratively (i.e. repeatedly) **stacked** in front of a noun they modify, in the sense that you can go on putting more and more adjectives in front of a given noun (as in *handsome strangers, dark handsome strangers, tall dark handsome strangers, sensitive tall handsome strangers* etc.). By contrast, neither determiners nor quantifiers can be stacked in this way (so that although we can have a quantifier+determiner+noun expression like *both the twins*, we cannot have a multiple determiner expression like **the these books* or a multiple quantifier expression such as **all both twins*). Moreover, determiners, quantifiers and adjectives can be used together to modify a noun, but when they do so, any determiner or quantifier modifying the noun has to precede any adjective(s) modifying the noun:

(19) (a)   **the** *same old* excuses [**determiner**+*adjective*+*adjective*+noun]
   (b)   **same* **the** *old* excuses [*adjective*+**determiner**+*adjective*+noun]
   (c)   **same old* **the** excuses [*adjective*+*adjective*+**determiner**+noun]

Thus, determiners and quantifiers seem to have a different distribution (and hence to be categorially distinct) from adjectives.

A further difference between determiners/quantifiers and adjectives can be illustrated in relation to what speaker B can – and cannot – reply in the following dialogue:

(20)   SPEAKER A: What are you looking for?
       SPEAKER B: **Chair/*Comfortable* chair/*A* chair/*Another* chair/*The* chair/*That* chair

As noted earlier, nouns like *chair* have the property that they are countable (in the sense that we can say *one chair, two chairs* etc.), and in this respect they differ from mass nouns like *furniture* which are uncountable (hence we can't say **one furniture, *two furnitures* etc). We see from (20) that a singular count noun like *chair* cannot stand on its own as a complete noun expression, nor indeed can it function as such even if modified by an adjective like *comfortable*; rather, a singular count noun requires a modifying determiner or quantifier like *a/another/the/that* etc. This provides us with clear evidence that determiners and quantifiers in English have a different categorial status from adjectives.

Indeed, a more general property which differentiates determiners/quantifiers from adjectives is that determiners/quantifiers tend to be restricted to modifying nouns which have specific number (or countability) properties. For example, *a* modifies a singular count noun, *much* modifies a (singular) mass noun, *several* modifies a plural count noun, *more* modifies either a plural count or a (singular) mass noun:

(21) (a)   Can you pass me **a** *chair/*****a** *chairs/*****a** *furniture?*
   (b)   He doesn't have **much** *furniture/*****much** *chair/*****much** *chairs* of his own
   (c)   He bought **several** *chairs/*****several** *chair/*****several** *furniture* in the sale
   (d)   Do we need **more** *furniture/****more** *chairs/*****more** *chair?*

By contrast, typical adjectives like *nice, simple, comfortable, modern* etc. can generally be used to modify all three types of noun:

(22) (a)   We need a **nice, simple, comfortable, modern** *chair*
   (b)   We need some **nice, simple, comfortable, modern** *chairs*
   (c)   We need some **nice, simple, comfortable, modern** *furniture*

(It should be noted, however, that a determiner like *the* can also be used to modify singular/plural count and non-count nouns alike.)

It seems reasonable to suppose that determiners and quantifiers are functional categories whereas adjectives are a lexical/substantive category. After all, there is an obvious sense in which adjectives (e.g. *thoughtful*) have descriptive content but determiners and quantifiers do not – as we can illustrate in terms of the following contrast (*?* and *!* are used to denote increasing degrees of semantic/pragmatic anomaly):

(23) (a)   a **thoughtful** *friend/?cat/??fish/?!pan/!problem*
   (b)   **a/another/every/the/this** *friend/cat/fish/pan/problem*

As (23a) illustrates, an adjective like *thoughtful* can only be used to modify certain types of noun; this is because its descriptive content is such that it is only compatible with (e.g.) an expression denoting a rational (mind-possessing) entity. By contrast, determiners/quantifiers like those bold-printed in (23b) lack specific descriptive content, and hence can be used to modify any semantic class of noun (the only restrictions being grammatical in nature – e.g. *a(n)/another* can only be used to modify a singular count noun expression). Thus, it seems appropriate to conclude that determiners and quantifiers are functional categories, and adjectives a lexical category.

Some linguists (e.g. Lyons 1999 and Adger 2003) treat quantifiers as a subtype of determiner and hence assign them to the category D: one possibility along these lines is to suppose that items like *the/this/that* are **definite determiners**, and those like *a/some/many* are **indefinite determiners** (and such a categorisation could be said to be implicit in the traditional claim that *the* is a 'definite article' and *a* an 'indefinite article'). However, the fact that a determiner like *the* can combine with a quantifier like *all/every* in a sentence like:

(24)   *All* **the** servile courtiers pandered to **the** *every* witless whim of King Kostas of Kostalotte

provides some syntactic evidence that the two have different distributions and hence may belong to different categories. Moreover, quantifiers and determiners exhibit different syntactic behaviour in respect of questions such as:

(25) (a)   Who didn't he want [*any* pictures of]?
     (b)   ??Who didn't he want [*the* pictures of]?

In both cases, *who* is the complement of the word *of* and is moved to the front of the sentence from its original position after *of*. But whereas fronting *who* when it is the complement of the quantifier expression *any pictures of* results in a grammatical sentence, fronting *who* when it is the complement of a determiner expression like *the pictures of* generally leads to a sentence of rather more questionable grammaticality (the relevant phenomenon being known as the **definiteness effect**. It should be noted, however, that there is quite a bit of variation between speakers as to how good or bad they judge sentences like (25b) to be). So, sentences like (24) and (25) could be said to provide evidence that quantifiers and determiners are syntactically distinct and so belong to different categories (though there is no general agreement on this).

2.6   Pronouns

Traditional grammars posit a category of **pronoun** (which we can abbreviate as **PRN**) to denote a class of words which are said to 'stand in place of' (the meaning of the prefix *pro-*) or 'refer back to' noun expressions. However, there are reasons to think that there are a number of different types of pronoun found in English and other languages (see Déchaine and Wiltschko 2002). One such type is represented by the word *one* in the use illustrated below:

(26) (a)   John has a red **car** and Jim has a blue *one*
     (b)   I'll take the green **apples** if you haven't got any red *ones*

From a grammatical perspective, *one* behaves like a regular count noun here in that it has the *s*-plural form *ones* and occurs in a position (after an adjective like *blue/red*) in which a count noun could occur. However, it is a *pronoun* in the sense that it has no descriptive content of its own, but rather takes its descriptive content from its antecedent (e.g. *one* in (26a) refers back to the noun *car* and so *one* is interpreted as meaning 'car'). Let's refer to this kind of pronoun as an **N-pronoun** (or pronominal noun).

By contrast, in the examples in (27) below, the bold-printed pronoun seems to serve as a pronominal quantifier. In the first (italicised) occurrence in each pair of examples, it is a **prenominal** (i.e. noun-preceding) quantifier which modifies a following noun expression (viz. *guests/miners/protesters/son/cigarettes/bananas*); in the second (bold-printed) occurrence it has no noun expression following it and so functions as a **pronominal** quantifier:

(27) (a)   *All guests* are welcome/**All** are welcome
(b)   *Many miners* died in the accident/**Many** died in the accident
(c)   *Several protesters* were arrested/**Several** were arrested
(d)   *Each son* was envious of the other/**Each** was envious of the other
(e)   I don't have *any cigarettes*/I don't have **any**
(f)   We have *no bananas*/We have **none**

We might therefore refer to pronouns like those bold-printed in (27) as **Q-pronouns** (or pronominal quantifiers). If (as will be suggested in chapter 6) question words like *which?/what?* in expressions like *which books?/what idea?* are interrogative quantifiers, it follows that interrogative pronouns like those italicised in the examples below:

(28) (a)   *What* have you been doing?
(b)   *Which* did you choose?
(c)   *Who* is she talking to?

are also Q-pronouns.
    A third type of pronoun are those bold-printed in the examples below:

(29) (a)   I prefer *this tie*/I prefer **this**
(b)   I haven't read *that book*/I haven't read **that**
(c)   I don't particularly like *these hats*/I don't particularly like **these**
(d)   Have you already paid for *those items*/Have you already paid for **those**?

Since the relevant words can also serve (in the italicised use) as prenominal determiners which modify a following noun, we can refer to them as **D-pronouns** (i.e. as pronominal determiners).
    A further type of pronoun posited in traditional grammar are so-called **personal pronouns** like *I/me/we/us/you/he/him/she/her/it/they/them*. These are called personal pronouns not because they denote people (the pronoun *it* is not normally used to denote a person), but rather because they encode the grammatical property of **person**. In the relevant technical sense, *I/me/my/we/us/our* are said to be **first-person pronouns**, in that they are expressions whose reference includes the person/s speaking; *you/your* are **second-person pronouns**, in that their reference includes the addressee/s (viz. the person/s being spoken to), but excludes the speaker/s; *he/him/his/she/her/it/its/they/them/their* are **third-person pronouns** in the sense that they refer to entities other than the speaker/s and addressee/s. Personal pronouns differ morphologically from nouns and other pronouns in modern English in that they generally have (partially) distinct **nominative**, **accusative** and **genitive** case forms, whereas nouns have a common nominative/accusative form and a distinct genitive *'s* form – as we see from the contrasts below:

(30) (a)   *John* snores/**He** snores
(b)   Find *John*!/Find **him**!
(c)   Look at *John's* trousers!/Look at **his** trousers!

Personal pronouns like *he/him/his* and nouns like *John/John's* change their morphological form according to the position which they occupy within the sentence, so that the nominative forms *he/John* are required as the subject of a **finite** verb like *snores*, whereas the accusative forms *him/John* are required when used as the complement of a **transitive** verb like *find* (or when used as the complement of a transitive preposition), and the genitive forms *his/John's* are required (inter alia) when used to express possession: these variations reflect different **case forms** of the relevant items.

Personal pronouns are **functors** by virtue of lacking descriptive content: whereas a noun like *dogs* denotes a specific type of animal, a personal pronoun like *they* denotes no specific type of entity, but has to have its reference determined from the linguistic or non-linguistic context. Personal pronouns encode the grammatical properties of (first, second or third) **person**, (singular or plural) **number**, (masculine, feminine or neuter/inanimate) **gender** and (nominative, accusative or genitive) **case**, as shown in the table in (31) below:

(31)   **Table of personal pronoun forms**

Person	Number	Gender	Nominative	Accusative	Genitive
1	SG	M/F	*I*	*me*	*my/mine*
1	PL	M/F	*we*	*us*	*our/ours*
2	SG/PL	M/F	*you*	*you*	*your/yours*
3	SG	M	*he*	*him*	*his*
3	SG	F	*she*	*her*	*her/hers*
3	SG	N	*it*	*it*	*its*
3	PL	M/F/N	*they*	*them*	*their/theirs*

(SG = singular; PL = plural; M = masculine; F = feminine; N = neuter. Note that some genitive pronouns have separate **weak** and **strong** forms, the weak form being used **prenominally** to modify a following noun expression – as in 'Take *my car*' – and the strong form being used **pronominally** – as in 'Take *mine*'.) On the nature of gender features in English, see Namai (2000).

But what grammatical category do personal pronouns belong to? Studies by Postal (1966), Abney (1987), Longobardi (1994) and Lyons (1999) suggest that they are D-pronouns. This assumption would provide us with a unitary analysis of the syntax of the bold-printed items in the bracketed expressions in sentences such as (32a,b) below:

(32) (a)   [**We** *republicans*] don't trust [**you** democrats]
       (b)   [**We**] don't trust [**you**]

Since *we* and *you* in (32a) modify the nouns *republicans/democrats* and since determiners like *the* are typically used to modify nouns, it seems reasonable to suppose that *we/you* function as prenominal determiners in (32a). But if this is so, it is plausible to suppose that *we* and *you* also have the categorial status of determiners (i.e. D-pronouns) in sentences like (32b). It would then follow that *we/you* have the categorial status of determiners in both (32a) and (32b), but differ in that they are used *prenominally* (i.e. with a following noun expression) in (32a), but *pronominally* (i.e. without any following noun expression) in (32b). Note, however, that third-person pronouns like *he/she/it/they* are typically used only pronominally – hence the ungrammaticality of expressions such as *they* *boys* in standard varieties of English (though this is grammatical in some non-standard varieties of English – e.g. that spoken in Bristol in South-West England). Whether or not such items are used prenominally, pronominally or in both ways is a **lexical** property of particular items (i.e. an idiosyncratic property of individual words).

Although the D-pronoun analysis has become the 'standard' analysis of personal pronouns over the past three decades, it is not entirely without posing problems. For example, a typical D-pronoun like *these/those* can be premodified by the universal quantifier *all*, but a personal pronoun like *they* cannot:

(33) (a)   *All* **these** are broken
     (b)   *All* **those** are broken
     (c)   **All* **they** are broken

Such a contrast is unexpected if personal pronouns like *they* are D-pronouns like *those/these*, and clearly raises questions about the true status of personal pronouns (an issue which we leave open here).

Because a number of aspects of the syntax of pronouns remain to be clarified and because the category **pronoun** is familiar from centuries of grammatical tradition, the label **PRN/pronoun** will be used throughout the rest of this book to designate pronouns. It should, however, be borne in mind that there are a number of different types of pronoun (including N-pronouns, Q-pronouns and D-pronouns), so that the term **pronoun** does not designate a unitary category. Some linguists prefer the alternative term **proform** (so that, for example, when used pronominally, *one* could be described as an **N-proform** or **pro-N**).

2.7   Auxiliaries

Having looked at the nominal functional category **pronoun**, we now turn to look at the verbal functional category **auxiliary**. Traditional grammarians use this term to denote a special class of items which once functioned simply as verbs, but in the course of the evolution of the English language have become sufficiently distinct from main verbs that they are now regarded as belonging to a different category of **auxiliary** (conventionally abbreviated to **AUX**).

Auxiliaries differ from main verbs in a number of ways. Whereas a typical main verb like *want* may take a range of different types of complement (e.g. an infinitival *to*-complement as in *I want [(you) to go home]*, or a noun expression as in *I want* [*lots of money*]), by contrast auxiliaries typically allow only a verb expression as their complement, and have the semantic function of marking grammatical properties associated with the relevant verb, such as **tense, aspect, voice**, or **mood**. The items italicised in (34) below (in the use illustrated there) are traditionally categorised as auxiliaries taking a [bracketed] complement containing a bold-printed non-finite verb:

(34) (a)   He *has/had* [**gone**]
      (b)   She *is/was* [**staying** at home]
      (c)   They *are/were* [**taken** away for questioning]
      (d)   He really *does/did* [**say** a lot]
      (e)   You *can/could* [**help** us]
      (f)   They *may/might* [**come** back]
      (g)   He *will/would* [**get** upset]
      (h)   I *shall/should* [**return**]
      (i)   You *must* [**finish** your assignment]
      (j)   You *ought* [to **apologise**]

In the uses illustrated here, *have/be* in (34a,b) are (perfect/progressive) **aspect** auxiliaries, *be* in (34c) is a (passive) **voice** auxiliary, *do* in (34d) a (present/past) **tense** auxiliary, and *can/could/may/might/will/would/shall/should/must/ought* in (34e–j) **modal** auxiliaries. As will be apparent, *ought* differs from other modal auxiliaries like *should* which take an infinitive complement in requiring use of infinitival *to*.

There are clear syntactic differences between auxiliaries and verbs. For example (as we saw in §1.5), auxiliaries can undergo **inversion** (and thereby be moved into pre-subject position) in questions such as (35) below, where the inverted auxiliary is italicised and the subject is bold-printed:

(35) (a)   *Can* **you** speak Japanese?
      (b)   *Does* **he** smoke?
      (c)   *Is* **it** raining?

By contrast, typical verbs do not themselves permit inversion, but rather require what is traditionally called **DO-support** (i.e. they have inverted forms which require the use of the auxiliary DO):

(36) (a)   **Intends* **he** to come?   (b) *Does* **he** intend to come?
      (c)   **Saw* **you** the mayor?   (d) *Did* **you** see the mayor?
      (e)   **Plays* **he** the piano?   (f) *Does* **he** play the piano?

A second difference between auxiliaries and verbs is that auxiliaries can generally be directly negated by a following *not* (which can usually attach to the auxiliary in the guise of its contracted form *n't*):

(37) (a)   John *could not/couldn't* come to the party
      (b)   I *do not/don't* like her much
      (c)   He *is not/isn't* working very hard
      (d)   They *have not/haven't* finished

By contrast, verbs cannot themselves be directly negated by *not/n't*, but require indirect negation through the use of DO-support:

(38) (a) 　*They *like not/liken't* me　　(b) They *do not/don't* like me
　　(c) 　*I *see not/seen't* the point　　(d) I *do not/don't* see the point
　　(e) 　*You *came not/camen't*　　　(f) You *did not/didn't* come

(Note that in structures such as *John decided not to stay* the negative particle *not* negates the infinitive complement *to stay* rather than the verb *decided*, as we see from the fact that the sentence can be paraphrased as 'John decided that he would not stay', not as 'John did not decide that he would stay.') And thirdly, auxiliaries can appear in sentence-final **tags**, as illustrated by the examples below (where the part of the sentence following the comma is traditionally referred to as a **tag**):

(39) (a) 　　You don't like her, *do* you?
　　(b) 　　He won't win, *will* he?
　　(c) 　　She isn't working, *is* she?
　　(d) 　　He can't drive, *can* he?

In contrast, verbs can't themselves be used in tags, but rather require the use of *do*-tags:

(40) (a) 　　You like her, *do/*like* you?
　　(b) 　　They want one, *do/*want* they?

So, on the basis of these (and other) syntactic properties, we can conclude that auxiliaries constitute a different category from verbs.

2.8　Infinitival *to*

　　　　A fourth type of functor found in English is the infinitive particle *to* – so called because the only kind of complement it allows is one containing a verb in the **infinitive** form (the infinitive form of the verb is its uninflected base form, i.e. the citation form found in dictionary entries). Typical uses of infinitival *to* are illustrated in (41) below:

(41) (a) 　　I wonder whether *to* [**go** home]
　　(b) 　　Many people want the government *to* [**change** course]
　　(c) 　　We don't intend *to* [**surrender**]

In each example in (41), the [bracketed] complement of *to* is an expression containing a (bold-printed) verb in the infinitive form. But what is the categorial status of infinitival *to*?

　　We are already familiar with an alternative use of *to* as a preposition, e.g. in sentences such as:

(42) (a) 　　He stayed *to* [the end of the film]
　　(b) 　　He went *to* [the police]

In (42), *to* behaves like a typical (transitive) preposition in taking a [bracketed] *the*-phrase (i.e. determiner phrase) as its complement (viz. *the end of the film* and *the police*). It might therefore seem that *to* is a preposition in both uses – one which takes a following determiner phrase complement (i.e. has a determiner expression as its complement) in (42) and a following verbal complement in (41).

However, infinitival *to* is very different in its behaviour from prepositional *to* in English: whereas prepositional *to* is a contentive with intrinsic lexical semantic content (e.g. it means something like 'as far as'), infinitival *to* seems to be a functor with no lexical semantic content. Because of its intrinsic lexical content, the preposition *to* can often be modified by intensifiers like *right/straight* (a characteristic property of prepositions), as in:

(43) (a)   He stayed *right* **to** the end of the film
     (b)   He went *straight* **to** the police

By contrast, infinitival *to* (because of its lack of lexical content) cannot be intensified by *right/straight*:

(44) (a)   *I wonder whether *right/straight* **to** go home
     (b)   *Many people want the government *right/straight* **to** change course
     (c)   *We don't intend *right/straight* **to** surrender

Moreover, what makes the prepositional analysis of infinitival *to* even more problematic is that it takes a different range of complements from prepositional *to* (and indeed different from the range of complements found with other prepositions). For example, prepositional *to* (like other prepositions) can have a noun expression as its complement, whereas infinitival *to* requires a verbal complement:

(45) (a)   I intend **to** *resign* [= **to**+*verb*]/*I intend **to** *resignation* [= **to**+*noun*]
     (b)   She waited for John **to** *arrive* [= **to**+*verb*]/She waited for John ***to** *arrival* [= **to**+*noun*]
     (c)   Try **to** *decide* [= **to**+*verb*]/*Try **to** *decision* [= **to**+*noun*]

Significantly, genuine prepositions in English (such as those bold-printed in the examples below) only permit a following verbal complement when the verb is in the -*ing* form (known as the **gerund** form in this particular use), not when the verb is in the uninflected base/infinitive form:

(46) (a)   I am **against** *capitulating/*capitulate*
     (b)   Try and do it **without** *complaining/*complain*
     (c)   Think carefully **before** *deciding/*decide*

By contrast, infinitival *to* can only take a verbal complement when the verb is in the infinitive form, never when it is in the gerund form:

(47) (a)   I want **to** *go/*going* there
     (b)   You must try **to** *work/*working* harder
     (c)   You managed **to** *upset/*upsetting* them

A further difference between infinitival and prepositional *to* (illustrated in (48) below) is that infinitival *to* permits **ellipsis** (i.e. omission) of its complement, whereas prepositional *to* does not:

(48)   SPEAKER A: Do you want to go to the cinema?
              SPEAKER B: No, I don't really want **to** (ellipsis of complement of infinitival **to**)
                        *No, I don't really want to go *to* (ellipsis of complement of prepositional *to*)

Thus, there are compelling reasons for assuming that infinitival *to* is a different **lexical item** (i.e. a different word) belonging to a different category from prepositional *to*. So what category does infinitival *to* belong to?

In the late 1970s, Chomsky suggested that there are significant similarities between infinitival *to* and a typical auxiliary like *should*. For example, they occupy a similar position within the clause:

(49) (a)   It's vital [that John *should* show an interest]
     (b)   It's vital [for John *to* show an interest]

We see from (49) that *to* and *should* are both positioned between the subject *John* and the verb *show*. Moreover, just as *should* requires after it a verb in the infinitive form (cf. 'You should *show/*showing/*shown* more interest in syntax'), so too does infinitival *to* (cf. 'Try to *show/*showing/*shown* more interest in syntax'). Furthermore, infinitival *to* behaves like typical auxiliaries (e.g. *should*) but unlike typical non-auxiliary verbs (e.g. *want*) in allowing ellipsis of its complement:

(50) (a)   I don't really want to go to the dentist's, but I know I *should*
     (b)   I know I should go to the dentist's, but I just don't want *to*
     (c)   *I know I should go to the dentist's, but I just don't *want*

The fact that *to* patterns like the auxiliary *should* in several respects strengthens the case for regarding infinitival *to* and auxiliaries as belonging to the same category. But what category?

Chomsky (1981, p. 18) suggested that the resulting category (comprising finite auxiliaries and infinitival *to*) be labelled **INFL** or **Inflection**, though (in accordance with the standard practice of using single-letter symbols to designate word categories) in later work (1986b, p. 3) he replaced **INFL** by the single-letter symbol **I**. The general idea behind this label is that finite auxiliaries are inflected forms (e.g. in 'He *doesn't* know', the auxiliary *doesn't* carries the third-person-singular present-tense inflection -*s*), and infinitival *to* serves much the same function in English as infinitive inflections in languages like Italian which have overtly inflected infinitives (so that Italian *canta-re* = English *to sing*). Under the INFL analysis, an auxiliary like *should* is a finite I/INFL, whereas the particle *to* is an infinitival I/INFL.

However, in work since the mid 1990s, a somewhat different categorisation of auxiliaries and infinitival *to* has been adopted. As the pairs of examples in (34a–h) show, finite auxiliaries typically have two distinct forms – a present-tense form and a corresponding past-tense form (cf. pairs such as *does/did, is/was, has/had, can/could* etc.). Thus, a common property shared by all finite auxiliaries is that they mark (present/past) **Tense**. In much the same way, it might be argued that infinitival *to* has Tense properties, as we can see from the contrast below:

(51) (a)   We believe [the President *may* have been lying]

    (b)   We believe [the President *to* have been lying]

In (51a), the bracketed complement clause has a present-tense interpretation (paraphraseable as 'We believe it *is* possible that the President has been lying'): this is because it contains the present-tense auxiliary *may*. However, the bracketed infinitive complement clause in (51b) can also have a present-tense interpretation, paraphraseable as 'We believe the President *has* been lying.' Why should this be? A plausible answer is that infinitival *to* carries Tense in much the same way as an auxiliary like *may* does. In a sentence like (51b), *to* is most likely to be assigned a present-tense interpretation. However, in a sentence such as (52) below:

(52)   The Feds believed [the junkies *to* have already stashed the hash in the trash-can by the time they were caught]

infinitival *to* seems to have a past-tense interpretation, so that (52) is paraphraseable as 'The Federal Agents believed the junkies *had* already stashed the hash in the trash-can by the time they were caught.' What this suggests is that *to* has abstract (i.e. invisible) tense properties, and has a present-tense interpretation in structures like (51b) when the bracketed *to*-clause is the complement of a present-tense verb like *believe*, and a past-tense interpretation in structures like (52) when the bracketed *to*-clause is the complement of a past-tense verb like *believed*. If finite auxiliaries and infinitival *to* both have (visible or invisible) tense properties, we can assign the two of them to the same category of **T/Tense-marker** – as is done in much contemporary work. The difference between them is sometimes said to be that auxiliaries carry **finite tense** (i.e. they are overtly specified for tense, in the sense that e.g. *does* is overtly marked as a present-tense form and *did* as a past-tense form) whereas infinitival *to* carries **non-finite tense** (i.e. it has an unspecified tense value which has to be determined from the context. For a more technical discussion of tense, see Julien 2001.)

2.9   Complementisers

The last type of functional category which we shall look at in this chapter is that of **complementiser** (abbreviated to **COMP** in earlier work and to **C** in more recent work): this is a term employed to describe the kind of (italicised) word which is used to introduce complement clauses such as those bracketed below:

(53) (a)   I think [*that* you may be right]
      (b)   I doubt [*if* you can help me]
      (c)   I'm anxious [*for* you to receive the best treatment possible]

Each of the bracketed clauses in (53) is a complement clause, in that it functions as the complement of the word immediately preceding it (*think/doubt/anxious*); the italicised word which introduces each clause is known in work since 1970 as a **complementiser** (but was known in more traditional work as a particular type of subordinating conjunction).

Complementisers are functors in the sense that they encode particular sets of grammatical properties. For example, complementisers encode (non-)finiteness by virtue of the fact that they are intrinsically finite or non-finite. More specifically, the complementisers *that* and *if* are inherently finite in the sense that they can only be used to introduce a finite clause (i.e. a clause containing a present- or past-tense auxiliary or verb), and not e.g. an infinitival *to*-clause; by contrast, *for* is an inherently infinitival complementiser, and so can be used to introduce a clause containing infinitival *to*, but not a finite clause containing a tensed auxiliary like (past-tense) *should*; compare the examples in (53) above with those in (54) below:

(54) (a)   *I think [*that* you **to** be right]
      (b)   *I doubt [*if* you **to** help me]
      (c)   *I'm anxious [*for* you **should** receive the best treatment possible]

(54a,b) are ungrammatical because *that/if* are finite complementisers and so cannot introduce an infinitival *to* clause; (54c) is ungrammatical because *for* is an infinitival complementiser and so cannot introduce a finite clause containing a past-tense auxiliary like *should*.

Complementisers in structures like (53) serve three grammatical functions. Firstly, they mark the fact that the clause they introduce is an **embedded clause** (i.e. a clause which is contained within another expression – in this case, within a main clause containing *think/doubt/anxious*). Secondly, they serve to indicate whether the clause they introduce is **finite** or **non-finite** (i.e. denotes an event taking place at a specified or unspecified time): *that* and *if* serve to introduce finite clauses, while *for* introduces non-finite (more specifically, infinitival) clauses. Thirdly, complementisers mark the **force** of the clause they introduce: typically, *if* introduces an **interrogative** (i.e. question-asking) clause, *that* introduces a **declarative** (statement-making) clause and *for* introduces an **irrealis** clause (i.e. a clause denoting an 'unreal' or hypothetical event which hasn't yet happened and may never happen).

However, an important question to ask is whether we really need to assign words such as *for/that/if* (in the relevant function) to a new category of C/complementiser, or whether we couldn't simply treat (e.g.) *for* as a preposition, *that* as a determiner and *if* as an adverb. The answer is 'No', because there are significant differences between complementisers and other apparently similar words. For example, one difference between the complementiser *for* and the preposition *for* is that the preposition *for* has substantive lexical semantic content and so (in some but not all of its uses) can be intensified by *straight/right*, whereas the complementiser *for* is a functor and can never be so intensified:

(55) (a)   He headed *straight/right* **for** the pub [*for* = preposition]
     (b)   The dog went *straight/right* **for** her throat [*for* = preposition]
     (c)   *He was anxious *straight/right* **for** nobody to leave [*for* = complementiser]
     (d)   *It is vital *straight/right* **for** there to be peace [*for* = complementiser]

Moreover, the preposition *for* and the complementiser *for* also differ in their syntactic behaviour. For example, a clause introduced by the complementiser *for* can be the subject of an expression like *would cause chaos*, whereas a phrase introduced by the preposition *for* cannot:

(56) (a)   *For him to resign* would cause chaos [= *for*-clause]
     (b)   *For him* would cause chaos [= *for*-phrase]

What makes it even more implausible to analyse infinitival *for* as a preposition is the fact that (bold-printed) prepositions in English aren't generally followed by a [bracketed] infinitive complement, as we see from the ungrammaticality of:

(57) (a)   *She was surprised **at** [*there to be nobody to meet her*]
     (b)   *I'm not sure **about** [*you to be there*]
     (c)   *I have decided **against** [*us to go there*]

On the contrary, as examples such as (46) above illustrate, the only verbal complements which can be used after prepositions are gerund structures containing a verb in the *-ing* form.

    A further difference between the complementiser *for* and the preposition *for* is that the noun or pronoun expression following the preposition *for* (or a substitute interrogative expression like *who?/what?/which one?*) can be preposed to the front of the sentence (with or without *for*) if *for* is a preposition, but not if *for* is a complementiser. For example, in (58) below, *for* functions as a preposition and the (distinguished) nominal *Senator Megabucks* functions as its complement, so that if we replace *Senator Megabucks* by *which senator?* the wh-expression can be preposed either on its own (in informal styles of English) or together with the preposition *for* (in formal styles):

(58) (a)   I will vote **for** *Senator Megabucks* in the primaries
     (b)   *Which senator* will you vote **for** in the primaries? [= informal style]
     (c)   **For** *which senator* will you vote in the primaries? [= formal style]

However, in (59a) below, the italicised expression is not the complement of the complementiser *for* (the complement of *for* in (59a) is the infinitival clause *Senator Megabucks to keep his cool*), but rather is the subject of the expression *to keep his cool*; hence, even if we replace *Senator Megabucks* by the interrogative wh-phrase *which senator*, the wh-expression can't be preposed (with or without *for*):

(59) (a) They were anxious **for** *Senator Megabucks* to keep his cool
    (b) **Which senator* were they anxious **for** to keep his cool?
    (c) **For which senator* were they anxious to keep his cool?

Furthermore, when *for* functions as a complementiser, the whole *for*-clause which it introduces can often (though not always) be substituted by a clause introduced by another complementiser; for example, the italicised *for*-clause in (60a) below can be replaced by the italicised *that*-clause in (60b):

(60) (a) Is it really necessary *for there to be a showdown*?
    (b) Is it really necessary *that there (should) be a showdown*?

By contrast, the italicised *for*-phrase in (61a) below cannot be replaced by a *that*-clause, as we see from the ungrammaticality of (61b):

(61) (a) We are heading *for a general strike*
    (b) **We are heading *that there (will) be a general strike*

So, there is considerable evidence in favour of drawing a categorial distinction between the preposition *for* and the complementiser *for*: they are different lexical items (i.e. words) belonging to different categories.

Consider now the question of whether the complementiser *that* could be analysed as a determiner. At first sight, it might seem as if such an analysis could provide a straightforward way of capturing the apparent parallelism between the two uses of *that* in sentences such as the following:

(62) (a) I refuse to believe **that** [*rumour*]
    (b) I refuse to believe **that** [*Randy Rabbit runs Benny's Bunny Bar*]

Given that the word *that* has the status of a prenominal determiner in sentences such as (62a), we might suppose that it has the function of a preclausal determiner (i.e. a determiner introducing the following italicised clause *Randy Rabbit runs Benny's Bunny Bar*) in sentences such as (62b).

However, there is evidence against a determiner analysis of the complementiser *that*. Part of this is phonological in nature. In its use as a complementiser (in sentences such as (62b) above), *that* typically has the **reduced** form /ðət/, whereas in its use as a determiner (e.g. in sentences such as (62a) above), *that* invariably has the **unreduced** form /ðæt/: the phonological differences between the two suggest that we are dealing with two different lexical items here (i.e. two different words), one of which functions as a complementiser and typically has a reduced vowel, the other of which functions as a determiner and always has an unreduced vowel.

Moreover, *that* in its use as a determiner (though not in its use as a complementiser) can be substituted by another determiner (such as *this/the*):

(63) (a) Nobody else knows about *that* incident/**this** incident/**the** incident (= determiner *that*)
    (b) I'm sure *that* it's true/***this** it's true/***the** it's true (= complementiser *that*)

Similarly, the determiner *that* can be used pronominally (without any complement), whereas the complementiser *that* cannot:

(64) (a)   Nobody can blame you for *that* mistake (prenominal determiner)
     (b)   Nobody can blame you for *that* (pronominal determiner)

(65) (a)   I'm sure *that* you are right (preclausal complementiser)
     (b)   *I'm sure *that* (pronominal complementiser)

The clear phonological and syntactic differences between the two argue that the word *that* which serves to introduce complement clauses is a different item (belonging to the category C/complementiser) from the determiner/D *that* which modifies noun expressions.

The third item which we earlier suggested might function as a complementiser in English is interrogative *if*. However, at first sight, it might seem as if there is a potential parallelism between *if* and interrogative wh-adverbs like *when/where/whether*, since they appear to occupy the same position in sentences like:

(66)   I don't know [*where/when/whether/if* he will go]

Hence we might be tempted to analyse *if* as an interrogative adverb.

However, there are a number of reasons for rejecting this possibility. For one thing, *if* differs from interrogative adverbs like *where/when/whether* not only in its form (it isn't a *wh*-word, as we can see from the fact that it doesn't begin with *wh*), but also in the range of syntactic positions it can occupy. For example, whereas typical wh-adverbs can occur in finite and infinitive clauses alike, the complementiser *if* is restricted to introducing finite clauses:

(67) (a)   I wonder [*when/where/whether/if* I should go] [= finite clause]
     (b)   I wonder [*when/where/whether/*if* to go] [= infinitive clause]

Moreover, *if* is different from interrogative wh-adverbs (but similar to other complementisers) in that it cannot be used to introduce a clause which serves as the complement of a (bold-printed) preposition:

(68) (a)   I'm not certain **about** [*whether/when/where* he'll go]
     (b)   *I'm concerned **over** [*if* taxes are going to be increased]
     (c)   *I'm puzzled **at** [*that* he should have resigned]
     (d)   *I'm not very keen **on** [*for* you to go there]

Finally, whereas a wh-adverb can typically be coordinated with (e.g. joined by a coordinating conjunction like *and/or* to) the adverb *not*, this is not true of *if*:

(69) (a)   I don't know [*whether* or *not* he'll turn up]
     (b)   *I don't know [*if* or *not* he'll turn up]

For reasons such as these, it seems more appropriate to categorise *if* as an interrogative complementiser, and *whether/where/when* as interrogative adverbs. More generally, our discussion in this section highlights the need to posit a category C of **complementiser**, to designate clause-introducing items such as *if/that/for* which serve the function of introducing specific types of finite or infinitival clause.

2.10   Labelled bracketing

Having looked at the characteristics of the major substantive/lexical and functional categories found in English, we are now in a position where we can start to analyse the grammatical structure of expressions. An important part of doing this is to categorise each of the words in the expression. A conventional way of doing so is to use the traditional system of labelled bracketing: each word is enclosed in a pair of square brackets, and the lefthand member of each pair of brackets is given an appropriate subscript category label to indicate what category the word belongs to. To save space (and printer's ink), it is conventional to use the following capital-letter abbreviations:

(70)   N = noun   V = verb
          A = adjective   ADV = adverb
          P = preposition   D/DET = determiner
          Q = quantifier   T = Tense-marker (e.g. auxiliary/infinitival *to*)
          C/COMP = complementiser   PRN = pronoun

Adopting the abbreviations in (70), we can represent the categorial status of each of the words in a sentence such as:

(71)   Any experienced journalist knows that he can sometimes manage to lure the unsuspecting politician into making unguarded comments

as in (72) below:

(72)   [$_Q$ Any] [$_A$ experienced] [$_N$ journalist] [$_V$ knows] [$_C$ that] [$_{PRN}$ he] [$_T$ can] [$_{ADV}$ sometimes] [$_V$ manage] [$_T$ to] [$_V$ lure] [$_D$ the] [$_A$ unsuspecting] [$_N$ politician] [$_P$ into] [$_V$ making] [$_A$ unguarded] [$_N$ comments]

What (72) tells us is that the words *journalist/politician/comments* belong to the category N/noun, *the* to the category D/determiner, *he* to the category PRN/pronoun (though if personal pronouns like *he* are analysed as D-pronouns, *he* would be assigned to the category D), *any* to the category Q/quantifier, *experienced/unsuspecting/unguarded* to the category A/adjective, *sometimes* to the category ADV/adverb, *into* to the category P/preposition, *knows/manage/lure/making* to the category V/verb, *can/to* to the category T/Tense-marker and *that* to the category C/complementiser. It is important to note, however, that the category labels used in (72) tell us only how the relevant words are being used in this particular sentence. For example, the N label on *comments* in (72) tells us that the item in question functions as a noun in this particular position in this particular sentence, but tells us nothing about the function it may have in other sentences. So, for example, in a sentence such as:

(73)   The president never comments on hypothetical situations

the word *comments* is a verb – as shown in (74) below:

(74)   [D The] [N president] [ADV never] [V comments] [P on] [A hypothetical] [N situations]

Thus, a labelled bracket round a particular word is used to indicate the grammatical category which the word belongs to in the particular position which it occupies in the phrase or sentence in question, so allowing for the possibility that (what appears to be) the same word may have a different categorial status in other positions in other structures.

2.11   Grammatical features

In the previous section, we suggested that we can assign words in sentences to categories on the basis of their grammatical properties. However, it should be pointed out that simply specifying what category a particular word in a particular sentence belongs to does not provide a full description of the grammatical properties of the relevant word. For example, categorising *he* as a pronoun in (72) doesn't tell us in what ways *he* differs from other pronouns like e.g. *I/us/you/her/it/them* – i.e. it doesn't tell us about the (third) person, (singular) number, (masculine) gender and (nominative) case properties of *he*. In other words, there is a great deal of additional grammatical information about words which is not represented by simply attaching a category label to the word – information which provides a finer level of detail than relatively coarse categorial descriptions. This information is generally described in terms of sets of **grammatical features**; by convention, features are enclosed in square brackets and often abbreviated (to save space). Using grammatical features, we can describe the person/number/gender/case properties of the pronoun *he* in terms of the features [3-Pers, Sg-Num, Masc-Gen, Nom-Case] i.e. 'Third-Person, Singular-Number, Masculine-Gender, Nominative-Case'. Each of these features comprises an **attribute** (i.e. a property like **person**, **number**, **gender** or **case**) and a **value** (which can be **first/second/third** for person, **singular/plural** for number, **masculine/feminine/neuter** for gender, and **nominative/accusative/genitive** for case).

An adequate description of syntax also requires us to specify the **selectional properties** of individual words (e.g. what kinds of complement they can take). We can illustrate the importance of selectional information by considering what kinds of word can occupy the position marked by — in the sentences below:

(75) (a)   He might — to Paris   (b) He is — to Paris   (c) He has — to Paris

A categorial answer would be 'A verb'. However, we can't just use *any* verb: for example, it's OK to use verbs like *go/fly*, but not verbs like *find/stay*. This is because different verbs **select** (i.e. 'take') different types of complement, and verbs like *go/fly* select a *to*-expression as their complement but verbs like *find/stay* do not. But the story doesn't end there, since each of the structures in (75) requires a different form of the verb: in (75a) we can use the infinitive form *go*, but not other forms of the verb (cf. *He might go/*going/*gone/*goes/*went to Paris*); in (75b) we can only use the progressive participle form *going* (cf. *He is going/*go/*gone/*goes/*went to Paris*); and in (75c) we can only use the perfect participle form *gone* (cf. *He has gone/*go/*going/*goes/*went to Paris*). This in turn is because the auxiliary *might* selects (i.e. 'takes') an infinitive complement, the progressive auxiliary *is* selects a progressive participle complement, and the perfect auxiliary *has* selects a perfect participle complement. In other words, a full description of the grammatical properties of words requires us to specify not only their categorial and subcategorial properties, but also their selectional properties. It is widely assumed that the selectional properties of words can be described in terms of **selectional features**. For example, the fact that progressive *be* selects a progressive participle complement might be described by saying that it has the selectional feature [V-*ing*] – a notation intended to signify that it selects a complement headed by a verb carrying the -*ing* suffix.

As far back as his 1965 book *Aspects of the Theory of Syntax*, Chomsky argued that all the grammatical properties of a word (including its categorial properties) can be described in terms of a set of grammatical features. In work in the 1970s, he argued that the categorial distinction between nouns, verbs, adjectives and prepositions can be handled in terms of two sets of **categorial features**, namely [±V] 'verbal/non-verbal' and [±N] 'nominal/non-nominal'. More specifically, he suggested that the categorial properties of nouns, verbs adjectives and prepositions could be described in terms of the sets of features in (76) below:

(76)   verb = [+V, −N]   adjective = [+V, +N]
            noun = [−V, +N]   preposition = [−V, −N]

What (76) claims is that verbs have verbal but not nominal properties, adjectives have both nominal and verbal properties, nouns have nominal but not verbal properties, and prepositions have neither nominal nor verbal properties. This analysis was designed to capture the fact that some grammatical properties extend across more than one category and so can be said to be **cross-categorial**. For example, Stowell (1981, p. 57 fn. 17) notes that verbs and adjectives in English share the morphological property that they alone permit *un*-prefixation (hence we find verbs like *undo* and adjectives like *unkind*, but not nouns like *unfriend or prepositions like *uninside): in terms of the set of categorial features in (76), we can account for this by positing that *un-* can only be prefixed to words which have the categorial feature [+V]. Likewise, as the following example kindly provided for me by Andrew Spencer shows, in Russian nouns and adjectives inflect for case, but not verbs or prepositions:

(77)   Krasiva*ya* dyevushk*a* vsunula chornu*yu* koshk*u* v pustu*yu* korobk*u*
         Beautiful girl   put   black   cat   in empty   box
         'The beautiful girl put the black cat in the empty box'

Thus, the nouns and adjectives in (77) carry (italicised) case endings (*-a* is a nominative suffix and *-u* an accusative suffix), but not the verb or preposition. In terms of the set of categorial features in (76) we can account for this by positing that case is a property of items which carry the categorial feature [+N].

An obvious drawback to the system of categorial features in (76) above is that it describes the categorial properties of a number of substantive/lexical categories, but not those of functional categories. Each functional category seems to be closely related to a corresponding lexical category: for example, auxiliaries appear to be related to verbs, determiners to adjectives, and the complementiser *for* to the preposition *for*. One way of handling both the similarities and differences between substantive categories and their functional counterparts is in terms of a functionality feature [±F], with functional categories carrying the feature [+F], and substantive categories carrying the feature [−F]. On this view, main verbs would have the feature specification [−N, +V, −F] whereas auxiliaries would have the feature specification [−N, +V, +F]; likewise, the complementiser *for* would have the feature specification [−N, −V, +F], and the preposition *for* would be specified as [−N, −V, −F]. We shall not speculate any further on this possibility here: for an attempt to motivate such an analysis, see Radford (1997a, pp. 65–68 and p. 84).

Although many details remain to be worked out, it seems clear that in principle, all grammatical properties of words (including their categorial properties) can be described in terms of sets of grammatical features. (See Ramat 1999 on categories and features.) However, in order to simplify our exposition, we shall continue to make use of traditional category labels throughout much of the book, gradually introducing specific features in later chapters where some descriptive purpose is served by doing so.

2.12   Summary

In this chapter, we have looked at the role played by categories in characterising the grammatical properties of words. In §2.2, we looked at the criteria used for categorising words, noting that semantic criteria have to be used with care, and that morphological criteria (relating to the inflectional and derivational properties of words) and syntactic criteria (relating to the range of positions which words can occupy within phrases and sentences) tend to be more reliable. In §2.3 we suggested that we can determine the categorial status of a word from its morphological and syntactic properties, with **substitution** being used as a test in problematic cases. In §2.4 we went on to draw a distinction between **substantive/lexical categories** (whose members have substantive lexical content) and **functional categories** (whose members have no substantive lexical content and serve only to mark grammatical properties such as number, person, case etc.). We then looked at a number of different types of functional category found in English. We began in §2.5 with determiners (= D) and quantifiers (= Q), arguing that they are categorially distinct from adjectives since they precede (but don't follow) adjectives, they can't be stacked, and they impose grammatical restrictions on the types of expression they can modify (e.g. *a* can only modify a singular count noun expression). In §2.6, we looked at pronouns and argued that English has at least three distinct types of pronoun, namely N-pronouns (like *one*), Q-pronouns (like *several*) and D-pronouns (like *this*). We went on to note that recent research has suggested that personal pronouns like *he* are also D-pronouns, but that this categorisation is not entirely unproblematic. In §2.7 we looked at the functional counterparts of verbs, namely auxiliaries: we argued that these are functors in that (unlike lexical verbs) they describe no specific action or event, but rather encode verb-related grammatical properties such as tense, mood, voice and aspect; we noted that auxiliaries are syntactically distinct from verbs in that (e.g.) they undergo inversion. In §2.8 we discussed the nature of infinitival *to*: we showed that it is distinct from the preposition *to*, and shares a number of properties in common with finite auxiliaries (e.g. auxiliaries and infinitival *to* allow ellipsis of their complements, but prepositional *to* does not). We noted the assumption made in much research over the past three decades that finite auxiliaries and infinitival *to* are different exponents of the same category (labelled **I/INFL/Inflection** in earlier work and **T/Tense-marker** in more recent work), with an auxiliary like *will* marking finite tense, and infinitival *to* marking non-finite tense. In §2.9 we argued that complementisers (= C or COMP) like *that/if/for* are a further category of functors, and that they mark the **force** of a complement clause (e.g. indicate whether it is **interrogative, declarative** or **irrealis**), and that (e.g.) *if* is distinct from interrogative adverbs like *how/when/whether* in that it can only introduce a finite clause, and cannot introduce a clause which is used as the complement of a preposition. In §2.10, we showed how the labelled bracketing technique can be used to categorise words in particular phrases and sentences. Finally, in §2.11 we noted that assigning words to grammatical categories provides a description of only some of their grammatical properties, and that a fuller description requires the use of **grammatical features** to describe their other grammatical properties. We went on to note Chomsky's claim that the categorial properties of words can also be described in terms of a set of grammatical features – bringing us to the conclusion that all grammatical properties of words can be characterised in terms of sets of features.

Workbook section

Exercise 2.1

Discuss the grammatical and categorial properties of the highlighted words in each of the following examples, giving arguments in support of your analysis:

1a   Nobody *need/dare* say anything
b   Nobody *needs/dares* to ask questions
c   John *is* working hard
d   John *may* stay at home
e   John *has* done it
f   John *has* to go there
g   John *used* to go there quite often

2a   Executives like *to* drive *to* work
b   I look forward *to* learning *to* drive
c   It's difficult *to* get him *to* work
d   I've never felt tempted *to* turn *to* taking drugs
e   Better *to* yield *to* temptation than *to* submit *to* deprivation!
f   Failure *to* achieve sometimes drives people *to* drink
g   Try *to* go *to* sleep.

3a   It is important *for* parents to spend time with their children
b   It would be disastrous *for* me *for* my driving-licence to be withdrawn
c   He was arrested *for* being drunk
d   We are hoping *for* a peace agreement to be signed
e   Ships head *for* the nearest port in a storm
f   Congress voted *for* the treaty to be ratified
g   It would be unfortunate *for* the students to fail their exams

Helpful hints

A particular problem arises (in the case of some of the examples in 3) in relation to words which allow a prepositional phrase complement (comprising a preposition and a noun or pronoun expression) in one use, and a *for*-infinitive clause in another – as with *arrange* in the examples below

(i) (a)   I can arrange **for** *immediate closure of the account*
(b)   I can arrange **for** *the account to be closed immediately*

In (ia) *for* is used with the noun expression *immediate closure of the account* as its complement, and is clearly a preposition – as we can see from the fact that (like the complement of a typical preposition) the relevant noun expression can be moved to the front of the sentence to highlight it:

(ii)   *Immediate closure of the account*, I can certainly arrange **for**

By contrast, *for* in (ib) seems to be a complementiser rather than a preposition. For one thing, prepositions don't allow an infinitival complement, as we see from examples like (57) in the main text. Moreover, the complement of *for* in (ib) cannot be preposed – as we see from the ungrammaticality of:

(iii)   *The account to be closed immediately*, I can certainly arrange **for**

What we might have expected to find is two occurrences of *for*, one serving as an (italicised) preposition introducing the complement of *arrange*, and the other serving as a (bold-printed) complementiser introducing the infinitive complement – much as we find in:

(iv)   What I can certainly arrange *for* is **for** the account to be closed immediately

But the expected *for* **for** sequence isn't grammatical in sentences like:

(v)   *I can certainly arrange *for* **for** the account to be closed immediately

The reason seems to be that words which take a prepositional complement generally drop the preposition when the (italicised) preposition has a complement introduced by a (bold-printed) complementiser:

(vi) (a)   What you can't be sure *of* is **that** he is telling the truth
  (b)   *You can't be sure *of* **that** he is telling the truth
  (c)   You can't be sure **that** he is telling the truth

Hence, although we might in principle expect to find a preposition+complementiser structure in (v), what seems to happen in practice is that the preposition is dropped in such structures – hence in (ib) the *for* which we find is the complementiser *for* rather than the (dropped) preposition *for*.

Model answer for sentences 1a, 2a and 3a

The main problem raised by the examples in 1 is whether the highlighted items have the categorial status of verbs or auxiliaries as they are used in each example – or indeed whether some of the items in some of their uses have a dual verb/auxiliary status (and so can function either as verbs or as auxiliaries). The words *need/dare* in 1a resemble modal auxiliaries like *will/shall/can/may/must* in that they lack the third-person-singular -*s* inflection, and take a bare infinitive complement (i.e. a complement containing the infinitive verb-form *say* but lacking the infinitive particle *to*). They behave like auxiliaries (in Standard English) in that they undergo inversion in questions, can appear in tags, and can be negated by *not/n't*:

(i) (a)   *Need/Dare* anyone say anything?
  (b)   He *needn't/daren't* say anything, *need/dare* he?

Conversely, they are not used with DO-support in any of these three constructions in Standard English:

(ii) (a)   *Does anyone need/dare say anything?
  (b)   *He *doesn't* need/dare say anything, does he?

Thus, *need/dare* when followed by a bare infinitive complement seem to have the status of (modal) auxiliaries. In 1a, *need/dare* are third-person-singular present-tense finite verb forms, as we see from the fact that the subject of *need* is the nominative pronoun *they* in (iii) below:

(iii)   Nobody need say anything, need *they*?

(Recall that finite verbs require nominative subjects.)

In 2a, the first *to* is an infinitive particle, and the second *to* is a preposition. Thus, the second *to* (but not the first) can be modified by the prepositional intensifier *straight* (cf. *Executives like to drive straight to work*, but not **Executives like straight to drive to work*). Moreover, the second *to* is a contentive preposition which has the antonym *from* (cf. *Executives like to drive from work*), whereas the first has no obvious antonym since it is an infinitive particle (cf. **Executives like from drive/driving to work*). In addition, like a typical transitive preposition, the second *to* (but not the first) can be followed by an accusative pronoun complement like *them* (cf. *Executives think the only way of getting to their offices is to drive to them*). Conversely, the first (infinitival) *to* allows ellipsis of its complement (cf. *Executives like to*), whereas the second (prepositional) *to* does not (cf. **Executives like to drive to*). Thus, in all relevant respects the first *to* behaves like an infinitive particle, whereas the second *to* behaves like a preposition.

In 3a, *for* could be either a complementiser (introducing the infinitival clause *parents to spend time with their children*), or a preposition (whose complement is the noun *parents*). The possibility that *for* might be used here as a preposition is suggested by the fact that the string *for parents* (or an interrogative counterpart like *for how many parents?*) could be preposed to the front of its containing sentence, as in:

(iv) (a)   *For parents*, it is important to spend time with their children
     (b)   *For how many parents* is it important to spend time with their children?

The alternative possibility that *for* might be used as a complementiser (with the infinitival clause *parents to spend time with their children* serving as its complement) is suggested by the fact that the *for*-clause here could be substituted by a *that*-clause, as in:

(v)   It is important *that parents should spend time with their children*

Thus, 3a is structurally ambiguous between one analysis on which *for* functions as a transitive preposition, and a second on which *for* functions as an infinitival complementiser which is irrealis in force.

Exercise 2.2

Use the labelled bracketing technique to assign each word in each of the sentences below to a grammatical category which represents how it is being used in the position in which it occurs in the sentence concerned. Give reasons in support of your proposed categorisation, highlight any analytic problems which arise, and comment on any interesting properties of the relevant words.

1   He was feeling disappointed at only obtaining average grades in the morphology
         exercises
2   Student counsellors know that money troubles can cause considerable stress
3   Opposition politicians are pressing for election debates to receive better television
         coverage
4   Seasoned press commentators doubt if the workers will ever fully accept that
         substantial pay rises lead to runaway inflation
5   Students often complain to their high school teachers that the state education system
         promotes universal mediocrity

6   Some scientists believe that climatic changes result from ozone depletion due to excessive carbon dioxide emission

7   Linguists have long suspected that peer group pressure shapes linguistic behaviour patterns in very young children

8   You don't seem to be too worried about the possibility that many of the shareholders may now vote against your revised takeover bid

Model answer for sentence 1

(i)   [PRN He] [T was] [V feeling] [A disappointed] [P at] [ADV only] [V obtaining] [A average] [N grades] [P in] [D the] [N morphology] [N exercises]

An issue of particular interest which arises in (i) relates to the status of the words *average* and *morphology*. Are these nouns or adjectives – and how can we tell? Since nouns used to modify other nouns are invariable in English (e.g. we say *skate boards*, not **skates boards*), we can't rely on morphological clues here. However, we can use syntactic evidence. If (as assumed here) the word *average* functions as an adjective in 1, we should expect to find that it can be modified by the kind of adverb like *relatively* which can be used to modify adjectives (e.g. *relatively good*); by contrast, if *morphology* serves as a noun in 1, we should expect to find that it can be modified by the kind of adjective (e.g. *inflectional*) which can be used to modify such a noun. In the event, both predictions are correct:

(ii)   He was feeling disappointed at only obtaining relatively average grades in the inflectional morphology exercises

Some additional evidence that *average* can function as an adjective comes from the fact that it has the *-ly* adverb derivative *averagely*, and (for some speakers at least) the noun derivative *averageness* – e.g. *The very averageness of his intellect made him the CIA's choice for president.* Moreover (like most adjectives), it can be used predicatively in sentences like *His performance was average.* (Note, however, that in structures such as *morphology exercises*, you will not always find it easy to determine whether the first word is a noun or adjective. Unless there is evidence to the contrary – as with *average* in (ii) above – assume that the relevant item is a noun if it clearly functions as a noun in other uses.)

3   Structure

3.1   Overview

In this chapter, we introduce the notion of **syntactic structure**, looking at how words are combined together to form phrases and sentences. We shall argue that phrases and sentences are built up by a series of **merger** operations, each of which combines a pair of constituents together to form a larger constituent. We show how the resulting structure can be represented in terms of a **tree diagram**, and we look at ways of testing the structure of phrases and sentences.

3.2   Phrases

To put our discussion on a concrete footing, let's consider how an elementary two-word phrase such as that produced by speaker B in the following mini-dialogue is formed:

(1)   SPEAKER A: What are you trying to do?
            SPEAKER B: *Help you*

As speaker B's utterance illustrates, the simplest way of forming a phrase is by **merging** (a technical term meaning 'combining') two words together: for example, by merging the word *help* with the word *you* in (1), we form the phrase *help you*. The resulting phrase *help you* seems to have verb-like rather than noun-like properties, as we see from the fact that it can occupy much the same range of positions as the simple verb *help*, and hence e.g. occur after the infinitive particle *to*:

(2) (a)   We are trying to *help*   (b) We are trying to *help you*

By contrast, the phrase *help you* cannot occupy the kind of position occupied by a pronoun such as *you*, as we see from (3) below:

(3) (a)   *You* are very difficult   (b) **Help you* are very difficult

So, it seems clear that the grammatical properties of a phrase like *help you* are determined by the verb *help*, and not by the pronoun *you*. Much the same can be said about the semantic properties of the expression, since the phrase *help you* describes an act of help, not a kind of person. Using the appropriate technical terminology, we can say that the verb *help* is the **head** of the phrase *help you*, and hence that *help you* is a **verb phrase**: and in the same way as we abbreviate category labels like **verb** to **V**, so too we can abbreviate the category label **verb phrase** to **VP**. If we use the traditional labelled bracketing technique to represent the category of the overall verb phrase *help you* and of its constituent words (the verb *help* and the pronoun *you*), we can represent the structure of the resulting phrase as in (4) below:

(4)   [VP [V help] [PRN you]]

An alternative (equivalent) way of representing the structure of phrases like *help you* is viá a **labelled tree diagram** such as (5) below (which is a bit like a family tree diagram – albeit for a small family):

(5)

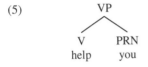

What the tree diagram in (5) tells us is that the overall phrase *help you* is a verb phrase (VP), and that its two **constituents** are the verb (V) *help* and the pronoun (PRN) *you*. The verb *help* is the **head** of the overall phrase (and so is the key word which determines the grammatical and semantic properties of the phrase *help you*); introducing another technical term at this point, we can say that conversely, the VP *help you* is a **projection** of the verb *help* – i.e. it is a larger expression formed by merging the head verb *help* with another constituent of an appropriate kind. In this case, the constituent which is merged with the verb *help* is the pronoun *you*, which has the grammatical function of being the **complement** (or **direct object**) of the verb *help*. The head of a projection/phrase determines the grammatical properties of its complement: in this case, since *help* is a **transitive** verb, it requires a complement with **accusative** case (e.g. a pronoun like *me/us/him/them*), and this requirement is satisfied here since *you* can function as an accusative form (as you can see from the table of pronoun forms given in (31) in §2.6).

The tree diagram in (5) is entirely equivalent to the labelled bracketing in (4), in the sense that the two provide us with precisely the same information about the structure of the phrase *help you*. The differences between a labelled bracketing like (4) and a tree diagram like (5) are purely notational: each category is represented by a single labelled **node** in a tree diagram (i.e. by a point in the tree which carries a category label like VP, V or PRN), but by a pair of labelled brackets in a labelled bracketing. In each case, category labels like V/verb and PRN/pronoun should be thought of as shorthand abbreviations for the set of grammatical features which characterise the overall grammatical properties of the relevant words (e.g. the pronoun *you* as used in (5) carries a set of features including [second-person] and [accusative-case], though these features are not shown by the category label PRN).

Since our goal in developing a theory of Universal Grammar is to uncover general structural principles governing the formation of phrases and sentences, let's generalise our discussion of (5) at this point and hypothesise that all phrases are formed in essentially the same way as the phrase in (5), namely by a **binary** (i.e. pairwise) merger operation which combines two constituents together to form a larger constituent. In the case of (5), the resulting phrase *help you* is formed by merging two words. However, not all phrases contain only two words – as we see if we look at the structure of the phrase produced by speaker B in (6) below:

(6)   SPEAKER A: What was your intention?
             SPEAKER B: *To help you*

The phrase in (6B) is formed by merging the infinitive particle *to* with the verb phrase *help you*. What's the head of the resulting phrase *to help you*? A reasonable guess would be that the head is the infinitival tense particle/T *to*, so that the resulting expression *to help you* is an **infinitival TP** (= infinitival tense projection = infinitival tense phrase). This being so, we'd expect to find that TPs containing infinitival *to* have a different distribution (and so occur in a different range of positions) from VPs/verb phrases – and this is indeed the case, as we see from the contrast below:

(7) (a)   They **ought** *to help you* (= **ought** + TP *to help you*)
    (b)   *They **ought** *help you* (= **ought** + VP *help you*)

(8) (a)   They **should** *help you* (= **should** + VP *help you*)
    (b)   *They **should** *to help you* (= **should** + TP *to help you*)

If we assume that *help you* is a VP whereas *to help you* is a TP, we can account for the contrasts in (7) and (8) by saying that *ought* is the kind of word which **selects** (i.e. 'takes') an infinitival TP as its complement, whereas *should* is the kind of word which selects an infinitival VP as its complement. Implicit in this claim is the assumption that different words like *ought* and *should* have different **selectional properties** which determine the range of complements they permit (as we saw in §2.11).

The infinitive phrase *to help you* is formed by merging the infinitive particle *to* with the verb phrase *help you*. If (as we argued in the previous chapter) infinitival *to* is a **non-finite tense particle** (belonging to the category T) and if *to* is the head of the phrase *to help you*, the structure formed by merging the infinitival T-particle *to* with the verb phrase/VP *help you* in (5) will be the TP (i.e. non-finite/infinitival tense projection/phrase) in (9) below:

(9)

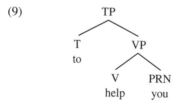

The **head** of the resulting infinitival tense projection *to help you* is the infinitive particle *to*, and the verb phrase *help you* is the **complement** of *to*; conversely, *to help you* is a **projection** of *to*. In keeping with our earlier observation that 'The head of a projection/phrase determines grammatical properties of its complement', the non-finite tense particle *to* requires an infinitival complement: more specifically, *to* requires the head V of its VP complement to be a verb in its **infinitive** form, so that we require the infinitive form *help* after infinitival *to* (and not a form like *helping/helped/helps*). Refining our earlier observation somewhat, we can therefore say that 'The head of a projection/phrase determines grammatical properties of the *head word of* its complement'. In (9), *to* is the head of the TP *to help you*, and the complement of *to* is the VP *help you*; the head of this VP is the V *help*, so that *to* determines the form of the V *help* (requiring it to be in the infinitive form *help*).

More generally, our discussion here suggests that we can build up phrases by a series of binary merger operations which combine successive pairs of constituents to form ever larger structures. For example, by merging the infinitive phrase *to help you* with the verb *trying*, we can form the even larger phrase *trying to help you* produced by speaker B in (10) below:

(10)   SPEAKER A: What are you doing?
          SPEAKER B: *Trying to help you*

The resulting phrase *trying to help you* is headed by the verb *trying*, as we see from the fact that it can be used after words like *be, start* or *keep* which select a complement headed by a verb in the *-ing* form (cf. *They were/started/kept trying to help you*). This being so, the italicised phrase produced by speaker B in (10) is a VP (= verb phrase) which has the structure (11) below:

(11)

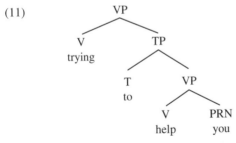

(11) tells us (amongst other things) that the overall expression *trying to help you* is a verb phrase/VP; its **head** is the verb/V *trying*, and the **complement** of *trying* is the TP/infinitival tense phrase *to help you*: conversely, the VP *trying to help you* is a **projection** of the V *trying*. An interesting property of syntactic structures illustrated in (11) is that of **recursion** – that is, the property of allowing a given structure to contain more than one instance of a given category (in this case, more than one verb phrase/VP – one headed by the verb *help* and the other headed by the verb *trying*).

Since our goal in developing a theory of Universal Grammar/UG is to attempt to establish universal principles governing the nature of linguistic structure, an important question to ask is whether there are any general principles of constituent structure which we can abstract from structures like (5), (9) and (11). If we look closely at the relevant structures, we can see that they obey the following two (putatively universal) constituent structure principles:

(12)   **Headedness Principle**
        Every syntactic structure is a projection of a head word

(13)   **Binarity Principle**
        Every syntactic structure is binary-branching

(The term *syntactic structure* is used here as an informal way of denoting an expression which contains two or more constituents.) For example, the structure (11) obeys the Headedness Principle (12) in that the VP *help you* is headed by the V *help*, the TP *to help you* is headed by the T *to*, and the VP *trying to help you* is headed by the V *trying*. Likewise, (11) obeys the Binarity Principle (13) in that the VP *help you* branches into two **immediate constituents** (in the sense that it has two constituents immediately beneath it, namely the V *help* and the PRN *you*), the TP *to help you* branches into two immediate constituents (the non-finite tense particle T *to* and the VP *help you*), and the VP *trying to help you* likewise branches into two immediate constituents (the V *trying* and the TP *to help you*). Our discussion thus leads us towards a **principled** account of constituent structure – i.e. one based on a set of principles of Universal Grammar.

There are several reasons for trying to uncover constituent structure principles like (12) and (13). From a learnability perspective, such principles reduce the range of alternatives which children have to choose between when trying to determine the structure of a given kind of expression: they therefore help us develop a more **constrained** theory of syntax. Moreover, additional support for the Binarity Principle comes from evidence that phonological structure is also binary, in that (e.g.) a syllable like *bat* has a binary structure, consisting of the **onset** |b| and the **rhyme** |at|, and the rhyme in turn has a binary structure, consisting of the **nucleus** |a| and the **coda**|t| (see Radford et al. 1999, pp. 88ff. for an outline of syllable structure). Likewise, there is evidence that morphological structure is also binary: for example (under the analysis proposed in Radford et al. 1999, p. 164), the noun *indecipherability* is formed by adding the prefix *de-* to the noun *cipher* to form the verb *decipher*; then adding the suffix *-able* to this verb to form the adjective *decipherable*; then adding the prefix *in-* to this adjective to form the adjective *indecipherable*; and then adding the suffix *-ity* to the resulting adjective to form the noun *indecipherability*. It would therefore seem that **binarity** is an inherent characteristic of the phonological, morphological and syntactic structure of natural languages. There is also a considerable body of empirical evidence in support of a binary-branching analysis of a range of syntactic structures in a range of languages (see e.g. Kayne 1984a) – though much of this work is highly technical and it would therefore not be appropriate to consider it here.

3.3   Clauses

Having considered how phrases are formed, let's now turn to look at how **clauses** and **sentences** are formed. By way of illustration, suppose that speaker B had used the simple (single-clause) sentence italicised in (14) below to reply to speaker A, rather than the phrase used by speaker B in (10):

(14)   SPEAKER A: What are you doing?
            SPEAKER B: *We are trying to help you*

What's the structure of the italicised clause produced by speaker B in (14)?
    In work in the 1960s, clauses were generally taken to belong to the category **S (Sentence/Clause)**, and the sentence produced by B in (14) would have been taken to have a structure along the following lines:

(15)

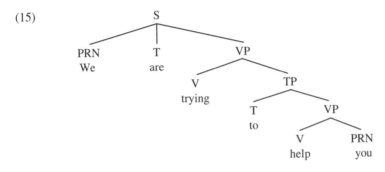

However, a structure such as (15) violates the two constituent structure principles which we posited in (12) and (13) above. More particularly, the S analysis of clauses in (15) violates the **Headedness Principle** (12) in that the S *we are trying to help you* is a structure which has no head of any kind. Likewise, the S analysis in (15) also violates the **Binarity Principle** (13) in that the S constituent *We are trying to help you* is not binary-branching but rather ternary-branching, because it branches into three immediate constituents, namely the PRN *we*, the T *are*, and the VP *trying to help you*. If our theory of Universal Grammar requires every syntactic structure to be a binary-branching projection of a head word, it is clear that we have to reject the S-analysis of clause structure in (15) as one which is not in keeping with UG principles.
    Let's therefore explore an alternative analysis of the structure of clauses which is consistent with the **headedness** and **binarity** requirements in (12) and (13). More specifically, let's make the unifying assumption that clauses are formed by the same binary merger operation as phrases, and accordingly suppose that the italicised clause in (14B) is formed by merging the (present) tense auxiliary *are* with the verb phrase *trying to help you*, and then subsequently merging the resulting expression *are trying to help you* with the pronoun *we*. Since *are* belongs to the category T of tense auxiliary, it might at first sight seem as if merging

are with the verb phrase *trying to help you* will derive (i.e. form) the **tense projection/tense phrase/TP** *are trying to help you*. But this can't be right, since it would provide us with no obvious account of why speaker B's reply in (16) below is ungrammatical:

(16)   SPEAKER A: What are you doing?
         SPEAKER B: *Are trying to help you*

If *are trying to help you* is a TP (i.e. a complete tense projection), how come it can't be used to answer speaker A's question in (16), since we see from sentences like (6B) that TP constituents like *to help you* can be used to answer questions.

An informal answer we can give is to say that the expression *are trying to help you* is somehow 'incomplete', and that only 'complete' expressions can be used to answer questions. In what sense is *Are trying to help you* incomplete? The answer is that finite T constituents require a subject, and the finite auxiliary *are* doesn't have a subject in (16). More specifically, let's assume that when we merge a tense auxiliary (= T) with a verb phrase (= VP), we form an **intermediate projection** which we shall here denote as T′ (pronounced 'tee-bar'); and that only when we merge the relevant T-bar constituent with a subject like *we* do we form a **maximal projection** – or, more informally a 'complete TP'. Given these assumptions, the italicised clause in (14B) will have the structure (17) below:

(17)

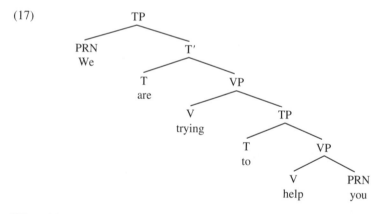

What this means is that a tense auxiliary like *are* has two projections: a smaller **intermediate projection** (T′) formed by merging *are* with its **complement** *trying to help you* to form the T-bar (intermediate tense projection) *are trying to help you*; and a larger **maximal projection** (TP) formed by merging the resulting T′ *are trying to help you* with its **subject** *we* to form the TP *We are trying to help you*. Saying that TP is the **maximal projection** of *are* in (17) means that it is the largest constituent headed by the tense auxiliary *are*.

Why should tense auxiliaries require *two* different projections, one in which they merge with a following complement to form a T-bar, and another in which the resulting T-bar merges with a preceding subject to form a TP? Following a suggestion made by Chomsky (1982, p. 10), the requirement for auxiliaries to

have two projections (as in (17) above) was taken in earlier work to be a consequence of a principle of Universal Grammar known as the **Extended Projection
Principle** (conventionally abbreviated to **EPP**), which can be outlined informally
as follows:

(18)   **Extended Projection Principle/EPP**
            A finite tense constituent T must be extended into a TP projection containing a subject

Given that (as we noted at the end of the previous chapter) the grammatical
properties of words are described in terms of sets of grammatical features, we
can say that tense auxiliaries like *are* carry an [EPP] **feature** which requires them
to have an extended projection into a TP which has a subject. If we posit that
all tense auxiliaries carry an [EPP] feature, it follows that any structure (like that
produced by speaker B in (16) above) containing a tense auxiliary which does
not have a subject will be ungrammatical by virtue of violating the Extended
Projection Principle (18).

The EPP requirement (for a finite auxiliary to have a subject) would seem
to be essentially syntactic (rather than semantic) in nature, as we can see from
sentences such as (19) below:

(19) (a)   *It* was alleged that he lied under oath
     (b)   *There* has been no trouble

In structures like (19), the italicised subject pronouns *it/there* seem to have no
semantic content (in particular, no referential properties) of their own, as we
see from the fact that neither can be questioned by the corresponding interrogative words *what?/where?* (cf. the ungrammaticality of **What was alleged that
he lied under oath?* and **Where has been no trouble?*), and neither can receive
contrastive focus (hence *it/there* cannot be contrastively stressed in sentences like
(19) above). Rather, they function as **expletive pronouns** – i.e. pronouns with
no intrinsic meaning which are used in order to satisfy the syntactic Projection
Principle/EPP. For example, the expletive subject *it* in (19a) might be argued to
serve the syntactic function of providing a subject for the auxiliary *was* to agree
with in person and number. (We deal with agreement in chapter 8 and so will have
nothing more to say about it for the time being.)

It is interesting to note that theoretical considerations also favour a binary-
branching TP analysis of clause structure like (17) over a ternary-branching S
analysis like (15). The essential spirit of Minimalism is to reduce the theoretical
apparatus which we use to describe syntactic structure to a minimum. For example,
it has been suggested (e.g. by Kayne 1994, Yang 1999 and Chomsky 2001) that
tree diagrams should only contain information about hierarchical structure (i.e.
containment/constituent structure relations), not about linear structure (i.e. left-
to-right word order), because linear information is redundant (in the sense that
it can be predicted from hierarchical structure by simple word-order rules) if
we use binary-branching trees. Suppose for example that we have a word-order
rule for English to the effect that 'Any constituent of a phrase HP which is the

sister of the head H is positioned to the right of H, but any other constituent of HP is positioned to the left of H.' This word-order rule will correctly predict (*inter alia*) that the VP *trying to help you* in (17) must be positioned to the right of the tense auxiliary/T *are* (because the relevant VP is the sister of *are*), and that the pronoun *we* must be positioned to the left of *are* (because *we* is not the sister of *are*). As you can see for yourself, it's not clear how we can achieve the same result (of eliminating redundant word-order information from trees) under a ternary-branching analysis like (15), since both the pronoun *we* and the verb phrase *trying to help you* are sisters of *are* in (15). It should be noted in passing that an important consequence of assuming that linear order is not a *syntactic* relation is that it entails that syntactic operations cannot be sensitive to word order (e.g. we can't handle subject–auxiliary agreement by saying that a finite auxiliary agrees with a *preceding* noun or pronoun expression): rather, all syntactic operations must be sensitive to hierarchical rather than linear structure. How this works in practice will become clearer as our exposition unfolds.

A question which we have not so far asked about the structure of clauses concerns what role is played by complementisers like *that*, *for* and *if*, e.g. in speaker B's reply in (20) below:

(20)   SPEAKER A: What are you saying?
            SPEAKER B: *That we are trying to help you*

Where does the C/complementiser *that* fit into the structure of the sentence? The answer suggested in work in the 1970s was that a complementiser merges with an S constituent like that in (15) above to form an **S'/S-bar** (pronounced 'ess-bar') constituent like that shown below (simplified by not showing the internal structure of the VP *trying to help you*, which is as in (11) above):

(21)

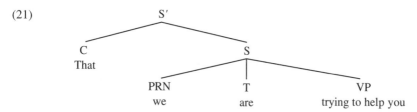

However, the claim that a clause introduced by a complementiser has the status of an S-bar constituent falls foul of the **Headedness Principle** (12), which requires that every syntactic structure be a projection of a *head word*. The principle is violated because S-bar in (21) is analysed as a projection of the S constituent *we are trying to help you*, and S is clearly not a word (but rather a string of words).

An interesting way round the *headedness* problem is to suppose that the head of a clausal structure introduced by a complementiser is the complementiser itself: since this is a single word, there would then be no violation of the Headedness Principle (12) requiring every syntactic structure to be a projection of a head word. Let's therefore assume that the complementiser *that* merges with the TP *we are trying to help you* (whose structure is shown in (17) above) to form the **CP/complementiser projection/complementiser phrase** in (22) below:

(22)

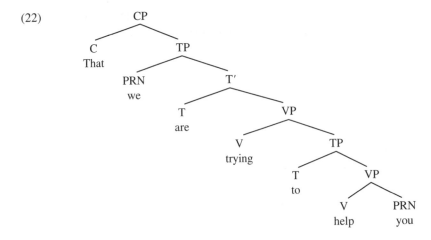

(22) tells us that the complementiser *that* is the **head** of the overall clause *that we are trying to help you* (and conversely, the overall clause is a **projection** of *that*) – and indeed this is implicit in the traditional description of such structures as *that*-clauses. (22) also tells us that the complement of *that* is the TP/tense phrase *we are trying to help you*. Clauses introduced by complementisers have been taken to have the status of CP/complementiser phrase constituents since the pioneering work of Stowell (1981) and Chomsky (1986b).

An interesting aspect of the analyses in (17) and (22) above is that clauses and sentences are analysed as **headed** structures – i.e. as projections of head words (in conformity with the Headedness Principle). In other words, just as phrases are projections of a head word (e.g. a verb phrase like *help you* is a projection of the verb *help*), so too a sentence like *We will help you* is a projection of the auxiliary *will*, and a complement clause like the bracketed *that*-clause in *I can't promise [that we will help you]* is a projection of the complementiser *that*. This enables us to arrive at a unitary analysis of the structure of phrases, clauses and sentences, in that clauses and sentences (like phrases) are projections of head words. More generally, it leads us to the conclusion that clauses/sentences are simply particular kinds of phrases (e.g. a *that*-clause is a complementiser phrase).

An assumption which is implicit in the analyses which we have presented here is that phrases and sentences are **derived** (i.e. formed) in a **bottom-up** fashion (i.e. they are built up from bottom to top). For example, the clause in (22) involves the following sequence of **merger** operations: (i) the verb *help* is merged with the pronoun *you* to form the VP *help you*; (ii) the resulting VP is merged with the non-finite T/tense particle *to* to form the TP *to help you*; (iii) this TP is in turn merged with the verb *trying* to form the VP *trying to help you*; (iv) the resulting VP is merged with the T/tense auxiliary *are* to form the T-bar *are trying to help* *you*; (v) this T-bar is merged with its subject *we* to form the TP *we are trying to help you*; and (vi) the resulting TP is in turn merged with the C/complementiser *that* to form the CP structure (22) *that we are trying to help you*. By saying that the structure (22) is derived in a **bottom-up** fashion, we mean that lower parts of the structure nearer the bottom of the tree are formed before higher parts of the structure nearer the top of the tree. (An alternative **top-down** model is presented in Phillips 2003.)

3.4   Specifiers

A question which arises from our analysis of tense auxiliaries in (17/22) above as having an immediate projection into T-bar and an extended projection into TP is whether there are other constituents which can have both an intermediate and an extended projection. The answer is 'Yes', as we can see by comparing the alternative answers (23i/ii) given by speaker B below:

(23)   SPEAKER A: Where did she hit him?
            SPEAKER B: (i) *On the nose*
                        (ii) *Right on the nose*

Let's first look at the structure of reply (i) *On the nose* in (23B), before turning to consider the structure of reply (ii) *Right on the nose*. *On the nose* in (23Bi) is a prepositional phrase/PP derived in the following fashion. The determiner *the* is merged with the noun *nose* to form the DP/determiner phrase *the nose* in (24) below:

(24)

DP
D   N
the   nose

(In work in the 1960s and 1970s, expressions like *the nose* were taken to have the categorial status of a NP/noun phrase; but here we follow more recent work dating from Abney 1987 which takes them to have the status of a DP/determiner phrase.) The preposition *on* is then merged with the resulting DP *the nose* to form the prepositional phrase/PP *on the nose*, which has the structure (25) below:

(25)
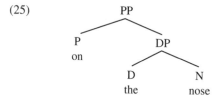

PP
P   DP
on
         D   N
         the   nose

The overall expression *on the nose* is a projection of the preposition *on* and so has the status of a prepositional phrase: the head of the PP *on the nose* is the preposition *on* and the complement of the preposition *on* is the DP *the nose*.

Given the traditional assumption that a verb or preposition which takes a noun or pronoun expression as its complement is **transitive**, *on* is a transitive preposition in this use, and *the nose* is its complement.

Now consider the structure of reply (ii) *Right on the nose* in (23B). This differs from the PP *on the nose* in that it also contains the adverb *right*. It seems implausible to suppose that the adverb *right* is the head of the overall expression, since this would mean that *right on the nose* was an adverbial phrase/ADVP: on the contrary, it seems more plausible to suppose that *right on the nose* is a prepositional phrase/PP in which the adverb *right* is a **modifier** of some kind which serves to extend the prepositional expression *on the nose* into the even larger prepositional expression *right on the nose* (so that the head of the structure is once again the preposition *on*). Some evidence that *right on the nose* is a PP (and not an ADVP) comes from **cleft sentences** (i.e. structures of the form 'It was *a car* that John bought', where the italicised constituent *a car* is said to be **focused**, and hence to occupy **focus** position in the cleft sentence structure). As we see from (26) below:

(26) (a)   It was *with great sadness* that he announced the resignation of the chairman
    (b)   *It was *very sadly* that he announced the resignation of the chairman

a prepositional phrase/PP like *with great sadness* can be **focused** in a cleft sentence, but not an adverbial phrase/ADVP like *very sadly*. In the light of this observation, consider the sentences below:

(27) (a)   It was *on the nose* that she hit him
    (b)   It was *right on the nose* that she hit him

The fact that both *on the nose* and *right on the nose* can occupy **focus** position in a cleft sentence suggests that both are PP/prepositional phrase constituents: *right on the nose* cannot be an ADVP/adverbial phrase since we see from (26b) above that adverbial expressions cannot be focused in cleft sentences.

The conclusion we reach from the data in (26)–(27) above is that the adverb *right* in *right on the nose* serves to extend the prepositional expression *on the nose* into the even larger prepositional expression *right on the nose*. Using the **bar notation** introduced in (17) above, we can analyse *right on the nose* in the following terms. The preposition *on* merges with its DP complement *the nose* to form the intermediate prepositional projection *on the nose* which has the categorial status of **P'** (or **P-bar**, pronounced 'pee-bar'); the resulting P-bar *on the nose* is then merged with the adverb *right* to form the PP below:

(28)

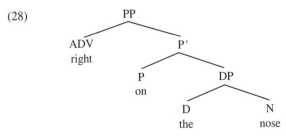

In other words, just as a tense auxiliary like *are* can be projected into a T′ like *are trying to help you* by merger with a following VP complement and then further projected into TP by merger with a preceding pronoun subject such as *we*, so too a preposition like *on* can be projected into a P′ like *on the nose* by merger with a following DP complement and then further projected into a PP like *right on the nose* by merger with a preceding adverbial modifier such as *right*.

Although *we* in (17) serves a different grammatical function from *right* in (28) (in that *we* is the **subject** of *are trying to help you*, whereas *right* is a **modifier** of *on the nose*), there is a sense in which the two occupy parallel positions within the overall structure containing them: just as *we* merges with a T′ to form a TP, so too *right* merges with a P′ to form a PP. Introducing a new technical term at this point, let's say that *we* serves as the **specifier** of the T *are*, of the T-bar *are trying to help you* and of the TP *we are trying to help you* in (17), and that *right* likewise serves as the **specifier** of the P *on*, of the P-bar *on the nose* and of the PP *right on the nose* in (28). More generally, we can say that a **specifier** is an expression which merges with an intermediate projection H-bar (where H-bar is a projection of some head word H) to project it into a maximal projection HP in the manner shown in (29) below:

(29)

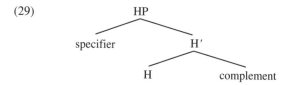

Given the informal word-order rule we suggested earlier ('Any constituent of a phrase HP which is the sister of the head H is positioned to the *right* of H, but any other constituent of HP is positioned to the *left* of H'), it follows that heads precede complements but specifiers precede heads in English: in other words, English is a language with **complement-last** and **specifier-first** word order.

The assumption that determiners can head projections of their own also has interesting theoretical implications. We see from (29) above that syntactic heads can typically be merged with both a complement *and a specifier*. If determiners function as heads, we should expect that they too will allow an appropriate kind of expression to function as their specifier (in an appropriate kind of structure). In this connection, consider the following contrast:

(30) (a)   I have never known a patient make **a** *quite so rapid* recovery
     (b)   I have never known a patient make *quite so rapid* **a** recovery

Modifiers in English are typically positioned between a determiner like *a* and a noun like *recovery* – and indeed this is the case with the modifying expression *quite so rapid* in (30a). However, in expressions like *quite so rapid* which contain a degree word like *so/too/how*, the whole degree expression can instead be positioned in front of a determiner like *a* – as in (30b). What syntactic position does the degree expression occupy in such cases? We can give a principled answer to this question if we assume that determiners can project into determiner phrases, since we can then say that a degree expression positioned in front of a determiner occupies **spec-DP** – i.e. the specifier position within the determiner phrase. On this view, (30b) would have the skeletal structure shown below (where we follow Abney 1987 in taking an expression like *quite so rapid* to be a projection of the **DEG**/degree word *so*, and hence to be a **DEGP** constituent):

(31)

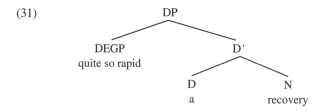

An analysis like (31) would mean that there is symmetry between the structure of determiner phrases and other types of phrase, in that (like other phrases), DPs allow a specifier of an appropriate kind. Indeed, although its internal structure is not shown in (31), the DEGP *quite so rapid* could be argued to have a similar *specifier+head+complement* structure, with the degree word *so* serving as its head, the adjective *rapid* as its complement, and the adverb *quite* as its specifier.

   As those of you familiar with earlier work will have noticed, the kind of structures we are proposing here are very different from those assumed in traditional grammar and in work in linguistics in the 1960s and 1970s. Earlier work implicitly assumed that only items belonging to **substantive/lexical categories** could project into phrases, not words belonging to **functional categories**. More specifically, earlier work assumed that there were noun phrases headed by nouns, verb phrases headed by verbs, adjectival phrases headed by adjectives, adverbial phrases headed by adverbs and prepositional phrases headed by prepositions. However, more recent work has argued that not only content words but also function words can project into phrases, so that we have tense phrases headed by a tense-marker, complementiser phrases headed by a complementiser, determiner phrases headed by a determiner – and so on. More generally, the assumption made in work over the last twenty years or so is that in principle *all* word-level categories can project into phrases. This means that some of the structures we make use of here may seem (at best) rather strange to those of you with a more traditional background, or (at worst) just plain *wrong*. However, the structure of a given phrase or sentence cannot be determined on the basis of personal prejudice or pedagogical precepts inculcated into you at secondary school, but rather has to be determined on the basis of syntactic evidence of the kind discussed in §3.6 below. I would therefore ask traditionalists to be prepared to be open to new ideas and new analyses (a necessary prerequisite for understanding in any discipline).

3.5   Intermediate and maximal projections

One aspect of our analysis of prepositional phrases which might at first sight seem puzzling is that the same expression *on the nose* is analysed as a PP in (23Bi/25), but as a P-bar in (23Bii/28). Why should this be? The answer is that the label PP denotes the **maximal projection** of (i.e. the largest expression headed by) the relevant preposition in a given structure. In (23Bi), speaker B replies *On the nose*: since the largest expression headed by *on* in (23Bi) is *On the nose*, it follows that *On the nose* has the status of a PP here. By contrast, in (23Bii) speaker B replies *Right on the nose*: here, *on the nose* is not the largest expression headed by *on*, and hence is not a PP but rather a P-bar; on the contrary, the largest expression headed by *on* in (23Bii) is *Right on the nose*, so it is this larger expression which has the status of PP.

Interestingly, there is some empirical evidence in support of the claim that *on the nose* is not a PP in (23Bii/28). As we see from examples like (32) below, a PP (like that italicised below) can generally be **preposed/fronted** (i.e. moved to the front of the sentence) in order to highlight it:

(32) (a)   They found a safe *under the floorboards*
     (b)   *Under the floorboards*, they found a safe

In the light of this observation, consider the following examples (where *right* in each case is to be interpreted as a modifier of *on the nose*):

(33) (a)   She hit him *right on the nose*
     (b)   *Right on the nose*, she hit him
     (c)   **On the nose*, she hit him *right*

The fact that *right on the nose* can be preposed in (33b) but not *on the nose* in (33c) provides evidence in support of the claim in (28) that *right on the nose* is a PP in (33a) but *on the nose* is not. If we assume that only **maximal projections** can be preposed, it follows that *right on the nose* can be preposed in (33) because it is the maximal projection of the preposition *on* (hence a PP), whereas *on the nose* cannot because it is an intermediate projection of the preposition *on* (hence a P-bar).

Although we have pointed out similarities between the structure of a PP like that in (28) and the structure of a TP like that in (17), there is a very important difference between the two. As we saw earlier from the grammaticality of *We are trying to help you* and the ungrammaticality of **Are trying to help you* as replies to the question *What are you doing?*, tense auxiliaries like *are* obligatorily require an appropriate specifier (e.g. a subject pronoun like *we*). By contrast, the fact that we can reply either *On the nose* or *Right on the nose* to a question like *Where did she hit him?* tells us that prepositions can be used either with or without an appropriate kind of specifier (e.g. an adverbial modifier like *right*). So, a significant difference between auxiliaries and prepositions is that it is *obligatory* for an auxiliary to have a specifier but *optional* for a preposition to have a specifier.

Just as prepositional phrases can have an (optional) adverbial modifier as their specifier, so too can adjectival phrases – as we see from the alternative replies given by speaker B in (34) below:

(34) SPEAKER A: How does your mother feel about your brother's success?
      SPEAKER B: (i) *Proud of him* (ii) *Very proud of him*

Reply (i) *Proud of him* in (34B) is an **adjectival phrase/AP** derived as follows. The preposition *of* merges with the pronoun *him* to form the PP/prepositional phrase *of him*. This is then merged with the adjective *proud* to form the AP/adjectival phrase *proud of him*, which has the structure (35) below:

(35)

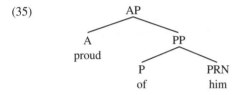

But what is the structure of reply (ii) *Very proud of him* in (34B)? This differs from *Proud of him* in that it contains the adverb *very*. It seems implausible that the adverb *very* could be the head of the overall expression *Very proud of him* since this would mean that *very proud of him* was an ADVP (adverbial phrase); but an ADVP analysis would be problematic because a question like *How does she feel?* can have an adjectival expression like *Happy* as an appropriate reply but not an adverbial expression like *Happily*. Since *Very proud of him* can be used to reply to the *how*-question asked by speaker A in (34), *very proud of him* must be an adjectival expression headed by the adjective *proud*. Using the **bar notation** introduced earlier, we can say that the A/adjective *proud* merges with its PP/prepositional phrase complement *of him* to form the A-bar (intermediate adjectival projection) *proud of him*, and that the resulting A-bar in turn merges with the adverbial specifier *very* to form the full AP/adjectival phrase in (36) below:

(36)

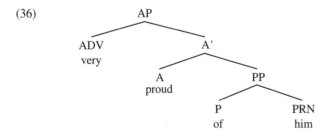

Evidence in support of the analysis in (36) comes from data relating to the preposing of adjectival expressions in sentences such as (37) below:

(37) (a)   She certainly seems to be *very proud of him*

    (b)   *Very proud of him*, she certainly seems to be

    (c)   **Proud of him*, she certainly seems to be *very*

If we assume (as we did in our earlier discussion of (33) above) that only maximal projections can be preposed in this way (not intermediate projections), we can provide a straightforward account of the data in (37) in terms of the analysis in (36). The structure in (36) tells us that *very proud of him* is the maximal projection of the adjective *proud*, and so is an AP/adjectival phrase constituent; hence it can be preposed in (37a) by virtue of its status as a maximal projection. By contrast, (36) tells us that *proud of him* is an intermediate projection of the adjective *proud* and hence an A-bar constituent: because only maximal projections like AP can be preposed, and because *proud of him* is only an intermediate A-bar projection, it cannot be preposed – hence the ungrammaticality of (37c).

A variety of other types of expression can also have extended projections via merger with an optional specifier of an appropriate kind. One such are adverbial expressions like those italicised in (38) below:

(38) (a)   She made up her mind *independently of me*

    (b)   She made up her mind *quite independently of me*

The adverb *independently* can be merged with a PP/prepositional phrase complement like *of me* to form the adverbial expression *independently of me*: this can serve either as a ADVP/adverbial phrase on its own – as in (38a) – or as an intermediate ADV-bar projection which can be extended into an ADVP by merger with an appropriate specifier (like the adverb *quite*) as in (38b).

Much the same might be said about the italicised noun phrases in (39) below (if the analysis of these structures in Radford 1993 is along the right lines):

(39) (a)   The opposition will oppose the/any *ban on imports*

    (b)   The opposition will oppose the/any *government ban on imports*

The noun *ban* can be merged with a following prepositional phrase complement like *on imports* to form the nominal expression *ban on imports*: this can either serve as a complete **noun phrase/NP** on its own, or can serve as an intermediate **N-bar** projection which is subsequently merged with an appropriate specifier (like the noun *government*) to form the larger noun phrase/NP *government ban on imports*. Because a noun expression headed by a singular count noun (like *ban*) must be modified by a determiner or quantifier, the resulting NP in either case must subsequently be merged with a determiner like *the* or a quantifier like *any*, so deriving a DP/determiner phrase like *the (government) ban on imports* or a QP/quantifier phrase like *any (government) ban on imports*.

In all of the structures which we have looked at so far which contain a specifier (i.e. in (17), (22), (28), (36), (38b) and (39b) above), the specifier has been a single word. However, this is by no means always the case, as we can see by comparing the two clauses in (40) below:

(40) (a)   *He* has resigned
    (b)   *The chairman* has resigned

(40a) is derived by merging the T/tense auxiliary *has* with its verb complement *resigned* to form the intermediate T-bar projection *has resigned*, and then merging the resulting T-bar with the pronoun *he* which serves as its specifier/subject to derive the extended TP projection in (41) below:

(41)

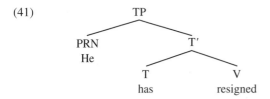

Now consider how we derive (40b) *The chairman has resigned*. As before, the tense auxiliary *has* merges with its verb complement *resigned* to form the T-bar *has resigned*; and as before, the resulting T-bar then merges with its subject specifier. However, this time the subject is not the single word *he* but rather a determiner phrase/DP *the chairman* which has itself been formed by merging the determiner *the* with the noun *chairman*. The result of merging the DP *the chairman* with the T-bar *has resigned* is to derive the TP (42) below:

(42)

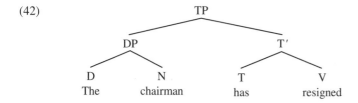

Evidence that *the chairman* is indeed the subject (and specifier) of *has* in (42) comes from auxiliary inversion facts in relation to sentences such as:

(43) (a)   *Has* **he** resigned?
    (b)   *Has* **the chairman** resigned?

As we see by comparing the statement (40a) *He has resigned* with the corresponding question (43a) *Has he resigned?* a question like (43a) is formed by moving a finite auxiliary (*has*) in front of its subject (*he*). Hence, the fact that the auxiliary *has* in (40b) moves in front of *the chairman* in (43b) *Has the chairman resigned?* suggests that *the chairman* is the subject of *has* in (40b) *The chairman has resigned* – precisely as is claimed in (42).

    If we compare (41) with (42), we can see that a specifier can be either a single word like *he* in (41) or a phrase like the DP *the chairman* in (42). In much the same way, a complement can be either a single word or a phrase. For example, in (42), the complement of *has* is the verb *resigned*; but in a more complex structure like (44) below:

(44)

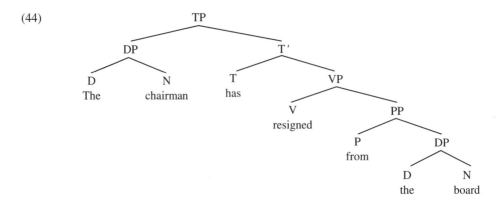

the complement of *has* is the verb phrase *resigned from the board*, which is formed
by merging the verb *resigned* with its PP/prepositional phrase complement *from
the board*.

3.6   Testing structure

Thus far, we have argued that phrases and sentences are built up by
merging successive pairs of constituents into larger and larger structures, and that
the resulting structure can be represented in terms of a labelled tree diagram. The
tree diagrams which we use to represent syntactic structure make specific claims
about how sentences are built up out of various different kinds of **constituent**
(i.e. syntactic unit): hence, trees can be said to represent the **constituent structure** of sentences. But this raises the question of how we know (and how we can
test) whether the claims made about syntactic structure in tree diagrams are true.
So far, we have relied mainly on *intuition* in analysing the structure of sentences –
we have in effect *guessed* at the structure. However, it is unwise to rely on intuition in attempting to determine the structure of a given expression in a given
language. For, while experienced linguists over a period of years tend to acquire
fairly strong intuitions about structure, novices by contrast tend to have relatively
weak, uncertain and unreliable intuitions; moreover, even the intuitions of supposed experts may ultimately turn out to be based on little more than personal
preference.

For this reason, it is more satisfactory (and more accurate) to regard constituent
structure as having the status of a *theoretical construct*. That is to say, it is part
of the theoretical apparatus which linguists find they need to make use of in
order to explain certain data about language (just as molecules, atoms and sub-
atomic particles are constructs which physicists find they need to make use of in
order to explain the nature of matter in the universe). It is no more reasonable
to rely wholly on intuition to determine syntactic structure than it would be to
rely on intuition to determine molecular structure. Inevitably, then, much of the

evidence for syntactic structure is of an essentially empirical character, based on the observed grammatical properties of particular types of expression. The evidence typically takes the form 'Unless we posit that such-and-such an expression has such-and-such a constituent structure, we shall be unable to provide a principled account of the observed grammatical properties of the expression.' Thus, structural representations ultimately have to be justified in empirical terms, i.e. in terms of whether or not they provide a principled account of the grammatical properties of phrases and sentences.

So, a tree diagram like (44) has the status of a hypothesis (i.e. untested and unproven assumption) about the structure of the corresponding sentence *The chairman has resigned from the board.* How can we test our hypothesis and determine whether (44) is or isn't an appropriate representation of the structure of the sentence? The answer is that there are a number of standard heuristics (i.e. 'tests') which we can use to determine structure. One such test relates to the phenomenon of **coordination**. English and other languages have a variety of **coordinating conjunctions** (which we might designate by the category label CONJ – or perhaps just J) like *and/but/or* which can be used to **coordinate** (= **conjoin** = join together) expressions such as those bracketed below:

(45) (a)   [fond of cats] *and* [afraid of dogs]
     (b)   [slowly] *but* [surely]
     (c)   [to go] *or* [to stay]

In each of the expressions in (45), an italicised coordinating conjunction has been used to conjoin the bracketed pairs of expressions. Clearly, any adequate grammar of English will have to provide a principled answer to the question: 'What kinds of strings (i.e. sequences of words) can and cannot be coordinated?'

Now, it turns out that we can't just coordinate any random set of strings, as we see by comparing the grammatical reply produced by speaker B in (46) below:

(46)   SPEAKER A: What does he do to keep fit?
              SPEAKER B: Run *up the hill* and *up the mountain*

with the ungrammatical reply produced by speaker B in (47) below:

(47)   SPEAKER A: What did he do about his bills?
              SPEAKER B: *Ring *up the phone company* and *up the electricity company*

Why should it be possible to coordinate the string *up the hill* with the string *up the mountain* in (46), but not possible to coordinate the string *up the phone company* with the string *up the electricity company* in (47)? We can provide a principled answer to this question in terms of constituent structure: the italicised string *up the hill* in (46) is a constituent of the phrase *run up the hill* (*up the hill* is a prepositional phrase, in fact), and so can be coordinated with another similar type of prepositional phrase (e.g. a PP such as *up the mountain*, or *down the hill*, or *along the path*, etc.). Conversely, however, the string *up the phone company* in (47) is not a constituent of the phrase *ring up the phone company*, and so cannot be coordinated with another similar string like *up the electricity company*. (Traditional grammarians say that *up* is associated with *ring* in expressions like *ring up someone*, and that the expression *ring up* forms a kind of complex verb which carries the sense of 'telephone'.) On the basis of contrasts such as these, we can formulate the following generalisation:

(48)   Only constituents of the same type can be coordinated

A **constraint** (i.e. principle imposing restrictions on certain types of grammatical operation) along the lines of (48) is assumed in much work in traditional grammar.

Having established the constraint (48), we can now make use of it as a way of testing the tree diagram in (44) above. In this connection, consider the data in (49) below (in which the bracketed strings have been coordinated by *and*):

(49) (a)   The chairman has resigned from [*the board*] and [*the company*]
    (b)   The chairman has resigned [*from the board*] and [*from the company*]
    (c)   The chairman has [*resigned from the board*] and [*gone abroad*]
    (d)   The chairman [*has resigned from the board*] and [*is living in Utopia*]
    (e)   *The [*chairman has resigned from the board*] and [*company has replaced him*]
    (f)   [*The chairman has resigned from the board*] and [*the company has replaced him*]

(49a) provides us with evidence in support of the claim in (44) that *the board* is a determiner phrase constituent, since it can be coordinated with another DP like *the company*; similarly, (49b) provides us with evidence that *from the board* is a prepositional phrase constituent, since it can be coordinated with another PP like *from the company*; likewise, (49c) provides evidence that *resigned from the board* is a verb phrase constituent, since it can be coordinated with another VP like *gone abroad*; in much the same way, (49d) provides evidence that *has resigned from the board* is a T-bar constituent, since it can be coordinated with another T′ like *is living in Utopia* (thereby providing interesting empirical evidence in support of the *binary-branching* structure assumed in the TP analysis of clauses, and against the ternary-branching analysis assumed in the S analysis of clauses); and in addition, (49f) provides evidence that *the chairman has resigned from the board* is a TP constituent, since it can be coordinated with another TP like *the company has replaced him*. Conversely, however, the fact that (49e) is ungrammatical suggests that (precisely as (44) claims) the string *chairman has resigned from the board* is not a constituent, since it cannot be coordinated with a parallel string like *company has replaced him* (and the constraint in (48) tells us that two strings of words can only be coordinated if both are constituents – and more precisely, if both are constituents of the same type). Overall, then, the coordination data in (49) provide empirical evidence in support of the analysis in (44). (It should be noted, however, that the coordination test is not always straightforward to apply, in part because there is more than one type of coordination – see e.g. Radford 1997a, pp. 104–7. Apparent complications arise in relation to sentences like 'He is *cross with her* and *in a filthy mood*', where the AP/adjectival phrase *cross with her* has been coordinated with the PP/prepositional phrase *in a filthy mood*: to say that these seemingly different AP and PP constituents are 'of the same type' requires a more abstract analysis than is implied by category labels like AP and PP, perhaps taking them to share in common the property of being predicative expressions. See Phillips 2003 for an alternative approach to coordination, and Johnson 2002 for problematic cases in German.)

There are a variety of other ways of testing structure, but we will not attempt to cover them all here (see Radford 1997a, pp. 102–16 for more detailed discussion). However, we will briefly mention two which are already familiar from earlier discussion. In §2.3, we noted that **substitution** is a useful tool for determining the categorial status of words. We can also use substitution as a way of testing whether a given string of words is a constituent or not, by seeing whether the relevant string can be replaced by (or serve as the antecedent of) a single word. In this connection, consider:

(50) (a)   *The chairman* has resigned from the board, and **he** is now living in Utopia
   (b)   The press say that the chairman has *resigned from the board*, and **so** he has
   (c)   If the Managing Director says the chairman has *resigned from the board*, he must have **done**
   (d)   If the chairman has *resigned from the board* (**which** you say he has), how come his car is still in the company car park?

The fact that the expression *the chairman* in (50a) can be substituted (or referred back to) by a single word (in this case, the pronoun *he*) provides evidence in support of the claim in (44) that *the chairman* is a single constituent (a DP/determiner phrase, to be precise). Likewise, the fact that the expression *resigned from the board* in (50b,c,d) can serve as the antecedent of *so/done/which* provides evidence in support of the claim in (44) that *resigned from the board* is a constituent (more precisely, a VP/verb phrase).

A further kind of constituent structure test which we made use of in §3.5 above relates to the possibility of **preposing** a constituent in order to highlight it in some way (i.e. in order to mark it out as a topic containing familiar/old information, or a focused constituent containing unfamiliar/new information). In our earlier discussion of (32), (33) and (37) above, we concluded that only a **maximal projection** can be highlighted in this way. This being so, one way we can test whether a given expression is a maximal projection or not is by seeing whether it can be preposed. In this connection, consider the following sentence:

(51)   The press said that the chairman would resign from the board, and *resigned from the board* he has

The fact that the italicised expression *resigned from the board* can be preposed in (51) indicates that it must be a maximal projection: this is consistent with the analysis in (44) which tells us that *resigned from the board* is a verb phrase which is the maximal projection of the verb *resigned*.

However, an important caveat which should be noted in relation to the preposing test is that particular expressions can sometimes be difficult (or even impossible) to prepose even though they are maximal projections. This is because there are **constraints** (i.e. restrictions) on such movement operations. One such constraint can be illustrated by the following contrast:

(52) (a)   I will certainly try to give up smoking
    (b)   *Give up smoking*, I will certainly try to
    (c)   **To give up smoking*, I will certainly try

Here, the VP/verb phrase *give up smoking* can be highlighted by being preposed, but the TP/infinitival tense phrase *to give up smoking* cannot – even though it is a maximal projection (by virtue of being the largest expression headed by infinitival *to*). What is the nature of the restriction on preposing *to+infinitive* expressions illustrated by the ungrammaticality of (52c)? The answer is not clear, but may be semantic in nature. When an expression is preposed, this is in order to highlight its semantic content in some way (e.g. for purposes of contrast – as in '*Syntax*, I don't like but *phonology* I do'). It may be that its lack of intrinsic lexical content makes infinitival *to* an unsuitable candidate for highlighting, and this may in turn be reflected in the fact that infinitival *to* cannot carry contrastive stress – as we see from the ungrammaticality of *'I don't want TO', where capitals mark contrastive stress. What this suggests is that:

(53)   The smallest possible maximal projection is moved which contains the highlighted material

So, if we want to highlight the semantic content of the VP *give up smoking*, we prepose the VP *give up smoking* rather than the TP *to give up smoking* because the VP is smaller than the TP containing it.

However, this is by no means the only constraint on preposing, as we see from (54) below (where *FBA* is an abbreviation for the *Federal Bureau of Assassinations* – a purely fictitious body, of course):

(54) (a)   Nobody had expected that the FBA would assassinate the king of Ruritania
    (b)   **King of Ruritania*, nobody had expected that the FBA would assassinate the
    (c)   *The king of Ruritania*, nobody had expected that the FBA would assassinate
    (d)   **The FBA would assassinate the king of Ruritania*, nobody had expected that
        (NB. *that* = ðət)
    (e)   *That the FBA would assassinate the king of Ruritania*, nobody had expected

The ungrammaticality of (54b,d) tells us that we can't prepose the NP *king of Ruritania* or the TP *the FBA would assassinate the king of Ruritania*. Why should this be? One possibility (briefly hinted at in Chomsky 1999) is that there may be a constraint on movement operations to the effect that a DP can be preposed but not an NP which is contained within a DP, and likewise that a CP can be preposed but not a TP which is contained within a CP. One implementation of this idea would be to posit a constraint like (55) below:

(55)   **Functional Head Constraint/FHC**
              The complement of a certain type of functional head F (e.g. a determiner or complementiser) cannot be moved on its own (without also moving F)

Suppose, then, that we want to highlight the NP *king of Ruritania* in (54) by preposing. (53) tells us to move *the smallest possible maximal projection containing the highlighted material*, and hence we first try to move this NP on its own: but the Functional Head Constraint tells us that it is not possible to prepose this NP on its own, because it is the complement of the determiner *the*. We therefore prepose the next smallest maximal projection containing the highlighted NP *king of Ruritania* – namely the DP *the king of Ruritania*; and as the grammaticality of (54c) shows, the resulting sentence is grammatical.

Now suppose that we want to highlight the TP *the FBA would assassinate the king of Ruritania*. (53) tells us to move the smallest maximal projection containing the highlighted material – but FHC (55) tells us that we cannot prepose a constituent which is the complement of a complementiser. Hence, we prepose the *next smallest* maximal projection containing the TP we want to highlight, namely the CP *that the FBA would assassinate the king of Ruritania* – as in (54e).

However, an apparent problem for the **Functional Head Constraint** (55) is posed by examples like:

(56) (a)   *Surrender to the enemy*, I never **will**
     (b)   *Surrender to the enemy*, he resolutely refused **to**

The preposed verb phrase *surrender to the enemy* is the complement of *will* in (56a), and the complement of *to* in (56b). Given the analysis in §2.7 and §2.8, *will* is a finite T/tense constituent and *to* is a non-finite T/tense particle. If (as we have assumed so far) T is a functional category, we would expect the Functional Head Constraint (55) to block preposing of the VP *surrender to the enemy* because this VP is the complement of the functional T constituent *will/to*. The fact that the resulting sentences (56a,b) are grammatical might lead us to follow Chomsky (1999) in concluding that T is a **substantive** category rather than a **functional category**, and hence does not block preposing of its complement. Alternatively, it may be that the constraint only applies to certain types of functional category (as hinted at in (55)) – e.g. D and C but not T (perhaps because D and C are the 'highest' heads within nominal and clausal structures respectively – and indeed in chapter 10 we shall reformulate this constraint along such lines).

It is interesting to note that alongside sentences like (56) above in which a phrase has been highlighted by being preposed, we also find sentences like (57) below in which a single word has been preposed:

(57) (a)   *Surrender*, I never will
     (b)   *Surrender*, he resolutely refused to

In (57) the verb *surrender* has been preposed on its own. At first sight, this might seem to contradict our earlier statement that only **maximal projections** can undergo preposing. However, more careful reflection shows that there is no contradiction here: after all, the maximal projection of a head H is *the largest expression headed by H*; and in a sentence like *I never will surrender*, the largest expression headed by the verb *surrender* is the verb *surrender* itself – hence, *surrender* in (57) is indeed a maximal projection. More generally, this tells us that an individual word can itself be a maximal projection, if it has no complement or specifier of its own.

The overall conclusion to be drawn from our discussion here is that the preposing test has to be used with care. If an expression can be preposed in order to highlight it, it is a maximal projection; if it cannot, this may either be because it is not a maximal projection, or because (even though it *is* a maximal projection) a syntactic **constraint** of some kind prevents it from being preposed, or because its head word has insufficient semantic content to make it a suitable candidate for highlighting.

3.7   Syntactic relations

Throughout this chapter, we have argued that phrases and sentences are formed by a series of binary merger operations, and that the resulting structures can be represented in the form of tree diagrams. Because they mark the way that words are combined together to form phrases of various types, tree diagrams are referred to in the relevant technical literature as **phrase-markers** (abbreviated to **P-markers**). They show us how a phrase or sentence is built up out of **constituents** of various types: hence, a tree diagram provides a visual representation of the **constituent structure** of the corresponding expression. Each **node** in the tree (i.e. each point in the tree which carries a category label like N, V, A′, T′, PP, CP etc.) represents a different constituent of the sentence; hence, there are as many different constituents in any given phrase-marker as there are nodes carrying category labels. Nodes at the very bottom of the tree are called **terminal nodes**, and other nodes are **non-terminal nodes**: so, for example, all the D, N, T, V and P nodes in (44) are terminal nodes, and all the DP, PP, VP, T′ and TP nodes are non-terminal nodes. The topmost node in any tree structure (i.e. TP in the case of (44) above) is said to be its **root**. Each terminal node in the tree carries a single **lexical item** (i.e. an item from the **lexicon**/dictionary, like *dog* or *go* etc.): lexical items are sets of phonological, semantic and grammatical features (with category labels like N, V, T, C etc. being used as shorthand abbreviations for the set of grammatical features carried by the relevant items).

It is useful to develop some terminology to describe the syntactic relations between constituents, since these relations turn out to be central to syntactic description. Essentially, a P-marker is a graph comprising a set of points

(= labelled nodes), connected by branches (= solid lines) representing **contain-ment** relations (i.e. telling us which constituents contain or are contained within which other constituents). We can illustrate what this means in terms of the following abstract tree structure (where A, B, C, D, E, F, G, H and J are different nodes in the tree, representing different constituents):

(58)

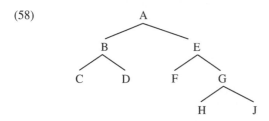

In (58), G **immediately contains** H and J (and conversely H and J are the two constituents immediately contained within G, and hence are the two **immediate constituents** of G): this is shown by the fact that H and J are the two nodes immediately beneath G which are connected to G by a **branch** (solid line). Likewise, E immediately contains F and G; B immediately contains C and D; and A immediately contains B and E. We can also say that E **contains** F, G, H and J; and that A contains B, C, D, E, F, G, H and J (and likewise that G contains H and J; and B contains C and D). Using equivalent kinship terminology, we can say that A is the **mother** of B and E (and conversely B and E are the two **daughters** of A); B is the mother of C and D; E is the mother of F and G; and G is the mother of H and J. Likewise, B and E are **sisters** (by virtue of both being daughters of A) – as are C and D; F and G; and H and J.

A particularly important syntactic relation is **c-command** (a conventional abbreviation of **constituent-command**), which provides us with a useful way of determining the relative position of two different constituents within the same tree (in particular, whether one is lower in the tree than the other or not). We can define this relation informally as follows (where X, Y and Z are three different nodes):

(59)   **C-command**
         A constituent X c-commands its sister constituent Y and any constituent Z
         which is contained within Y

A more concrete way of visualising this is to think of a tree diagram as representing a network of train stations, with each of the labelled nodes representing the name of a different station in the network, and the branches representing the rail tracks linking the stations. We can then say that one node X c-commands another node Y if you can get from X to Y on the network by taking a northbound train, getting off at the first station, changing trains there and then travelling one or more stops south *on a different line*.

In the light of the definition of **c-command** given above, let's consider which constituents each of the nodes in (58) c-commands. A doesn't c-command any of the other nodes, since A has no sister. B c-commands E, F, G, H and J because B's sister is E, and E contains F, G, H and J. C c-commands only D, because C's sister is D, and D does not contain any other constituent; likewise, D c-commands only C. E c-commands B, C and D because B is the sister of E and B contains C and D. F c-commands G, H and J, because G is the sister of F and G contains H and J. G c-commands only F, because G's sister is F, and F does not contain any other constituents. H and J likewise c-command only each other because they are sisters which have no daughters of their own.

We can illustrate the importance of the c-command relation in syntactic description by looking at the distribution of a class of expressions which are known as **anaphors**. These include **reflexives** (i.e. *self/selves* forms like *myself/yourself/themselves* etc.) and **reciprocals** like *each other* and *one another*. Such anaphors have the property that they cannot be used to refer directly to an entity in the outside world, but rather must be **bound** by (i.e. take their reference from) an **antecedent** elsewhere in the same phrase or sentence. Where an anaphor has no (suitable) antecedent to bind it, the resulting structure is ungrammatical – as we see from contrasts such as those in (60) below:

(60) (a)   **He** must feel proud of *himself*
    (b)   *****She** must feel proud of *himself*
    (c)   **Himself* must feel proud of you

In (60a), the third-person-masculine-singular anaphor *himself* is bound by a suitable third-person-masculine-singular antecedent (*he*), with the result that (60a) is grammatical. But in (60b), *himself* has no suitable antecedent (the feminine pronoun *she* is not a suitable antecedent for the masculine anaphor *himself*), and so is **unbound** (with the result that (60b) is ill-formed). In (60c), there is no antecedent of any kind for the anaphor *himself*, with the result that the anaphor is again unbound and the sentence ill-formed.

There are structural restrictions on the binding of anaphors by their antecedents, as we see from:

(61) (a)   **The president** may blame *himself*
    (b)   **Supporters of **the president** may blame *himself*

(62) (a)   **They** may implicate *each other*
    (b)   **The evidence against **them** may implicate *each other*

As a third-person-masculine-singular anaphor, *himself* must be bound by a third-person-masculine-singular antecedent like *the president*; similarly, as a plural anaphor, *each other* must be bound by a plural antecedent like *they/them*. However, it would seem from the contrasts above that the antecedent must occupy the right kind of position within the structure in order to bind the anaphor or else the resulting sentence will be ungrammatical. The question of what is the right position for the antecedent can be defined in terms of the following structural condition:

(63)   **C-command condition on binding**
A bound constituent must be c-commanded by an appropriate antecedent

The relevant bound constituent is the reflexive anaphor *himself* in (61), and its antecedent is *the president*; the bound constituent in (62) is the reciprocal anaphor *each other*, and its antecedent is *they/them*. Sentence (61a) has the structure (64) below:

(64)

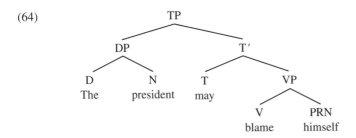

The reflexive pronoun *himself* can be bound by the DP *the president* in (64) because the sister of the DP node is the T-bar node, and the pronoun *himself* is contained within the relevant T-bar node (by virtue of being one of the grand-children of T-bar): consequently, the DP *the president* c-commands the anaphor *himself* and the binding condition (63) is satisfied. We therefore correctly specify that (61a) *The president may blame himself* is grammatical, with *the president* interpreted as the antecedent of *himself*.

But now consider why a structure like (65) below is ungrammatical (cf. (61b) above):

(65)

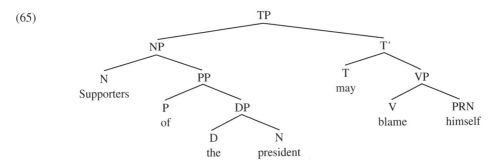

The answer is that the DP node containing *the president* doesn't c-command the PRN node containing *himself*, because the sister of the DP node is the P node *of*, and *himself* is not contained within (i.e. not a daughter, granddaughter, or great-granddaughter etc. of) the preposition *of*. Since there is no other appropri-ate antecedent for *himself* within the sentence (e.g. although the NP *supporters of the president* c-commands *himself*, it is not a suitable antecedent because it is a plural expression, and *himself* requires a singular antecedent), the anaphor *himself* remains unbound – in violation of the binding requirement on anaphors.

This is the reason why (61b) *Supporters of the president may blame himself* is ungrammatical.

Our brief discussion of anaphor binding here highlights the fact that the relation **c-command** has a central role to play in syntax. It also provides further evidence for positing that sentences have a hierarchical constituent structure, in that the relevant restriction on the binding of anaphors in (63) is characterised in structural terms. There's much more to be said about binding, though we shan't pursue the relevant issues here: for technical discussion, see Reuland (2001a) and Reuland and Everaert (2001).

3.8   Bare phrase structure

In this chapter, we have used a system of category labels based on the **bar notation** which has been widely adopted since the 1970s. Within this framework, a sentence like (the title of Gloria Gaynor's immortal song) *I will survive* has the structure (66) below:

(66)

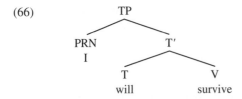

The bar notation used in (66) posits that there are three different **levels** of projection (i.e. types of expression): (i) **heads** (also called **minimal projections**) like the T/tense auxiliary *will*; (ii) **intermediate projections** like the T-bar *will survive*; and (iii) **maximal projections** like the TP *I will survive*. However, Chomsky (1999, p. 2) argues that a system of category labels which posits three different types of category label for projections of a given head H (viz. H, H-bar and HP) violates a UG principle which he terms the **Inclusiveness Condition** – outlined informally below:

(67)   **Inclusiveness Condition**
          No new information can be introduced in the course of the syntactic computation

The reason why the bar notation used in trees like (66) violates inclusiveness is as follows. When the word *will* is taken out of the lexicon, its lexical entry specifies that it has a set of properties which include the grammatical properties represented by the category label T in (66). But the tree in (66) tells us that when *will* is merged with its complement *survive*, the resulting string *will survive* belongs to the category T-bar – in other words, it is an **intermediate projection** of *will*. Likewise, the tree in (66) also tells us that the larger string *I will survive* is a TP – in other words, it is the **maximal projection** of *will*. But this information about intermediate and maximal projections is not part of the lexical entry for *will*, and hence must be added in the course of the syntactic computation. However, adding such information about projection levels violates the **Inclusiveness Condition** (67).

One way of avoiding violation of inclusiveness is to remove all information about projection levels from trees, and hence replace a tree like (66) above by one like (68) below:

(68)

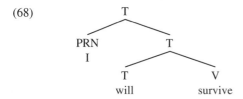

What our revised tree (68) says is that *will, will survive* and *I will survive* are all projections of the tense auxiliary *will* and hence are all **tense expressions**. Moreover, information about projection levels turns out to be entirely redundant, since it is predictable from looking at the relative positions of constituents within a given structure. Simply by looking at the positions they occupy in the tree (68) we can tell that *will* is the minimal projection of *will* (i.e. it is the smallest expression headed by *will*), that *will survive* is an intermediate projection of *will* (by virtue of being neither the smallest nor the largest expression headed by *will*) and that *I will survive* is the maximal projection of *will* (by virtue of being the largest expression headed by *will*). Similarly, we can tell that the V *survive* is both a minimal and a maximal projection, in that it is both the smallest and the largest expression headed by *survive*: hence (e.g.) it can behave like a maximal projection and undergo preposing (as in *Survive, I will*). In much the same way, we know from looking at the structure in (68) that the pronoun *I* is likewise both a minimal and a maximal projection: given their status as maximal projections, it follows that pronouns can undergo preposing (as with the pronoun *him* in *Him, I would never trust*). Since the information about projection levels in the bar notation is redundant, Chomsky reasons, such information should not be represented in the system of category labels used in tree diagrams: after all, the goal of **Minimalism** is to reduce theoretical apparatus to the minimum which is conceptually necessary.

Given the possibility (mentioned in §2.11) that categorial information (i.e. information about the category that an item belongs to) can be represented in terms of grammatical features (and hence subsumed within the set of features which characterise the idiosyncratic properties of individual words), a further possibility is that category labels like those in (68) can be entirely replaced by sets of features, so opening up the possibility of developing a theory of **bare phrase structure** – i.e. a theory in which there are no category labels in syntactic trees. An even more radical possibility along these lines would be for the structure of *I will survive* to be represented in terms of an **unlabelled tree diagram** like (69) below:

(69)

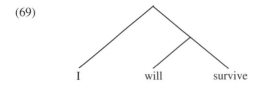

An unlabelled tree diagram like (69) tells us that the constituents of (69) are *I*, *will*, *survive*, *will survive* and *I will survive*. The lexical entries for the items *I*, *will* and *survive* comprise sets of features which include information about their grammatical and selectional properties: for example, the entry for *will* tells us that it is a finite auxiliary which selects an infinitival complement. The fact that *will* selects an infinitive complement (and that *survive* is an infinitive form and is the sister of *will*) means that *survive* must be the complement of *will* and hence that *will survive* is a projection of *will*. Likewise, the fact that *will* has an [EPP] feature requiring it to project a subject means that the nominative pronoun *I* must be the subject of *will*, and hence that *I will survive* is an extended projection of *will*. As before, the relative position of the relevant constituents within the overall structure tells us that *will* is a minimal projection (of itself), *will survive* is an intermediate projection of *will*, and *I will survive* is the maximal projection of *will*. The overall conclusion we arrive at is that the information about category labels and projection levels in a conventional labelled tree diagram like (66) above may well be redundant.

If the kind of reasoning outlined here is along the right lines, it opens up the possibility of developing a theory of **bare phrase structure** such as that outlined in a skeletal form in Chomsky (1995) and Uriagereka (1998) – though it should be noted that the relevant discussion in these two works is highly technical and not suitable for those who don't have some mathematical background in set theory. However, we shall continue to use traditional labelled trees and the bar notation to represent structure, category membership and projection levels throughout the rest of this book, since this remains the notation most widely used in contemporary work in syntax.

3.9   Summary

In this chapter, we have looked at how words are combined together to form phrases and sentences. In §3.2 we showed how more and more complex phrases can be built up by successive binary **merger** operations, each of which combines a pair of constituents to form a larger constituent. In §3.3 we argued that clauses containing a finite tense auxiliary are formed by merging the tense auxiliary with a verbal complement to form an intermediate T-bar projection which is then merged with a subject to form an extended TP/tense phrase projection. On this view, a sentence like *It may rain* would be formed by merging the present-tense auxiliary *may* with the verb *rain* to form the T-bar constituent *may rain*, and then merging the resulting T-bar with the pronoun *it* to derive the TP

It may rain. We also noted the claim made by Chomsky in earlier work that the requirement for tense auxiliaries to have a subject is a consequence of a principle of Universal Grammar called the **Extended Projection Principle/EPP**, which requires a finite T to have an extended projection into a TP containing a subject; and we noted that in more recent work this subject-requirement is described by saying that a finite T has an [EPP] feature requiring it to have an extended projection into a TP containing a subject. We went on to suggest that clauses introduced by a complementiser/C are formed by merging C with a TP complement to form a CP/complementiser phrase. In §3.4 we argued that a prepositional phrase like *right on the nose* has a similar internal structure to a TP like *He has resigned*, and that in both cases the head P/T *on/has* merges with a following complement to form the intermediate P-bar/T-bar projection *on the nose/has resigned* which in turn is merged with a preceding **specifier** to form the extended PP/TP projection *right on the nose/he has resigned*. In §3.5 we went on to argue that other types of head (e.g. adjectives, adverbs, and nouns) can likewise project both into an intermediate projection via merger with a following complement, and into an extended projection via merger with a preceding specifier. We introduced the term **maximal projection** to denote the largest expression headed by a particular word in a given structure. In §3.6, we looked at ways of testing constituent structure, outlining tests relating to coordination, substitution, and preposing. We noted that a variety of factors can sometimes prevent constituents from being preposed in order to highlight them; for example, items with little or no substantive lexical content generally cannot be preposed, and there are also syntactic restrictions on preposing – e.g. such movement operations are subject to a **Functional Head Constraint** which bars the complement of a certain type of functional head (e.g. determiner or complementiser) from being moved on its own. In §3.7, we looked at the syntactic relations between constituents within tree diagrams, noting that the relation **c-command** plays a central role in syntax, e.g. in relation to anaphor binding. In §3.8 we discussed the potential redundancy in the system of labels used to represent categories and projection levels in traditional phrase structure trees, and noted that Chomsky has been seeking to develop a theory of **bare phrase structure** in recent work.

For those of you familiar with work in traditional grammar, it will be clear that the assumptions made about syntactic structure within the Minimalist framework are somewhat different from those made in traditional grammar. Of course, there are some similarities: within both types of framework, it is assumed that lexical categories project into phrases, so that by combining a noun with one or more other constituents we can form a noun phrase, and likewise by combining a verb/preposition/adjective/adverb with one or more other constituents we can form a verb phrase/prepositional phrase/adjectival phrase/adverbial phrase. But there are two major differences between the two types of framework. One is that Minimalism (unlike traditional grammar) assumes that function words also project into phrases (so that by combining a determiner with a noun expression we form a determiner phrase, by combining a (present- or past-tense) auxiliary/T with a complement and a subject we form a Tense Projection/TP, and by combining a complementiser with a TP we form a complementiser projection/CP). This in some cases results in an analysis which is rather different from that found in traditional grammar (e.g. in that *the nose* would be considered a noun phrase in traditional grammar, but is taken to be a determiner phrase within the framework adopted here). A further difference between the two frameworks is that Minimalism assumes that all syntactic structure is binary-branching, whereas traditional grammar (implicitly) does not.

Workbook section

Exercise 3.1

Discuss the derivation of the following sentences, showing how their structure is built up in a pairwise fashion by successive binary merger operations.

1	He has become very fond of Mary
2	She must be quite pleased to see you
3	He may need to ask for help
4	They are expecting to hear from you
5	You should try to talk to the president
6	Inflation is threatening to undermine the growth of the economy
7	Nobody could believe that Sam was working for the government
8	He may refuse to admit that he was defrauding the company

Show how evidence from coordination and pronoun substitution can be used in support of your analysis. In addition, say which constituents can (and cannot) be preposed – and why.

Helpful hints

Assume that the sentences are derived in a **bottom-up** fashion by first merging the last two words in the sentence to form a constituent, then merging the constituent thereby formed with the third-from-last word to form an even larger constituent, then merging this even larger constituent with the fourth-from-last word . . . and so on. (It should be noted, however, that while this simple procedure will work for most of the sentences in the two exercises in this chapter, it requires modification to handle more complex sentences – e.g. those with phrasal specifiers like sentences 1, 2, 5, 16 and 18 in exercise 3.2.)

Model answer for sentence 1

Merging the preposition *of* with the noun *Mary* which serves as its complement derives the PP (prepositional phrase) in (i) below:

(i)
```
        PP
       /  \
      P    N
      of  Mary
```

Merging the adjective *fond* with the resulting PP (which is the complement of *fond*) forms the intermediate adjectival projection (A-bar) *fond of Mary* in (ii) below:

(ii)

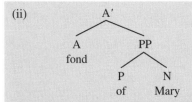

Merging the A-bar in (ii) with the adverb *very* which serves as its specifier (in that it modifies *fond of Mary*) forms the AP/adjectival phrase in (iii) below:

(iii)

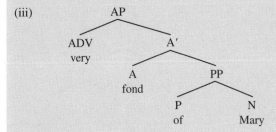

Merging the verb *become* with the AP *very fond of Mary* which serves as the complement of *become* forms the VP/verb phrase in (iv) below:

(iv)

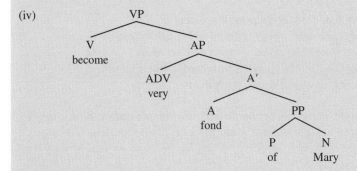

Merging the tense auxiliary (T constituent) *has* with its verb phrase complement *become very fond of Mary* forms the intermediate T-bar projection (v) below:

(v)

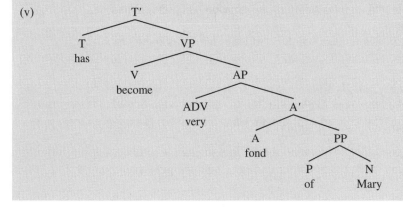

Merging the T-bar in (v) with the pronoun *he* which serves as its subject/specifier will derive the TP:

(vi)

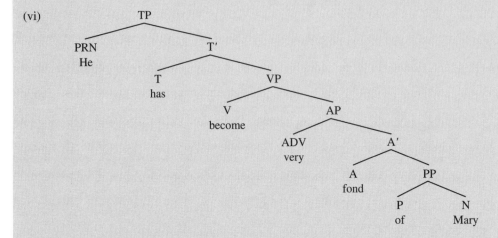

Evidence in support of the analysis in (vi) comes from coordination data in relation to sentences such as:

(vii) (a)   He has become very fond [*of Mary*] and [**of her sister**]
    (b)   He has become very [*fond of Mary*] and [**proud of her achievements**]
    (c)   He has become [*very fond of Mary*] but [**less fond of her sister**]
    (d)   He has [*become very fond of Mary*] and [**grown used to her mother**]
    (e)   He [*has become very fond of Mary*] and [**is hoping to marry her**]

The fact that each of the italicised strings can be coordinated with another similar (bold-printed) string is consistent with the claim made in (vi) that *of Mary* is a PP, *fond of Mary* is an A-bar, *very fond of Mary* is an AP, *become very fond of Mary* is a VP and *has become very fond of Mary* is a T-bar.

    Additional evidence in support of the analysis in (vi) comes from the use of the proforms *so/which* in:

(viii) (a)   He is apparently *very fond of Mary*, though nobody expected him to become **so**
     (b)   If he has *become very fond of Mary* (**which** he has), why doesn't he ask her out?

The fact that *very fond of Mary* is the antecedent of *so* in (viiia) is consistent with the claim made in (vi) that *very fond of Mary* is an AP; likewise, the fact that *become very fond of* Mary is the antecedent of *which* in (viiib) is consistent with the claim made in (vi) that *become very fond of Mary* is a VP.

    If we look at the question of which expressions in the sentence can and cannot be preposed in order to highlight them, we find the following picture (*?* indicates questionable grammaticality):

(ix) (a)   *Mary*, he (certainly) has become very fond of
   (b)   *?Of Mary*, he (certainly) has become very fond
   (c)   **Fond of Mary*, he (certainly) has become very
   (d)   *Very fond of Mary*, he (certainly) has become
   (e)   *Become very fond of Mary*, he (certainly) has
   (f)   **Has become very fond of Mary*, he (certainly)

(Adding the adverb *certainly* improves the acceptability of some of the relevant sentences, for discourse reasons which need not concern us.) In (53) in the main text, we suggested that highlighting involves preposing the smallest possible maximal projection containing the focused material. Suppose that we want to highlight *Mary* via preposing. Since *Mary* is a maximal projection in (vi) by virtue of being the largest expression headed by the word *Mary*, preposing *Mary* in (ixa) yields a grammatical outcome, as expected. By contrast, preposing the prepositional phrase *of Mary* yields a somewhat degraded sentence, as we see from (ixb): this may be because if we want to highlight *Mary* alone, we prepose the *smallest* maximal projection containing *Mary*, and this is clearly the N *Mary* not the PP *of Mary*. There would only be some point in preposing *of Mary* if we wanted to highlight *of* as well as *Mary*; but since the preposition *of* (rather like infinitival *to*) has little or no semantic content (some linguists suggesting that it is a **genitive case particle** in this kind of use and hence a functor), an *of*-phrase is not a good candidate for highlighting. The string *fond of Mary* cannot be preposed in (ixc) because it is an intermediate (A-bar) projection of the adjective *fond*, not its maximal projection (the maximal projection of the adjective *fond* being the AP *very fond of Mary*). By contrast, the string *very fond of Mary* can be preposed in (ixd) by virtue of its status as the maximal projection of *fond* (i.e. the largest expression headed by *fond*). In (ixe) we see that *become very fond of Mary* can also be preposed by virtue of being the maximal projection of the verb *become* – even though it is the complement of the T constituent *has*; hence, either T is not a functional category (as suggested in Chomsky 1999), or else the Functional Head Constraint applies only to some functional categories (e.g. those like D and C which are the highest heads in nominal/clausal structures respectively). By contrast, the string *has become very fond of Mary* cannot be preposed in (ixf) because of its status as an intermediate (T-bar) projection of *has* – the corresponding maximal projection of *has* being the TP *He has become very fond of Mary*.

Exercise 3.2

In §3.7, we showed how the relation **c-command** plays an important role in accounting for the use of reflexive and reciprocal anaphors. The same can be argued to be true of two other types of expression, namely non-anaphoric pronominals like *he/him/her/it/them* etc. and referential noun expressions like *John* or *the president*. Chomsky (1981) developed a **Theory of Binding** which incorporated the three binding principles outlined in a slightly revised form below:

(i)   Binding Principles
      Principle A: an anaphor must be bound within its local domain
      Principle B: a (non-anaphoric) pronominal (expression) must be free within its local domain
      Principle C: an R-expression (i.e. referring noun expression) must be free within the overall structure containing it

Although there is controversy about how best to define the notion of **local domain** in relation to binding, for present purposes assume that this corresponds to the notion of TP, and that the three binding principles in (i) thus amount to the following:

(ii)   A: An anaphor (like *himself*) must be bound by (i.e. must refer to) a c-commanding constituent within the closest TP immediately containing it

B: A pronominal (like *him*) must not be bound by (i.e. must not refer to) any c-commanding constituent within the closest TP immediately containing it

C: An R-expression (i.e. a referring noun expression like *John/the president*) must not be coreferential to (i.e. must not refer to the same entity as) any c-commanding expression within the overall tree structure containing it

In the light of the Binding Principles outlined informally in (ii), discuss the binding properties of the expressions *Fred*, *John*, *he/him* and *himself* in sentences 1–6 below, drawing trees to represent the structure of the sentences.

1a	The rumours about Fred have upset him
b	*The rumours about Fred have upset himself
2a	The rumours about him have upset Fred
b	*The rumours about himself have upset Fred
3a	John must feel that Fred has disgraced himself
b	*John must feel that himself has disgraced Fred
4a	John must feel that he has disgraced Fred
b	John must feel that Fred has disgraced him
5a	John may wonder if the rumours about Fred will affect him
b	John may wonder if the rumours about him will affect Fred
6a	John may suspect that Fred has taken some pictures of him
b	John may suspect that Fred has taken some pictures of himself

In addition to its role in *Binding Theory*, the notion c-command has traditionally been assumed to play an important part in accounting for the syntax of so-called (negative/interrogative) **polarity expressions** – i.e. expressions which are said to be restricted to occurring in negative or interrogative contexts. One way of characterising this restriction is to suppose that the relevant expressions are restricted to occurring in a position where they are c-commanded by what Klima (1964) termed an **affective** constituent (e.g. a negative, interrogative or conditional expression – conditional expressions including *if/unless* in structures like 'I will shut him up *if he tries to say anything*'). Polarity expressions include the **partitive** quantifier *any* (and related compounds like *anyone/anything*), the items *need* and *dare* when serving as auxiliaries which don't take third-person singular *-s* in the present tense and which have a bare (*to*-less) infinitive complement, and idioms like *lift a finger*. Show how the c-command condition accounts for the (un)grammaticality of the following:

7	You mustn't talk to anyone
8	Nobody need do anything
9	Who dare blame anyone?
10	She has refused to sign anything
11	She should know if anyone has made any changes
12	I don't think that anyone dare lift a finger

13   He may have no desire to change anything
14   Nobody will think that anything has changed
15   He may feel unable to do anything
16   No politician dare offend anyone
17   *Anyone isn't helping me
18   *The fact that nothing has happened will change anything
19   John will deny that anything has happened
20   *John has denied anything
21   John has denied any involvement
22   John has denied involvement in any fraud

In relation to 17 (intended to be synonymous with *There isn't anyone helping me*) show how the traditional ternary-branching analysis of clauses as S-constituents (whereby 17 would be analysed as an S constituent comprising the pronoun/PRN *anyone*, the present-tense auxiliary/T *isn't* and the verb phrase/VP *helping me*) would be unable to provide a principled account of the ungrammaticality of 17 in terms of the c-command condition on polarity items. In relation to 19 and 20, consider why some linguists (e.g. Landau 2002) have claimed that it is not the verb *deny* which is negative, but rather the complementiser *that*, and say why sentences like 21 and 22 cast doubt on this. Consider an alternative account of data like 19–22 under which we assume that a polarity item must be **asymmetrically c-commanded** by an affective item, and we define asymmetric c-command as follows:

(iii)   X asymmetrically c-commands Y if X c-commands Y but Y does not c-command X

(A different approach to polarity items can be found in Acquaviva 2002.)

Helpful hints

Assume that *need/dare* (when they take a bare *to*-less infinitive complement) are modal auxiliaries which occupy the head T position of TP, and that they take a VP complement: assume also that they are polarity items in this use. Assume that *no* in 13 and 16 is a quantifier (= Q) which heads a quantifier phrase (= QP) constituent and has a noun phrase as its complement: assume that when the head Q of QP is negative, the overall QP is negative as well (because a phrase carries the same features as its head by virtue of being a projection of the relevant head). In addition, assume that *mustn't/don't/isn't* are (inherently negative) T/tense auxiliaries. Finally, assume that *anyone/anything/nobody/nothing* are pronouns (more specifically, they are Q-pronouns, i.e. pronominal quantifiers). [A descriptive detail which you might care to note is that the quantifier *any* has two uses. It can serve as a **universal** (or 'free choice') **quantifier** with a meaning similar to *every* (as in *He'll do anything for a laugh*): in this use, the initial *a-* of *any* is stressed, and the relevant word is not a polarity item – i.e. is not restricted to occurring in affective contexts. The second use of *any* is as a **partitive** (or **existential**) **quantifier**: in this use, it has a meaning similar to *some* and can be unstressed (with its initial vowel reduced to schwa or even being truncated in rapid colloquial speech styles – e.g. *He wouldn't do 'nything*), and is indeed a polarity item restricted to occurring in affective contexts. Assume that in the examples in 7–22 above, you are dealing with partitive *any*, and that this is a polarity item.]

Model answer for sentence 1a

Although we will not attempt to argue this here, there are good reasons for thinking that sentence 1a has the structure (i) below:

(i)

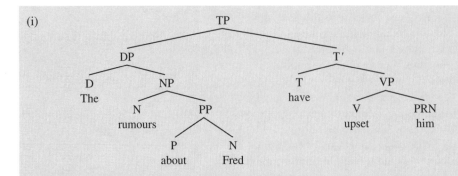

Him is a pronominal (i.e. a non-anaphoric pronoun), and hence subject to Principle B of Binding Theory. This specifies that a pronominal like *him* cannot refer to any expression c-commanding it within the closest TP containing it; and from this it follows that such a pronominal can (a) refer to an expression contained in a different TP within the same sentence, or (b) refer to an expression within the same TP as long as that expression does not c-command *him*, or (c) refer to some entity in the domain of discourse (e.g. some person not mentioned in the relevant sentence, but present in the discourse context). The second of these possibilities (b) allows for *him* to refer to *Fred* in (i), since although *him* and *Fred* are contained within the same TP, *Fred* does not c-command *him* (the only constituent which *Fred* c-commands being the preposition *about*) so that principle B is satisfied if *him* refers to *Fred* (or if indeed *him* refers to some other person not mentioned in the sentence).

The noun *Fred* is an R-expression by virtue of being a referring noun expression, and hence is subject to Principle C of Binding Theory. This specifies that an R-expression like *Fred* cannot be coreferential to any expression which c-commands it anywhere within the overall structure containing it. However, there is no violation of Principle C in (i) if *Fred* and *him* are coreferential, since *Fred* is not c-commanded by *him*. (The only constituent which *him* c-commands is the V *upset*). There is likewise no violation of Principle C if *Fred* refers to some person not mentioned within the sentence. Overall, then, principles B and C allow for the twin possibilities that *him* can either refer to *Fred* or refer to someone other than Fred who is not directly mentioned in the sentence.

Model answer for sentence 7

Given the assumptions made in the text, sentence 7 will have the structure (ii) below:

(ii)

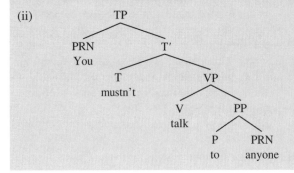

The T node containing the negative auxiliary *mustn't* here c-commands the PRN node containing the polarity item *anyone* because the sister of [T *mustn't*] is [VP *talk to anyone*], and *anyone* is contained within this VP, since the PRN node is one of the grandchildren of the VP node. If you prefer to use the alternative train metaphor suggested in §3.7 (under which X c-commands Y if you can get from X to Y on a train by going one stop north, then taking a southbound train on a different line and travelling as many stops south as you choose), you can say that [T *mustn't*] c-commands [PRN *anyone*] because if you travel one stop north from the T station you arrive at the T-bar station, and if you then change trains at the T-bar station you can get a southbound train on a different line which will take you to the PRN station containing *anyone* (at the end of the line) via the VP and PP stations. Since the polarity item *anyone* is c-commanded by the negative auxiliary *mustn't*, the c-command condition on the use of polarity items is satisfied, and sentence 7 is therefore grammatical.

4   Null constituents

4.1   Overview

So far, our discussion of syntactic structure has tacitly assumed that all constituents in a given structure are **overt** (in the sense that they have overt phonetic features, as well as grammatical and semantic features). However, in this chapter we argue that syntactic structures may also contain **null constituents** (also known as **empty categories**) – i.e. constituents which have grammatical and semantic features but lack phonetic features (and so are 'silent' or 'inaudible').

4.2   Null subjects

We are already familiar with one kind of null constituent from the discussion of the **Null-Subject Parameter** in §1.6. There, we saw that alongside finite clauses like that produced by speaker A in the dialogue in (1) below with an overt subject like *Maria*, Italian also has finite clauses like that produced by speaker B, with a null subject pronoun conventionally designated as *pro* (and referred to affectionately as 'little *pro*'):

(1)   SPEAKER A: Maria è tornata?
                      Maria is returned?
                      'Has Maria returned?'
         SPEAKER B: Sì,   *pro* è tornata
                      Yes, *pro* is returned
                      'Yes, she has returned'

One reason for positing that the sentence in (1B) has a null *pro* subject is that *tornare* 'return' (in the use illustrated here) is a one-place predicate which requires a subject: this requirement is satisfied by the overt subject *Maria* in (1A), and by the null *pro* subject in (1B). A second reason relates to the agreement morphology carried by the auxiliary *è* 'is' and the participle *tornata* 'returned' in (1). Just as the form of the (third-person-singular) auxiliary *è* 'is' and the (feminine-singular) participle *tornata* is determined via agreement with the overt (third-person-feminine-singular) subject *Maria* in (1A), so too the auxiliary and participle agree in exactly the same way with the null *pro* subject in (1B), which (as used here) is third person feminine singular by virtue of referring to *Maria*. If the sentence in (1B) were subjectless, it is not obvious how we would account for the relevant agreement facts. Since all finite clauses in Italian allow a null *pro* subject, we can refer to *pro* as a **null finite subject**.

Although English is not an Italian-style null-subject language (in the sense that it is not a language which allows any and every kind of finite clause to have a null *pro* subject), it does have three different types of null subject (briefly discussed in exercise 1.1). One of these are **imperative null subjects**. As the examples in (2) below illustrate, an imperative sentence in English can have an overt subject which is either a second-person expression like *you*, or a third-person expression like *anyone*:

(2) (a)   Don't *you* dare lose your nerve!
    (b)   Don't *anyone* dare lose their nerve!

However, imperative null subjects are intrinsically second person, as the contrast in (3) below shows:

(3) (a)   Don't lose your nerve!
    (b)   *Don't lose their nerve!

In other words, imperative null subjects seem to be a silent counterpart of *you*. One way of describing this is to say that the pronoun *you* can have a **null spellout** (and thereby have its phonetic features not spelled out – i.e. deleted/omitted) when it is the subject of an imperative sentence.

A second type of null subject found in English are **truncated null subjects**. In cryptic styles of colloquial spoken English (and also in diary styles of written English) a sentence can be *truncated* (i.e. shortened) by giving a subject pronoun like *I/you/he/we/they* a null spellout if it is the first word in a sentence. So, in sentences like those in (4) below:

(4) (a)   *I* can't find my pen
    (b)   *I* think I left it at home
    (c)   Why do I always lose things?

the two italicised occurrences of the subject pronoun *I* can be given a null spellout because in each case *I* is the first word in the sentence, but not other occurrences of *I* – as we see from (5) below:

(5) (a)   Can't find my pen
    (b)   Think I left it at home/*Think left it at home
    (c)   *Why do always lose things?

However, not all sentence-initial subjects can be truncated (e.g. we can't truncate *He* in a sentence like *He is tired*, giving **Is tired*): the precise nature of the constraints on **truncation** is unclear.

A third type of null subject found in English are **non-finite null subjects**, found in non-finite clauses which don't have an overt subject. In this connection, compare the structure of the bracketed infinitive clauses in the (a) and (b) examples below:

(6) (a)   We would like [*you* to stay]
    (b)   We would like [to stay]

(7) (a)   We don't want [*anyone* to upset them]
    (b)   We don't want [to upset them]

Each of the bracketed infinitive complement clauses in the (a) examples in (6) and (7) contains an overt (italicised) subject. By contrast, the bracketed complement clauses in the (b) examples appear to be subjectless. However, we shall argue that apparently subjectless infinitive clauses contain a **null subject**. The particular kind of null subject found in the bracketed clauses in the (b) examples has the same grammatical and referential properties as a pronoun, and hence appears to be a null pronoun. In order to differentiate it from the null ('little *pro*') subject found in finite clauses in null-subject languages like Italian, it is conventionally designated as **PRO** and referred to as 'big PRO'. Given this assumption, a sentence such as (6b) will have a parallel structure to (6a), except that the bracketed TP has an overt pronoun *you* as its subject in (6a), but a null pronoun PRO as its subject in (6b) – as shown below:

(8)

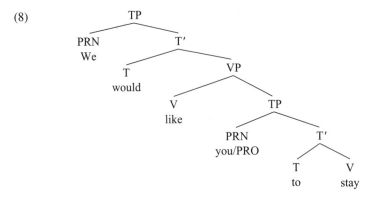

Using the relevant technical terminology, we can say that the null PRO subject in (8) is **controlled** by (i.e. refers back to) the subject *we* of the **matrix** (= containing = next highest) clause – or, equivalently, that *we* is the **controller** or **antecedent** of PRO: hence, a structure like 'We would like PRO to stay' has an interpretation akin to that of 'We would like *ourselves* to stay'. Verbs (such as *like*) which allow an infinitive complement with a PRO subject are said to function (in the relevant use) as **control verbs**; likewise, a complement clause with a null PRO subject is known as a **control clause**.

　　An obvious question to ask at this juncture is why we should posit that apparently subjectless infinitive complements like those bracketed in (6b) and (7b) above have a null PRO subject. Part of the motivation for PRO comes from considerations relating to argument structure. The verb *stay* (as used in (6b) above) is a one-place predicate which requires a subject argument – and positing a PRO subject for the *stay* clause satisfies the requirement for *stay* to have a subject. The null PRO subject of a control infinitive becomes overt if the infinitive clause is substituted by a finite clause, as we see from the paraphrases for the (a) examples given in the (b) examples below:

(9) (a)   I am sorry [*PRO* to have kept you waiting]
     (b)   I am sorry [*I* have kept you waiting]

(10) (a)   Jim promised [*PRO* to come to my party]
     (b)   Jim promised [*he* would come to my party]

The fact that the bracketed clauses in the (b) examples contain an overt (italicised) subject makes it plausible to suppose that the bracketed clauses in the synonymous (a) examples have a null PRO subject. (Note, however, that only verbs which select both an infinitive complement and a finite complement allow a control clause to be substituted by a finite clause with an overt subject – hence, not a control verb like *want* in *I want to go home* because *want* does not allow a *that*-clause complement, as we see from the ungrammaticality of **I want that I should leave*. Interestingly, Xu 2003 claims that all control verbs in Chinese allow an overt subject pronoun in place of PRO in control clauses.)

Further evidence in support of positing a null PRO subject in such clauses comes from the syntax of **reflexive anaphors** (i.e. *self/selves* forms such as *myself/yourself/himself/themselves* etc.). As examples such as the following indicate, reflexives generally require a **local antecedent** (the reflexive being italicised and its antecedent bold-printed):

(11) (a)   They want [**John** to help *himself*]
     (b)   ****They** want [John to help *themselves*]

In the case of structures like (11), a local antecedent means 'an antecedent contained within the same [bracketed] clause/TP as the reflexive'. (11a) is grammatical because it satisfies this locality requirement: the antecedent of the reflexive *himself* is the noun *John*, and *John* is contained within the same (bracketed) *help*-clause as *himself*. By contrast, (11b) is ungrammatical because the reflexive *themselves* does not have a local antecedent (i.e. it does not have an antecedent within the bracketed clause containing it); its antecedent is the pronoun *they*, and *they* is contained within the *want* clause, not within the [bracketed] *help* clause. In the light of the requirement for reflexives to have a local antecedent, consider now how we account for the grammaticality of the following:

(12)   John wants [PRO to prove himself]

Given the requirement for reflexives to have a local antecedent, it follows that the reflexive *himself* must have an antecedent within its own [bracketed] clause. This requirement is satisfied in (12) if we assume that the bracketed complement clause has a PRO subject, and that PRO is the antecedent of *himself*. Since PRO in turn is controlled by *John* (i.e. *John* is the antecedent of PRO), this means that *himself* is **coreferential** to (i.e. refers to the same individual as) *John*.

We can formulate a further argument in support of positing a PRO subject in apparently subjectless infinitive clauses in relation to the syntax of **predicate nominals**: these are nominal (i.e. noun-containing) expressions used as the complement of a copular (i.e. linking) verb such as *be, become, remain* (etc.) in expressions such as *John was/became/remained my best friend*, where the predicate nominal is *my best friend*, and the property of *being/becoming/remaining my best friend* is **predicated** of *John*. Predicate nominals of the relevant type have to agree in number with the subject of their own clause in copular constructions, as we see from examples such as the following:

(13) (a)   They want [**their son** to become *a millionaire/*millionaires*]
     (b)   He wants [**his sons** to become *millionaires/*a millionaire*]

The italicised predicate nominal has to agree with the (bold-printed) subject of its own [bracketed] *become* clause, and cannot agree with the subject of the *want* clause. In the light of this local (clause-internal) agreement requirement, consider now how we account for the agreement pattern in (14) below:

(14) (a)   They want [PRO to become *millionaires/*a millionaire*]
     (b)   He wants [PRO to become *a millionaire/*millionaires*]

If we posit that the *become* clause has a PRO subject which is controlled by (i.e. refers back to) the subject of the *want* clause, the relevant agreement facts can be accounted for straightforwardly: we simply posit that the predicate nominal (*a*) *millionaire(s)* agrees with PRO (since PRO is the subject of the *become* clause), and that PRO in (14a) is plural because its controller/antecedent is the plural pronoun *they*, and conversely that PRO in (14b) is singular because its antecedent/controller is the singular pronoun *he*.

A further argument in support of positing that control clauses have a silent PRO subject can be formulated in theoretical terms. In the previous chapter, we noted that finite auxiliaries have an [EPP] feature which requires them to have a subject specifier. Since finite auxiliaries belong to the category T of tense-marker, we can generalise this conclusion by positing that all finite T constituents have an [EPP] feature requiring them to have a subject. However, since we argued in chapter 2 that infinitival *to* also belongs to the category T (by virtue of its status as a non-finite tense-marker), we can suggest the broader generalisation that not only a finite T but also a non-finite T containing the infinitive particle *to* has an [EPP] feature and hence must likewise project a subject. The analysis in (8) above is consistent with this generalisation, since it posits that the *stay* clause either has an overt *you* subject or a null PRO subject, with either type of subject satisfying the [EPP] feature of *to*.

The overall conclusion which our discussion here leads us to is that just as infinitive complements like *you to stay* in (6a) have an overt subject (*you*), so too seemingly subjectless infinitive complements like *to stay* in (6b) have a null

PRO subject – as shown in (8) above. In structures like (8), PRO has an explicit **controller**, which is the subject of the matrix clause (i.e. of the clause which immediately contains the control verb). However, this is not always the case, as we can see from structures like (15) below:

(15) (a)   It is important [PRO to take regular exercise]
     (b)   It's difficult [PRO to learn a foreign language]
     (c)   It's unwise [PRO to mix business with pleasure]

It is clear from examples like (16) below that apparently subjectless clauses like those bracketed in (15) and (16) must have a null PRO subject:

(16) (a)   It's important [PRO to prepare *myself* properly for the exam]
     (b)   It's important [PRO not to take *oneself* too seriously]

since the reflexives *myself/oneself* require a local antecedent within the bracketed clause containing them, and PRO serves the function of being the antecedent of the reflexive. However, PRO itself has no explicit antecedent in structures like (15) and (16). In such cases (where PRO lacks an explicit controller), PRO can either refer to some individual outside the sentence (e.g. the speaker in (16a)) or can have **arbitrary reference** (as in (16b)) and refer to 'any arbitrary person you care to mention' and hence have much the same interpretation as arbitrary *one* in sentences like '*One* can't be too careful these days'. (See Landau 1999, 2001 for further discussion of *control* structures.)

4.3   Null auxiliaries

So far, all the clauses we have looked at in this chapter and the last have contained a TP projection headed by a finite auxiliary or infinitival *to*. The obvious generalisation suggested by this is that all clauses contain TP. An important question begged by this assumption, however, is how we are to analyse finite clauses which contain no overt auxiliary. In this connection, consider the construction illustrated in (17) below:

(17)   He could have helped her, or [she have helped him]

Both clauses here (viz. the *he* clause and the bracketed *she* clause) appear to be finite, since both have nominative subjects (*he/she*). If all finite clauses contain a TP projection headed by a finite T constituent, it follows that both clauses in (17) must be TPs containing a finite T. This is clearly true of the *he* clause, since this contains the finite modal auxiliary *could*; however, the *she* clause doesn't seem to contain any finite auxiliary constituent, since *have* is an infinitive form in (17) (the corresponding finite form which would be required with a third-person subject like *she* being *has*). How can we analyse finite clauses as projections of a finite T constituent when clauses like that bracketed in (17) contain no finite auxiliary?

An intuitively plausible answer is to suppose that the string *she have helped him* in (17) is an **elliptical** (i.e. abbreviated) variant of *she could have helped him*, and that the T constituent *could* in the second clause undergoes a particular form of ellipsis called **gapping**. (**Gapping** is a grammatical operation by which the head of a phrase is given a **null spellout** – and so has its phonetic features deleted – when the same item occurs elsewhere within the sentence, and is so called because it leaves an apparent 'gap' in the phrase where the head would otherwise have been.) If so, the second clause will have the structure (18) below (where ~~could~~ marks an ellipsed counterpart of *could*, and *have* is treated as a non-finite AUX/Auxiliary heading an AUXP/Auxiliary Phrase – the rationale for AUXP will be discussed in §5.7):

(18)

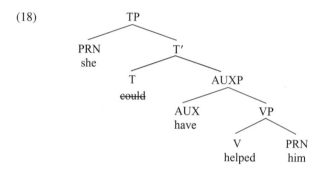

The head T position of TP in a structure like (18) is filled by the ellipsed auxiliary ~~could~~. Although an ellipsed item loses its phonetic features, it retains its grammatical and semantic features, so that ~~could~~ in (18) is a silent counterpart of *could*. The **null T** analysis in (18) provides a principled account of three observations. Firstly, the bracketed clause in (17) is interpreted as an elliptical form of *she could have helped him*: this can be straightforwardly accounted for under the analysis in (18) since T contains a null counterpart of *could*. Secondly, the subject is in the nominative case form *she*: this can be attributed to the fact that the T position in (18) is filled by a 'silent' counterpart of the finite auxiliary *could*, so that (like other finite auxiliaries) it requires a nominative subject. Thirdly, the perfect auxiliary *have* is in the infinitive form: this is because ~~could~~ (being a null copy of *could*) has the same grammatical properties as *could*, and so (like *could*) requires a complement headed by a word (like *have*) in the infinitive form.

A further argument in support of the null T analysis in (18) comes from facts relating to **cliticisation** (a process by which one word attaches itself in a leech-like fashion to another). The perfect auxiliary *have* has a range of variant forms in the spoken language. When unstressed, it can lose its initial /h/ segment and have its vowel reduced to schwa /ə/, and so be pronounced as /əv/ e.g. in sentences such as *You should have been there*. (Because *of* is also pronounced /əv/ when unstressed, some people mistakenly write this as *You should of been there* – not *you*, of course!) However, when *have* is used with a pronominal subject ending in a vowel or diphthong (e.g. a pronoun like *I/we/you/they*), it can lose its vowel entirely and be contracted down to /v/; in this weak form, it is phonetically too insubstantial to survive as an independent word and **encliticises** onto (i.e. attaches to the end of) its subject, resulting in structures such as:

(19) (a) *You've* done your duty
     (b) *They've* retired General Gaga
     (c) *I've* forgotten to lock the door
     (d) *We've* saved you a place

However, note that *have* cannot cliticise onto *she* in (20) below:

(20)   *He could have helped her or *she've* helped him

so that *she've* is not homophonous with the invented word *sheeve*. Why should cliticisation of *have* onto *she* be blocked here? Let's suppose that *have*-cliticisation is subject to the following structural conditions:

(21)   *Have* can encliticise onto a pronoun ending in a vowel or diphthong provided that
         (i) the pronoun asymmetrically c-commands *have* (i.e. the pronoun c-commands *have* but is not itself c-commanded by *have*)
         (ii) the two are immediately adjacent, in the sense that there is no constituent intervening between the two (i.e. no constituent which c-commands *have* and which is in turn c-commanded by the pronoun)

The **asymmetric c-command condition** (21i) in effect requires the pronoun to be 'higher up' in the structure than *have*. (In the relevant technical sense, one constituent X asymmetrically c-commands another constituent Y if X c-commands Y, but Y does not c-command X.) The **adjacency condition** (21ii) requires *have* to be immediately adjacent to the pronoun which it cliticises to. (A descriptive detail which we set aside here is that (21) applies specifically to encliticisation of *have*: encliticisation of the *'s* variant of *has* is subject to far less restrictive conditions on its use – but this will not be pursued here.)

To see how (21) works, consider the structure below:

(22)

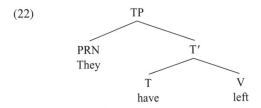

Here, the pronoun *they* ends in a diphthong and so is the kind of pronoun that *have* can cliticise onto. The asymmetric c-command condition (21i) is met in that *they* c-commands *have*, but *have* does not c-command *they*. The adjacency condition

(21ii) is also met in that there is no constituent intervening between *they* and *have*. Since both its structural conditions are met, (21) correctly predicts that *have* can encliticise onto *they*, so deriving *They've left*. The kind of cliticisation involved here is essentially phonological (rather than syntactic), so that *they* and *have* remain separate words in the syntax, but are fused together in the PF component (i.e. the component responsible for determining Phonetic Form) once the structure **generated** (i.e. formed) by the syntax has been handed over to the PF component for morphological and phonological processing.

In the light of our discussion of *have* cliticisation, now consider why cliticisation of *have* onto *she* is not possible in (20) **He could have helped her or she've helped him*. Under the *null T* analysis suggested above, the second clause in (20) contains a null variant of *could* and has the structure shown in (18) above, repeated as (23) below:

(23)

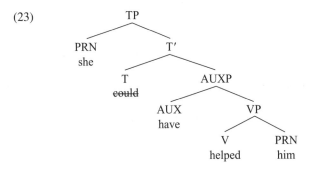

Although the asymmetric c-command condition (21i) is met in (23) in that *she* c-commands but is not c-commanded by *have*, the adjacency condition (21ii) is not met in that *she* is not immediately adjacent to *have* because the null auxiliary *could* intervenes between the two (in the sense that ~~could~~ c-commands *have*, and ~~could~~ is in turn c-commanded by *she*). Thus, the presence of the intervening null auxiliary ~~could~~ blocks cliticisation of *have* onto *she* in (23), thereby accounting for the ungrammaticality of (20) **He could have helped her or she've helped him*. Turning this conclusion on its head, we can say that the ungrammaticality of (20) provides us with empirical evidence that the bracketed clause in (17) contains a null counterpart of *could* intervening between *she* and *have* – as is claimed in the analysis in (23) above.

Our discussion so far in this section has suggested that some seemingly auxiliariless clauses are TPs headed by a T containing an auxiliary which (via ellipsis) is given a null phonetic spellout. A rather different kind of null-auxiliary structure is found in African American English (AAE), in sentences such as the following (from Labov 1969, p. 717):

(24)   He just feel like he gettin' cripple up from arthritis

In AAE, specific forms of the auxiliary BE have null variants, so that we find null forms of *are* and *is* in contexts where Standard English (SE) would require the contracted forms *'s* and *'re*. Hence, in place of SE *he's getting crippled* we find AAE *he gettin cripple* (with a null counterpart of *'s*). Evidence in support of the assumption that AAE sentences like (24) incorporate a null variant of *is* comes from the fact that the missing auxiliary *is* may surface in a **tag**, as in sentences such as the following (where the sequence following the comma is the tag) (from Fasold 1980, p. 29):

(25)   He gonna be there, I know he *is*

In tag sentences, the auxiliary found in the tag is a copy of the auxiliary used in the main clause. This being so, it follows that the main *gonna* clause in (25) must contain a null variant of the progressive auxiliary *is*. In other words, the main clause in (25) must be a TP with the structure shown in skeletal form in (26) below (s̶t̶r̶i̶k̶e̶t̶h̶r̶o̶u̶g̶h̶ indicating that the phonetic features of the auxiliary are not spelled out):

(26)   [TPHe [T i̶s̶] gonna be there]

Interestingly, the form *am* (contracted to *'m*) has no null counterpart in AAE, nor do the past-tense forms *was/were*. It would seem, therefore, that the only finite forms of BE which have a null counterpart in AAE are the specific auxiliary forms *are* and *is*. No less interestingly, Wolfram (1971, p. 149) reports that in non-standard Southern White American English the use of null auxiliaries is even more restricted, and that the only form of BE with a null counterpart is *are*; cf. the parallel observation by Fasold (1980: 30) that 'There are many southern whites who delete only *are*.'

4.4   Null T in auxiliariless finite clauses

Our analysis of the kind of auxiliariless clauses discussed in §4.3 as TPs headed by a T which has a null phonetic spellout suggests the more general hypothesis that:

(27)   All finite clauses are TPs headed by an (overt or null) T constituent

Such a hypothesis has interesting implications for finite clauses such as the following which contain a finite verb but no auxiliary:

(28) (a)   He enjoys syntax
     (b)   He enjoyed syntax

It implies that we should analyse auxiliariless finite clauses like those in (28a,b) above as TP constituents which have the respective structures shown in (29a,b) below:

(29)   (a)

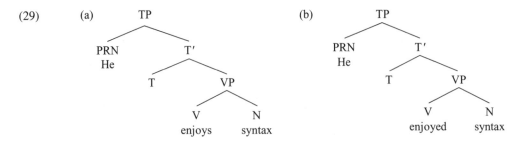

Structures like those in (29) would differ from null-auxiliary structures like (23) *He could have helped her or she ~~could~~ have helped him* and (26) *He ~~is~~ gonna be there* in that they don't contain a silent counterpart of a specific auxiliary like *could* or *is*, but rather simply don't contain any auxiliary at all.

However, there's clearly something very odd about a *null T* analysis like (29) if we say that the relevant clauses are TPs which are headed by a T constituent which contains absolutely *nothing*. For one thing, a category label like T is an abbreviation for a set of features carried by a lexical item – hence, if we posit that structures like (29) are TPs, the head T position of TP has to be occupied by some kind of lexical item. Moreover, the structures which are generated by the syntactic component of the grammar are eventually handed over to the semantic component to be assigned a semantic interpretation, and it seems reasonable to follow Chomsky (1995) in requiring all constituents in a syntactic structure to play a role in determining the meaning of the overall structure. If so, it clearly has to be the case that the head T of TP contains some item which contributes in some way to the semantic interpretation of the sentence. But what kind of item could T contain?

In order to try and answer this question, it's instructive to contrast auxiliariless structures like those in (29) above with auxiliary-containing structures like those in (30) below:

(30)   (a)

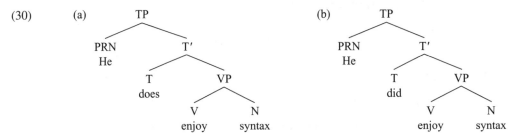

The head T position in TP is occupied by the present-tense auxiliary *does* in (30a), and by the past-tense auxiliary *did* in (30b). If we examine the internal morphological structure of these two words, we see that *does* contains the present-tense affix -*s*, and that *did* contains the past-tense affix -*d* (each of these affixes being attached to an irregular stem form of the auxiliary DO). In schematic terms, then, we can say that the head T constituent of TP in structures like (30) is of the form *auxiliary+tense affix*.

If we now look back at the auxiliariless structures in (29), we see that the head V position of VP in these structures is occupied by the verbs *enjoys* and *enjoyed*, and that these have a parallel morphological structure, in that they are of the form *verb+tense affix*. So, what finite clauses like (29) and (30) share in common is that in both cases they contain an (auxiliary or main) verb carrying a tense affix. In structures like (30) which contain an auxiliary like DO, the tense affix is attached to the auxiliary; in structures like (29) which contain no auxiliary, the tense affix attaches instead to the main verb *enjoy*. If we make the reasonable assumption that (as its label suggests) T is the **locus** of the tense properties of a finite clause (in the sense that T is the constituent which carries its tense features), an interesting possibility to consider is that the relevant tense affix (in both types of clause structure) originates in the head T position of TP. Since tensed verbs agree with their subjects in person and number, let us suppose that the tense affix (below abbreviated to *Tns*) also carries person and number properties. On this view, sentences like *He does enjoy syntax* and *He enjoys syntax* would have the respective syntactic structures indicated in (31a,b) below, where [*3SgPr*] is an abbreviation for the features [third-person, singular-number, present-tense]:

(31)　　(a)　　TP　　　　　　　　　　(b)　　　TP

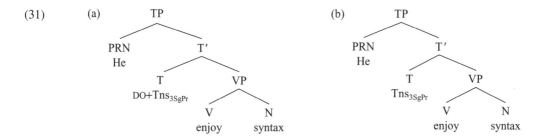

The two structures share in common the fact that they both contain a tense affix (*Tns*) in T; they differ in that the tense affix is attached to the auxiliary DO in (31a), but is unattached in (31b) because there is no auxiliary in T for the affix to attach to.

Under the analysis in (31), it is clear that T in auxiliariless clauses like (31b) would not be empty, but rather would contain a tense/agreement affix whose semantic contribution to the meaning of the overall sentence is that it marks tense. But what about the phonetic spellout of the tense affix? In a structure like (31a), it is easy to see why the (third-person-singular-present) tense affix is ultimately spelled out as an *s*-inflection on the end of the auxiliary *does*, because the affix is directly attached to the auxiliary DO in T. But how come the affix ends up spelled out as an *s*-inflection on the main verb *enjoys* in a structure like (31b)? We can answer this question in the following terms. Once the syntax has formed a clause structure like (31), the relevant syntactic structure is then sent to the **semantic component** to be assigned a semantic interpretation, and to the **PF component** to be assigned a phonetic form. In the PF component, a number of morphological and phonological operations apply. One of these morphological operations is traditionally referred to as **Affix Hopping**, and can be characterised informally as follows:

(32)   **Affix Hopping**
        In the PF component, an unattached tense affix is lowered onto the closest head c-commanded by the affix (provided that the lower head is a verb, since tense affixes require a verbal host to attach to)

Because the closest head c-commanded by T in (31b) is the verb *enjoy* (which is the head V of VP), it follows that (in the PF component) the unattached affix in T will be lowered onto the verb *enjoy* via the morphological operation of Affix Hopping, in the manner shown by the arrow in (33) below:

(33)

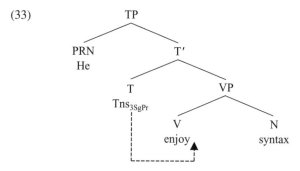

Since inflections in English are **suffixes**, we can assume that the tense affix will be lowered onto the *end* of the verb *enjoy*, to derive the structure [*enjoy*+*Tns₃SgPr*]. Since *enjoy* is a regular verb, the resulting structure will ultimately be spelled out in the phonology as the form *enjoys*.

What we have done so far in this section is sketch out an analysis of auxiliariless finite clauses as TPs headed by a T constituent containing an abstract tense affix which is subsequently lowered onto the verb by an **Affix Hopping** operation in the PF component (so resulting in a clause structure which looks as if it contains no T constituent). However, an important question to ask at this juncture is why we should claim that auxiliariless clauses contain an abstract T constituent. From a theoretical point of view, one advantage of the abstract T analysis is that it provides a unitary characterisation of the syntax of clauses, since it allows us to say that all clauses contain a TP projection, that the subject of a clause is always in **spec-TP** (i.e. always occupies the specifier position within TP), that a finite clause always contains an (auxiliary or main) verb carrying a tense affix, and so on. Lending further weight to theory-internal considerations such as these is a substantial body of empirical evidence, as we shall see.

One argument in support of the **tense affix** analysis comes from coordination facts in relation to sentences such as:

(34) (a)   He *enjoys syntax*, and **has learned a lot**
     (b)   He *enjoyed syntax*, and **is taking a follow-up course**

In both sentences, the italicised string *enjoys syntax/enjoyed syntax* has been coordinated with a bold-printed constituent which is clearly a T-bar in that it comprises a present-tense auxiliary (*has/is*) with a verb phrase complement (*learned a lot/taking a follow-up course*). On the assumption that only the same kinds of constituent can be conjoined by *and*, it follows that the italicised (seemingly T-less) strings *enjoys syntax/enjoyed syntax* must also be T-bar constituents; and since they contain no overt auxiliary, this means they must contain an abstract T constituent of some kind – precisely as the tense affix analysis in (33) claims.

A direct consequence of the tense affix analysis (33) of auxiliariless finite clauses is that finite auxiliaries and finite main verbs occupy different positions within the clause: finite auxiliaries occupy the head T position of TP, whereas finite main verbs occupy the head V position of VP. An interesting way of testing this hypothesis is in relation to the behaviour of items which have the status of auxiliaries in some uses, but of verbs in others. One such word is HAVE. In the kind of uses illustrated in (35) below, HAVE is a **perfect** auxiliary (and so requires the main verb to be in the perfect participle form *seen/been*):

(35) (a)   They *have* seen the ghost
     (b)   They *had* been warned about the ghost

However, in the uses illustrated in (36) below, HAVE is **causative** or **experiential** in sense (and so has much the same meaning as *cause* or *experience*):

(36) (a)   The doctor *had* an eye-specialist examine the patient
     (b)   The doctor *had* the patient examined by an eye-specialist
     (c)   The teacher *had* three students walk out on her
     (d)   I've never *had* anyone send me flowers

By traditional tests of auxiliarihood, perfect *have* is an auxiliary, and causative/experiential *have* is a main verb: e.g. perfect *have* can undergo inversion (*Has she gone to Paris?*) whereas causative/experiential *have* cannot (**Had the doctor an eye specialist examine the patient?*). In terms of the assumptions we are making here, this means that finite forms of HAVE are positioned in the head T position of TP in their perfect use, but in the head V position of VP in their causative or experiential use.

Evidence in support of this claim comes from facts about cliticisation. We noted earlier in (21) above that the form *have* can cliticise onto an immediately adjacent pronoun ending in a vowel/diphthong which asymmetrically c-commands *have*. In the light of this, consider contrasts such as the following:

(37) (a)   *They've* seen a ghost (= perfect *have*)
     (b)   **They've* their car serviced regularly (= causative *have*)
     (c)   **They've* students walk out on them sometimes (= experiential *have*)

How can we account for this contrast? If we assume that perfect *have* in (37a) is a finite (present-tense) auxiliary which occupies the head T position of TP, but that causative *have* in (37b) and experiential *have* in (37c) are main verbs occupying the head V position of a VP complement of a null T, then prior to cliticisation the three clauses will have the respective simplified structures indicated by the partial labelled bracketings in (38a–c) below (where *Tns* is an abstract tense affix):

(38) (a)   [$_{TP}$ They [$_T$ *have+Tns*] [$_{VP}$ [$_V$ seen] a ghost]]

   (b)   [$_{TP}$ They [$_T$ *Tns*] [$_{VP}$ [$_V$ *have*] their car serviced regularly]]

   (c)   [$_{TP}$ They [$_T$ *Tns*] [$_{VP}$ [$_V$ *have*] students walk out on them sometimes]]

(Here and throughout the rest of the book, *partial* labelled bracketings are used to show those parts of the structure most relevant to the discussion at hand, omitting other parts. In such cases, we generally show relevant heads and their maximal projections but omit intermediate projections, as in (38) above where we show T and TP but not T-bar.) Since we claimed in (21) above that cliticisation of *have* onto a pronoun is blocked by the presence of an intervening constituent, it should be obvious why *have* can cliticise onto *they* in (38a) but not in (38b,c): after all, there is no intervening constituent separating the pronoun *they* from *have* in (38a), but *they* is separated from the verb *have* in (38b,c) by an intervening T constituent containing a tense affix (*Tns*), so blocking contraction. It goes without saying that a crucial premise of this account is the assumption that (in its finite forms) *have* is positioned in the head T position of TP in its use as a perfect auxiliary, but in the head V position of VP in its use as a causative or experiential verb. In other words, *have* cliticisation facts suggest that finite clauses which lack a finite auxiliary are TPs headed by an abstract T constituent containing a tense affix.

A further piece of empirical evidence in support of the TP analysis comes from **tag questions**. As we see from the examples below, sentences containing (a finite form of) perfect *have* are tagged by *have*, whereas sentences containing (a finite form of) causative *have* are tagged by *do*:

(39) (a)   Mary *has* gone to Paris, *has/*does* she?

   (b)   Jules *has* his hair styled by Quentin Quiff, *does/*has* he?

Given the T-analysis of perfect *have* and the V-analysis of causative *have* and the assumption that all clauses contain a TP constituent, the main clauses in (39a,b) will have the respective (simplified) structures indicated in (40a,b) below:

(40) (a)   [$_{TP}$ Mary [$_T$ has] [$_{VP}$ [$_V$ gone] to Paris]]

   (b)   [$_{TP}$ Jules [$_T$ *Tns*] [$_{VP}$ [$_V$ has] his hair styled by Quentin Quiff]]

(A complication which we overlook here and throughout is that HAVE will only be spelled out as the form *has* in the PF component, and hence should more properly be represented as the abstract item HAVE in the syntax.) If we assume that the T constituent which appears in the tag must be a copy of the T constituent in the main clause, the contrast in (39) can be accounted for in a principled fashion. In (39a), the head T position of TP is filled by the auxiliary *has*, and so the tag contains a copy of *has*. In (39b), however, T contains only an abstract tense affix, hence we would expect the tag to contain a copy of this affix. Now, in the main clause, the affix can be lowered from T onto the verb *have* in the head V position of VP, with the resulting verb eventually being spelled out as *has*. But in the tag, there is no verb for the affix to be lowered onto. Accordingly, DO-*support* is used: in other words, the (meaningless) dummy auxiliary stem *do* is attached to the affix in order to provide an overt verbal stem for the affix to attach to. The lexical entry for the irregular verb DO specifies that the string [DO+*Tns*] is spelled out as *does* when the tense affix carries the features [third-person, singular-number, present-tense].

In this section, we have argued that a finite T always contains a tense affix. In clauses containing an auxiliary, the auxiliary is directly merged with the tense affix to form an *auxiliary+affix* structure; in auxiliariless clauses, the tense affix is lowered onto the main verb by an **Affix Hopping** operation in the PF component, so forming a *verb+affix* structure. However, in order to avoid our exposition becoming too abstract, we will generally show auxiliaries and verbs in their orthographic form – as indeed we did in (40) above, where the relevant form of the word HAVE was represented as *has* rather than as [HAVE+Affix$_{3SgPr}$].

4.5   Null T in bare infinitive clauses

In the previous section, we argued that auxiliariless finite clauses are TP constituents headed by an abstract T containing a tense affix. Given that clauses containing a finite auxiliary are also TPs, a plausible conclusion to draw is that all finite clauses are TPs. Since *to* infinitive clauses are also TPs (with *to* serving as a non-finite tense particle) we can generalise still further and say that all finite and infinitival clauses are TPs. This in turn has implications for how we analyse **bare** (i.e. *to*-less) infinitive complement clauses such as those bracketed below (where the italicised verb is infinitival in form):

(41) (a)   I have never known [Tom *criticise* anyone]
     (b)   A reporter saw [Senator Sleaze *leave* Benny's Bunny Bar]
     (c)   You mustn't let [the pressure *get* to you]

If (as we are suggesting) all finite and infinitival clauses are indeed TPs, bare infinitive clauses like those bracketed in (41) will be TPs headed by a null T constituent. Since the relevant null T constituent resembles infinitival *to* in requiring the (italicised) verb in the bracketed complement clause to be in the infinitive form, we can take it to be a null counterpart of infinitival *to* (below symbolised as *to̸*). This in turn will mean that the bracketed infinitive clause in (41a) has the structure (42) below:

(42)

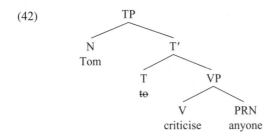

We could then say that verbs like *know*, *see* and *let* (as used in (41) above) take an infinitival TP complement headed by an infinitive particle with a null spellout, whereas verbs like *expect, judge, report, believe* etc. take a TP complement headed by an infinitive particle which is overtly spelled out as *to* in structures like those below:

(43) (a)   I expect [him *to* win]
    (b)   I judged [him *to* be lying]
    (c)   They reported [him *to* be missing]
    (d)   I believe [him *to* be innocent]

This means that all infinitive clauses are TPs headed by an infinitival T which is overtly spelled out as *to* in infinitive clauses like those bracketed in (43), but which has a null spellout in infinitive clauses like those bracketed in (41).

From a historical perspective, the null infinitive particle analysis is far from implausible since many bare infinitive clauses in present-day English had *to* infinitive counterparts in earlier varieties of English – as is illustrated by the following Shakespearean examples:

(44) (a)   I saw [her coral lips *to* move] (Lucentio, *The Taming of the Shrew*, I.i)
    (b)   My lord your son made [me *to* think of this] (Helena, *All's Well That Ends Well*, I.iii)
    (c)   What would you have [me *to* do]? (Lafeu, *All's Well That Ends Well*, V.ii)
    (d)   I had rather hear [you *to* solicit that] (Olivia, *All's Well That Ends Well*, III.i)

Moreover, some bare infinitive clauses have *to* infinitive counterparts in present-day English:

(45) (a)   I've never known [Tom (to) criticise anyone]
    (b)   Tom has never been known [*to* criticise anyone]

(46) (a)   A reporter saw [Senator Sleaze leave Benny's Bunny Bar]
    (b)   Senator Sleaze was seen [*to* leave Benny's Bunny Bar]

The infinitive particle which heads the bracketed infinitival TP in sentences like (45) and (46) must be overtly spelled out as *to* when the relevant TP is used as the complement of a passive participle like *known* in (45b) or *seen* in (46b), but can have a null spellout when the relevant TP is the complement of an active transitive verb like the perfect participle *known* in (45a) or the past-tense form *saw* in (46a) – a key difference being that a null spellout for the infinitive particle is optional in structures like (45a) but obligatory in structures like (46a). Although data like (44)–(46) are suggestive rather than conclusive, they make it plausible to suppose that bare infinitive clauses are TPs headed by a null variant of infinitival *to*.

Additional support for the **null infinitive particle** analysis of bare infinitive clauses comes from cliticisation facts in relation to sentences such as the following:

(47) (a)   I can't let [*you have* my password]
     (b)   *I can't let [*you've* my password]

If we suppose that the bracketed infinitive complement in (47b) is a TP headed by a null variant of infinitival *to* as in:

(48)   I can't let [$_{TP}$ you [$_T$ *to*] have my password]

we can account for the fact that *have* cannot cliticise onto *you* by positing that the presence of the null infinitive particle *to* intervening between *you* and *have* blocks cliticisation of *have* onto *you*.

A further argument leading to the same conclusion comes from structures like:

(49) (a)   Let [there be peace]
     (b)   I've never known [there be complaints about syntax]

It has been argued by Safir (1993) that the pronoun *there* (in this use as an **expletive pronoun**) is restricted to occurring in the specifier/subject position within TP. Such a restriction would account for contrasts such as:

(50) (a)   I consider [*there* to be an economic crisis]
     (b)   *I consider [*there* an economic crisis]

since the first bracketed complement is a TP headed by infinitival *to*, and the second is a type of verbless clause sometimes referred to as a **small clause** which appears not to be headed by T (since it contains no auxiliary or infinitival *to*, and no VP). If expletive *there* can only occur in spec-TP, it follows that the bracketed infinitive complement clauses in (49) must be TPs headed by a null infinitival T.

Our discussion here leads us to the wider conclusion that both *to* infinitive clauses and bare (*to*-less) infinitive clauses are TP constituents headed by an infinitive particle which has the overt spellout *to* in most types of infinitive clause, but has a null spellout in bare infinitive clauses. Given that we earlier argued that all finite clauses contain a TP projection (headed by a T which contains a tense affix, and may or may not also contain an auxiliary), the overall conclusion which we reach is that all finite and infinitival clauses contain a TP, and that T is overt in clauses containing a finite auxiliary or infinitival *to*, but is null elsewhere (because *to* in bare infinitive clauses has a null spellout, and the *Tns* affix in auxiliariless finite clauses is lowered onto the main verb in the PF component). One advantage of this analysis is that it enables us to attain a uniform characterisation of the syntax of (finite and infinitival) clauses as TP structures headed by a T with a V or VP complement. (For alternative analyses of the types of structure discussed in this section, see Felser 1999a,b and Basilico 2003.)

4.6   Null C in finite clauses

The overall conclusion to be drawn from our discussion in §4.3–§4.5 is that all finite and infinitive clauses contain an overt or null T constituent which projects into TP (with the subject of the clause occupying the specifier position within TP). However, given that clauses can be introduced by complementisers such as *if/that/for*, a natural question to ask is whether apparently complementiser-less clauses can likewise be argued to be CPs headed by a null complementiser. In this connection, consider the following:

(51) (a)   We didn't know [*if* he had resigned]
    (b)   We didn't know [*that* he had resigned]
    (c)   We didn't know [he had resigned]

The bracketed complement clause is interpreted as interrogative in force in (51a) and declarative in force in (51b), and it is plausible to suppose that the force of the clause is determined by force features carried by the italicised complementiser introducing the clause: in other words, the bracketed clause is interrogative in force in (51a) because it is introduced by the interrogative complementiser *if*, and is declarative in force in (51b) because it is introduced by the declarative complementiser *that*.

But now consider the bare (i.e. seemingly complementiserless) clause in (51c): this can only be interpreted as declarative in force (not as interrogative), so that (51c) is synonymous with (51b) and not with (51a). Why should this be? One answer is to suppose that the bracketed bare clause in (51c) is a CP headed by a null variant of the declarative complementiser *that* (below symbolised as *that*), and that the bracketed complement clauses in (51a–c) have the structure (52) below:

(52)

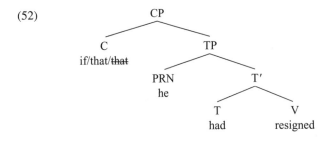

Given the analysis in (52), we could then say that the force of each of the bracketed complement clauses in (51) is determined by the force features carried by the head C of the overall CP; in (51a) the clause is a CP headed by the interrogative complementiser *if* and so is interrogative in force; in (51b) it is a CP headed by the declarative complementiser *that* and so is declarative in force; and in (51c) it is a CP headed by a null variant of the declarative complementiser *that* and so is likewise declarative in force. More generally, the **null complementiser** analysis would enable us to arrive at a uniform characterisation of all finite clauses as CPs in which the force of a clause is indicated by force features carried by an (overt or null) complementiser introducing the clause.

Empirical evidence in support of the null complementiser analysis of bare complement clauses like that bracketed in (51c) comes from coordination facts in relation to sentences such as:

(53)   We didn't know [*he had resigned*] or [**that he had been accused of corruption**]

In (53), the italicised bare clause has been coordinated with a bold-printed clause which is clearly a CP since it is introduced by the overt complementiser *that*. If we make the traditional assumption that only constituents of the same type can be coordinated, it follows that the italicised clause *he had resigned* in (53) must be a CP headed by a null counterpart of *that* because it has been coordinated with a bold-printed clause headed by the overt complementiser *that* – as shown in simplified form in (54) below:

(54)   We didn't know [~~that~~ *he had resigned*] or [**that he had been accused of corruption**]

What such an analysis implies is that the complementiser *that* can optionally be given a null phonetic spellout by having its phonetic features deleted in the PF component under certain circumstances: such an analysis dates back in spirit more than four decades (see e.g. Stockwell, Schachter and Partee 1973, p. 599).

There are a number of conditions governing *that*-deletion. Lexical factors seem to play a part here, in that just as only some predicates which select an infinitival TP complement allow the infinitive particle to have a null spellout (as we saw in the previous section), so too only some predicates which select a *that*-clause complement allow *that* to have a null spellout. Hornstein (2000) suggests that passive participles and adjectives resist *that*-deletion, but the real situation seems rather more complex. For example, the adjective *clear* readily allows *that*-deletion, but the adjective *undeniable* does not:

(55) (a)   It is **clear** [*that* he was framed]
     (b)   It is **clear** [he was framed]

(56) (a)   It is **undeniable** [*that* he was framed]
     (b)   ?*It is **undeniable** [he was framed]

(Irrelevantly, (56b) is grammatical if taken to be two separate sentences – e.g. *It is undeniable. He was framed.*) There are also structural constraints on *that*-deletion. As Hawkins (2001, p. 13) notes, there is a strong adjacency effect insofar as *that* can generally only be deleted when it is asymmetrically c-commanded by and immediately adjacent to the relevant (bold-printed) predicate – as can be seen by comparing the examples in (55) above with those in (57) and (58) below:

(57) (a)   It is **clear** to everyone [*that* he was framed]
     (b)   ??It is **clear** to everyone [he was framed]

(58) (a)   [*That* he was framed] is **clear** to everyone
     (b)   *[He was framed] is **clear** to everyone

In (57), the adjectival predicate *clear* asymmetrically c-commands but is not immediately adjacent to *that* (the two being separated by the intervening prepositional phrase *to everyone*), and so *that* cannot be given a null spellout. In (58), *that* is neither c-commanded by nor immediately adjacent to *clear*, so that once again *that* cannot be given a null spellout. The adjacency requirement might suggest that complementiser deletion involves cliticisation of the null complementiser onto the head immediately above it – but precisely how, when and why complementisers receive a null spellout remains shrouded in mystery.

So far in this section, we have argued that seemingly complementiserless finite declarative complement clauses are introduced by a null C constituent (here analysed as a null counterpart of the complementiser *that*). However, the null C analysis can be extended from finite embedded clauses to **main (= root = principal = independent) clauses** like those produced by speakers A and B in (59) below:

(59)   SPEAKER A: I am feeling thirsty
            SPEAKER B: Do you feel like a Coke?

The sentence produced by speaker A is declarative in force (by virtue of being a statement). If force is marked by a force feature carried by the head C of CP, this suggests that such declarative main clauses are CPs headed by a null complementiser carrying a declarative force feature. However, it seems unlikely that the null complementiser introducing declarative main clauses is a null counterpart of *that*, since *that* in English is only used to introduce embedded clauses, not main clauses. Let's therefore suppose that declarative main clauses in English are introduced by an inherently null complementiser (below symbolised as ø), and hence that the sentence produced by speaker A in (59) has the structure shown in (60) below:

(60)

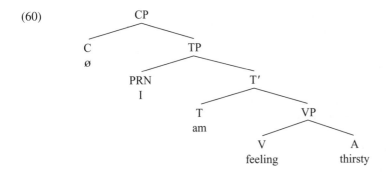

Under the CP analysis of main clauses in (60), the declarative force of the overall sentence is attributed to the fact that the sentence is a CP headed by a null complementiser ø which carries a declarative force feature which we can represent as [Dec-Force]. (The purists among you may object that it's not appropriate to call a null declarative particle introducing a main clause a complementiser when it doesn't introduce a complement clause: however, in keeping with work over the past four decades, we'll use the term complementiser/C in a more general sense here, to designate a category of word which can introduce both complement clauses and other clauses, and which serves to mark properties such as force and finiteness.)

From a cross-linguistic perspective, an analysis such as (60) which posits that main clauses are CPs headed by a force-marking complementiser is by no means implausible in that we find languages like Arabic in which both declarative and interrogative main clauses can be introduced by an overt complementiser, as the examples below illustrate (adapted from Ross 1970, p. 245):

(61) (a)   *?inna* lwalada taraka lbayta
            That the.boy left   the.house
            'The boy left the house' (declarative)

     (b)   *Hal* taraka lwaladu lbayta?
            If   left   the.boy the.house
            'Did the boy leave the house?' (interrogative)

Moreover (as we will see in more detail in §5.2), there is some evidence from sentences like (62) below that inverted auxiliaries in main-clause yes–no questions occupy the head C position of CP in English:

(62)   SPEAKER A: What were you going to ask me?
            SPEAKER B: (a) *If* **you** feel like a Coke
                       (b) *Do* **you** feel like a Coke?
                       (c) **If do* **you** feel like a Coke?

The fact that the inverted auxiliary *do* in (62b) occupies the same pre-subject position (in front of the bold-printed subject **you**) as the complementiser *if* in (62a), and the fact that *if* and *do* are mutually exclusive (as we see from the fact that structures like (62c) are ungrammatical) suggests that inverted auxiliaries (like complementisers) occupy the head C position of CP. This in turn means that main-clause questions are CPs headed by a C which is interrogative in force by virtue of containing an interrogative force feature which can be represented as [Int-Force].

Interestingly, an interrogative main clause can be coordinated with a declarative main clause, as we see from sentences like (63) below:

(63)   [I am feeling thirsty], but [*should I save my last Coke till later*]?

In (63) we have two (bracketed) main clauses joined together by the coordinating conjunction *but*. The second (italicised) conjunct *should I save my last Coke till later?* is an interrogative CP containing an inverted auxiliary in the head C position of CP. Given the traditional assumption that only constituents which belong to the same category can be coordinated, it follows that the first conjunct *I am feeling thirsty* must also be a CP; and since it contains no overt complementiser, it must be headed by a null complementiser – precisely as assumed in (60) above.

The more general conclusion which our discussion in this section leads us to is that all finite clauses have the status of CP constituents which are introduced by a complementiser. Finite complement clauses are CPs headed either by an overt complementiser like *that* or *if* or by a null complementiser (e.g. a null variant of *that* in the case of declarative complement clauses). Finite main clauses are likewise CPs headed by a C which contains an inverted auxiliary if the clause is interrogative, and an inherently null complementiser otherwise.

4.7   Null C in non-finite clauses

The overall conclusion to be drawn from our discussion in §4.6 is that all finite clauses (whether main clauses or complement clauses) are CPs headed by an (overt or null) complementiser which marks the force of the clause. But what about non-finite clauses? It seems clear that *for-to* infinitive clauses such as that bracketed in (64) below are CPs since they are introduced by the infinitival complementiser *for*:

(64)   I will arrange [*for* them to see a specialist]

But what about the type of (bracketed) infinitive complement clause found after verbs like *want* in sentences such as (65) below?

(65)   She wanted [*him* to apologise]

At first sight, it might seem as if the bracketed complement clause in sentences like (65) can't be a CP, since it isn't introduced by the infinitival complementiser *for*. However, it is interesting to note that the complement of *want* is indeed introduced by *for* when the infinitive complement is separated from the verb *want* in some way – e.g. when there is an intervening adverbial expression like *more than anything* as in (66a) below, or when the complement of *want* is in **focus position** in a **pseudo-cleft sentence** as in (66b):

(66) (a)   She wanted **more than anything** *for him to apologise*
     (b)   What she really wanted was *for him to apologise*

(Pseudo-cleft sentences are sentences such as 'What John bought was *a car*', where the italicised expression is said to be **focused** and to occupy **focus** position within the sentence.) This makes it plausible to suggest that the complement of *want* in structures like (65) is a CP headed by a null variant of *for* (below symbolised as ~~for~~), so that (65) has the skeletal structure (67) below (simplified by showing only those parts of the structure immediately relevant to the discussion at hand):

(67)   She wanted [$_{CP}$ [$_C$ ~~for~~] [$_{TP}$ him [$_T$ to] apologise]]

We can then say that the infinitive subject *him* is assigned accusative case by the complementiser ~~for~~ in structures like (67) in exactly the same way as the accusative subject *them* is assigned accusative case by the complementiser *for* in the bracketed complement clause in (64). (How case-marking works will be discussed in §4.9.) One way of accounting for why the complementiser isn't overtly spelled out as *for* in structures like (67) is to suppose that it is given a null spellout (and thereby has its phonetic features deleted) when introducing the complement of a verb like *want*: we can accordingly refer to verbs like *want* as *for*-deletion verbs. For speakers of varieties of English such as mine, *for*-deletion is obligatory when the *for*-clause immediately follows a verb like *want*, but cannot apply when the *for*-clause is separated from *want* in some way – as the examples below illustrate:

(68) (a)   *More than anything, she **wanted** *for him to apologise*
     (b)   More than anything, she **wanted** *him to apologise*
     (c)   She **wanted** more than anything *for him to apologise*
     (d)   *She **wanted** more than anything *him to apologise*

(69) (a)   What she **wanted** was *for him to apologise*
     (b)   *What she **wanted** was *him to apologise*

It would seem, therefore, that *for*-deletion is subject to much the same strict adjacency requirement as *that*-deletion (discussed earlier in §4.6). Since *have*-cliticisation is subject to much the same conditions, it may be that *for*-deletion somehow involves the complementiser cliticising to the verb *want* and thereby being given a null spellout (in much the same way as in African American English/AAE sentences like (25) *He gonna be there, I know he is*, the form *is* has a null spellout only in contexts where in Standard English/SE it would cliticise to a host, so that SE *He's gonna* corresponds to AAE *He gonna*).

Interestingly, not all *for*-deletion verbs behave exactly like *want*: for example, in my variety of English the verb *prefer* optionally (rather than obligatorily) allows deletion of *for* when it immediately follows *prefer* – cf.:

(70) (a)   We would very much **prefer** *for you to be there*
     (b)   We would very much **prefer** *you to be there*

The precise conditions on when *for* can or cannot be deleted are unclear: there are complex lexical factors at work here (in that e.g. words like *want* and *prefer* may behave differently in a particular variety of English) and also complex socio-linguistic factors (in that there is considerable dialectal variation with respect to the use of *for* in infinitive complement clauses).

Having looked at *for*-deletion verbs which select an infinitival complement with an accusative subject, let's now consider the syntax of **control** infinitive clauses with a null PRO subject like that bracketed in (71) below:

(71)   I will arrange [PRO to see a specialist]

What we shall argue here is that control clauses which have a null PRO subject are introduced by a null infinitival complementiser. However, the null complementiser introducing control clauses differs from the null complementiser found in structures like *want/prefer someone to do something* in that it never surfaces as an overt form like *for*, and hence is inherently null. There is, however, parallelism between the structure of a *for* infinitive clause like that bracketed in (64) above, and that of a control infinitive clause like that bracketed in (71), in that they are both CPs and have a parallel internal structure, as shown in (72a,b) below (simplified by not showing the internal structure of the verb phrase *see a specialist*):

(72)   (a)   (b)

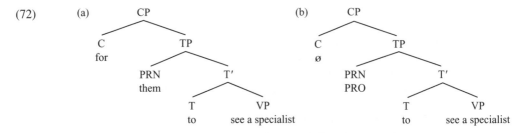

The two types of clause thus have essentially the same CP+TP+VP structure, and differ only in that a *for* infinitive clause like (72a) has an overt *for* complementiser and an overt accusative subject like *them*, whereas a control infinitive clause like (72b) has a null *ø* complementiser and a null PRO subject.

Some evidence in support of claiming that a control clause with a null PRO subject is introduced by a null complementiser comes from coordination facts in relation to sentences such as the following:

(73)   I will arrange [*to see a specialist*] and [**for my wife to see one at the same time**]

The fact that the italicised control infinitive can be conjoined with the bold-printed CP headed by *for* suggests that control infinitives must be CPs (if only the same types of constituent can be conjoined).

Further evidence in support of the CP status of control infinitives comes from the fact that they can be focused in **pseudo-cleft sentences**. In this connection, consider the contrast below:

(74) (a)　　What I'll try and arrange is [*for you to see a specialist*]
　　　(b)　　*What I'll try and arrange for is [*you to see a specialist*]
　　　(c)　　What I'll try and arrange is [*PRO to see a specialist*]

The grammaticality of (74a) suggests that a CP like *for you to see a specialist* can occupy focus position in a pseudo-cleft sentence, whereas conversely the ungrammaticality of (74b) suggests that a TP like *you to see a specialist* cannot. If CP can be focused in pseudo-clefts but TP cannot, then the fact that a control infinitive like *PRO to see a specialist* can be focused in a pseudo-cleft like (74c) suggests that it must have the same CP status as (74a) – precisely as the analysis in (74b) above claims.

Overall, the conclusion which our analysis in this section leads us to is that infinitive complements containing the complementiser *for* (or its null counterpart *for*) are CPs, and so are control infinitives (which contain a null complementiser ø as well as a null PRO subject).

4.8　　Defective clauses

In §4.6, we argued that all finite clauses are CPs, and in §4.7 we went on to argue that *for* infinitives with accusative subjects and control infinitives with null PRO subjects are likewise CPs. These two assumptions lead us to the more general conclusion that:

(75)　　　　All canonical (i.e. 'normal') clauses are CPs

And indeed this is an assumption made by Chomsky in recent work. However, there is one particular type of clause which is exceptional in that it lacks the CP layer found in canonical clauses – namely infinitival complement clauses like those bracketed in (76) below which have (italicised) accusative subjects:

(76) (a)　　They believe [*him* to be innocent]
　　　(b)　　We didn't intend [*you* to get hurt]

Complement clauses like those bracketed in (76) are exceptional in that their subjects are assigned accusative case by the transitive verb (*believe/intend*) immediately preceding them: what's exceptional about this is that the verb is in a different clause from the subject which it assigns accusative case to. For this reason, such clauses are known as **exceptional case-marking clauses** (or **ECM clauses**); and verbs (like *believe*) when used with an ECM clause as their complement are known as **ECM verbs**.

ECM complement clauses seem to be TPs which lack the CP layer found in canonical clauses, and for this reason Chomsky (1999) terms them **defective clauses**. One reason for thinking that the bracketed ECM clauses in sentences like (76) are not full CPs is that they cannot readily be coordinated with *for*-infinitives, as we see from the ungrammaticality of (77) below:

(77)   *We didn't intend [*you to hurt him*] or [**for him to hurt you**]

Although (for speakers like me) the verb *intend* can take either a bare ECM infinitive complement or a *for* infinitive complement, the fact that the two cannot be conjoined suggests that the bare ECM infinitive clauses have the status of TPs while *for-to* infinitive clauses have the status of CPs. By contrast, coordination is indeed possible in sentences like:

(78)   We didn't intend [*you to hurt him*] or [**him to hurt you**]

and this is because both bracketed clauses in (78) are infinitival TPs.

Further evidence that ECM infinitive clauses like those bracketed in (76) are TPs rather than CPs comes from the fact that they cannot occur in focus position in pseudo-clefts, as we see from the ungrammaticality of the sentences below:

(79) (a)   *What they believe is [*him to be innocent*]
     (b)   *What we hadn't intended was [*you to get hurt*]

If ECM clauses are TPs, this follows from the restriction noted in (75) that only CPs (not TPs) can occur in focus position in a pseudo-cleft sentence. Moreover, a further property of sentences like (76) which would be difficult to account for if the bracketed complement clause were a CP is the fact that its (italicised) subject can be **passivised** and thereby made into the subject of the main clause, as in (80) below:

(80) (a)   *He* is believed to be innocent
     (b)   *You* weren't intended to get hurt

This is because it is a property of the subject of an infinitival CP complement clause like that bracketed in (81a) below that its subject cannot be passivised – as we see from the ungrammaticality of (81b):

(81) (a)   We didn't intend [for *you* to get hurt]
     (b)   *You* weren't intended [for to get hurt]

Likewise, the subject of the infinitival CP complement of a *for*-deletion verb like *want* cannot be passivised either:

(82) (a)   She wanted [*John* to apologise]
     (b)   *John* was wanted [to apologise]

– and indeed this is precisely what we expect if the subjects of CPs cannot passivise, and if the bracketed complement clauses in (82) are CPs headed by a null counterpart of *for*, as claimed in §4.7. However, the fact that the passive sentences in (80) are grammatical suggests that the bracketed complement clauses in (76) are TPs rather than CPs (since the subject of an infinitival TP can be passivised, but not the subject of an infinitival CP). Hence, complement clauses like those bracketed in (76) above are defective clauses which have no CP layer, and (76a) *They believe him to be innocent* accordingly has the structure (83) below:

(83)

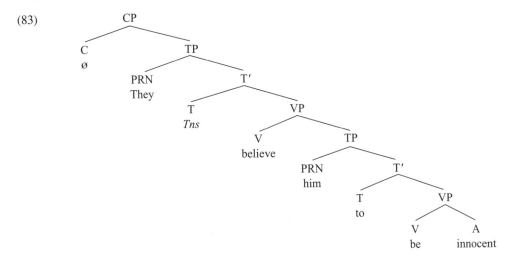

The particular aspect of the analysis in (83) most relevant to our discussion in this section is the claim that the complement clause *him to be innocent* is an infinitival TP headed by *to*, and its subject *him* is assigned accusative case by the transitive verb *believe*: how this happens, we shall look at in the next section.

We can extend the analysis of ECM predicates like *believe* proposed in this section to verbs like those discussed in §4.5 which select a bare infinitive complement. On this view, a sentence like *I have never known him be rude to anyone* would be analysed as containing a transitive perfect participle *known* which selects a TP complement headed by a null counterpart of infinitival *to* – as shown in skeletal form in (84) below:

(84)   I have never known [TP him [T t̶o̶] be rude to anyone]

Since the subject of a TP complement can passivise, the analysis in (84) predicts that the subject of the bracketed infinitive complement in (84) can passivise, and this is indeed the case as we see from examples like (85) below:

(85)   He has never been known to be rude to anyone

Because infinitival *to* can only have a null spellout when the TP complement it heads is the complement of an active transitive verb-form like the perfect participle *known* in (84) and not when the relevant TP is the complement of a passive participle like *known* in (85), it follows that infinitival *to* must be given an overt spellout in sentences like (85).

Under the analysis proposed here, verbs which take a bare infinitive complement with an accusative subject are analysed as ECM predicates which select a TP complement headed by an infinitival T which has an overt spellout as *to* in passive structures like (85) and a null spellout in active structures such as (84). However, one predicate which is problematic to classify in such terms is *let*, since it allows a bare infinitive complement in active structures like (86a) below but doesn't allow the subject of the infinitive to passivise, as we see from the ungrammaticality of sentences like (86b):

(86) (a)   You shouldn't let [him upset you]
      (b)   *He shouldn't be let [(to) upset you]

We can't describe the relevant facts by saying that *let* is a defective verb which has no passive participle form, since *let* is used as a passive participle in sentences like *The prisoners were let out of jail*. An alternative analysis is to suppose that whereas typical ECM predicates select an infinitival TP complement in both active and passive uses, *let* is irregular in that it only selects an infinitival TP complement in active uses, not when used as a passive participle. Similar lexical idiosyncrasies are found with a number of other verbs: for example, *know* only allows a bare infinitival complement with an accusative subject when used as a perfect participle in structures like (84) above. (An alternative way of accounting for the impossibility of passivisation in sentences like (86b) which we won't adopt here is to take *let* to be a verb selecting a CP complement headed by an inherently null complementiser which in turn selects an infinitival TP complement headed by a null counterpart of infinitival *to*: the ungrammaticality of (86b) then follows from the impossibility of passivising the subject of a CP complement.)

4.9   Case properties of subjects

A question which we haven't addressed so far is how subjects are case-marked. In this connection, consider how the italicised subject of the bracketed infinitive complement clause in (87) below is assigned accusative case:

(87)   She must be keen [for *him* to meet them]

Since *for* is a transitive complementiser, it seems plausible to suppose that the infinitive subject *him* is assigned accusative case by the transitive complementiser *for* – but *how*? We've already seen that the relation **c-command** plays a central role in our characterisation of a wide range of disparate phenomena, including the binding of anaphors, morphological operations like Affix Hopping, phonological operations like *have*-cliticisation, and so on. Let's therefore explore the possibility that c-command is also central to case assignment. More particularly, let's suppose that:

(88)   A transitive head assigns accusative case to a noun or pronoun expression which it c-commands

In addition, let's follow Pesetsky (1995) in positing the following UG principle governing the application of grammatical (and other kinds of linguistic) operations:

(89)   **Earliness Principle**
         Operations apply as early in a derivation as possible

In the light of (88) and (89), let's look at the derivation of the bracketed complement clause in (87). The first step is for the verb *meet* to be merged with its pronoun complement *them* to form the VP shown in (90) below:

(90)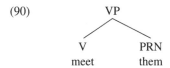

Meet is a transitive verb which c-commands the pronoun *them*. Since (88) specifies that a transitive head assigns accusative case to a pronoun which it c-commands, and since the Earliness Principle specifies that operations like case assignment must apply as early as possible in a derivation, it follows that the pronoun *them* will be assigned accusative case by the transitive verb *meet* at the stage of derivation shown in (90).

The derivation then continues by merging the infinitive particle *to* with the VP in (90), so forming the T-bar *to meet them*. The resulting T-bar is merged with its subject *him* to form the TP *him to meet them*. This TP in turn is merged with the complementiser *for* to form the CP shown in (91) below:

(91)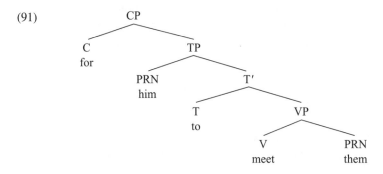

For is a transitive complementiser and c-commands the infinitive subject *him*. Since (88) specifies that a transitive head assigns accusative case to a pronoun which it c-commands, and since the Earliness Principle specifies that operations like case assignment must apply as early as possible in a derivation, it follows that the pronoun *him* will be assigned accusative case by the transitive complementiser *for* at the stage of derivation shown in (91). This account of the case-marking of infinitive subjects can be extended from accusative subjects of *for* infinitives in structures like (91) to accusative subjects of ECM infinitives in structures like (83) *They believe [him to be innocent]*, since the transitive verb *believe* c-commands the infinitive subject *him* in (83). (As we shall see in chapter 8, a tacit assumption underlying the case assignment analysis is that noun and pronoun expressions enter the derivation carrying a case feature which is initially unvalued, and which is then valued as nominative, accusative or genitive by a c-commanding head of an appropriate kind.)

Having looked at how accusative subjects are case-marked, let's now turn to look at the case-marking of nominative subjects. In this connection, consider the case-marking of the italicised subjects in (92) below:

(92)   *He* may suspect [that *she* is lying]

Consider first how the complement clause subject *she* is assigned case. The bracketed complement clause in (92) has the structure (93) below:

(93)

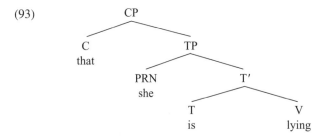

If we are to develop a unitary theory of case-marking, it seems plausible to suppose that nominative subjects (just like accusative subjects) are assigned case under c-command by an appropriate kind of head. Since the finite complementiser *that* in (93) c-commands the subject *she*, let's suppose that *she* is assigned nominative case by the complementiser *that* (in much the same way as the infinitive subject *him* in (91) is assigned accusative case by the transitive complementiser *for*). More specifically, let's assume that

(94)   A finite complementiser assigns nominative case to a noun or pronoun
         expression which it c-commands

In (93), the only noun or pronoun expression c-commanded by the finite complementiser *that* is the clause subject *she*, which is therefore assigned nominative case in accordance with (94).

But how can we account for the fact that the main-clause subject *he* in (92) is also assigned nominative case? The answer is that (as we argued in §4.6) all canonical clauses – including all main clauses – are CPs introduced by a complementiser, and that if the clause contains no overt complementiser, it is headed by a null complementiser. This being so, the main clause in (92) will have the structure (95) below:

(95)

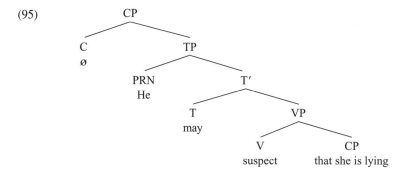

Thus, the overall clause is headed by a null finite declarative complementiser [c ø] in much the same way as the Arabic main clauses in (61) are headed by an overt complementiser, and it is this null finite complementiser which assigns nominative case to the subject *he* in (95) in accordance with (94) above, since the complementiser *ø* c-commands the pronoun *he*. (On the possibility of a finite C being a nominative case assigner, see Chomsky 1999, p. 35, fn.17.)

However, an interesting complication arises in relation to the Arabic data in (61) above. Sentence (61a) is introduced by the **transitive** finite complementiser *?inna* 'that' and the subject *lwalada* 'the boy' is assigned **accusative** case in accordance with (88). By contrast, sentence (61b) is introduced by the finite complementiser *hal* 'if': this is not transitive and assigns **nominative** case to the subject *lwaladu* (which therefore carries the nominative ending -*u* rather than the accusative ending -*a*). Such considerations suggest that we need to revise (94) by adding the italicised condition shown in (96) below:

(96)   An *intransitive* finite complementiser assigns nominative case to a noun or
          pronoun expression which it c-commands

Since none of the English finite complementisers (e.g. *if, that, ~~that~~* and the null finite complementiser found in main clauses) are transitive, all finite clauses in English will have nominative subjects.

Having looked at accusative and nominative subjects, let's now turn to consider the null PRO subjects found in control clauses. If we suppose that it is a defining characteristic of all pronouns that they carry case, then PRO too must carry case – and indeed there is some evidence that this is so. Part of the relevant evidence comes from structures like (97) below which contain a (bold-printed) **floating quantifier** which modifies the (italicised) subject of its clause, but is separated from (and positioned lower than) the subject:

(97)   *They* have **all** gone home

In a language like Icelandic which has a richer morphology than English, float-ing quantifiers agree in case with their antecedent (i.e. with the expression which they modify). In a structure like (98) below (from Sigurðsson 1991, p. 331) the verb *leiðist* 'got bored' requires a subject with **dative** (= DAT) case, and hence a floating quantifier modifying the subject also has dative case:

(98)   *Strákarnir*   leiðist **öllum** í skóla
         the.boys.DAT bored all.DAT in school
         'The boys all got bored in school'

Interestingly, when the relevant verb is used in a control clause, a floating quantifier modifying the subject of the control clause has dative case, as the following example (from Sigurðsson ibid.) shows:

(99)   *Strákarnir*   vonast til [að PRO leiðast ekki **öllum** í skóla]
         The.boys.NOM hoped for [to PRO bore   not all.DAT at school]
         'The boys hoped to not all get bored at school'

Why should the floating quantifier in (99) be dative? It doesn't carry the same case as the main-clause subject *strákarnir* 'the boys', since the latter has nominative (= NOM) case. On the contrary, the floating quantifier carries the same case as (and is construed as quantifying) the null PRO subject of its clause, and PRO has dative case because it is an idiosyncratic property of the relevant verb in Icelandic that it requires a dative subject. (Icelandic is said to be a language with **quirky-case subjects** in that some verbs require dative subjects, others require accusative subjects and so on. On dative and quirky subjects, see Moore and Perlmutter 2000, and Sigurðsson 2002.)

In short, the syntax of floating quantifiers in Icelandic makes it clear that PRO has case properties of its own. But what case does PRO carry in a morphologically impoverished language like English? Chomsky and Lasnik (1995, pp. 119–20) suggest that the subject of a control clause carries what they call **null case**. The morphological effect of null case is to ensure that a pronoun is unpronounced – just as the morphological effect of nominative case is to ensure that (e.g.) a third-person-masculine-singular pronoun is pronounced as *he*. But how is PRO assigned null case? If we are to attain a unitary account of case-marking under which a noun or pronoun expression is case-marked by a head which c-commands it, a plausible answer is the following:

(100)   A null intransitive non-finite complementiser assigns null case to a noun or
         pronoun expression which it c-commands

It follows from (100) that PRO in a structure like (72b) above will be assigned null case by the null (non-finite, intransitive) complementiser which c-commands PRO.

We can conflate the various claims made about case-marking above into (101) below:

(101)   **Case Assignment Conditions**
          A noun or pronoun expression is assigned case by the closest case-assigner which
          c-commands it (in consequence of the **Earliness Principle**) and is assigned
             (i)   accusative case if c-commanded by a transitive head (e.g a transitive verb like *meet*,
                   or a transitive preposition like *with* or a transitive complementiser like *for* or ~~*for*~~)
            (ii)   nominative case if c-commanded by an intransitive finite complementiser (like *that,*
                   ~~*that*~~, *if* or the null declarative main-clause complementiser *Ø*)
           (iii)   null case if c-commanded by a null intransitive non-finite complementiser *Ø*

If we assume that PRO is the only exponent of null case in English, it follows
from (101iii) that control infinitive clauses (which are headed by a null-case-
assigning complementiser under the analysis in §4.7) will always require a PRO
subject.

What is particularly interesting about our discussion of case-marking here from
a theoretical point of view is that it provides yet more evidence for the centrality
of the relation **c-command** in syntax. (See Frank and Vijay-Shanker 2001 for a
technical defense of the primitive nature of c-command.) An important theoretical
question to ask at this juncture is why c-command should be such a fundamental
relation in syntax. From a Minimalist perspective (since the goal of Minimalism
is to utilise only theoretical apparatus which is conceptually necessary), the most
principled answer would be one along the following lines. It is clear that the
operation **Merge** (which builds phrases out of words, and sentences out of phrases)
is conceptually necessary, in that (e.g.) to form a prepositional phrase like *to Paris*
out of the preposition *to* and the noun *Paris*, we need some operation like Merge
which combines the two together. In order to achieve the Minimalist goal of
developing a constrained theory of Universal Grammar/UG which makes use only
of concepts and constructs which are **conceptually necessary**, we can suppose
that the only kind of syntactic relations which UG permits us to make use of are
those created by the operation Merge. Now, two structural relations created by
the operation Merge are **contain(ment)** and **c-command** in that if we merge a
head X with a complement YP to form an XP projection, XP **contains** X, YP and
all the constituents of YP, and X c-commands YP and all the constituents of YP.
Minimalist considerations therefore lead us to hypothesise that the containment
and c-command relations created by merger are the only primitive relations in
syntax.

Our discussion in this section shows that case-marking phenomena can be
accounted for in a principled fashion within a highly constrained Minimalist
framework which makes use of the **c-command** relation which is created by
the operation Merge. Note that a number of other grammatical relations which
traditional grammars make use of (e.g. relations like **subjecthood** and **objecthood**) are not relations which can be used within the Minimalist framework. For
example, a typical characterisation of accusative case assignment in traditional
grammar is that a transitive verb or preposition assigns accusative case to its

object. There are two problems with carrying over such a generalisation into the framework we are using here. The first is that Minimalism is a constrained theory which does not allow us to appeal to the relation objecthood, only to the relations **contain** and **c-command**; the second is that the traditional objecthood account of accusative case assignment is empirically inadequate, in that it fails to account for the accusative case-marking of an infinitive subject by a transitive complementiser in structures like (91), because *him* is not the object of the complementiser *for* but rather the subject of *to meet them* (and the same holds for accusative subjects of ECM infinitive structures like (83) above). As our discussion in later chapters unfolds, it will become clear that there are a number of other syntactic phenomena which can be given a principled description in terms of the relations **contain** and **c-command**.

4.10   Null determiners

Thus far, we have argued that empty categories play an important role in the syntax of clauses in that clauses may contain a null subject, a null T constituent and a null C constituent. We now turn to argue that the same is true of the syntax of **nominals** (i.e. noun expressions), and that many **bare nominals** (i.e. noun expressions which contain no overt determiner or quantifier) are headed by a null determiner or null quantifier. The assumption that bare nominals contain a null determiner/quantifier has a long history – for example, Chomsky (1965, p. 108) suggests that the noun *sincerity* in a sentence such as *Sincerity may frighten the boy* is modified by a null determiner. Chomsky's suggestion was taken up and extended in later work by Abney (1987), Longobardi (1994, 1996, 2001) and Bernstein (2001).

In this connection, consider the syntax of the italicised bare nominals in (102) below:

(102)   *Italians* love *opera*

As we see from (103a) below, the French counterpart of the bare nominals in (102) are DPs headed by the determiner *les/l'* ('the') – and indeed as (103b) shows, this type of structure is also possible in English:

(103) (a)   *Les Italiens* adorent *l'opéra*
             The Italians adore   th'opera
             'Italians love opera'
       (b)   *The Italians* love *the opera*

This suggests that bare nominals like those italicised in (102) above are DPs headed by a null determiner, so that the overall sentence in (102) has the structure (104) below:

(104)

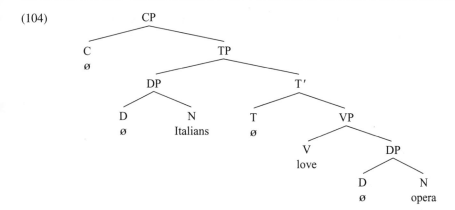

Given the analysis in (104), there would be an obvious parallelism between the syntax of clauses and nominals, in that just as canonical clauses are CPs headed by an overt or null C constituent, so too canonical nominals are DPs headed by an overt or null D constituent.

One piece of empirical evidence in support of analysing bare nouns as DPs comes from sentences like:

(105) (a) *Italians* and [**the majority of Mediterraneans**] love opera
       (b) Italians love [*opera*] and [**the finer things in life**]

The fact that the bare nouns *Italians* and *opera* can be coordinated with determiner phrases/DPs like *the majority of Mediterraneans/the finer things in life* (both headed by the determiner *the*) provides us with empirical evidence that bare nouns must be DPs, if only similar kinds of categories can be coordinated.

If (as we are suggesting here) there are indeed a class of null determiners, we should expect these to have specific grammatical, selectional and semantic properties of their own: and, as we shall see, there is indeed evidence that this is so. For one thing, the null determiner carries **person** properties – in particular, it is a third-person determiner. In this respect, consider sentences such as:

(106) (a) We linguists take **ourselves/*yourselves/*themselves** too seriously, don't *we/*you/*they*?
       (b) You linguists take **yourselves/*ourselves/*themselves** too seriously, don't *you/*we/*they*?
       (c) Linguists take **themselves/*ourselves/*yourselves** too seriously, don't *they/*we/*you*?

(106a) shows that a first-person expression such as *we linguists* can only bind (i.e. serve as the antecedent of) a first-person reflexive like *ourselves*, and can only be tagged by a first-person pronoun like *we*. (106b) shows that a second-person expression like *you linguists* can only bind a second-person reflexive like *yourselves*, and can only be tagged by a second-person pronoun like *you*. (106c) shows that a bare nominal like *linguists* can only bind a third-person reflexive like *themselves* and can only be tagged by a third-person pronoun like *they*. One way of accounting for the relevant facts is to suppose that the nominals *we linguists/you linguists/linguists* in (106a–c) are DPs with the respective structures shown in (107a–c):

(107)   (a) 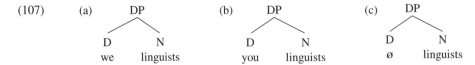   (b)   (c)

and that the person properties of a DP are determined by the person features carried by its head determiner. If *we* is a first-person determiner, *you* is a second-person determiner and *ø* is a third-person determiner, the grammaticality judgments in (106a–c) above are precisely as the analysis in (107a–c) would lead us to expect.

In addition to having specific person properties, the null determiner *ø* also has specific selectional properties – as can be illustrated by the following set of examples:

(108) (a)   I wrote *poems*
    (b)   I wrote *poetry*
    (c)   *I wrote *poem*

If each of the italicised bare nouns in (108) is the complement of a null (quantifying) determiner *ø*, the relevant examples show that *ø* can select as its complement an expression headed by a plural count noun like *poems*, or by a singular mass noun like *poetry* – but not by a singular count noun like *poem*. The complement-selection properties of the null determiner *ø* mirror those of the overt quantifier *enough*:

(109) (a)   I've read **enough** *poetry*
    (b)   I've read **enough** *poems*
    (c)   *I've read **enough** *poem*

The fact that *ø* has much the same selectional properties as a typical overt (quantifying) determiner such as *enough* strengthens the case for positing the existence of a null determiner *ø*, and for analysing bare nominals as DPs headed by a null determiner (or QPs headed by a null quantifier).

Moreover, there is evidence that the null determiner *ø* has specific semantic properties of its own – as we can illustrate in relation to the interpretation of the italicised nominals in the sentences below:

(110) (a)   *Eggs* are fattening
    (b)   *Bacon* is fattening
    (c)   I had *eggs* for breakfast
    (d)   I had *bacon* for breakfast

The nouns *eggs* and *bacon* in (110a/b) have a **generic** interpretation, paraphraseable as 'eggs/bacon in general'. In (110c,d) *eggs* and *bacon* have a **partitive** interpretation, paraphraseable as 'some eggs/bacon'. If we say that the italicised bare nominals are DPs/determiner phrases headed by a null determiner, as shown below:

(111)

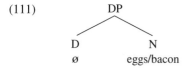

we can say that the null determiner has the semantic property of being a generic or partitive quantifier, so that bare nominals are interpreted as generic or partitive expressions.

The claim that null determiners have specific semantic properties is an important one from a theoretical perspective in the light of the principle suggested by Chomsky (1995) that all constituents (or at any rate, all heads and maximal projections) must be **interpretable** at the **semantics interface** (i.e. must be able to be assigned a semantic interpretation by the semantic component of the grammar, and hence must contribute something to the meaning of the sentence containing them). This principle holds for null constituents as well as overt constituents, so that e.g. a seemingly null T constituent contains an abstract affix carrying an interpretable tense feature, and a null C constituent contains an abstract morpheme carrying an interpretable force feature. If the null D constituent found in structures like (110) and (111) is interpreted as a (generic or partitive) quantifier, the null D analysis will satisfy the relevant requirement.

The assumption that bare nominals are headed by a null determiner allows us to arrive at a unitary characterisation of the syntax of nominals. We can then say that nominals like *the president* which are modified by an overt determiner are DPs, bare nominals like *Italians* are DPs headed by a null determiner, and personal pronouns like *they* (if analysed as D-pronouns, as in §2.6) are determiners used without a complement – as shown below:

(112)

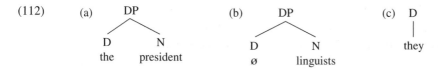

This means that all nominal and pronominal expressions are D-expressions – i.e. projections of an (overt or null) D constituent – an assumption widely referred to as the **DP hypothesis**. Indeed, the DP hypothesis can be further extended if we follow Freidin and Vergnaud (2001) in supposing that a pronoun like *they* (if used to refer to *linguists*) in a sentence such as:

(113)   Linguists think *they* are undervalued

is a DP comprising a head determiner *they* with a noun complement *linguists* which is given a null spellout in the PF component, as shown in (114) below:

(114)

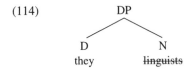

However, Radford (1993) argued that while a phrasal analysis along the lines of (114) may be appropriate for some pronouns (e.g. *which?*), other pronouns (e.g. *who?*) seem to be simple heads. This difference of status is reflected in syntactic differences between the two: e.g. *who* can be modified by *else* but *which* and overtly phrasal expressions cannot (cf. *Who else? *Which else? *How many people else?*), and *who* can be positioned immediately in front of a preposition, but *which* and phrases cannot (cf. *Who to? *Which to? *How many people to?*). While an analysis like (114) may be appropriate for some types of pronoun in some languages (see Wiltschko 2002), it does not seem appropriate for English personal pronouns.

We have argued in this section that canonical nominal expressions are DPs headed by an (overt or null) determiner. However, there is evidence that this is true only of nominal expressions used as **arguments** (i.e. nominals used as the subject or complement of a predicate), not of non-argument nominals (e.g. nominals which have a **vocative**, **predicative** or **exclamative** use). More specifically (as Longobardi 1994 argues), non-argument nominals such as those italicised in (115) below can be N-projections lacking a determiner:

(115) (a)   Do all syntacticians suffer from asteriskitis, *doctor*?
    (b)   Dr DoLittle is *head of department*
    (c)   *Poor fool*! He thought he'd passed the syntax exam

The italicised nominal expression serves a **vocative** function (i.e. is used to address someone) in (115a), a **predicative** function in (115b) (in that the property of being head of department is predicated of the unfortunate Dr DoLittle), and an **exclamative** function in (115c). Each of the italicised nominals in (115) is headed by a singular count noun (*doctor/head/fool*): in spite of the fact that such nouns require an overt determiner when used as arguments, here they function as non-arguments and are used without any determiner. This suggests that non-argument nominals can be N-expressions, whereas argument nominals are always D-expressions.

Chomsky (1999, fn. 10) maintains that only referential nominal arguments (i.e. nominal arguments which are referring expressions) have the status of true DPs, not 'nonspecifics, quantified and predicate nominals, etc.' If so, bare nominals with a quantificational interpretation would more appropriately be analysed as QPs headed by a null quantifier: on this view, the noun *eggs* in (110c) *I had eggs for breakfast* would be a QP headed by a null partitive quantifier (rather than a DP headed by a null determiner).

4.11   Summary

In this chapter, we have seen that null constituents (i.e. constituents which have no overt phonetic form but have specific grammatical and semantic properties) play a central role in syntax. We began by looking at null (finite, imperative, truncated and non-finite) subjects in §4.2, arguing in particular that control infinitive clauses have a null PRO subject which can refer to some expression within a higher clause, or refer to some entity in the domain of discourse, or have arbitrary reference. In §4.3 we showed that elliptical clauses like that bracketed in *He could have helped her or* [*she have helped him*] are TPs headed by a null (ellipsed) tense auxiliary. In §4.4 we extended this *null T* analysis to auxiliariless finite clauses like *He enjoys syntax*, arguing that they contain a TP headed by an abstract tense affix which is lowered onto the main verb by the morphological operation of *Affix Hopping* in the PF component. In §4.5 we argued that bare (*to*-less) infinitive clauses like that bracketed in *I have never known* [*him tell a lie*] are TPs headed by a null variant of infinitival *to*. We concluded that all finite and infinitive clauses contain a TP headed by an overt or null T constituent carrying finite or non-finite tense. In §4.6, we argued that all finite clauses are CPs, and that those which are not introduced by an overt complementiser are CPs headed by a null complementiser which encodes the force of the clause (so that a sentence like *He enjoys syntax* is declarative in force by virtue of being a CP headed by a null declarative C). In §4.7 we saw that *for* infinitives, the infinitive complements of *want*-class verbs and control infinitives are also CPs, and went on to posit that all canonical clauses are CPs. However, in §4.8 we argued that ECM (Exceptional Case-Marking) clauses with accusative subjects like that bracketed in *I believe* [*him to be innocent*] are defective clauses which have the status of TPs rather than CPs. In §4.9 we examined case-marking, arguing that a transitive head assigns accusative case to a noun or pronoun expression which it c-commands, an intransitive finite complementiser assigns nominative case to a noun or pronoun expression which it c-commands, and a null intransitive non-finite complementiser assigns null case to a pronoun expression which it c-commands. We also noted that in consequence of Pesetsky's Earliness Principle, noun and pronoun expressions are case-marked by the closest case-assigner which c-commands them. In §4.10, we looked briefly at the syntax of nominals, arguing that bare nominal arguments (like *Italians* and *opera* in *Italians love opera*) are DPs headed by a null determiner which has the grammatical property of being a third-person determiner, the selectional property of requiring as its complement a nominal headed by a singular mass noun or plural count noun, and the semantic property that it has a generic or partitive interpretation. We concluded that canonical nominals (more particularly, nominal arguments) are D-expressions, comprising either an overt or null D-pronoun (like *he* or *PRO*) used without a complement, or an overt or null determiner (like *the* or *ø*) used with a noun expression as its complement; however, we noted the claims by Chomsky and Longobardi that only referential nominal arguments are DPs, not quantified nominals, vocatives, exclamatives or predicate nominals.

Workbook section

Exercise 4.1

Draw tree diagrams to represent the structure of the following sentences, presenting arguments in support of your analysis and commenting on any null constituents they contain and the reasons for positing them. In addition, say how each of the noun or pronoun expressions is case-marked.

1	Students enjoy the classes
2	We have fun
3	Voters know politicians lie
4	John promised to behave himself
5	She sees no need for him to apologise
6	They would prefer students to do exams
7	Economists expect salaries to rise
8	He might like you to talk to her
9	I have known you have a tantrum
10	John wanted to help him

In addition, say why *have*-cliticisation is or is not permitted in 11b,12b,13b,14B and 15b below:

11a	They have suffered hardship
b	They've suffered hardship
12a	The Sioux have suffered hardship
b	*The Sioux've suffered hardship
13a	Sioux have suffered hardship
b	*Sioux've suffered hardship
14	SPEAKER A: How are students coping with your *Fantasy Syntax* course?
	SPEAKER B: *Two've given up
15a	They may have left
b	*They may've left

Helpful hints

Bear in mind that in the main text we argued that all clauses other than non-finite clauses used as the complement of an ECM verb are CPs, and that bare nominal arguments are DP or QP constituents headed by a null determiner or quantifier. For the purposes of this exercise, assume the following:

(i)   *Have* can cliticise onto a word W provided that
        – W is a noun or pronoun ending in a vowel or diphthong
        – W asymmetrically c-commands *have*
        – there is no intervening constituent c-commanded by W and
        c-commanding *have*

In relation to 3, consider what case *politicians* has, and how you can use this to determine whether the complement of *know* is a TP or a CP. In 4, use Binding Principle A from exercise 3.2 to help you account for why *himself* is coreferential to *John*. In 5, assume that *no* is a negative quantifier which has a noun phrase complement. In 10, use Binding Principle B from exercise 3.2 to help you account for why *him* cannot be coreferential to *John*. In relation to the (b,B) examples in 11–15, draw trees to represent the structure of the sentences immediately prior to cliticisation, and then show whether or not the analysis of *have*-cliticisation given in (i) above predicts that cliticisation is possible; note that the noun *Sioux* is pronounced |su:|. Show how the ungrammaticality of 13b can be used to evaluate the hypothesis that a bare noun like *Sioux* in 13 is a DP headed by a null determiner. In addition, say how sentences like 11b can be used to evaluate the plausibility of analyses (such as that proposed by Freidin and Vergnaud 2001) which take pronouns like *they* to be determiners which have a nominal complement whose phonetic features are given a null spellout in the PF component, so that e.g. if *they* refers to *Sioux*, the pronoun *they* would be a DP with the structure shown in (ii) below:

(ii)

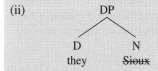

Would it be any more or less plausible to suppose that the (numeral) quantifier *two* in sentences like that produced by speaker B in 14 has an N complement containing a null copy of the noun *students*? In relation to 15, assume that *have left* is an AUXP comprising the AUX *have* and the V *left*.

Model answer for sentence 1

Given the arguments in the main text that all finite clauses contain a TP headed by a T constituent containing an affix which encodes tense and (person and number) agreement features, the sentence *Students enjoy the classes* will contain a TP headed by a tense affix which carries the features [third-person, plural-number, present-tense], which we can abbreviate to Tns_{3PLPR}. Likewise, given the arguments in the main text that ordinary finite clauses are CPs headed by an (overt or null) complementiser which marks the force of the clause, the overall sentence will be a CP headed by a null finite declarative complementiser [C ø]. Finally, in accordance with the DP hypothesis, both nominal arguments containing an overt determiner (like *the classes*) and bare nominal arguments like *students* will be determiner phrases, differing only in whether they are headed by the overt third-person determiner *the* or the null third-person determiner [D ø]. Given these assumptions, sentence 1 will have the structure below:

(i)

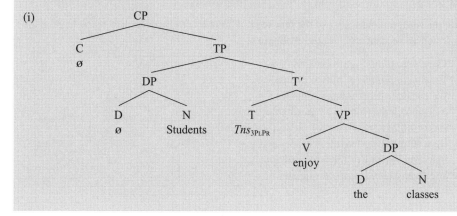

Because there is no auxiliary in T for it to attach to, the *Tns* affix in T is lowered onto the verb *enjoy* by the morphological operation of **Affix Hopping** in the PF component, forming *enjoy*+*Tns*$_{3PLPR}$ (which is ultimately spelled out as the third-person-plural present-tense form *enjoy*). Evidence that the overall clause *Students enjoy the classes* is a CP headed by a null complementiser comes from coordination facts in relation to sentences such as:

(ii)   [*Students enjoy the classes*] but [**do they like the lectures**]?

In (ii) the declarative clause *Students enjoy the classes* has been coordinated with the interrogative clause *do they like the lectures?* which contains the inverted auxiliary *do*. If (as claimed in the main text) inverted auxiliaries occupy the head C position of CP, it follows that the second of the two coordinate clauses in (ii) must be a CP; and if only constituents of the same type can be coordinated, it follows that the first clause must also be a CP – as in (i) above. Evidence in support of positing a null present-tense T constituent in (i) comes from the fact that the T-bar *ø enjoy the classes* can be coordinated with another T-bar like *don't like the lectures*, as we see from (iii) below:

(iii)   Students *enjoy the classes*, but *don't like the lectures*

Evidence that the bare nominal *students* is a DP headed by a null third-person determiner [$_D$ ø] comes from the fact that sentence 1 can only be tagged by a third-person pronoun like *they*:

(iv)   Students enjoy the lectures, don't *they/*we/*you*?

The null determiner is interpreted as a generic quantifier in (i).

The DP *the classes* in (i) is assigned accusative case by virtue of being c-commanded by the transitive verb *enjoy* (and *enjoy* is the closest case-assigner c-commanding *the classes*). Accordingly, the DP *the classes* can be substituted by an accusative pronoun, as in:

(v)   Students enjoy *them*

By contrast, the DP *ø students* is assigned nominative case by virtue of being c-commanded by the intransitive finite complementiser *ø* (which is the closest – and indeed only – case-assigner c-commanding the DP *ø students*). We therefore correctly predict that this DP can be substituted by a nominative pronoun, as in:

(vi)   *They* enjoy the classes

Exercise 4.2

Account for the (un)grammaticality of the bracketed infinitive complement clause structures in the following sentences in standard varieties of English:

1 a   They were *planning* [to escape]
  b   *They were *planning* [him to escape]
2 a   We *consider* [him to be unsuitable]
  b   *It is *considered* [him to be unsuitable]
3 a   He would *like* [me to leave]
  b   He would *like* [to leave]
4 a   She seems *keen* [for them to participate]
  b   *She seems *keen* [for to participate]

5 a	I received a *request* [to resign]
b	*I received a *request* [him to resign]
6 a	It was *agreed* [to review the policy]
b	*It was *agreed* [us to review the policy]
7 a	Congress *decided* [to ratify the treaty]
b	*Congress *decided* [for him to ratify the treaty]
8 a	She *expected* [to win the nomination]
b	She *expected* [him/*he to win the nomination]
9 a	He should *let* [you have a break]
b	*He should *let* [have a break]
10 a	*He *said* [her to like oysters]
b	*He *said* [to like oysters]

In addition, say how you would analyse structures like (4b) in varieties of English (like Belfast English) in which they are grammatical and have a meaning roughly paraphraseable as 'She seems keen for herself to participate.' What if *for-to* can serve as a compound T constituent in such sentences in the relevant varieties (and likewise in sentences such as *I wanted Jimmy for to come with me*, from Henry 1995, p. 85)?

Helpful hints

Note that (1b) is intended to have an interpretation paraphraseable as 'They were planning for him to escape', (9b) to have an interpretation paraphraseable as 'He should let himself have a break', (10a) to have an interpretation paraphraseable as 'He said she liked oysters', and (10b) to have an interpretation paraphraseable as 'He said he liked oysters' (where the two occurrences of *he* refer to the same individual). Assume that each of the italicised words in the above examples has its own idiosyncratic selectional properties, and that the selectional properties of any word W are described by saying: 'W selects as its complement an expression headed by . . .' (where in place of the dots you insert the features characterising the relevant head). So, you might say e.g. that a verb like *arrange* can select a complement headed by an infinitival complementiser (either the transitive infinitival complementiser *for* or the null intransitive infinitival complementiser *Ø*), whereas an ECM verb like *believe* selects a complement headed by the infinitival T *to*. By contrast, other verbs (it might turn out) don't select a particular kind of infinitive complement – or indeed *any* kind of infinitive complement. Assume that the seemingly subjectless clauses in 1–10 (whether grammatical or not) have a null PRO subject. Pay attention (i) to the selectional properties of the italicised words and (ii) to the case properties of the subjects of the bracketed complement clauses. In the case of the ungrammatical examples, consider whether the ungrammaticality is attributable to a **selectional error** (in that the italicised word is used with a kind of complement which it does not select/allow) or a **case error** (in that the subject of the bracketed complement clause has a case which it cannot be assigned in accordance with the case assignment conditions given in (101) in the main text) – or both.

Model answer for sentences 1a and b

Given the CP analysis of finite clauses and control clauses in the text, 1a will have the structure (i) below:

(i)

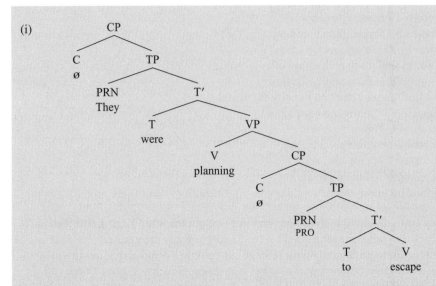

The null complementiser introducing the CP complement of the verb *planning* is intransitive and non-finite, and accordingly assigns null case to the PRO subject which it c-commands. Support for the CP analysis of the bracketed complement clause *to escape* in 1a comes from the fact that (like other CPs, but unlike TPs) it can serve as the focused constituent in pseudo-cleft sentences like:

(ii)   What they were planning (to do) was *to escape*

The fact that it is also possible to say:

(iii)   They were planning *for him to escape*

suggests that *plan* can also select a complement headed by the transitive infinitival complementiser *for*. This leads to the greater generalisation that *plan* can select a CP complement headed by an infinitival complementiser (either the transitive infinitival complementiser *for* or the null intransitive infinitival complementiser Ø). The ungrammaticality of 1b *They were planning him to escape* could be attributable to a case error (if the null complementiser heading the complement clause is intransitive and so assigns null case to the infinitive subject), or to a spellout error (if the complementiser heading the complement clause is the kind of *for* complementiser which can never be given a null spellout – unlike the *for* introducing an infinitival complement of a verb like *want*).

5   Head movement

5.1   Overview

So far, we have examined a range of syntactic structures which are derived by a series of **merger** operations. We now go on to look at structures whose derivation involves not only merger but also a movement operation called **head movement**. In this chapter, we focus mainly on two specific types of head movement operation, one which affects auxiliaries in present-day English, and another which affected main verbs in earlier stages of English; we also look briefly at how head movement can apply to nouns.

5.2   T-to-C movement

In chapters 3 and 4, we saw that complementisers are positioned in front of subjects in the clauses they introduce. More specifically, we suggested that complementisers head a separate projection in clauses which we termed a **complementiser phrase/CP**, with the head C position of CP being filled by a complementiser like *that/for/if*. However, complementisers are not the only kind of word which can precede subjects in clauses. As we saw in our brief discussion of questions in §4.6, auxiliaries can also precede subjects in yes–no questions such as *Do you feel like a Coke?* In this respect, inverted auxiliaries seem to resemble complementisers – as the following (love-struck, soap-operesque) dialogue illustrates:

(1)   SPEAKER A: Honey-buns, there's something I wanted to ask you
           SPEAKER B: What, sweetie-pie?
           SPEAKER A: **If you will marry me**
           SPEAKER B (*pretending not to hear*): What d'you say, darlin'?
           SPEAKER A: **Will you marry me?**

What's the structure of the two bold(-printed) proposals which speaker A makes in (1)? The answer is straightforward enough in the case of *If you will marry me*: it's a clause introduced by the interrogative complementiser/C *if*, and so is a complementiser phrase/CP constituent with the structure (2) below:

(2)

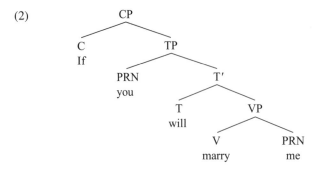

But now consider the structure of the second proposal *Will you marry me?* What position is occupied by the inverted auxiliary *will*? Since *will* appears to occupy the same pre-subject position that the complementiser *if* occupies in (2), a plausible suggestion to make is that the inverted auxiliary actually occupies the head C position of CP. If this is so, we'd expect *will* and *if* to be mutually exclusive (on the assumption that we can only insert one word in a given head position like C, not two words): in other words, if both complementisers and inverted auxiliaries occupy the head C position of CP, we'd expect to find that a question can be introduced either by a complementiser or by a preposed auxiliary – but not by the two together. This is indeed the case, as we see from the ungrammaticality of speaker B's reply in (3) below:

(3)   SPEAKER A: What d'you want to ask me?
        SPEAKER B: *If will you marry me

The fact that questions can't contain both a complementiser and an inverted auxiliary provides us with empirical evidence that inverted auxiliaries occupy the same structural position as complementisers – i.e. that both occupy the head C position of CP.

But how can a finite auxiliary (which normally occupies the head T position of TP) come to be positioned in the head C position of CP? The conventional answer is that auxiliaries in questions move out of their normal post-subject position into pre-subject position by a movement operation which in chapter 1 we referred to as **auxiliary inversion**. Given our assumption that an inverted auxiliary occupies the head C position of CP, this means that the auxiliary moves from the head T position in TP into the head C position in CP, as shown by the arrow in (4) below:

(4)

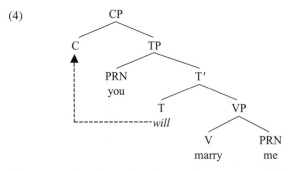

Hence, auxiliary inversion in questions involves **T-to-C movement**.

An important question which is begged by the T-to-C movement analysis is *why* auxiliaries should move from T to C in questions. Using a metaphor adopted by Chomsky (1995), we can say that C is a **strong** head in questions in English and that a strong head position has to be filled (i.e. occupied) by an overt constituent of an appropriate kind. In a complement-clause yes–no question like that bracketed in:

(5)   He asked [*if* I would marry him]

C is filled by the complementiser *if* – and indeed speaker A's first proposal in (1) might be regarded as an elliptical form of *I wanted to ask you* [*if you will marry me*], with *if* introducing the bracketed complement clause, and constituents other than those of the bracketed clause undergoing ellipsis. However, complementisers like *if* can't be used to introduce main clauses in English, so some other way has to be found of filling the strong C position in main-clause questions. Adapting an analysis dating back to Baker (1970), let's suppose that in main clauses, an interrogative C is filled by a null question particle **Q**, and that Q **attracts** an auxiliary like *will* to move from T to C to attach to it, so filling the strong C position.

But why should the null interrogative complementiser Q attract an auxiliary to move from T to C? One possibility is to follow Chomsky (1995) in supposing that Q is **affixal** in nature, and attracts an overt head to attach to it. Since affixes generally only attach to a particular kind of word (e.g. the past-tense-*d* affix can attach to verbs but not nouns, prepositions or adjectives), and since only **tensed** (i.e. present- or past-tense) auxiliaries move to C, one implementation of this idea (suggested in Chomsky 1993) is to suppose that Q carries a strong **tense** feature, and hence attracts the head T constituent of TP to move from T to C. On this view, the tensed auxiliary *will* in (4) moves from T to attach to the invisible Q affix in C – as shown in (6) below:

(6)

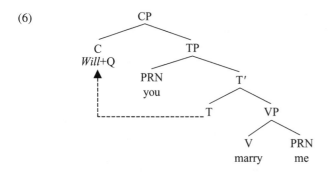

The auxiliary *will* moves from T to C in order to satisfy the requirement for the null question affix Q to have an appropriate kind of item (i.e. a present- or past-tense T constituent) affixed to it. The Q-affix analysis is far from implausible from a cross-linguistic point of view: for example, yes–no questions in Latin could be formed using the overt question suffix *-ne*. If we adopt the question-affix analysis, we can say that it is the affixal status of an interrogative C (viz. the fact that C in main-clause questions contains a null affix Q) which triggers T-to-C movement. Given that English is a largely *suffixal* language (in that it mainly utilises derivational and inflectional suffixes), we can take Q to be suffixal in nature, so that the attracted auxiliary will end up positioned to the left of Q.

5.3   Movement as copying and deletion

An interesting question which arises from the T-to-C movement analysis is what it means for the auxiliary to *move out of T*. If movement of an auxiliary from T to C were to result in the head T position of TP vanishing without trace, a sentence such as *Will you marry me?* would have the structure below:

(7)

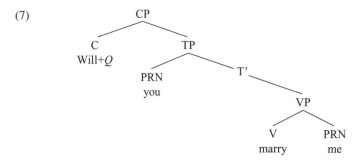

But a structure such as (7) is problematic in that it violates two constituent structure principles which we posited in §3.2, namely:

(8)   **Headedness Principle**
        Every syntactic structure is a projection of a head word

(9)   **Binarity Principle**
        Every (non-terminal node in a) syntactic structure is binary-branching

A tree such as (7) would violate the headedness requirement (8) in that neither TP nor T-bar has a head T constituent; (7) would also violate the binarity requirement (9) in that T-bar is a non-terminal node in the tree (by virtue of not being one of the nodes at the very bottom of the tree) yet is not binary-branching (since T-bar does not have two daughters) but rather unary-branching (since T-bar has only one daughter).

It seems clear, then, that movement of an auxiliary from T to C cannot result in the loss of the original T constituent which heads TP: so, T must remain in place in the form of a **null** constituent of some kind as shown in (10) below (with *?* indicating that the identity of the null constituent is yet to be determined):

(10)

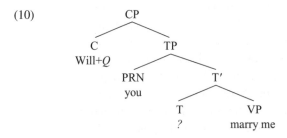

(The internal structure of the VP *marry me* is as in (6) above, but is not shown here in order to save space, and because it is not relevant to the point at hand.) The structure in (10) satisfies both the **headedness** requirement (in that TP and T-bar are headed by a null T), and the **binarity** requirement (in that T-bar is a binary-branching constituent whose two daughters are a null T and its VP complement). However, the question posed by the analysis in (10) is: 'What is the nature of the mysterious T constituent (= ?) which heads TP and T-bar after *will* moves to C?'

Our discussion of **gapping** (i.e. head ellipsis) in the previous chapter suggests a possible answer. In §4.3 we suggested that ellipsis of the second (italicised) occurrence of *could* in a sentence such as (11a) below results in a structure such as (11b) containing a null occurrence of *could* (designated as ~~could~~):

(11) (a)   He **could** have helped her, or she *could* have helped him
     (b)   He **could** have helped her, or she ~~could~~ have helped him

This raises the possibility that T-to-C movement could be a composite operation by which a **copy** of an auxiliary in T is first moved into C, and then the original occurrence of the auxiliary in T is **deleted** (by which we mean that its phonetic features are given a **null spellout** and so are unpronounced), leaving a null copy of the auxiliary in T. The assumption that movement is a composite operation involving two suboperations of copying and deletion is the cornerstone of Chomsky's **copy theory of movement**.

If we consider the copying component of movement more carefully, we see that it involves a form of **merger** operation by which a copy of a constituent which has already been merged in one position is subsequently merged in another position. To see what this means, let's look rather more closely at the derivation of *Will you marry me?* The first stage of derivation involves merging the verb *marry* with the pronoun *me* to form the VP *marry me*; the tense auxiliary *will* then merges with this VP to form the T-bar *will marry me*; this in turn merges with the subject *you* to form the TP *you will marry me*; the resulting TP merges with a C constituent containing the null question suffix Q, so that at this stage of derivation we have the simplified structure (12) below:

(12)

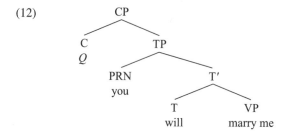

A copy of the T constituent *will* is then merged with the interrogative complementiser, so forming a complex C constituent which comprises both the original C constituent (containing Q) and the T constituent containing *will*. Subsequent deletion of the phonetic features of the original occurrence of *will* in T derives the structure (13) below:

(13)

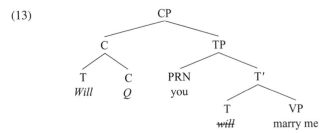

On this view, the inverted auxiliary *will* undergoes two separate merger operations in (13): first of all it is merged in T with its VP complement *marry me*, forming the T-bar *will marry me*; then (a copy of) *will* is merged with the null question particle Q in C, deriving *Will+Q you will marry me*; subsequent deletion of the phonetic features of the original occurrence of *will* in T in turn derives *Will+Q you will marry me*.

An interesting source of evidence in support of the copy theory of movement comes from the study of language acquisition. Young children sometimes produce **auxiliary copying** structures like the following (produced by a boy called Sam at age 2 years and 9 months: thanks to Ian Crookston for the data):

(14) (a)   *Can* its wheels *can* spin?
     (b)   *Did* the kitchen light *did* flash?
     (c)   *Is* the steam *is* hot?
     (d)   *Was* that *was* Anna?

What is Sam doing here? The answer seems to be that he has mastered the **copy-merge** component of auxiliary inversion and so is able to merge a copy of *will* in C: but he has not yet mastered the **copy-deletion** component of auxiliary inversion and so fails to delete the phonetic features of the original occurrence of the auxiliary in T. Accordingly, (14a) above has the simplified structure (15) below for Sam (in which the structure of the DP *its wheels* is not shown because it is irrelevant to the point at hand):

(15)

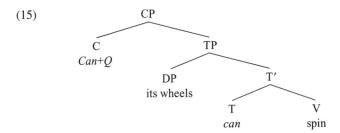

The fact that Sam seems to have mastered the **merger** operation involved in auxiliary inversion (i.e. merging an auxiliary in T and then merging a copy of the auxiliary in C) but not the **copy-deletion** operation (in that he fails to delete the original occurrence of the auxiliary in T) suggests that it is plausible to analyse a movement operation like **auxiliary inversion** as a composite operation involving the two separate operations of **copy-merge** (i.e. merging a copy of a T-auxiliary in C) and **copy-deletion**.

In addition to evidence from child grammars we also have evidence from adult grammars in support of the claim that a moved auxiliary leaves behind a null copy of itself. Part of this evidence comes from the phenomenon of *have*-cliticisation which we touched on in §4.4 and in exercise 4.1. In this connection, note that *have* cannot cliticise onto the pronoun I/*we*/*you*/*they* in inversion structures such as:

(16) (a)   Should **they have**/*they 've* called the police?
     (b)   Will **we have**/*we 've* finished the rehearsal by 9pm?
     (c)   Would **you have**/*you 've* come with me?
     (d)   Could **I have**/*I 've* done something to help?

(*'ve* represents the vowel-less clitic form /v/ here.) The sequence *they 've* in (16a) does not rhyme with *grave* in careful speech styles, since it is pronounced /ðeɪəv/ not /ðeɪv/. Likewise, the sequence *we 've* in (16b) is not homophonous with *weave* in careful speech styles, since *we have* in (16b) can be reduced to /wiəv/ but not /wi:v/. Similarly, *you 've* doesn't rhyme with *groove* in (16c), nor *I 've* with *hive* in (16d). Why should cliticisation of *have* onto the pronoun be blocked here? We can give a straightforward answer to this question if we posit that when an inverted auxiliary moves from T to C, it leaves behind a null copy of itself in the T position out of which it moves. Given this assumption, a sentence such as (16a) will have the simplified structure shown below (if we assume that *have* is an AUX heading AUXP – see §5.6):

(17)

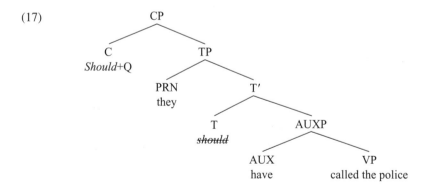

In the previous chapter, we characterised *have*-cliticisation along the following lines:

(18)   *Have* can encliticise onto a pronoun which asymmetrically c-commands
              have if the pronoun ends in a vowel or diphthong, and if there is no
              intervening constituent separating the two (i.e. if there is no intervening
              constituent c-commanding *have* and c-commanded by the pronoun).

Although in (17) the pronoun *they* ends in a diphthong and asymmetrically c-commands *have* (in the sense that *they* c-commands *have* but *have* does not c-command *they*), the two are separated by the intervening null auxiliary ~~should~~ which occupies the head T position of TP: since ~~should~~ c-commands *have* and is in turn c-commanded by *they*, it intervenes between the two in the relevant technical sense and hence blocks *have*-cliticisation, thereby accounting for the ungrammaticality of (16a) **Should they've called the police?* Note that a crucial plank in the argumentation here is the assumption that T-to-C movement leaves behind a null copy of the moved auxiliary in the head T position of TP, and this null auxiliary serves to block cliticisation of *have* onto a c-commanding pronoun.

Our discussion of auxiliary inversion here has interesting implications for the derivation of sentences. In this connection, consider how we derive a sentence such as:

(19)   Can you swim?

The first stage is to go to the **lexicon** (= dictionary) and choose a **lexical array** (i.e. a selection of lexical items out of which the sentence is going to be built). In the case of (19), the lexical array will consist of the verb *swim*, the pronoun *you*, the auxiliary *can*, and the null interrogative complementiser Q. The next stage is for the auxiliary *can* and the verb *swim* to be taken out of the lexical array and merged, so deriving the T-bar *can swim*. The pronoun *you* is then taken from the lexical array, and merged with the T-bar *can swim* to form the TP *you can swim*. The null interrogative complementiser Q is then taken from the lexical array and merged with the TP *you can swim* to form the CP *Q you can swim*. Since Q is affixal and has a *tense* feature attracting a tensed head, Q triggers merger of a copy of the present-tense auxiliary *can* with Q, forming *Can+Q you can swim*. Subsequent deletion of the original occurrence of *can* in T derives *Can+Q you ~~can~~ swim*.

5.4   V-to-T movement

Having looked at T-to-C movement in English, we now turn to look at a rather different kind of movement operation, which involves **V-to-T movement** – more specifically, movement of a finite main verb from the head V position of VP into the head T position of TP. We shall see that this kind of verb movement operation was productive in **Elizabethan English** (i.e. the English used during the reign of Queen Elizabeth I, when Shakespeare was writing), but is no longer productive in present-day English. Since part of the evidence for V-to-T movement involves negative sentences, we begin by looking at the syntax of negation.

In Elizabethan English, clauses containing a finite auxiliary are typically negated by positioning *not* between the auxiliary and the verb:

(20) (a)   She *shall* not **see** me (Falstaff, *The Merry Wives of Windsor*, III.iii)
     (b)   I *will* not **think** it (Don Pedro, *Much Ado About Nothing*, III.ii)
     (c)   Thou *hast* not **left** the value of a cord (Gratiano, *The Merchant of Venice*, IV.i)

Let's suppose (for the time being, pending a reanalysis of negation in §5.7) that *not* in Elizabethan English is an adverb which functions as the specifier of the verbal expression following it (so that e.g. *not* is the specifier of *see me* in (20a) above, and hence modifies *see me*). If so, (20a) will have a structure along the lines of (21) below (where ø is a null complementiser marking the declarative force of the sentence):

(21)

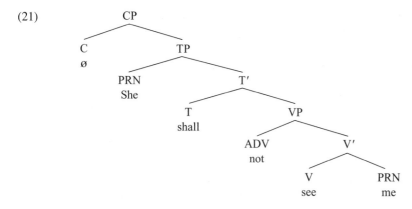

An analysis such as (21) provides a straightforward account of the position which *not* occupies in front of the verb *see*.

In negative questions, the auxiliary moves from T to C (as in present-day English), leaving *not* in front of the verb:

(22) (a)   **Have** I *not* heard the sea rage like an angry boar? (Petruchio, *The Taming of the Shrew*, I.ii)
   (b)   **Didst** thou *not* hear somebody? (Borachio, *Much Ado About Nothing*, III.iii)
   (c)   **Will** you *not* dance? (King, *Love's Labour's Lost*, V.ii)

If questions involve movement of a finite auxiliary from T to C, then a sentence such as (22a) will involve the T-to-C movement operation shown in (23) below (where we take the string *the sea rage like an angry boar* to be an ECM clause headed by a null counterpart of infinitival *to*, symbolised as *t̶o̶*):

(23)

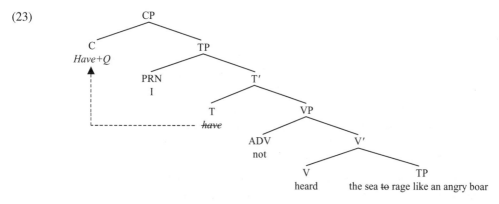

The auxiliary *have* is first merged in T and then moved to C (i.e. a copy of the auxiliary is merged with the question suffix Q in C), leaving behind a copy of *have* in T which is ultimately deleted. The assumption that *not* is a VP-specifier provides a straightforward account of the fact that *not* remains positioned in front of the verb *heard* after *have* moves to C.

However, an interesting aspect of negative sentences in Shakespearean English is that in auxiliariless finite clauses like those in (24) below, the (bold-printed) main verb is positioned in front of *not*:

(24) (a)   I **care** *not* for her (Thurio, *The Two Gentlemen of Verona*, V.iv)
    (b)   He **heard** *not* that (Julia, *The Two Gentlemen of Verona*, IV.ii)
    (c)   My master **seeks** *not* me (Speed, *The Two Gentlemen of Verona*, I.i)
    (d)   I **know** *not* where to hide my head (Trinculo, *The Tempest*, II.ii)

If *not* in Elizabethan English is a VP-specifier which is positioned at the leftmost edge of the verb phrase, how can we account for the fact that the verb (which would otherwise be expected to follow the negative particle *not*) ends up positioned in front of *not* in sentences like (24)? The answer we shall give here is that when a finite T in Elizabethan English contains no auxiliary, the verb moves out of the head V position of VP into the head T position of TP in order to fill T. If so, a sentence like (24a) *I care not for her* will involve the V-to-T movement operation represented by the dotted arrow in (25) below:

(25)

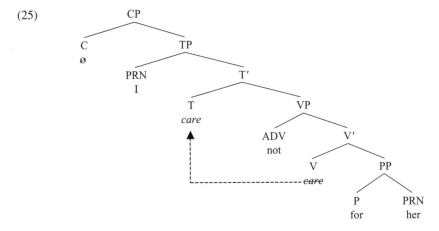

Thus, the verb *care* is first merged in the head V position within VP, and then moves into the head T position in TP, thereby ending up positioned in front of *not* (with the original occurrence of *care* in V being given a null spellout).

An important theoretical question to ask at this juncture is *why* the verb *care* should move from V to T. Using Chomsky's *strength* metaphor, we can suppose that a finite T is **strong** in Elizabethan English and so must be filled: this means that in a sentence in which the T position is not filled by an auxiliary, the verb moves from V to T in order to fill the strong T position. One way of characterising what it means for T to be strong is to suppose that T contains a *Tns* affix with a strong V-feature which requires it to have an (auxiliary or non-auxiliary) verb attached to it as its host. Let's suppose that a strong affix is one which can find a host either by merger, or by attracting an appropriate item to attach to the affix. So, in a structure like (21), the strong (second-person-singular present-tense) *Tns* affix in T is provided with a host by directly merging the auxiliary *may* with the *Tns* affix in T, forming *may+Tns* (although the *Tns* affix is not shown in the simplified structure in (21) above); but in a structure like (25), the strong *Tns* affix in T attracts the closest verb which it c-commands (namely the verb *care*) to move to T and attach to the *Tns* affix, so that the affix is provided with a verbal host via movement – as shown in (26) below:

(26)

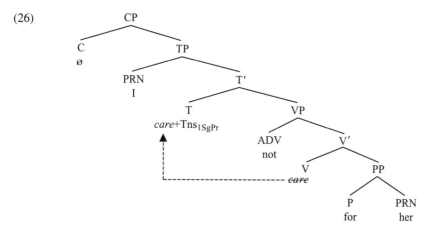

By contrast, T in present-day English contains a **weak** *Tns* affix (more specifically, an affix with a weak V-feature), and a weak *Tns* affix cannot attract a verb to move from V to T, but rather can only be attached to a verbal host either by merger of an auxiliary like *may* directly with the null *Tns* affix in T, or by lowering of the *Tns* affix onto the main verb, e.g. in auxiliariless finite clauses such as *He enjoys the classes*. In such auxiliariless clauses, the weak *Tns* affix in T undergoes the morphological operation of **Affix Hopping** in the PF component, lowering the affix onto the main verb in the manner shown by the arrow in (27) below:

(27)

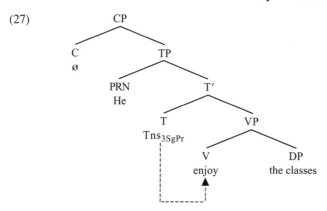

On this view, both strong and weak *Tns* affixes can be directly merged with an auxiliary in T; the two differ in how the affix comes to be attached to a main verb;

a strong *Tns* affix (like that found in Elizabethan English) triggers movement of the verb from V to T in structures like (26) above; a weak *Tns* affix (like that found in present-day English) is lowered onto the main verb in the PF component by **Affix Hopping** in structures like (27) above.

5.5   Head movement

There seem to be significant parallels between the kind of movement operation involved in **T-to-C movement** in (23) on the one hand, and **V-to-T movement** in (25) on the other. Both operations involve movement of a word from the head position in one phrase into the head position in a higher phrase. Accordingly, in (23) the auxiliary *have* moves from the head T position of TP into the head C position of CP; and in (25) the verb *care* moves from the head V position of VP into the head T position of TP. This suggests that T-to-C movement and V-to-T movement are two different instances of a more general **head movement** operation by which an item occupying the head position in a lower phrase is moved into the head position in a higher phrase.

As we see from (23) above, questions in Elizabethan English involved the same inversion operation as in present-day English. Given our assumption that inversion involves movement from T to C, an obvious prediction made by the assumption that verbs move from V to T in Elizabethan English is that they can subsequently move from T to C in interrogatives – and this is indeed the case, as we see from the fact that the (italicised) moved verb ends up positioned in front of its (bold-printed) subject in questions like:

(28) (a)   *Saw* **you** my master? (Speed, *The Two Gentlemen of Verona*, I.i)

   (b)   *Speakest* **thou** in sober meanings? (Orlando, *As you Like It*, V.ii)

   (c)   *Know* **you** not the cause? (Tranio, *The Taming of the Shrew*, IV.ii)

   (d)   *Spake* **you** not these words plain? (Grumio, *The Taming of the Shrew*, I.ii)

On the account given here, the derivation of a negative question such as (28c) *Know you not the cause?* will involve the two head movement operations shown in simplified form in (29) below:

(29)

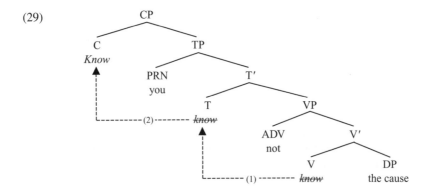

(The structure in (29) is simplified for expository purposes by not showing the verb *know* attaching to a strong *Tns* affix in T, and by not showing movement of the resulting *know+Tns* structure to attach to a strong Q affix in C, forming the structure *know+Tns+Q*.) The verb *know* moves from V to T because a finite T is strong in Elizabethan English, by virtue of containing a *Tns* affix with a strong V-feature; and *know* subsequently moves from T to C because an interrogative C is likewise strong by virtue of containing a question particle Q with a strong T-feature. Consequently, *know* moves through T into C by two successive applications of **head movement** (numbered (1) and (2) above): *know* is first merged in V, then moved to T and from there moved to C. In structures like (29), head movement is said to apply in a **successive-cyclic** fashion, moving the verb *know* (in successive **cycles** or steps) first from V to T, and then from T to C. Each time the verb moves, it leaves behind a copy of itself which is eventually deleted.

A key assumption made in (29) is that the verb *know* moves to C via the intermediate step of moving to T. This raises the question of why *know* can't move directly from V to C in the manner shown in simplified form in (30) below:

(30)   [CP [C *Know*] [TP you [T ø] [VP not [V *know*] the cause]]]

One way of ruling out the kind of long-distance head movement operation illustrated in (30) is in terms of a locality principle suggested by Travis (1984), which we can outline in the following terms:

(31)   **Head Movement Constraint/HMC**
              Movement from one head position to another is only possible between a
              given head and the closest head which asymmetrically c-commands it (i.e.
              between a given head and the next highest head in the structure containing it)

If we look at the two movement operations in (29), we see that both obey HMC: operation (1) involves local movement of the verb *know* from the head V position of VP into the next highest head position in the structure, namely the head T position of TP; and operation (2) involves local movement of *know* from the head T position of TP into the next highest head position in the structure, namely the head C position of CP. Since both head movement operations are strictly local, there is no violation of HMC. By contrast, direct movement of *know* from V to C in (30) is non-local and violates HMC in that the verb *know* moves from the head V position of VP directly into the head C position of CP, in spite of the fact that C is not the next highest head above V. (On the contrary, T is the next highest head above V.) HMC therefore provides a principled account of why (28c) *Know you not the cause?* is ungrammatical in present-day English: the verb *know* cannot move directly to C (because this would violate the HMC requirement for movement to be local), and cannot move through T into C (because verbs can no longer move from V to T in present-day English).

However, such an analysis raises the question of why finite verbs should be able to move from V to T in Elizabethan English, but not in present-day English. Using Chomsky's **strength** metaphor, we can say that the *Tns* affix carried by a finite T was **strong** in Elizabethan English, but is **weak** in present-day English. Because the affix was strong in finite clauses in Elizabethan English, it could attract a verb to move from V to T; but because the affix is weak in present-day English, T can only be filled by an auxiliary which is directly merged in T, not by a verb moving from V to T. More generally, we can suppose that there is parametric variation with respect to the relative strength of a given type of head, so that (e.g.) a finite T was strong in Elizabethan English but is weak in present-day English. We can refer to the relevant parameter as the **Head-Strength Parameter**. Note that the parameter may have different settings for different types of head in a given language: e.g. a finite T is weak in present-day English, but a finite C is strong in interrogative main clauses.

But why should a finite *Tns* affix be strong in Elizabethan English and weak in present-day English? A suggestion which has been made by a number of linguists (e.g. Platzack and Holmberg 1989, Roberts 1993, Rohrbacher 1999, Vikner 1997 and Koeneman 2000) is that the relative strength or weakness of a tense affix in a language is correlated with the relative richness of the system of subject-agreement inflections which it encodes, in the sense that a tense affix is strong in languages in which finite auxiliaries and verbs carry **rich** subject-agreement inflections (i.e. in which they carry a wide range of different agreement affixes) and weak in languages in which finite auxiliaries and verbs carry **impoverished** subject-agreement inflections. In this connection, it is interesting to note that whereas third-person-singular -*s* is the only regular agreement inflection found on (present-tense) verbs in present-day Standard English, in Shakespearean English we find four present-tense inflections, viz. second-person-singular -*st*, third-person-singular -*th* or -*s* (the two being dialectal variants) and third-person-plural -*n*:

(32) (a)   Thou *sayst* true (Petruchio, *The Taming of the Shrew*, IV.iii)
     (b)   The sight of love *feedeth* those in love (Rosalind, *As You Like It*, III.v)
     (c)   It *looks* ill, it *eats* drily (Parolles, *All's Well That Ends Well*, I.i)
     (d)   And then the whole quire hold their lips and laugh, and *waxen* in their mirth (Puck, *A Midsummer Night's Dream*, II.i)

If a *Tns* affix is strong in rich agreement languages and weak in poor agreement languages, we can correlate the strength of T in Elizabethan English with the relative richness of its subject-agreement morphology; and conversely, we can correlate the weakness of T in present-day English with the impoverished nature of its subject-agreement morphology. (See Vikner 1995 and Rohrbacher 1999 for attempts to do this, and Bobaljik 2000 for a dissenting view.)

The relative richness of the agreement features carried by finite verbs in Elizabethan times, as compared to present-day English, is reflected in a further syntactic difference between them. Elizabethan English was a **null-subject language**, and hence allowed finite verbs and finite auxiliaries (like those italicised below) to have null subjects (whether in root/main clauses or not, and whether the subject is sentence-initial or not):

(33) (a)   *Sufficeth*, I am come to keep my word (Petruchio, *The Taming of the Shrew*, III.ii)

(b)   *Would* you would bear your fortunes like a man (Iago, *Othello*, IV.i)

(c)   *Lives*, sir (Iago, *Othello*, IV.i, in reply to 'How does Lieutenant Cassio?')

(d)   *Hast* any more of this? (Trinculo, *The Tempest*, II.ii)

(e)   After some question with him, *was* converted (Jacques de Boys, *As You Like It*, V.iii)

(f)   Had it stretched so far, *would* have made nature immortal (Countess of Rousillon, *All's Well That Ends Well*, I.i)

(g)   You must be so too, if *heed* me (Antonio, *The Tempest*, II.i)

Since the null subject in sentences like (33) occurs in a nominative position (by virtue of being the subject of a finite clause), it has nominative case and so is different from the 'big PRO' subject of infinitives (which has null case), and hence seems to be an instance of the finite 'little pro' subject found in null-subject languages like Italian – recall our brief discussion of null subjects in §4.2. By contrast, present-day English is a non-null-subject (i.e. *pro*-less) language, so that the present-day counterparts of (33) generally require (italicised) overt subjects:

(34) (a)   *It* is enough that I have come to keep my word

(b)   *I* wish you would bear your fortunes like a man

(c)   *He* is alive, sir

(d)   Have *you* any more of this?

(e)   After some discussion with him, *he* was converted

(f)   Had it stretched so far, *it* would have made nature immortal

(g)   You ought to be like that as well, if *you* ask me

It would seem, therefore, that a finite T can have a null nominative *pro* subject in a language like Elizabethan English where finite verbs carry rich agreement morphology (and raise to T), but not in a language like present-day English where finite verbs have impoverished agreement morphology (and remain **in situ** – i.e. in the position in which they were originally merged, hence in the head V position of VP). Why should this be? One possibility is that in a language with a rich system of agreement inflections, the agreement inflections on the verb serve to **identify** the null subject (e.g. the *-st* inflection on *hast* in (33d) is a second-person-singular inflection, and hence allows us to identify the null *pro* subject as a second-person-singular subject with the same properties as *thou*). But in a weak-agreement language like contemporary English, agreement morphology is too impoverished to allow identification of a null *pro* subject (e.g. if we asked **Can help*? we'd have no way of telling from the agreementless form *can* whether the missing subject is *I*, *you*, *he*, *they* or whatever).

Our discussion here suggests the possibility that there is parametric variation across languages in respect of whether finite verbs carry rich or impoverished subject-agreement morphology, and that the relative richness of agreement morphology correlates with whether the *Tns* affix in T in finite clauses is strong (and can trigger V-to-T raising) or weak, and with whether a finite T can have a null nominative *pro* subject or not. In rich-agreement languages, a finite T contains a strong *Tns* affix and the main verb raises to T if there is no auxiliary to host the affix in T; in poor agreement languages, T contains a weak *Tns* affix which is lowered onto the main verb by **Affix Hopping** if there is no auxiliary in T. (A minor complication is that poor-agreement languages may have other kinds of null subject: e.g. Japanese and Korean have no agreement morphology except in so-called 'honorific' constructions, but allow subjects and objects to be null if they can be discourse-identified – i.e. if their reference can be determined from the discourse context.)

5.6   Auxiliary raising

Although we assumed in the previous section that no verbs in present-day English can move from V to T, the picture is complicated by the behaviour of *be* in examples like (35) below:

(35) (a)   She may not *be* suitable   (b) She *is* not suitable

In (35a) the copular verb *be* seems to occupy the head V position in VP, and so follows *not*: but in (35b) *is* precedes *not* and so seems to occupy the head T position of TP. This suggests that the copula *be* originates as a main verb (in the head V position of VP) and remains in situ when non-finite as shown in simplified form in (36a) below, but moves into the head T position of TP when finite as shown in (36b):

(36) (a)   [cp [c ø] [TP she [T may] [VP not [V *be*] suitable]]]
     (b)   [cp [c ø] [TP she [T *is*] [VP not [V *i̶s̶*] suitable]]]

A similar conclusion is suggested by examples such as the following:

(37) (a)   She may not *be* enjoying syntax   (b) She *is* not enjoying syntax

In (37a), the head T position of TP is occupied by the modal auxiliary *may*, and the head V position of VP is occupied by the verb *enjoying*; *be* therefore seems to occupy some intermediate position between the two. Since *be* (in this use) is an aspectual auxiliary (marking progressive aspect), let's suppose that *be* in (37) occupies the head AUX/Auxiliary position of an AUXP (i.e. Auxiliary Phrase). However, in (37b) progressive *is* occupies the head T position of TP and hence precedes *not*. One analysis of the relevant data is to suppose that aspectual *be* originates as the head AUX constituent of AUXP and remains in situ when non-finite as shown in (38a) below, but moves from AUX to T when finite – as shown in (38b) (where *not* is taken to occupy a position to the left of AUXP – see the discussion in the next section):

(38) (a)   [cp [c ø] [TP she [T may] not [AUXP [AUX *be*] [VP [V enjoying] syntax]]]]
     (b)   [cp [c ø] [TP she [T *is*] not [AUXP [AUX *i̶s̶*] [VP [V enjoying] syntax]]]]

On this view, present-day English would have a BE-raising operation moving finite forms of *be* from the head V position in VP (or the head AUX position in AUXP) into the head T position in TP (an idea which dates back to Klima 1964). This would mean that present-day English retains a last vestige of raising-to-T.

The different positions occupied by finite and non-finite forms of *be* are mirrored by the perfect auxiliary *have* – as the examples below illustrate:

(39) (a)   He may not *have* done it   (b) He *has* not done it

The head T position of TP in (39a) is occupied by *may* and the head V position of VP by *done*; hence the infinitive form *have* must occupy some position intermediate between the two, e.g. the head AUX position of an AUXP/Auxiliary Phrase, as in (40a) below. However the fact that the finite form *has* in (39b) is positioned in front of *not* suggests that finite forms of the perfect auxiliary *have* raise from AUX to T in the manner shown informally in (40b) below:

(40) (a)   [CP [C ø] [TP He [T may] not [AUXP [AUX have] [VP [V done] it]]]]
     (b)   [CP [C ø] [TP He [T *has*] not [AUXP [AUX *has*] [VP [V done] it]]]]

So far, we have suggested that the auxiliaries *be* and *have* may raise to T from a lower AUX/V position within the clause in present-day English. Roberts (1998) argues that the same is true of some modal auxiliaries as well. In this connection, consider the interpretation of the following negative sentences:

(41) (a)   You must not do that (= 'It is *necessary* for you *not* to do that')
     (b)   You need not do that (= 'It is *not necessary* for you to do that')

In (41a) the modal *must* has **wide scope** with respect to negation (i.e. *must* has semantic scope over *not*) whereas in (41b) the modal *need* has **narrow scope** with respect to negation (i.e. *need* falls within the semantic scope of *not*). Roberts suggests that in sentences like (41) above, wide-scope modals like *must* are directly generated in T (as in (42a) below) whereas narrow-scope modals like *need* are initially generated in some position below T (perhaps the head AUX position of an AUXP) and from there move to T (as in (42b) below):

(42) (a)   [CP [C ø] [TP you [T must] not [VP [V do] that]]]
     (b)   [CP [C ø] [TP you [T *need*] not [AUXP [AUX *need*] [VP [V do] that]]]]

Roberts's analysis implies that present-day English has an operation by which narrow-scope auxiliaries raise from AUX to T. An interesting aspect of (42b) is that the polarity item *need* originates in a position where it is c-commanded by *not* (so satisfying the *c-command* requirement on polarity items discussed in exercise 3.2, if we assume that the relevant requirement is that a polarity item must be c-commanded by a negative/interrogative item *at some stage of derivation*). The two different T/AUX positions for auxiliaries can be occupied by different modals in Scots English structures such as *He must no can do it* (= 'It must be the case that he does not have the capability to do it', from Brown 1991, p. 98), with *must* located in T and having scope over *not* and *can* located in AUX and falling within the scope of *not*.

If finite forms of *be* (in all uses) and *have* (in its use as a perfect auxiliary) and narrow-scope modals like *need* all raise to T, it is clear that the suggestion made in the previous section that T in present-day English is a weak head which does not trigger any form of V-raising is untenable. Rather, the appropriate generalisation would appear to be that in present-day English, only a highly restricted set of verbs can raise to T. In traditional grammars, the items which can raise to T are all said to function as **auxiliaries** in the relevant use. Adopting this intuition, we can say that a finite T in present-day English can trigger movement of an auxiliary verb to T (but not movement of a main verb to T). One mechanism by which we can describe the relevant phenomenon is to suppose that whereas a finite V in Elizabethan English had a strong V-feature enabling it to attract a finite auxiliary or non-auxiliary verb, a finite T in present-day English has a strong AUX-feature which enables it to attract an auxiliary verb to raise to T, but not a main verb. Of course, this raises the question of how precisely we characterise auxiliaries: one possibility is that we can define auxiliaries as verbs which do not function as **predicates**. Bearing in mind that canonical predicates have nominal, prepositional or clausal (CP/TP) arguments, we can suppose that *be* is not a predicate in structures like (36), since its complement is the adjective *suitable*, and adjectival expressions are not arguments – suggesting in turn that *be* in this use is not a predicate. (Indeed, one view of *be* in such structures is that it is a **dummy** or **expletive** verb used simply in order to satisfy the grammatical requirement that *may* requires a complement headed by a verb in the infinitive form, and an adjective like *suitable* is therefore not an appropriate kind of complement for *may*.) Likewise, the fact that *be* in (38), *have* in (40) and *need* in (42b) all have a VP complement may suggest that they are not predicates, if predicates require a nominal, prepositional or clausal complement. Clearly, careful consideration needs to be given to the question of what are the defining characteristics of an auxiliary – but we shall not pursue this issue here. (See Ackema 2001 for an alternative account of auxiliary raising in a different framework.)

On the analysis suggested here, a finite T in present-day English contains a *Tns* affix with a strong AUX feature. If the closest verbal head c-commanded by T is an auxiliary (as in (36b, 38b, 40b, 42b) above), the affix attracts it; but if the closest verbal head c-commanded by T is a main verb (as in (27) above), the affix is instead lowered onto the main verb in the PF component by **Affix Hopping**.

The assumption that auxiliaries may originate in a position lower than negation raises interesting questions about the syntax of infinitival *to*, given the similarities between auxiliaries and infinitival *to*. In this connection, it is interesting to note that although auxiliaries are positioned above *not* in finite clauses, infinitival *to* is generally positioned below *not* – as we see from sentences like (43) below:

(43)   John ought not to say anything

Here, *ought* is a modal auxiliary which occupies the head T position of TP; we can see that it is an auxiliary from the fact that like typical auxiliaries, it allows negative cliticisation (giving rise to *oughtn't*). However, if (43) is a single clause and no clause can contain more than one T constituent, and if *ought* occupies the head T position of TP, it follows that infinitival *to* cannot occupy the head T position of TP but rather must occupy some lower position. One possibility is that *to* originates in the same AUX position as narrow-scope modals, so that (43) has the structure shown in skeletal form in (44) below:

(44)   [CP [C ø] [TP John [T ought] not [AUXP [AUX to] say anything]]]

However, although *not to* is the normal word order in negative infinitives, the alternative order *to not* is also found, as the examples below illustrate:

(45) (a)   He decided [not to co-operate with the police]
     (b)   He decided [to not co-operate with the police]

It seems reasonable to suppose that the two different word orders in the bracketed complement clauses in (45a,b) reflect two different positions occupied by infinitival *to*, as suggested in (46a,b) below:

(46) (a)   [CP [C ø] [TP PRO [T ø] not [AUXP [AUX to] co-operate with the police]]]
     (b)   [CP [C ø] [TP PRO [T to] not co-operate with the police]]

There is a subtle meaning difference between the two examples: (45b) implies a much more deliberate act of defiance than (45a). Given the analysis suggested in (46), this meaning difference can be attributed to a **scope** difference, with *not* c-commanding and so having scope over *to* in (46a), and *to* c-commanding and having scope over *not* in (46b). A similar scope difference is found between *will* and *not* in sentences like:

(47) (a)   He almost certainly won't co-operate with the police
     (b)   He will almost certainly not co-operate with the police

In (47a), *not* has semantic scope over *will* and the sentence is paraphraseable as 'It is almost certainly *not* the case that he *will* co-operate with the police', whereas in (47b) *will* has scope over *not* and the sentence is paraphraseable as 'It *will* almost certainly be the case that he does *not* co-operate with the police.'

Although there are in principle two distinct positions which auxiliaries and infinitival *to* can occupy within clauses (viz. the head AUX position of AUXP, and the head T position of TP), if these two positions correlate directly with scope, it is plausible to assume that a given lexical item L (where L is a finite auxiliary or infinitival *to*) is only projected in the head AUX position of AUXP if L falls within the scope of an element like *not* which has scope over L but not over T, and that otherwise L is directly projected in the head T position of TP (and the sentence then contains no AUXP projection associated with L). In other words, in negative clauses like (42b) and (46b) in which the negative adverb *not* has scope over a narrow-scope auxiliary like *need* or infinitival *to*, the relevant item is generated in the head AUX position of AUXP; but in non-negative structures like (48) below:

(48)   [He may decide [to quit his job]]

the auxiliary *may* and the infinitival particle *to* are directly generated in the head T position of TP of the bracketed clause containing them, and neither clause contains an AUXP constituent (if AUX is only projected where required for scope purposes). One way of thinking of this is to suppose that AUX and T are **syncretised** (i.e. collapsed into a single T head) in structures in which there is no constituent intervening between the two. By contrast, non-finite auxiliaries (e.g. like *be* in *He may be lying* or *He seems to be lying*) always occupy the head AUX position of AUXP and never move into T.

5.7   Another look at negation

In §5.4 and §5.5 we assumed that the negative particle *not* is a VP-specifier which occupies initial position within VP. However, this assumption is problematic in a number of respects, as should be apparent if you look back at (38), (40), (42), (44) and (46b) in §5.6. For example, in a sentence such as (37a) *She may not be enjoying syntax*, it is clear that *not* does not occupy a VP-initial position immediately in front of the verb *enjoying*: on the contrary, *not* appears to occupy some position between the modal auxiliary *may* and the aspectual auxiliary *be* – as shown in (38a). Moreover, we shall argue in chapter 7 that only an **argument** of a verb can occupy the specifier position within VP – and *not* in a negative sentence like *She may not sell it* is not an argument of the verb *sell* (because *not* isn't one of the participants in the act of selling). It is clear, therefore, that we need to rethink our earlier analysis of negation. One alternative analysis which has been proposed in work dating back to Pollock (1989) is that *not* is contained within a separate **NEGP/Negation Phrase** projection, and that *not* serves as the specifier of NEGP (and hence is positioned in spec-NEGP): this has subsequently become a standard analysis of negation. (See Ingham 2000 for evidence of a NEGP constituent in Late Middle English; and see Haegeman 1995 for a wide-ranging account of the syntax of negation.)

Such an analysis is far from implausible from a historical perspective: in earlier varieties of English, sentences containing *not* also contained the negative particle *ne* (with *ne* arguably serving as the head NEG constituent of NEGP and *not* as its specifier). This can be illustrated by the following Middle English example taken from Chaucer's *Wife of Bath's Tale*:

(49)   A lord in his houshold *ne* hath *nat* every vessel al of gold (lines 99–100)
         'A lord in his household does not have all his vessels made entirely of gold'

A plausible analysis of a sentence like (49) is to suppose that *ne* originates as the head NEG constituent of NEGP, with *nat* (= 'not') as its specifier: the verb *hath* originates in the head V position of VP and from there moves to the head NEG position of NEGP, attaching to the negative prefix *ne* to form the complex head *ne+hath* as shown in simplified form in (50) below:

(50)   [$_{NEGP}$ nat [$_{NEG}$ ne+*hath*] [$_{VP}$ [$_V$ ~~hath~~] every vessel al of gold]]

The resulting complex head *ne+hath* then attaches to a present-tense affix *Tns* in T, as shown in simplified (and abbreviated) form in (51) below:

(51)   [$_{TP}$ A lord . . . [$_T$ ne+hath+*Tns*] [$_{NEGP}$ nat [$_{NEG}$ ~~ne+hath~~] [$_{VP}$ [$_V$ ~~hath~~] every vessel al of gold]]]

Merger of the TP in (51) with a null declarative complementiser will derive the CP structure associated with (49) *A lord in his houshold ne hath nat every vessel al of gold.*

By Shakespeare's time, *ne* had dropped out of use, leaving the head NEG position of NEGP null (just as in *ne . . . pas* 'not . . . . at.all' negatives in present-day French, *ne* has dropped out of use in colloquial styles). Positing that *not* in Elizabethan English is the specifier of a NEGP headed by a null NEG constituent opens up the possibility that V moves through NEG into T, so that (24a) *I care not for her* has the derivation shown (in simplified form) in (52) below:

(52)

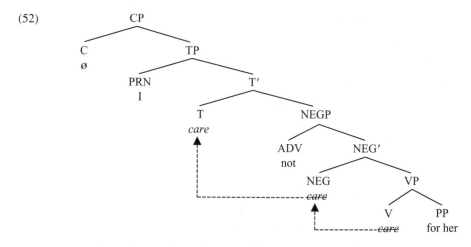

This would mean that head movement applies in a **successive-cyclic** (two-step) fashion. Each of the two head movement operations in (52) – viz. movement of *care* from V to NEG, and then from NEG to T – is local in the sense that it satisfies the **Head Movement Constraint** (31), since in each case movement is from one head position into the next highest head position in the structure. If head movement is driven by affixal properties of heads, and if both T and NEG contain an affix with a strong V-feature which can trigger movement of a main verb, the verb *care* will first move from V to NEG in order to attach to a null negative affix (in much the same way as the verb *hath* in (50) moves from V to Neg to attach to the overt negative affix *ne*), and the resulting complex NEG head (comprising a null negative affix with a verb attached to it) in turn will move from NEG to T in order to attach to a strong tense affix in T.

An important question posed by the analysis in (52) is why sentences like (24a) *I care not for her* are ungrammatical in present-day English. The answer is that neither T nor NEG has a strong V-feature in present-day English, and so they are unable to attract a main verb like *care* to move through NEG into T. Still, this assumption in turn raises the question of why we can't simply leave the present-tense verb *care* in situ (in the head V position of VP) in present-day English – as in (53) below:

(53)   [$_{CP}$ [$_C$ ø] [$_{TP}$ I [$_T$ *Tns*] [$_{NEGP}$ not [$_{NEG}$ ø] [$_{VP}$ [$_V$ care] for her]]]]

One answer is the following. Let's suppose that (just like syntactic operations), morphological and phonological operations in the PF component apply in a **bottom-up** fashion, and process structures in a **cyclic** fashion (i.e. in a step-wise fashion, one projection at a time). What this means is that when the syntax hands over the structure in (53) to the PF component, the lowest maximal projection in the structure (the VP *care for her*) will be processed first, then the next lowest maximal projection (the NEGP *not ø care for her*), then the next lowest maximal projection (the TP *I Tns not ø care for her*) and finally the overall CP (*ø I Tns not ø care for her*). Let's also posit that all operations (whether syntactic, morphological, or phonological) are subject to Pesetsky's (1995) **Earliness Principle**, which we outlined informally in §4.9 as follows:

(54)   **Earliness Principle**
          Operations must apply as early as possible in a derivation

All of this means that **Affix Hopping** will apply to the *Tns* affix in (53) on the TP cycle – i.e. at the point where we have already processed VP and NEGP, and are now beginning to process TP. The structure which the PF component can 'see' on the TP cycle is (55) below:

(55)   [$_{TP}$ I [$_T$ *Tns*] [$_{NEGP}$ not [$_{NEG}$ ø] [$_{VP}$ [$_V$ care] for her]]]

At this point, we might expect Affix Hopping to apply to lower the *Tns* affix in T onto the verb *care*. There are two possible ways in which we might seek to achieve this. One is by lowering the affix directly from T onto V as in (56a) below, and the other is to lower the affix first onto null NEG head and then onto V in the manner shown in (56b):

(56) (a)   [$_{TP}$ I [$_T$ *Tns*] [$_{NEGP}$ not [$_{NEG}$ ø] [$_{VP}$ [$_V$ care] for her]]]

     (b)   [$_{TP}$ I [$_T$ *Tns*] [$_{NEGP}$ not [$_{NEG}$ ø] [$_{VP}$ [$_V$ care] for her]]]

However, a movement operation like (56a) which lowers the affix directly from T onto V would violate the **Head Movement Constraint** (31), since it involves lowering the head T of TP onto the head V of VP; and yet V is not the next lowest head in the structure (rather, NEG is), and HMC only allows a head to be lowered onto the head immediately beneath it in the structure. Accordingly, we might suppose that Affix Hopping applies in a successive cyclic fashion, lowering the affix first from T onto NEG, and then from NEG onto V – as in (56b). However, there are two problems posed by any such successive-cyclic lowering operation. The first is that NEG doesn't seem to be the kind of head which is an appropriate host for a *Tns* affix (at least, if we assume that a tense affix attaches to an overt verb, since NEG is neither overt nor a verb): hence, the first step of the two-step movement arrowed in (56b) – namely lowering the affix onto NEG – may perhaps be ruled out for this reason. To make matters worse, the second step of lowering the *Tns* affix from NEG onto V in (56b) is also ruled out, because it violates a UG principle traditionally referred to as the **Strict Cyclicity Principle**, outlined informally below:

(57)   **Strict Cyclicity Principle/SCP**
          At a stage of derivation where a given projection HP is being cycled/processed, only operations affecting the head H of HP and some other constituent of HP can apply

Lowering the *Tns* affix from T onto NEG in (56a) does not violate **SCP**, since T-to-NEG lowering clearly affects T (by moving the *Tns* affix in T) and also affects a NEG constituent which is contained within TP (since this ends up having a *Tns* affix attached to it). But the subsequent operation of lowering the affix from NEG onto V is **anticyclic**, since NEG-to-V lowering does not affect T (in violation of SCP), but rather affects only NEG and V. We therefore correctly predict that sentences like **I not care for her* are ungrammatical in present-day English. (See also Lasnik 1995, 2000 and Ochi 1999.)

A final point to be made here is that we have excluded from our discussion negative interrogatives like *Shouldn't you be at work?* Cormack and Smith (2000a) argue that in such sentences the negative particle *n't* has scope over the modal (so that the sentence has a meaning paraphraseable as 'Is it not the case that you should be at work?') and hence originates in a position above TP. One proposal along these lines would be to suppose that NEGP in such sentences is positioned between CP and TP, and that the auxiliary *should* raises from T through NEG into C, with *n't* cliticising onto the auxiliary. This would allow for the possibility of two types of negation occurring in a sentence such as *Mightn't he not have seen her?* where *not* originates within a NEGP immediately above VP, and *n't* within a NEGP immediately above TP.

5.8   DO-support

In present-day English, the negative counterpart of a sentence like *I care for her* requires DO-support, as we see from (58) below:

(58)   I do not care for her

But how does *do* come to be introduced into the derivation – and why? In order to answer this question, let's look rather more closely at the derivation of sentence (58). Suppose that (as before) the syntactic component of our grammar generates the structure (53) above. Suppose (again as before) that this structure is then handed over to the PF component (where morphological and phonological operations apply in a bottom-up, cyclic fashion) and that we reach the point where the TP shown in (55) above (and repeated as (59) below) is being cycled in the PF component:

(59)   [$_{TP}$ I [$_T$ *Tns*] [$_{NEGP}$ not [$_{NEG}$ ø] [$_{VP}$ [$_V$ care] for her]]]

Since T contains an unattached *Tns* affix with a weak V-feature, we would expect the affix to be lowered onto an overt verbal stem by Affix Hopping. But if Affix Hopping is a purely *local* operation which lowers an unattached *Tns* affix onto the closest head c-commanded by T (hence onto the head word of the expression which is the complement of T), then it follows that all Affix Hopping can do is lower the affix onto the head NEG constituent of NEGP. But, as we have already seen, NEG is arguably not an appropriate host for the affix, since it is neither overt nor verbal. In order to avoid the derivation crashing, the 'dummy' auxiliary DO is merged with the unattached affix in T, forming the structure:

(60)   [$_{TP}$ I [$_T$ DO+*Tns*] [$_{NEGP}$ not [$_{NEG}$ ø] [$_{VP}$ [$_V$ care] for her]]]

If (as here) the *Tns* affix carries the features [first-person, singular-number, present-tense], the string DO+*Tns* will eventually be spelled out as *do*.

What is implicitly being assumed here is that **Affix Hopping** and **DO-Support** are complementary PF operations which provide two different ways of ensuring that an affix attaches to an appropriate host. We can therefore see them as two types of **Affix Attachment** operation, as in (61) below:

(61)   **Affix Attachment**
         When the PF component processes a structure whose head H contains an (undeleted) Tense affix which is not attached to a verb:
         (i) H is attached to the head immediately below it if that is an overt verb – i.e. if H has a complement headed by an overt verb [= **Affix Hopping**]
         (ii) if not (i.e. if H does not have a complement headed by an overt verb), the expletive (i.e. semantically **contentless**) stem DO is attached to the Tense affix [= **DO-Support**]

We can illustrate how (61) works in terms of the italicised structures below:

(62) (a)   *He won the race*
     (b)   He said he would win the race, and *he did*
     (c)   He said he would win the race, and *win the race, he did*
     (d)   *Did he win the race?*
     (e)   *Didn't he win the race?*
     (f)   Some people don't believe he won the race, but *he DID win it*

Consider first (62a), which is derived as follows. The determiner *the* merges with the noun *race* to form the DP *the race*; the verb *win* merges with this DP to form the VP *win the race*. This VP is merged with a T constituent containing a (past-tense) affix *Tns* to form the T-bar *Tns win the race*. This T-bar merges with the pronoun *he* to form the TP *he Tns win the race*; and the resulting TP in turn is merged with a null declarative complementiser *ø* to form the CP shown in skeletal form in (63) below:

(63)   [CP [C ø] [TP He [T *Tns*] [VP [V win] the race]]]

The syntactic structure (63) is then sent to the PF component (and the semantic component) to be processed. PF operations apply in a bottom-up, cyclic fashion. On the TP cycle, the *Tns* affix in T is lowered onto the verb *win* in accordance with (61i), so that the verb has the form *win+Tns*: since the lexical entry for the irregular verb *win* specifies that it is spelled out as *won* when it has a past-tense affix attached to it, the overall structure is eventually spelled out as (62a) *He won the race*.

Now consider why *do* is used in the elliptical clause *he did* in (62b). This would appear to have the syntactic structure shown in (64) below, with the italicised material undergoing ellipsis:

(64)   [CP [C ø] [TP he [T *Tns*] [VP [V ~~win~~] ~~the race~~]]]

The *Tns* affix in T cannot subsequently be lowered onto the verb *win* in the PF component via the **Affix Hopping** operation (61i) because the verb is not overt (by virtue of having undergone ellipsis); hence the **DO-support** operation in (61ii) has to apply, attaching DO to the *Tns* affix, with the resulting DO+*Tns* string eventually being spelled out as *did*.

Now consider the clause *Win the race, he did* in (62c). Let's suppose that (in the syntax) the VP *win the race* undergoes preposing in order to highlight it, and is thereby moved to the front of the overall clause (to become the specifier of the null complementiser), and that the phonetic features of the original occurrence of the VP *win the race* are given a null spellout, as shown informally in (65) below:

(65)   [CP [VP *win the race*] [C ø] [TP he [T *Tns*] [VP ~~win the race~~]]]

Once again, in the PF component the *Tns* affix cannot be lowered onto the verb *win* because the complement of T is a VP which contains a null copy of the verb *win* (the overall VP having moved to the front of the sentence, leaving a null copy behind). Accordingly, **DO-support** (61ii) applies once again, and T is eventually spelled out as *did*.

Let's turn now to look at the derivation of the yes–no question (62d) *Did he win the race?* Let's suppose that a series of syntactic merger operations have applied to generate the structure (66) below:

(66)   [CP [C Q] [TP he [T *Tns*] [VP [V win] *the race*]]]

Let's further suppose that the Q morpheme/question particle which occupies the head C position of CP has a strong T-feature and hence attracts whatever is contained within T to adjoin to Q. Since T in (66) contains only a *Tns* affix, this affix will adjoin to Q (and the original occurrence of the affix in T will be deleted), so deriving the structure (67) below:

(67)   [CP [C *Tns*+Q] [TP he [T *T̶n̶s̶*] [VP [V *win*] *the race*]]]

The resulting syntactic structure is then sent to the PF component to undergo morphological and phonological processing. Since the *Tns* affix in T gets deleted, it does not undergo Affix Hopping. By contrast, the *Tns* affix in C is not deleted and is unattached (in the sense that it is not attached to an overt verbal stem), and hence must undergo **Affix Attachment** (61). However, since the complement of the C constituent which contains the tense affix is not a VP headed by an overt verb (but rather is a TP headed by a null T), Affix Hopping (61i) cannot apply; consequently, **do-support** (61ii) must apply instead, attaching the dummy stem DO to the unattached affix, to form the string *do*+*Tns*+*Q*, which is eventually spelled out as *did*.

Now, consider the negative question (62e) *Didn't he win the race?* In keeping with the NEGP analysis of negation outlined in the previous section, let's suppose that after the VP *win the race* has been formed, it is merged with a null NEG head *ø* to form a NEG-bar constituent, and that this in turn is merged with a negative adverb *n't* which serves as its specifier, forming the NEGP *n't ø win the race*. This NEGP is then merged with a T containing an abstract *Tns* affix, forming the T-bar *Tns n't ø win the race*. Suppose that the clitic negative *n't* then attaches to the end of the *Tns* affix, with the original occurrence of *n't* in spec-NEGP being deleted, so forming the string *Tns*+*n't* *n̶'̶t̶* *ø win the race*. The resulting T-bar is in turn merged with the subject *he*, forming the TP *He Tns*+*n't* *n̶'̶t̶* *ø win the race*. This is then merged with an interrogative C constituent containing a Q morpheme, forming the CP (68) below:

(68)   [CP [C Q] [TP he [T *Tns*+*n't*] [NEGP *n̶'̶t̶* [NEG *ø*] [VP [V *win*] *the race*]]]]

Since Q has a strong T-feature, it attracts all the material contained in T to adjoin to Q, so deriving:

(69)   [CP [C *Tns*+*n't*+Q] [TP he [T *T̶n̶s̶*+*n̶'̶t̶*] [NEGP *n̶'̶t̶* [NEG *ø*] [VP [V *win*] *the race*]]]]

The resulting syntactic structure is then handed over to the PF component. On the CP cycle, the *Tns* affix in C will be subject to **Affix Attachment** (61). However, since the complement of C is not a VP headed by an overt verb, Affix Hopping (61i) cannot apply, and **do-support** (61ii) applies instead, creating the complex head DO+*Tns*+*n't*+Q, which is ultimately spelled out as *didn't*.

An interesting descriptive implication of the analysis presented in (69) is that it is in principle possible that the interrogative form of some auxiliaries may have a different spellout from their non-interrogative counterparts. This is because in their interrogative form they attach to a null question complementiser Q, whereas in their non-interrogative form they do not. A case in point is *be*. When used with a first person singular subject (= *I*), this has the negative interrogative form *aren't* – a form which is not found with an *I* subject (in varieties of English like mine) in non-interrogative uses, as the following contrast shows:

(70) (a)   *Aren't* I entitled to claim Social Security benefits?
     (b)   *I *aren't* entitled to claim Social Security benefits (= *I'm not . . .*)

This can be accounted for by positing that the string $be+Tns_{1SgPr}+n't+Q$ found in (70a) can be spelled out as *aren't* – but not the Q-less string $be+Tns_{1SgPr}+n't$ in (70b) because this is not interrogative (by virtue of having no Q affix attached to it).

Finally, let's turn to consider the clause *He DID win it* in (62f), where capitals mark contrastive stress (and the utterance is used to deny any suggestion that he didn't win the race). One way of handling the relevant phenomenon is to suppose that T is the locus of contrastive stress in such structures, and hence contains an abstract EMP(hasis) marker of some kind which is spelled out as contrastive stress, and which must be attached to a verbal stem – so requiring **DO-support** in contrastive structures like (62f). Such an analysis would require us to suppose that EMP (perhaps by virtue of having phonological but not morphological content) is not an affix and so cannot be lowered from T onto V. An alternative possibility is that EMP is a clitic-like constituent which originates within the complement of T and (rather like the negative clitic *n't*) requires the use of **DO-support** to provide a host for the clitic EMP. We shall not speculate further on these (and other) analyses of emphatic *do* here. (On DO-support, see Halle and Marantz 1993, Lasnik 1995, Bobaljik 2002; see also Embick and Noyer 2001 for a different view.)

The analysis of DO-support outlined here has interesting theoretical implications. The structures generated by the syntactic component of the grammar are sent not only to the PF component (where they are assigned a phonetic form) but also to the semantic component (where they are assigned a semantic interpretation). Chomsky in recent work (1995, 1998, 1999, 2001) has proposed a constraint on grammars to the effect that syntactic structures must not contain constituents which are not legible at the semantics interface or at the PF interface (i.e. grammars must not contain constituents which do not contribute to determining the meaning or phonetic form of expressions). Under the analysis of **DO-support** presented here, the dummy auxiliary DO is analysed as a meaningless 'chunk' of morphology which is not present in the syntax, but rather is added in the PF component in order to provide a host for an unsupported tense affix. Since syntactic structures which contain 'meaningless' constituents will cause the derivation to crash at the semantics interface (because meaningless constituents cannot be assigned any semantic interpretation), this is a welcome result since if the dummy auxiliary DO is not present in the syntax, it will not be processed by the semantic component: all the semantic component 'sees' in DO-support structures is a tense affix which is clearly interpretable by virtue of the fact that it encodes present or past tense.

5.9   Head movement in nominals

Our discussion so far has focused entirely on head movement in clauses. To end this chapter, we look briefly at head movement in nominals – more particularly, at **N-movement** (i.e. the movement of a noun out of the head N position of NP into a higher head position within the nominal expression containing it). In this connection, consider the syntax of the English nominal (71a) below and its Italian counterpart (71b) (from Cinque 1994, p. 86):

(71) (a)   the Italian invasion of Albania
     (b)   l'invasione   italiana dell'Albania
            the invasion Italian   of.the Albania

If the adjective *Italian* is the specifier of the noun *invasion*, (71a) will have the simplified structure:

(72)

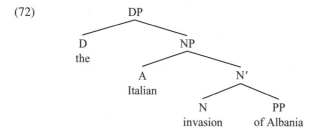

On this view, the noun *invasion* merges with its PP complement *of Albania* to form the N-bar (intermediate nominal projection) *invasion of Albania*, and this in turn merges with the adjectival specifier *Italian* to form the NP (maximal nominal projection) *Italian invasion of Albania*; the resulting NP is then merged with the determiner *the* to form the DP *the Italian invasion of Albania*. The adjective *Italian* in (72) can be thought of as being (in an informal sense) the 'subject' of *invasion*, since it identifies the people who are doing the invading – and if *subjects* are typically specifiers, it is appropriate to analyse the kind of adjective found in (72) as the specifier of the N *invasion*, of the N-bar *invasion of Albania* and of the NP *Italian invasion of Albania*.

In the corresponding Italian structure (71b) *l'invasione italiana dell'Albania*, the head noun *invasione* ends up occupying a position to the left of the adjective *italiana*. Cinque (1994) argues that this is the result of the noun moving out of the head N position within NP into some higher head position within the nominal (via **Head Movement**). At first sight, it might seem as if the noun attaches to the right of the head D constituent of DP: but – argues Cinque – any such assumption is falsified by nominals like (73) below:

(73)   la grande invasione italiana dell'   Albania
              the great   invasion Italian of.the Albania
              'the great Italian invasion of Albania'

The fact that the noun *invasione* ends up positioned after the adjective *grande* 'great' in (73) suggests that the noun cannot move to some position immediately to the right of the determiner *la* 'the'. Instead, the noun must 'move to a head intermediate between N and D' (Cinque 1994, p. 87). If this intervening head is the locus of the number properties of nominals (as suggested by Picallo 1991 and Ritter 1991), we can label this intermediate head **Num** (= **Number**). If the adjective *grande* 'great' serves as the specifier of Num, this will mean that the derivation of (73) involves the movement operation shown in (74) below:

(74)

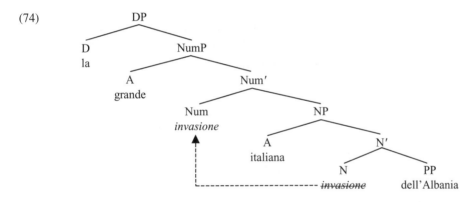

The noun *invasione* originates in the head N position of NP and then (via **head movement**) moves into the head Num position of NumP, with the original occurrence of *invasione* in N being deleted. It may be that Num is a strong head in Italian (perhaps an affix with a strong N-feature triggering movement of N to Num) by virtue of the richness of the number morphology carried by nouns and adjectives in Italian, whereas Num is a weak head in present-day English by virtue of the impoverished nature of number morphology in English (e.g. adjectives no longer inflect for number). If Num is also the locus of **gender** properties in nouns, we can further correlate the strength of Num in Italian and its weakness in English with the fact that Italian has gender in nouns but English does not. It should also be noted that an assumption embodied in the analysis in (74) is that adjectives serve as specifiers of the expressions they modify, and that different types of adjective serve as specifiers to different types of head (e.g. *italiana* in (74) is the specifier of N, and *grande* is the specifier of Num): see Cinque (1994) for a more extensive implementation of the idea that different kinds of adjectives serve as the specifiers of different kinds of heads, and Cinque (1999) for an extension of the specifier analysis to clausal adverbs.

While the kind of N-movement operation found in Italian is not found in present-day English, it did occur in earlier varieties of English. For example, in Chaucer's *Troilus and Criseyde* we find nominals such as those in (75) below where the italicised noun precedes the bold-printed adjective:

(75) (a)   hire own *brother* **dere** (= her own brother dear)
   (b)   a *thing* **immortal** (= a thing immortal)
   (c)   blosmy *bowes* **grene** (= blossomy branches green)
   (d)   hire *hornes* **pale** (= her horns pale)

The italicised noun in such structures has moved from the head N position of NP into the head Num position of NumP, so moving in front of the bold-printed adjective. (See Kishimoto 2000 for arguments that present-day structures like *something nice* are a last vestige of this once-productive N-to-Num movement operation, deriving from *some nice thing* via movement of *thing* from N to Num.)

Although nouns generally move only as far as Num in Italian, in some other languages nouns can move above Num into the head D position of DP (if the head D of DP is strong/affixal in nature). Consider in this regard the following Norwegian examples (from Taraldsen 1990):

(76) (a)   hans bøker om   syntaks   (b) bøkene   hans om   syntaks
          his   books about syntax   books+the his   about syntax

Taraldsen argues that (76b) is derived via movement of the noun *bøker* 'books' from the head N position of NP to the head D position of DP, where it attaches to the left of the affixal determiner +*ne* 'the'.

Longobardi (1994, p. 623) argues that proper nouns (i.e. names) in Italian can raise from N to D across an intervening adjective (like the possessive adjective *mio*) in structures like (77b) below:

(77) (a)   *Il   mio Gianni* ha finalmente telefonato
          The my Gianni has finally   phoned
          'My Gianni has finally phoned'
   (b)   *Gianni mio* ha finalmente telefonato
          Gianni mine has finally   phoned
          'My Gianni has finally phoned'

In (77a) the head D position of DP is filled by the determiner *il* 'the', and there is no movement of the proper noun *Gianni* from N to D. However, in (77b) the head D position of DP is filled by a null affixal determiner, and the proper noun *Gianni* raises from N to D to attach to the null determiner, in the process crossing the possessive adjective *mio*. In earlier varieties of English, a similar type of movement operation seems to be found in **vocative** expressions used to address someone, as the italicised vocative in (78b) below illustrates (from Chaucer's *Troilus and Criseyde*):

(78) (a)   'Iwis, *myn uncle*,' quod she
             'Certainly, my uncle,' said she
    (b)   'And whi so, *uncle myn*? whi so?' quod she
             'And why so, uncle mine, why so?' said she

. As these examples show, the noun *uncle* can be positioned either before or after the possessive *myn* in vocative expressions. How can we account for this? One possibility (suggested in relation to Italian vocatives like *mio caro Gianni* 'my dear Gianni' and *Gianni mio caro* 'Gianni my dear' by Longobardi 1994, p. 626) is that vocative structures like *uncle myn* are DPs in which the noun *uncle* has raised from N to D, whereas structures like *myn uncle* are 'smaller' nominals which lack a DP projection and hence cannot trigger N-to-D movement. (See Longobardi 1994, 1996, 2001 for an insightful discussion of the syntax and semantics of N-to-D movement in nominals. See also Vikner 1995 and Roberts 2001b for more general discussion of head movement.)

The general conclusion to be drawn from this section is that we find evidence from languages other than present-day English (and from earlier varieties of English) that **head movement** may apply in nominal as well as clausal structures. In particular, we find evidence of two types of N-movement operation: (i) movement of a noun to a Num position intermediate between D and N; and (ii) movement of a noun to the head D position of DP (with the noun first moving to Num before moving to D, in order for movement of the noun to be successive-cyclic and thereby satisfy the **Head Movement Constraint**).

5.10   Summary

In this chapter, we have been concerned with the syntax of **head movement**. We began by looking at **auxiliary inversion** in questions in English in §5.2, arguing that this involves a T-to-C movement operation whereby an auxiliary moves from the head T position of TP into the head C position of CP. We suggested that auxiliaries move to C in main clause questions because C in such structures is **strong** (perhaps by virtue of containing a null question particle Q which is affixal and has a strong tense feature) and so **attracts** an auxiliary in T to move to C. In §5.3 we argued that movement operations like auxiliary inversion involve two separate **copying** and **deletion** operations: a copy of the auxiliary in T is merged with an affixal Q constituent/question particle in C, and then the original occurrence of the auxiliary in T is deleted. In §5.4 we saw that finite main verbs in Elizabethan English could move from V to T by an operation of V-to-T movement (as is shown by word-order in negative sentences like *I care not for her*), but that this kind of movement is no longer possible in present-day

English. We suggested that a null finite T was strong in Elizabethan English (perhaps containing an abstract *Tns* affix with a strong V-feature triggering the raising of verbs to T) but that its counterpart in present-day English is weak (so that a *Tns* affix in T is lowered onto the main verb by the morphological operation of **Affix Hopping**). In §5.5 we argued that T-to-C movement and V-to-T movement are two different reflexes of a more general **Head Movement** operation, and that head movement is subject to a strict locality condition (imposed by the **Head Movement Constraint**) which requires it to apply in a successive cyclic (stepwise) fashion, so that movement is only possible between a given head and the next highest head within the structure containing it. We noted that finite verbs in Elizabethan English carried a richer system of agreement inflections than their counterparts in present-day English (allowing them to be used with a null nominative **pro** subject), and conjectured that T is strong in languages with rich subject–verb agreement morphology and weak in languages with poor subject–verb agreement morphology. In §5.6 we argued that present-day English has a last vestige of V-to-T raising in finite clauses whereby the auxiliaries BE and HAVE and narrow-scope modal auxiliaries raise from a lower AUX/V position into the head T position of TP. We suggested that a finite T in present-day English contains a *Tns* affix which can only attract an auxiliary to move to T, not a main verb: we noted that one possible implementation of this idea would be that a finite T has a strong AUX-feature in present-day English. We also suggested that infinitival *to* occupies the head AUX position of AUXP in negative infinitives of the form . . . *not to* . . . but that in non-negative structures both infinitival *to* and finite auxiliaries are directly merged in the head T position of TP. In §5.7, we took a closer look at negation. Revising our earlier analysis of *not* as a VP-specifier, we outlined an alternative analysis under which *not* is the specifier of a NEGP constituent which was headed by *ne* in Chaucerian English, but which is null in present-day English. On this view, Shakespearean negatives like *He heard not that* involve movement of the verb from V through NEG into T. Because NEG and T don't have a strong V-feature in present-day English, they can no longer trigger movement of a main verb. In §5.8 we outlined a morphological account of **Affix Hopping** and **DO-Support**. We suggested that once the syntactic component of the grammar has generated a given syntactic structure (e.g. a complete CP), the relevant structure is then sent to the PF component for morphological and phonological processing. If a structure being processed by the PF component contains an unattached *Tns* affix, this is lowered onto the closest head below it by **Affix Hopping** if this is an overt verb; if not, the dummy item DO is attached to the affix by **DO-Support**. In §5.9, we presented evidence that head movement can also apply in nominal structures. We argued that nouns in Italian raise to a head **Num**(ber) position intermediate between D and N in structures like *la grande invasione italiana dell'Albania* 'the great invasion Italian of.the Albania'. We noted that in some languages, nouns can raise still further to attach to D – e.g. in Norwegian nominals such as *bøkene hans* 'books.the his'.

Workbook section

Exercise 5.1

Discuss the derivation of each of the following (declarative or interrogative) sentences, drawing a tree diagram to represent the structure of each sentence and saying why the relevant structure is (or is not) grammatical (in the case of 4, saying why it is ungrammatical as a main clause):

1	He helps her	9	*He helps not her
2	*He d's help her	10	*He not helps her
3	*Helps he her?	11	He does not help her
4	*If he helps her?	12	He doesn't help her
5	Does he help her?	13	Doesn't he help her?
6	I wonder if he helps her	14	He might not help her
7	*I wonder if does he help her	15	He dare not help her
8	*I wonder if helps he her		

(Note that *d's* in 2 represents unstressed *does*, /dəz/.) Say what is archaic about the syntax of 16 below (the second line of the nursery rhyme *Baa Baa Black Sheep*) – and why such structures are no longer grammatical in many varieties of English:

16   Have you any wool?

Then, discuss the derivation of each of the following questions produced by a number of different children aged two to four years, and identify the nature of the child's error in each case:

17   Is the clock is working?
18   Does it opens?
19   Don't you don't want one?
20   Does it doesn't move?

Consider, also, the derivation of the following questions reported (by Akmajian and Heny 1975, p. 17) to have been produced by an unnamed three-year-old girl:

21   Is I can do that?
22   Is you should eat the apple?
23   Is the apple juice won't spill?

And finally, say why you think negative imperatives like 24 (which were grammatical in Elizabethan English) are ungrammatical in present-day English, and why we find 25 instead:

24   *Be not afraid!
25   Don't be afraid!

Helpful hints

In 13, account for the fact that the sentence is ambiguous between one interpretation paraphraseable as 'Is it the case that he doesn't help her' and another paraphraseable as 'Isn't it the case that he helps her?' In 14 and 15, consider the scope relations between the auxiliary and *not*, and bear in mind the suggestion made in the main text that finite auxiliaries normally originate in T, but originate in an AUX position below NEG if they fall within the scope of *not*.

In 17–20, consider the possibility that children sometimes fail to delete the original occurrence of a moved T constituent. In 19 and 20, consider the possibility that attachment of the clitic *n't* to a *Tns* affix in T may either be treated by the child as a syntactic operation, or as a phonological operation which applies *after* the relevant syntactic structure has been formed. In relation to 24, consider the possibility that although a T in finite declarative and interrogative clauses has a strong AUX feature, T in imperatives is weak and so can attract neither main verbs nor auxiliaries.

Model answer for sentence 1

Given the assumptions made in the text, 1 will have the simplified syntactic structure (i) below:

(i)

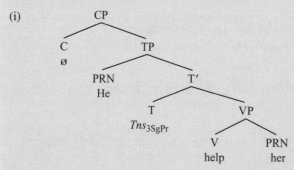

The overall clause is a CP headed by a null declarative complementiser ∅ which has a TP complement headed by a T constituent which carries a present-tense *Tns* affix which is third-person singular by agreement with the subject *he*, and which needs an overt verb stem to attach to. Since T does not have a strong V-feature in present-day English, the verb *help* cannot be raised to provide a host for the affix in T. After the syntactic structure in (i) has been formed, it is handed over to the PF component, where it is processed in a bottom-up, cyclic fashion. On the TP cycle, the *Tns* affix in T is lowered onto the end of the verb *help* by Affix Hopping, which specifies that a weak affix in T is lowered onto the head V of a VP complement of T. Affix Hopping results in the form [*help*+*Tns*$_{3SgPr}$], which is ultimately spelled out as *helps*. The complement pronoun *her* is assigned accusative case in the syntax by the c-commanding transitive verb *help*, and the subject pronoun *he* is assigned nominative case by the c-commanding null intransitive finite complementiser ∅.

Exercise 5.2

Discuss the derivation of the following Shakespearean sentences:

1	Thou marvell'st at my words (Macbeth, *Macbeth*, III.ii)
2	Macbeth doth come (Third Witch, *Macbeth*, I.iii)
3	He loves not you (Lysander, *A Midsummer Night's Dream*, III.ii)
4	You do not look on me (Jessica, *The Merchant of Venice*, II.vi)
5	Wilt thou use thy wit? (Claudio, *Much Ado About Nothing*, V.i)
6	Wrong I mine enemies? (Brutus, *Julius Caesar*, IV.ii)
7	Knows he not thy voice? (First Lord, *All's Well That Ends Well*, IV.i)
8	Didst thou not say he comes? (Baptista, *The Taming of the Shrew*, III.ii)
9	Canst not rule her? (Leontes, *The Winter's Tale*, II.iii)
10	Hath not a Jew eyes? (Shylock, *The Merchant of Venice*, III.i)

11   Do not you love me? (Benedick, *Much Ado About Nothing*, V.iv)
12   Buy thou a rope! (Antipholus, *The Comedy of Errors*, IV.i)
13   Fear you not him! (Tranio, *The Taming of the Shrew*, IV.iv)
14   Speak not you to him! (Escalus, *Measure for Measure*, V.i)
15   Do not you meddle! (Antonio, *Much Ado About Nothing*, V.i)
16   She not denies it (Leonato, *Much Ado About Nothing*, IV.i)

Helpful hints

Assume that 9 has a null finite *pro* subject. Assume also that sentences 12–15 are **imperative** in force, and consider the possibility that V raises to C in imperatives in Elizabethan English (see Han 2001), perhaps attaching to a strong imperative affix *Imp*. Consider also the possibility that *not* had a dual status and could either function as an independent word (like present-day English *not*) or could serve as an enclitic particle (like present-day English *n't*) which attached to an immediately adjacent finite T constituent. Finally, say in what way(s) sentence 16 proves problematic in respect of the assumptions made in the main text (and in the model answer below), and see if you can think of possible solutions (e.g. What if the verb raised as far as NEG but not as far as T?).

Model answer for sentences 1 and 2

Relevant aspects of the derivation of 1 (here presented in simplified form) are as follows. The verb *marvel* merges with its PP complement *at my words* to form the VP *marvel at my words*. This in turn is merged with a T constituent containing a present-tense *Tns* affix to form the T-bar *Tns marvel at my words*, which is in turn merged with its subject *thou*. The *Tns* affix agrees with *thou* and thus carries the features [second-person, singular-number, present-tense], below abbreviated to *2SgPr*. The resulting TP is merged with a null intransitive finite C which marks the declarative force of the sentence and which assigns nominative case to *thou* by virtue of being the closest case-assigning head c-commanding *thou*. 1 thus has the syntactic structure shown in simplified form in (i) below, with the dotted arrow indicating movement of the verb *marvel* from V to T:

(i)

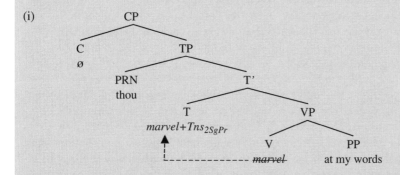

The string *marvel+Tns₂SgPr* is ultimately spelled out as *marvell'st* in the PF component.

  Sentence 2 is derived as follows. The verb *come* merges with a weak *Tns* affix in T, forming the T-bar *Tns come*. This will in turn be merged with its subject *Macbeth*, which we can take to be a DP headed by a null determiner, in accordance with the **DP hypothesis** (and indeed, proper names in many languages can be premodified by an overt determiner – cf. e.g. Italian *la Callas*, literally 'the Callas'). Merging the resulting TP with a null declarative complementiser will derive the syntactic structure shown in (ii) below:

(ii)

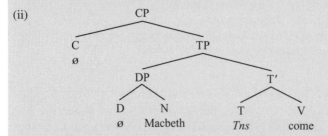

It would seem that the *Tns* affix undergoes DO-support in the PF component, and is ultimately spelled out as *doth* (which is a dialectal variant of *does*). What is surprising about this is that the dummy auxiliary DO is used only to support a *Tns* affix which is unable to find a host by any other means. So what we'd expect to happen when the structure in (ii) is handed over to the PF component is for the *Tns* affix to be lowered onto the verb *come* in the PF component by **Affix Hopping**, with the resulting verb being spelled out as *cometh* (a dialectal variant of *comes*). However, this is clearly not what happens.

One alternative possibility which this might lead us to consider is that DO is not a dummy auxiliary with a morphological support function in Elizabethan English, but rather has independent semantic content of some kind and so is directly generated in T in the syntax, just like (e.g.) the aspectual auxiliaries HAVE (marking perfect aspect) and BE (marking progressive aspect). In this connection, it is interesting to note that in Caribbean Creoles (according to Rickford 1986 and Harris 1986), DO is used to mark habitual aspect in sentences such as:

(iii)   He does be sick (= 'He is usually sick')

Likewise, DO functions as a habitual aspect marker in Irish English (see Guilfoyle 1983, Harris 1986) and in south-western varieties of British English (see Wakelin 1977, pp. 120–21). However, sentence 2 doesn't seem to have a habitual interpretation paraphraseable as 'Macbeth usually comes' (but rather has an interpretation more akin to 'Macbeth is coming'), so it is not clear that this is a credible approach. Let's therefore continue to explore the possibility outlined in (ii) that DO is not generated in the syntax, but rather serves to support an unattached affix in the PF component.

One suggestion along these lines is that the *Tns* affix in a finite T in a structure like (ii) could be either strong or weak in Elizabethan English. Where it is strong, the *Tns* affix will trigger raising of the main verb from V to T; where it is weak, the verb will remain in situ, and the *Tns* affix will remain unattached in the syntax. The resulting structure (ii) will then be handed over to the PF component, where it is processed in a bottom-up fashion. Although in present-day English DO-**support** is only used where **Affix Hopping** cannot apply, let's suppose that in Shakespearean English the two are in free variation, in the sense that either can be used as a way of providing a host for an unattached affix in T. Applying **Affix Hopping** will lower the (third-person-singular present-tense) affix in (ii) onto the verb deriving the string *come+Tns$_{3SgPr}$* (which is ultimately spelled out as *cometh*). Applying DO-**support** instead will result in the dummy stem DO being attached to the *Tns* affix in T, so forming the string *do+Tns$_{3SgPr}$* (which is ultimately spelled out as *doth*). If an analysis along the lines outlined here is tenable, it implies that there was considerably more morphosyntactic variation in Shakespearean English than we find in present-day varieties of Standard English – for example, in respect of a finite *Tns* affix being either strong or weak, and an unattached *Tns* affix either being lowered onto the verb, or having DO attached to it. Given that Shakespeare's writing contains a mixture of different dialect forms (as we see from the alternation between dialectal variants like *comes/cometh* and *does/doth*), this may not be implausible. However, as noted by Tieken-Boon van Ostade (1988), the origin of DO is 'one of the great riddles of English linguistic history'.

6   Wh-movement

6.1   Overview

In the previous chapter, we looked at the **head movement** operation by which a head can move into the next highest head position within the structure containing it. In this chapter, we look at a very different kind of movement operation traditionally termed **wh-movement**, by which a wh-expression like *who* or *what languages* moves into the specifier position within CP. We begin by looking at the syntax of wh-questions, and then go on to probe the syntax of other types of wh-clause, including exclamative clauses and relative clauses.

6.2   Wh-questions

So far, we have implicitly assumed that CP comprises a head C constituent (which can be filled by a complementiser or a preposed auxiliary) and a TP complement. However, one question which such an analysis begs is what position is occupied by the bold-printed constituent which precedes the italicised auxiliary in **root interrogatives** (i.e. main-clause questions) such as (1) below:

(1) (a)   **What languages** *can* you speak?
    (b)   **Which one** *would* you like?
    (c)   **Who** *was* she dating?
    (d)   **Where** *are* you going?

Each of the sentences in (1) contains an italicised inverted auxiliary occupying the head C position of CP, preceded by a bold-printed interrogative **wh-expression** – i.e. an expression containing an interrogative word beginning with *wh-* like *what/which/who/where/when/why*. (Note that *how* in questions like *How are you? How well did he behave?* etc. is also treated as a wh-word because it exhibits the same syntactic behaviour as interrogative words beginning with *wh-*.) Each of the wh-expressions in (1) functions as the complement of the verb at the end of the sentence – as we see from the fact that each of the examples in (1) has a paraphrase in which the wh-expression occupies complement position after the italicised verb:

(2) (a)   You can *speak* **what languages**?
    (b)   You would *like* **which one**?
    (c)   She was *dating* **who**?
    (d)   You are *going* **where**?

Structures like (2) are termed **wh-in-situ questions**, since the bold-printed wh-expression does not get preposed, but rather remains **in situ** (i.e. 'in place') in the canonical position associated with its grammatical function (e.g. *what languages* in (2a) is the direct object complement of *speak*, and complements are normally positioned after their verbs, so *what languages* is positioned after the verb *speak*). In English, wh-in-situ questions are used primarily as **echo questions**, to echo and question something previously said by someone else – as we can illustrate in terms of the following dialogue:

(3)   SPEAKER A: I just met Lord Lancelot Humpalot
            SPEAKER B: You just met *who*?

Echo questions such as that produced by speaker B in (3) suggest that the wh-expressions in (1) originate as complements of the relevant verbs, and subsequently get moved to the front of the overall clause. But what position do they get moved into?

The answer is obviously that they are moved into some position preceding the inverted auxiliary. Since inverted auxiliaries occupy the head C position of CP, let's suppose that preposed wh-expressions are moved into a position preceding the head C of CP. Given that **specifiers** are positioned before heads, a plausible suggestion to make is that preposed wh-expressions move into the *specifier position within CP* (= **spec-CP**). If so, a sentence like (1c) *Who was she dating?* will involve the arrowed movement operations shown in (4) below:

(4)

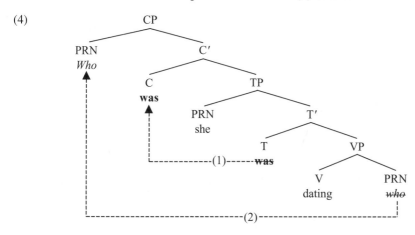

(To be more precise, interrogative pronouns like *who* are Q-pronouns and hence pronominal quantifiers.) Two different kinds of movement operation (indicated by the numbered arrows) are involved in (4): the movement arrowed in (1) involves the familiar operation of **head movement** by which the bold-printed auxiliary

was moves from the head T position of TP into the head C position of CP; by contrast, (2) involves movement of an italicised wh-expression from the complement position within VP into the specifier position in CP, and this very different kind of movement operation is known as **wh-movement**. Note that unlike head movement (which, as its name suggests, moves only heads which are minimal projections), wh-movement moves maximal projections; for instance, in (1a) *What languages can you speak?* wh-movement moves the quantifier phrase *what languages* which is the maximal projection of the interrogative quantifier *what?* by virtue of being the largest expression headed by the word *what*; and in (1c) *Who was she dating?* it moves the interrogative Q-pronoun *who* (which is a maximal projection by virtue of being the largest expression headed by the word *who*). Following Cheng (1997), we might suppose that every clause must be **typed** (i.e. identified as declarative or interrogative etc. in type) in the syntax, and that a clause is typed as interrogative if it contains an interrogative head or specifier: on this view, movement of the interrogative pronoun *who* to spec-CP serves to type the CP in (4) as interrogative.

Evidence in support of the assumption that preposed wh-expressions move into spec-CP comes from varieties of English in which a preposed wh-expression can precede a complementiser like *that*. This is true, for example, of interrogative complement clauses like those bracketed below in Belfast English (from Henry 1995, p. 107):

(5) (a)   I wonder [*which dish* **that** they picked]
    (b)   They didn't know [*which model* **that** we had discussed]

Since the complementiser *that* occupies the head C position in the bracketed CP, it seems reasonable to suppose that the wh-expressions *which dish/which model* in front of *that* occupy the specifier position within CP, and this is what Alison Henry argues. (See Seppänen and Trotta 2000 and Zwicky 2002 for discussion of the syntax of *wh+that* structures.)

6.3   Wh-movement as a copying operation

A tacit assumption made in our analysis of wh-movement in (4) is that just as a moved head (e.g. an inverted auxiliary) leaves behind a null copy of itself in the position out of which it moves, so too a moved wh-expression leaves behind a copy at its **extraction site** (i.e. in the position out of which it is **extracted**/moved). In earlier work in the 1970s and 1980s, moved constituents were said to leave behind a **trace** in the positions out of which they move (informally denoted as *t*), and traces of moved nominal constituents were treated as being like pronouns in certain respects. A moved constituent and its trace(s) were together said to form a (movement) **chain**, with the highest member of the chain (i.e. the moved constituent) being the **head** of the movement chain, and the lowest trace being the

foot of the chain. Within the framework of Chomsky's more recent **copy theory of movement**, a trace is taken to be a full copy (rather than a pronominal copy) of a moved constituent. Informally, however, we shall sometimes refer to the null copies left behind by movement as **traces** or **trace copies** in later sections and chapters.

The assumption that moved wh-expressions leave a copy behind can be defended not only on theoretical grounds (in terms of our desire to develop a unified theory of movement in which both minimal and maximal projections leave behind copies when they move), but also on empirical grounds. One such empirical argument comes from a phenomenon known as ***wanna-contraction***. In colloquial English, the sequence *want to* can sometimes contract to *wanna*, as in (6) below:

(6) (a)   I *want to* go home   (b) I *wanna* go home

Given the claim made in §4.7 that control infinitive clauses are CPs headed by a null complementiser, the complement clause in (6a) will have the skeletal structure shown in (7) below:

(7)   I want [$_{CP}$ [$_C$ ø] [$_{TP}$ PRO [$_T$ to] go home]]

The fact that *wanna*-contraction is possible in (6b) suggests that neither the intervening null complementiser ø nor the intervening null subject PRO prevents *to* from cliticising onto *want* in the phonological component, forming *want+to* – which is ultimately spelled out as *wanta* or *wanna*.

What is of particular interest to us is that (in non-sloppy speech styles) the sequence *want to* cannot contract to *wanna* in sentences like:

(8) (a)   Who don't you *want to* win the game?
    (b)   *Who don't you *wanna* win the game?

Why should this be? Well, let's assume that *who* in (8) originates as the subject of the infinitive clause *to win the game* – as seems plausible in view of the fact that (8a) has the echo-question counterpart:

(9)   You don't want *who* to win the game?

Let's also assume that (for reasons outlined in §4.7) the complement of *want* in structures like (8) and (9) is a CP headed by a null complementiser (perhaps a null variant of *for*). On this view, (9) will have the skeletal structure (10) below:

(10)   You don't want [$_{CP}$ [$_C$ ø] [$_{TP}$ who [$_T$ to] win the game]]

Movement of *who* to the front of the overall sentence (together with auxiliary inversion) will result in the structure shown below (simplified, inter alia, by not showing the trace of the inverted auxiliary):

(11)   *Who* don't you want [$_{CP}$ [$_C$ ø] [$_{TP}$ ~~who~~ [$_T$ to] win the game]]

However, *wanna*-contraction is not possible in a structure like (11) – as we see from the ungrammaticality of (8b) **Who don't you wanna win the game?* Why should this be? This is unlikely to be because of the presence of the null complementiser ø between *want* and *to*, since we see from the fact that structures like (7) allow *wanna*-contraction in sentences like (6b) that *wanna*-contraction is not blocked by an intervening null complementiser. So what blocks contraction in structures like (11)? The **copy theory of movement** provides us with a principled answer, if we assume that when *who* moves to the front of the overall sentence in (11), it leaves behind a copy of itself (which is ultimately given a null phonetic spellout), and it is the presence of this copy intervening between *want* and *to* which prevents *wanna*-contraction in (8b).

A different kind of evidence in support of the claim that preposed wh-expressions leave behind a null copy when they move comes from a phenomenon which we can call **preposition copying**. In this connection, consider the following Shakespearean wh-structures:

(12) (a)   *In what enormity* is Marcius poor **in**? (Menenius, *Coriolanus*, II.i)
     (b)   *To what form but that he is* should wit larded with malice and malice forced with wit turn him **to**? (Thersites, *Troilus and Cressida*, V.i)
     (c)   . . . that fair [*for which* love groan'd **for**] (Prologue to Act II, *Romeo and Juliet*)

(12a,b) are interrogative clauses, and the bracketed structure in (12c) is a **relative clause** – so called because it contains a relative wh-pronoun *which* relating (more specifically, referring back) to the preceding noun expression *that fair*. In these examples, an italicised prepositional wh-phrase (i.e. a prepositional phrase containing a wh-word like *what/which*) has been moved to the front of the relevant clause by wh-movement. But a (bold-printed) copy of the preposition also appears at the end of the clause. In case you think that this is a Shakespearean quirk (or – Heaven forbid – a slip of the quill on the part of Will), the examples in (13) below show much the same thing happening in (bracketed) **relative clauses** in present-day English:

(13) (a)   But if this ever-changing world [*in which* we live **in**] makes you give in and cry, say 'Live and Let Die' (Sir Paul McCartney, theme song from the James Bond movie *Live and Let Die*)
     (b)   IKEA only actually has ten stores [*from which* to sell **from**] (Economics reporter, BBC Radio 5)
     (c)   Israeli soldiers fired an anti-tank missile and hit a police post [*in which* the Palestinian policeman who was killed had been **in**] (News reporter, BBC Radio 5)
     (d)   Tiger Woods (*about whom* this Masters seems to be all **about**) is due to tee off shortly (Sports reporter, BBC Radio 5)
     (e)   The hearing mechanism is a peripheral, passive system *over which* we have no control **over** (undergraduate exam paper)

How can we account for preposition copying in structures like (12) and (13)?

The **copy theory of movement** enables us to provide a principled answer to this question. Let's suppose that wh-movement (like **head movement**) is a composite operation involving two suboperations of **copying** and **deletion**: the first stage is for a copy of the moved wh-expression to be moved into spec-CP; the second stage is for the original occurrence of the wh-expression to be deleted. From this perspective, preposition copying arises when the preposition at the original extraction site undergoes copying but not deletion. To see what this means in more concrete terms, consider the syntax of (12a) *In what enormity is Marcius poor in?* This is derived as follows. The wh-quantifier *what* merges with the noun *enormity* to derive the quantifier phrase/QP *what enormity*. This in turn is merged with the preposition *in* to form the prepositional phrase/PP *in what enormity*. This PP is then merged with the adjective *poor* to form the adjectival phrase/AP *poor in what enormity*. This AP is merged with the copular verb *is* to form the verb phrase/VP *is poor in what enormity*. This VP is merged with a finite T constituent which triggers raising of the verb *is* from V to T; the resulting T-bar constituent is merged with its subject *Marcius* (which is a DP headed by a null determiner) to form the tense phrase/TP *ø Marcius is poor i̶s̶ in what enormity*. Merging this with a strong C into which *is* moves forms the C-bar *Is ø Marcius i̶s̶ poor i̶s̶ in what enormity?* Moving a copy of the PP *in what enormity* into spec-CP in turn derives the structure shown in simplified form in (14) below (with copies of moved constituents shown in italics):

(14)

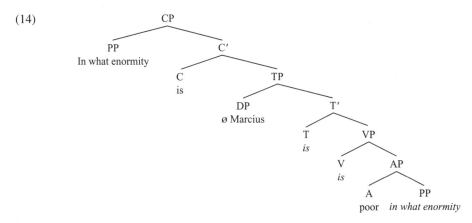

The two italicised copies of the moved copular verb *is* are deleted by operation of **copy-deletion**. But consider how copy-deletion affects the copy left behind by movement of the PP *in what enormity* to spec-CP. If we suppose that copy-deletion in (12a) deletes the smallest phrase containing the wh-word *what*, it will delete the quantifier phrase *what enormity* rather than the prepositional phrase *in what enormity*, so deriving (12a) *In what enormity is Marcius poor in?* Thus, preposition copying structures like (12) and (13) provide evidence that wh-movement is a composite operation involving wh-copying and wh-deletion.

A related piece of evidence in support of wh-movement involving a copying operation comes from sentences such as those below:

(15) (a)   *What hope* **of finding survivors** could there be?
   (b)   *What hope* could there be **of finding survivors**?

(16) (a)   *What proof* **that he was implicated** have you found?
   (b)   *What proof* have you found **that he was implicated**?

In order to try and understand what's going on here, let's take a closer look at the derivation of (15). The expression *what hope of finding survivors* is a QP comprising the quantifier *what* and an NP complement which in turn comprises the noun *hope* and its PP complement *of finding survivors*. The overall QP *what hope of finding survivors* is initially merged as the complement of the verb *be*, but ultimately moves to the front of the overall sentence in (15a): this is unproblematic, since it involves wh-movement of the whole QP. But in (15b), it would seem as if only part of this QP (= the string *what hope*) undergoes wh-movement, leaving behind the PP *of finding survivors*. The problem with this is that the string *what hope* is not a constituent, only a *subpart* of the overall QP *what hope of finding survivors*. Given the standard assumption that only complete constituents can undergo movement, we clearly cannot maintain that the non-constituent string *what hope* gets moved on its own. So how can we account for sentences like (15b)? Copy theory provides us with an answer, if we suppose that wh-movement places a copy of the complete QP *what hope of finding survivors* at the front of the overall sentence, so deriving the structure shown in skeletal form in (17) below:

(17)   **What hope of finding survivors** could there be *what hope of finding survivors*

If we further suppose that the PP *of finding survivors* is spelled out in its original position (i.e. in the italicised position it occupied before wh-movement applied) but the remaining constituents of the QP (the quantifier *what* and the noun *hope*) are spelled out in the superficial (bold-printed) position in which they end up after wh-movement, (15b) will have the superficial structure shown in simplified form below after copy-deletion has applied (with ~~strikethrough~~ indicating constituents which receive a null spellout):

(18)   **What hope** ~~**of finding survivors**~~ could there be ~~*what hope*~~ *of finding survivors*

As should be obvious, such an analysis relies crucially on the assumption that moved constituents leave behind full copies of themselves. It also assumes the possibility of **split spellout/discontinuous spellout**, in the sense that (in sentences like (15) and (16) above) a PP or CP which is the complement of a particular type of moved constituent can be spelled out in one position (in the position where it originated), and the remainder of the constituent spelled out in another (in the position where it ends up). More generally, it suggests that (in certain structures) there is a choice regarding which part of a movement chain gets deleted (an idea developed in Bobaljik 1995; Brody 1995; Groat and O'Neil 1996; Pesetsky 1997, 1998; Richards 1997; Roberts 1997; Runner 1998; Nunes 1999; Cormack and Smith 1999; and Bošković 2001). A further possibility which this opens up is that wh-in-situ structures may involve a moved wh-expression being spelled out in its initial position (at the foot of the movement chain) rather than in its final position (at the head of the movement chain): see Pesetsky (2000) and Reintges, LeSourd and Chung (2002) for analyses of this ilk, and Watanabe (2001) for a more general discussion of wh-in-situ structures.

A further piece of evidence in support of the copy account of wh-movement comes from the fact that an overt copy of a moved pronoun may sometimes appear at its extraction site – as (19) below illustrates (the % sign indicating that only a certain percentage of speakers accept such sentences):

(19) (a)   *He is someone [**who** I don't know anyone [that likes ~~who~~]]
      (b)   %He is someone [**who** I don't know anyone [that likes *him*]]

The sentences in (19) contain two bracketed relative clauses, one modifying *some-one* and the other modifying *anyone*. The word *who* here is a **relative pronoun** which is initially merged as the complement of the verb *likes*, but undergoes wh-movement and is thereby moved out of the relative clause containing *likes* to the front of the relative clause containing *know*. What we'd expect to happen is that the copy of *who* left behind at the extraction site receives a null spellout: but this leads to ungrammaticality in (19a), for the following reason. To use a colourful metaphor developed by Ross (1967), relative clauses are **islands**, in the sense that they are structures which are impervious to certain types of grammatical operation. Let's suppose that islands have the property that a copy of a moved constituent cannot be given a null spellout if the copy is inside an island and its antecedent lies outside the island: this condition prevents the italicised copy of ~~who~~ from receiving a null spellout in (19a), because it is contained within a relative clause island (namely the *that*-clause) and its bold-printed moved counterpart **who** lies outside the island. Some speakers resolve this problem by spelling out the copy overtly as *him*. Still, this raises the question of why they should spell out a copy of *who* as *him* rather than as *who*. Pesetsky (1997, 1998) argues that this is because of a principle which requires copies of moved constituents to be as close to unpronounceable as possible. Where islandhood constraints prevent a completely null spellout, the minimal overt spellout is simply to spell out the person/number/gender/case properties of the expression – hence the use of the third-person-masculine-singular accusative pronoun *him* in (19b).

Further evidence that wh-movement leaves behind a copy which is subsequently deleted comes from speech errors involving **wh-copying**, e.g. in relative clauses such as that bracketed below:

(20)   It's a world record [**which** many of us thought *which* wasn't on the books at all] (Athletics commentator, BBC2 TV)

What's the nature of the speech error made by the tongue-tied (or brain-drained) BBC reporter in (20)? The answer is that when moving the relative pronoun *which* from its initial italicised position to its subsequent bold-printed position, our intrepid reporter successfully merges a copy of *which* in the bold-printed position, but fails to delete the original occurrence of *which* in the italicised position. Such speech errors provide us with further evidence that wh-movement is a composite operation involving both copying and deletion.

A different kind of argument in support of positing that a moved wh-expression leaves behind a null copy comes from the semantics of wh-questions. Chomsky (1981, p. 324) argues that a wh-question like (21a) below has a semantic representation (more precisely, a **Logical Form/LF representation**) which can be shown informally as in (21b) below, with (21b) being paraphraseable as 'Of which x (such that x is a person) is it true that she was dating x?':

(21) (a)   Who was she dating?
    (b)   Which x (x a person), she was dating x

In the **LF representation** (21b), the quantifier *which* functions as an interrogative **operator** which serves to **bind** the **variable** x. Since a grammar must compute a semantic representation for each syntactic structure which it **generates/** forms, important questions arise about how syntactic representations are to be **mapped**/converted into semantic representations. One such question is how a syntactic structure like (21a) can be mapped into an LF representation like (21b) containing an operator binding a variable. If a moved wh-expression leaves behind a copy, (21a) will have the syntactic structure (4) above which is repeated in simplified form (omitting all details not immediately relevant to the discussion at hand) in (22) below (where ~~who~~ is a null trace copy of the preposed wh-word *who*):

(22)   *Who* was she dating ~~who~~?

The LF-representation for (21a) can be derived from the syntactic representation (22) in a straightforward fashion if the copy ~~who~~ in (22) is given an LF interpretation as a variable bound by the quantifier *which*.

The assumption that a wh-copy (i.e. a copy of a moved wh-expression) has the semantic function of a variable which is bound by a wh-quantifier has interesting implications for the syntax of wh-movement. In §3.8, we noted that there is a c-command condition on binding to the effect that one constituent X can only bind another constituent Y if X c-commands Y. If we look at the structure produced by wh-movement, we find that it always results in a structure in which the moved wh-expression c-commands (by virtue of occurring higher up in the structure than) its copy. For example, in our earlier structure (4) above, the moved wh-pronoun *who* c-commands its copy ~~who~~ by virtue of the fact that *who* is contained within (and hence a constituent of) the C-bar *was she ~~was~~ dating ~~who~~* which is the sister of the PRN-node containing the moved wh-pronoun *who*. It would therefore seem that a core syntactic property of wh-movement (namely the fact that it always moves a wh-expression into a *higher* position within the structure containing it) follows from a semantic requirement – namely the requirement that a wh-copy (by virtue of its semantic function as a variable) must be bound by a c-commanding wh-expression (which has the semantic function of an operator expression). Given their semantic function as operators, wh-words are sometimes referred to as **wh-operators**; likewise, wh-expressions are sometimes referred to as **operator expressions**, and wh-movement as **operator movement**.

A related semantic argument in support of the copy theory of movement is formulated by Chomsky (1995) in relation to the interpretation of sentences such as:

(23)   Joe wonders which picture of himself Jim bought

In (23), the reflexive anaphor *himself* can refer either to *Joe* or to *Jim*. An obvious problem posed by the latter interpretation is that a reflexive has to be c-commanded by a local antecedent (one contained within the same TP, as we saw in §3.7), and yet *Jim* does not c-command *himself* in (23). How can we account for the dual interpretation of *himself*? Chomsky argues that the copy theory of movement provides a principled answer to this question. The QP *which picture of himself* is initially merged as the complement of the verb *bought* but is subsequently moved to the front of the *bought* clause, leaving behind a copy in its original position, so deriving the structure shown in skeletal form in (24) below:

(24)   [CP [TP Joe wonders [CP **which picture of himself** [TP Jim bought *which picture of himself*]]]]

Although the italicised copy of the QP *which picture of himself* gets deleted in the PF component, Chomsky argues that copies of moved constituents remain visible in the semantic component, and that binding conditions apply to LF representations. If (24) is the LF representation of (23), the possibility of *himself* referring to *Jim* can be attributed to the fact that the italicised occurrence of *himself* is c-commanded by (and contained within the same TP as) *Jim* at LF. On the other hand, the possibility of *himself* referring to *Joe* can be attributed to the fact that the bold-printed occurrence of **himself** is c-commanded by (and occurs within the same TP as) *Joe*.

In this section, we have seen that there is a range of empirical evidence which supports the claim that a constituent which undergoes wh-movement leaves behind a copy at its extraction site. This copy is normally given a null spell-out in the PF component, though we have seen that copies may sometimes have an overt spellout, or indeed part of a moved phrase may be spelled out in one position, and part in another. We have also seen that copies of moved wh-constituents are visible in the semantic component, and play an important role in relation to the interpretation of anaphors.

6.4   Wh-movement, EPP and the Attract Closest Principle

An important question raised by the analysis outlined above is what triggers wh-movement. Chomsky (1998, 1999, 2001) suggests that an [**EPP**] **feature** is the mechanism which drives movement of wh-expressions to spec-CP.

More specifically, he maintains that just as T in finite clauses carries an [EPP] feature requiring it to be extended into a TP projection containing a subject as its specifier, so too C in wh-questions carries an [EPP] feature requiring it to be extended into a CP projection containing a wh-expression as its specifier. Some evidence that complementisers can indeed have an [EPP] feature comes from sentences like (25b) below:

(25) (a)   *There* has been a riot
     (b)   He prevented *there* from being a riot

If we suppose that expletive *there* is inserted in a sentence like (25a) in order to satisfy an [EPP] feature carried by T, and if we further suppose (in the light of arguments offered by Landau 2002) that *from* is a complementiser in structures like (25b), it seems plausible to suppose that *there* is used in (25b) to satisfy an [EPP] feature carried by the complementiser *from*. More generally, the [EPP] feature of a head H requires H to have a specifier which matches one or more of the features carried by H: so, for example, since a finite T carries person and number features, its [EPP] feature requires it to have a subject with matching person and/or number features; and if we assume that C in a wh-clause contains a [WH] feature, this will mean that its [EPP] feature requires it to have a wh-specifier.

We can illustrate how the EPP analysis of wh-movement works by looking at the derivation of the bracketed interrogative complement clause in (26) below:

(26)   He wants to know [where you are going]

The bracketed wh-question clause in (26) is derived as follows. The verb *going* is merged with its complement *where* (which is a locative adverbial pronoun) to form the VP *going where*. The present-tense auxiliary *are* is then merged with the resulting VP to form the T-bar *are going where*. The pronoun *you* is in turn merged with this T-bar to form the TP *you are going where*. A null complementiser [c ø] is subsequently merged with the resulting TP. Since the relevant clause is a wh-question, C contains a [WH] feature. In addition, since English (unlike Chinese) is the kind of language which requires wh-movement in ordinary wh-questions, C also has an [EPP] feature requiring it to have a specifier. Given these assumptions, merging C with its TP complement will form the C-bar in (27) below (where features are CAPITALISED and enclosed within square brackets):

(27)

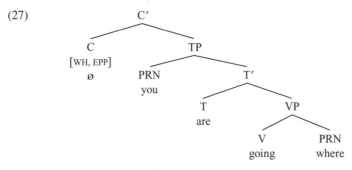

(A minor descriptive detail is that the locative adverbial pronoun *where* is categorised here as a PRN/pronoun, though it could equally be assigned to the category ADV/adverb.) The [WH] feature of C allows C to attract a wh-expression. The [EPP] feature of C requires C to project as its specifier an expression which has a feature which **matches** some feature of C: since C carries a [WH] feature, this amounts to a requirement that C must project a wh-specifier. On the assumption that the wh-pronoun *where* carries a [WH] feature, this means that C will **attract** the wh-pronoun *where* to move from the VP-complement position which it occupies in (27) above to CP-specifier position. If we suppose that the [WH] and [EPP] features carried by C are deleted (and thereby inactivated) once their requirements are satisfied (deletion being indicated by ~~strikethrough~~), we derive the structure (28) below (assuming, too, that the phonological features of the trace of the moved wh-constituent *where* are also deleted):

(28)

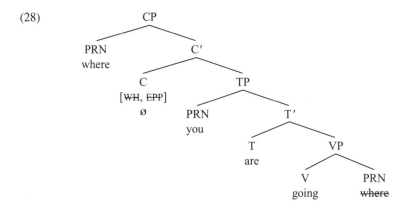

There is no auxiliary inversion (hence no movement of the auxiliary *are* from T to C) because (28) is a complement clause, and an interrogative C only carries a [TNS] feature triggering auxiliary inversion in main clauses.

Chomsky (2001) maintains that *movement* is simply another form of *merger*. He refers to merger operations which involve taking an item out of the **lexical array** and merging it with some other constituent as **external merge**, and to movement operations by which an item contained within an existing structure is moved to a new position as **internal merge**. Accordingly, the structure (27) is created by a series of external merger operations, and is then mapped into (28) by an internal merger operation (namely wh-movement).

The EPP analysis of wh-movement has interesting implications for the syntax of **multiple wh-questions** which contain two or more separate wh-expressions. (See Dayal 2002 for discussion of the semantic properties of such questions.) A salient syntactic property of such questions in English is that only *one* of the wh-expressions can be preposed – as we see from the fact that in the bracketed interrogative clauses in (29) below, only *who* can be preposed and not *what*:

(29) (a)   I wonder [*who* he might think has done **what**]
     (b)   *I wonder [*who* **what** he might think has done]
     (c)   *I wonder [**what** *who* he might think has done]
     (d)   *I wonder [**what** might he think *who* has done]

In order to get a clearer picture of what is going on in the bracketed complement clause here, let's consider what happens when we arrive at the stage of derivation shown in (30) below:

(30)

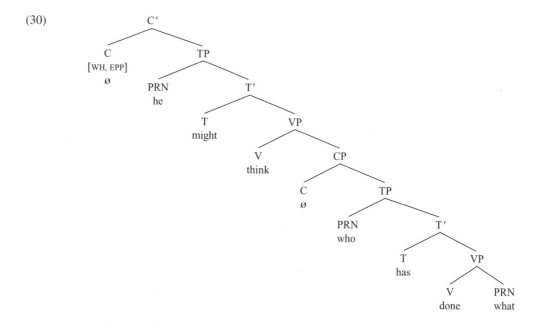

By hypothesis, the null complementiser [c ø] at the root/top of the tree contains a [WH] feature requiring the clause to contain a wh-expression, and an [EPP] feature requiring it to have a specifier matching the [WH] feature carried by C (i.e. to have a wh-specifier). In order to satisfy this requirement, C searches for a wh-expression within the C-bar structure immediately containing it in (30). Since it is *who* rather than *what* which is preposed in (30) and since *who* is closer to C than *what*, let's suppose that C attracts the *closest* wh-expression which it c-commands. This requirement is a consequence of a principle of Universal Grammar (adapted from Chomsky 1995, p. 297) which we can outline informally as follows:

(31)   **Attract Closest Principle/ACP**
         A head which attracts a given kind of constituent attracts the *closest*
         constituent of the relevant kind

(Chomsky 1995, p. 311 proposes an analogous principle which he terms the **Minimal Link Condition** and formulates it thus: 'K attracts α only if there is no β, β closer to K than α, such that K attracts β.') It follows from **ACP** that a C carrying [WH, EPP] features will trigger movement of the **closest** constituent carrying a wh-feature to C. So, since *who* appears to be closer to C than *what* in (30), it is *who* which is attracted to move to spec-CP. Using rather different but equivalent terminology, sentences like (29) can be said to show a **superiority effect** in that C has to attract the 'highest' constituent of the relevant type. An alternative to the ACP account is to suppose that the relevant effect is a consequence of an **Intervention Constraint** to the effect that in a structure of the form [...X...[...Y...[...Z...]]] X cannot attract Z if there is a constituent Y of the same type as Z which intervenes between X and Z: on this view, the presence of *who* intervening between C and *what* in (30) prevents C from attracting *what* to move to spec-CP.

One question this raises, however, is how we determine whether *who* or *what* is closer to C. At first sight, it might seem as if there is a simple way of doing this – namely by counting the number of nodes you have to go through if you try and get from one constituent to the other by climbing along the branches of the tree. In order to get from the C node containing the null complementiser to the PRN node containing *who*, we have to go through six other nodes (C-bar, TP, T-bar, VP, CP, TP), whereas in order to get from C to the PRN node containing *what* we have to go through eight other nodes (C-bar, TP, T-bar, VP, CP, TP, T-bar, VP): hence, this simple node-counting procedure tells us that *who* is closer to C than *what*, and consequently it is *who* which is attracted by C in (30) and not *what*, in accordance with the **Attract Closest Principle**.

However, the idea that grammars might employ a counting algorithm of some kind in order to determine how syntactic operations apply is implausible, since counting otherwise seems to play no part in syntax – for instance, we find no syntactic operations which target (e.g.) the fourth constituent in a sentence, or which invert the second and third constituents. Moreover, the notion of counting is alien to the spirit of Minimalism, which assumes that the only primitive relations in syntax are structural relations like **contain** and **c-command** which come about via merger. From a theoretical perspective, it is therefore preferable to define relative closeness in terms of structural relations. There are a variety of ways of doing this (see Fitzpatrick 2002), but for present purposes we can make the following assumption (where X, Y and Z are three different constituents):

(32)   X is closer to Y than to Z if X c-commands both Y and Z, and Z is
              contained within some maximal projection which does not contain Y.

If we take X to be the main clause C in (30), Y to be *who* and Z to be *what*, we can see that *who* is closer to the main-clause C than *what* in terms of the definition of closeness in (32) because C c-commands both *who* and *what* but *what* is contained within a maximal projection (= the VP *done what*) which does not contain *who*. In consequence, the **Attract Closest Principle** (31) correctly predicts that *what* cannot undergo wh-movement in (30), but *who* can, with *who* thereby moving into spec-CP and deriving the structure shown below (assuming deletion of the [WH] and [EPP] features of C, and of the trace copy of the moved pronoun *who*):

(33)

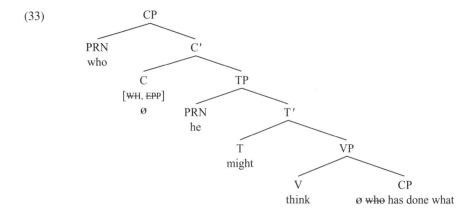

In short, the assumption that C carries [WH] and [EPP] features, in conjunction with the **Attract Closest Principle** (31) and the ancillary assumption that the [EPP] and [WH] features of C are deleted (and thereby inactivated) once a wh-expression has been moved to spec-CP, accounts for the pattern of grammaticality found in multiple wh-questions like (29). (Note that our focus on English here means that we do not deal with languages like Bulgarian which allow multiple wh-fronting: see Grewendorf 2001 and Bošković 2002a for alternative accounts of multiple wh-fronting.)

6.5   Explaining what moves where

Our discussion in the previous section looked at wh-movement in interrogative complement clauses which involve movement of a wh-word (rather than a wh-phrase), and which don't involve auxiliary inversion. But now consider how we handle the syntax of main-clause wh-questions like (34) below which involve both movement of a wh-phrase and movement of an auxiliary:

(34)   Which assignment have you done?

Let's suppose that the derivation of (34) proceeds as follows. The quantifier *which* merges with the noun *assignment* to form the QP *which assignment*. This in turn is merged with the verb *done* to form the VP *done which assignment*. The resulting VP is subsequently merged with the present-tense auxiliary *have* to form the T-bar *have done which assignment*, which is itself merged with the pronoun *you* to form the TP *you have done which assignment*. TP is then merged with a null interrogative C. Since (34) is a wh-question, C will carry a [WH] feature and an [EPP] feature. Since (34) is a main-clause question, we can assume (as in the previous chapter) that C also carries a [TNS] feature which triggers movement of a tensed auxiliary from T to C. Given these assumptions, merging C with the TP *you have done which assignment* will derive the following structure:

(35)

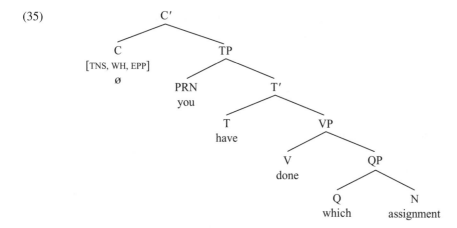

At first sight, the derivation might seem straightforward from this point on: the [TNS] feature of C attracts the present-tense auxiliary *have* to attach to a null question affix in C; the [WH, EPP] features of C trigger movement of the wh-expression *which assignment* to the specifier position within CP. Assuming that all the features of C are deleted (and thereby inactivated) once their requirements are satisfied, the relevant movement operations will derive the structure shown in simplified form below:

(36)

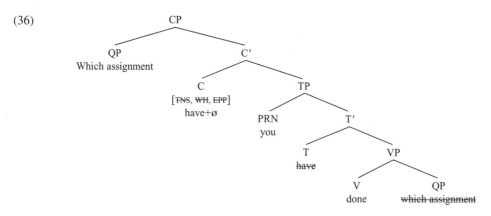

Since the resulting sentence (34) *Which assignment have you done?* is grammatical, things appear to work out exactly as required.

But if we probe a little deeper, we'll see that there are a number of questions raised by the derivation outlined above. The core assumptions underlying it are the following:

(37) (i)   The [TNS] and [WH] features of C attract a constituent whose head carries a matching [TNS] and [WH] feature respectively

   (ii)   The [EPP] feature of C requires a constituent matching one of the features of C to be merged in spec-CP

   (iii)   Minimal and maximal projections (though not intermediate projections) can undergo movement

But while the assumptions made in (37) are perfectly compatible with the derivation assumed in (36), they raise important questions about what kind of constituent moves to what kind of position and why.

One such question is why the [TNS] feature of C in (35) attracts [T *have*] rather than [TP *you have done which assignment*]. We can offer a principled answer to this question by supposing that a head which carries a feature [F] can freely attract either a minimal or a maximal projection carrying [F], but that UG principles rule out certain possibilities. From this perspective, we would expect that the [TNS] feature of C can in principle attract either T or TP (and indeed both are equally close to C in terms of the definition of closeness in (32) above), and if in practice C cannot attract TP, this is because some UG principle rules out this possibility. One reason why C cannot attract its TP complement may be that movement is an operation by which a head attracts (and is thereby merged with) a constituent *which it is not already merged with*. Since TP is already merged with C by virtue of being the complement of C, it follows that C cannot attract TP. The tacit assumption underlying our reasoning here is that UG incorporates a principle such as the following:

(38)   **Remerger Constraint**
No constituent can be merged more than once with the same head.

As we saw earlier, [TP *you have done which assignment*] is initially merged with C at the stage of derivation when the structure shown in (35) above is formed. To subsequently move TP into spec-CP would involve merging TP as the specifier of C – and this would violate the **Remerger Constraint** (38), since it would mean that TP was initially merged with C as its complement, and subsequently remerged with C as its specifier. By contrast, the Remerger Constraint would not prevent C from attracting [T *have*], since *have* is not merged with C prior to T-to-C movement: on the contrary, *have* was initially merged with its VP complement *done which assignment* and its pronoun specifier *you*, so that merging (a copy of) *have* with C does not violate the constraint against remerger. In short, we can account for why C attracts T rather than TP in terms of a UG principle like (38) barring remerger operations.

A follow-up question is why a tensed auxiliary attracted by C moves into C rather than into spec-CP. A plausible answer to this question is that UG principles determine the **landing site** of moved constituents (i.e. determine where they end up being positioned). For concreteness, let's assume that UG incorporates a principle along the lines of (39) below:

(39)   **Constituent Structure Constraint**
(i) Only a head (i.e. minimal projection) can occupy a head position
(ii) Only a maximal projection can occupy a specifier or complement position

(39i) would mean that the head T constituent of TP (by virtue of being a minimal projection) can only move to the head C position of CP, not to the specifier position within CP. (Chomsky 1995, p. 253 offers an alternative account based on chain uniformity, and Carnie 2000 discusses attendant problems.)

Now consider the question of why the [WH] feature of C attracts the QP *which assignment* rather than the Q *which*. Given our earlier assumptions, we'd expect that the [WH] feature carried by C can in principle attract either a wh-word or a wh-phrase. However, the [EPP] feature carried by C requires C to project a specifier, and (39ii) tells us that a specifier position can only be filled by a maximal projection. Since we have already seen that the **Remerger Constraint** (38) prevents C from attracting TP to move to spec-CP, the only way of satisfying the [EPP] requirement is for a wh-constituent to be moved into spec-CP; and since (39ii) tells us that only a maximal projection can occupy a specifier position, it follows that the [WH] feature of C attracts a wh-marked maximal projection like *which assignment* to move into spec-CP, not a wh-marked minimal projection like *which*. (Note, however, that the story told here for English needs to be modified for languages which allow certain types of wh-word to move to C, as would seem to be the case for Polish data in Borsley 2002, German data in Kathol 2001, and North Norwegian data in Radford 1994: it may be that C in such languages has an [EDGE] feature requiring a wh-expression to move to the **edge** of C rather than an [EPP] feature requiring a wh-expression to move to spec-CP.)

The story told above assumes that UG principles like the **Remerger Constraint** (38) and the **Constituent Structure Constraint** (39) determine that the [TNS] feature of C attracts movement of a tensed auxiliary to C, and that the [WH, EPP] features of C attract movement of a wh^{MAX} (i.e. a wh-marked maximal projection) to spec-CP. However, an entirely different approach to the problem of accounting for why the [TNS] and [WH] features of C attract different types of constituent to move to different positions in English is to posit that they are different types of feature which trigger different types of movement operation in different components of the grammar. For example, if the [TNS] feature on C is essentially affixal in nature, we could conclude that head movement operations like T-to-C movement are intrinsically morphological in nature (in that they are designed to provide an affix with a host), and hence take place in the PF component rather than the syntactic component – a possibility explored by Chomsky (1999, pp. 30–1). Chomsky notes that some evidence in support of such a hypothesis comes from the fact that head movement has rather different properties from typical syntactic movement operations like wh-movement. For example, head movement can attract only heads whereas wh-movement can attract maximal projections; head movement is a strictly local operation (whereby a head can attract the head of its complement), whereas wh-movement can attract more distant constituents (e.g. C can attract a wh-constituent which originates within a lower clause, as in (30) and (33) above); head movement involves a form of affixation operation by which one head is affixed to another (forming a compound head), whereas wh-movement is a merger operation by which a moved constituent is merged as the specifier of C; and conversely wh-movement has an effect on semantic interpretation (in that it creates an operator-variable configuration as we noted in relation to (21) above), whereas auxiliary inversion does not. These differences (Chomsky reasons) suggest that features like the [WH] feature of C are syntactic features triggering movement of a maximal projection in the syntax, whereas features like the [TNS] feature of C are morphological features triggering movement of a minimal projection in the PF component. (See Boeckx and Stjepanović 2001 for an additional argument for head movement being a PF operation, and Baltin 2002 for a rebuttal.)

Perceptive though Chomsky's observations are, they are suggestive rather than conclusive (see Embick and Noyer 2001 for a sceptical view). For example, his claim that head movement is a PF operation because it has no effect on semantic interpretation has little force if we assume that the semantic component interprets the tense properties of clauses by looking at the tense properties of the head T constituent of TP – and cares little whether what is in T is an overt auxiliary or a null copy of a moved auxiliary. Likewise, the argument that head movement is subject to a strict locality constraint like HMC is called into question by Hagstrom's (1998) analysis of wh-questions in wh-in-situ languages (like Japanese, Okinawan, Navajo and Sinhala) in which he claims that they involve long-distance head movement of a question particle to C. Hagstrom proposes to abandon HMC, and argues that the apparent locality of head movement is an artefact of the **Attract Closest Principle/ACP** (31). On this view, local (successive-cyclic) movement of the verb *say* from V to T to C in a Shakespearean sentence such as:

(40)   What said she? (Proteus, *The Two Gentlemen of Verona*, I.i)

will be a consequence of ACP rather than HMC. For example, if T has a strong V-feature and C has a strong T-feature (as we assumed in the previous chapter), T will attract the closest verb (i.e. the head V *said* of the VP *said what*) to move to T, and C will attract the closest tensed head (i.e. the head T constituent of TP, with T containing the moved verb *said* at the relevant stage of derivation) to move to C – thereby guaranteeing local head movement without the need for positing HMC. In short, the question of whether head movement is a syntactic operation (as argued by Roberts 2002) or a PF operation (as argued by Chomsky 1999) or has facets of both (as argued by Zwart 2001) is one which remains open at present.

6.6   Wh-subject questions

Underlying the analyses we have presented so far in this chapter is the assumption that questions in English have the following syntactic properties:

(41) (i)   Interrogative clauses are CPs headed by a C with [WH, EPP] features
     (ii)   C in root/main interrogative clauses also has an affixal [TNS] feature

The [WH, EPP] features of C trigger movement of a wh-expression to spec-CP; and the affixal [TNS] feature carried by C in main-clause questions triggers movement of an auxiliary or tense affix from T to C (with a moved tense affix requiring concomitant DO-support, as we saw in §5.8).

However, the assumptions made in (41) raise interesting questions about how we account for the contrast in (42) below:

(42) (a)   Who'd the police call? ('$d = did$)   (b) *Who the police called?
     (c)   Who called the police?   (d) *Who'd call the police? ('$d = did$)

(42a,b) are wh-object questions, in the sense that the preposed interrogative expression *who* is the direct object complement of the verb *call*; as would be expected from the assumption in (41ii) that C in main-clause questions carries an affixal [TNS] feature, they require T-to-C movement and concomitant DO-support. By contrast, (42c,d) are wh-subject questions, in the sense that *who* is the subject of the verb *call*; contrary to what (41ii) would lead us to expect, wh-subject questions do not allow T-to-C movement and DO-support. (More precisely, DO can be used if it is emphatic, receives contrastive stress and is spelled out as the full form *did* – as in *Who DID call the police?* with capitals marking contrastive stress.) Why should this be?

One answer to this question (different versions of which are suggested in Radford 1997a and Agbayani 2000) is the following. Let's suppose that T-to-C movement (and concomitant DO-support) is only found in questions in which a wh-expression moves to spec-CP. In wh-object questions like (42a,b) it is clear that the wh-pronoun *who* moves to spec-CP, since it is the object of the verb *call* and if it had not moved to spec-CP, it would have been positioned after the verb (as in the echo question *The police called who?*). But in wh-subject questions like (42c,d) it is by no means clear that the wh-pronoun *who* has moved into spec-CP, since even if it remained in situ in spec-TP it would still end up as the first overt constituent in the sentence. Let's therefore consider the possibility that in sentences like (42c,d) where a wh-expression is the subject of the overall interrogative clause, the wh-expression remains in situ in spec-TP and does not move to spec-CP. If T-to-C movement and concomitant DO-support are only found in questions which involve movement of a wh-expression to spec-CP, and if wh-subject questions do not involve wh-movement to spec-CP, we can seemingly account for the absence of DO-support in wh-subject questions like (42c,d).

On this view, the derivation of (42c) would proceed as follows. The determiner *the* merges with the noun *police* to form the DP *the police*. This DP is then merged with the verb *call* to form the VP *call the police*. The resulting VP is in turn merged with a past-tense affix *Tns*, forming the T-bar *Tns call the police*. This T-bar is then merged with the pronoun *who*, forming the TP *who Tns call the police*. If we follow Agbayani (2000) in supposing that all interrogative clauses are CPs, the resulting TP will be merged with an interrogative C to form the CP shown in simplified form below:

(43)

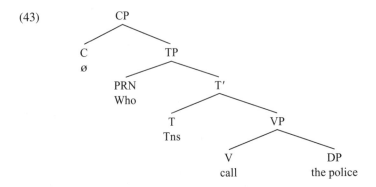

The past-tense affix in T will be lowered onto the main verb by Affix Hopping in the PF component, so that the verb is spelled out as *called* in (42c) *Who called the police?*

However, the spec-TP analysis of wh-subjects outlined in (43) above raises a number of questions. For example, why isn't the wh-pronoun *who* in (43) attracted to move to spec-CP and why isn't there any T-to-C movement if C always has [TNS, WH, EPP] features in main-clause questions as claimed in (41) above? Maintaining the claim in (41) that C in main-clause questions always has [TNS, WH, EPP] features at the same time as maintaining the wh-in-situ analysis of wh-subject questions in (43) is going to require considerable ingenuity: for example, we might suppose that the [TNS, WH, EPP] features of C only trigger wh-movement and T-to-C movement when the relevant wh-expression is c-commanded by T. This would mean that C triggers both wh-movement and T-to-C movement in a structure like (35) because the closest wh-expression to C (= *which assignment*) is c-commanded by T; but it would also mean that there is neither wh-movement nor T-to-C movement in a structure like (43) because the closest wh-expression to C (= *who*) is not c-commanded by T. However, even this (somewhat contrived) analysis leaves us without a principled explanation of how the [TNS, WH, EPP] features of C are deleted in a structure like (43) which shows neither wh-movement nor T-to-C movement.

Moreover, the core assumption underlying the analysis in (43) above (viz. that the wh-subject remains in spec-TP in wh-subject questions like (42c) *Who called the police?*) is called into question by the observation by Pesetsky and Torrego (2001) that *who* in (42c) can be substituted by *who on earth* or *who the hell*:

(44) (a)   *Who on earth* called the police?
    (b)   *Who the hell* called the police?

As Pesetsky (1987) notes (and as the examples in (45) below illustrate), wh-expressions like *who on earth* and *who the hell* have the property that they cannot remain in situ, but rather must move to spec-CP:

(45) (a)   *Who on earth/Who the hell* is she going out with?
    (b)   *She is going out with *who on earth/who the hell*?

If wh-expressions like those italicised in (45) always move to spec-CP, it follows that the italicised subjects in (44) must likewise have moved to spec-CP – and hence it is plausible to suppose that the same is true of the subject *who* in (42c) *Who called the police?* (See den Dikken and Giannakidou 2002 for more detailed discussion of the syntax and semantics of expressions like *who the hell?*)

Let's therefore follow Pesetsky and Torrego in taking all wh-questions (including wh-subject questions) to be CPs which show movement of a wh-expression to spec-CP. In particular, let's suppose that after the TP *who Tns call the police* has been formed, it is merged with an interrogative C constituent which carries [TNS, WH, EPP] features, so forming the structure in (46) below (cf. (43) above):

(46)

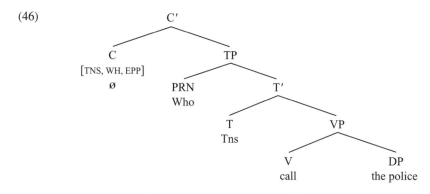

What we might expect to happen at this point is for the [WH, EPP] features of C to attract *who* to move to spec-CP, and for the [TNS] feature of C to attract movement of the *Tns* affix from T to C, with the dummy auxiliary *do* being attached to the affix in the PF component in order to provide it with a host. But such a derivation would wrongly predict that (42d) *Who'd call the police?* is grammatical on the relevant interpretation (where *'d* is a contracted form of *did*). So it would seem that the [TNS] feature of C does not attract the head T constituent of TP. So what does it attract?

The answer given by Pesetsky and Torrego is that the [WH] and [TNS] features of C *both* attract the nominative wh-pronoun *who*, with the [EPP] feature of C ensuring that *who* moves to spec-CP. A key assumption underlying Pesetsky and Torrego's analysis is that the word *who* (by virtue of being the subject of a tensed clause) carries a *tense* feature as well as a wh-feature. More specifically, they posit that agreement between T and its subject involves not only copying the person/number features of the subject onto T but also (conversely) copying the tense feature of T onto the subject. This is far from implausible from a cross-linguistic perspective, since in languages like Chamicuro, tense is overtly marked on subjects, as the following example (from Parker 1999, p. 552) shows:

(47)   Y-alíyo ka   ké:ni
        3-fall   the$_{PAST}$ rain
        'The rain fell' = 'It rained'

In (47), the head D *ka* 'the' of the subject DP *ka ké:ni* 'the rain' is a *past-tense* determiner (the corresponding non-past determiner being *na*), providing clear evidence of tense-marking on the subject. If tense-marking of subjects also takes place in English, we can assume that a tensed T will have a tensed subject, so that *who* in *Who called the police?* will be a *past-tense* subject by virtue of being the subject of a past-tense T. Now, at first sight this might seem implausible, since *who* doesn't carry the regular past-tense suffix *-d*: however, this is because *-d* is a *verbal* suffix which attaches only to (regular) verbs, hence not to a pronoun like *who*. Pesetsky and Torrego claim that the tense feature carried by the subject of a tensed clause in English is manifested as *nominative case*, so that a *nominative* subject is really a subject carrying a tense feature. On this view, *who* in (42c) *Who called the police?* will carry a tense feature which causes the subject pronoun to be spelled out as the tensed (nominative) form *who*, rather than as the accusative form *whom* or the genitive form *whose*.

In the light of these assumptions, let's return to the stage of derivation we reached in (46) above. As assumed in (41), C in a main-clause question carries [TNS], [WH] and [EPP] features: the [TNS] feature of C requires C to attract a tensed constituent to move to the edge of CP, its [WH] feature requires the relevant structure to contain a wh-marked constituent, and its [EPP] feature requires C to project a specifier carrying a feature matching one of the features of C. One way of satisfying these requirements would be to move *who* from spec-TP to spec-CP, and move (a copy of) the tense affix in T to C (using DO-support to provide a host for the affix). However (as we have already seen), this would wrongly predict that a sentence like (42d) **Who'd call the police?* should be grammatical (where *'d* is a clitic form of *did*). Why should such a derivation (involving two movement operations, WH-MOVEMENT and T-TO-C MOVEMENT) lead to ungrammaticality? Pesetsky and Torrego's answer is that simply moving *who* from spec-TP to spec-CP on its own (without T-to-C movement) can satisfy the requirements of all three [TNS, WH, EPP] features of C, and economy considerations dictate that a derivation involving a single movement operation O should be preferred to one involving both O and an additional movement operation. Movement of *who* to spec-CP can satisfy the [WH] and [EPP] features of C because *who* carries a wh-feature and moves to spec-CP, and can at the same time satisfy the [TNS] feature of C because *who* carries a tense feature (by virtue of being the subject of a tensed clause). The resulting derived structure is as follows (with the arrow showing how wh-movement applies):

(48)

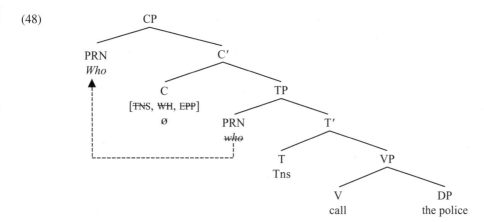

Since movement of the tensed wh-pronoun *who* to spec-CP is sufficient to satisfy the requirements of all three features carried by C, economy considerations dictate that T-TO-C MOVEMENT is unnecessary (hence not permitted) in wh-subject question structures, Pesetsky and Torrego reason. (An incidental detail is that the past-tense affix in T will subsequently be lowered onto the head V of VP in the PF component, with the result that the verb *call* is ultimately spelled out as the past-tense form *called*.)

Pesetsky and Torrego's analysis allows us to maintain the generalisation in (41) that all main-clause questions are CPs headed by a C constituent carrying [TNS, WH, EPP] features. In non-subject questions, the requirements of the [WH, EPP] features of C are met by moving a wh-expression into spec-CP, and the requirements of its [TNS] feature are met by T-to-C movement. But in questions where the attracted wh-expression is the subject of the interrogative clause, the requirements of all three features are met by moving the wh-subject *who* (which carries a tense feature by virtue of being the subject of a tensed T) into spec-CP.

6.7   Pied-piping

Our discussion of wh-movement in structures like (26/28) suggested that a C carrying [WH, EPP] features attracts a constituent headed by a wh-word to move to spec-CP. An interesting problem posed by this assumption is how we account for what happens in clauses like those bracketed in (49) below where an (italicised) wh-expression is the complement of a (bold-printed) preposition:

(49) (a)   They asked [*who* he was referring **to**]
     (b)   They asked [**to** *whom* he was referring]

In these examples, the wh-pronoun *who(m)* is the complement of the preposition *to* (*whom* being the accusative form of the pronoun in formal styles, *who* in other styles). In informal styles, the wh-pronoun *who* is preposed on its own, leaving the preposition *to* **stranded** or **orphaned** at the end of the bracketed complement clause – as in (49a). However, in formal styles, the preposition *to* is **pied-piped** (i.e. dragged) along with the wh-pronoun *whom*, so that the whole PP *to whom* moves to spec-CP position within the bracketed clause – as in (49b). (The **pied-piping** metaphor was coined by Ross 1967, based on a traditional fairy story in which the pied-piper in the village of Hamelin enticed a group of children to follow him out of a rat-infested village by playing his pipe.)

   Given the assumptions we have made hitherto, the bracketed interrogative complement clause in (49a) will be derived as follows. The preposition *to* merges with its pronoun complement *who* to form the PP *to who*. This in turn is merged with the verb *referring* to form the VP *referring to who*. This VP is then merged with the past-tense auxiliary *was*, forming the T-bar *was referring to who* which in turn is merged with its subject *he* to form the TP *he was referring to who*. Merging the resulting TP with a null interrogative complementiser carrying [WH, EPP] features will derive the structure shown in (50) below:

(50)

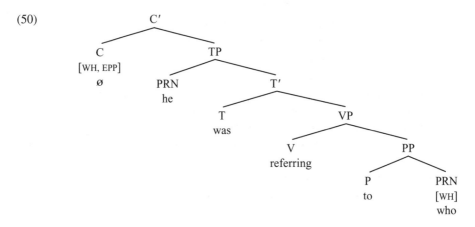

The [WH, EPP] features of C attract a wh-marked maximal projection to move to the specifier position within CP. Since the only wh-marked maximal projection in (50) is the wh-pronoun *who* (which is a maximal projection by virtue of being the largest expression headed by *who*) it follows that *who* will move to spec-CP (thereby deleting the [WH] and [EPP] features of C), so deriving the CP shown in simplified form below:

(51)

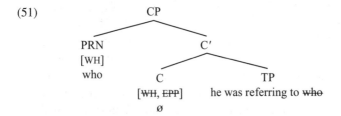

And (51) is the structure of the bracketed interrogative complement clause in (49a).

But what about the derivation of the bracketed complement clause in the formal-style sentence (49b) *They asked [to whom he was referring]*? How can we account for the fact that the whole prepositional phrase *to whom* is moved to the front of the complement clause in (49b), with the preposition *to* being pied-piped along with the wh-pronoun *whom*? One approach to preposition pied-piping is to assume that the head P *to* of the PP *to whom* carries a wh-feature which it acquires from the wh-word *whom* via some form of feature-copying: by virtue of being a projection of *to*, the PP *to whom* will then carry the same wh-feature as its head preposition *to*, and so can be attracted by the [WH] feature of C. This is a traditional idea underlying metaphorical claims in earlier work that a wh-feature can **percolate** from a complement onto a preposition, or conversely (to use the more funereal metaphor adopted by Sag 1997) that a preposition can **inherit** a wh-feature from its complement. Let's suppose that this kind of feature-copying comes about via merger, and that (in formal styles of English) a preposition is wh-marked when merged with a wh-complement (in the sense that the wh-feature on the pronoun is thereby copied onto the preposition).

In the light of this assumption, we can return to consider the derivation of the formal-style bracketed complement clause in (49b) *They asked [to whom he was referring]*. Since the complement of the preposition *to* in (49b) is the pronoun *whom* which contains a wh-feature, *to* will inherit this wh-feature via merger with *whom* in formal styles, and if it does, the bracketed complement clause in (49b) will have the structure shown in (52) below at the stage of derivation when C merges with its TP complement:

(52)

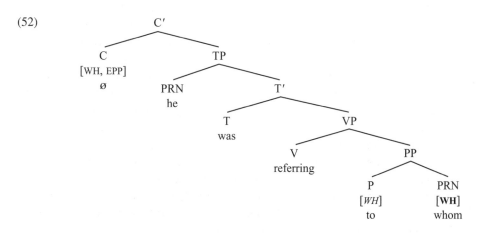

The PP *to whom* will consequently carry a [WH] feature (not shown here), by virtue of being the maximal projection of the wh-marked preposition *to*. Given the **Attract Closest Principle/ACP**, the [WH] feature of C will attract the *closest* wh-marked maximal projection c-commanded by C. Since the PP *to whom* is closer to C than the PRN *whom*, this means that the wh-marked PP *to whom* moves to spec-CP, so deriving the structure shown in simplified form below:

(53)

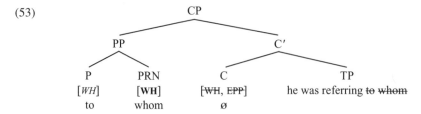

If wh-copying (between a preposition and its wh-object) and use of *whom* are both associated with formal styles of English, it follows that preposition pied-piping will occur with *whom* but not *who*. (But see Lasnik and Sobin 2000 for fuller discussion of the use of *whom* in present-day English.) Some evidence which might seem to support a feature-copying analysis of pied-piping comes from the observation made by Kishimoto (1992) that in Sinhala, a PP comprising a P and a wh-word has the question-particle *də* suffixed to the (P head of the) overall PP, even though the relevant particle normally attaches to a wh-word: if *də* attaches to a wh-marked constituent, this would be consistent with the view that the wh-feature on the wh-word percolates up to the head P of PP. (However, see Hagstrom 1998 for an alternative account.)

The feature-copying analysis of pied-piping outlined above has interesting ramifications for more complex cases of pied-piping, e.g. in sentences such as

(54)   *In the capital of which province* had the rebels hidden?

If (as we assumed in (37i) above) only a constituent with a wh-marked head can be attracted by a C carrying [WH, EPP] features, the story which we will have to tell about how the string *in the capital of* comes to be pied-piped along with the wh-QP *which province* will be the following. The preposition *of* is wh-marked by merger with its wh-complement *which province*, and the PP *of which province* thereby comes to carry the same wh-feature as its head. The noun *capital* is in turn wh-marked by merger with its wh-complement *of which province*, and the NP *capital of which province* carries the same wh-feature as its head. The determiner *the* is then wh-marked by merger with its wh-complement *capital of which province*, and the DP *the capital of which province* is thereby wh-marked as well. The preposition *in* is subsequently wh-marked by merger with its wh-complement *the capital of which province*, with the result that the whole PP *in the capital of which province* is wh-marked – and hence can be attracted by a C with a [WH] feature.

However, there are aspects of this feature-copying analysis which seem questionable. For example, the assumption that the wh-feature on the word *which* (via a series of merger operations) percolates onto *of, capital, the* and *in* raises the question of why none of these words shows any visible sign of being wh-marked. The proliferation of wh-features entailed by the analysis seems not only morphologically unmotivated but also (from the Minimalist perspective of trying to eliminate unnecessary descriptive apparatus) conceptually unattractive. More-over, if a [WH] feature can percolate from a complement to a head via merger, there seems nothing to prevent the [WH] feature on the preposition *in* spreading onto the verb *hidden* in (54) and thence onto its VP projection *hidden in the cap-ital of which province*, so triggering wh-movement of the VP headed by *hidden* and wrongly predicting that sentences like (55) below are ungrammatical:

(55)   *Hidden in the capital of which province* had the rebels?

Clearly, constraints have to be put on wh-percolation, but the nature of these constraints is not clear. For example, is it just nominal and prepositional heads which can be wh-marked via merger with a wh-complement – and if so, why?

Furthermore, it is by no means clear that the core assumption underlying the analysis (namely that a wh-marked C attracts a constituent with a wh-marked *head*) can be defended in relation to sentences like:

(56) (a)   *Whose car* did he borrow?
     (b)   *How many cars* do you own?

At first sight, there might seem to be no problem here: after all, why not simply assume that *whose* in (56a) is the head of *whose car* and that *how* in (56b) is the head of *how many cars* and hence that wh-movement targets a maximal projection headed by a wh-word like *whose/how*? However, the problem is that *whose* cannot be the head of *whose car* because *whose* carries genitive case and yet *whose car* is the complement of the transitive verb *borrow* and so must be accusative; and likewise *how* cannot be the head of *how many cars* because *how* is a degree adverb and yet *how many cars* is not an adverbial phrase but rather a quantifier phrase. It seems more plausible to take *whose* and *how* to be the specifiers of the expressions containing them, so that the relevant expressions have the structures shown in simplified form below:

(57)   (a)   DP   (b)   QP

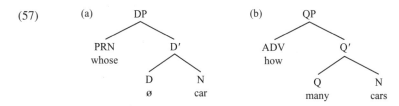

(57a) is adapted from Chomsky (1995, p. 263) and assumes that the head of the overall DP is a null definite determiner (a null counterpart of the D constituent *the*), so that (57a) has an interpretation paraphraseable as 'the car belonging to who'. (57b) claims that the overall structure is a plural nominal expression headed by the quantifier *many*, with *cars* serving as its complement and *how* as its specifier.

The crucial aspect of the analyses in (57a,b) from our perspective is that the wh-word *whose/how* is not the *head* of the overall DP/QP structure, but rather its *specifier*. This challenges the core assumption (37i) underlying the feature-copying analysis of pied-piping – namely that a wh-marked C attracts a constituent with a wh-marked *head*. Such an assumption would provide us with no account of why the overall nominals *whose car* and *how many cars* undergo wh-movement in (56), and not *who* and *how* on their own. Note that we cannot simply suppose that a phrase is a projection of the features carried by its specifier as well as those carried by its head, since this would wrongly predict (e.g.) that *whose car* (by virtue of having a genitive specifier) should be genitive – when it is accusative as used in (56a).

Let's therefore explore an entirely different approach to pied-piping – one which dispenses with the feature-copying apparatus we used above. Chomsky (1995, pp. 262–5) offers such an approach based on a principle which we can outline informally as follows:

(58)   **Convergence Principle**
A head which attracts a constituent containing a feature [F] attracts movement of the smallest accessible constituent containing [F] which will lead to a convergent (i.e. well-formed) derivation

This means that the [WH] feature on C attracts the smallest constituent containing a word carrying a [WH] feature whose movement will lead to a well-formed sentence. In the case of a sentence like (34) *Which assignment have you done?* the smallest constituent carrying a wh-feature is the wh-word *which* that is the head Q of the QP *which assignment*, and hence a minimal projection; but since the [EPP] feature of C requires C to project a specifier, and the Constituent Structure Constraint (39ii) tells us that only a maximal projection can occupy a specifier position, *which* cannot move on its own, so the next smallest constituent containing *which* has to move, namely the QP *which assignment*. Since this is a maximal projection, it can move to spec-CP without violation of any constraints.

Now consider how the convergence account handles preposition pied-piping in the bracketed relative clauses in (49a) *They asked [who he was referring to]* and (49b) *They asked [to whom he was referring]*. These would both have the structure (50) above at the point where C is merged with its TP complement, and the [WH] feature of C would attract the smallest constituent containing a wh-word which will ensure convergence. Since the smallest such constituent is the wh-pronoun *who*, it is *who* which is preposed in informal-style relative-clause structures like *who he was referring to* in (49a). But let's suppose that in formal styles of English, there is a **Stranding Constraint** which 'bars preposition stranding' (Chomsky 1995, p. 264). This means that (in formal styles) the wh-pronoun *whom* cannot be preposed on its own, since this would lead to violation of the Stranding Constraint. So, instead, the next smallest constituent containing the wh-word is preposed, namely the PP *to whom*.

The assumption that pied-piping of additional material along with a wh-word occurs only when it is forced by the need to ensure convergence offers us an interesting account of pied-piping in sentences such as (59b–e) below, which are wh-movement counterparts of the wh-in-situ question in (59a):

(59) (a)   You had thought a picture of whose mother was on the mantelpiece?
    (b)   *Whose had you thought a picture of mother was on the mantelpiece?
    (c)   ??Whose mother had you thought a picture of was on the mantelpiece?
    (d)   ??Of whose mother had you thought a picture was on the mantelpiece?
    (e)   *Picture of whose mother had you thought a was on the mantelpiece?
    (f)   A picture of whose mother had you thought was on the mantelpiece?

At the stage of derivation where the main-clause C is merged with its TP complement, (59b–f) will have the structure shown in simplified form below (if we take the indefinite article *a* to be a determiner rather than a quantifier):

(60)

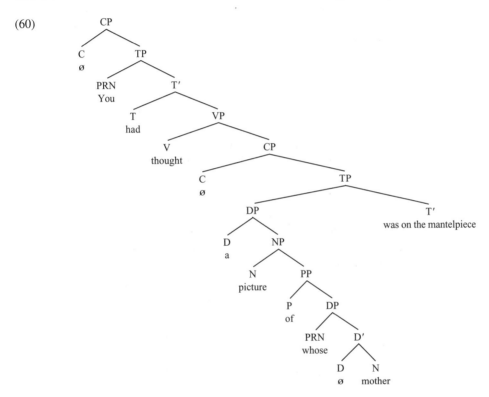

The main-clause C constituent at the top of the tree contains an affixal [TNS] feature which attracts the tensed auxiliary *had* to move to C, and [WH, EPP] features which attract the smallest convergent constituent containing a wh-word to move to spec-CP. Let's look carefully at what happens.

Movement of the pronoun *whose* on its own in (59b) leads to ungrammaticality, and the obvious question to ask is why this should be. (Part of) the answer lies in a constraint identified by Ross (1967), termed the **Left Branch Condition**, which we can paraphrase loosely as in (61) below:

(61)   **Left Branch Condition/LBC**
        In languages like English, the leftmost constituent of a nominal, adjectival, or adverbial expression cannot be extracted out of the expression containing it

(The term *nominal expression* can be taken to refer to DP/QP. Within an order-free theory of syntax, the term *leftmost* should be reformulated in terms of some hierarchical counterpart like *daughter* – but this is a detail we set aside here.) **LBC** accounts for the ungrammaticality of structures such as those below in English (where the italicised wh-word is intended to modify the bold-printed expression):

(62) (a)   **Whose* are you dating **girlfriend**?
   (b)   **Which* did she choose **dress**?
   (c)   **How* are you **happy with it**?
   (d)   **How* does she work **independently of you**?

(Irrelevantly, (62c,d) are grammatical if *how* is construed as an independent adverb which does not modify the bold-printed material.) Since LBC blocks extraction of *whose* on its own in (60), the **Convergence Principle** (58) tells us to try preposing the next smallest constituent containing *whose*, namely the DP *whose mother*. But movement of this DP is not possible either, as we see from the ungrammaticality of (59c). How come?

   One reason for the ungrammaticality of (59c) is that it violates a constraint on movement operations posited by Huang (1982) which we can outline informally as follows:

(63)   **Constraint on Extraction Domains/CED**
         Only complements allow material to be extracted out of them, not specifiers or adjuncts.

We can illustrate Huang's CED constraint in terms of the following contrasts:

(64) (a)   He was taking [pictures of *who*]?
   (b)   *Who* was he taking [pictures of ~~who~~]?

(65) (a)   [Part of *what*] has broken?
   (b)   **What* has [part of ~~what~~] broken?

(66) (a)   He was angry [when she hid *what*]?
   (b)   *What was he angry [when she hid ~~what~~]?

(64a), (65a) and (66a) are echo questions in which the wh-pronoun *who/what* remains in situ, while (64b), (65b) and (66b) are their wh-movement counterparts. In (64), *who* is extracted out of a bracketed nominal expression which is the complement of the verb *taking*, and yields the grammatical outcome (64b) since there is no violation of CED (extraction out of complement expressions being permitted by CED). By contrast, in (65) *what* is extracted out of a bracketed expression which is the subject (and hence specifier) of the auxiliary *has*, and since CED blocks extraction out of specifiers, the resulting sentence (65b) is ungrammatical. Likewise in (66), *what* is extracted out of a bracketed adjunct clause, and since CED blocks extraction out of adjuncts, (66b) is ungrammatical. (See Nunes and Uriagereka 2000 and Sabel 2002 for attempts to devise a Minimalist account of CED effects.)

In the light of Huang's CED constraint, the reason why extraction of *whose mother* leads to ungrammaticality in (59c) should be clear. This is because *whose mother* is contained within [DP *a picture of whose ø mother*] in (60), and since this DP is the specifier of the T-bar *was on the mantelpiece*, CED blocks extraction of any material out of this DP. As should be obvious, movement of *whose* on its own in (59b) will also violate CED (as well as LBC) – hence (59b) shows a higher degree of ill-formedness (by virtue of violating both CED and LBC) than (59c) (which violates only CED).

In conformity with the Convergence Principle, we therefore try and prepose the next smallest constituent containing *whose* in (60), namely the PP *of whose ø mother*. But extraction of this PP out of the containing [DP *a picture of whose ø mother*] is again blocked by CED. Accordingly, we try and prepose the next smallest constituent containing *whose*, namely [NP *picture of whose ø mother*]: once again, however, this is blocked by CED – as well as by the **Functional Head Constraint/FHC** (discussed in §3.6) which forbids extraction of the complement of a functional head like D or C (and hence blocks extraction of the complement of the determiner *a*). Because it violates two constraints (CED and FHC), (59e) induces a higher degree of ungrammaticality than (59d) (which violates only CED). We therefore prepose the next smallest constituent containing *whose*, namely [DP *a picture of whose ø mother*]. This is permitted by CED, since CED only blocks *extraction out of a specifier*, not *extraction of a specifier*. Since this DP is the smallest maximal projection containing *whose* which can be preposed without violating any constraint, the convergence analysis correctly predicts the grammaticality of (59f) *A picture of whose mother had you thought was on the mantelpiece?*

We began our analysis of pied-piping in this section by assuming that the [WH] feature on C can only attract a maximal projection carrying a wh-feature, and that a phrase only carries a wh-feature if it has a wh-head. We saw that one analysis of pied-piping consistent with this assumption is that it is the result of a **feature-copying** operation by which a head acquires a copy of a wh-feature carried by a constituent which it merges with. However, we noted that this account runs into problems in relation to wh-movement structures where the wh-word is the specifier of the head containing it. We sketched Chomsky's alternative **convergence** view under which the [WH] feature on C attracts the smallest constituent containing a wh-word whose movement will lead to a convergent derivation.

The convergence view is not entirely without posing problems however, as we can illustrate in terms of the following Polish examples kindly provided by Bob Borsley:

(67) (a) *Którego* Jan widział **mężczyzną**?
          Which Jan saw   **man**?
          'Which man did Jan see?'

     (b) *Którego* **mężczyzną** Jan widział?
          Which **man**   Jan saw?
          'Which man did Jan see?'

If convergence requires us to move the *smallest* wh-marked constituent, then the fact that movement of the quantifier *którego* 'which' on its own is permitted would lead us to suppose that it should not be possible to move the larger QP *którego mężczyzną* 'which man?'. It is not clear how such data can best be dealt with under the convergence account: perhaps (as briefly mentioned in a parenthetical remark in §6.5) Polish allows either movement of a wh-head to C or movement of a wh-phrase to spec-CP, and hence permits either the smallest wh-marked head to move to C, or the smallest wh-phrase to move to spec-CP. Other solutions can be envisaged, but a book on English syntax is not the place to speculate on Polish syntax.

6.8   Yes–no questions

Implicit in our earlier claim (41) is the following assumption about wh-questions in English:

(68)   Main-clause questions are CPs headed by a C which carries [TNS, WH, EPP] features.

This assumption has interesting implications for the syntax of yes–no questions such as:

(69)   Is it raining?

It implies that not only wh-questions but also yes–no questions are CPs containing an interrogative specifier. But what kind of specifier could yes–no questions contain? The answer suggested in Grimshaw (1993) and Roberts (1993) is that they contain a **null question operator** which is directly generated in spec-CP (i.e. which is positioned in spec-CP by simple merger rather than movement). From a historical perspective, the null-operator analysis is by no means implausible, since in Elizabethan English we found main-clause yes–no questions introduced by the overt question word *whether*, as illustrated below:

(70) (a)   Whether had you rather lead mine eyes or eye your master's heels? (Mrs Page, *The Merry Wives of Windsor*, III.ii)

(b)   Whether dost thou profess thyself a knave or a fool? (Lafeu, *All's Well That Ends Well*, IV.v)

Given the null-operator analysis of yes–no questions, we can posit that yes–no questions have essentially the same syntax in present-day English as in Elizabethan English, save that yes–no questions could be introduced by the overt interrogative operator *whether* in Elizabethan English, but are introduced by a null interrogative operator (a null counterpart of *whether*) in present-day English.

A second piece of evidence in support of the null-operator analysis comes from the fact that yes–no questions can be introduced by *whether* when they are transposed into reported speech (and so occur in a complement clause), as we see from the examples below:

(71) (a)   'Are you feeling better?' he asked
     (b)   He asked *whether* I was feeling better

A third piece of evidence is that yes–no questions with auxiliary inversion resemble *whether* questions in that in both cases *yes/no* are appropriate answers:

(72) (a)   When he asked 'Did you vote for Larry Loudmouth?', I said 'Yes' and you said 'No'
     (b)   When he asked whether we voted for Larry Loudmouth, I said 'Yes' and you said 'No'

A fourth argument is that main-clause yes–no questions can be tagged by *or not* in precisely the same way as complement-clause *whether* questions:

(73) (a)   Has he finished *or not*?
     (b)   I can't say whether he has finished *or not*

If yes–no questions are CPs containing a null yes–no question operator (a null counterpart of *whether*) in spec-CP, we can arrive at a unitary characterisation of questions as *CPs with an interrogative specifier*.

   What all of this means is that (69) *Is it raining?* will be derived as follows. The present-tense auxiliary *is* merges with the verb *raining* to form the T-bar *is raining*. The resulting T-bar merges with the subject *it* to form the TP *it is raining*. This TP in turn merges with a null C which has [TNS, WH, EPP] features. The [TNS] feature of C attracts (a copy of) the T constituent *is* to merge with C; the requirement imposed by the [WH, EPP] features of C for CP to contain a wh-specifier is satisfied by merging a null yes–no question operator in spec-CP (which, for concreteness, we can take to be a null counterpart of the adverb *whether*, below symbolised as ~~whether~~), ultimately deriving the structure shown below (after deletion of the features of C and of the original occurrence of *is*):

(74)

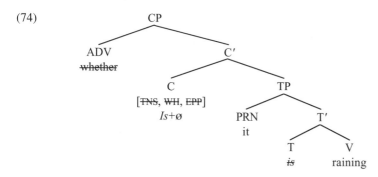

If we take the yes–no question operator to be a null counterpart of *whether*, the lexical entry for *whether* will need to specify that it receives a null spellout in main clauses but is spelled out as |weðə| elsewhere.

6.9   Wh-exclamatives

Although we have so far concentrated on interrogative clauses, there are a number of other types of wh-clause found in English. One of these are **exclamative** clauses like:

(75) (a)   *What fun* we have had!
    (b)   *What a pain in the neck* he must be!
    (c)   *How badly* he is behaving!
    (d)   *How* he longed to see her again!

These show wh-movement of an (italicised) exclamative wh-expression (containing *what!* or *how!*) but no auxiliary inversion. Within the framework adopted here, one way of accounting for this is to suppose that wh-exclamative clauses are CPs headed by an exclamative C – i.e. by a C containing an exclamative force feature, [EXCL-FORCE] – and that an exclamative C carries [WH] and [EPP] features but no [TNS] feature (because the only kind of wh-clause whose head C contains a [TNS] feature is a main-clause question). This means that when C merges with its TP complement, (75a) will have the following structure:

(76)

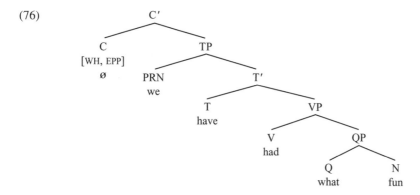

The [WH] feature of C attracts the closest maximal projection with a wh-word (i.e. the QP *what fun*) and moves it into spec-CP, simultaneously deleting the [WH, EPP] features on C. The resulting derived structure is that shown in simplified form below:

(77)

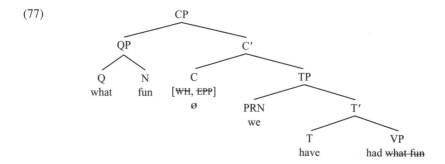

The auxiliary *have* remains in situ in the head T position of TP, since C in (76) and (77) does not have a [TNS] feature and hence cannot attract *have* to move from T to C.

6.10   Relative clauses

A further type of wh-clause (briefly touched on earlier in relation to (12c), (13), (19) and (20) above) are **relative clauses** like those bracketed below:

(78) (a)   It's hard to find *someone* [**who** you can relate to]
     (b)   It's hard to find *someone* [**to whom** you can relate]
     (c)   Can you think of *things* [**which** she might need]?
     (d)   Is there *anybody* [**whose car** I can borrow]?

They are called **relative clauses** because they contain a **relative pronoun** (*who/whose/which*) that 'relates' (i.e. refers back) to an (italicised) **antecedent** in a higher clause (generally one which immediately precedes the bold-printed relative wh-expression). Each of the bracketed relative clauses in (78) contains a bold-printed wh-expression which has undergone wh-movement and thereby been positioned at the front of the bracketed relative clause. In (78b) the preposition *to* has been pied-piped along with the (relative) wh-pronoun *whom*, so that *to whom* is preposed rather than *whom* on its own; likewise, in (78d) the noun *car* is pied-piped along with the genitive wh-pronoun *whose*.

Relative wh-clauses resemble exclamative wh-clauses in that they too show wh-movement without auxiliary inversion. We can therefore analyse them in a similar way, namely as CPs containing a C with [WH, EPP] features but no [TNS] feature. On this view, the bracketed relative clause in (78a) would have the simplified structure shown below at the point where C is merged with its TP complement:

(79)   [$_C$ ∅$_{WH, EPP}$] [$_{TP}$ you [$_T$ can] [$_{VP}$ [$_V$ relate] [$_{PP}$ [$_P$ to] **who**]]]

The [WH, EPP] features of the null C attract the closest maximal projection with a wh-word – i.e. the bold-printed relative pronoun *who* (which is the maximal projection of the wh-word *who*). *Who* then moves to spec-CP, thereby deleting the [WH, EPP] features of C and so forming the CP (80) below:

(80)   [$_{CP}$ **who** [$_C$ ∅~~WH, EPP~~] [$_{TP}$ you [$_T$ can] [$_{VP}$ [$_V$ relate] [$_{PP}$ [$_P$ to] ~~who~~]]]]

An alternative possibility found in more formal styles is for the whole PP to be preposed, so that *to* is pied-piped along with the relative pronoun, deriving the structure shown in simplified form below:

(81)   [$_{CP}$ **to whom** [$_C$ ∅~~WH, EPP~~] [$_{TP}$ you [$_T$ can] [$_{VP}$ [$_V$ relate] ~~to whom~~]]]

The relative pronoun in structures like (81) is spelled out as the accusative form *whom* in formal styles.

Although the relative pronoun is overtly spelled out as *who/whom* in structures like (80) and (81) above, relative pronouns in English can also be given a null spellout, so resulting in **bare relative clauses** (i.e. relative clauses which contain no overt relative pronoun) like those bracketed in the (b) examples below:

(82) (a)   It's hard to find people [*who* you can trust]
     (b)   It's hard to find people [you can trust]

(83) (a)   This is something [*which* I will treasure]
     (b)   This is something [I will treasure]

(84) (a)   I know a place [*where* you can stay]
     (b)   I know a place [you can stay]

(85) (a)   I remember the time [*when* we first met]
     (b)   I remember the time [we first met]

(86) (a)   That's the reason [*why* I was late]
     (b)   That's the reason [I was late]

Although the bare relative clauses in the (b) examples don't contain an overt relative pronoun, there is reason to believe that they contain a null relative pronoun – and hence (e.g.) that (82b) contains a null counterpart of *who*. For example, the verb *trust* in (82b) is a two-place transitive predicate which requires a noun or pronoun expression as its complement: since *trust* has no overt object, it must have a null object of some kind. On the assumption that all relative clauses contain a relative pronoun, the object must be a relative pronoun (or **relative operator**, to use alternative technical terminology). For concreteness, let's suppose that the object of the verb *trust* in (82b) is the relative pronoun *who*. If so, the bracketed relative clauses in (82a,b) will both have the structure shown below at the point where the null complementiser C is merged with its TP complement:

(87)   [c ∅$_{WH, EPP}$] [TP you [T can] [VP [v trust] *who*]]

The [WH, EPP] features of the complementiser will attract the relative pronoun *who* to move to spec-CP and are thereafter deleted (along with the trace copy of the moved pronoun *who*), so deriving the CP (88) below:

(88)   [CP *who* [c ∅$_{WH, EPP}$] [TP you [T can] [VP [v trust] ~~who~~]]]

If we further suppose that the PF component permits a relative pronoun which occupies spec-CP position in a relative clause to be given a null spellout, then *who* in (88) can be given a null spellout in the PF component, so deriving:

(89)   [CP ~~who~~ [c ∅$_{WH, EPP}$] [TP you [T can] [VP [v trust] ~~who~~]]]

One reason why the relative pronoun can be given a null spellout may be that its person/number/gender features can be **identified** by its antecedent: e.g. *who* refers back to *people* in (82a) and so is identifiable as a third-person-plural animate pronoun even if deleted.

While the analysis of bare relative clauses sketched above is plausible, an important question to ask is whether there is any empirical evidence in support of the key assumption that bare relative clauses contain a relative pronoun which undergoes wh-movement in the same way as overt relative pronouns do. An interesting piece of evidence in support of a wh-movement analysis comes from **islandhood effects**. As we noted earlier in §6.3, Ross (1967) argued that certain types of syntactic structures are **islands** – i.e. they are structures out of which no subpart can be moved via any kind of movement operation (the general idea behind his metaphor being that any constituent which is on an island is marooned there and can't be removed from the island by any movement operation of any kind). One type of island identified by Ross are wh-clauses (i.e. clauses beginning with a wh-expression). In this connection, note the ungrammaticality of sentences like:

(90)   *He is someone [**who** nobody knows [*what* the FBA did to]]

(intended to have a meaning which can be paraphrased somewhat clumsily as 'He is someone such that nobody knows what the FBA did to him'). In (90), the relative pronoun *who* is the object of the preposition *to*, and is moved out of the bracketed *did*-clause to the front of the *knows*-clause. However, the *did*-clause is a wh-clause (by virtue of being introduced by *what*) and wh-clauses are islands: this means that moving *who* out of the *did*-clause will lead to violation of Ross's **wh-island constraint** (forbidding any constituent from being moved out of a wh-clause: see Sabel 2002 for a more detailed account of the constraint).

What is of more immediate relevance to our claim that bare relative clauses contain a relative pronoun which undergoes wh-movement is that bare relative clauses exhibit the same islandhood effect, as we see from the ungrammaticality of:

(91)   *He is someone [nobody knows [*what* the FBA did to]]

How can we account for this? Given our assumption that bare relative clauses contain a relative pronoun which moves to spec-CP and is subsequently given a null spellout in the PF component, (91) will have the structure (92) below (simplified in numerous respects, including by not showing trace copies of moved constituents):

(92)   *He is someone [$_{CP}$ **who** [$_{C}$ ø] nobody knows [$_{CP}$ *what* [$_{C}$ ø] the FBA did to]]

The relative pronoun *who* is initially merged as the complement of the preposition *to* and is then moved out of the *did*-clause to the front of the *knows*-clause, and receives a null spellout in the PF component. But since the *did*-clause is a wh-clause (by virtue of containing the preposed wh-word *what*) and since wh-clauses are islands, movement of the relative pronoun out of the *did*-clause will lead to violation of the **wh-island constraint**. Thus, our assumption that bare relative clauses contain a relative pronoun which undergoes wh-movement provides a principled account of the ungrammaticality of structures like (92).

In finite relative clauses like those bracketed in (82)–(86) above, the (italicised) relative pronoun can *optionally* be given a null spellout. But in infinitival relative clauses like those bracketed below, it is *obligatory* for the relative pronoun to have a null spellout:

(93) (a)   *Everyone needs someone [*who* to love]
    (b)   Everyone needs someone [to love]

(94) (a)   *I have no comment [*which* to make]
    (b)   I have no comment [to make]

(95) (a)   *I need a place [*where* to stay]
    (b)   I need a place [to stay]

(96) (a)   *It's the right time [*when* to act]
    (b)   It's the right time [to act]

(97) (a)   *There's no reason [*why* to complain]
    (b)   There's no reason [to complain]

The bracketed structures in (93)–(97) above are control clauses, hence CPs containing a null intransitive complementiser and a null PRO subject. Given the assumptions made here, (93b) will have the partial, simplified structure shown in (98) below:

(98)   Everyone needs someone [$_{CP}$ ~~who~~ [$_C$ ∅$_{WH, EPP}$] [$_{TP}$ PRO [$_T$ to] [$_{VP}$ [$_V$ love] ~~who~~]]]

The relative pronoun will move from VP-complement position to CP-specifier position, and obligatorily be given a null spellout.

It is also obligatory for a relative pronoun to be given a null spellout in infinitival relative clauses containing the transitive complementiser *for* – as we see from the examples below:

(99) (a)   *Find someone [*who* for them to play with]!
    (b)   Find someone [for them to play with]!

(100) (a)   *Find a pen [*which* for me to write with]!
    (b)   Find a pen [for me to write with]!

(101) (a)   *I've got a place [*where* for him to stay]
    (b)   I've got a place [for him to stay]

(102) (a)   *This is the time [*when* for you to leave]
    (b)   This is the time [for you to leave]

(103) (a)   *There's no reason [*why* for her to cry]
    (b)   There's no reason [for her to cry]

Accordingly, an infinitival relative clause like that bracketed in (99b) will contain a relative pronoun like *who* which is initially merged as the complement of the preposition *with* and then moves to become the specifier of the complementiser *for*, ultimately being given a null spellout.

So far, we have seen that relative pronouns are optionally given a null spell-out in finite relative clauses, and obligatorily given a null spellout in non-finite (infinitival) relative clauses. However, there is an important complication which we have overlooked so far, which relates to **pied-piping**. In (both finite and non-finite) relative clauses in which other material is pied-piped along with the relative pronoun when it moves to the front of the relative clause, the relative pronoun cannot be null but rather must be overtly spelled out – as we see from the contrast below (where ~~strikethrough~~ is used to denote a 'silent' relative pronoun with a null spellout, and traces of moved wh-pronouns are omitted):

(104) (a)   I need something [*which* I can write with]
      (b)   I need something [*~~which~~* I can write with]
      (c)   I need something [*with which* I can write]
      (d) *I need something [*with ~~which~~* I can write]

(105) (a)   He is someone [*who* you can rely on]
      (b)   He is someone [*~~who~~* you can rely on]
      (c)   He is someone [*on whom* you can rely]
      (d) *He is someone [*on ~~whom~~* you can rely]

Why should it be that relative pronouns can have a null spellout in structures like (104b) and (105b), but not in structures like (104d) and (105d)?

The reason seems to be related to a difference in the superficial position occupied by the relative pronoun in the two types of clause. This positional difference becomes apparent if we compare the superficial structure of the bracketed relative clauses in (104a,b) with that of the relative clauses in (104c,d), shown in (106) below:

(106)   (a)   CP   (b)   CP

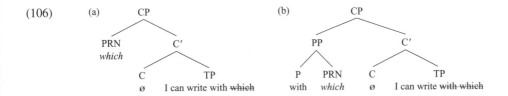

In (106a), the italicised relative pronoun *which* ends up (at the end of the syntactic derivation) as the specifier of the null complementiser heading the relative clause, and can be given a null spellout. By contrast, in (106b) the relative pronoun remains the complement of the preposition *with* throughout the derivation, and it is the whole PP *with which* that is in spec-CP. The descriptive generalisation which this suggests is the following:

(107)   **Relative Pronoun Spellout Condition/RPSC**
          A relative pronoun occupying spec-CP position in a relative clause is given a null spellout at PF (optionally in a finite clause, obligatorily in a non-finite clause)

In accordance with RPSC, *which* can receive a null spellout in (106a) by virtue of occupying CP-specifier position, but not in (106b) by virtue of occupying PP-complement position.

Since it is obligatory for a relative pronoun in spec-CP to receive a null spellout in a non-finite relative clause, relative pronouns in non-finite relative clauses are spelled out differently from their finite counterparts – as we can see by comparing the examples in (104) above with those in (108) below:

(108) (a)   *I need something [*which* to write with]
   (b)   I need something [~~which~~ to write with]
   (c)   I need something [*with which* to write]
   (d)   *I need something [*with* ~~which~~ to write]

The key difference is that whereas a relative pronoun which occupies the specifier position in a finite relative clause can either have an overt spellout as in (104a) or a null spellout as in (104b), a relative pronoun which occupies spec-CP in an infinitival relative clause obligatorily receives a null spellout as in (108b), and cannot be overtly spelled out – as we see from the ungrammaticality of (108a).

6.11   *That*-relatives

A type of relative clause which we have not so far looked at are *that*-relatives (i.e. relative clauses introduced by *that*) like those bracketed below:

(109) (a)   It's hard to find *people* [**that** you can trust]
   (b)   There is *little* [**that** anyone can do]
   (c)   We now have *computers* [**that** even a child can use]

What's the status of *that* in such clauses? One answer (suggested by Sag 1997) is that the word *that* is a relative pronoun which behaves in much the same way as other relative pronouns like *who* and *which*. However, an alternative analysis which we will adopt here is to take *that* to be a relative clause complementiser (= C). The C analysis accounts for several properties of relative *that*. Firstly, it is homophonous with the complementiser *that* found in declarative clauses like that bracketed in:

(110)   I said [*that* you were right]

and has the same phonetically reduced exponent /ðət/. Secondly, (unlike a typical wh-pronoun) it can only occur in finite relative clauses like those bracketed in (109) above, not in infinitival relative clauses like those bracketed below:

(111) (a)   The director is looking for *locations* [**in which** to film a documentary about the FBA]
   (b)   *The director is looking for *locations* [**that** to film a documentary about the FBA in]

Thirdly, unlike a typical wh-pronoun such as *who* (which has the formal-style accusative form *whom* and the genitive form *whose*), relative *that* is invariable and has no variant case forms – e.g. it lacks the genitive form *that's* in standard varieties of English, as we see from (112) below:

(112) (a)   Lord Lancelot Humpalot is *someone* [**whose** ego is even bigger than his libido]
      (b)   *Lord Lancelot Humpalot is *someone* [**that's** ego is even bigger than his libido]

Fourthly, unlike a typical wh-pronoun, *that* does not allow pied-piping of a preposition:

(113) (a)   There are still *diseases* [**for which** there is no cure]
      (b)   *There are still *diseases* [**for that** there is no cure]

Observations such as these suggest that relative *that* is a complementiser rather than a relative pronoun. If so, *that*-relative clauses will be headed by an overt complementiser in the same way as infinitival relative clauses containing the transitive complementiser *for* in sentences such as (99–103) above.

However, given the assumption that all relative clauses contain a relative pronoun, it is plausible to conclude that relative clauses headed by *that* contain a relative pronoun which moves to spec-CP and which is ultimately given a null spellout in the PF component. The analysis of relative clause *that* as a complementiser which attracts a wh-pronoun to become its specifier is lent some plausibility by the fact that in earlier varieties of English we found relative clauses containing an overt (preposed) wh-pronoun followed by the complementiser *that* – as the following examples illustrate:

(114) (a)   In every peril [*which that* is to drede] . . . (Chaucer, *Troilus and Criseyde*)
      (b)   He hathe seyd that he woold lyfte them [*whom that* hym plese] (Middle English, from Traugott 1972, p. 156)

Moreover, we have syntactic evidence from **island constraints** in support of analysing *that*-relatives in present-day English as involving movement of a relative pronoun to spec-CP. For example, relative clauses containing *that* show the same wh-island sensitivity as relative clauses containing an overt wh-pronoun like *who*:

(115) (a)   *He is someone [**who** nobody knows [*what* the FBA did to]]
      (b)   *He is someone [**that** nobody knows [*what* the FBA did to]]

This parallelism suggests that the derivation of *that*-relatives involves a relative pronoun moving to the spec-CP position within the relative clause and subsequently being given a null spellout at PF, with the ungrammaticality of (115a,b) being attributed to the fact that the relative pronoun originates as the complement of the preposition *to* and is extracted out of the bracketed *what*-clause in violation of the **wh-island constraint**.

This being so, the bracketed relative clause in (109a) *It's hard to find people [that you can trust]* will involve merging a relative pronoun like *who* as the object of the verb *trust*, so that the relative clause has the structure shown below at the point where the complementiser *that* is merged with its TP complement:

(116)   [c that_{WH, EPP}] [TP you [T can] [VP [V trust] *who*]]

The [WH, EPP] features of the complementiser *that* will attract the relative pronoun *who* to become the specifier of *that* and are thereby deleted (along with the trace copy of the moved pronoun *who*), so deriving the CP (117) below:

(117)   [CP *who* [c that~~WH, EPP~~] [TP you [T can] [VP [V trust] ~~who~~]]]

The spellout condition (107) will allow the relative pronoun to be given a null spellout in the PF component, so deriving:

(118)   [CP ~~who~~ [c that~~WH, EPP~~] [TP you [T can] [VP [V trust] ~~who~~]]]

and (118) is the structure of the bracketed relative clause in (109a).

   However, an important complication arises at this point. After all, our Relative Pronoun Spellout Condition/RPSC (107) tells us that a relative pronoun is *optionally* given a null spellout in a finite clause. So, while we would expect a structure like (118) in which the relative pronoun has a null spellout to be grammatical, we would also expect a structure like (117) in which the relative pronoun is overtly spelled out as *who* to be grammatical. It might at first sight seem as if we can get round this problem by modifying RPSC so as to specify that a relative pronoun is obligatorily given a null spellout in a relative clause headed by the complementiser *that*. However, this will not account for the fact that relative clauses headed by *that* are also ungrammatical if other material is pied-piped along with the relative pronoun:

(119) (a)   *Colombo has found the weapon [*with which* **that** she was killed]
      (b)   *She is someone [*on whom* **that** you can rely]

And indeed, the same is true of infinitival relative clauses headed by the complementiser *for*:

(120) (a)   *Try and find something [*with which* **for** me to write]
      (b)   *There must be someone [*in whom* **for** me to confide]

Why should sentences like (119) and (120) be ungrammatical?

   The answer given to this question by Chomsky and Lasnik (1977) is that such sentences violate a constraint operating in present-day English they call the **Multiply Filled COMP Filter/MFCF**, and which we can outline informally as follows:

(121)   **Multiply Filled COMP Filter/MFCF**
          Any CP which contains an overt complementiser (*that/if/for*) with an overt specifier is ungrammatical

The relevant 'filter' is arguably reducible to a lexical property of overt complementisers (namely that they don't allow an overt specifier). Be that as it may, **MFCF** helps us account for contrasts such as the following in present-day English:

(122) (a) *They're looking for places [CP **which** [C that] FBA agents can hide in]
  (b) *They're looking for places [CP **in which** [C that] FBA agents can hide]
  (c) They're looking for places [CP ~~which~~ [C that] FBA agents can hide in]

(123) (a) *They're looking for places [CP **which** [C for] FBA agents to hide in]
  (b) *They're looking for places [CP **in which** [C for] FBA agents to hide]
  (c) They're looking for places [CP ~~which~~ [C for] FBA agents to hide in]

Sentences like (122a,b) and (123a,b) violate MFCF because they contain an overt wh-expression (*which* or *in which*) which serves as the specifier of an overt complementiser (*that* or *for*): (123b) is also ruled out by the spellout condition (107) which requires a relative pronoun which occupies the specifier position in a non-finite relative clause to have a null spellout. By contrast, (122c) and (123c) involve no violation of MFCF because they contain a *null* relative pronoun which serves as the specifier of an overt complementiser.

In some varieties of English, MFCF seems to have a rather different form, permitting *wh+that* clauses like that bracketed (124a) below, but not those like that bracketed in (124b):

(124) (a) %I really don't know [*what kind of plan* **that** he has in mind]
  (b) *I really don't know [*what* **that** he has in mind]

As noted by Zwicky (2002), the relevant varieties permit *wh+that* structures when the wh-expression is a wh-phrase like *what kind of plan*, but not when it is a wh-pronoun like *what*. Such varieties seem to have a somewhat different version of MFCF from that which operates in Standard English.

Since our discussion in this section and the last has made much use of null relative pronouns, it is interesting to explore the question of whether there are parallels between these and other null pronouns – e.g. null subject pronouns like 'big PRO' and 'little pro'. The answer seems to be that there are indeed potential parallels. For example, we claimed in §4.9 that in a control clause like that bracketed below:

(125)   I tried [CP [C ø] [TP PRO [T to] help him]]

the null complementiser [C ø] in the bracketed control clause obligatorily assigns null case to the subject of its TP complement. What this means is that the only type of subject which TP permits in a control clause is a null 'big PRO' subject. Let's suppose that just as the complementiser in a control clause requires the null spellout of a constituent which it case-marks (with the result that the only kind of subject allowed in a control clause is PRO), so too an overt relative-clause complementiser like *for/that* requires the null spellout of the wh-marked constituent which it attracts (with the result that relative clauses headed by *for/that* must contain a null relative pronoun). This assumption would account for the pattern of data found in *for/that* relative clauses like those bracketed in (122) and (123) above.

But what about relative clauses headed by a null infinitival complementiser? Here the distribution of null relative pronouns seems more akin to that of 'little pro' subjects in a null-subject language like Italian. In Italian, the subject of a finite clause is only null if it is a weak pronoun (e.g. one which is not focused or used contrastively), not if it is a DP like *il presidente della repubblica* 'the president of the republic' or *Maria*: hence, we find both overt and null subjects in finite clauses in Italian. If we suppose that relative pronouns are weak (as seems plausible since they cannot carry contrastive stress), we can draw a parallel between *pro* subjects in a null-subject language and English relative pronouns in a relative clause introduced by a null infinitival complementiser: if the wh-moved expression in the relative clause comprises a relative pronoun on its own (as in structures like (108a,b) above), it must obligatorily be given a null spellout (in the same way as a weak subject pronoun in a finite clause in Italian must be given a null spellout). But if the moved wh-expression is a larger structure (e.g. a PP comprising a preposition and a relative pronoun as in 108c,d), the wh-expression cannot be given a null spellout (in the same way as a DP subject like *il presidente della repubblica* 'the president of the republic' in a finite clause in Italian cannot be given a null spellout).

Finally, consider *finite* relative clauses headed by a null complementiser like those in (104a,b) and (105a,b) above, where a relative pronoun in spec-CP *optionally* receives a null spellout. There seem to be wider parallels here with the phenomenon of **Topic Drop** in finite clauses in languages like German. In German, an expression which is the topic of a sentence can be moved into the specifier position within CP (with concomitant movement of an auxiliary or non-auxiliary verb into C) and can *optionally* be given a null spellout if it is a pronoun – as we see from the optionality of the pronominal topic *das* 'that' in structures like that below (from Rizzi 1992, p. 105):

(126)   (*Das*) habe ich gestern   gekauft
          (*That*) have I   yesterday bought
          'I bought *that* yesterday'

If the preposed pronominal topic *das* 'that' in (126) occupies spec-CP position, the conditions under which it optionally receives a null spellout can be assimilated to those under which a relative pronoun in spec-CP optionally receives a null spellout in a finite clause headed by a null complementiser in English. Of course, important theoretical questions remain about how and why certain types of pronoun in spec-CP in certain types of clause receive a null spellout – but we shall not pursue these here. And the null spellout of *whether* in root main clauses may be a related phenomenon, given the observation by Rizzi (2000) that (in some languages) the specifier of a root clause can have a null spellout in certain types of structure.

A final descriptive detail which should be noted is that our discussion of relative clauses in this section and the last has concentrated on **restrictive relative clauses**, so called because in a sentence such as:

(127)   I saw the man [(who/that) they arrested] on TV

the bracketed relative clause restricts the class of men being referred to in the sentence to the one who they arrested. A different type of relative clause are **appositive relative clauses** like those italicised below:

(128) (a)   John (*who used to live in Cambridge*) is a very good friend of mine
      (b)   Yesterday I met my bank manager, *who was in a filthy mood*
      (c)   Mary has left home – *which is very upsetting for her parents*

They generally serve as 'parenthetical comments' or 'afterthoughts' set off in a separate intonation group from the rest of the sentence in the spoken language (this being marked by parentheses, or a comma, or a hyphen in the written language). Unlike restrictives, appositives can be used to qualify unmodified proper nouns (i.e. proper nouns like *John* which are not modified by a determiner like *the*). Moreover, they are always introduced by an overt relative pronoun, as we see in relation to the parenthesised appositive relative clauses below:

(129) (a)   John (*who you met last week*) is a good friend of mine
      (b)   *John (*that you met last week*) is a good friend of mine
      (c)   *John (*you met last week*) is a good friend of mine

Furthermore, whereas a restrictive relative clause like that bracketed in (130a) below can be **extraposed** (i.e. moved) to the end of the containing clause and thereby be separated from its italicised antecedent, an appositive relative clause like that bracketed in (130b) does not allow **extraposition**:

(130) (a)   *A man* has been arrested [who the police want to interview about a series of burglaries]
      (b)   **John* has been arrested [who the police want to interview about a series of burglaries]

A third type of relative clause are so-called **free relative clauses** such as those italicised in:

(131) (a)   *What you say* is true
      (b)   I will go *where you go*
      (c)   I don't like *how he behaved towards her*

They are characterised by the fact that the wh-pronoun *what/where/how* appears to be antecedentless, in that it doesn't refer back to any other constituent in the sentence. Moreover, the set of relative pronouns found in free relative clauses is different from that found in restrictives or appositives: e.g. *what* and *how* can serve as free relative pronouns, but not as appositive or restrictive relative pronouns; and conversely *which* can serve as a restrictive or appositive relative pronoun but not as a free relative pronoun. Appositive relatives (discussed in Citko 2002) and free relatives are interesting in their own right, but we shall not attempt to explore their syntax here.

Although there are many interesting aspects of relative clauses which we will not go into here, the brief outline given in this section and the preceding one suffices for the purpose of underlining that it is not only interrogative wh-expressions which undergo wh-movement, but also exclamative wh-expressions and relative wh-expressions (with the latter showing null spellout of a wh-pronoun in certain

types of relative clause). Indeed, there are a range of other constructions which
have been claimed to involve wh-movement of a null wh-operator, including comparative clauses like (132a) below, *as*-clauses like (132b), and so-called *tough*-
clauses like (132c):

(132) (a)   It is bigger than *I expected it to be*
    (b)   Ames was a spy, *as the FBI eventually discovered*
    (c)   Syntax is tough *to understand*

It is interesting to note that (132a) has a variant form containing the overt wh-word
what in some (non-standard) varieties of English, where we find *It is bigger than*
what *I expected it to be*: see Kennedy and Merchant (2000), Lechner (2001) and
Kennedy (2002) for discussion of comparative structures; see also Potts (2002)
for discussion of *as*-structures like (132b). We will not attempt to fathom the
syntax of constructions like those in (132) here, however.

6.12   Summary

We began this chapter in §6.2 by arguing that main-clause wh-
questions are CPs headed by a C constituent which attracts a tensed auxiliary
to move to C via **head movement** and a wh-expression to move into spec-CP
via **wh-movement**. In §6.3 we argued that a moved wh-expression leaves behind
a null copy of itself at its extraction site (i.e. in the position out of which it is
extracted/moved); we presented arguments to this effect from *wanna*-contraction,
preposition-copying, wh-copying, split spellout and operator-variable binding;
and we noted that in earlier work, copies were analysed as **traces**. In §6.4 we
outlined an analysis of complement-clause wh-questions, under which C carries
[WH] and [EPP] features which attract a wh-expression c-commanded by C to
move to spec-CP. We noted that in consequence of the **Attract Closest Principle**, C in multiple wh-questions attracts movement of the *closest* wh-expression
which it c-commands. In §6.5 we looked at main-clause wh-questions, arguing
that C in such cases carries not only [WH, EPP] features but also a [TNS] feature.
We asked why the [TNS] feature of C attracts movement of T rather than TP,
and concluded that movement of TP is ruled out by a **Remerger Constraint**
which bars a head from being merged with the same constituent more than once;
we argued that movement of an inverted auxiliary from T to C rather than to
spec-CP is the consequence of a **Constituent Structure Constraint** to the effect
that only a head can occupy a head position, and only a maximal projection can
occupy a specifier position. We also asked why the [WH] feature of C attracts
movement of a wh^{MAX} (i.e. a maximal projection containing a wh-word) rather
than a minimal projection, and concluded that this is because the [EPP] feature of
C requires C to project a specifier, and the Constituent Structure Constraint will
only allow a maximal projection to occupy a specifier position. We looked briefly
at an alternative account developed by Chomsky under which the [TNS] feature
of C is an affixal feature which triggers head movement in the PF component,

whereas the [WH] feature of C is a syntactic feature which triggers movement of a wh^{MAX} to spec-CP. In §6.6 we discussed the syntax of wh-subject questions like *Who called the police?* which contain a wh-word which is the subject of the interrogative clause. We noted that such questions do not involve auxiliary inversion, and outlined Pesetsky and Torrego's account under which the relevant clauses are CPs, with the [WH] and [TNS] features of C jointly attracting the wh-subject to move from spec-TP to spec-CP (the relevant wh-subject being assumed to carry a copy of the tense feature carried by T). In §6.7 we noted that although the [WH, EPP] features of C (in simple cases) attract the closest maximal projection with a wh-head to move to spec-CP in English, wh-movement in formal styles of English may result in a preposition being **pied-piped** along with the wh-expression. We outlined a **feature-copying** account under which (in formal but not informal styles of English) a transitive preposition inherits a wh-feature carried by its complement, with the result that the preposition itself carries a [WH] feature, and its containing PP thereby becomes the closest wh^{MAX} to C (and hence moves to spec-CP). We noted, however, that this account runs into problems in relation to structures which involve movement of a wh-phrase in which the wh-word is the specifier rather than the head of the phrase. We outlined Chomsky's alternative **convergence** account under which a C with a [WH] feature attracts the smallest constituent containing a wh-word which will lead to convergence (i.e. which will ensure a grammatical outcome). In §6.8 we looked briefly at the syntax of yes–no questions, arguing that these contain a null question operator (a null counterpart of *whether*) in spec-CP. In §6.9 we discussed the syntax of exclamative clauses, arguing that these are CPs in which the head C constituent carries [WH, EPP] features, but no [TNS] feature: hence, exclamative clauses involve wh-movement without auxiliary inversion. In §6.10, we looked at the derivation of relative clauses, arguing that this involves movement of a wh-expression containing a relative pronoun to spec-CP, with a relative pronoun receiving a null spellout when occupying spec-CP – optionally in finite clauses, obligatorily in infinitival clauses. In §6.11, we looked at *that*-relatives, arguing that these too involve movement of a wh-pronoun to spec-CP, with the wh-pronoun obligatorily receiving a null spellout in consequence of the **Multiply Filled COMP Filter**. We explored typological similarities between null relative pronouns and other types of null pronoun (including null *pro* and *PRO* subjects and null topics).

Overall, the main point of this chapter has been to look at the syntax of preposed (interrogative, exclamative and relative) wh-expressions. All three types of expression end up (via movement) in an **A-bar position** – i.e. a specifier position which can be occupied by either an argument or an adjunct. Because it moves wh-expressions into spec-CP and spec-CP is an A-bar position, wh-movement can be regarded as a particular instance of a more general **A-bar movement** operation. (As should be obvious, the term *A-bar* here is used in an entirely different manner from the way we employed it in §3.5, when we claimed that in an adjectival phrase like *very proud of him*, the string *proud of him* is an A-bar constituent and thus an intermediate projection of the adjective *proud*.)

Workbook section

Exercise 6.1

Discuss the derivation of the wh-clauses below, drawing tree diagrams to show their superficial structure and saying why they are grammatical or ungrammatical in standard varieties of English:

1a	Which film have you seen?
b	*Which have you seen film?
2a	Dare anyone say anything?
b	Who interrupted him?
3a	Who/?Whom were you talking to?
b	To whom/?To who were you talking?
4a	Who have they spoken to?
b	Who've they spoken to?
c	?To who have they spoken?
d	*To who've they spoken?
5a	Which picture of you have they published?
b	*Which picture of you've they published?
6a	What excuse has he given?
b	*What has he given excuse?
c	*What excuse he has given?
d	*What he has given excuse?
7a	In whose mother has he confided?
b	Whose mother has he confided in?
c	*Whose has he confided in mother?
d	*In whose has he confided mother?
8a	What courage he has shown!
b	*What he has shown courage!
c	*What courage has he shown!
d	*What has he shown courage!
9a	How proud of him you must be!
b	How proud you must be of him!
10a	The leader of which party has resigned?
b	*Leader of which party has the resigned?
c	?Of which party has the leader resigned?
d	?Which party has the leader of resigned?
e	*Which has the leader of party resigned?

In addition, comment on relevant aspects of the syntax of the interrogative/exclamative Shakespearean sentences in (11) below, the African American English interrogatives in (12) (from Green 1998, pp. 98–9) and the bracketed complement clauses in Belfast English (adapted from Henry 1995) in (13) and (14):

11a	What sayst thou? (Olivia, *Twelfth Night*, III.iv)
b	What dost thou say? (Othello, *Othello*, III.iii)
c	What didst not like? (Othello, *Othello*, III.iii)
d	What visions have I seen! (Titania, *A Midsummer Night's Dream*, V.i)

12a	What I'm gon' do? (= 'What am I going to do?')
b	How she's doing? (= 'How is she doing?')
13a	They wondered [which one that he chose]
b	They wondered [which one did he choose]
c	*They wondered [which one that did he choose]
14a	They wondered [if/whether (*that) we had gone]
b	*They wondered [if/whether had we gone]
c	They wondered [had we gone]

Helpful hints

In 2a, assume that *dare, anyone* and *anything* are **polarity items**, and that *dare* originates in T. In 3–4, the prefixed question mark ? indicates that the use of *who(m)* in the relevant sentence (for speakers like me) leads to stylistic incongruity (in that the accusative form *whom* and preposition pied-piping are used in more formal styles, and the accusative form *who* and preposition stranding in less formal styles). In 4–5, bear in mind the claim made in §4.3 that *have* can cliticise onto another word W as long as W is a pronoun ending in a vowel or diphthong, W asymmetrically c-commands *(ha)ve*, and there is no overt or null constituent intervening between W and *have* (= no intervening constituent c-commanding *have* and c-commanded by W). In 6–10, compare how well the **convergence** and **feature-copying** accounts of pied-piping would handle the relevant data. In 14, consider the possibility that both *if* and *whether* are complementisers in Belfast English (though only *if* is a complementiser in Standard English).

Model answer for sentence 1a

Sentence 1a is derived as follows. The quantifier *which* is merged with the noun *film* to form the QP *which film*. This in turn is merged with the (perfect participle) verb *seen* to form the VP *seen which film*. This is merged with the (present-) tense auxiliary *have* to form the T-bar *have seen which film*. The resulting T-bar is in turn merged with the pronoun *you* to form the TP *you have seen which film*. This is merged with a null C constituent containing [TNS, WH, EPP] features, so forming the C-bar in (i) below:

(i)

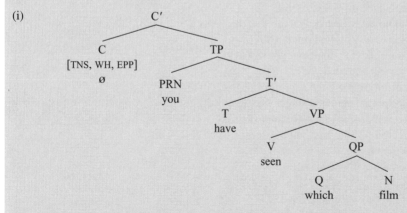

In principle, we would expect the [TNS] feature of C to be able to attract either T or TP to move to the edge of CP; but movement of TP is ruled out by the **Remerger Constraint** (because TP is already merged as the complement of C and hence cannot be remerged as the specifier of C), and hence the [TNS] feature of C attracts the present-tense auxiliary *have* to move to the edge of CP.

Since the **Constituent Structure Constraint** only allows a head to occupy a head position, *have* adjoins to the null complementiser in C. In principle, we would expect the [WH] feature of C to be able to attract either movement of a wh-head like *which* or movement of a wh-phrase like *which film* (and we see in the main text that both possibilities are found in languages like Polish). However, since the [EPP] feature of C requires C to project a specifier and the Constituent Structure Constraint requires a specifier position to be filled by a maximal projection, the [WH, EPP] features of C attract the closest maximal projection containing a wh-word (namely the QP *which film*, whose head is the wh-quantifier *which*) to move to spec-CP. Assuming that the features of C are deleted after their requirements are satisfied, the structure which results after head movement and wh-movement have applied is that shown in simplified form below:

(ii)

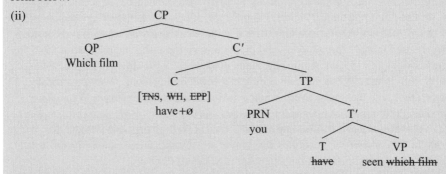

Exercise 6.2

Discuss the derivation of the bracketed restrictive relative clauses in the sentences below, drawing tree diagrams to show their superficial structure and saying why they are grammatical or ungrammatical in standard varieties of English:

1a	He is someone [who you can talk to]
b	He is someone [you can talk to]
c	He is someone [to whom you can talk]
d	*He is someone [to you can talk]
2a	*He is someone [who that you can talk to]
b	He is someone [that you can talk to]
c	*He is someone [to whom that you can talk]
d	*He is someone [to that you can talk]
3a	They recruit people [who have got a degree]
b	They recruit people [who've got a degree]
c	They recruit people [that have got a degree]
d	*They recruit people [have got a degree]
4a	*This is the way [how he behaved]
b	This is the way [he behaved]
c	*This is the way [how that he behaved]
d	This is the way [that he behaved]
5a	*I need someone [who to love me]
b	I need someone [to love me]
c	*I need someone [who to love]
d	I need someone [to love]

6a	I need a place [in which to stay]
b	*I need a place [in to stay]
c	*I need a place [which to stay in]
d	I need a place [to stay in]
e	*I need a place [where to stay]
f	I need a place [to stay]
7a	*I need a place [in which for her to stay]
b	*I need a place [in for her to stay]
c	*I need a place [which for her to stay in]
d	I need a place [for her to stay in]
e	*I need a place [where for her to stay]
f	I need a place [for her to stay]
8a	*This is no way [how to behave]
b	This is no way [to behave]
c	*This is no way [how for you to behave]
d	This is no way [for you to behave]

Helpful hints

In relation to 3b,d and 5a,b, consider whether a relative pronoun which is the subject of the relative clause is in spec-CP or in spec-TP (and whether the answer you come up with for 3b,d may be different to that you come up with for 5a,b), and how data relating to *have*-cliticisation and the null spellout of relative pronouns could have a bearing on this. (See the note on *have*-cliticisation in the helpful hints to the previous exercise.) In relation to 4 and 8, assume that *how* is a manner pronoun/PRN which originates as the complement of the verb *behave*: try and identify the way in which *how* differs from other restrictive relative pronouns like *who/which/where/why*.

Model answer for sentence 1a,b

Sentence 1a is derived as follows. The preposition *to* merges with the wh-pronoun *who* to form the PP *to who*. This is merged with the verb *talk* to form the VP *talk to who*. The resulting VP is merged with the present-tense auxiliary *can* to form the T-bar *can talk to who*, and this is then merged with the subject *you* to form the TP *you can talk to who*. This TP is subsequently merged with a null complementiser (perhaps a null counterpart of *that*) which carries [WH, EPP] features, so deriving the structure shown in (i) below:

(i)

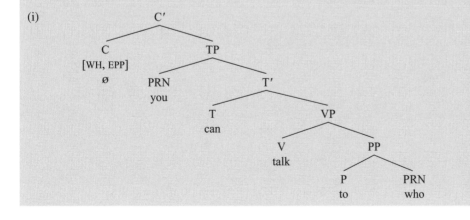

The [WH] feature of C attracts the closest expression containing a wh-feature to move to the edge of CP. Since the [EPP] feature of C requires it to project a specifier, and since the Constituent Structure Constraint requires a specifier position to be filled by a maximal projection, the [WH, EPP] features of C attract the closest maximal projection containing a wh-word to move to spec-CP. The wh-marked pronoun *who* is a maximal projection by virtue of being the largest expression headed by the wh-word *who*. Hence, *who* moves to spec-CP, and thereby erases the [WH, EPP] features of C, so deriving the structure shown in simplified form below, which is the superficial structure of the bracketed relative clause in 1a:

(ii)

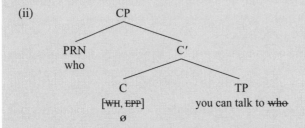

Given that the **Relative Pronoun Spellout Condition** specifies that a relative pronoun occupying the specifier position in a finite relative clause can optionally have a null spellout in the PF component, an alternative possibility is for the relative pronoun *who* in spec-CP to be given a null spellout at PF, so deriving (iii) below, which is the superficial structure associated with the bracketed relative clause in 1b:

(iii)

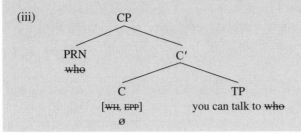

7 A-movement

7.1 Overview

In this chapter, we look at the syntax of **subjects**. So far, we have assumed that subjects originate in the specifier position within TP and remain *in situ* (except where the subject undergoes wh-movement and moves to spec-CP, e.g. in sentences like *Who did he say was coming?*). However, in this chapter we shall argue that subjects originate internally within the Verb Phrase as arguments of verbs, and are subsequently raised into the specifier position within TP, with the relevant movement operation being triggered by an [EPP] feature carried by T. Since spec-TP is an **A-position** (i.e. a position which can generally only be occupied by argument expressions), the operation by which subjects move into spec-TP is traditionally known as **A-movement**.

7.2 Subjects in Belfast English

Let's begin our discussion of the syntax of subjects by looking at some interesting data from Belfast English (kindly supplied to me by Alison Henry). Alongside Standard English constructions like (1a,b) below:

(1) (a)   *Some students* should get distinctions
   (b)   *Lots of students* have missed the classes

Belfast English also has structures like (2a,b):

(2) (a)   There should *some students* get distinctions
   (b)   There have *lots of students* missed the classes

Sentences like (2a,b) are called *expletive* structures because they contain the **expletive** pronoun *there*. (The fact that *there* is not a **locative** pronoun in this kind of use is shown by the impossibility of replacing it by locative *here* or questioning it by the interrogative locative *where?* or contrastively focusing it by assigning it contrastive stress.) For the time being, let's focus on the derivation of Belfast English sentences like (2a,b) before turning to consider the derivation of Standard English sentences like (1a,b).

One question to ask about the sentences in (2a,b) is where the expletive pronoun *there* is positioned. Since *there* immediately precedes the tensed auxiliary *should/have*, a reasonable conjecture is that *there* is the subject of *should/have* and hence occupies the spec-TP position. If this is so, we'd expect to find that the (bold-printed) auxiliary can move in front of the (italicised) expletive subject (via T-to-C movement) in questions – and this is indeed the case in Belfast English, as the sentences in (3) below illustrate:

(3) (a)   **Should** *there* <u>some students</u> get distinctions?
    (b)   **Have** *there* <u>lots of students</u> missed the classes?

But what position is occupied by the underlined quantified expressions *some students/lots of students* in (3)? Since they immediately precede the verbs *get/missed* and since subjects precede verbs, it seems reasonable to conclude that the expressions *some students/lots of students* function as the subjects of the verbs *get/missed* and (since subjects are typically specifiers) occupy **spec-VP** (i.e. specifier position within VP). If these assumptions are correct, (2a) will have the structure (4) below (simplified by not showing the internal structure of the expressions *some students/distinctions*: we can take both of these to be QP/Quantifier Phrase expressions, headed by the overt quantifier *some* in one case and by a null quantifier [$_Q$ ø] in the other):

(4)

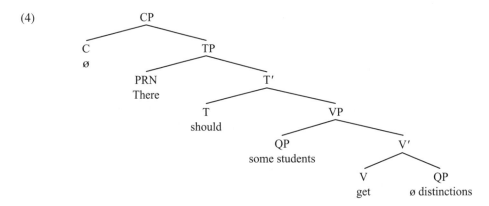

The analysis in (4) claims that the sentence contains two subjects/specifiers: *there* is the specifier (and syntactic subject) of *should*, and *some students* is the specifier (and semantic subject) of *get*.

Given the assumptions in (4), sentence (2a) will be derived as follows. The noun *distinctions* merges with a null quantifier [$_Q$ ø] to form the QP *ø distinctions*. By virtue of being the complement of the verb *get*, this QP is merged with the V *get* to form the **V-bar** (incomplete verb expression) *get ø distinctions*. The resulting V-bar is then merged with the subject of *get*, namely the QP *some students* (itself formed by merging the quantifier *some* with the noun *students*), so deriving the VP *some students get ø distinctions*. This VP is in turn merged with the tense auxiliary *should*, forming the T-bar *should some students get* *ø distinctions*. Let's suppose that a finite T has an [EPP] feature requiring it to have a specifier with person/number properties. In sentences like (2a,b) in Belfast English, the requirement for T to have such a specifier can be satisfied by merging expletive *there* with the T-bar *should some students get ø distinctions*, so forming the TP *There should some students get ø distinctions*. The resulting TP is then merged with a null declarative complementiser, forming the CP shown in (4) above.

But what about the derivation of the corresponding Standard English sentence (1a) *Some students should get distinctions*? Let's suppose that the derivation of (1a) runs parallel to the derivation of (2a) until the point where the auxiliary *should* merges with the VP *some students get ø distinctions* to form the T-bar *should some students get ø distinctions*. As before, let's assume that [T *should*] has an [EPP] feature requiring it to project a structural subject/specifier. But let's also suppose that the requirement for [T *should*] to have a specifier of its own cannot be satisfied by merging expletive *there* in spec-TP because in standard varieties of English *there* can generally only occur in structures containing an intransitive verb like *be, become, exist, occur, arise, remain* etc. Instead, the [EPP] requirement for T to have a subject with person/number properties is satisfied by moving the subject *some students* from its original position in spec-VP into a new position in spec-TP, in the manner shown by the arrows below:

(5)

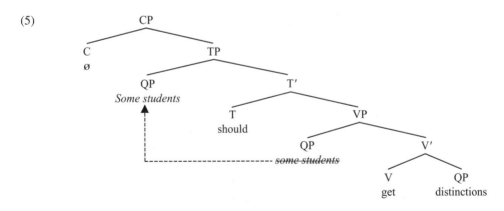

Since spec-TP is an A-position which can only be occupied by an argument expression, the kind of movement operation illustrated by the dotted arrow in (5) is called **A-movement**.

Given the arguments presented in chapters 5 and 6 that head movement and A-bar movement are composite operations involving copying and deletion, we would expect the same to be true of A-movement. One piece of evidence in support of a copying analysis of A-movement comes from **scope** facts in relation to sentences such as (6a) below, which will have the syntactic structure shown in simplified form in (6b) if *everyone* originates as the subject of the verb *finished* and is then raised up (by A-movement) to become the subject of the present-tense auxiliary HAVE:

(6) (a)   Everyone hasn't finished the assignment yet

    (b)   [CP [C ø] [TP *Everyone* [T has] [NegP not [Neg ø] [VP ~~everyone~~ [V finished] the assignment yet]]]]

For many speakers, sentences like (6a) are ambiguous between (i) a reading on which the quantifier expression *everyone* has **scope** over *not* so that the sentence means much the same as 'Everyone is in the position of not having finished the assignment yet', and (ii) another reading on which *everyone* falls within the scope of *not* (so that the sentence means much the same as 'Not everyone has finished the assignment yet'). We can account for this scope ambiguity in a principled fashion if we suppose that A-movement involves copying, that scope is defined in terms of c-command (so that a scope-bearing constituent has scope over constituents which it c-commands), and that the scope of a universally quantified expression like *everyone* in negative structures like (6b) can be determined either in relation to the initial position of *everyone* or in relation to its final position. In (6b) *everyone* is initially merged in a position (marked by ~~strikethrough~~) in which it is c-commanded by (and so falls within the scope of) *not*; but via A-movement it ends up in an (italicised) position in which it c-commands (and so has scope over) *not*. The scope ambiguity in (6a) therefore reflects the two different positions occupied by *everyone* in the course of the derivation. (See Lebeaux 1995, Hornstein 1995, Romero 1997, Sauerland 1998, Lasnik 1998/1999, Fox 2000, and Boeckx 2000, 2001 for discussion of scope in A-movement structures.)

The claim that (non-expletive) subjects like *some students/lots of students* in sentences like (1a, b) originate internally within the VP containing the relevant verb (and from there move into spec-TP in sentences like (1a, b) above) is known in the relevant literature as the **VP-Internal Subject Hypothesis** (= **VPISH**), and has been widely adopted in research since the mid 1980s. An extensive body of evidence was adduced in support of the hypothesis from a variety of sources and languages in the 1980s and early 1990s, e.g. in Kitagawa (1986), Speas (1986), Contreras (1987), Zagona (1987), Kuroda (1988), Sportiche (1988), Rosen (1990), Ernst (1991), Koopman and Sportiche (1991), Woolford (1991), Burton and Grimshaw (1992), McNally (1992), Guilfoyle, Hung and Travis (1992), and Huang (1993). Since then, it has become a standard analysis. In §§7.3–7.6 below, we look at some of the evidence in support of VPISH.

7.3   Quotatives and idioms

An interesting piece of evidence in support of the VP-Internal Subject Hypothesis comes from **quotative inversion** structures like (7) below:

(7)   'Sentences like this are called quotatives', **said** *Leon*

The relevant structures are called **quotative** because they involve a direct quotation (the underlined quoted material being enclosed within inverted commas);

they involve **inversion** in the sense that the bold-printed main verb *said* in (7) ends up positioned in front of its italicised subject *Leon*. Collins (1997), Collins and Branigan (1997) and Suñer (2000) argue that the italicised subject in such structures remains in situ in the specifier position within the verb phrase, and that the bold-printed verb moves to some higher head position above the VP in which it originates.

But what evidence is there that the subject remains in spec-VP in quotative inversion structures like (7)? Part of the evidence comes from the syntax of **floating quantifiers**. In structures in which the subject raises out of spec-VP into spec-TP in English, the moved subject in spec-TP can serve as the antecedent for a floating quantifier like *all/both/each* (i.e. for a quantifier which is positioned after the subject and forms a separate constituent, but is nonetheless interpreted as modifying the subject). We can illustrate this in terms of structures like (8) below:

(8) (a)   **The students** should *all/both/each* get distinctions
    (b)   **The students** *all/both/each* got distinctions

In (8a) the bold-printed subject DP *the students* is in spec-TP and hence precedes the auxiliary *should*. The italicised floating quantifiers *all/both/each* are c-commanded by the subject DP *the students*, and are construed as modifying the subject DP. Hence, examples like (8a) tell us that a moved subject in spec-TP can serve as the antecedent of a floating quantifier positioned between the moved subject and the verb. By hypothesis, the bold-printed subject is likewise in spec-TP in (8b) and so can again occur as the antecedent of the italicised quantifier between the moved subject and the verb.

In the light of this restriction, consider the following contrast (noted by Collins and Branigan 1997):

(9) (a)   'We must do this again', **the guests** *all* declared to Tony
    (b)   *'We must do this again', declared **the guests** *all* to Tony

In the uninverted structure (9a), the subject *the guests* occupies the canonical spec-TP position associated with subjects, and hence can serve as the antecedent of the floating quantifier *all*. Now, if the subject were also in spec-TP in (9b), we'd again expect the quantifier *all* to be able to be positioned after the subject. The fact that this is not possible leads Collins and Branigan to conclude that the subject in quotative inversion structures like (9b) remains in situ in spec-VP. If so, this provides empirical evidence in support of VPISH.

However, the assumption that the postverbal subject in quotative inversion structures like (7) and (9b) remains in situ in spec-VP raises the question of where the verb and the quoted material (both of which end up in front of the subject) move to, since if they remained in situ within the verb phrase, they would be expected to follow the subject. Collins (1997) argues that the quoted material moves to spec-TP (a position which is normally occupied by the subject, but which is available for some other constituent to move into if the subject remains in spec-VP). As for where the verb moves to, Suñer (2000) argues that it does not move to T (since T is not strong enough to attract main verbs to move to T in present-day English), but rather moves to the head **Asp** (= Aspect) position of an **AspP** (= Aspect Phrase) projection which is positioned below T but above VP. On this view, a sentence like (7) would have the structure (10) below (with arrows showing movement, and *t* indicating trace copies of moved constituents):

(10)

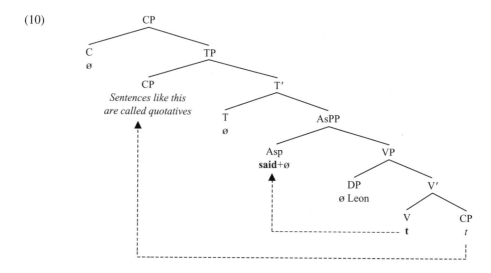

Suñer notes that an interesting prediction made by the assumption that the verb undergoes short verb movement to Asp (rather than long verb movement to T) is that inversion of verb and subject will be blocked in structures containing an aspectual auxiliary like perfect *have* or progressive *be*, and she notes that contrasts like that in (11) below provide empirical support for her claim:

(11) (a)   'What time is it?' John was asking of Mona
     (b)   *'What time is it?' was John asking of Mona
     (c)   *'What time is it?' was asking John of Mona

If finite aspectual auxiliaries originate in Asp and raise to T, *was* will originate in Asp in structures like (11) and hence will block movement of the verb *asking* to Asp – so accounting for the ungrammaticality of quotative inversion in structures like (11b,c). (See Alexiadou and Anagnostopoulou 2001 for discussion of other subject-in-situ structures.)

Further empirical evidence in support of the VP-Internal Subject Hypothesis comes from the syntax of **idioms**. We can define idioms as expressions (like those italicised below) which have an idiosyncratic meaning which is not a purely compositional function of the meaning of their individual parts:

(12) (a)   Let's have a couple of drinks to *break the ice*
     (b)   Be careful not to *upset the applecart*
     (c)   The president must *bite the bullet*

There seems to be a constraint that only a string of words which forms a unitary constituent can be an idiom. So, while we find idioms like those in (12) which are of the form *verb+complement* (but where the subject isn't part of the idiom), we don't find idioms of the form *subject+verb* where the verb has a complement which isn't part of the idiom: this is because in *subject+verb+complement* structures, the verb and its complement form a unitary constituent (a V-bar), whereas the subject and the verb do not – and only unitary constituents can be idioms.

In the light of the constraint that an idiom is a unitary constituent with an idiosyncratic interpretation, consider idioms such as the following:

(13) (a)   All hell broke loose
     (b)   The shit hit the fan
     (c)   The cat got his tongue

In (13), not only is the choice of verb and complement fixed, but so too is the choice of subject. In such idioms, we can't replace the subject, verb or complement by near synonyms – as we see from the fact that sentences like (14) below are ungrammatical (on the intended idiomatic interpretation):

(14) (a)   *The whole inferno escaped
     (b)   *Camel dung was sucked into the air conditioning
     (c)   *A furry feline bit his lingual articulator

However, what is puzzling about idioms like (13) is that one or more auxiliaries can freely be positioned between the subject and verb:

(15) (a)   All hell *will* break loose
     (b)   All hell *has* broken loose
     (c)   All hell *could have* broken loose

(16) (a)   The shit *might* hit the fan
     (b)   The shit *has* hit the fan
     (c)   The shit *must have* hit the fan

How can we reconcile our earlier claim that only a string of words which form a unitary constituent can constitute an idiom with the fact that *all hell . . . break loose* is a discontinuous string in (15), since the subject *all hell* and the predicate *break loose* are separated by the intervening auxiliaries *will/has/could have*? To put the question another way: how can we account for the fact that although the choice of subject, verb and complement is fixed, the choice of auxiliary is not?

The VP-Internal Subject Hypothesis provides a straightforward answer, if we suppose that subjects originate internally within VP, and that clausal idioms like those in (13) are *VP idioms* which require a fixed choice of head, complement and specifier in the VP containing them. For instance, in the case of (13a), the relevant VP idiom requires the specific word *break* as its head verb, the specific adjective *loose* as its complement, and the specific quantifier phrase *all hell* as its subject/specifier. We can then account for the fact that *all hell* surfaces in front of the auxiliary *will* in (15a) by positing that the QP *all hell* originates in spec-VP as the subject of *break loose*, and is then raised (via A-movement) into spec-TP to become the subject of *will break loose*. Given these assumptions, (15a) will be derived as follows. The verb *break* merges with the adjective *loose* to form the idiomatic V-bar *break loose*. This is then merged with its QP subject *all hell* to form the idiomatic VP *all hell break loose*. The resulting VP is merged with the tense auxiliary *will* to form the T-bar *will all hell break loose*. Since finite auxiliaries carry an [EPP] feature requiring them to have a subject specifier with person/number features, the subject *all hell* moves from being the subject of *break* to becoming the subject of *will* – as shown in simplified form in (17) below:

(17)

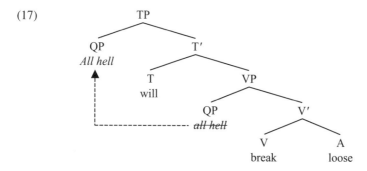

We can then say that (in the relevant idiom) *all hell* must be the sister of *break loose*, and that this condition will be met only if *all hell* originates in spec-VP as the subject (and sister) of the V-bar *break loose*. We can account for how the subject *all hell* comes to be separated from its predicate *break loose* by positing that subjects originate internally within VP and from there raise to spec-TP (via **A-movement**) across an intervening T constituent like *will*, so that the subject and predicate thereby come to be separated from each other – movement of the subject to spec-TP being driven by an [EPP] feature carried by [T *will*] requiring *will* to have a subject with person/number features. Subsequently, the TP in (17) is merged with a null declarative complementiser, so deriving the structure associated with (15a) *All hell will break loose*.

7.4   Argument structure

The assumption that subjects originate internally within VP ties up in interesting ways with traditional ideas from predicate logic which we touched on briefly in §1.2. As we saw there, traditional work in logic maintains that **propositions** (which can be thought of as representing the substantive semantic content of clauses) comprise a **predicate** and a set of **arguments**. Simplifying somewhat, we can say that a predicate is an expression denoting an activity or event, and an argument is an expression denoting a participant in the relevant activity or event. For example, in sentences such as those below, the italicised verbs are predicates and the bracketed expressions represent their arguments.

(18) (a)   [The guests] have *arrived*
     (b)   [The police] have *arrested* [the suspect]

In other words, the arguments of a verb are typically its subject and complement(s). It has been widely assumed in work spanning more than half a century that complements of verbs are contained within a projection of the verb – e.g. *the suspect* in (18b) is the direct-object complement of *arrested* and is contained within the verb phrase headed by *arrested* (so that *arrested the suspect* is a VP). Under the VP-Internal Subject Hypothesis, we can go further than this and make the following (more general) claim:

(19)   **Predicate-Internal Argument Hypothesis**
            All the arguments of a predicate originate within a projection of the predicate

Such an assumption allows us to maintain that there is a uniform **mapping** (i.e. relationship) between syntactic structure and semantic argument structure – more specifically, between the position in which arguments are initially merged in a syntactic structure and their semantic function.

To see what this means in practice, consider the derivation of (18b) *The police have arrested the suspect.* The verb *arrested* merges with its direct-object complement *the suspect* (a DP formed by merging the determiner *the* with the noun *suspect*) to form the V-bar *arrested the suspect.* The resulting V-bar is in turn merged with the subject DP *the police* (formed by merging the determiner *the* with the noun *police*) to form the VP shown in (20) below (simplified by not showing the internal structure of the two DPs):

(20)

In a structure such as (20), the complement *the suspect* is said to be the **internal argument** of the verb *arrested* (in the sense that it is the argument contained within the immediate V-bar projection of the verb, and hence is a sister of the verb), whereas the subject *the police* is the **external argument** of the verb *arrested* (in that it occupies a position external to the V-bar constituent which is the immediate projection of the verb *arrested*). The VP in (20) is then merged with the present-tense auxiliary [T *have*], forming the T-bar *have the police arrested the suspect.* Since a finite T has an [EPP] feature requiring it to have a subject of its own, the DP *the police* moves from being the subject of *arrested* to becoming the subject of [T *have*], forming *The police have the police arrested the suspect.* Merging the resulting TP with a null declarative complementiser in turn derives the structure shown in simplified form in (21) below:

(21)

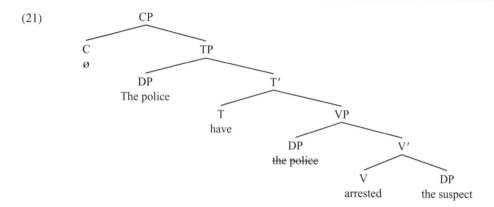

Under the analysis in (21), the argument structure of the verb *arrest* is directly reflected in the internal structure of the VP which it heads, since *the suspect* is the internal (direct-object) argument of *arrested* and *the police* was initially merged as its external (subject) argument – and indeed a null copy of *the police* is left behind in spec-VP, marking the spec-VP position as associated with *the police*.

7.5   Thematic roles

In the previous section, we concluded that the argument structure of clauses is directly reflected in the internal syntactic structure of verb phrases. However, there is an important sense in which it is not enough simply to say that in a sentence such as (18b) *The police have arrested the suspect* the verb *arrest* is a predicate which has two arguments – the internal argument *the suspect* and the external argument *the police*. After all, such a description fails to account for the fact that these two arguments play very different semantic roles in relation to the act of *arrest* – i.e. it fails to account for the fact that *the police* are the individuals who perform the act (and hence get to verbally and physically abuse the suspect), and that *the suspect* is the person who suffers the consequences of the act (e.g. being manhandled, handcuffed, thrown into the back of a windowless vehicle and beaten up). Hence, any adequate account of argument structure should provide a description of the semantic role which each argument plays.

In research spanning half a century – beginning with the pioneering work of Gruber (1965), Fillmore (1968) and Jackendoff (1972) – linguists have attempted to devise a universal typology of the semantic roles played by arguments in relation to their predicates. In the table in (22) below are listed a number of terms used to describe some of these roles (the convention being that terms denoting semantic roles are CAPITALISED), and for each role an informal gloss is given, together with an illustrative example (in which the italicised expression has the semantic role specified):

(22)   List of roles played by arguments with respect to their predicates

Role	Gloss	Example
THEME	Entity undergoing the effect of some action	*Mary* fell over
AGENT	Entity instigating some action	*Debbie* killed Harry
EXPERIENCER	Entity experiencing some psychological state	*I* like syntax
LOCATIVE	Place in which something is situated or takes place	He hid it *under the bed*
GOAL	Entity representing the destination of some other entity	John went *home*
SOURCE	Entity from which something moves	He returned *from Paris*
INSTRUMENT	Means used to perform some action	He hit it *with a hammer*

We can illustrate how the terminology in (22) can be used to describe the semantic roles played by arguments in terms of the following examples

(23) (a)   [The FBI] arrested [Larry Luckless]
            [AGENT]   [THEME]
     (b)   [The suspect] received [a caution]
            [GOAL]   [THEME]
     (c)   [The audience] enjoyed [the play]
            [EXPERIENCER]   [THEME]
     (d)   [The president] went [to Boston]
            [THEME]   [GOAL]
     (e)   [They] stayed [in a hotel]
            [THEME]   [LOCATIVE]
     (f)   [The noise] came [from the house]
            [THEME]   [SOURCE]

Given that – as we see from these examples – the THEME role is a central one, it has become customary over the past two decades to refer to the relevant semantic roles as **thematic roles**; and since the Greek letter θ (= *theta*) corresponds to *th* in English and the word *thematic* begins with *th*, it has also become standard practice to abbreviate the expression *thematic role* to **θ-role** (pronounced *theeta-role* by some and *thayta-role* by others). Using this terminology, we can say (e.g.) that in (23a) *the FBI* is the AGENT argument of the predicate *arrested*, and that *Larry Luckless* is the THEME argument of *arrested*.

Thematic relations (like AGENT and THEME) have been argued to play a central role in the description of a range of linguistic phenomena. For example, it has been argued that the distribution of certain types of adverb is thematically determined. Thus, Gruber (1976) argues that adverbs like *deliberately* can only be used to modify AGENT arguments:

(24) (a)   *John* (= AGENT) **deliberately** rolled the ball down the hill
     (b)   **The ball* (= THEME) **deliberately** rolled down the hill

Likewise, Fillmore (1972, p. 10) argues that the adverb *personally* can only be associated with EXPERIENCER arguments:

(25) (a)   **Personally**, *I* (= EXPERIENCER) don't like roses

   (b)   **Personally**, your proposal doesn't interest *me* (= EXPERIENCER)

   (c)   ***Personally**, *I* (= AGENT) hit you

   (d)   ***Personally**, you hit *me* (= THEME)

In a similar vein, Fillmore (1968, p. 10) argues that only constituents with the same thematic function can be coordinated:

(26) (a)   *John* (= AGENT) broke the window

   (b)   *A hammer* (= INSTRUMENT) broke the window

   (c)   ??*John* (= AGENT) **and** *a hammer* (= INSTRUMENT) broke the window

And Jackendoff (1972) argues at length that a number of constraints on **passive** structures can be accounted for in thematic terms. For example, he argues (1972, p. 44) that the ill-formedness of passive sentences like:

(27) (a)   *Five dollars are cost by this book

   (b)   *Two hundred pounds are weighed by Bill

is attributable to violation of the following condition (formulated in thematic terms):

(28)   **Passive Thematic Hierarchy Condition**
            The passive *by*-phrase must be higher on the Thematic Hierarchy than the superficial subject

The hierarchy referred to in (28) is that in (29) below:

(29)   **Thematic Hierarchy**
            AGENT > LOCATIVE/SOURCE/GOAL > THEME

Jackendoff maintains that the *by*-phrase in both examples in (27) is a THEME argument of the relevant verb, whereas the superficial subject is a LOCATIVE argument. Since THEME is lower on the hierarchy (29) than LOCATIVE, sentences like (27) violate the condition (28) and so are ungrammatical.

   If we look closely at the examples in (23), we see a fairly obvious pattern emerging. Each of the bracketed argument expressions in (23) carries one and only one θ-role, and no two arguments of any predicate carry the same θ-role. Chomsky (1981) suggested that these thematic properties of arguments are the consequence of a principle of Universal Grammar traditionally referred to as the **θ-criterion**, and outlined in (30) below:

(30)   **Theta-criterion/θ-criterion**
            Each argument bears one and only one θ-role, and each θ-role is assigned to one and only one argument (Chomsky 1981, p. 36)

A principle along the lines of (30) has been assumed (in some form or other) in much subsequent work.

   However, a question which arises from (30) is how θ-roles are assigned to arguments. It seems clear that in V-bar constituents of the form *verb+complement*, the thematic role of the complement is determined by the semantic properties of the verb. As examples like (23a–c) illustrate, the θ-role associated with complements is often that of THEME (though this is not always the case – e.g. the complement *me* of the verb *bother* in *Personally, it doesn't bother me* has the thematic role of EXPERIENCER). However, the question of how subjects are assigned θ-roles is more complex.

Marantz (1984, pp. 23ff.) and Chomsky (1986a, pp. 59–60) argue that although verbs directly assign θ-roles to their internal arguments (i.e. complements), it is not the verb but rather the whole verb+complement (i.e. V-bar) expression which determines the θ-role assigned to its external argument. The evidence they adduce in support of this conclusion comes from sentences such as:

(31) (a)   John threw a ball
     (b)   John threw a fit

(32) (a)   John broke the window
     (b)   John broke his arm

Although the subject of the verb *threw* in both (31a) and (31b), *John* plays a different thematic role in the two sentences – that of AGENT in the case of *threw a ball*, but that of EXPERIENCER in *threw a fit*. Likewise, although the subject of the verb *broke* in both (32a) and (32b), *John* plays the role of AGENT in (32a) but that of EXPERIENCER on the most natural (accidental arm-breaking) interpretation of (32b). From examples such as these, Marantz and Chomsky conclude that the thematic role of the subject is not determined by the verb alone, but rather is compositionally determined by the whole verb+complement structure – i.e. by V-bar. On this view, a verb assigns a θ-role *directly* to its internal argument, but only *indirectly* (as a compositional function of the semantic properties of the overall V-bar) to its external argument. To use the relevant technical terminology, we can say that predicates **directly θ-mark** their complements, but **indirectly θ-mark** their subjects/specifiers.

A related observation is that auxiliaries seem to play no part in determining the assignment of θ-roles to subjects. For example, in sentences such as:

(33) (a)   He will throw the ball/a fit
     (b)   He was throwing the ball/a fit
     (c)   He had been throwing the ball/a fit
     (d)   He might have been throwing the ball/a fit

the thematic role of the subject *he* is determined purely by the choice of V-bar constituent (i.e. whether it is *throw the ball* or *throw a fit*), and is not affected in any way by the choice of auxiliary. Clearly, any theory of θ-marking should offer us a principled answer to questions such as the following: how are θ-roles assigned? Why do some constituents (e.g. verbs) play a key role in θ-marking, while others (e.g. auxiliaries) do not?

We can provide a principled answer to these questions in the following terms. Let us assume that θ-roles are assigned to arguments via merger with a predicative expression (i.e. an expression headed by an item which functions as a predicate – e.g. a verb). In the light of this observation, consider our earlier sentence (18b) *The police have arrested the suspect*. Since the verb *arrested* is a predicate which selects a THEME complement, the complement *the suspect* will be assigned the θ-role of THEME argument of *arrest* when the verb merges with its complement. Since *arrest* is a predicate which (in addition to requiring a THEME complement) also requires an AGENT external argument, the subject *the police* will be assigned the θ-role of AGENT argument of *arrest* when it merges with the V-bar *arrested the suspect*. The resulting VP *the police arrested the suspect* is then merged with the auxiliary *have* to form the T-bar *have the police arrested the suspect*. Because a finite T has an [EPP] feature requiring it to have a specifier, the subject *the police* raises to spec-TP, deriving *The police have ~~the police~~ arrested the suspect*. However, the subject *the police* does not receive any θ-role from the auxiliary *have*, since auxiliaries are not predicates (unlike main verbs) and hence do not θ-mark their subjects. The resulting TP is ultimately merged with a null declarative complementiser to derive the structure associated with (18b) *The police have arrested the suspect*.

Our discussion here suggests that thematic considerations lend further support to the VP-Internal Subject Hypothesis. By positing that subjects originate internally within VP, we can arrive at a unitary and principled account of θ-marking in terms of *sisterhood*, in that an argument is θ-marked by a predicative expression which is its sister: e.g. the verb *arrested* in (21) θ-marks its sister argument (complement) *the suspect*, and the V-bar *arrested the suspect* θ-marks its sister (subject) argument *the police*.

7.6   Unaccusative predicates

The overall conclusion to be drawn from our discussion so far is that subjects originate internally within VP, as θ-marked arguments of the verb. In all the structures we have looked at until now, the verb phrase has contained both a complement and a specifier (the specifier being the subject of the verb). However, in this and subsequent sections we look at VPs containing a verb and a complement *but no specifier*, and where it is the complement of the verb which subsequently moves to spec-TP.

One such type of VP are those headed by a special subclass of intransitive verbs which are known as **unaccusative predicates** for reasons which will become apparent shortly. In this connection, consider the syntax of the italicised arguments in structures such as the following:

(34) (a)   There have **arisen** *several complications*
    (b)   There could have **occurred** *a diplomatic incident*
    (c)   There **remains** *little hope of finding survivors*

The fact that the italicised expressions are positioned after the bold-printed verbs suggests that they function as the complements of the relevant verbs – and indeed there is syntactic evidence in support of this view. Part of the evidence comes from their behaviour in relation to a constraint on movement operations discovered by Huang (1982) which we discussed in §6.7 and characterised as follows:

(35)   **Constraint on Extraction Domains/CED**
        Only complements allow material to be extracted out of them, not specifiers or adjuncts.

In the light of Huang's CED constraint, consider a sentence such as:

(36)   *How many survivors* does there remain [some hope of finding ~~how many survivors~~]?

Here, the wh-phrase *how many survivors* has been extracted (via **wh-movement**) out of the bracketed expression *some hope of finding how many survivors*. Given that the Condition on Extraction Domains tells us that only complements allow material to be extracted out of them, it follows that the bracketed expression in (36) must be the complement of the verb *remain*. By extension, we can assume that the italicised expressions in (34) are likewise the complements of the bold-printed verbs.

A further argument supporting the claim that unaccusative subjects are initially merged as complements comes from observations about **quantifier stranding** in the West Ulster variety of English. McCloskey (2000) notes that West Ulster English allows wh-questions such as (37) below which have the interpretation 'What are all the things that you got for Christmas?':

(37) (a)   **What** *all* did you get for Christmas?
     (b)   **What** did you get *all* for Christmas?

He argues that when the universal quantifier *all* is used to modify a wh-word like *what*, wh-movement can either move the whole expression *what all* to the front of the sentence (as in 37a), or can move the word *what* on its own, thereby **stranding** the quantifier in situ (as in 37b). In the light of his observation, consider the following sentence:

(38)   **What** happened *all* at the party last night?

The fact that the quantifier *all* is stranded in a position following the unaccusative verb *happened* suggests that the wh-expression *what all* originates in postverbal position as the complement of the verb *happened*. More generally, sentences like (38) provide empirical evidence in support of positing that unaccusative subjects are initially merged as complements.

However, the unaccusative complements italicised in structures like (34) differ in an important respect from the complements of typical transitive verbs. A typical transitive verb has a thematic subject and a thematic complement, and assigns accusative case to its complement (as in *She hit him*, where *hit* has the nominative AGENT subject *she* and the accusative THEME complement *him*). However, unaccusative structures like (34) differ from transitive structures in that they have a non-thematic *there* subject (which is non-thematic in the sense that it isn't a theta-marked argument of the verb, but rather is a pure expletive), and (in languages which have a richer case system than English) the italicised complement receives *nominative* (= NOM) case, as the following Icelandic example (which Matthew Whelpton kindly asked Johannes Gisli Jónsson to provide for me) illustrates:

(39)   það   hafa komið *nokkrir*_{NOM} *gestir*_{NOM}
         There have come some   guests

Because they don't assign accusative case to their complements, such verbs are known as **unaccusative predicates**.

Not all intransitive verbs allow their arguments to be positioned after them, however – as we see from the ungrammaticality of sentences such as (40) below:

(40) (a)   *When the Snail Rail train arrived five hours late, there complained *many passengers*
     (b)   *In the dentist's surgery, there groaned *a toothless patient*
     (c)   *Every time General Wynott Nukem goes past, there salutes *a guard at the gate*

Intransitive verbs like *complain/groan/salute* are known as **unergative verbs**: they differ from unaccusatives in that the subject of an unergative verb has the thematic role of an AGENT argument, whereas the subject of an unaccusative verb has the thematic property of being a THEME argument.

In addition to the contrast illustrated in (34) and (40) above, there are a number of other important syntactic differences between unaccusative verbs and other types of verb (e.g. unergative verbs or transitive verbs). For example, Alison Henry (1995) notes that in one dialect of Belfast English (which she calls dialect A) unaccusative verbs can have (italicised) postverbal subjects in imperative structures like:

(41) (a)   Leave *you* now!
     (b)   Arrive *you* before 6 o'clock!
     (c)   Be going *you* out of the door when he arrives!

By contrast, other (e.g. unergative or transitive) verbs don't allow postverbal imperative subjects, so that imperatives such as (42) below are ungrammatical in the relevant dialect:

(42) (a)   *Read *you* that book!
     (b)   *Eat *you* up!
     (c)   *Always *laugh* you at his jokes!

Additional evidence for positing that unaccusative verbs are syntactically distinct from other verbs comes from **auxiliary selection** facts in relation to earlier stages of English when there were two perfect auxiliaries (*have* and *be*), each taking a complement headed by a specific kind of verb. Unaccusative verbs differed from transitive or unergative verbs in being used with the perfect auxiliary *be*, as the sentences in (43) below (taken from various plays by Shakespeare) illustrate:

(43) (a)   Mistress Page *is* **come** with me (Mrs Ford, *The Merry Wives of Windsor*, V.v)

(b)   *Is* the duke **gone**? Then *is* your cause **gone** too (Duke, *Measure for Measure*, V.i)

(c)   How chance thou *art* **returned** so soon? (Antipholus, *The Comedy of Errors*, I.ii)

(d)   She *is* **fallen** into a pit of ink (Leonato, *Much Ado About Nothing*, IV.i)

We find a similar contrast with the counterparts of perfect *have/be* in a number of other languages – e.g. Italian and French (cf. Burzio 1986), Sardinian (cf. Jones 1994), German and Dutch (cf. Haegeman 1994), and Danish (cf. Spencer 1991): see Sorace (2000) for further discussion. A last vestige of structures like (43) survives in present-day English structures such as *All hope of finding survivors is now gone*.

A further difference between unaccusative predicates and others relates to the adjectival use of their perfect-participle forms. As the examples below indicate, perfect-participle (*-n/-d*) forms of unaccusative verbs can be used adjectivally (to modify a noun), e.g. in sentences such as:

(44) (a)   The train *arrived* at platform 4 is the delayed 8.28 for London Euston

(b)   The vice squad arrested a businessman recently *returned* from Thailand

(c)   Several facts recently *come* to light point to his guilt

(d)   Brigadier Bungle is something of a *fallen* hero

By contrast, perfect-participle forms of (active) transitive verbs or unergative verbs cannot be used in the same way, as we see from the ungrammaticality of examples like (45) below:

(45) (a)   *The man *committed* suicide was a neighbour of mine

(b)   *The thief *stolen* the jewels was never captured

(c)   *The man *overdosed* was Joe Dough

(d)   *The *yawned* student eventually fell asleep in class

In this respect, unaccusative verbs resemble passive participles, which can also be used adjectivally (cf. *a changed man, a battered wife, a woman arrested for shoplifting* etc.). Additional syntactic differences between unaccusative verbs and others have been reported for other languages (see e.g. Burzio 1986 on *ne* cliticisation in Italian, and Contreras 1986 on bare nominals in Spanish).

We thus have a considerable body of empirical evidence that unaccusative subjects behave differently from subjects of other (e.g. unergative or transitive) verbs. Why should this be? The answer given in work dating back to Burzio (1986) is that the subjects of unaccusative verbs do not originate as the subjects of their associated verbs at all, but rather as their *complements*, and that unaccusative structures with postverbal arguments involve leaving the relevant argument *in situ* in VP-complement position – e.g. in unaccusative expletive structures such as (34) above, and in Belfast English unaccusative imperatives such as (41). This being so, a sentence such as (34a) *There have arisen several complications* will be derived as follows. The quantifier *several* merges with the noun *complications* to form the QP *several complications*. This is merged as the complement of the unaccusative verb *arisen*, forming the VP *arisen several complications*. The resulting VP is merged with the auxiliary *have* to form the T-bar shown in simplified form below:

(46)

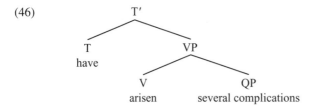

The [EPP] feature carried by the finite T constituent *have* requires it to have a nominal expression as its specifier. This requirement is satisfied by merging expletive *there* in spec-TP. The resulting TP *there have arisen several complications* is then merged with a null declarative-force complementiser to form the CP (47) below:

(47)

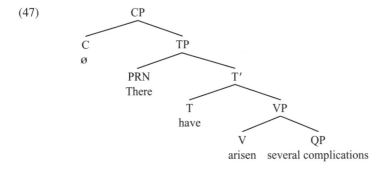

And (47) is the structure of (34a) *There have arisen several complications*.

However, an alternative way for the T constituent in (46) to satisfy the [EPP] requirement to have a nominal specifier is for T to attract a nominal to move to spec-TP. In accordance with the **Attract Closest Principle**, T will attract the closest nominal within the structure containing it. Since the only nominal in (46) is the QP *several complications*, T therefore attracts this QP to move to spec-TP in the manner shown in simplified form in (48) below:

(48)

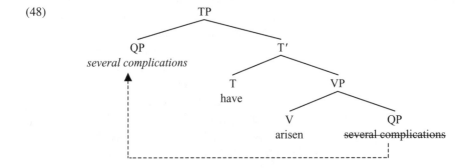

The type of movement involved is the familiar **A-movement** operation which moves an argument from a position lower down in a sentence to become the structural subject (and specifier) of TP. The resulting TP in (48) is subsequently merged with a null complementiser marking the declarative force of the sentence, so generating the structure associated with *Several complications have arisen*.

The A-movement analysis of unaccusative subjects outlined in (48) above allows us to provide an interesting account of sentence pairs like that in (49) below:

(49) (a)   All hope of finding survivors has gone
    (b)   All hope has gone of finding survivors

Since GO is an unaccusative verb, the QP *all hope of finding survivors* will originate as the complement of *gone*. Merging *gone* with this QP will derive the VP *gone all hope of finding survivors*. The resulting VP is merged with the T constituent *has* to form the T-bar *has gone all hope of finding survivors*. Since T has an [EPP] feature requiring it to project a specifier, the QP *all hope of finding survivors* is raised to spec-TP, leaving an (italicised) copy behind in the position in which it originated. Merging the resulting TP with a null complementiser marking the declarative force of the sentence derives the structure shown in simplified form in (50) below:

(50)   [CP [C ø] [TP [QP **All hope of finding survivors**] [T has] [VP [V gone]
       [QP *all hope of finding survivors*]]]]

In the case of (49a), the whole of the QP *all hope of finding survivors* is spelled out in the bold-printed spec-TP position it moves to, and the italicised copy of the moved QP in VP-complement position is deleted in its entirety – as shown in simplified form in (51) below:

(51)   [CP [C ø] [TP [QP **All hope of finding survivors**] [T has] [VP [V gone]
      [QP ~~*all hope of finding survivors*~~]]]]

In the case of (49b), the quantifier *all* and the noun *hope* are spelled out in the bold-printed position they move to in (50), and the PP *of finding survivors* is spelled out in the VP-complement position in which it originates – as shown in (52) below:

(52)   [CP [C ø] [TP [QP **All hope ~~of finding survivors~~**] [T has] [VP [V gone]
      [QP ~~*all hope*~~ *of finding survivors*]]]]

(52) thus presents us with another example of the **discontinuous/split spellout** phenomenon highlighted in §6.3. It also provides evidence in support of taking A-movement (like other movement operations) to be a composite operation involving copying and deletion.

7.7   Passive predicates

A class of predicates which are similar in some respects to unaccusative predicates are **passive predicates**. Traditional grammarians maintain that the bold-printed verbs in sentences such as the (a) examples in (53)–(55) below are in the **active voice**, whereas the italicised verbs in the corresponding (b) sentences are in the **passive voice** (and have the status of **passive participles**):

(53) (a)   Hundreds of passers-by **saw** the attack
     (b)   The attack was *seen* by hundreds of passers-by

(54) (a)   Lex Luthor **stole** the kryptonite
     (b)   The kryptonite was *stolen* by Lex Luthor

(55) (a)   They **took** everything
     (b)   Everything was *taken*

There are four main properties which differentiate passive sentences from their active counterparts. One is that passive (though not active) sentences generally require the auxiliary BE. Another is that the main verb in passive sentences is in the passive participle form (cf. *seen/stolen/taken*), which is generally homophonous with the perfect-participle form. A third is that passive sentences may (though need not) contain a *by*-phrase in which the complement of *by* plays the same thematic role as the subject in the corresponding active sentence: for example, *hundreds of passers-by* in the active structure (53a) serves as the subject of *saw the attack*, whereas in the passive structure (53b) it serves as the complement of the preposition *by* (though in both cases it has the thematic role of EXPERIENCER argument of *see*). The fourth difference is that the expression which serves as the complement of an active verb surfaces as the subject in the corresponding passive construction: for example, *the attack* is the complement of *saw* in the active structure (53a), but is the subject of *was* in the passive structure (53b). Since this chapter is concerned with A-movement (and hence the syntax of subjects), we focus on the syntax of the superficial subjects of passive sentences (setting aside the derivation of *by*-phrases).

Passive predicates resemble unaccusatives in that alongside structures like those in (56a)–(58a) below containing preverbal subjects they also allow expletive structures like (56b)–(58b), in which the italicised argument can be postverbal (providing it is an indefinite expression):

(56) (a)   *No evidence of any corruption* was found
     (b)   There was found *no evidence of any corruption*

(57) (a)   *Several cases of syntactophobia* have been reported
     (b)   There have been reported *several cases of syntactophobia*

(58) (a)   *A significant change of policy* has been announced
      (b)   There has been announced *a significant change of policy*

How can we account for the dual position of the italicised expression in such structures?

The answer given within the framework outlined here is that a passive subject is initially merged as the thematic complement of the main verb (i.e. it originates as the complement of the main verb as in (56b)–(58b) and so receives the θ-role which the relevant verb assigns to its complement), and subsequently moves from VP-complement position into TP-specifier position in passive sentences such as (56a)–(58a). On this view, the derivation of sentences like (56) will proceed as follows. The noun *corruption* merges with the quantifier *any* to form the QP *any corruption*. The resulting QP then merges with the preposition *of* to form the PP *of any corruption*. This PP in turn merges with the noun *evidence* to form the NP *evidence of any corruption*. The resulting NP is merged with the negative quantifier *no* to form the QP *no evidence of any corruption*. This QP is merged as the complement of the passive verb *found* (and thereby assigned the thematic role of THEME argument of *found*) to form the VP *found no evidence of any corruption*. The VP thereby formed is merged with the auxiliary *was* forming the T-bar *was found no evidence of any corruption*. The auxiliary [$_T$ *was*] carries an [EPP] feature requiring it to have a specifier. This requirement can be satisfied by merging the expletive pronoun *there* in spec-TP, deriving the TP *There was found no evidence of any corruption*. Merging this TP with a null complementiser marking the declarative force of the sentence will derive the structure shown in simplified form in (59) below:

(59)

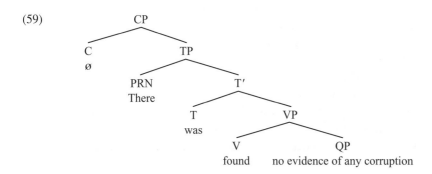

However, an alternative way of satisfying the [EPP] feature of T is not to merge *there* in spec-TP but rather to **passivise** the QP *no evidence of any corruption* – i.e. to move it from being the thematic object of *found* to becoming the structural subject of *was*. Merging the resulting TP with a null complementiser which marks the sentence as declarative in force derives the CP shown in simplified form in (60) below (with the dotted arrow showing the movement which took place on the TP cycle):

(60)

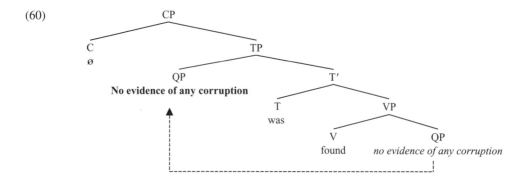

The arrowed movement operation (traditionally called **passivisation**) by which QP moves from thematic complement position into structural subject position turns out to be a particular instance of the more general **A-movement** operation which serves to create structural subjects (i.e. to move arguments into spec-TP in order to satisfy the [EPP] feature of T). Note that an assumption implicit in the analyses in (59) and (60) is that verb phrases headed by intransitive passive participles remain subjectless throughout the derivation, because the T constituent *was* is the head which requires a structural subject by virtue of its [EPP] feature, not the verb *found* (suggesting that it is functional heads like T and C which trigger movement, not lexical heads like V).

In the case of (56a) *No evidence of any corruption was found*, the whole of the QP *no evidence of any corruption* is spelled out in the bold-printed spec-TP position in (60) at the **head** of the movement chain, and all the material in the italicised VP-complement position at the **foot** of the movement chain is deleted. However, in §6.3 we saw that some structures in which a moved noun has a prepositional complement may allow **discontinuous spellout**, with the noun and any preceding expressions modifying it being spelled out at the head of the movement chain, and its prepositional or clausal complement being spelled out at the foot of the movement chain. Discontinuous spellout is also permitted in (60), allowing for the possibility of the quantifier *no* and the noun *evidence* being spelled out in the bold-printed position at the head of the movement chain, and the PP *of any corruption* being spelled out in the italicised VP-complement position at the foot of the movement chain, so deriving the structure associated with the sentence in (61) below:

(61)   **No evidence** was found *of any corruption*

Sentences such as (61) thus provide us with empirical evidence that passive subjects originate as complements, on the assumption that *of any corruption* is a remnant of the preposed complement *no evidence of any corruption*.

Further evidence that passive subjects originate as complements comes from the distribution of idiomatic nominals like those italicised below:

(62) (a)   They **paid** *little heed* to what he said

   (b)   *Little heed* was **paid** to what he said

(63) (a)   They **paid** *due homage* to General Ghouly

   (b)   *Due homage* was **paid** to General Ghouly

(64) (a)   The FBI **kept** *close tabs* on the CIA

   (b)   *Close tabs* were **kept** on the CIA by the FBI

In expressions such as *pay heed/homage to* and *keep tabs on*, the verb *pay/keep* and the noun expression containing *heed/tabs/homage* together form an idiom. Given our arguments in §7.3 that idioms are unitary constituents, it is apparent that the bold-printed verb and the italicised noun expression must form a unitary constituent when they are first introduced into the derivation. This will clearly be the case if we suppose that the noun expression originates as the complement of the associated verb (as in (62a)–(64a)), and becomes the subject of the passive auxiliary *was/were* in (62b)–(64b) via passivisation/A-movement.

Additional evidence that passive subjects are initially merged as complements comes from quantifier stranding in West Ulster English structures such as the following (from McCloskey 2000, p. 72):

(65)   **What** was said *all* at the meeting?

Recall from our earlier discussion of sentences like (37) that McCloskey argues that stranded quantifiers modifying wh-expressions are left behind via movement of the wh-expression without the quantifier. This being so, sentences such as (65) provide evidence that *what all* originates as the complement of the passive participle *said* (with *what* subsequently being passivised on its own, stranding *all*) – and more generally, that passive subjects are initially merged as thematic objects.

A claim which is implicit in the hypothesis that passive subjects originate as thematic objects is that the subjects of active verbs and the complements of passive verbs have the same thematic function. Evidence that this is indeed the case comes from the traditional observation that the two are subject to the same pragmatic restrictions on the choice of expression which can occupy the relevant position, as we see from sentences such as the following (where ?, ?! and ! mark increasing degrees of pragmatic anomaly):

(66) (a)   *The students/?the camels/?!The flowers/!The ideas* were arrested

   (b)   They arrested *the students/?the camels/?!the flowers/!the ideas*

We can account for this if we suppose that pragmatic restrictions on the choice of admissible arguments for a given predicate depend jointly on the semantic properties of the predicate and the thematic role of the argument: it will then follow that two expressions which fulfil the same thematic role in respect of a given predicate will be subject to the same pragmatic restrictions on argument choice.

Since passive subjects like those italicised in (66a) originate as complements, they will have the same θ-role (and hence be subject to the same pragmatic restrictions on argument choice) as active complements like those italicised in (66b).

We can arrive at the same conclusion (that passive subjects originate as thematic complements) on theoretical grounds. It seems reasonable to suppose that principles of UG correlate thematic structure with syntactic structure in a uniform fashion: this assumption is embodied in the **Uniform Theta Assignment Hypothesis/UTAH** argued for at length in Baker (1988). Given **UTAH**, it follows that two arguments which fulfil the same thematic function with respect to a given predicate will occupy the same initial position in the syntax. Hence if passive subjects have the same θ-role as active objects, it is plausible to suppose that passive subjects originate in the same VP-complement position as active objects.

7.8   Long-distance passivisation

Thus far, the instances of passivisation which we have looked at have been clause-internal in the sense that they have involved movement from complement to subject position within the same clause/TP. However, passivisation can also apply across certain types of clause boundary – as can be illustrated in relation to structures such as (67) and (68) below:

(67) (a)   There are alleged to have been **stolen** *a number of portraits of the queen*

    (b)   *A number of portraits of the queen* are alleged to have been **stolen**

(68) (a)   There are believed to have **occurred** *several riots*

    (b)   *Several riots* are believed to have **occurred**

It seems clear that the italicised expression in each case is the thematic complement of the bold-printed verb in the infinitive clause, so that *a number of portraits of the queen* is the thematic complement of the passive verb *stolen* in (67), and *several riots* is the thematic complement of the unaccusative verb *occurred* in (68). In (67a) and (68a), the italicised argument remains *in situ* as the complement of the bold-printed verb; but in (67b) and (68b) the italicised argument moves to become the structural subject of the auxiliary *are*. Let's look rather more closely at the derivation of sentences like (68a) on the one hand and (68b) on the other.

(68a) is derived as follows. The quantifier *several* merges with the noun *riots* to form the QP *several riots*. This QP merges with (and is θ-marked by) the unaccusative verb *occurred* to form the VP *occurred several riots*. The resulting VP merges with the perfect auxiliary *have* to form the AUXP *have occurred several riots*. This in turn merges with the infinitival tense particle *to*, so forming the TP *to have occurred several riots*. The resulting TP merges with the passive verb *believed* to form the VP *believed to have occurred several riots*. This then merges with the auxiliary *are* to form the T-bar *are believed to have occurred several riots*. A finite T like *are* has an [EPP] feature requiring it to have a specifier, and one way of satisfying this requirement is for expletive *there* to be merged in spec-TP, forming the TP shown in (69) below (simplified by not showing intermediate projections, and by not showing the internal structure of the QP *several riots*):

(69)   [TP There [T are] [VP [V believed] [TP [T to] [AUXP [AUX have]
         [VP [V occurred] [QP several riots]]]]]]

However, an alternative way of satisfying the [EPP] requirement for *are* to have a structural subject is for the closest nominal expression it c-commands (namely, *several riots*) to **passivise** (i.e. undergo A-movement) and thereby move into spec-TP, as shown by the dotted arrow in (70) below (where *t* is a trace copy of the moved QP *several riots*):

(70)   [TP *Several riots* [T are] [VP [V believed] [TP [T to] [AUXP [AUX have] [VP [V occurred] [QP *t*]]]]]]

The kind of passivisation operation shown by the dotted arrow in (70) is sometimes termed **long-distance passivisation**, since it involves moving an argument out of a lower TP into the specifier position in a higher TP. Since operations which move a nominal into spec-TP are instances of A-movement, long-distance passivisation is yet another instance of the familiar **A-movement** operation. The TPs in (69,70) will subsequently be merged with a null complementiser marking the declarative force of the sentence, so deriving the overall structure associated with (68a,b).

A key assumption made in (69, 70) is that the *to*-infinitive complement of the verb *believed* is a TP and not a CP. This is in line with our assumption in §4.8 that *believe* is an ECM verb when used with an infinitival complement, and that its complement is a defective clause (lacking the CP layer found in canonical clauses) and hence a TP. Recall that we have independent evidence from contrasts such as the following:

(71) (a)   Nobody intended [*you* to get hurt]
     (b)   *You* weren't intended [to get hurt]

(72) (a)   Nobody intended [for *you* to get hurt]
     (b)   **You* weren't intended [for to get hurt]

that an (italicised) expression contained within a TP complement like that bracketed in (71) can passivise, but an expression contained within a CP complement like that bracketed in (72) cannot. Consequently, the fact that *several riots* can passivise in (70) suggests that the *to*-infinitive complement of *believed* must be a TP, not a CP.

Evidence that we need to posit a long-distance passivisation operation comes from the fact that idiomatic nominals can undergo long-distance passivisation, as in the following examples:

(73) (a)   *Little heed* is thought to have been **paid** to what he said
   (b)   *Close tabs* are alleged to have been **kept** on the FBI
   (c)   *All hell* is expected to **break loose**
   (d)   *The shit* is said to have **hit the fan**

The italicised idiomatic nominals are normally used as the complement of the bold-printed verbs in (73a,b) and as the subject of the bold-printed expressions in (73c,d). So how do they come to be used as the subject of a higher passive clause in sentences like (73)? The answer is that they undergo long-distance passivisation. Note, incidentally, that sentences like (73c,d) suggest that long-distance passivisation can move *subjects* as well as *objects*. This is because (in conformity with the **Attract Closest Principle**), passivisation involves movement of the closest nominal which the relevant tense auxiliary c-commands. In a clause like (73a) in which the verb *paid* projects a complement but no subject, the auxiliary will trigger preposing of the complement *little heed* on the TP cycle because this is the closest nominal c-commanded by the auxiliary *is* – the relevant movement being shown in skeletal form in (74a) below; by contrast, in a clause like (73c) in which the verb *break* projects a subject *all hell*, the auxiliary *is* will trigger passivisation of *all hell* because this is the closest nominal c-commanded by *is* – as shown in (74b) below:

(74) (a)   [TP *Little heed* [T is] [VP [V thought] [TP [T to] have been [VP [V paid] ~~little heed~~ to what he said]]]]

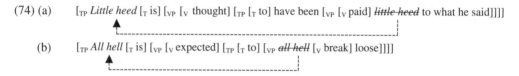

   (b)   [TP *All hell* [T is] [VP [V expected] [TP [T to] [VP ~~all hell~~ [V break] loose]]]]

Although we have referred to the movement operation involved in structures like (74) as long-distance passivisation, it is in fact our familiar **A-movement** operation by which T attracts the closest nominal expression which it c-commands to move to spec-TP. (An incidental detail to note is that the TPs in (74) are subsequently merged with a null complementiser marking the declarative force of the sentence.)

7.9   Raising

A further type of structure which involves movement of an argument expression out of one clause to become the subject of another clause is illustrated by the (b) examples in (75)–(78) below:

(75) (a)   There does **seem** [to remain *some hope of peace*]
   (b)   *Some hope of peace* does **seem** [to remain]

(76) (a)   There does **appear** [to have been made *remarkably little progress on disarmament*]
   (b)   *Remarkably little progress on disarmament* does **appear** [to have been made]

(77) (a)   It would **seem** [that *Senator Slyme* has been lying to Congress]
     (b)   *Senator Slyme* would **seem** [to have been lying to Congress]

(78) (a)   It would **appear** [that *they* have underestimated her]
     (b)   *They* would appear [to have underestimated her]

In (75), the italicised expression *some hope of peace* is the thematic complement of the unaccusative predicate *remain*; it remains *in situ* in the expletive structure (75a), but raises to become the subject of the *seem*-clause in (75b). In (76), the italicised expression *remarkably little progress on disarmament* is the thematic complement of the passive verb *made*; it remains in situ in the expletive structure (76a) but raises to become the subject of the *appear*-clause in (76b). In (77), the italicised expression *Senator Slyme* is the thematic subject of the verb *lying*: if the complement clause is a finite clause as in (77a), it surfaces as the subject of the complement clause; but if the complement clause is infinitival as in (77b), it surfaces as the subject of the *seem* clause. Likewise, in (78), the italicised pronoun *they* is the thematic subject of the verb *underestimate*: if the complement clause is finite as in (78a), it surfaces as the subject of the complement clause; if the complement clause is infinitival as in (78b), it surfaces as the subject of the *appear* clause.

   Examples like (75)–(78) suggest that verbs like *seem* and *appear* resemble passive predicates in that they allow an expression which is a theta-marked argument of a predicate in a lower clause to raise to become the subject of the *seem/appear*-clause. Given this assumption, a sentence such as (75b) will have the following simplified derivation. At the point where the QP *some hope of ø peace* has been formed (the noun *peace* having been merged with a null quantifier), it will be merged with (and θ-marked by) the verb *remain* to form the VP *remain some hope of ø peace*. This VP is then merged with the infinitival tense particle *to* to form the TP *to remain some hope of ø peace*. The resulting infinitival TP is subsequently merged with the verb *seem* to form the VP *seem to remain some hope of ø peace*. This in turn is merged with the finite tense auxiliary DO to form the T-bar *does seem to remain some hope of ø peace*. A finite T has an [EPP] feature requiring it to have a subject; one way of satisfying this requirement is to merge expletive *there* with the resulting T-bar, to form the TP shown in simplified form in (79) below:

(79)   [TP *There* [T does] [VP [V seem] [TP [T to] [VP [V remain] some hope of ø peace]]]]

An alternative way of satisfying the [EPP] feature of [T *does*] is to move the closest nominal c-commanded by *does* (= the QP *some hope of ø peace*) from being the thematic complement of *remain* to becoming the structural subject of *does*, as shown in simplified form in (80) below:

(80)   [TP *Some hope of ø peace* [T does] [VP [V seem] [TP [T to] [VP [V remain] ~~some hope of ø peace~~]]]]

The type of movement operation arrowed in (80) is traditionally known as **raising** (because it *raises* an argument out of a lower clause to become the subject of a higher clause) but in reality it turns out to be yet another instance of the more general **A-movement** operation by which T attracts the closest nominal which it c-commands to move to spec-TP. Words like *seem/appear* (when used with an infinitival complement) have the property that the subject of the *seem/appear*-clause is created by being raised out of a complement clause, and so (for this reason) are known as **raising predicates**. The parallels between raising in structures like (80) and long-distance passivisation in structures like (70) should be obvious. (A minor detail to be tidied up is that the TPs in (79) and (80) are subsequently merged with a null complementiser marking the sentence as declarative in force.)

7.10   Comparing raising and control predicates

It might at first sight seem tempting to conclude from our discussion of long-distance passivisation structures like (74) and raising structures like (80) that all clauses containing a structure of the form *verb+to+infinitive* have a similar derivation to that in (74) and (80) in which some expression is raised out of the infinitive complement to become the subject of the main clause. However, any such conclusion would be undermined by our claim in §4.2 and §4.7 that some verbs which take *to+infinitive* complements are **control predicates**. In this connection, consider the difference between the two types of infinitive structure illustrated below:

(81) (a)   He does seem [to scare them]
     (b)   He does want [to scare them]

As used in (81), the verb *seem* is a **raising predicate**, but the verb *want* is a **control predicate**. We will see that this reflects the fact that the verbs *seem* and *want* differ in respect of their argument structure. We can illustrate this by sketching out the derivation of the two sentences.

In the raising structure (81a), the verb *scare* merges with (and assigns the EXPERIENCER θ-role to) its internal argument/thematic complement *them*. The resulting V-bar *scare them* then merges with (and assigns the AGENT θ-role to) its external argument/thematic subject *he*. The resulting VP *he scare them* is then merged with the infinitival tense particle *to*, so forming the TP *to he scare them*. This in turn merges with the raising verb *seem* to form the VP *seem to he scare them*. The resulting VP *seem to he scare them* is subsequently merged with the (emphatic) auxiliary *does*. The [EPP] feature carried by [T *does*] requiring it to have a structural subject triggers raising of the closest nominal c-commanded by *does* (namely *he*) from being thematic subject of *scare them* to becoming structural subject of *does* – as shown in schematic form below:

(82)   [$_{TP}$ *He* [$_T$ does] [$_{VP}$ [$_V$ seem] [$_{TP}$ [$_T$ to] [$_{VP}$ ~~he~~ [$_V$ scare] them]]]]

The resulting TP is then merged with a null complementiser marking the sentence as declarative in force.

A key assumption made in the raising analysis in (82) is that the verb *seem* (as used there) is a one-place predicate whose only argument is its infinitival TP complement, to which it assigns an appropriate θ-role – perhaps that of THEME argument of *seem*. This means that the VP headed by *seem* has no thematic subject: note, in particular, that the verb *seem* does not θ-mark the pronoun *he*, since *he* is θ-marked by *scare*, and the θ-CRITERION (30) rules out the possibility of any argument being θ-marked by more than one predicate. Nor does the VP headed by *seem* have a structural subject at any stage of derivation, since *he* raises to become the subject of the TP containing *does*, not of the VP containing *seem*.

Now let's turn to consider the derivation of the control infinitive structure (81b) *He does want to scare them*. As before, the verb *scare* merges with (and assigns the EXPERIENCER θ-role to) its internal argument (i.e. thematic complement) *them*. The resulting V-bar *scare them* then merges with (and assigns the AGENT θ-role to) its external argument. Given the assumption we made in §4.2 that control infinitives have a particular kind of null pronominal subject known as 'big PRO', the thematic subject of *scare them* will be PRO, and this will be merged in spec-VP (in accordance with the VP-Internal Subject Hypothesis), and thereby be assigned the θ-role of AGENT argument of *scare*. The resulting VP *PRO scare them* then merges with infinitival *to*, forming the TP *to PRO scare them*. Given the conclusion we drew in §4.8 that control infinitives are CPs, this TP will in turn merge with a null infinitival complementiser to form the CP *ø to PRO scare them*. The CP thereby formed serves as the internal argument (and thematic complement) of the verb *want*, so is merged with *want* and thereby assigned the θ-role of THEME argument of *want*. The resulting V-bar *want ø to PRO scare them* then merges with its external argument (and thematic subject) *he*, assigning *he* the thematic role of EXPERIENCER argument of *want*. The resulting VP *he want ø to PRO scare them* is then merged with the tense auxiliary DO, forming the T-bar *does he want ø to PRO scare them*. The [EPP] feature carried by [$_T$ does] requires it to have a structural subject, and this requirement is satisfied by moving the closest noun or pronoun expression c-commanded by *does* (namely the pronoun *he*) to become the structural subject of *does*, as shown in simplified form below:

(83)   [$_{TP}$ *He* [$_T$ does] [$_{VP}$ ~~he~~ [$_V$ want] [$_{CP}$ [$_C$ ø] [$_{TP}$ [$_T$ to] [$_{VP}$ PRO [$_V$ scare] them]]]]]

The TP in (83) is then merged with a null complementiser marking the sentence as declarative in force. The resulting structure satisfies the **θ-criterion** (which requires each argument to be assigned a single θ-role, and each θ-role to be assigned to a single argument), in that *he* is the EXPERIENCER argument of *want*, the bracketed CP in (83) is the THEME complement of *want*, PRO is the AGENT argument of *scare*, and *them* the EXPERIENCER argument of *scare*.

The analysis of control predicates presented here differs from that presented in chapter 4 in that it assumes that the PRO subject of a control infinitive like that bracketed in (81b) *He does want to scare them* is merged in spec-VP, and not (as assumed in chapter 4) in spec-TP. As we have seen, the requirement for PRO to be generated in spec-VP follows from the **Predicate-Internal Argument Hypothesis** (19) which posits that arguments are generated internally to a projection of their predicate, so that PRO (by virtue of being the thematic subject of *scare*) is generated as the specifier of the VP headed by *scare*. Baltin (1995, p. 244) provides an empirical argument in favour of claiming that the PRO subject is positioned in spec-VP in control infinitives. He notes that under the spec-VP analysis in (83), PRO will be positioned between *to* and *scare* rather than between *want* and *to* (as would be the case if PRO were in spec-TP), and hence PRO will not block *to* from cliticising onto *want* forming *wanta/wanna*. The fact that the contraction is indeed possible – as we see from (84) below:

(84)   He does *wanta/wanna* scare them

leads Baltin to conclude that PRO is merged in spec-VP, and remains there throughout the derivation – at no point becoming the subject of infinitival *to*. Of course, an ancillary assumption which has to be made is that the null C which intervenes between *want* and *to* in (83) does not block contraction. One way of accounting for this might be to assume that *to* first cliticises onto the null C constituent introducing the complement clause in (83), and then subsequently (together with the null complementiser to which it has attached) cliticises onto the verb *want*.

An important conclusion which Baltin draws from his analysis of *wanna* contraction is that infinitival *to* in control structures does not have an [EPP] feature, and hence does not have a specifier at any stage of derivation. In much the same way, we can argue that the possibility of *gonna* contraction in raising structures such as (85) below:

(85)   Little heed is *gonna* be paid to my proposal

provides evidence in support of positing that infinitival *to* in raising structures does not have an [EPP] feature either. Prior to passivisation, (85) will have the structure shown informally in (86) below:

(86)   [$_T$ is] [$_{VP}$ [$_V$ going] [$_{TP}$ [$_T$ to] be paid little heed to my proposal]]

If the idiomatic nominal *little heed* is raised directly to become the subject of *is* without first becoming the subject of *to*, (85) will have the structure shown in (87) below after passivisation has applied:

(87)   [$_{TP}$ *little heed* [$_T$ is] [$_{VP}$ [$_V$ going] [$_{TP}$ [$_T$ to] be paid ~~little heed~~ to my proposal]]]

The absence of any constituent intervening between *to* and *going* means that *to* can cliticise onto *going*, forming *gonna*. But if *to* in raising/passive infinitive structures has an [EPP] feature, the idiomatic nominal *little heed* will have to raise to become the specifier of infinitival *to* before becoming the subject of *is*, so that after passivisation we will have the structure (88) below:

(88)   [TP *little heed* [T is] [VP [V going] [TP ~~little heed~~ [T to] be paid ~~little heed~~ to my proposal]]]

We would then expect that the presence of a trace copy of *little heed* intervening between *going* and *to* should block contraction, and we would therefore wrongly predict that *gonna* contraction is not possible, and hence that (85) is ungrammatical. The fact that contraction is indeed possible suggests that infinitival *to* does not have an [EPP] feature in passive infinitive structures. Moreover, Bošković (2002b) argues that the ungrammaticality of *double there* structures like:

(89) (a)   *There seems [there to be a problem]
     (b)   *There was reported [there to be a problem]

provides further evidence that infinitival *to* in raising/passive structures does not have an [EPP] feature, since if it did we should expect the bracketed infinitive complements to allow an expletive subject of their own. Epstein and Seeley (1999) likewise argue that A-movement always takes place in a single step, and not in multiple (successive-cyclic) steps. Given Baltin's argument that *to* does not have an [EPP] feature in control infinitives either, the more general conclusion which these two sets of claims invite is that:

(90)   A finite T has an [EPP] feature, but infinitival *to* does not

And indeed this assumption is implicit in the analyses outlined in (79), (80), (82), (83) and (87) above.

There are interesting parallels between the derivation of unaccusative structures like (91a) below (sketched in (48) above), passive structures like (91b) (sketched in (70) above) and raising structures like (91c) (sketched in (82) above):

(91) (a)   [TP [T have] [VP [V **arisen**] *several complications*]]

     (b)   [TP [T are] [VP [V **believed**] [TP [T to] [AUXP [AUX have] [VP [V occurred] [QP *several riots*]]]]]]

     (c)   [TP [T does] [VP [V **seem**] [TP [T to] [VP *he* [V scare] them]]]]

In each of these structures, a (bold-printed) one-place predicate which has no external argument (and which therefore projects into an intransitive VP which has a complement but no subject) allows movement of the closest (italicised) constituent c-commanded by the underlined T constituent out of the containing VP into spec-TP. For instance, the VP headed by the unaccusative verb *arisen* in (91a) has no subject and consequently allows its complement *several complications* to move out of its containing VP into spec-TP. Likewise, the VPs headed by the passive verb *believed* and the unaccusative verb *occurred* in (91b) have no subject of their own, and so allow *several riots* to move out of both VPs into spec-TP in the main clause. Similarly, the VP headed by the raising verb *seem* in (91c) has no subject of its own and so allows the pronoun *he* to move into the main-clause spec-TP position.

What all of this points to is that an intransitive (subjectless) VP allows a nominal c-commanded by its head verb to be attracted by a higher T constituent to move into spec-TP. However where a VP has a thematic subject of its own, it is this subject which raises to spec-TP (because the **Attract Closest Principle** requires T to attract the closest nominal which it c-commands to raise to spec-TP). So, for example, in (91c) above, it is the subject *he* of the VP headed by *scare* which raises to spec-TP and thereby becomes the subject of the present-tense auxiliary *does*. The same is true of a control structure like (92) below (repeated from (83) above):

(92)   [TP *He* [T does] [VP *he* [V want] [CP [C ∅] [TP [T to] [VP PRO [V scare] them]]]]]

Here, the pronoun *he* originates as the thematic subject of *want*, and hence raises to spec-TP by virtue of being the closest nominal c-commanded by [T *does*].

What this suggests is that the particular property of passive, unaccusative and raising predicates which enables them to permit A-movement of a nominal argument which they c-command is that they are intransitive and therefore do not project an external argument (so that the VP they head is subjectless). By contrast, verbs which project an external argument of their own (and hence occur in a VP which has a thematic subject) require this subject to be attracted by a higher T constituent to move into spec-TP. These distinct patterns of movement are a consequence of the **Attract Closest Principle**. (See Culicover and Jackendoff 2001 for arguments that control and raising predicates have a distinct syntax.)

Having looked at the syntax of control predicates on the one hand and raising predicates on the other, we end this chapter by looking briefly at the question of how we can determine whether a given predicate which selects an infinitival *to* complement is a control predicate or a raising predicate. In this connection, it should be noted that there are a number of syntactic differences between raising and control predicates which are a direct reflection of the different thematic properties of these two types of predicate. For example, raising predicates like *seem* can have expletive *it/there* subjects, whereas control predicates like *want* cannot:

(93) (a)   *It* **seems/*wants** to be assumed that he lied to Congress
     (b)   *There* **seem/*want** to remain several unsolved mysteries

(The expletive nature of *it* in (93a) is shown by the fact that it cannot be substituted by a referential pronoun like *this/that*, or questioned by *what?* Likewise, the expletive nature of *there* in (93b) is shown by the fact that it cannot be substituted by a referential locative adverb like *here*, or questioned by *where?*) This is because control predicates like *want* are two-place predicates which project a thematic subject (an EXPERIENCER in the case of *want*, so that the subject of *want* must be an expression denoting an entity capable of experiencing desires), and non-referential expressions like expletive *it/there* are clearly not thematic subjects and so cannot be assigned a θ-role. By contrast, raising predicates like *seem* have no thematic subject, and hence impose no restrictions on the choice of structural subject in their clause, so allowing a (non-thematic) expletive subject.

Similarly, raising predicates like *seem* (but not control predicates like *want*) allow idiomatic subjects such as those italicised below:

(94)   Whenever they meet, . . .
   (a)   *all hell* **seems/*wants** to break loose
   (b)   *the fur* **seems/*wants** to fly
   (c)   *the cat* **seems/*wants** to get his tongue

The ungrammaticality of sentences like **All hell wants to break loose* can be attributed to the fact that *want* is a control predicate, and hence (in order to derive such a structure) it would be necessary to assume that *all hell* originates as the subject of *want*, and that *break loose* has a separate *PRO* subject of its own: but this would violate the requirement that (on its idiomatic use) *all hell* can only occur as the subject of *break loose*, and conversely *break loose* (in its idiomatic use) only allows *all hell* as its subject. By contrast, *All hell seems to break loose* is grammatical because *seem* is a raising predicate, and so *all hell* can originate as the subject of *break loose* and then be raised up to become the subject of the null tense constituent [$_T$ ø] in the *seem* clause. The null T agrees in person and number with the 3Sg expression *all hell*, but because there is no overt auxiliary in the head T position of TP to spell out the relevant features, the tense and agreement features of T are spelled out on the verb *seem* (via the morphological operation of **Affix Hopping**), with the consequence that the main verb ultimately surfaces in the third-person-singular present-tense form *seems*.

A further property which differentiates the two types of predicate is that raising predicates like *seem* preserve truth-functional equivalence under passivisation, so that (95a) below is cognitively synonymous with (95b):

(95) (a)   John seems to have helped Mary
     (b)   =Mary seems to have been helped by John

By contrast, control predicates like *want* do not preserve truth-functional equivalence under passivisation, as we see from the fact that (96a) below is not cognitively synonymous with (96b):

(96) (a)   John wants to help Mary

(b)   ≠Mary wants to be helped by John

Moreover, there are pragmatic restrictions on the choice of subject which control predicates like *want* allow (in that the subject generally has to be a rational being, not an inanimate entity) – as we see from (97) below (where ! marks pragmatic anomaly):

(97)   *My cat/!My gesture* wants to be appreciated

By contrast, raising predicates freely allow animate or inanimate subjects:

(98)   *My cat/My gesture* seems to have been appreciated

The different properties of the two types of predicate stem from the fact that control predicates like *want* θ-mark their subjects, whereas raising predicates like *seem* do not: so, since *want* selects an EXPERIENCER subject as its external argument (and prototypical EXPERIENCERS are animate beings), *want* allows an animate subject like *my cat*, but not an inanimate subject like *my gesture*. By contrast, since raising predicates like *seem* do not θ-mark their subjects, they allow a free choice of subject.

A final remark to be made is that although our discussion of **raising** and **control** predicates has revolved around verbs, a parallel distinction is found in adjectives. For example, in sentences such as:

(99) (a)   *John* is **likely** to win the race

(b)   *John* is **keen** to win the race

the adjective *likely* is a raising predicate and *keen* a control predicate. We can see this from the fact that *likely* allows expletive and idiomatic subjects, but *keen* does not:

(100) (a)   *There* is **likely/*keen** to be a strike

(b)   *All hell* is **likely/*keen** to break loose

This is one reason why throughout this chapter we have talked about different types of *predicate* (e.g. drawing a distinction between raising and control predicates) rather than different types of *verb*.

7.11   Summary

This chapter has primarily been concerned with the syntax of subjects. In §7.2 we argued that Belfast English structures such as *There should some students get distinctions* provide us with evidence that subjects originate internally within VP, and we noted that the claim that subjects originate internally within VP is known as the **VP-Internal Subject Hypothesis/VPISH**. We also maintained that sentences such as *Some students should get distinctions* involve movement of *some students* from the specifier position within VP to the specifier position within TP, and we noted that the relevant movement operation is known as **A-movement**. In §7.3 we claimed that the syntax of quotative structures like *'It wasn't me', said Mary* provides support for VPISH, if *Mary* remains in situ in the specifier position within VP. We suggested that idioms like *All hell will break loose* provide further empirical support for the VPISH, since the assumption that idioms are unitary constituents requires us to suppose that *all hell* originates as the subject of *break loose* (in the specifier position within VP) and from there is raised up (by application of A-movement) to become the subject/specifier of the TP headed by *will*. In §7.4 we argued that the VP-Internal Subject Hypothesis allows us to posit a uniform mapping between (semantic) argument structure and (initial) syntactic structure, if we suppose that all arguments of a predicate originate internally within a projection of the predicate. It then follows that in a sentence such as *The police have arrested the suspect*, the predicate *arrested* is merged with its internal argument (= complement) *the suspect* to form the V-bar *arrested the subject*, and then the resulting structure is merged with the external argument (= subject) of *arrested* to form the VP *the police arrested the suspect*. Because finite auxiliaries have an [EPP] feature requiring them to project a specifier, the subject *the police* then moves (via A-movement) from spec-VP to spec-TP, thereby becoming the subject of *have*. In §7.5 we saw that different arguments play different semantic roles with respect to their predicates, and that these have traditionally been described in terms of a set of **thematic roles** (= **θ-roles**) such as THEME, AGENT, EXPERIENCER, LOCATIVE, GOAL, SOURCE etc. We suggested that an argument is assigned a θ-role (= **θ-marked**) via merger with a predicative expression. Hence, in *The police have arrested the suspect*, the internal argument *the suspect* is assigned the θ-role of THEME argument of the predicate *arrested* via merger with *arrested*; likewise, the external argument *the police* is assigned the θ-role of AGENT via merger with the V-bar *arrested the suspect*. We noted that there are constraints on θ-marking imposed by the **θ-criterion**, which requires each argument to bear one and only one θ-role, and each θ-role assigned by a given predicate to be assigned to one and only one argument. In §7.6, we looked at the syntax of **unaccusative predicates** like *arise/remain/occur* etc. and argued that the argument of an unaccusative verb originates as its complement but differs from the complement of a transitive verb in that it receives nominative rather than accusative case. We highlighted a number of further differences between unaccusative predicates and other types of predicate (e.g. in relation to the position of subjects in Belfast English imperatives, and auxiliary selection in earlier varieties of English). In §7.7, we looked at the structure of simple passive clauses, arguing that a passive subject originates as the thematic complement of a subjectless passive participle, and is raised into spec-TP (via A-movement) in order to satisfy the [EPP] feature of T. In §7.8 we saw that passivisation can be a **long-distance** operation involving movement of an argument contained within an infinitival TP which is the complement of a passive participle. We noted that the position of idiomatic subjects in sentences like *Little heed is thought to have been paid to their proposal* provides empirical support for positing long-distance passivisation (as a particular instance of a more general A-movement operation whereby T attracts the closest noun or pronoun expression it c-commands to move to spec-TP). In §7.9 we argued that predicates like *seem/appear* function as **raising predicates** in the sense that their subjects originate internally within their infinitive complement, and from there are raised to spec-TP position within the *seem/appear*-clause: hence, in a sentence such as *All hell would appear to have broken loose*, the idiomatic expression *all hell* originates as the subject of *broken loose* and from there is raised up to become the subject of *would* by A-movement. In §7.10, we contrasted raising predicates with control predicates, noting that they differ in that control predicates θ-mark their subjects (and hence generally require an animate subject) and have a CP complement, whereas raising predicates do not θ-mark their subjects (and hence freely allow inanimate, expletive and idiomatic subjects) and have a TP complement. We also noted that (unlike control predicates), raising predicates preserve truth-functional equivalence under passivisation.

Workbook section

Exercise 7.1

Say whether the italicised verbs as used in the type of construction illustrated in the examples below function as raising or control predicates (or are ambiguous and can serve as both), and what evidence there is to support your analysis. Provide a detailed outline of the derivation of any *one* of the control sentences and any *one* of the raising sentences, giving arguments in support of your answer.

1	Employers *tend* to exploit employees
2	John has *decided* to quit the university
3	We *came* to appreciate the classes
4	You *have* to help me
5	They *failed* to hit the target
6	He *tried* to rectify the situation
7	He *refused* to sign the petition
8	He's *beginning* to irritate me
9	They *attempted* to pervert the course of justice
10	I *happened* to be passing your house
11	He is *going* to quit his job
12	He *stands* to lose a fortune
13	John *promises* to be a good student
14	He *needs* to have a shave
15	They *managed* to open the door

16	We *intend* to close the store
17	The weather is *threatening* to ruin the weekend
18	We are *hoping* to get a visa
19	She has *chosen* to ignore him
20	They are *planning* to visit London

Model answer for sentence 1

There are a number of reasons for suggesting that *tend* functions as a raising predicate when it takes an infinitive complement. For one thing (as we would expect if *tend* is a one-place raising predicate which does not θ-mark its subject), *tend* imposes no restrictions on its choice of subject, and so freely allows either an expression like *Professor Peabrain* (denoting an animate being) or an expression like *Syntax* (denoting an inanimate entity) as the subject of its containing clause – as illustrated in (i) below:

(i)   *Professor Peabrain/Syntax* tends to baffle people

Moreover, *tend* allows a non-thematic subject like expletive *there/it* – as in the examples below:

(ii)   *There* tends to be a lot of confusion about syntax
(iii)   *It* tends to be assumed that syntax is hard

(We can tell that *there* is an expletive pronoun in (ii) from the fact that it cannot be substituted by *here* or questioned by *where?* Likewise, *it* must be expletive in (iii) because it cannot be substituted by *this/that* or questioned by *what?*) Moreover, *tend* can have an idiomatic subject, as in (iv) below:

(iv)   *All hell* tends to break loose

Given that *all hell* can serve only as the subject of *break loose* in the relevant idiom in (iv), it is clear that we could not analyse *tend* as a control predicate in (iv) and claim that *all hell* originates as the subject of *tend* and PRO as the subject of *break loose*, since this would violate the requirement that *all hell* can occur only as the subject of *break loose* and conversely that *break loose* can only have the subject *all hell* (in the relevant idiom). By contrast, if *tend* is a raising predicate, we can claim that *all hell* originates as the subject of *break loose* and then raises up to become the subject of the (null T constituent in the) *tend* clause. Furthermore, *tend* preserves truth-functional equivalence under passivisation, as we can see from the fact that (v) and (vi) are truth-functionally equivalent:

(v)   Employers tend to exploit employees
(vi)   = Employees tend to be exploited by employers

Given the assumption that *tend* is a raising predicate, sentence 1 will be derived as follows. The noun *employees* merges with a null determiner (which has much the same generic sense as *the* in *The Italians love pasta*) to form the DP *ø employees*. The resulting DP merges with (and is assigned the θ-role of THEME argument of) the verb *exploit* to form the V-bar *exploit ø employees*. The DP *ø employers* (itself formed by merging a null determiner with the noun *employers*) is then

merged with (and assigned the θ-role of AGENT argument of) this V-bar, forming the VP *ø*
employers exploit ø employees. This VP is merged as the complement of the infinitival tense
particle *to*, forming the TP *to ø employers exploit ø employees*. The relevant TP is in turn merged
with the verb *tend*, forming the VP *tend to ø employers exploit ø employees*: we can perhaps take
the TP complement of *tend* to have the thematic function of being a THEME argument of *tend*. The
resulting VP is merged with a null present tense T, forming [T *ø*] *tend to ø employers exploit ø*
employees. By virtue of being finite, [T *ø*] has an [EPP] feature requiring it to have a specifier. In
accordance with the **Attract Closest Principle**, this requirement is satisfied by moving the closest
nominal c-commanded by [T *ø*] – namely the DP *ø employers* – into spec-TP in the manner shown
by the dotted arrow below:

(vii)   [TP *ø employers* [T *ø*] [VP [V tend] [TP [T to] [VP *ø employers* [V exploit] employees]]]]

The resulting structure (vii) is merged with a null complementiser marking the declarative force of
the sentence, so forming the structure (viii) below:

(viii)   [CP [C *ø*] [TP *ø employers* [T *ø*] [VP [V tend] [TP [T to] [VP *ø employers* [V exploit]
         employees]]]]]

The derivation satisfies the **θ-criterion** by virtue of the fact that each argument carries one and
only one θ-role: i.e. *ø employees* is the THEME argument of *exploit*, *ø employers* is the AGENT
argument of *exploit* and the TP complement of *tend* is its THEME argument.

Exercise 7.2

Discuss the derivation of the following sentences:

1 a   There are certain to remain some problems
  b   There were reported to remain some problems
  c   There were thought likely to remain some problems
2 a   A change of policy was envisaged
  b   A change of policy seems to be envisaged
  c   A change of policy is thought likely to be envisaged
3 a   Differences of opinion are emerging
  b   Differences of opinion are beginning to emerge
  c   Differences of opinion appear to be starting to emerge
4 a   He is leaving the country
  b   He is planning to leave the country
  c   He is thought to be planning to leave the country
5 a   No details are going to be revealed
  b   No details of any threats seem likely to be revealed
  c   No details are expected to be revealed of any threats
6 a   What has happened?
  b   What is expected to happen?
  c   What seems to be likely to happen?

Helpful hints

Assume that the infinitive form *be* is a copular verb occupying the head V position of VP when immediately followed by an adjective, but is an auxiliary occupying the head AUX position of AUXP when immediately followed by a passive or progressive participle. For the purposes of this exercise, assume that a finite T has an [EPP] feature, but that infinitival *to* does not. Assume that *he* has the thematic role of an EXPERIENCER argument of the relevant predicates in 4, but that all other arguments in 1–6 are THEME arguments of their associated predicates. In relation to 5a, consider the significance of the fact that *going to* can contract to *gonna*; in 5b,c assume that *any* is a partitive quantifier which has the property of being a polarity item (in the sense specified in exercise 3.2); in relation to 5c, bear in mind the discussion of discontinuous spellout in the text. In relation to 6, bear in mind the discussion of the syntax of wh-subjects in §6.6.

Model answer for sentence 1a

The quantifier *some* merges with the noun *problems* to form the QP *some problems*. This QP is merged with (and assigned the θ-role of THEME complement of) the unaccusative predicate *remain* to form the VP *remain some problems*. This in turn is merged with the infinitival tense particle *to*, forming the TP *to remain some problems*. This is then merged with the raising adjective *certain* to form the AP *certain to remain some problems*. This in turn is merged with the copular verb *be* to form the VP *be certain to remain some problems*. The resulting VP is merged with a null finite T which attracts the copula *be* to move from V to T in the manner indicated by the dotted arrow in (i), so forming the structure shown in simplified form below:

(i)

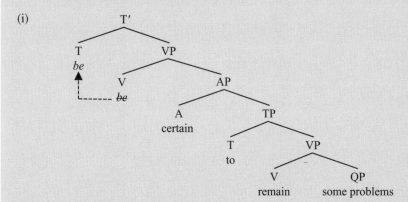

T (by virtue of being finite) has an [EPP] feature requiring it to project a subject, and this requirement is satisfied by merging *there* in spec-TP, forming the structure shown in abbreviated form in (ii) below (where *t* is a trace of the moved copula *be*):

(ii)

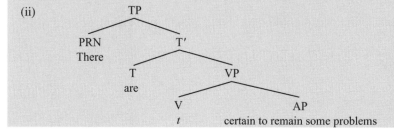

The TP in (ii) is subsequently merged with a null declarative complementiser.

The analysis presented here assumes that *certain* is a raising adjective. Evidence that this is so comes from the fact that clauses containing *certain* allow expletive and idiomatic subjects, as in:

(iii) (a)   *It* is certain to be raining in Manchester

    (b)   *The fur* is certain to fly

The expletive nature of *it* in (iiia) is shown by the fact that it cannot be substituted by referential pronouns like *this/that* or questioned by *what?*

8   Agreement, case and movement

8.1   Overview

In this chapter, we take a look at the syntax of agreement. We begin by outlining the claim made by Chomsky in recent work that agreement involves a relation between a **probe** and a **goal** (though it should be noted that the term **goal** in this chapter is used in an entirely different way from the term GOAL which was used to denote the thematic role played by a particular kind of argument in relation to its predicate in §7.5). We look at the nature of agreement, and go on to show that nominative and null case-marking involve agreement with T. Finally, we explore the relationship between the [EPP] feature carried by T and agreement, and look at the consequences of this for control infinitives on the one hand and raising infinitives on the other.

8.2   Agreement

In traditional grammars, finite auxiliaries are said to agree with their subjects. Since (within the framework used here) finite auxiliaries occupy the head T position of TP and their subjects are in spec-TP, in earlier work agreement was said to involve a specifier–head relationship (between T and its specifier). However, there are both theoretical and empirical reasons for doubting that agreement involves a spec–head relation. From a theoretical perspective (as we saw in §4.9), Minimalist considerations lead us to the conclusion that we should restrict the range of syntactic relations used in linguistic description, perhaps limiting it to the relation **c-command** created by merger. From a descriptive perspective, a spec–head account of agreement is problematic in that it fails to account for agreement between the auxiliary *are* and the nominal *several prizes* in passive structures such as:

(1)   There **are** thought likely to be awarded *several prizes*

Since the auxiliary *are* occupies the head T position of TP in (1) and the expletive pronoun *there* is in spec-TP, a spec–head account of agreement would lead us to expect that *are* should agree with *there*. But instead, *are* agrees with the in situ complement *several prizes* of the passive participle *awarded*. What is going on here? In order to try and understand this, let's take a closer look at the derivation of (1).

The quantifier *several* merges with the noun *prizes* to form the QP *several prizes*. This is merged as the thematic complement of the passive verb *awarded* to form the VP *awarded several prizes*. This in turn is merged with the passive auxiliary *be* to form the AUXP *be awarded several prizes*. This is then merged with the infinitival tense particle *to*, forming the TP *to be awarded several prizes*. The resulting TP is merged with the raising adjective *likely* to derive the AP *likely to be awarded several prizes*. This AP is subsequently merged with the passive verb *thought* to form the VP *thought likely to be awarded several prizes*. This in turn merges with the passive auxiliary *be*, forming the T-bar shown in simplified form in (2) below (where the notation BE indicates that the morphological form of the relevant item hasn't yet been determined):

(2)

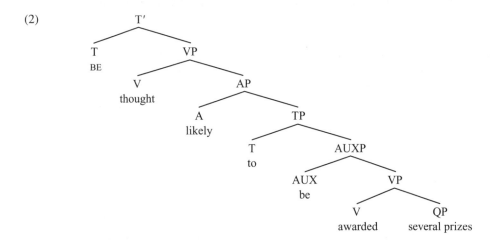

The tense auxiliary [T BE] needs to agree with an appropriate nominal within the structure containing it. Given Pesetsky's **Earliness Principle** (which requires operations to apply as early as possible in a derivation), T-agreement must apply as early as possible in the derivation, and hence will apply as soon as BE is introduced into the structure. On the assumption that c-command is central to syntactic operations, T will agree with a nominal (i.e. a noun or pronoun expression) which it c-commands. Accordingly, as soon as the structure in (2) is formed, [T BE] searches for a nominal which it c-commands to agree with.

To use the terminology introduced by Chomsky (1998, 1999, 2001), by virtue of being the highest head in the overall structure at this point in the derivation, BE serves as a **probe** which searches for a c-commanded nominal **goal** to agree with. The only nominal goal c-commanded by [T BE] within the structure in (2) is the QP *several prizes*: [T BE] therefore agrees in person and number with *several prizes*, and so is ultimately spelled out as the third-person-plural form *are* in the PF component. Chomsky refers to person and number features together as

φ-features (where φ is the Greek letter *phi*, pronounced in the same way as *fie* in English): using this terminology, we can say that the probe [T BE] agrees in φ-features with the goal *several prizes*. Subsequently, expletive *there* is merged in spec-TP to satisfy the [EPP] requirement for T to project a specifier, and the resulting TP is in turn merged with a null declarative complementiser to form the CP shown in simplified form below (which is the structure of (1) above):

(3)   [CP [C ∅] [TP There [T are] [VP [V thought] [AP [A likely] [TP to be awarded several prizes]]]]]

However, there are a number of details which we have omitted in (3); one relates to the **case** assigned to the complement (*several prizes*) of the passive participle *awarded*. Although case is not overtly marked on the relevant noun expressions in English, evidence from languages like Icelandic with a richer case system suggests that the complement of a passive participle in finite expletive clauses is assigned nominative case via agreement with T – as the following contrast (from Sigurðsson 1996, p. 12) illustrates:

(4) (a)   það   voru lesnar *fjórar   bækur*
           There were read   four_{NOM.PL} books_{NOM.PL}
    (b)   það   var skilað *fjórum   bókum*
           There was returned four_{DAT.PL} books_{DAT.PL}

In (4a), the auxiliary *voru* is a third-person-plural form which agrees with the NOM.PL/nominative plural complement *fjórar bækur* 'four books'. In (4b), the auxiliary is the agreementless form *var* 'was', and the complement of the passive participle is DAT.PL/dative plural. (*Var* is a third-person-singular form, but can be treated as an agreementless form if we characterise agreement by saying that 'An auxiliary is first/second person if it agrees with a first/second-person subject, but third person otherwise; it is plural if it agrees with a plural subject, but singular otherwise.' This means that a third-person-singular auxiliary can arise either by agreement with a third-person-singular expression or – as here – can be a **default** form used as a fall-back when the auxiliary doesn't agree with anything.) Sigurðsson argues that it is an inherent lexical property of the participle *skila* 'returned' that (like around a quarter of transitive verbs in Icelandic) it assigns so-called **inherent** dative case to its complement (see Svenonius 2002a,b on dative complements), and (because it can't agree with a non-nominative complement) the auxiliary surfaces in the agreementless form *var*; by contrast, the participle *lesnar* 'read' in (4a) does not assign inherent case to its complement, and instead the complement is assigned (so-called) **structural** nominative case via agreement with the past-tense auxiliary *voru* 'were'.

Icelandic data like (4) suggest that there is a systematic relationship between nominative case assignment and T-agreement: they are two different reflexes of an **agreement** relationship between a finite T probe and a nominal goal. In consequence of the agreement relationship between the two, the T probe agrees with a nominal goal which it c-commands, and the nominal goal is assigned nominative case. Accordingly, *several prizes* in (3) receives nominative case via agreement with [$_T$ *are*]. (It should be noted in passing that throughout this chapter, we focus on characterising syntactic agreement. On so-called 'semantic agreement' in British English structures like *The government are ruining the country*, see den Dikken 2001 and Sauerland and Elbourne 2002.)

The approach to case assignment outlined here (in which subjects are assigned nominative case via agreement with a finite T) is different from that outlined in §4.10, where we suggested that subjects are case-marked by a c-commanding C constituent. But in one sense, our revised hypothesis that finite subjects are case-marked by T is consistent with our earlier analysis. In chapter 4, we argued that (in consequence of the Earliness Principle) a noun or pronoun expression is case-marked by the closest case-assigner which c-commands it: since we also assumed in chapter 4 that subjects originate in spec-TP, it was natural to assume that they are case-marked by the closest functional head above them, namely C. But once we move to an analysis like that in chapter 7 in which subjects originate internally within VP, our assumption that they are case-marked by the closest case-assigning head above them opens up the possibility that nominative subjects may be case-marked by T rather than by C – and indeed this is the assumption which we will make from now on (an assumption widely made in current research).

8.3   Feature valuation

Let's think through rather more carefully what it means to say that case is systematically related to agreement, and what the mechanism is by which case and agreement operate. To illustrate our discussion, consider the derivation of a simple passive such as that produced by speaker B below:

(5)   SPEAKER A: What happened to the protestors?
           SPEAKER B: *They were arrested*

Here, discourse factors determine that a third-person-plural pronoun is required in order to refer back to the third-person-plural expression *the protestors*, and that a past-tense auxiliary is required because the event described took place in the past. So (as it were) the person/number features of *they* and the past-tense feature of *were* are determined in advance, before the items enter the derivation. By contrast the case feature assigned to *they* and the person/number features assigned to *were* are determined via an agreement operation in the course of the derivation: e.g. if the subject had been the singular pronoun *one*, the auxiliary would have been third person singular via agreement with *one* (as in *One was arrested*); and if THEY had been used as the object of a transitive verb (as in *The police arrested them*), it would have surfaced in the accusative form *them* rather than the nominative form *they*.

Generalising at this point, let's suppose that noun and pronoun expressions like THEY enter the syntax with their (person and number) φ-features already

valued, but their case feature as yet **unvalued**. (The notation THEY is used here to provide a case-independent characterisation of the word which is variously spelled out as *they/them/their* depending on the case assigned to it in the syntax.) Using a transparent feature notation, let's say that THEY enters the derivation carrying the features [3-Pers, Pl-Num, u-Case], where *Pers* = person, *Pl* = plural, *Num* = number, and *u* = unvalued. Similarly, let's suppose that finite T constituents (like the tense auxiliary BE) enter the derivation with their tense feature already valued, but their person and number φ-features as yet unvalued (because they are going to be valued via agreement with a nominal goal). This means that BE enters the derivation carrying the features [Past-Tns, u-Pers, u-Num]. In the light of these assumptions, let's see how the derivation of (5B) proceeds.

The pronoun THEY is the thematic complement of the passive verb *arrested* and so merges with it to form the VP *arrested THEY*. This is in turn merged with the tense auxiliary BE, forming the structure (6) below (where already-valued features are shown in **bold**, and unvalued features in *italics*):

(6)

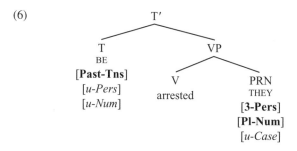

Given Pesetsky's **Earliness Principle**, T-agreement will apply at this point. Let's suppose that agreement in such structures involves a c-command relation between a probe and a goal in which unvalued φ-features on the probe are valued by the goal, and an unvalued case feature on the goal is valued by the probe. (In Chomsky's use of these terms, it is the unvalued person/number features which serve as the probe rather than the item BE itself, but this is a distinction which we shall overlook throughout, in order to simplify exposition.) Since [T BE] is the highest head in the structure (6), it serves as a probe which searches for a c-commanded goal with an unvalued case feature, and locates the pronoun THEY. Accordingly, an agreement relation is established between the probe BE and the goal THEY. One reflex of this agreement relation is that the unvalued person and number features carried by the probe BE are valued by the goal THEY. Valuation here involves a **Feature-Copying** operation which we can sketch in general terms as follows (where α and ß are two different constituents contained within the same structure, and where one is a probe and the other a goal):

(7)   **Feature-Copying**
           If α is valued for some feature [F] and β is unvalued for [F] and if β agrees with α, the
           feature-value for [F] on α is copied onto ß

In consequence of the Feature-Copying operation (7), the values of the person/
number features of THEY are copied onto BE, so that the unvalued person and
number features [*u-Pers, u-Num*] on BE in (6) are assigned the [*3-Pers, Pl-Num*]
values carried by THEY – as shown in (8) below, where the underlined features
are those which have been valued via the Feature-Copying operation (7):

(8)

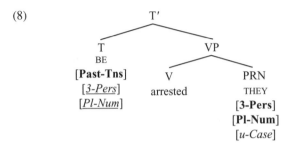

A second reflex of the agreement relation between BE and THEY is that the unvalued
case feature [*u-Case*] carried by the goal THEY is valued by the probe BE. Since
only auxiliaries with finite (present/past) tense have nominative subjects (and
not e.g. infinitival auxiliaries), we can suppose that it is the finite tense features
of the probe which are responsible for assigning nominative case to the goal.
Accordingly, we can posit that nominative case assignment involves the kind of
operation sketched informally below:

(9)   **Nominative Case Assignment**
       An unvalued case feature on a goal is valued as nominative by a probe
       carrying finite tense if probe and goal match in φ-features (i.e. in person and
       number)

Since the person/number features of the probe BE match those of the goal THEY
in (8), and since BE carries finite tense (by virtue of its [Past-Tns] feature), the
unvalued case feature on THEY is valued as nominative, resulting in the structure
shown in (10) below (where the underlined feature is the one valued as nominative
in accordance with (9) above):

(10)

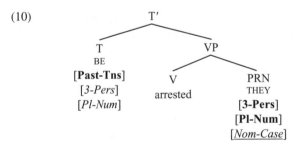

Since all the features carried by BE are now valued, BE can ultimately be spelled out
in the phonology as the third-person-plural past-tense form *were*. Likewise, since
all the features carried by THEY are also valued, THEY can ultimately be spelled out
as the third-person-plural nominative form *they*. However, the derivation in (8) is
not yet terminated: the [EPP] feature of T will subsequently trigger A-movement

of *they* to become the structural subject of *were*, and the resulting TP *they were arrested ~~they~~* will then be merged with a null declarative complementiser to form the structure *ø they were arrested ~~they~~*: but since our immediate concern is with case and agreement, we skip over these details here.

Although we have given an essentially Chomskyan account of nominative case-marking in (9) and will continue to use it throughout the rest of the book, a theoretically more elegant account would be to make use of Pesetsky and Torrego's assumption (discussed in §6.6) that nominative case is a manifestation of a *tense* feature on T. On this alternative view, the [*u-Case*] feature on THEY in (8) would be replaced by a [*u-Tense*] feature which is valued as [*Past-Tense*] by the Feature-Copying operation in (7), with any (present- or past-) tensed form of the pronoun being spelled out as *they*. This solution is more elegant in two respects. Firstly, it eliminates the need for a **Nominative Case Assignment** operation, since nominative case assignment becomes a tense-copying operation which is simply a particular instance of the **Feature-Copying** operation in (7). Secondly, it avoids a potential violation of a UG principle which Chomsky terms the **Inclusiveness Condition** and which he says (1999, p. 2) 'bars introduction of new elements (features) in the course of a derivation'. Under the analysis sketched in (8), THEY enters the derivation with an *unvalued* case feature which is then assigned the value *nominative* via agreement with a T constituent which has *person, tense and number* features. So it would seem that the value *nominative* is introduced into the derivation via a case-valuation operation like (9), leading to a potential violation of the **Inclusiveness Condition**. By contrast, under the alternative tense-copying analysis of nominative case, no new feature value is introduced into the derivation: instead, the existing [Past] value for the [Tns] feature on T is copied onto the subject.

8.4   Uninterpretable features and feature-deletion

Our discussion of how case and agreement work in a sentence such as (5B) has wider implications. One of these is that items may enter the derivation with some of their features already **valued** and others as yet **unvalued**: e.g. BE enters the derivation in (6) with its tense feature valued, but its φ-features unvalued; and THEY enters with its φ-features valued but its case feature unvalued. This raises the question of which features are initially valued when they first enter the derivation, which are initially unvalued – and why. Chomsky (1998) argues that the difference between valued and unvalued grammatical features correlates with a further distinction between those grammatical features which are **interpretable** (in the sense that they play a role in semantic interpretation), and those which are **uninterpretable** (and hence play no role in semantic interpretation). For example, it seems clear that the case feature of a pronoun like THEY is uninterpretable, since a subject pronoun surfaces as nominative, accusative or genitive depending on the type of [bracketed] clause it is in, without any effect on meaning – as the examples in (11) below illustrate:

(11) (a)   It is said [*they* were arrested]
   (b)   He expected [*them* to be arrested]
   (c)   He was shocked at [*their* being arrested]

By contrast, the (person/number) φ-features of pronouns are interpretable, since e.g. a first-person-singular pronoun like *I* clearly differs in meaning from a third-person-plural pronoun like *they*. In the case of finite auxiliaries, it is clear that their tense features are interpretable, since a present-tense form like *is* differs in meaning from a past-tense form like *was*. By contrast, the (person/number) φ-features of auxiliaries are uninterpretable, in that they serve purely to mark agreement with a particular nominal. This suggests a correlation such as (12) below between whether or not features are interpretable and whether or not they are initially valued:

(12)   **Feature Value Correlation**
   (i)   Interpretable features enter the derivation already valued
   (ii)   Features which enter the derivation unvalued are uninterpretable

The correlation between valuedness and interpretability turns out to be an important one. (It should be noted that Chomsky 1998 offers a rather different formulation of (12ii) to the effect that uninterpretable features enter the derivation unvalued, but his claim seems problematic e.g. for languages in which nouns may enter the derivation with an uninterpretable gender φ-feature with a fixed but arbitrary value: e.g. the noun *Mädchen* 'girl' is inherently neuter in gender in German, though it denotes a feminine entity.)

As we saw in the simplified model of grammar which we presented in §1.3, each structure generated by the syntactic component of the grammar is subsequently sent to the **PF component** of the grammar to be **spelled out** (i.e. assigned a **PF representation** which provides a representation of its **Phonetic Form**). If we assume that unvalued features are **illegible** to (and hence cannot be processed by) the **PF component**, it follows that every unvalued feature in a derivation must be valued in the course of the derivation, or else the derivation will **crash** (i.e. fail) because the PF component is unable to **spell out** unvalued features. In more concrete terms, this amounts to saying that unless the syntax specifies whether we require e.g. a first-person-singular or third-person-plural present-tense form of BE, the derivation will crash because the PF component cannot determine whether to spell out BE as *am* or *are*.

In addition to being sent to the PF component, each structure generated by the syntactic component of the grammar is simultaneously sent to the **semantic component**, where it is converted into an appropriate **semantic representation**. Clearly, interpretable features play an important role in the computation of semantic representations. Equally clearly, however, uninterpretable features play no role whatever in this process: indeed, since they are illegible to the semantic component, we need to devise some way of ensuring that uninterpretable features do not input into the semantic component. How can we do this?

Chomsky's answer is to suppose that uninterpretable features are **deleted** in the course of the syntactic derivation, in the specific sense that they are marked as being invisible in the semantic component while remaining visible in the syntax and in the PF component. To get a clearer idea of what this means in concrete terms, consider the uninterpretable nominative case feature on *they* in (5B) *They were arrested*. Since this case feature is uninterpretable, it has to be deleted in the course of the syntactic derivation, so that the semantic component cannot 'see' it. However, the PF component must still be able to 'see' this case feature, since it needs to know what case has been assigned to the pronoun THEY in order to determine whether the pronoun should be spelled out as *they*, *them* or *their*. This suggests the following convention:

(13)　　　**Feature Visibility Convention**
　　　　　Any uninterpretable feature deleted in the syntax is invisible to the semantic component, but remains visible in the syntactic component and in the PF component

The next question to ask at this juncture is what kind of syntactic operation is involved in the deletion of uninterpretable features. Let's suppose (following Chomsky) that feature-deletion involves the kind of operation outlined informally below (where α and ß enter into an agreement relation, and one is a probe and the other a goal):

(14)　　　**Feature-Deletion**
　　　　　α deletes any uninterpretable (person/number/case) feature(s) carried by ß if α is φ-complete and if the value(s) of any φ-feature(s) carried by ß match those of the corresponding φ-feature(s) of α

Here, α and ß are two different constituents contained within the same structure, and one is a probe and the other a goal. In a language like English where finite verbs agree with their subjects in person and number (but not gender), ß is φ-**complete** if it carries both person and number features (though in a language like Arabic where finite verbs agree in person, number and gender with their subjects, ß is φ-complete if it carries person, number and gender: see Nasu 2001, 2002 for discussion). For ß to delete the person/number/case features of α, the φ-features of ß must **match** the φ-features carried by α. Let's define the relation 'match' in the following terms:

(15)　　　**The relation 'match'**
　　　　　α and β *match* in respect of some feature [F] either if both have the same value for [F], or if one is valued for [F] and the other unvalued for [F] – but not if they have different values for [F].

To make a rather abstract discussion more concrete, let's consider how feature-deletion applies in the case of our earlier structure (10) above. Here, both BE and THEY are φ-complete, since both are specified for person as well as number. Moreover, the two *match* in respect of their φ-features, since the two have the same value for person and number (in that both are third person plural). Let's assume that (in consequence of the **Earliness Principle**), feature-deletion applies as early as possible in the derivation, and hence applies at the point where the structure in (10) has been formed. In accordance with Feature-Deletion (14), φ-complete BE can delete the uninterpretable case feature carried by THEY; and conversely φ-complete THEY can delete the uninterpretable person/number features carried by BE. Feature-Deletion therefore results in the structure (16) below (where ~~strikethrough~~ indicates deletion):

(16)

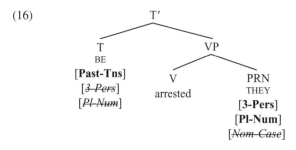

The deleted features will now be invisible in the semantic component – in accordance with (13). The rest of the derivation proceeds as before.

Chomsky sees uninterpretable features as being at the very heart of agreement, and posits (1999, p. 4) that 'Probe and Goal must both be active for Agree to apply' and that a constituent α (whether Probe or Goal) is **active** only if α contains one or more **uninterpretable** features. In other words, it is the presence of uninterpretable features on a constituent that makes it active (and hence able to serve as a probe or goal, and to play a part in feature-valuation and feature-deletion).

As should be obvious, the **Feature-Deletion** operation posited in (14) is very different from the **(Trace) Copy-Deletion** operation we assumed in earlier chapters by which a trace copy of a moved constituent is deleted. Feature-Deletion is an operation which renders the affected features invisible to the semantic component, while leaving them visible to the phonological component. By contrast, Copy-Deletion is an operation which renders traces of moved constituents invisible to the phonological component (in the sense that they are not given any phonetic spellout), while leaving them visible in the semantic component. The reason why traces must remain visible in the semantic component is that they play an important role in semantic interpretation, as we can see in relation to a sentence such as (17a) below, which has the simplified structure (17b) (assuming that *a famous politician* originates as the object of the passive participle *seen* and raises to become the subject of *has*):

(17) (a)   A famous politician has not been seen in the Hotel Casanova for weeks
     (b)   *A famous politician* has not been seen ~~a famous politician~~ in the Hotel
             Casanova for weeks

(17a) exhibits a **scope ambiguity** in respect of whether *a famous politician* has scope over *not* (so that the sentence is paraphraseable as 'There is a specific famous politician, Gerry Attrick, who has not been seen in the Hotel Casanova for weeks') or conversely whether *not* has scope over *a famous politician* (so that the sentence is paraphraseable as 'Not a single famous politician has been seen in the Hotel Casanova for weeks'). If the semantic component is able to 'see' traces, it will 'see' the structure represented in skeletal form in (17b) above. One way of handling the scope ambiguity of sentences like (17a) is to posit that scope is defined in terms of c-command and that the scope ambiguity correlates with the fact that in the structure (17b), *not* is c-commanded by (so falls within the scope of) the moved constituent *a famous politician*, but conversely *not* c-commands (and hence has scope over) its trace *a famous politician*. A plausible conclusion to draw is that trace-deletion takes place in the phonological component, so that traces remain in the syntax and hence are visible in the semantic component, and can play a role in determining scope in relevant types of structure. The assumption that trace-deletion is a phonological operation is implicit in Chomsky's remark (1999, p. 11) that 'Phonological rules . . . eliminate trace.'

8.5   Expletive *it* subjects

So far, all the constructions we have looked at have involved a finite T agreeing with a noun or pronoun expression which carries interpretable person/number φ-features. However, English has two **expletive pronouns** which (by virtue of being non-referential) carry no interpretable φ-features. One of these is *expletive it* in sentences such as:

(18) (a) *It* is said that he has taken bribes
  (b) *It* can be difficult to come to terms with long-term illness
  (c) *It*'s a pity that she can't come
  (d) *It*'s a long way from here to Lands End

The pronoun *it* in sentences like these appears to be an **expletive**, since it cannot be replaced by a referential pronoun like *this* or *that*, and cannot be questioned by *what*. Let's examine the syntax of expletive *it* by looking at the derivation of a sentence like (18a).

Suppose that we have reached the stage of derivation where the (passive participle) verb *said* has been merged with its CP complement *that he has taken bribes* to form the VP *said that he has taken bribes*. Merging this VP with the tense auxiliary BE forms the structure shown in simplified form below:

(19)

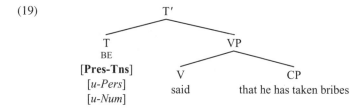

In accordance with Pesetsky's **Earliness Principle**, we might expect T-agreement to apply at this point. Accordingly, the probe BE (which is active by virtue of its uninterpretable person/number φ-features) searches for an active goal to value its unvalued φ-features. It might at first sight seem as if the CP headed by *that* is an appropriate goal, and is a third-person-singular expression which can value the person/number features of BE. However, it seems unlikely that such clauses have person/number features. One reason for thinking this is that even if the *that*-clause in (19) is coordinated with another *that*-clause as in (20) below, the verb BE remains in the singular form *is*:

(20)   It is said [*that he has taken bribes* and *that he has embezzled company funds*]

If each of the italicised clauses in (20) were singular in number, we would expect the bracketed coordinate clause to be plural (in the same way as the coordinate structure *John and Mary* is a plural expression in a sentence like *John and Mary are an item*): but the fact that the passive auxiliary *is* remains singular in (20) suggests that the CP has no number properties of its own. Nor indeed does the *that*-clause in (19) have an unvalued case feature which could make it into an active goal, since *that*-clauses appear to be caseless (as argued by Safir 1986), in that a *that*-clause cannot be used in a position like that italicised in (21) below where it would be assigned accusative case by a transitive preposition such as *of*:

(21)   *There have been reports of *that he has taken bribes*

If the CP in (19) has no uninterpretable case feature, it is inactive and so cannot value the φ-features of BE.

   However, a question we might ask about (19) is whether BE could instead agree with the subject of the *that*-clause, namely *he*: after all, *he* has an uninterpretable case feature (making it active), and is a third-person-singular expression and so could seemingly value the unvalued person/number features of BE. Yet it is clear that BE does not in fact agree with *he*, since if we replace *he* by the first-person-plural subject *we*, BE still surfaces in the third-person-singular form *is* – as (22) below illustrates:

(22)   It *is* said [CP that [TP **we** have taken bribes]]

Something, then, must prevent BE from agreeing with *we* – but what? The answer lies in a constraint developed by Chomsky termed the **Phase Impenetrability Condition/PIC**. Since understanding PIC requires a prior understanding of the notion of **phase** developed by Chomsky in recent work (1998, 1999, 2001), let's first take a look at what phases are.

   In §1.5 we suggested that a fundamental principle of UG is a **Locality Principle** which requires all grammatical operations to be local. Using the **probe–goal** terminology introduced in this chapter, we can construe this as meaning that all grammatical operations involve a relation between a probe P and a **local** goal G which is sufficiently 'close' to the probe. However, an important question to ask is why probe–goal relations must be local. In this connection, Chomsky (2001,

p. 13) remarks that 'the P, G relation must be local' in order 'to minimise search' (i.e. in order to ensure that a minimal amount of searching will enable a probe to find an appropriate goal). His claim that locality is forced by the need 'to minimise search' suggests a processing explanation: the implication is that the Language Faculty can only process limited amounts of structure at one time – and, more specifically, can only hold a limited amount of structure in its 'active memory' (Chomsky 1999, p. 9). In order to ensure a 'reduction of computational burden' (1999, p. 9) Chomsky proposes that 'the derivation of EXP[ressions] proceeds by *phase*' (ibid.), so that syntactic structures are built up one *phase* at a time. He maintains (2001, p. 14) that 'phases should be as small as possible, to minimise memory'. More specifically, he suggests (1999, p. 9) that phases are 'propositional' in nature, and hence include CPs. His rationale for taking CP to be phases is that CP represents a complete clausal complex (including a specification of **force**).

In what sense do phases ensure that grammatical operations are purely local? The answer given by Chomsky is that any goal within the (c-command) **domain** of the phase (i.e. any goal c-commanded by the head of the phase) is **impenetrable** to further syntactic operations. He refers to this condition as the **Phase Impenetrability Condition/PIC** – and we can state it as follows (cf. Chomsky 2001, p. 5, ex. 6):

(23)   **Phase Impenetrability Condition/PIC**
          Any goal in the (c-command) domain of a phase head is impenetrable to a
          probe outside the phase

Stated in a form like (23), the relevant condition clearly begs the question of *why* a goal positioned 'below' a phase head should be impenetrable to a probe positioned 'above' the phase. Chomsky's answer (2001, p. 5) is that once a complete phase has been formed, the domain of the phase head (i.e. its complement) undergoes a **transfer** operation by which it is simultaneously sent to the phonological component to be assigned an appropriate phonetic representation, and to the semantic component to be assigned an appropriate semantic representation – and hence no constituent in the relevant domain is thereafter able to undergo any further syntactic operations. So, for example, once the operations which take place on the CP cycle have been completed, the TP which is the domain/complement of the phase head C will be sent to the phonological and semantic components for processing. As a result, TP is no longer accessible in the syntax, and hence neither TP itself nor any constituent of TP can subsequently serve as a goal for a higher probe of any kind in the syntax.

In the light of the Phase Impenetrability Condition (23), let's return to our earlier structure (19) and ask why the auxiliary *is* in the main clause can't agree with the subject *he* of the complement clause. The answer is as follows. The complement clause *that he has taken bribes* is a CP, hence a phase. The domain of that CP (i.e. the constituent which is the complement of the head C of CP) is the TP *he has taken bribes*. This means that neither this TP nor any of its constituents can serve as a goal for a probe outside CP. Since *is* in (19) lies outside the bracketed

CP phase, and *he* lies inside its bracketed TP domain, PIC prevents agreement between the two. (See Polinsky and Potsdam 2001, and Branigan and MacKenzie 2002 for an analysis of apparent long-distance agreement in terms of PIC.)

So far, what we have established in relation to the structure in (19) is that BE cannot agree with the *that*-clause because the latter is inactive and has no φ-features or case feature; nor can BE agree with *he*, because PIC makes *he* impenetrable to BE. It is precisely because BE cannot agree with CP or with any of its constituents that expletive *it* has to be used, in order to satisfy the [EPP] requirement of T, and to value the φ-features of T. In keeping with the Minimalist spirit of positing only the minimal apparatus which is conceptually necessary, let's further suppose that expletive *it* has 'a full complement of φ-features' (Chomsky 1998, p. 44) but that (as Martin Atkinson (pc) suggests) these are the only features carried by *it* in its expletive use. More specifically, let's assume that expletive *it* carries the features [third-person, singular-number]. Since expletive *it* is a 'meaningless' expletive pronoun, these features will be *uninterpretable*. Given this assumption, merging *it* as the specifier of the T-bar in (19) above will derive the structure (24) below (with interpretable features shown in bold, and uninterpretable features in italics):

(24)

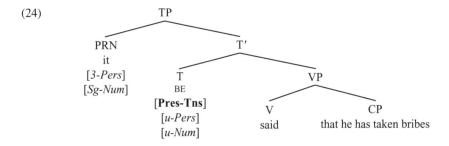

At this stage in the derivation, the pronoun *it* can serve as a probe because it is the highest head in the structure, and because *it* is active by virtue of its uninterpretable φ-features. Likewise, the auxiliary BE can serve as a goal for *it* because BE is c-commanded by *it* and BE is active by virtue of its uninterpretable φ-features. Feature-Copying (7) can therefore apply to value the unvalued φ-features on BE as third person singular (via agreement with *it*), and Feature-Deletion (14) can apply to delete the uninterpretable φ-features of both *it* and BE, so deriving:

(25)

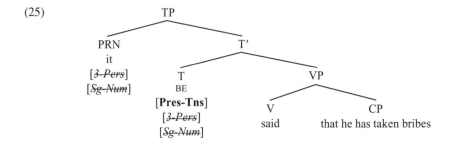

As required, all unvalued features have been valued at this point (BE ultimately being spelled out in the PF component as *is*), and all uninterpretable features deleted. The resulting structure (25) is subsequently merged with a null declarative complementiser. The deleted uninterpretable person/number features of *it* and BE will be visible in the PF component and the syntax, but not in the semantic component; the undeleted [**Pres-Tns**] feature of BE will be visible in all three components. Hence, BE will be spelled out as *is* in the PF component, since the phonology can 'see' the third-person, singular-number, present-tense features carried by BE.

There are two particular features of the analysis outlined above which merit further comment. One is that we have assumed that expletive *it* carries person and number features, but no gender feature and no case feature. While *it* clearly carries an interpretable (neuter/inanimate) gender feature when used as a referential pronoun (e.g. in a sentence like *This book has interesting exercises in it*, where *it* refers back to *this book*), it has no semantic interpretation in its use as an expletive pronoun, and so can be assumed to carry no interpretable gender feature in such a use. The reason for positing that expletive *it* is a caseless pronoun is that it is already active by virtue of its uninterpretable φ-features, and hence does not 'need' a case feature to make it active for agreement (unlike subjects with interpretable φ-features). Some suggestive evidence that expletive *it* may be a caseless pronoun comes from the fact that it has no genitive form *its* – at least for speakers like me who don't say (e.g.) **He was annoyed at its raining*.

A further assumption worth commenting on is that we have assumed that expletive *it* is intrinsically third person singular, and that this is why BE ends up in the third-person-singular form *is* in sentences like (18a) *It is said that he has taken bribes*. However, if we were to accept Chomsky's view that all uninterpretable features enter the derivation unvalued, we'd have to say that the pronoun *it* enters the derivation with unvalued person/number features, as in (26) below:

(26)

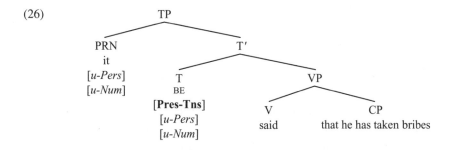

The obvious question which such an analysis would raise is how a pronoun with unvalued person/number features can value the unvalued person/number features of T (and conversely). To answer this question, we'd have to invoke default number/person valuation conditions such as those italicised below:

(27)   **Person/Number Valuation**
Where α and β enter into an agreement relation and β has one or more
unvalued φ-features which match corresponding φ-features carried by α,
α values β as:
(i) first person if α is first person, second person if α is second person, and
third person otherwise
(ii) plural if α is plural and *singular otherwise*

(27i) would ensure that the person features of both *it* and BE are assigned the default
(*otherwise*) value [*3-Pers*]; and (27ii) would ensure that the number features of
both *it* and BE are assigned the default value [*Sg-Num*]. We will not attempt to
choose between the analyses in (24) and (26) here, but for concreteness we will
henceforth assume (24).

Let's now turn to consider the question of how we handle sentences like the
following, which contain so-called *weather it*:

(28) (a)   It is raining   (b) It has been snowing

One way of analysing a sentence like (28a) is to treat RAIN as a predicate which has
no θ-marked argument, and to take *it* to be a non-referential (expletive) pronoun.
This would mean that the first stage in the derivation of (28a) is for the tense
auxiliary BE to be merged with the verb RAIN (which is ultimately spelled out
as the form *raining* because the progressive auxiliary BE requires a complement
headed by a verb in the *ing*-form). Merging expletive *it* as the specifier of the
resulting T-bar BE *raining* would derive the structure (29) below, if we assume
(for expository purposes) that *it* is intrinsically third person singular:

(29)

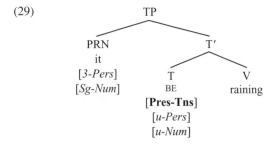

At this point, *it* is the highest head in the overall structure, and is active (by
virtue of its uninterpretable φ-features) and so can serve as a probe. [T BE] is
c-commanded by *it* and is also active (by virtue of its own uninterpretable φ-
features), and so can serve as a goal for the probe *it*. Accordingly, the unvalued
person/number features on BE are valued via the **Feature-Copying** operation (7),
with the result that the φ-features of BE are assigned the same values as those of
it. Since both *it* and BE are φ-complete (by virtue of carrying both person and
number features), and since their φ-features have matching values, each can delete
the uninterpretable φ-features of the other in accordance with **Feature-Deletion**
(14), so deriving:

(30)

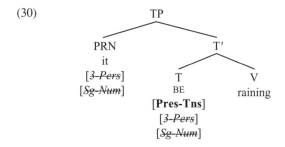

The deleted uninterpretable person/number features of *it* and BE will be visible in the PF component and the syntax, but not in the semantic component; the undeleted [**Pres-Tns**] feature of BE will be visible in all three components. Hence, BE will be spelled out as *is* in the PF component, since PF can 'see' the third-person, singular-number, present-tense features carried by BE. The resulting TP will subsequently be merged with a null declarative-force complementiser.

A key assumption in the analysis outlined above is that expletive *it* is a meaningless 'filler', and so non-referential. However, this assumption would seem to be called into question by the observation that expletive *it* can serve as the antecedent of PRO: cf.

(31) (a)   It sometimes rains after PRO snowing (Chomsky 1981, p. 324)
      (b)   It can seem that someone is guilty without [PRO seeming that they actually committed the crime] (Williams 1994, p. 91)

If we suppose that only a referential pronoun can serve as the controller of PRO, a plausible conclusion to draw is that expletive *it* is referential (in a sense made precise by Chomsky 1981, who suggests that expletive *it* is a **quasi-argument**). And if weather *it* in sentences like (28a,b) is referential, it is also plausible to suppose that it is initially merged as a (quasi-)argument of the weather predicate with which it is associated. If we suppose that weather verbs like *rain/snow* are unaccusative (as is suggested by the fact that in Italian they can be used with the auxiliary *essere* 'be' in perfect-participle forms), this would mean that *it* in (28a,b) originates as the complement of the verb *rain/snow*. If weather *it* is indeed referential and if this means that its person/number features are interpretable, then it follows that weather *it* will also need an unvalued case feature to make it active in the syntax. Assuming all of this, we will have the structure shown in simplified form in (32) below at the stage when T is merged with its complement:

(32)

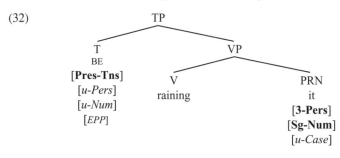

The unvalued person/number features of BE will be valued as third person sin-gular in accordance with **Feature-Copying** (7), and deleted in accordance with Feature-Deletion (14). The unvalued case feature on *it* will be valued as nom-inative by Nominative Case Assignment (9), and deleted by Feature-Deletion (14). The [EPP] feature of T will simultaneously trigger movement of *it* (which is active by virtue of its unvalued case feature) to spec-TP, so deriving the struc-ture in (33) below (simplified by not showing features carried by the trace copy of *it*):

(33)

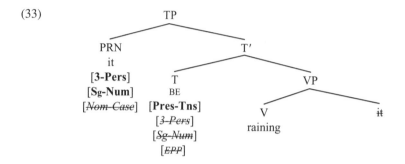

As required, all uninterpretable features have been deleted, so the resulting deriva-tion is convergent. If the analysis of expletive *it* outlined here is along the right lines it suggests that (contrary to what we assumed earlier) expletive *it* is not a pure 'dummy' element inserted in spec-TP to satisfy the [EPP] requirement of T, but rather is a (quasi-)argument which originates internally within VP. Of course, if expletive *it* carries case, we have to ask why (as noted above) it has no genitive form: however, this is arguably just a lexical idiosyncrasy, since even in its refer-ential use *it* has no strong genitive form (Peter Evans (pc) points out), as we see from the ungrammaticality of ?**Its watering the flowers is something I don't like about my cat*.

8.6   Expletive *there* subjects

Having looked at the syntax of expletive *it* in the previous section, we now turn to look at expletive *there*. As a starting point for our discussion, we'll go back to the very first sentence we looked at in this chapter, namely (1) *There are thought likely to be awarded several prizes*. Let's suppose that the derivation proceeds as before, until we reach the stage in (2) above. However, let's additionally assume that *several prizes* carries interpretable φ-features (marking it as a third-person-plural expression) and an uninterpretable (and unvalued) case-feature. Let's also assume (as in earlier discussions) that BE carries an interpretable present-tense feature, and uninterpretable (and unvalued) φ-features. This being so, the structure formed when BE is merged with its VP complement will be that shown in simplified form below:

(34)

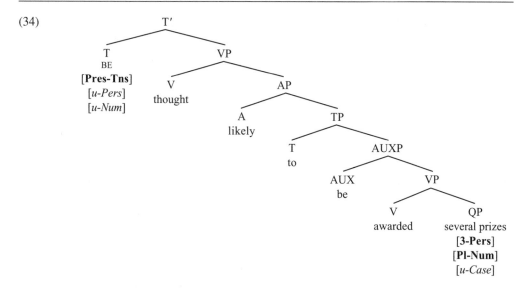

Given the **Earliness Principle**, T-agreement will apply at this point in the deriva-tion. Because BE is the highest head in the structure (in that it is the only head in the structure which is not c-commanded by another head), and because BE is active (by virtue of its uninterpretable φ-features), BE serves as a probe which searches for a nominal goal within the structure containing it. The nominal *several prizes* can serve as a goal for the probe BE, since *several prizes* is active by virtue of carrying an uninterpretable case feature. By application of Feature-Copying (7), the unvalued person and number features on BE are given the same values as those on *several prizes* – as shown in simplified form in (35) below:

(35)   [BE]   thought likely to be awarded [several prizes]
          [Pres-Tns]   **[3-Pers]**
          [3-Pers]   **[Pl-Num]**
          [Pl-Num]   *[u-Case]*

By application of Nominative Case Assignment (9), the unvalued case feature of the goal *several prizes* in (35) is assigned the value nominative as shown in (36) below, since the probe BE carries finite tense (more specifically, present tense), and since the probe [BE] and the goal *several prizes* have matching φ-feature values because both are third person plural:

(36)   [BE]   thought likely to be awarded [several prizes]
          [Pres-Tns]   **[3-Pers]**
          [3-Pers]   **[Pl-Num]**
          [Pl-Num]   *[Nom-Case]*

Via Feature-Deletion (14), the probe BE deletes the uninterpretable nominative case feature on *several prizes*, since BE is φ-complete (by virtue of carrying both person and number features) and the φ-features of the probe BE match those of the goal *several prizes*. Conversely, via the same Feature-Deletion operation

(14), the goal *several prizes* deletes the uninterpretable person/number features
on the probe BE, since the goal is φ-complete (carrying both person and number
features), and probe and goal have matching φ-feature values. Feature-Deletion
yields:

(37)   [BE]   thought likely to be awarded [several prizes]
        [Pres-Tns]   **[3-Pers]**
        [~~3-Pers~~]   **[Pl-Num]**
        [~~Pl-Num~~]   [~~Nom-Case~~]

We have thus deleted all uninterpretable case/agreement features on both probe
and goal, as required.

However, BE also has an [EPP] feature (not shown above) requiring it to project
a structural subject. In (1) *There are thought likely to be awarded several prizes*,
the [EPP] requirement of [T BE] is satisfied by merging expletive *there* in spec-TP.
Let's assume that (like expletive *it*), expletive *there* carries no case feature (and
hence has no genitive form, as we see from the ungrammaticality of *She was
upset by there's being nobody to help her*). More precisely, let's follow Chomsky
(1998, 1999, 2001) in positing that the only feature carried by expletive *there* is an
uninterpretable person feature, and let's further suppose that *there* is intrinsically
third person (consistent with the fact that a number of other words beginning
with *th-* are third person – e.g. *this, that, these, those* and *the*). Accordingly,
merging *there* in spec-TP will derive the structure shown in abbreviated form
below:

(38)

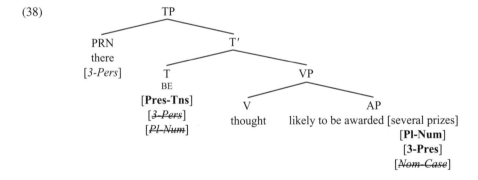

The pronoun *there* serves as a probe because it is the highest head in the structure,
and because it is active by virtue of carrying an uninterpretable third-person φ-
feature. It therefore searches for a c-commanded goal to agree with. Let's suppose
that agreement (of the kind we are concerned with here) involves a T–nominal
relation (i.e. a relation between T and a noun/pronoun expression): this being so,
there (being a pronominal probe) will search for an active T constituent to serve
as its goal, and find [T BE]. BE is an active goal for the probe *there* in (38) because
be contains uninterpretable person/number features: these have been marked as
invisible to the semantic component (via Feature-Deletion), but remain visible

and active in the syntax in accordance with the Feature Visibility Convention (13). Accordingly, Feature-Deletion (14) applies, and the goal BE deletes the matching uninterpretable third-person feature carried by the probe *there*. This is possible because *there* is active as a probe and BE is active as a goal (as we have just seen), and because the goal BE is φ-complete (having both person and number features), and the third-person feature carried by the probe *there* matches the third-person feature carried by the goal BE. Deleting the uninterpretable person feature of *there*, and merging the resulting TP with a null complementiser carrying an interpretable declarative force feature [**Dec-Force**], derives the CP shown in skeletal form below:

(39)   ø   there   BE   thought likely to be awarded [several prizes]
       [**Dec-Force**]   [3-Pers]   [**Pres-Tns**]   [**3-Pers**]
                                     [3-Pers]   [**Pl-Num**]
                                     [Pl-Num]   [Nom-Case]

Only the bold-printed interpretable features will be processed by the semantic component, not the barred italicised uninterpretable features (since these have all been deleted and deletion makes features invisible to the semantic component, while leaving them visible to the syntactic and phonological components); both the interpretable and uninterpretable features will be processed by the phonological component where BE will be spelled out as *are*. (On colloquial structures like *There's lots of people in the room*, see den Dikken 2001.)

An important question to ask in the context of our discussion of expletive *it* in the previous section and expletive *there* in this section is what factors determine the choice of expletive in a particular sentence. In this connection, let's ask why expletive *there* can't be used in place of expletive *it* in sentences like (40b) below:

(40) (a)   *It* is said that he has taken bribes
     (b)   **There* is said that he has taken bribes

Let's suppose that merging BE with the VP headed by the verb *said* forms the structure shown in (19) above, and that subsequently merging *there* in spec–TP derives the structure shown in (41) below:

(41)

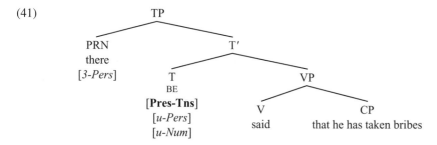

Because it is the highest head in the structure, and because it is active by virtue of its uninterpretable person feature, *there* serves as a probe. BE serves as the goal for *there* because BE is c-commanded by *there*, and BE itself is active by virtue of its uninterpretable person/number features. Via Feature-Copying (7), the unvalued person feature of BE will be assigned the same third-person value as *there* – as shown in schematic form below:

(42)   there   BE   said that he has taken bribes
          [*3-Pers*] [**Pres-Tns**]
                    [*3-Pers*]
                    [*u-Num*]

Via Feature-Deletion (14), BE can delete the uninterpretable person feature of *there*, because BE is φ-complete and the person features of BE and *there* have matching values. However, *there* cannot delete the person feature of BE, since *there* is φ-incomplete (in that it has person but not number), and only a φ-complete α can delete one or more features of ß. Accordingly, the structure which results after Feature-Deletion applies is:

(43)   there   BE   said that he has taken bribes
          [~~3-Pers~~] [**Pres-Tns**]
                    [*3-Pers*]
                    [*u-Num*]

However, the resulting derivation will ultimately crash, for two reasons. Firstly, the number feature on BE has remained unvalued, and the PF component cannot process unvalued features. And secondly, the uninterpretable person and number features on BE have not been deleted, and the semantic component cannot process uninterpretable features. In other words, our assumptions about the differences between expletive *it* and expletive *there* allow us to provide a principled account of why (40a) *It is said that he has taken bribes* is grammatical, but (40b) **There is said that he has taken bribes* is not.

Now let's ask why expletive *it* can't be used in place of *there* in a sentence like (44b) below:

(44) (a)   *There* are thought likely to be awarded several prizes
     (b)   **It* is thought likely to be awarded several prizes

One way of answering this question is by making the assumption outlined below:

(45)   **EPP Generalisation**
            When T carries an [EPP] feature, this can be deleted
                        (i) by merging expletive *there* in spec-TP if T c-commands a matching indefinite goal (i.e. an indefinite noun or pronoun expression which matches T in person/number)
            or   (ii) by merging expletive *it* in spec-TP if T c-commands no matching goal
            or   (iii) by moving the closest matching active goal c-commanded by T into spec-TP

The requirement in (45iii) for T to attract the closest matching goal is a consequence of the **Attract Closest Principle**. (45i) stipulates the indefiniteness requirement without explaining it. An interesting possibility to explore would be that in expletive *there* structures, the associate is indefinite because it has no person properties, so that *there* is inserted in order to value the person properties of T (though see Frampton and Gutmann 1999 for an alternative explanation. See also Lasnik 2001 on the nature of EPP.)

It follows from (45) that in structures like (34) where [$_T$ BE] c-commands (and agrees in person and number with) an indefinite nominal (*several prizes*), expletive *there* can be used but not expletive *it*, so deriving (44a) *There are thought likely to be awarded several prizes*. Conversely in structures like (19) where there is no matching goal accessible to the probe [$_T$BE], *it* can be used but not *there* – so deriving (18a) *It is said that he has taken bribes*. It also follows from (45) that neither expletive can be used in structures like the following:

(46) (a) *There was impeached the president
     (b) *It was impeached the president

This is because *was* in (46) c-commands and agrees in person and number with the definite goal *the president*, so that the conditions for the use of either expletive in (45i,ii) are not met. The only way of deleting the [EPP] feature of T in such a case is to passivise the definite DP *the president*, so deriving:

(47)   The president was impeached

So, we see that the **EPP Generalisation** in (45) provides a descriptively adequate characterisation of data like (40), (44), (46) and (47). (See Bowers 2002 for an alternative account of the *there/it* distinction in expletives.)

However, our so-called 'generalisation' in (45) is little more than a descriptive stipulation, and begs the question of why the relevant restrictions on the use of expletives should hold. A preferable solution would be to see the choice between expletive *there* and expletive *it* as one rooted in UG principles. Reasoning along these lines, one possibility would be to posit that economy considerations dictate that we use an expletive carrying as few uninterpretable features as possible. In a structure like (19), the expletive has to serve two functions: (i) to satisfy the [EPP] requirement for T to have a specifier with person and/or number properties; and (ii) to value the unvalued person/number features of [$_T$ BE]. Hence only expletive *it* can be used, since this carries both person and number. But in a structure like (2), the expletive is not needed to value the person/number features of [$_T$BE] since these are valued by *several prizes*; rather, the expletive serves only to satisfy the requirement for T to have a specifier with person and/or number features. In this situation, we might suppose, *there* is preferred to *it* because *there* carries only person, and economy considerations dictate that we use as few uninterpretable features as possible.

Throughout this section, we have followed Chomsky in assuming that expletive *there* is a 'dummy' pronoun directly merged in spec-TP. However, just as there are some who believe that expletive *it* originates internally within VP, so too there are some who believe that expletive *there* originates internally within VP, perhaps with a locative function (as suggested by Moro 1997). Bowers (2002, p. 195) argues that the ungrammaticality of transitive expletive structures such as the following in Standard English:

(48)   *There has [someone eaten a bagel]

cannot be accounted for under Chomsky's spec-TP analysis of expletive *there*, since nothing in the spec-TP account prevents *has* from agreeing with (and assigning nominative case to) *someone*, with expletive *there* being inserted in spec-TP in order to delete the [EPP] feature of T. A principled way of ruling out sentences like (48), Bowers argues, is by supposing that expletive *there* originates in spec-VP as a nonthematic subject – and hence it can only occur in intransitive VPs which (by their very nature) do not have a thematic subject.

We can illustrate how such an analysis might work in terms of a sentence such as (49) below:

(49)   There have arisen several problems

The verb *arise* is an unaccusative predicate which projects a complement, but no thematic subject. Precisely because it projects no thematic subject, it can project an expletive subject (on Bowers's assumption that a predicate only allows an expletive subject if it has no thematic subject). This means that expletive *there* will initially be merged as the specifier of the VP headed by *arisen* in (49), so that at the stage of derivation when HAVE is merged with its VP complement, we have the structure shown in (50) below:

(50)

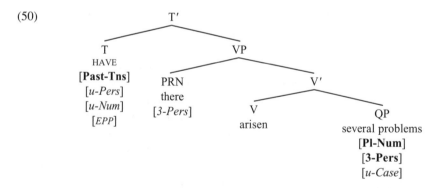

[T HAVE] will then probe for active matching goals which carry person and/or number features, and locates *two* such active goals, *there* and *several problems*. Accordingly, T simultaneously agrees with both *there* and *several problems* – resulting in **multiple agreement** (i.e. agreement between a probe and more than one matching goal). Clearly, this will only yield a successful outcome if the associate carries the same third-person feature as *there* – thereby accounting for the observation by Sigurðsson (1996) that expletive associates must be third-person expressions. The [EPP] feature of T simultaneously attracts the closest active goal, so triggering movement of *there* to spec-TP. We can assume that all the various operations affecting a given probe (like T in (50) above) apply simultaneously, so that agreement with *there*, agreement with *several problems* and movement of *there* to spec-TP all apply at the same time.

A potential problem posed by analysing expletive *there* as a (perhaps locative) quasi-argument initially merged in spec-VP is that (unlike expletive *it* in sentences such as (31) above) expletive *there* cannot serve as a controller for PRO – as we see from (51) below:

(51)   There occurred three more accidents without [there/*PRO being any
              medical help available on the premises]   (Haegeman 1994, p. 279)

If quasi-arguments have the property of being able to serve as controllers of PRO, sentences like (51) might be thought to argue against a VP-internal origin for expletive *there*. However, a straightforward way of accounting for the contrast between (31) and (51) is to suppose that PRO requires an antecedent with both person and number features, and that expletive *it* carries both of these features, but expletive *there* carries only person.

A VP-internal analysis of expletives like that in (50) also offers significant theoretical advantages over Chomsky's TP analysis, in that it provides us with a way of avoiding two potentially problematic aspects of Chomsky's analysis. One is that although a probe is generally the *head* of a containing projection (so that the head T of TP is the probe in most of the structures we have looked at in this chapter), Chomsky's TP analysis of expletives has to stipulate that a *specifier* can also serve as a probe when it is an expletive pronoun like *there/it* – a claim which is hard to square with his (2001) view that specifier–head agreement should be eliminated from the set of operations permitted by UG. By contrast, the VP-internal analysis of expletives allows us to maintain the stronger claim that only a *head* can be a probe. A second feature of Chomsky's analysis (illustrated in (38) above) is that he needs to assume that a T which has already had its person/number features valued and deleted by agreement with an indefinite associate can nonetheless serve as an active goal for agreement with an expletive probe. One way round this problem (suggested by Pesetsky and Torrego 2001) is to say that the relevant features are **marked for deletion** (or metaphorically speaking, sentenced to death) on the TP cycle, but not actually deleted (or, metaphorically speaking, executed) until a later stage of derivation (at the end of the CP cycle/phase). However, any such intrinsically undesirable splitting of deletion into two processes can be avoided under the account suggested here, which allows us to posit a unitary treatment of deletion along the lines of (52) below:

(52)   **Feature Inactivation Hypothesis**
              An uninterpretable feature becomes inactive in the syntax (and invisible to
              the semantic component) immediately it is deleted

However, it should be noted that while (52) is compatible with a VP analysis of expletives, it is not compatible with Chomsky's claim that expletive *there* is directly merged in spec-TP.

A crucial premise of our alternative account of expletives is that in structures like (50), a T-probe can agree simultaneously with multiple goals (so that *have* simultaneously agrees in person with *there* and in person and number with *several problems*). However, this assumption raises interesting questions about how agreement works in transitive sentences like:

(53)   We are helping him

Given the assumptions we are making here, (53) will be derived as follows. The verb *helping* merges with its THEME complement *him* to form the V-bar *helping him*. This V-bar is in turn merged with its AGENT argument *we* to form the VP *we helping him*. The resulting VP is then merged with a present-tense T constituent to form the T-bar shown in simplified form in (54) below:

(54)

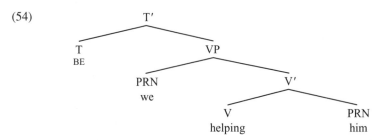

Given the Earliness Principle, T will serve as a probe at this point and look for one or more nominal goals to value (and delete) its unvalued person/number features. However, if (as we assumed in our discussion of (50) above) a probe can agree with multiple goals, an important question to ask is why T can't agree with both the subject *we* and the complement *him*. If (contrary to fact) multiple agreement were permitted in structures like (54), it would cause the derivation to crash because the person/number features of BE would have to be valued as first person plural in order to agree with the subject *we* and as third person singular in order to agree with the object *him*, and this would clearly lead to conflicting requirements on how the person/number features of BE should be valued. In reality, T agrees with the subject *we* in transitive structures like (54) and not with the object *him*. But in a framework which allows a probe to agree with multiple goals, how can we rule out agreement between T and the object of a transitive verb?

One answer to this question is provided by the Phase Impenetrability Condition, which we formulated in (23) above in the manner set out in (55) below:

(55)   **Phase Impenetrability Condition/PIC**
          Any goal c-commanded by a phase head is impenetrable to any probe outside the phase

In our earlier discussion of PIC in §8.5, we noted Chomsky's (1999, p. 9) claim that phases are 'propositional' in nature, and that accordingly CPs are phases. However, Chomsky claims that **transitive verb phrases** (but not intransitive VPs) are also propositional in nature and hence phases, by virtue of the fact that transitive VPs contain a complete thematic (argument structure) complex, including an external argument in spec-VP.

If transitive VPs are phases, and PIC allows only constituents on the **edge** (i.e. in the head or specifier position) of a phase to be accessible to a higher probe, it follows that in a structure like (54) above, the T constituent BE will only be able to agree with the subject *we* on the edge of the transitive VP phase, not with the object *him* which lies within the (c-command) domain of the transitive phase head *helping*. By contrast, in expletive structures like (50), PIC will not prevent the T constituent *have* from agreeing with both *there* and *several problems*, since the VP headed by the unaccusative verb *arisen* is intransitive (its specifier *there* not being an external argument but rather being a non-referential expletive pronoun).

If we adopt the Feature Inactivation Hypothesis (52), there is also another way in which we can prevent agreement between T and the object of a transitive verb in structures like (54). If the object *him* enters the derivation with an unvalued case feature and (in accordance with the Earliness Principle) the relevant case feature is valued as accusative (and deleted) as soon as *him* is merged with the transitive verb *helping*, it follows that once we reach the stage of derivation shown in (54) above, the accusative case feature carried by *him* will have been deleted, so making *him* inactive for agreement with T. (We look at accusative case assignment in the next chapter, so will say no more about it for the time being.)

8.7   Agreement and A-movement

So far, we have seen that agreement plays an important role not only in valuing the φ-features of T but also in valuing the case features of nominals. Chomsky (1998, 1999, 2001) goes further and suggests that agreement also plays an important role in A-movement operations. To see why, let's return to consider the derivation of our earlier sentence (5B) *They were arrested*. Assume that the derivation proceeds as sketched earlier, with THEY being merged as the thematic complement of *arrested*, and the resulting VP in turn being merged with the tense auxiliary BE to form the structure (56) below:

(56)

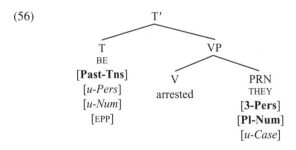

In (56), [$_T$BE] is an active probe (by virtue of its uninterpretable person and number features) and has an uninterpretable [EPP] feature. It therefore searches for active nominal goals which can value and delete its person/number features, locating the pronoun THEY (which is active by virtue of its uninterpretable case feature and which has person and number features which match those of BE). Since the matching goal THEY is a definite pronoun, the [EPP] feature of [T BE] cannot be deleted by merging an expletive in spec-TP, but rather can only be deleted by movement of the goal to spec-TP, in accordance with (45iii): accordingly, THEY moves to become the specifier of BE, thereby deleting the uninterpretable [EPP] feature of BE. Assuming that Feature-Copying, Nominative Case Assignment and Feature-Deletion work as before, the structure which is formed at the end of the TP cycle will be that shown below:

(57)

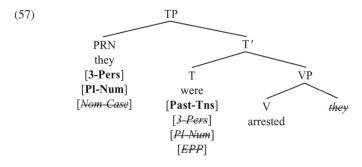

(To avoid excessive visual clutter, the trace copy of *they* left behind in VP-complement position is shown here simply as *they*, but is in fact an identical copy of *they*, containing the same features as *they*. The same typographical convention will be used throughout the rest of this chapter.) The TP in (57) will subsequently be merged with a null declarative-force C, so terminating the syntactic derivation. Since all uninterpretable features have been deleted, the derivation **converges** – i.e. results in a syntactic structure which can subsequently be mapped into well-formed phonetic and semantic representations.

A key assumption underlying the analysis sketched here is that T triggers movement of a nominal goal with which it agrees in person and number. Interesting empirical support for this claim comes from European Portuguese. Costa (2001) notes that in colloquial Portuguese, an intransitive verb used in an unaccusative structure like that below can be either third person singular or third person plural if used with an in-situ postverbal argument as in (58) below:

(58) (a)   Fecharam *muitas fábricas*   (b) Fechou   *muitas fábricas*
           Closed-3Pl many   factories   Closed-3Sg many   factories
           'Many factories closed'   'Many factories closed'

However, the postverbal argument (which originates as the complement of the verb) can only move in front of the verb into spec-TP if the verb (or, more accurately, the associated T-constituent) agrees with the subject in both person and number: cf.

(59) (a)   *Muitas fábricas* fecharam   (b) *Muitas fábricas fechou
           Many   factories closed-3Pl   Many   factories closed-3Sg
           'Many factories closed'   'Many factories closed'

This suggests that movement of the italicised nominal from VP-complement position to spec-TP is dependent on full person/number agreement between T and the nominal which it attracts. Costa follows Belletti (1988) in positing that in agreementless sentences like (58b), the postverbal argument is assigned partitive case by the verb (which, in a language in which nouns have a limited case morphology will surface in a form homophonous with the accusative); assignment of case to the complement makes it inactive, and so ineligible to undergo T-agreement – with the result that T surfaces in the agreementless default (third-person-singular) form. It may be that we find a related phenomenon in English sentence pairs such as:

(60) (a)   There is *only me* considered suitable
     (b)   *Only I* am considered suitable

In (60a) the italicised pronoun expression follows the verb *be*, is not assigned nominative case, does not trigger T-agreement and is not raised to spec-TP; by contrast in (60b) the italicised nominal is assigned nominative case, triggers T-agreement, and is moved to spec-TP. Accordingly, sentences like (60) provide empirical support for Chomsky's claim that there is a close association between case, agreement and A-movement.

8.8   EPP in control infinitives

The analysis presented in the previous section assumes that a finite T carries an [EPP] feature which drives A-movement. But what about the kind of infinitival [$_T$ *to*] constituent found in **control** clauses? In the previous chapter, we assumed that infinitival *to* never has an [EPP] feature, and hence that the PRO subject of a control clause like that bracketed in (61a) below remains in situ in spec-VP as in (61b), rather than raising to spec–TP as in (61c):

(61) (a)   They don't want [to see you]
     (b)   They don't want [$_{CP}$ [$_C$ ø] [$_{TP}$ [$_T$ to] [$_{VP}$ PRO [$_V$ see] you]]]
     (c)   They don t want [$_{CP}$ [$_C$ ø] [$_{TP}$ PRO [$_T$ to] [$_{VP}$ ~~PRO~~ [$_V$ see] you]]]

We noted Baltin's (1995) claim that the *in-situ* analysis (61b) under which PRO remains in situ would account for why *wanna*-contraction is possible in such sentences (yielding *They don't wanna see you*), since there would be no PRO intervening between *want* and *to*. However, Baltin's argument is not entirely convincing. After all, if intervening null constituents block *to* from cliticising onto *want* and if control clauses are CPs, why doesn't the intervening null complementiser in (61b,c) block *wanna*-contraction? If we answer this question (as we did in the previous chapter) by suggesting that *to* first cliticises onto the null complementiser and then the two of them together subsequently cliticise onto *want*, we can handle the relevant data by supposing that only an *overt* subject in spec-TP (like *who* at the relevant stage of derivation in **Who don't they want to see you?*) in spec-TP blocks cliticisation of *to* onto C, not a null subject like PRO in (61c). What weakens the contraction argument still further is that this kind of contraction is idiosyncratic to the verb WANT (and indeed to the form *want* rather than *wants*, *wanted*, or *wanting*) rather than being associated with all control predicates, and this has led some linguists to suggest that *wanna* should simply be listed in the lexicon as an idiosyncratic form of *want* rather than being the product of a cliticisation operation. (See Boeckx 2000 for an alternative account of *wanna*-contraction.)

In short, the *wanna*-cliticisation argument for saying that PRO remains in situ is potentially flawed. Indeed, there seems to be counter-evidence in support of claiming that PRO *does* in fact move to spec-TP in control infinitives (and hence that control *to* has an EPP feature). Part of the evidence comes from the syntax of constituents like those italicised in (62) below which have the property that they are construed as modifying a bold-printed antecedent which is not immediately adjacent to them in the relevant structure:

(62) (a)   **They** were *both* priding themselves on their achievements
   (b)   **I** don't *myself* think that Svengali was the best choice for England manager
   (c)   **He** was *personally* held responsible

Both in (62a) is a **floating quantifier** (and *each/all* can be used in a similar fashion); *myself* in (62b) is a **floating emphatic reflexive**; and *personally* in (62c) is an **argument-oriented adverb** (construed as modifying an argument, in this case *he*). In each sentence in (62), the italicised expression is construed as modifying the bold-printed subject of the clause. Contrasts such as those in (63) and (64) below:

(63) (a)   **Two republican senators** were *themselves* thought to have been implicated
   (b)   *There were *themselves* thought to have been implicated **two republican senators**

(64) (a)   **Two republican senators** are *both* thought to have been implicated
   (b)   *There are *both* thought to have been implicated **two republican senators**

suggest that a floating modifier must be c-commanded by its bold-printed antecedent.

In the light of the requirement for a floating modifier to be c-commanded by its antecedent, consider the syntax of the bracketed clauses in the following sentences:

(65) (a)   [To *both* be betrayed by their friends] would be disastrous for Romeo and Juliet
   (b)   [To *themselves* be indicted] would be unfair on the company directors
   (c)   It was upsetting [to *personally* have been accused of corruption]

In each of these examples, the bracketed clause is a control clause containing a PRO argument. In each case, PRO is the thematic complement of a passive participle (viz. *betrayed/indicted/accused*). Hence, if control *to* has no [EPP] feature and PRO remains in situ, the TP in the bracketed infinitive complement in

(65b) will have the skeletal structure (66a) below, but if control *to* has an [EPP] feature, this will trigger movement of PRO to become the structural subject of *to* – as in (66b):

(66) (a)   [cp [c ø] [TP [T to] [AUXP *themselves* [AUX be] [VP [V indicted] **PRO**]]]]
     (b)   [cp [c ø] [TP **PRO** [T to] [AUXP *themselves* [AUX be] [VP [V indicted] ~~PRO~~]]]]

Given the requirement for a floating emphatic reflexive to be c-commanded by its antecedent, and given that PRO is the intended antecedent of *themselves* in (66), it is clear that (66a) cannot be the right structure, since PRO does not c-command *themselves* in (66a). By contrast, movement of PRO to spec-TP in (66b) means that PRO will indeed c-command *themselves*, so correctly predicting that (66b) is grammatical.

Let's therefore follow Chomsky (1998, 1999, 2001) in positing that control *to* does indeed have an [EPP] feature, triggering raising of PRO to spec-TP. Let's also follow Chomsky in positing that PRO is assigned null case by agreement with a c-commanding T with null (non-finite) tense in much the same way as subjects in tensed clauses are assigned nominative case by agreement with a c-commanding T which has finite (present or past) tense. More specifically, let's assume that *to* in control infinitives contains not only an abstract non-finite tense feature, but also abstract φ-features; and let's further suppose that null case assignment can be characterised informally as follows:

(67)   **Null Case Assignment**
        An unvalued case feature on a goal is valued as **null** by a probe carrying null (non-finite) tense if probe and goal match in (person and number) φ-features

See Stowell (1982) and Martin (2001) on the tense properties of control *to*, and Martin (2001) for evidence that control *to* has agreement features; but see Bowers (2002) for a different analysis of the case-marking of PRO subjects.

In the light of these assumptions, consider the derivation of the bracketed control clause in:

(68)   They have decided [PRO to help you]

Decide is a control predicate (as we see from the fact that (68) is paraphraseable as *They have decided that they will help you*, and from the fact that *decide* does not allow an expletive subject in a sentence like **There has decided to be an enquiry*). Given the VP-Internal Subject Hypothesis, the PRO subject of the bracketed infinitive clause will originate in spec-VP, as the specifier of *help you*. More specifically, the derivation proceeds as follows. The verb *help* merges with its complement *you*, and the resulting V-bar *help you* in turn merges with its PRO subject to form the VP *PRO help you*. Merging control *to* with this VP forms the TP *to help you*. Let's suppose that since PRO refers back to *they* in (68), PRO (as used here) carries the interpretable features [**3-Pers, Pl-Num**]; let's also suppose that PRO enters the derivation with an unvalued case feature [*u*-Case]. In addition, let's assume that control *to* carries an interpretable non-finite-tense feature [**Nf-Tns**] (denoting an irrealis event which has not yet happened but may happen in the future), and also has uninterpretable (and unvalued) person/number features. Finally (for the reasons given above), let's assume that *to* carries an [EPP] feature in control clauses. Given all these assumptions, merging *to* with [$_{VP}$ *PRO help you*] will form the T-bar (69) below (simplified by showing only features on constituents of immediate concern to us):

(69)

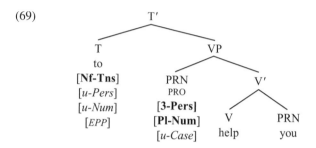

Since *to* is the highest head in the structure and is active (by virtue of its uninterpretable φ-features), it serves as a probe which searches for a goal to value and delete its φ-features. Since *to* c-commands PRO and PRO is active by virtue of its uninterpretable case feature, PRO can serve as a goal for the probe *to*. The unvalued φ-features on the probe are assigned the same third-person-plural values as those on the goal by Feature-Copying (7) and are deleted by Feature-Deletion (14). The unvalued case feature on PRO is assigned the value [*Null-Case*] by Null Case Assignment (67) and deleted by Feature-Deletion (14). Since PRO is a definite pronoun, the [EPP] feature of *to* is deleted by movement of PRO to spec-TP in accordance with the EPP Generalisation (45iii). The result of applying these various operations is to derive the TP (70) below (simplified in a number of ways, e.g. by showing the trace of PRO simply as *t* rather than as a deleted copy of PRO):

(70)

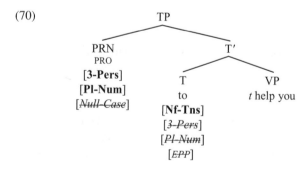

The resulting TP is subsequently merged with the null non-finite complementiser which introduces control clauses. As required, the structure which will serve as input to the semantic component will contain only (bold-printed) interpretable features – all uninterpretable features having been deleted.

A question of incidental detail which arises from the assumption made above that control T assigns null case to a nominal or pronominal expression which it c-commands is why T in (69) cannot assign null case to the pronoun *you* which is the object of the transitive verb *help*, since T c-commands *you* as well as PRO. One answer to this question is that (as we saw in §8.6), transitive verb phrases are **phases**, and hence the Phase Impenetrability Condition (55) allows a T probe to locate a goal on the edge of a transitive VP (like the PRO subject of the VP in (69) above), but not to locate a goal in the c-command domain of a transitive verb (hence not a pronoun like *you* in (69) since this is c-commanded by the transitive phase head *help*). A second answer is that the **Earliness Principle** requires *you* to be assigned case as early as possible in the derivation; and given our assumption in §4.9 that a transitive head assigns accusative case to a noun or pronoun expression which it c-commands, it follows that the case feature carried by *you* will be valued as accusative (and, we suppose, deleted) at the stage of derivation where it is merged as the complement of the transitive verb *help*: and our **Feature Inactivation Hypothesis** (52) tells us that once its case feature is deleted, *you* thereafter becomes inactive for agreement.

In the previous section, we suggested that a finite T has an [EPP] feature which triggers movement of the closest active matching goal to spec-TP, in conformity with the Attract Closest Principle. In this section, we have suggested that control *to* likewise carries an [EPP] feature triggering movement of the closest active goal to spec-TP. This suggests that we should look to see whether there is some property which finite T and control T share in common which will account for why both of them have an [EPP] feature. One possibility suggested by Chomsky (1999, p. 6) is 'to associate EPP with φ-completeness'. What this would mean is that T has an [EPP] feature only if it has a complete set of φ-features – an idea explored in Nasu (2001, 2002). On the assumption that in a language like English where T probes agree in person and number but not gender with appropriate goals T is φ-complete if it carries person and number features, we can say that a finite T is φ-complete by virtue of carrying person and number features, and the same is true of control *to* under the formulation of Null Case Assignment given in (67) above. However, a natural question to ask in relation to the φ-completeness analysis of [EPP] is whether raising *to* also has an [EPP] feature, and if so whether it is φ-complete or not. This is the question we explore in the next section.

8.9 EPP in other infinitives

In the previous chapter, we posited that raising *to* does not carry an [EPP] feature. This would mean that a sentence such as (71a) below has the skeletal structure (71b), with *he* originating as the thematic subject of *admire* and being raised directly to become the structural subject of *does* (as shown by the dotted arrow):

(71) (a)   He does seem to admire her

    (b)   [CP [C Ø] [TP *he* [T does] [VP [V seem] [TP [T to] [VP ~~he~~ [V admire] her]]]]]

More specifically, we assumed that *to* in raising structures like (71b) does not have an [EPP] feature, so that *he* does not become the subject of *to* at any stage of derivation. If *to* in raising clauses is assumed to be defective (and hence to lack person and/or number φ-features), this is entirely consistent with Chomsky's suggested generalisation that only a φ-complete T carries an [EPP] feature.

However, Chomsky (2001, fn. 56) argues that (somewhat contrived) sentences like (72) below provide empirical evidence that raising *to* does after all have an [EPP] feature:

(72)   John seems to Fred [to appear to himself [to like Mary]]

Here, *himself* refers to *John*, not to *Fred*. This is puzzling if we assume that the antecedent of a reflexive must be an argument locally c-commanding the reflexive (and hence contained within the same TP as the reflexive), since if raising *to* has no [EPP] feature and *John* moves directly from being the subject of the *like* clause to becoming the subject of the *seem* clause, the lefthand bracketed TP containing the reflexive will contain no antecedent for *himself*, and hence we will wrongly predict that sentences like (72) are ill-formed. By contrast, argues Chomsky, if we posit that raising *to* does indeed have an [EPP] feature, *John* will move from being subject of *like Mary* to becoming subject of *to like Mary*, then later becoming subject of *to appear to himself to like Mary*, before finally moving to become the subject of the null T constituent in the *seem* clause. This will mean that a null trace copy of *John* is left behind as the subject of each of the two infinitive clauses, as shown in skeletal form in (73) below:

(73)   *John* seems to Fred [***John*** to appear to himself [***John*** to like Mary]]

Since the reflexive *himself* is locally c-commanded by the bold-printed trace ***John*** in (73) within the lefthand bracketed TP containing the reflexive, (73) correctly predicts that *himself* will be interpreted as referring to *John*. (Recall that Chomsky posits that traces are deleted in the phonological component but remain visible in the syntactic and semantic components.) Further evidence that A-movement in raising structures is successive-cyclic is presented in Bošković (2002b).

Sentences like (73) suggest that raising *to* must have an [EPP] feature triggering movement of an argument to spec-TP. But it's important to bear in mind that the [EPP] feature on T works in conjunction with the person/number φ-features of T: more specifically, the [EPP] feature on T triggers movement to spec-TP of an expression which matches one or more of the φ-features of T. It therefore follows that T in raising clauses must carry one or more φ-features if it is to trigger movement of a nominal carrying φ-features of its own. Now it clearly cannot be the case that raising *to* carries both person and number, since if it did we would wrongly predict that raising clauses require a null PRO subject (given that infinitival *to* assigns null case to its subject by (67) when carrying both person and number). The conclusion we reach, therefore, is that raising *to* must carry only *one* φ-feature. But which φ-feature – person or number?

The answer is provided by raising sentences such as the following:

(74)   There do seem to remain several problems

On the assumption that raising *to* carries an [EPP] feature requiring it to project a subject, it seems reasonable to posit that expletive *there* will become the specifier of *to remain several problems* at some stage of derivation, and thereafter be raised up (in the manner shown by the arrow in the skeletal structure in (75) below) to become the specifier of *do* on the main-clause TP cycle:

(75)   [TP *There* [T do] [VP [V seem] [TP ~~there~~ [T to] [VP [V remain] several problems]]]]

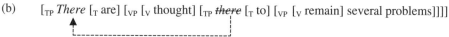

This being so, merging *there* as the specifier of raising *to* on the subordinate clause TP cycle must satisfy the [EPP] feature of *to*. It follows that the φ-feature carried by *to* in (75) must match that carried by expletive *there*. Since we argued in §8.6 that expletive *there* carries person (but not number), it also follows that *to* in (75) must carry a person feature. This being so, the [EPP] feature of raising *to* will require it to project a specifier carrying a person feature, and expletive *there* clearly satisfies this requirement. (Note that the argument goes through irrespective of whether we follow Chomsky 2001 in positing that *there* originates as the specifier of *to*, or Bowers 2002 in assuming that *there* originates as the specifier of *remain* and is subsequently raised up to become the specifier of *to*.)

Our conclusion can be generalised from raising sentences like (74/75) to long-distance passives like (76a) below, involving the movement operation arrowed in (76b):

(76) (a)   There are thought to remain several problems
     (b)   [TP *There* [T are] [VP [V thought] [TP ~~there~~ [T to] [VP [V remain] several problems]]]]

Passive *to* (i.e. the kind of *to* found in long-distance passives) cannot carry both person and number features, since otherwise it would wrongly be predicted to require a subject with null case. Since the derivation of (76a) involves a stage at which *there* is the specifier of *to* and since *there* carries person but not number, it seems reasonable to conclude that passive *to* (like raising *to*) likewise carries person but not number.

We can generalise our finding still further to infinitival TPs such as those bracketed in (77) and (78) below:

(77) (a)   They were expecting [TP *the visitors* to be met at the airport]

    (b)   They were expecting [TP *there* to be someone to meet the visitors at the airport]

(78) (a)   I will arrange [CP for [TP *the visitors* to be met at the airport]]

    (b)   I will arrange [CP for [TP *there* to be someone to meet the visitors at the airport]]

The bracketed TPs in (77) are ECM clauses (with the properties noted in §4.8). Since *the visitors* originates as the thematic complement of the passive verb *met* in (77a) but ends up as the subject of [T *to*], it is clear that the head T of the bracketed complement-clause TP must contain an [EPP] feature and at least one φ-feature. Since the infinitive subject can be expletive *there* in (77b), and since *there* carries only person, it follows that the head T of an ECM clause must carry a person feature as well as an [EPP] feature. But if we suppose that a non-finite T which carries a full set of person and number features (like the head T of a control clause) assigns null case to its subject, then it is apparent from the fact that the subject of an ECM clause is an overt constituent and hence does not have null case that the head T of an ECM clause must also be defective, and so carry an [EPP] feature and a person feature, but no number feature. Our conclusion can be generalised in a straightforward fashion to *for*-infinitive structures like those bracketed in (78): if we define ECM structures as structures in which a constituent within TP is assigned case by an external head lying outside the relevant TP, it follows that *for*-infinitives are also ECM structures.

    Our argumentation here leads us to the following more general conclusions:

(79)   **Feature composition of T in English**

    (i)   T always carries an [EPP] feature in all types of (finite and non-finite, main and complement) clauses

    (ii)   T carries a complete set of (person and number) φ-features in finite clauses and non-finite **control** clauses

    (iii)   T is defective in respect of its φ-features in other types of non-finite clause (e.g. in raising clauses, long-distance passives, and ECM clauses) and carries only person (not number).

And these are essentially the assumptions made in Chomsky (2001).

    In the light of the assumptions in (79), consider the derivation of the following sentence:

(80)   Several prizes are thought likely [to be awarded]

Since the bracketed infinitive complement in (80) is a defective clause, [T *to*] will carry uninterpretable [EPP] and person features (but no number feature) in accordance with (79i,iii). This means that at the point where *to* is merged with its complement we have the structure shown in skeletal form below:

(81)   [T to]   be awarded [several prizes]

        [*u-Pers*]   **[3-Pers]**

         [*EPP*]   **[Pl-Num]**

                           [*u-Case*]

Since [T *to*] is the highest head in the structure at this point and is active by virtue of its uninterpretable person feature, [T *to*] serves as a probe which searches for an active goal and locates *several prizes*, which is active by virtue of its unvalued case feature. The goal *several prizes* values the unvalued person feature of *to* as third person and (by virtue of being φ-complete) deletes it. The unvalued case feature of *several prizes* cannot be valued or deleted by *to*, since *to* is φ-incomplete (by virtue of having no number feature), and only a finite/nonfinite φ-complete T can assign nominative/null case to a goal, and only a φ-complete α can delete a matching feature of ß. The [EPP] feature of *to* is deleted by movement of *several prizes* to spec-TP in accordance with the EPP Generalisation (45iii), thereby deriving the structure (82) below (simplified in various ways, including by showing the deleted trace of *several prizes* without its features):

(82)   [several prizes]   [T to]   be awarded ~~several prizes~~
        [3-Pers]   [*3-Pers*]
        [Pl-Num]   [*EPP*]
        [*u-Case*]

Merging the structure (82) with the raising adjective *likely*, merging the resulting AP with the passive verb *thought* and then merging the resulting VP with a finite present-tense T constituent containing BE will derive:

(83)   [T BE]   thought likely [several prizes]   [T to] be awarded ~~several prizes~~
        [Pres-Tns]   **[3-Pers]**   [*3-Pers*]
        [*u-Pers*]   **[Pl-Num]**   [*EPP*]
        [*u-Num*]   [*u-Case*]
        [*EPP*]

Because it is the highest head in the structure and is active by virtue of its uninterpretable φ-features, BE serves as a probe which searches for an active goal and locates *several prizes*. By virtue of being φ-complete, the goal *several prizes* values and deletes the uninterpretable person/number features of the probe BE. By virtue of being finite and φ-complete, BE values the unvalued case feature of *several prizes* as nominative, and deletes it. The [EPP] feature of BE is deleted by moving *several prizes* to spec-TP in accordance with (45iii), so deriving:

(84) [several prizes]   [T BE]   thought likely ~~several prizes~~   [T to]   be awarded ~~several prizes~~
     [3-Pers]   **[Pres-Tns]**   [*3-Pers*]
     [Pl-Num]   [*3-Pers*]   [*EPP*]
     [*Nom-Case*]   [*Pl-Num*]
                       [*EPP*]

The resulting TP is subsequently merged with a null declarative complementiser, and BE is ultimately spelled out as *are*. Since all unvalued features have been valued and all uninterpretable features have been deleted, the derivation **converges** (i.e. results in a well-formed structure which can be assigned an appropriate phonetic representation and an appropriate semantic representation).

Now let's return to take another look at the derivation of our earlier sentence
(1) *There are thought likely to be awarded several prizes*. Let's adopt Chomsky's
TP analysis of expletives and suppose that we have reached the stage of derivation
in (81) above, repeated as (85) below:

(85)   [$_T$ to]   be awarded [several prizes]
         [*u-Pers*]   [**3-Pers**]
         [*EPP*]   [**Pl-Num**]
                                   [*u-Case*]

As before, *to* serves as a probe and identifies *several prizes* as an active goal. Since
several prizes is φ-complete, it can not only value the unvalued person feature of
to but also delete it, yielding:

(86)   [$_T$ to]   be awarded [several prizes]
         [~~3-Pers~~]   [**3-Pers**]
         [*EPP*]   [**Pl-Num**]
                                   [*u-Case*]

Since the goal *several prizes* is an indefinite expression, the [EPP] feature of *to*
can be deleted by merging expletive *there* in spec-TP in accordance with the EPP
Generalisation (45i), deriving:

(87)   there   [$_T$ to]   be awarded [several prizes]
         [*3-Pers*] [~~3-Pers~~]   [**3-Pers**]
                 [~~EPP~~]   [**Pl-Num**]
                                     [*u-Case*]

Since *there* is the highest head in the structure and is active by virtue of its
uninterpretable person feature, it serves as a probe, and picks out *to* as a matching
goal containing a person feature. However, since *to* is defective (in that it has no
number feature), it cannot delete the uninterpretable person feature on *there*. (We
assume here that *several prizes* cannot serve as a possible goal for *there*, because
agreement is a relation between a noun/pronoun expression like *there* and a T
constituent like *to*, not a relation between two noun/pronoun expressions like
there and *several prizes*.)

Merging the TP in (87) with the raising adjective *likely*, merging the resulting
AP with the passive verb *thought* and merging the resulting VP with a present-
tense T containing BE will derive:

(88)   [$_T$ BE]   thought likely [there]   [$_T$ to]   be awarded [several prizes]
         [**Pres-Tns**]   [*3-Pers*] [~~3-Pers~~]   [**3-Pers**]
         [*u-Pers*]   [~~EPP~~]   [**Pl-Num**]
         [*u-Num*]   [*u-Case*]
         [*EPP*]

At this point, [$_T$ BE] is the highest head in the structure and so serves as a probe.
Its uninterpretable person and number features make it active, and mean that
[$_T$ BE] looks for active nominal goals which have person and/or number features.

However, there are two such active nominal goals which are accessible to the probe [T BE] in (88) – namely the expletive pronoun *there* (active by virtue of its uninterpretable third-person feature) and the quantifier phrase *several prizes* (active by virtue of its uninterpretable case feature, and carrying both person and number features). Both are accessible to [T BE] in terms of the Phase Impenetrability Condition (55) since neither is c-commanded by a phase head (i.e. by a complementiser or by a transitive verb). Let's suppose (consistent with Chomsky 2001 and with our earlier discussion of (50) above) that when a probe locates more than one active goal, it undergoes simultaneous **multiple agreement** with all active goals accessible to it – in other words, the probe BE simultaneously agrees with both *there* and *several prizes*. The unvalued person feature of BE will be valued as third person via Feature Matching with the third-person goals *there* and *several prizes*; the unvalued number feature of BE will be valued as plural via agreement with the plural goal *several prizes*. The unvalued case feature on the goal *several prizes* will be valued as nominative (and deleted) by the φ-complete probe BE because the two match in person and number and BE carries finite tense. The uninterpretable person/number features of the probe BE can in turn be deleted by the φ-complete goal *several prizes*. In accordance with (45iii) and the Attract Closest Principle, the [EPP] feature of BE attracts the closest active goal (namely *there*) to move to become the specifier of BE (movement resulting in deletion of the [EPP] feature on BE), deriving:

(89)   there   [T BE]   thought likely ~~there~~ [T to]   be awarded [several prizes]
           [~~3-Pers~~] [**Pres-Tns**]   [~~3-Pers~~]   [**3-Pers**]
                [~~3-Pers~~]   [~~EPP~~]   [**Pl-Num**]
                [~~Pl-Num~~]   [~~Nom-Case~~]
                [~~EPP~~]

The resulting structure will then be merged with a null declarative complementiser, and BE will ultimately be spelled out as the third-person-plural present-tense form *are*. As required, all uninterpretable features have been deleted from (89), so only the bold interpretable features are seen by the semantic component.

Note that an important assumption which is incorporated into the analysis presented here is that the φ-features of T agree with every goal which is accessible to them (giving rise to multiple agreement), but that (in consequence of the Attract Closest Principle) the [EPP] feature of T only triggers movement of the **closest** goal to spec-TP.

Under the analysis presented in this section (in which all instances of infinitival *to* carry an [EPP] feature), an important question which arises is how we account for the ungrammaticality of sentences like:

(90)   *There are thought likely several prizes to be awarded

Consider first how (90) might be derived, before considering why it is ill-formed. The derivation proceeds along familiar lines until we reach the stage of derivation in (83) above, repeated as (91) below:

(91)   [T BE]   thought likely [several prizes]   [T to]   be awarded ~~several prizes~~
         [Pres-Tns]   **[3-Pers]**   [*3-Pers*]
         [*u-Pers*]   **[Pl-Num]**   [*EPP*]
         [*u-Num*]   [*u-Case*]
         [*EPP*]

As before, the case feature of *several prizes* is valued as nominative and deleted
by [T BE], and conversely the person/number features of BE are valued and deleted
by *several prizes*. Let's suppose that the lexical array contains expletive *there* and
that the [EPP] feature of BE is deleted by merging *there* in spec-TP, and that the
uninterpretable third-person feature of *there* is deleted by the φ-complete [T BE],
so deriving:

(92)   there   [T BE]   thought likely [several prizes]   [T to]   be awarded ~~several prizes~~
         [*3-Pers*] **[Pres-Tns]**   **[3-Pers]**   [*3-Pers*]
                   [*3-Pers*]   **[Pl-Num]**   [*EPP*]
                   [*Pl-Num*]   [*u-Case*]
                   [*EPP*]

(92) is then merged with a null declarative complementiser, and BE is ultimately
spelled out as *are*. Since the resulting structure contains no unvalued or uninterpretable features, we expect the corresponding sentence (90) to be well-formed.
But it is ungrammatical. Why should this be?

Chomsky's answer is that Merge is a more primitive and less complex operation
than Move and that 'Simple operations preempt more complex ones' (Chomsky
1998, p. 18). Merge is a more primitive relation than Move in that other combina-
torial systems (like the artificial languages used in mathematics, logic or computer
science) employ Merge but not Move. Move is more complex than Merge because
it is a composite *agree+copy+merge+pied-pipe* operation. It therefore follows
from 'complexity considerations' (Chomsky 1998, p. 18) that spec-TP must be
filled by merger if the lexical array (i.e. the set of items taken out of the lexicon
to build the relevant sentence structure) contains an expletive, with movement to
spec-TP being used only as a last resort (i.e. where the lexical array contains no
expletive). As Chomsky (1998, p. 17) puts it, 'Merge preempts the more complex operation Move' (though see Shima 2000 for a dissenting view). Since the
sentence in (90) contains expletive *there*, it is clear that the lexical array for (90)
includes an expletive. In the light of this observation, let's return to the earlier
stage of derivation represented in (81) above, repeated as (93) below:

(93)   [T to]   be awarded [several prizes]
         [*u-Pers*]   **[3-Pers]**
         [*EPP*]   **[Pl-Num]**
                                   [*u-Case*]

Complexity considerations – more explicitly what Chomsky (1999, p. 5) refers
to as 'preference of Merge over (more complex) Move' – will require the [EPP]
feature of [T *to*] be satisfied by merging expletive *there* in spec-TP, so resulting
in (87) above, repeated as (94) below:

(94)   there   [T to]   be awarded [several prizes]
            [3-Pers] [3-Pers]   [**3-Pers**]
                    [*EPP*]   [**Pl-Num**]
                                              [*u-Case*]

Subsequently, the derivation will proceed through the steps discussed in (88) and
(89) above, ultimately deriving the CP structure associated with *There are thought
likely to be awarded several prizes*.

   To revert to terminology used in earlier chapters, if T in English always has an
[EPP] feature, A-movement will always be a **local** operation which (in complex
structures where an argument moves out of one or more lower TP constituents to
become the subject of a higher TP) applies in a **successive-cyclic** fashion, with the
relevant argument moving to become the subject of a lower TP before going on to
become the subject of a higher TP. Since we saw in §5.6 that head movement is also
successive-cyclic (in that a moved head moves into the next highest head position
within the structure immediately containing it), the greater generalisation would
appear to be that all movement is local (and hence successive-cyclic in complex
structures), so that any moved constituent moves into the closest appropriate
landing site above it (as argued in Rizzi 2001a). If so, we would expect to find
that wh-movement is also a local (hence successive-cyclic) operation. And indeed,
theoretical considerations suggest that it must be.

   In this chapter, we have seen that CPs and transitive VPs are phases, and that
the Phase Impenetrability Condition/PIC (55) prevents a constituent which is c-
commanded by a complementiser or a transitive verb from being attracted by
an external head which c-commands the CP/VP containing the relevant comple-
mentiser/transitive verb. PIC turns out to have important consequences for how
wh-movement operates in complex sentences such as:

(95)   What will they think that he has done?

The wh-pronoun *what* originates as the thematic complement of the transitive verb
done, and it might at first sight seem as if it moves from being the complement of
the transitive verb *done* to becoming the specifier of the C constituent containing
the inverted auxiliary *will* in a single step like that shown in highly simplified
form in (96) below:

(96)   [CP *What* [C *will+ø*] they *will* think that he has done *what*]

And indeed, this is precisely what we tacitly assumed in chapter 6. However, a
single-step movement operation like that shown in (96) will involve three violations of the Phase Impenetrability Condition, since it involves the bracketed C
constituent serving as a probe which attracts the wh-pronoun *what* to move out of
a transitive VP headed by *done*, out of a CP headed by *that*, and out of a further
transitive VP headed by *think*. The only way of avoiding violation of PIC is for
wh-movement to apply in a successive-cyclic fashion, moving *what* first to the

front of the transitive VP headed by *do*, then to the front of the complement clause CP headed by *that*, then to the front of the transitive VP headed by *think*, and finally to the front of the main-clause CP headed by the null complementiser to which the inverted auxiliary *will* adjoins. It would not be appropriate for us to look in more detail at the successive-cyclic nature of wh-movement at this point, until we have taken a closer look at the internal structure of verb phrases in chapter 9 and at the nature of phases in chapter 10: hence we postpone discussion of this until chapter 10.

8.10   Summary

In this chapter, we have taken a look at Chomsky's recent work on case, agreement and A-movement. In §8.2 we saw that agreement plays an integral role in nominative case assignment, in that nominative case is assigned to a nominal which agrees in person and number with a finite T. In §8.3 we argued that some features enter the derivation already valued (e.g. the tense feature of T and the person/number φ-features of nominals), whereas others (e.g. the φ-features of T and the case feature of nominals) are initially unvalued and are assigned values in the course of the derivation by operations like Feature-Copying (7) and Nominative Case Assignment (9). In §8.4, we claimed that interpretable features enter the derivation already valued, whereas those features which are initially unvalued are uninterpretable. We saw that agreement and case-marking involve a relation between an active probe and an active goal, and that probe and goal are only active if they carry one or more uninterpretable features (e.g. uninterpretable φ-features or case features). We also saw that uninterpretable features have to be deleted in the course of the derivation by a Feature-Deletion operation (14), in order to ensure that they do not feed into the semantic component and thereby cause the derivation to crash (because they are **illegible** in the semantic component), and that only a φ-complete α can delete an uninterpretable feature of ß. In §8.5, we suggested that expletive *it* enters the derivation with uninterpretable third-person and singular-number features, and that these value, delete and in turn are deleted by those of the auxiliary in sentences such as *It is said that he has taken bribes*. However, we noted that weather *it* is quasi-referential, and may originate as an argument internally within VP. In §8.6, we looked at Chomsky's claim that *there* is merged directly in spec-TP, and serves as a probe whose uninterpretable third-person feature is deleted via agreement with a φ-complete T. We noted that such an analysis has consequences (for the nature of probes and the inactivation of features) which may not seem desirable, and outlined an alternative analysis of expletives as originating within VP. In §8.7 we outlined Chomsky's agreement-based theory of movement under which movement involves an agreement relation between an active probe with an [EPP] feature and an active goal, and we suggested in (45) that the [EPP] feature of T can be satisfied either by merger of an expletive in spec-TP, or by movement of the closest active matching goal to spec-TP, with merger/movement of the relevant constituent in spec-TP deleting the [EPP] feature of T. In §8.8 we looked at the syntax of control infinitives, claiming that their PRO subject is assigned null case via agreement with a φ-complete T carrying null (non-finite) tense. We went on to argue that data relating to the distribution of floating modifiers suggest that T in control clauses has an [EPP] feature which triggers movement of PRO to spec-TP. In §8.9 we argued that T in other kinds of infinitive clause (e.g. the infinitival complements of raising, passive and ECM predicates) is defective in that although it carries uninterpretable [EPP] and person features (the latter serving to make T **active**), it lacks the number feature carried by a φ-complete T in finite and control clauses. We saw that such an analysis entails that A-movement takes place in a successive-cyclic fashion, with the moved argument being raised to become the subject of a lower TP before raising to become the subject of a higher TP. We went on to consider the possibility that all movement operations are local (and hence apply in a successive-cyclic fashion in complex structures) and noted that this implies that A-bar movement operations like wh-movement are also successive-cyclic in complex sentences (but said we would postpone detailed discussion of this until chapter 10).

Workbook section

Exercise 8.1

Discuss the derivation of the following sentences.

1   There remains little hope of finding any survivors
2   There are expected to remain some problems
3   Several mineworkers are thought to have died
4   They are considered likely to want to enter the race
5   It would be unthinkable to compromise yourself
6   He appears to be thought to be certain to win the race
7   He is hoping to be promoted
8   It is rumoured that there have been several riots
9   It is thought to be likely that some houses have collapsed
10   There seem certain to remain some problems

In addition, say why the derivation of each of the following sentences crashes (informal paraphrases of the intended meaning being given where this may be unclear):

11   *There are expected some problems to remain (= 'There are expected to remain some problems')
12   *Some problems are expected there to remain (= 'There are expected to remain some problems')
13   *It is expected there to remain some problems (= 'There are expected to remain some problems')
14   *There are rumoured that several prisoners were recaptured
15   *They appear were detained (= 'It appears that they were detained')
16   *He is believed has quit his job (= 'It is believed that he has quit his job')

Helpful hints

Assume (as in §§4.6–4.7) that all finite clauses and all control infinitive clauses (i.e. infinitive clauses which are the complement of a CONTROL predicate like *decide*) are canonical clauses and hence CPs containing a T headed by a φ-complete T with person, number and [EPP] features. By contrast, assume (as in §4.8) that seemingly subjectless infinitive clauses which are the complement of a raising predicate like *seem/likely* or a passive participle like *expected* are defective clauses, and hence are TPs headed by a defective T which has person and [EPP] features, but no number feature. Be careful not to confuse raising structures like *It's likely to rain* with control structures like *It's easy to make a mistake*: note that in the first structure we can have an expletive *there* subject (*There's likely to be a strike*), but not in the second (**There's easy to be a mistake*). Assume that infinitival *be* is the head AUX constituent of an AUXP when followed by a passive participle, but the head V of a VP when followed by an adjective. Finally, assume that the preference for Merge over Move holds only internally within a given CP (i.e. where an expletive and a nominal which are competing for the same spec-TP position are both contained in the same CP). Do any of these sentences prove problematic for the analysis in the text – and if so, why?

Model answer for sentence 1

If we assume Chomsky's TP analysis of expletives, sentence 1 will be derived as follows. The noun *hope* is merged with its PP complement *of finding any survivors* (whose structure need not concern us here) to form the NP *hope of finding any survivors*. This NP is merged with the quantifier *little* to form the QP *little hope of finding any survivors*. This QP is merged as the complement of the unaccusative verb *remain* to form the VP *remain little hope of finding any survivors*. This in turn is merged with an affixal finite T constituent (below denoted as AFF) to form the structure shown in simplified form in (i) below:

(i)

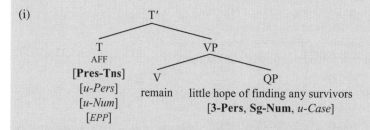

The affixal T serves as a probe because it is the highest head in the structure, and because its uninterpretable person/number features make it active. In accordance with the Earliness Principle, T immediately searches for an active goal, locating the QP *little hope of finding any survivors* (which is active by virtue of having an uninterpretable case feature). The T probe values the case feature on the QP goal as nominative via the Nominative Case Assignment operation (9) in the main text, and deletes it via Feature-Deletion (14). Conversely, the QP goal values the unvalued φ-features on the T probe as third person singular via Feature-Copying (7) and deletes them via Feature-Deletion (14). If the lexical array for the relevant CP (i.e. the set of constituents out of which the CP in question is formed) includes expletive *there*, preference of Merge over Move will mean that the [EPP] requirement for T to have a specifier must be satisfied by merging *there* in spec-TP, thereby deleting the [EPP] feature of T in accordance with (45i); the uninterpretable third-person feature of *there* will be deleted by the φ-complete affix in T. Merging the resulting TP with a null complementiser marking the sentence as declarative in force derives:

(ii)

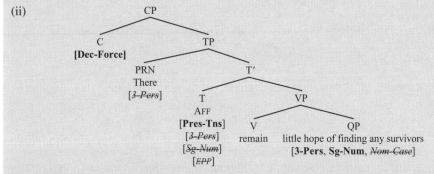

All the features in (ii) feed into the PF component, and since there are no unvalued features in (ii), the relevant structure can be assigned an appropriate PF representation: since there is no overt auxiliary in T on which the Tense Affix (AFF) containing the person/number/tense features of T can be spelled out, the relevant affix is lowered onto the verb *remain* (by the morphological operation of Affix Hopping) in the PF component, so that the verb ultimately surfaces in the third-person-singular present-tense form *remains*. Since all features in (ii) are valued, (ii) can be mapped into an appropriate PF representation; and since all (italicised) uninterpretable features have been deleted, (ii) can also be mapped into an appropriate semantic representation.

Exercise 8.2

Discuss the derivation of following Belfast English sentences (kindly supplied to me by Alison Henry):

1   There should have been lots of students taking the course
2   There should have lots of students been taking the course
3   There should lots of students have been taking the course
4   There have seemed to be lots of students enjoying the course
5   There have seemed lots of students to be enjoying the course
6   There have lots of students seemed to be enjoying the course

Model answer for sentence 1

If we assume Chomsky's TP analysis of expletive *there*, sentence 1 will have the following (simplified) derivation. The transitive verb *taking* merges with its DP complement *the course* to form the V-bar *taking the course*. This is in turn merged with its subject QP *lots of students* (whose internal structure need not concern us here) to form the VP *lots of students taking the course*. This then merges with the progressive auxiliary *been* to form the progressive auxiliary projection (PROGP) *been lots of students taking the course*. This in turn is merged with the perfect auxiliary *have* to form the Perfect Auxiliary Projection (PERFP) *have been lots of students taking the course*. The resulting PERFP is in turn merged with a finite T constituent containing the past-tense modal auxiliary *should*, so deriving the T-bar shown in simplified form in (i) below (where only the features of those constituents of immediate interest to us are shown):

(i)
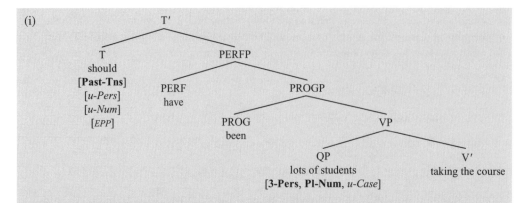

By virtue of its uninterpretable person and number features, [T *should*] serves as a probe and identifies the QP *lots of students* as the only accessible active goal. (Since a transitive VP is a phase, the Phase Impenetrability Condition prevents T from accessing any constituent of a transitive VP other than its specifier and head – and hence prevents the VP complement *the course* from being a goal for T.) Accordingly, *lots of students* values (as third person plural) and deletes the person/number features of *should*, and conversely *should* values (as nominative) and deletes the case feature of *lots of students*. Since the goal *lots of students* is an indefinite expression, the [EPP] feature carried by [T *should*] can be deleted by merging expletive *there* in spec-TP in accordance with the EPP Generalisation (45i) in the main text – and indeed, preference of Merge over Move would dictate that we need to use an expletive subject if (as in 1) we have an expletive pronoun in our lexical array. Merging expletive *there* in spec-TP will delete the [EPP] feature of T, and conversely the uninterpretable person feature carried by *there* can be deleted by the φ-complete T constituent *should*, so deriving the simplified structure:

(ii)   *There*   *should*   have been *lots of students* taking the course
        [~~3-Pers~~] **[Past-Tns]**   **[3-Pers]**
                      [~~3-Pers~~]   **[Pl-Num]**
                      [~~Pl-Num~~]   [~~Nom-Case~~]
                      [~~EPP~~]

The resulting TP will subsequently be merged with a null declarative C. Since all unvalued features have been valued and all uninterpretable features deleted, the resulting derivation is convergent (in that it can be mapped into appropriate phonetic and semantic representations).

Helpful hints on sentences 2–6

Discuss the problems posed for Chomsky's Prefer-Merge-Over-Move principle by some of the sentences 2–6, and also the problems posed for the assumption made throughout our text so far that only C (in wh-clauses) and T (in all types of clause) have an [EPP] feature. Consider the possibility of an alternative account under which languages (and language varieties) may differ in respect of an EPP parameter in relation to what kind of heads carry an [EPP] feature.

9 Split projections

9.1 Overview

Hitherto, we have assumed a simple model of clause structure in which canonical clauses are CP+TP+VP structures. However, in §5.6 we suggested that it is necessary to 'split' TP into two different auxiliary-headed projections in sentences like *He may be lying* – namely a TP projection headed by the T constituent *may* and an AUXP projection headed by the AUX constituent *be*; and in §7.3 we suggested that it may be necessary to posit a further **Asp**(ect) head in clauses to house the preposed verb in quotative structures like *'We hate syntax', said the students*. In this chapter, we go on to suggest that CPs, VPs and NPs should likewise be *split* into multiple projections – hence the title of the chapter. We begin by looking at arguments that the CP layer of clause structure should be split into a number of separate projections: **Force Phrase**, **Topic Phrase**, **Focus Phrase** and **Finiteness Phrase**. We then go on to explore the possibility of splitting verb phrases into two or more separate projections – an inner core headed by a lexical verb, and an outer shell headed by a **light verb** (with perhaps an additional projection between the two in transitive verb phrases). Finally we turn to look at evidence for a split projection analysis of NPs.

9.2 Split CP: Force, Topic and Focus projections

Our discussion of wh-movement in chapter 6 was concerned with movement of (interrogative, exclamative and relative) wh-expressions to the periphery of clauses (i.e. to a position above TP). However, as examples like (1) below illustrate, it is not simply wh-constituents which undergo movement to the clause periphery:

(1)   *No other colleague* would he turn to

In (1), *no other colleague* (which is the complement of the preposition *to*) has been **focused/focalised** – i.e. moved to the front of the sentence in order to **focus** it (and thereby give it special emphasis). At first sight, it would appear that the focused object moves into spec-CP and that the pre-subject auxiliary *would* moves from

T to C in the manner shown in (2) below (simplified *inter alia* by not showing *he* originating within VP):

(2)   [_{CP} *No other colleague* [_C **would**] [_{TP} he [_T ~~would~~] [_{VP} [_V turn] [_{PP} [_P to] ~~no other colleague~~]]]]

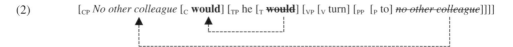

However, one problem posed by the CP analysis of **focusing/focalisation** sketched in (2) is that a structure containing a preposed focused constituent can occur after a complementiser like *that*, as in:

(3)   I am absolutely convinced [**that** *no other colleague would he turn to*]

This suggests that there must be more than one type of CP projection 'above' TP in clauses: more specifically, there must be one type of projection which hosts preposed focused constituents, and another type of projection which hosts complementisers. Reasoning along these lines, Luigi Rizzi (1997, 2001b, 2003) suggests that CP should be *split* into a number of different projections – an analysis widely referred to as the **split CP hypothesis**. More specifically, he suggests that complementisers (by virtue of their role in specifying whether a given clause is declarative, interrogative, imperative, or exclamative in **force**) should be analysed as **Force** markers heading a **ForceP** (= Force Phrase) projection, and that focused constituents should be analysed as contained within a separate **FocP** (= Focus Phrase) headed by a **Foc** constituent (= Focus marker).

On this view, the bracketed complement clause in (3) would have the structure shown in simplified form below:

(4)

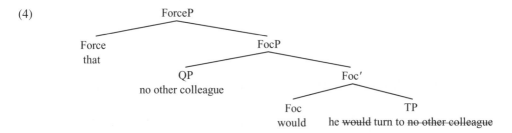

The focused QP/quantifier phrase *no other colleague* originates as the complement of the preposition *to* and (by virtue of being focused) moves from complement position within PP into specifier position within FocP. The auxiliary *would* originates in T and from there moves into the head Foc position of FocP. One way of describing the relevant data is to suppose that the head Foc constituent of FocP carries an [EPP] feature and an uninterpretable focus feature which together attract the focused object *no other colleague* (which itself contains a matching interpretable focus feature) to move into spec-FocP, and that Foc is a strong head carrying an affixal [TNS] feature which attracts the auxiliary *would* to move from T into Foc.

From a discourse perspective, a focused constituent typically represents **new information** (i.e. information not previously mentioned in the discourse and assumed to be unfamiliar to the hearer). In this respect, focused constituents differ from another class of preposed expressions which serve as the **topic** of the clause immediately containing them. Topics typically represent **old information** (i.e. information which has already been mentioned in the discourse and hence is assumed to be known to the hearer). In this connection, consider the sentence produced by speaker B below:

(5)   SPEAKER A: The demonstrators have been looting shops and setting fire to cars
         SPEAKER B: *That kind of behaviour*, we cannot tolerate in a civilised society

Here, the italicised phrase *that kind of behaviour* refers back to the activity of looting shops and setting fire to cars mentioned earlier by speaker A, and so is the **topic** of the discourse. Since the topic *that kind of behaviour* is the complement of the verb *tolerate* it would be expected to occupy the canonical complement position following *tolerate*. Instead, it ends up at the front of the overall sentence, and so would seem to have undergone a movement operation of some kind. Since the relevant movement operation serves to mark the preposed constituent as the topic of the sentence, it is widely known as **topicalisation**. (On differences between focusing and topicalisation, see Rizzi 1997; Cormack and Smith 2000b; Smith and Cormack 2002; Alexopoulou and Kolliakou 2002; and Drubig 2003.) However, since topicalisation moves a maximal projection to a specifier position on the periphery of the clause, it can (like focusing and wh-movement) be regarded a particular instance of the more general **A-bar movement** operation we looked at in chapter 7 whereby a moved constituent is attracted into an A-bar specifier position (i.e. the kind of specifier position which can be occupied by arguments and adjuncts alike).

Rizzi (1997) and Haegeman (2000) argue that just as focused constituents occupy the specifier position within a Focus Phrase, so too topicalised constituents occupy the specifier position within a **Topic Phrase**. This in turn raises the question of where Topic Phrases are positioned relative to other constituents within the clause. In this connection, consider the italicised clause in (6) below:

(6)   He had seen something truly evil – prisoners being ritually raped, tortured and mutilated.
         He prayed *that atrocities like those, never again would he witness*

In the italicised clause in (6), *that* marks the declarative force of the clause; *atrocities like those* is the object of the verb *witness* and has been preposed in order to mark it as the topic of the sentence (since it refers back to the acts of rape, torture and mutilation mentioned in the previous sentence); the preposed negative adverbial phrase *never again* is a focused constituent, and hence requires auxiliary inversion. Thus, the italicised *that*-clause in (6) will have the simplified structure shown below:

(7)

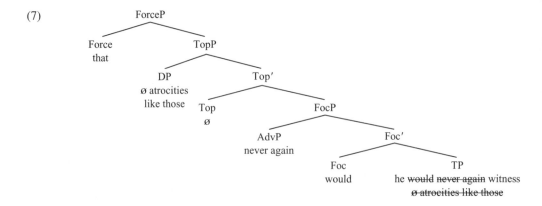

We can assume that the head Top constituent of the Topic Phrase contains an [EPP] feature and an uninterpretable topic feature, and that these attract a maximal projection which carries a matching interpretable topic feature to move to the specifier position within the Topic Phrase. If we further assume that Top is a weak head (and so does not carry an affixal [TNS] feature), we can account for the fact that the auxiliary *would* remains in the strong Foc position and does not raise to the weak Top position.

Rizzi's **split CP** analysis raises interesting questions about the syntax of the kind of wh-movement operation which we find (inter alia) in interrogatives, relatives and exclamatives. Within the unitary (unsplit) CP analysis outlined in chapter 7, it was clear that wh-phrases moved into spec-CP; but if CP can be split into a number of distinct projections (including a Force Phrase, a Topic Phrase and a Focus Phrase), the question arises as to which of these projections serves as the landing site for wh-movement. Rizzi (1997, p. 289) suggests that 'relative operators occupy the highest specifier position, the spec of Force'. In this connection, consider the syntax of the bracketed relative clauses in (8) below:

(8) (a)   A university is the kind of place [in which, that kind of behaviour, we cannot tolerate]
    (b)   Syntax is the kind of subject [which only very rarely will students enjoy]

In (8a), the preposed wh-expression *in which* precedes the preposed topic *that kind of behaviour*; in (8b) the preposed relative pronoun *which* precedes the preposed focused expression *only very rarely*. If Rizzi is right in suggesting that preposed relative operator expressions occupy specifier position within the Force Phrase, the bracketed relative clauses in (8a,b) above will have the simplified structures shown below:

(9) (a)   [ForceP *in which* [Force ∅] [TopP **that kind of behaviour** [Top ∅] [TP we cannot tolerate **t** *t*]]]
    (b)   [ForceP *which* [Force ∅] [FocP **only very rarely** [Foc *will*] [TP students *t* enjoy *t* **t**]]]

(Trace copies of moved constituents are shown as *t* and printed in the same type-face as their antecedent.)

By contrast, Rizzi argues (1997, p. 299) that a preposed wh-operator expression 'ends up in Spec of Foc in main questions'. If (as he claims) clauses may contain only a single Focus Phrase constituent, such an assumption will provide a straightforward account of the ungrammaticality of main-clause questions such as (10) below:

(10) (a)   *What never again will you do?
     (b)   *What will never again you do?

If both *what* and *never again* (when preposed) move into the specifier position within FocP, if Foc allows only one focused constituent as its specifier, and if no clause may contain more than one FocP constituent, it follows that (10a) will be ruled out by virtue of Foc having two specifiers (*what* and *never again*) and that (10b) will be ruled out by virtue of requiring two Focus Phrase constituents (one hosting *what* and another hosting *never again*). Likewise, multiple wh-movement questions (i.e. questions in which more than one wh-expression is preposed) like (11) below will be ruled out in a similar fashion:

(11) (a)   *Who where did he send?
     (b)   *Who did where he send?

The assumption that preposed wh-phrases occupy spec-FocP has interesting implications for our claim in §6.8 that yes–no questions contain an interrogative operator ~~whether~~ (a null counterpart of *whether*). If this null operator (like other interrogative expressions) occupies spec-FocP, and if Foc is a strong head, it follows that inverted auxiliaries in main-clause yes–no questions like *Has he left?* will involve movement of the inverted auxiliary *has* into the head Foc position within FocP, with the specifier position in FocP being filled by a null counterpart of *whether*. This assumption would account for the ungrammaticality of sentences such as the following:

(12) (a)   *Will never again things be the same?
     (b)   *Can *that kind of behaviour* we tolerate in a civilised society?

If *never again* is the specifier of a FocP constituent in (12a), the inverted auxiliary must be in a higher FocP projection whose specifier is ~~whether~~. However, we have already seen in relation to sentences like (10) and (11) above that clauses may only contain one FocP constituent, so the ungrammaticality of (12a) can be attributed to the impossibility of stacking one FocP on top of another. Likewise, if *that kind of behaviour* is a topicalised constituent occupying the specifier position within a Topic Phrase in (12b) and if an inverted auxiliary like *can* in a yes–no question occupies the head Foc position of a FocP containing ~~whether~~ as its specifier, this means that FocP is positioned above TopP in (12b). Given the Head Movement Constraint, *can* will have to move through Top to get into Foc; but since Top is a weak head, *can* is prevented from moving through Top into Foc; and since Foc is a strong affixal head, the affix in Foc ends up being stranded without any verb to attach to. If we reverse the order of the two projections and position TopP above FocP, the resulting structure is fine, as we see from (13) below:

(13)   That kind of behaviour, can we tolerate in a civilised society?

In (13), the topic *that kind of behaviour* occupies the specifier position of a TopP which has a weak head, while the inverted auxiliary *can* occupies the strong head Foc position in a FocP which has the null operator ~~whether~~ as its specifier.

Although Rizzi argues that a preposed interrogative wh-expression moves into spec-FocP in main clauses, he maintains that a preposed wh-expression moves into a different position (spec-ForceP) in complement-clause questions. Some evidence in support of this claim comes from sentences such as the following (from Culicover 1991):

(14) (a)   Lee wonders [whether under no circumstances at all would Robin volunteer]
     (b)   Lee wonders [why under no circumstances at all would Robin volunteer]

Here, the wh-expressions *whether/why* occur to the left of the focused negative phrase *under no circumstances*, suggesting that *whether/why* do not occupy specifier position within FocP but rather some higher position – and since ForceP is the highest projection within the clause, it is plausible to suppose that *whether/why* occupy spec-ForceP in structures like (14).

A question raised by Rizzi's analysis of relative and interrogative wh-clauses is where preposed wh-expressions move in exclamative clauses. In this connection, consider (15) below:

(15) (a)   *How many of their policies* **only rarely** do politicians get around to implementing!
     (b)   *In how many countries*, <u>that kind of behaviour</u>, autocratic leaders would simply not tolerate!

In (15a), the italicised exclamative wh-expression *how many of their policies* precedes the bold-printed focused constituent **only rarely**, while in (15b) the exclamative wh-phrase *in how many countries* precedes the underlined topic *that kind of behaviour*. And in (16) below:

(16)   *In how many countries of the world*, <u>such behaviour</u>, **under no circumstances** would autocratic leaders tolerate!

an italicised exclamative expression precedes both an underlined topicalised expression and a bold-printed focused expression – though the resulting sentence is clearly highly contrived. All of this suggests that exclamative wh-expressions (like relative wh-expressions) move into the specifier position within ForceP.

9.3   Split CP: Finiteness projection

In the previous section, we argued that above TP there may be not just a single CP projection but rather at least three different types of projection – namely a Force Phrase, a Topic Phrase and a Focus Phrase (the latter two being found only in clauses containing focused or topicalised constituents). However, Rizzi argues that below FocP (and above TP) there is a fourth functional projection which he terms **FinP/Finiteness Phrase**, whose head **Fin** constituent serves the function of marking a clause as finite or non-finite. He argues that Fin is the position occupied by prepositional particles like *di* 'of' which introduce infinitival control clauses in languages like Italian in structures such as (17) below:

(17)   Gianni pensa, *il   tuo   libro, di PRO conoscerlo bene*
         Gianni thinks, the your book, of PRO know.it   well
         'Gianni thinks that your book, he knows well'

Rizzi maintains that the italicised clause which is the complement of *pensa* 'thinks' in (17) has the simplified structure (18) below:

(18)

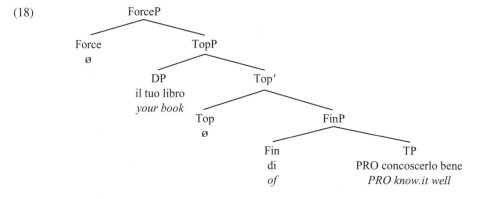

Under his analysis, *il tuo libro* 'the your book' is a topic and *di* 'of' is a Fin head which marks its clause as non-finite (more specifically, as infinitival). Moreover, Rizzi maintains that the Fin head *di* 'of' assigns null case to the PRO subject of its clause (an account of null case assignment in keeping with our account in §4.9, but not with the Chomskyan account given in §8.8).

While present-day English has no overt counterpart of infinitival particles like Italian *di* in control clauses, it may be that *for* served essentially the same function in Middle English control infinitives such as those bracketed below:

(19) (a)   Al were it good [*no womman* for to touche] (Chaucer, *Wife of Bath's Tale*, line 85)
            Although it would be good to touch *no woman*
     (b)   I wol renne out, [*my borel* for to shewe] (Chaucer, *Wife of Bath's Tale*, line 356)
            I will run out, in order to show *my clothing*

In (19a,b) the italicised expression is the direct object of the verb at the end of the line, but has been focalised/topicalised and thereby ends up positioned in front of *for*. This is consistent with the possibility that *for* occupies the same *Fin* position in Middle English as *di* in Modern Italian, and that the italicised complements in (19a,b) move into specifier position within a higher Focus Phrase/Topic Phrase projection. Since the *for* infinitive complement in (19) has a null subject rather than an overt accusative subject, we can suppose that it is intransitive in the relevant use.

An interesting possibility raised by this analysis is that *for* in overt-subject infinitives in present-day English also functions as a non-finite Fin head – though an obligatorily transitive one. In this regard, consider the two different replies given by speaker B below:

(20)   SPEAKER A: What was the advice given by the police to the general public?
         SPEAKER B: (i) *Under no circumstances* **for** anyone to approach the escaped convicts
                    (ii) **That** *under no circumstances* should anyone approach the escaped
                    convicts

What is particularly interesting about speaker B's replies in (20) is that the focused prepositional phrase *under no circumstances* precedes the complementiser *for* in (20Bi), but follows the complementiser *that* in (20Bii). This suggests that *for* occupies the head Fin position of FinP, but *that* occupies the head Force position of ForceP. On this view, the two answers given by speaker B would have the respective skeletal structures shown in (21a,b) below:

(21)   (a)

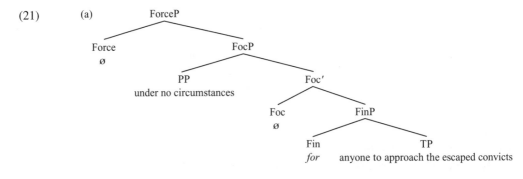

         (b)

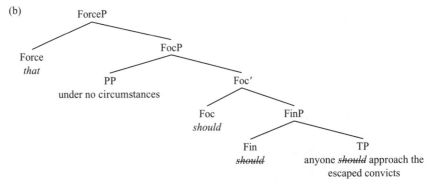

If Foc is a strong head in finite (though not infinitival) clauses, it follows that the auxiliary *should* in (21b) will raise from the head T position of TP into the head Foc position of FocP; and if we assume the **Head Movement Constraint**, it also follows that *should* must move first to Fin before moving into Foc. We can suppose that the reply given by speaker B in (22) below:

(22)   SPEAKER A: What was the advice given by the police to the general public?
         SPEAKER B: *Under no circumstances* to approach the escaped convicts

has essentially the same structure as that shown in (21a), save that in place of the overt Fin head *for* we have a null Fin head, and that in place of the overt subject *anyone* we have a null PRO subject. In addition, if Foc is only a strong head in finite clauses, the Fin head remains in situ rather than raising to Foc.

The overall gist of Rizzi's **split** CP hypothesis is that in structures containing a topicalised and/or focalised constituent, CP splits into a number of different projections. In a clause containing both a topicalised and a focalised constituent, CP splits into four separate projections – namely a Force Phrase, Topic Phrase, Focus Phrase and Finiteness Phrase. In a sentence containing a topicalised but no focalised constituent, CP splits into three separate projections – namely into a Force Phrase, Topic Phrase and Finiteness Phrase. In a sentence containing a focalised but no topicalised constituent, CP again splits into three projections – namely into a Force Phrase, Focus Phrase and Finiteness Phrase. However, in a structure containing no focalised or topicalised constituents, Rizzi posits that Force and Finiteness features are **syncretised** (i.e. collapsed) onto a single head, with the result that CP does not split in this case: in other words, rather than being realised on two different heads, the relevant force and finiteness features are realised on a single head corresponding to the traditional C constituent (so that C is in effect a composite force/finiteness head). In simple terms, what this means is that C only splits into multiple projections in structures containing a topicalised and/or focalised constituent.

We can illustrate the conditions under which CP does (or does not) split in terms of the syntax of the *that*-clauses in (23) below:

(23) (a)   You must know that *this kind of behaviour* we cannot tolerate
     (b)   You must know that we cannot tolerate *this kind of behaviour*

In (23a) the object *this kind of behaviour* has been topicalised, so forcing CP to split into three projections (ForceP, TopP and FinP) as shown in simplified form in (24) below:

(24)   [$_{ForceP}$ [$_{Force}$ that] [$_{TopP}$ *this kind of behaviour* [$_{Top}$ ø] [$_{FinP}$ [$_{Fin}$ ø] [$_{TP}$ we [$_{T}$ cannot] tolerate *t*]]]]

By contrast, in (23b) there is no topicalised or focalised constituent, hence CP does not split into multiple projections. Accordingly, only a single C constituent is projected which carries both finiteness and force features, as in (25) below (where DEC is a declarative force feature and FIN is a finiteness feature):

(25)   [$_{CP}$ [$_{C}$ that$_{DEC, FIN}$] [$_{TP}$ we [$_{T}$ cannot] tolerate this kind of behaviour]]

Rizzi posits that (in finite clauses) the relevant types of head are spelled out in the manner shown informally in (26) below:

(26)   A head in a split CP projection can be spelled out in English as:
     (i)   *that* in a complement clause if it carries a declarative force feature (with or without a finiteness feature)
     (ii) ø if it carries a finiteness feature (with or without a declarative force feature)

It follows from (26) that the Force head in (24) can be spelled out as *that* but not as *ø*, and that Fin can be spelled out as *ø* but not as *that*, so accounting for the ungrammaticality of:

(27) (a)   *You must know *ø* this kind of behaviour *that* we cannot tolerate

    (b)   *You must know *that* this kind of behaviour *that* we cannot tolerate

    (c)   *You must know *ø* this kind of behaviour *ø* we cannot tolerate

(Irrelevantly, (27c) is grammatical if written with a colon between *know* and *this kind of behaviour* and read as two separate sentences.) It also means that the syncretised (force/finiteness) C constituent in (25) can either be spelled out as *that* in accordance with (26i), or be given a null spellout in accordance with (26ii) as in (28) below:

(28)   You must know [c *ø*DEC, FIN] we cannot tolerate this kind of behaviour

In other words, Rizzi's analysis provides a principled account of the (overt/null) spellout of finite declarative complementisers in English (though see Sobin 2002 for complications). (Complementiser spellout may be different in other languages – see e.g. Alexopoulou and Kolliakou 2002 on Greek.)

Before leaving the split CP analysis, an important technical complication should be pointed out (highlighted in relation to wh-movement at the end of §8.8). If we adopt Chomsky's **Phase Impenetrability Condition/PIC** (under which the complement of a phase head is impenetrable to an external probe) and if we assume that not only CPs but also transitive VPs are phases, it follows that topicalisation or focalisation of the complement of a transitive verb will mean that the object must first move to the edge of the verb phrase before moving to the clause periphery. For the time being we set this issue aside here, returning to it in chapter 10 because Chomsky's work on phases assumes that verb phrases are analysed as split projections in the manner outlined below.

9.4   Split VPs: VP shells in ergative structures

Having looked at evidence that CP can be split into a number of different projections, we now turn to look at evidence arguing that VPs should be split into two distinct projections – an outer **VP shell** and an inner VP core. For obvious reasons, this has become known as the **VP shell** analysis.

The sentences we have analysed throughout this book so far have generally contained simple verb phrases headed by a verb with a single complement. Such single-complement structures can easily be accommodated within the binary-branching framework adopted here, since all we need say is that a verb merges with its complement to form a (binary-branching) V-bar constituent. However, a particular problem for the binary-branching framework is posed by three-place

predicates like those italicised in (29) below which have a (bold-printed) subject
and two (bracketed) complements:

(29 (a)   **He** *rolled* [the ball] [down the hill]
   (b)   **He** *filled* [the bath] [with water]
   (c)   **He** *broke* [the vase] [into pieces]
   (d)   **They** *withdrew* [the troops] [from Ruritania]

If we assume that complements are sisters to heads, it might seem as if the V-bar
constituent headed by *rolled* in (29a) has the structure (30) below:

(30)

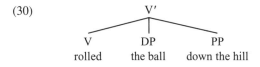

| V | DP | PP |
| rolled | the ball | down the hill |

However, a structure such as (30) is problematic within the framework adopted
here. After all, it is a ternary-branching structure (V-bar branches into the three
separate constituents, namely the V *rolled*, the DP *the ball* and the PP *down
the hill*), and this poses an obvious problem within a framework which assumes
that the merger operation which forms phrases is an inherently **binary** operation which can only combine constituents in a *pairwise* fashion. Moreover, a
ternary-branching structure such as (30) would wrongly predict that the string
the ball down the hill does not form a constituent, and so cannot be coordinated
with another similar string (given the traditional assumption that only identical
constituents can be conjoined) – yet this prediction is falsified by sentences such
as:

(31)   He rolled *the ball down the hill* and *the acorn up the mountain*

How can we overcome these problems?

   One answer is to suppose that transitive structures like *He rolled the ball down
the hill* have a complex internal structure which is parallel in some respects to
causative structures like *He made the ball roll down the hill* (where MAKE has
roughly the same meaning as CAUSE). On this view *the ball roll down the hill*
would serve as a VP complement of a null causative verb (which can be thought
of informally as an invisible counterpart of MAKE). We can further suppose that
the null causative verb is affixal in nature and so triggers raising of the verb *roll*
to adjoin to the causative verb, deriving a structure loosely paraphraseable as *He
made + roll [the ball roll down the hill]*, where *roll* is a trace copy of the moved
verb *roll*. We could then say that the string *the ball down the hill* in (31) is a
VP remnant headed by a trace copy of the moved verb *roll*. Since this string is a
VP constituent, we correctly predict that it can be coordinated with another VP
remnant like *the acorn up the mountain* – as is indeed the case in (31).

   Analysing structures like *roll the ball down the hill* as transitive counterparts
of intransitive structures is by no means implausible, since many three-place
transitive predicates like *roll* can also be used as two-place intransitive predicates

in which the (italicised) DP which immediately follows the (bold-printed) verb in the three-place structure functions as the subject in the two-place structure – as we see from sentence-pairs such as the following:

(32) (a)   They will **roll** *the ball* down the hill
     (b)   *The ball* will **roll** down the hill

(33) (a)   He **filled** *the bath* with water
     (b)   *The bath* **filled** with water

(34) (a)   He **broke** *the vase* into pieces
     (b)   *The vase* **broke** into pieces

(35) (a)   They **withdrew** *the troops* from Ruritania
     (b)   *The troops* **withdrew** from Ruritania

(36) (a)   They **closed** *the store* down
     (b)   *The store* **closed** down

(37) (a)   They **moved** *the headquarters* to Brooklyn
     (b)   *The headquarters* **moved** to Brooklyn

(Verbs which allow this dual use as either three-place or two-place predicates are sometimes referred to as **ergative predicates**.) Moreover, the italicised DP seems to play the same thematic role with respect to the bold-printed verb in each pair of examples: for example, *the ball* is the THEME argument of *roll* (i.e. the entity which undergoes a rolling motion) both in (32a) *They will roll the ball down the hill* and in (32b) *The ball will roll down the hill*. Evidence that *the ball* plays the same semantic role in both sentences comes from the fact that the italicised argument is subject to the same pragmatic restrictions on the choice of expression which can fulfil the relevant argument function in each type of sentence: cf.

(38) (a)   *The ball/the rock/!the theory/!sincerity* will **roll** down the hill
     (b)   They will **roll** *the ball/the rock/!the theory/!sincerity* down the hill

If principles of UG correlate thematic structure with syntactic structure in a uniform fashion (in accordance with Baker's 1988 **Uniform Theta Assignment Hypothesis/UTAH**), then it follows that two arguments which fulfil the same thematic function with respect to a given predicate must be merged in the same position in the syntax.

An analysis within the spirit of UTAH would be to assume that since *the ball* is clearly the subject of *roll* in (32a) *The ball will roll down the hill*, then it must also be the case that *the ball* originates as the subject of *roll* in (32b) *They will roll the ball down the hill*. But if this is so, how come *the ball* is positioned after the verb *roll* in (32b), when subjects are normally positioned before their verbs? A plausible answer to this question within the framework we are adopting here is to suppose that the verb *roll* moves from its initial (post-subject) position after *the ball* into a higher verb position to the left of *the ball*. More specifically, adapting ideas put forward by Larson (1988, 1990), Hale and Keyser (1991, 1993,

1994) and Chomsky (1995), let's suppose that the (b) examples in sentences like (32)–(37) are simple VPs, but that the (a) examples are split VP structures which comprise an outer **shell** and an inner core.

More concretely, let's make the following assumptions. In (32b) *The ball will roll down the hill*, the V *roll* is merged with its PP complement *down the hill* to form the V-bar *roll down the hill*, and this is then merged with the DP *the ball* to form the VP structure (39) below:

(39)

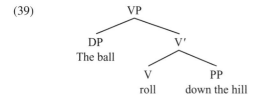

In the case of (32b), the resulting VP will then be merged with the T constituent *will* to form the T-bar *will roll down the hill*; the [EPP] and φ-features of [T *will*] trigger raising of the subject *the ball* into spec-TP to become subject of *will* (in the manner shown by the dotted arrow below), deriving:

(40)

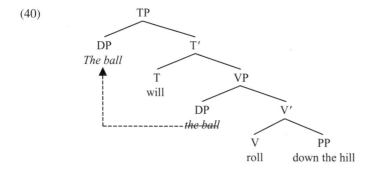

The resulting TP is subsequently merged with a null declarative C constituent. (Throughout this chapter, we simplify exposition by omitting details like this which are not directly relevant to the point at hand.)

Now consider how we derive (32a) *They will roll the ball down the hill*. Let's suppose that the derivation proceeds as before, until we reach the stage where the VP structure (39) *the ball roll down the hill* has been formed. But this time, let's assume that the VP in (39) is then merged as the complement of an abstract causative **light verb** (v) – i.e. a null verb with much the same causative interpretation as the verb MAKE (so that *They will roll the ball down the hill* has a similar interpretation to *They will make the ball roll down the hill*). Let's also suppose that this causative light verb is affixal in nature (or has a strong V-feature), and that the verb *roll* adjoins to it, forming a structure which can be paraphrased literally as 'make+roll the ball down the hill' – a structure which has an overt counterpart in French structures like *faire rouler la balle en bas de la colline* (literally 'make roll the ball into bottom of the hill'). The resulting v-bar structure is then merged with the subject *they* (which is assigned the θ-role of AGENT argument of the causative light verb), to form the complex vP (41) below (lower-case letters being used to denote the light verb, and the dotted arrow showing movement of the verb *roll* to adjoin to the null light verb *ø*):

(41)

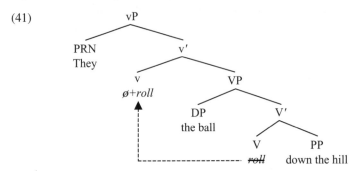

Subsequently, the vP in (41) merges with the T constituent *will*, the subject *they* raises into spec-TP, and the resulting TP is merged with a null declarative complementiser, forming the structure (42) below (where the dotted arrows show movements which have taken place in the course of the derivation):

(42)

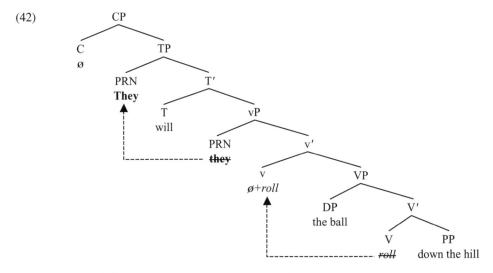

The analysis in (42) correctly specifies the word order in (32a) *They will roll the ball down the hill.* (See Stroik 2001 for arguments that *do* is used to support a null light verb in elliptical structures such as *John will roll a ball down the hill and Paul will do so as well.*)

The VP-shell analysis in (42) provides an interesting account of an otherwise puzzling aspect of the syntax of sentences like (32a) – namely the fact that adverbs like *gently* can be positioned either before *roll* or after *the ball*, as we see from:

(43) (a)   They will *gently* **roll** *the ball* down the hill
      (b)   They will **roll** *the ball gently* down the hill

Let's suppose that adverbs like *gently* are **adjuncts**, and that **adjunction** is a different kind of operation from **merger**. Merger extends a constituent into a larger type of projection, so that (e.g.) merging T with an appropriate complement extends T into T-bar, and merging T-bar with an appropriate specifier extends T-bar into TP. By contrast, adjunction extends a constituent into a larger projection of the same type, e.g. merging a moved V with a minimal projection like T forms a larger T constituent; merging an adjunct with an intermediate projection like T-bar extends T-bar into another T-bar constituent; merging an adjunct with a maximal projection like TP forms an even larger TP – and so on. (See Stepanov 2001 and Chomsky 2001 for technical accounts of differences between adjunction and merger.) Let's suppose that *gently* is the kind of adverb which can adjoin to an intermediate verbal projection. Given this assumption and the light-verb analysis in (42), we can then propose the following derivations for (43a,b).

In (43a), the verb *roll* merges with the PP *down the hill* to form the V-bar *roll down the hill*, and this V-bar in turn merges with the DP *the ball* to form the VP *the ball roll down the hill*, with the structure shown in (39) above. This VP then merges with a null causative light verb *ø* to which the verb *roll* adjoins, forming the v-bar *ø+roll the ball r̶o̶l̶l̶ down the hill*. The resulting v-bar merges with the adverb *gently* to form the larger v-bar *gently ø+roll the ball r̶o̶l̶l̶ down the hill*; and this v-bar in turn merges with the subject *they* to form the vP *they gently ø+roll the ball r̶o̶l̶l̶ down the hill*. The vP thereby formed merges with the T constituent *will*, forming the T-bar *will they gently ø+roll the ball r̶o̶l̶l̶ down the hill*. The subject *they* raises to spec-TP forming the TP *they will t̶h̶e̶y̶ gently ø+roll the ball r̶o̶l̶l̶ down the hill*. The resulting TP is then merged with a null declarative complementiser to derive the structure shown in simplified form in (44) below (with arrows showing movements which have taken place):

(44)

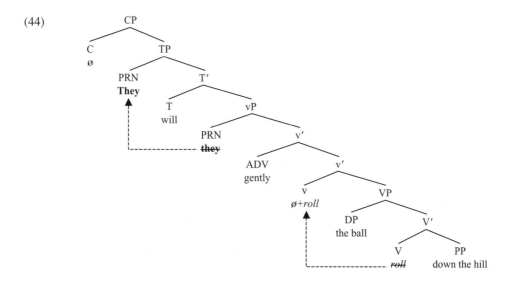

The analysis in (44) correctly specifies the word order in (43a) *They will gently roll the ball down the hill*.

Now consider how (43b) *They will roll the ball gently down the hill* is derived. As before, the verb *roll* merges with the PP *down the hill*, forming the V-bar *roll down the hill*. The adverb *gently* then merges with this V-bar to form the larger V-bar *gently roll down the hill*. This V-bar in turn merges with the DP *the ball* to form the VP *the ball gently roll down the hill*. The resulting VP is merged with a causative light verb [ᵥ ø] to which the verb *roll* adjoins, so forming the v-bar *ø+roll the ball gently ~~roll~~ down the hill*. This v-bar is then merged with the subject *they* to form the vP *they ø+roll the ball gently ~~roll~~ down the hill*. The vP thereby formed merges with [T *will*], forming the T-bar *will they ø+roll the ball gently ~~roll~~ down the hill*. The subject *they* raises to spec-TP, and the resulting TP is merged with a null declarative C to form the CP (45) below (with arrows showing movements which have taken place):

(45)

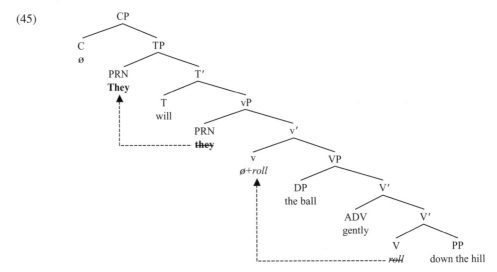

The different positions occupied by the adverb *gently* in (44) and (45) reflect a subtle meaning difference between (43a) and (43b): (43a) means that the action which initiated the rolling motion was gentle, whereas (43b) means that the rolling motion itself was gentle.

A light-verb analysis also offers us an interesting account of adverb position in sentences like:

(46) (a)   He had *deliberately* rolled the ball **gently** down the hill
     (b)   *He had **gently** rolled the ball *deliberately* down the hill

Let's suppose that *deliberately* (by virtue of its meaning) can only be an adjunct to a projection of an agentive verb (i.e. a verb whose subject has the thematic role of AGENT). If we suppose (as earlier) that the light verb [ᵥ ø] is a causative verb with an AGENT subject, the contrast in (46) can be accounted for straightforwardly: in (46a) *deliberately* is contained within a vP headed by a null agentive causative

light verb; but in (46b) it is contained within a VP headed by the non-agentive verb
roll. (The verb *roll* is a non-agentive predicate because its subject has the θ-role
THEME, not AGENT.) We can then say that adverbs like *deliberately* are adverbs
which adjoin to a v-bar headed by an agentive light verb, but not to V-bar.

This in turn might lead us to expect to find a corresponding class of adverbs
which can adjoin to V-bar but not v-bar. In this connection, consider the following
contrasts (adapted from Bowers 1993, p. 609):

(47) (a)   Mary jumped the horse *perfectly* over the last fence
   (b)   *Mary *perfectly* jumped the horse over the last fence

Given the assumptions made here, the derivation of (47a) would be parallel to
that in (45), while the derivation of (47b) would be parallel to that in (44). If
we assume that the adverb *perfectly* (in the relevant use) can function only as an
adjunct to a V-projection, the contrast between (47a) and (47b) can be accounted
for straightforwardly: in (47a), *perfectly* is adjoined to a V-bar, whereas in (47b)
it is merged with a v-bar (in violation of the requirement that it can only adjoin
to a V-projection).

As we have seen, the VP shell analysis outlined here provides an interesting
solution to the problems posed by three-place predicates which have two complements. However, the problems posed by verbs which take two complements arise
not only with transitive verbs which have intransitive counterparts (like those in
(32)–(37) above), but also with verbs such as those bold-printed in (48) below
(the complements of the verbs being bracketed):

(48) (a)   They will **load** [the truck] [with hay]
   (b)   He **gave** [no explanation] [to his friends]
   (c)   They **took** [everything] [from her]
   (d)   Nobody can **blame** [you] [for the accident]

Verbs like those in (48) cannot be used intransitively, as we see from the ungrammaticality of sentences such as:

(49) (a)   *The truck will load with hay
   (b)   *No explanation gave to his friends
   (c)   *Everything took from her
   (d)   *You can blame for the accident

However, it is interesting to note that in structures like (48) too we find that
adverbs belonging to the same class as *gently* can be positioned either before the
verb or between its two complements:

(50) (a)   They will *carefully* load the truck with hay
   (b)   They will load the truck *carefully* with hay

This suggests that (in spite of the fact that the relevant verbs have no intransitive
counterpart) a **shell** analysis is appropriate for structures like (48) too. If so, a
sentence such as (48a) will have the structure shown in simplified form in (51)
below (with arrows showing movements which take place):

(51)

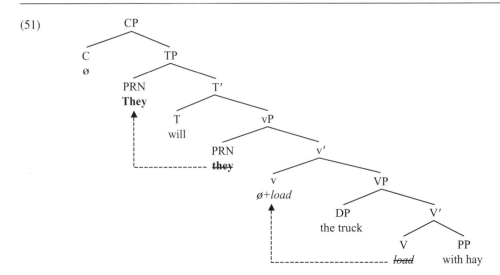

We can then say that the adverb *carefully* adjoins to v-bar in (50a), and to V-bar in (50b). If we suppose that verbs like *load* are essentially affixal in nature (in the sense that they must adjoin to a null causative light verb with an AGENT external argument) we can account for the ungrammaticality of intransitive structures such as (49a) **The truck will load with hay*.

9.5   VP shells in resultative, double-object and object-control structures

The VP shell analysis outlined above can be extended from predicates like *load* which have both nominal and prepositional complements to so-called **resultative predicates** which have both nominal and adjectival complements – i.e. to structures such as those below:

(52) (a)   The acid will turn the litmus-paper red
     (b)   They may paint the house pink

In (52a), the verb *turn* originates in the head V position of VP, with the DP *the litmus-paper* as its subject and the adjective *red* as its complement (precisely as in *The litmus-paper will turn red*); *turn* then raises to adjoin to a strong causative light verb *ø* heading vP; the subject of this light verb (the DP *the acid*) in turn raises from spec-vP to spec-TP, and the resulting TP merges with a null declarative complementiser – as shown informally in (53) below:

(53)   [CP [C ø [TP **the acid** [T will] [vP **the acid** [v ø+*turn*] [VP the litmus-paper [V *turn*] red]]]]

(For alternative analyses of resultative structures like (52), see Keyser and Roeper 1992; Carrier and Randall 1992; and Oya 2002.)

We can extend the vP shell analysis still further, to take in **double-object** structures. such as:

(54) (a)   They will get [the teacher] [a present]
   (b)   Could you pass [me] [the salt]?
   (c)   I showed [them] [my passport]
   (d)   She gave [me] [a hat]

For example, we could suggest that (54a) has the structure (55) below (with arrows indicating movements which take place in the course of the derivation):

(55)

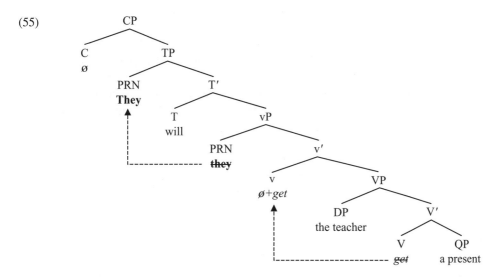

That is, *get* originates as the head V of VP (with *the teacher* as its subject and *a present* as its complement, much as in *The teacher will get a present*), and then raises up to adjoin to the strong causative light verb ø heading vP; the subject *they* in turn originates in spec-vP (and has the thematic role of AGENT argument of the null causative light verb ø), and subsequently raises to spec-TP. (For a range of alternative analyses of the double-object construction, see Larson 1988; 1990; Johnson 1991; Bowers 1993; and Pesetsky 1995.)

The VP shell analysis outlined above also provides us with an interesting solution to the problems posed by so-called **object-control predicates**. In this connection, consider the syntax of the infinitive structure in (56) below:

(56)   What decided you to take syntax?

For reasons given below, *decide* functions as a three-place predicate in this use, taking *what* as its subject, *you* as its object, and the clause *to take syntax* as a further complement. If we suppose that the infinitive complement *to take syntax* has a PRO subject (and is a CP headed by a null complementiser ø), (56) will have the skeletal structure (57) below (simplified e.g. by ignoring traces: the three arguments of *decide* are bracketed):

(57)   [What] decided [you] [ø PRO to take syntax]?

Since PRO is **controlled** by the object *you*, the verb *decide* (in such uses) is an object-control predicate.

There are a number of reasons for thinking that the verb *decide* in sentences like (56) is indeed a three-place object-control predicate, and that *you* is the object of *decide* (rather than the subject of *to take syntax*). Thus, (56) can be paraphrased (albeit a little clumsily) as:

(58)   What decided *you* [that **you** should take syntax]?

We can then say that *you* in (57) corresponds to the italicised object *you* in (58), and the PRO subject in (57) corresponds to the bold-printed **you** subject of the complement clause in (58). Moreover, the verb *decide* imposes pragmatic restrictions on the choice of expression following it (which must be a rational, mind-possessing entity – not an irrational, mindless entity like *the exam*):

(59)   !What decided *the exam* to be difficult?

This suggests that the relevant expression must be an argument of *decide*. Furthermore, the expression following *decide* cannot be an expletive pronoun such as *there*:

(60)   *What decided *there* to be an election?

A plausible conclusion to draw from observations such as these is that the (pro)nominal following *decide* is an (object) argument of *decide* in sentences such as (56), and serves as the controller of a PRO subject in the following *to* infinitive. However, this means that *decide* has two complements in structures such as (56) – the pronoun *you* and the control infinitive *to take syntax*. Within a binary-branching framework, we clearly can't assume that the V-bar headed by *decide* in (56) has a ternary-branching structure like:

(61)

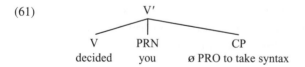

However, we can avoid a structure like (61) if we suppose that (56) has a structure more akin to that of:

(62)   What made you decide to take syntax?

but differing from (62) in that in place of the overt causative verb *make* is an affixal causative light verb *ø*, with the verb *decide* raising to adjoin to the light verb as in (63) below:

(63)

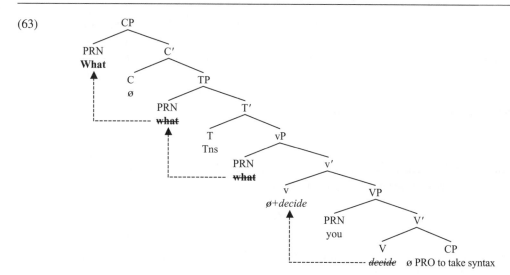

The wh-pronoun *what* moves from spec-vP to spec-TP by A-movement, and then from spec-TP to spec-CP by A-bar movement. There is no T-to-C movement here for reasons which should be familiar from §6.6 (where we saw that questions with a wh-subject do not trigger auxiliary inversion). Instead, the past-tense affix (*Tns*) in T which carries person/number/tense features is lowered onto the light-verb complex *ø+decide*, which is ultimately spelled out as the past-tense form *decided*.

The light-verb analysis in (63) offers two main advantages over the analysis in (61). Firstly, (63) is consistent with the view that the merger operation by which phrases are formed is binary; and secondly, (63) enables us to attain a more unitary theory of **control** under which the controller of PRO is always a subject/specifier, never an object (since PRO in (63) is controlled by *you*, and *you* is the subject of the VP which was originally headed by the verb *decide*). This second result is a welcome one, since the verb *decide* clearly functions as a subject-control verb in structures such as:

(64)   Who decided PRO to take syntax?

where the PRO subject of *to take syntax* is controlled by the thematic subject of *decided* (i.e. by *who*).

Although the verb *decide* can be used both as a so-called object-control predicate in sentences like *What decided you to take syntax?* and as a subject-control predicate in sentences like *Who decided to take syntax?*, most object-control predicates (like *persuade*) have no subject-control counterpart – as we see from (65) below:

(65) (a)   He *persuaded* Mary to come to his party
     (b)   *Mary persuaded to come to his party

This means that the analysis of sentences like (65a) will involve a greater level of abstraction, since it involves claiming that *persuade* originates in the head V position of VP and that *Mary* is the thematic subject of *persuade* (so that *persuade* originates in the same position as *decide* in (63) above, and *Mary* in the same position as *you*). We will also have to say that *persuade* is an obligatorily transitive affixal verb which must adjoin to the kind of abstract light verb which we find in structures like (63) – so accounting for the ungrammaticality of structures like (65b). (For further discussion of so-called object-control verbs, see Bowers 1993; for an analysis of the control verb *promise*, see Larson 1991.)

9.6   VP shells in transitive, unergative, unaccusative, raising and locative inversion structures

In §9.4 and §9.5, we looked at how to deal with the complements of three-place transitive predicates. But now we turn to look at the complements of simple (two-place) transitive predicates (which have subject and object arguments) like *read* in (66) below:

(66)   He read the book

Chomsky (1995) proposes a light-verb analysis of two-place transitive predicates under which (66) would (at the end of the vP cycle) have a structure along the lines of (67) below (with the arrow showing movement of the verb *read* from V to adjoin to a null light verb in v):

(67)

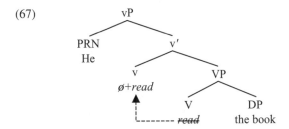

That is, *read* would originate as the head V of VP, and would then be raised to adjoin to a null agentive light verb ø. (A different account of transitive complements as VP-specifiers is offered in Stroik 1990 and Bowers 1993.)

Chomsky's light-verb analysis of two-place transitive predicates can be extended in an interesting way to handle the syntax of a class of verbs which are known as **unergative predicates**. These are verbs like those italicised in (68) below which have agentive subjects, but which appear to have no complement:

(68) (a)   Shall we *lunch*?   (d) Why not *guess*?
     (b)   Let's *party*!   (e) He *apologised*
     (c)   Don't *fuss*!   (f) She *overdosed*

Such verbs pose obvious problems for our assumption in the previous chapter that agentive subjects originate as *specifiers* and merge with an intermediate verbal projection which is itself formed by merger of a verb with its complement. The reason should be obvious – namely that unergative verbs like those italicised in (68) appear to have no complements. However, it is interesting to note that unergative verbs often have close paraphrases involving an overt light verb (i.e. a verb such as *have/make/take* etc. which has little semantic content of its own in the relevant use) and a nominal complement:

(69) (a) Shall we *have* lunch   (d) Why not *make* a guess?
     (b) Let's *have* a party!   (e) He *made* an apology
     (c) Don't *make* a fuss!   (f) She *took* an overdose

This suggests a way of overcoming the problem posed by unergative verbs – namely to suppose (following Baker 1988 and Hale and Keyser 1993) that unergative verbs are formed by incorporation of a complement into an abstract light verb. This would mean (for example) that the verb *lunch* in (68a) is an implicitly transitive verb, formed by incorporating the noun *lunch* into an abstract light verb which can be thought of as a null counterpart of *have*. Since the incorporated object is a simple noun (not a full DP), we can assume (following Baker 1988) that it does not carry case. The VP thereby formed would serve as the complement of an abstract light verb with an external argument (the external argument being *we* in the case of (68a) above). Under this analysis, unergatives would in effect be transitives with an incorporated object: hence we can account for the fact that (like transitives) unergatives require the use of the perfect auxiliary HAVE in languages (like Italian) with a HAVE/BE contrast in perfect auxiliaries.

  Moreover, there are reasons to suppose that a light-verb analysis is required for **unaccusative** structures as well, and that the syntax of unaccusative predicates like *come/go* is rather more complex than we suggested in §7.6, where we noted Burzio's claim that the arguments of unaccusative predicates originate as their complements. An immediate problem posed by Burzio's assumption is how we deal with two-place unaccusative predicates which take two arguments. In this connection, consider unaccusative imperative structures such as the following in (dialect A of) Belfast English (see Henry 1995: note that *youse* is the plural form of *you* – corresponding to American English *y'all*):

(70) (a) Go you to school!
     (b) Run youse to the telephone!
     (c) Walk you into the garden!

If postverbal arguments of unaccusative predicates are **in-situ** complements, this means that each of the verbs in (70) must have two complements. But if we make the traditional assumption that complements are sisters of a head, this means that if both *you* and *to school* are complements of the verb *go* in (70a), they must be sisters of *go*, and hence the VP headed by *go* must have the (simplified) structure (71) below:

(71)

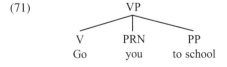

          VP
         / | \
        V   PRN   PP
        Go you   to school

However, a ternary-branching structure such as (71) is obviously incompatible with a framework such as that used here which assumes that the merger operation by which phrases are formed is inherently binary.

Since analysing unaccusative subjects in such structures as underlying complements proves problematic, let's consider whether they might instead be analysed as specifiers. On this view, we can suppose that the inner VP core of a Belfast English unaccusative imperative structure such as (70a) *Go you to school!* is not (71) above, but rather (72) below:

(72)

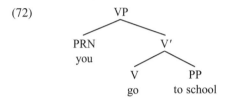

We can then say that it is a property of unaccusative predicates that all their arguments originate within VP. But the problem posed by a structure like (72) is that it provides us with no way of accounting for the fact that unaccusative subjects like *you* in (70a) *Go you to school!* surface postverbally. How can we overcome this problem? One answer is the following. Let us suppose that VPs like (72) which are headed by an unaccusative verb are embedded as the complement of a null light verb, and that the unaccusative verb raises to adjoin to the light verb in the manner indicated by the arrow in (73) below:

(73)

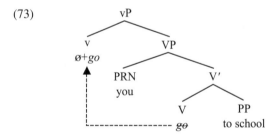

If (as Alison Henry argues) subjects remain in situ in imperatives in dialect A of Belfast English, the postverbal position of unaccusative subjects in sentences such as (70) can be accounted for straightforwardly. And the shell analysis in (73) is consistent with the assumption that the merger operation by which phrases are formed is intrinsically binary.

Moreover, the shell analysis enables us to provide an interesting account of the position of adverbs like *quickly* in unaccusative imperatives (in dialect A of Belfast English) such as:

(74)   Go you quickly to school!

If we suppose that adverbs like *quickly* are adjuncts which merge with an intermediate verbal projection (i.e. a single-bar projection comprising a verb and its complement), we can say that *quickly* in (74) is adjoined to the V-bar *go to school* in (73). What remains to be accounted for (in relation to the syntax of imperative subjects in dialect A of Belfast English) is the fact that subjects of transitive and unergative verbs occur in preverbal (not postverbal) position: cf.

(75) (a)   *You* read that book!
     (b)   *Read *you* that book!

(76) (a)   *Youse* tell the truth!
     (b)   *Tell *youse* the truth

(77) (a)   *You* protest!
     (b)   *Protest *you*!

Why should this be? If we assume (as in our discussion of (66) above) that transitive verbs originate as the head V of a VP complement of a null agentive light verb, an imperative such as (75a) will contain a vP with the simplified structure shown in (78) below (where the dotted arrow indicates movement of the verb *read* to adjoin to the null light verb heading vP):

(78)

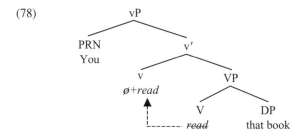

The AGENT subject *you* will originate in spec-vP, as the subject of the agentive light verb *ø*. Even after the verb *read* adjoins to the null light verb, the subject *you* will still be positioned in front of the resulting verbal complex *ø+read*. As should be obvious, we can extend the light-verb analysis from transitive verbs like *read* to unergative verbs like *protest* if we assume (as earlier) that such verbs are formed by incorporation of a noun into the verb (so that *protest* is analysed as having a similar structure to *make (a) protest*), and if we assume that unergative subjects (like transitive subjects) originate as specifiers of an agentive light verb.

  Given these assumptions, we could then say that the difference between unaccusative subjects and transitive/unergative subjects is that unaccusative subjects originate within VP (as the argument of a lexical verb), whereas transitive/unergative subjects originate in spec-vP (as the external argument of a light verb). If we hypothesise that verb phrases always contain an outer vP shell headed by a strong (affixal) light verb and an inner VP core headed by a lexical verb, and that lexical verbs always raise from V to v, the postverbal position of unaccusative subjects can be accounted for by positing that the subject remains in situ in such structures. Such a hypothesis will clearly require us to modify our earlier assumptions about the intransitive use of ergative predicates in sentences like (32)–(37) above, and to analyse intransitive ergatives in a parallel fashion to unaccusatives.

The light-verb analysis sketched here also offers us a way of accounting for the fact that in Early Modern English, the perfect auxiliary used with unaccusative verbs was *be* (as we saw in §7.6), whereas that used with transitive and unergative verbs was *have*. We can account for this by positing that the perfect auxiliary *have* selected a vP complement headed by a transitive light verb with an external argument, whereas the perfect auxiliary *be* selected a complement headed by an intransitive light verb with no external argument. The distinction has been lost in present-day English, with perfect *have* being used with both types of vP complement.

A class of predicates which are related to unaccusatives (in that they project no external argument) are **raising** predicates like *seem*. In this connection, consider the syntax of a raising sentence such as:

(79)   The president does seem to me to have upset several people

Given the assumptions made in this chapter, (79) will be derived as follows. The verb *upset* merges with its QP complement *several people* to form the VP *upset several people*. This in turn merges with a null causative light verb, which (by virtue of being affixal in nature) triggers raising of the verb *upset* to adjoin to the light verb (as shown by the dotted arrow below); the resulting v-bar merges with its external AGENT argument *the president* to form the vP in (80) below (paraphraseable informally as 'The president caused-to-get-upset several people'):

(80)

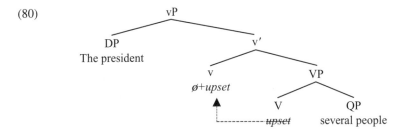

The resulting vP is then merged with the auxiliary *have* to form an AUXP, and this AUXP is in turn merged with [$_T$ *to*]. If we follow Chomsky (2001) in supposing that T in raising infinitives has an [EPP] feature and an unvalued person feature, the subject *the president* will be attracted to move to spec-TP, so deriving the structure shown in simplified form below (with the arrow marking A-movement):

(81)

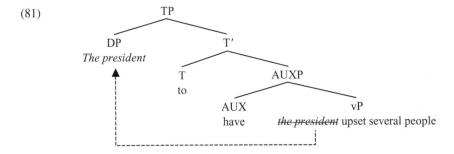

The TP in (81) is then merged as the complement of *seem*, forming the V-bar *seem the president to have upset several people* (omitting traces and other empty categories, to make exposition less abstract). Let's suppose that *to me* is the EXPERIENCER argument of *seem* and is merged as the specifier of the resulting V-bar, forming the VP shown in (82) below (once again simplified by not showing traces and other empty categories):

(82)

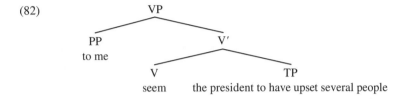

On the assumption that all verb phrases contain an outer vP shell, the VP in (82) will then merge with a null (affixal) light verb, triggering raising of the verb *seem* to adjoin to the light verb. Merging the resulting vP with a finite T constituent containing (emphatic) DO will derive the structure shown in simplified form below (with the arrow showing the verb movement that took place on the vP cycle):

(83)

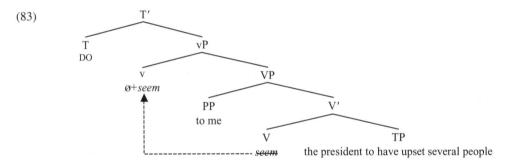

[$_T$ DO] serves as a probe looking for an active nominal goal. The **Phase Impenetrability Condition** (which renders the object of a transitive verb impenetrable to a c-commanding T constituent) makes the nominal *several people* impenetrable to T, since it is the object of the transitive verb *upset*: and let's assume that the pronoun *me* is likewise inaccessible to T (perhaps because a nominal goal is only active if it has an unvalued case feature, and the case feature of *me* has already been valued as accusative by the transitive preposition *to*; or perhaps because *me* serves as the goal of a closer probe, namely the transitive preposition *to*). If so, *the president* (which is active by virtue of having an unvalued case feature) will be the only nominal which can serve as the goal of [$_T$ DO] in (83). Accordingly, DO assigns nominative case to *the president* (and conversely agrees with *the president*, with DO ultimately being spelled out at PF as *does*), and the [EPP] and uninterpretable person/number features of DO ensure that *the president* moves into spec-TP, so deriving the structure shown in simplified form below:

(84)

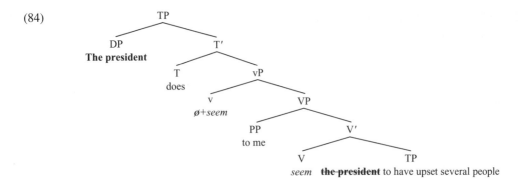

The resulting TP will then be merged with a null declarative complementiser, forming the CP structure associated with (79) *The president does seem to me to have upset several people*. We can assume that the related sentence (85) below:

(85)   The president does seem to have upset several people

has an essentially parallel derivation, except that the verb *seem* in (85) projects no EXPERIENCER argument, so that the structure formed when *seem* is merged with its TP complement will not be (82) above, but rather [$_{VP}$ [$_V$ *seem*] [$_{TP}$ *the president* [$_T$ *to*] *have upset several people*]].

An interesting corollary of the light-verb analysis of raising verbs like *seem* is that the Italian counterpart of *seem* is used with the perfect auxiliary *essere* 'be' rather than *avere* 'have' – as we can illustrate in relation to:

(86)   Maria mi è sempre sembrata essere simpatica
        Maria me is always seemed   be   nice
        'Maria has always seemed to me to be nice'

(The position of the EXPERIENCER argument *mi* 'to me' in (86) is accounted for by the fact that it is a clitic pronoun, and clitics attach to the left of a finite auxiliary or verb in Italian – in this case attaching to the left of *è* 'is'.) Earlier, we suggested that in languages with the HAVE/BE contrast, HAVE typically selects a vP complement with an external argument, whereas BE selects a vP complement with no external argument. In this context, it is interesting to note (e.g. in relation to structures like (84) above) that the light verb found in clauses containing a raising predicate like *seem* projects no external argument, and hence would be expected to occur with (the relevant counterpart of) the perfect auxiliary BE in a language with the HAVE/BE contrast. Data such as (86) are thus consistent with the light-verb analysis of raising predicates like *seem* outlined here. (It should be noted, however, that the HAVE/BE contrast is somewhat more complex than suggested here: see Sorace 2000 for a cross-linguistic perspective.)

The assumption made in this section that intransitive clauses have a split vP+VP structure in which the verb raises from V to v provides us with a way of analysing **locative inversion** structures such as (87) below, so called because the locative expression *down the hill* precedes the auxiliary *will*:

(87)   Down the hill will roll the ball

We can derive this as follows. The verb *roll* merges with its complement *down the hill* and its specifier *the ball* to form the VP *the ball roll down the hill* shown in (39) above. This is then merged with an intransitive light verb which (being strong) triggers movement of the verb *roll* from V to v, so deriving the structure shown in simplified form below:

(88)

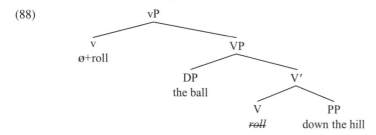

The resulting vP is then merged with a finite T constituent *will* which has an [EPP] feature. Let's suppose that T (in addition to its person/number/tense and [EPP] features) in this kind of structure carries some additional feature which enables it to attract the PP *down the hill* and that as a result, *down the hill* moves to spec-TP, so deriving the structure:

(89)

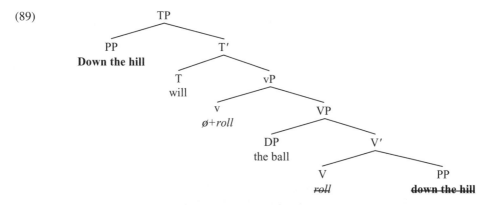

Such an analysis leaves the subject *the ball* in situ in spec-VP (hence following the raised verb *roll*), thereby accounting for the word order we find in (87) *Down the hill will roll the ball*. Interestingly, a locative inversion structure can occur as the complement of a complementiser like *that*, as we see from:

(90)   He was startled to find **that** *down the hill was rolling an enormous snowball*

This is precisely what would be expected if locative inversion involves movement of a locative to spec-TP, as in (89) above. (See Levin and Rappaport Hovav

1995; Collins 1997; Nakajima 2001; and Bowers 2002 on locative inversion; see Culicover and Levins 2001 for arguments that locative inversion structures are different in nature from structures like 'Into the room walked carefully *the students in the class who had heard about the social psych experiment that we were about to perpetrate*' containing a long italicised postverbal subject.)

9.7   Transitive light verbs and accusative case assignment

In the previous chapter, we saw that nominative and null case are assigned to a goal by a matching φ-complete probe (the probe being a finite T for nominative case, and a non-finite control T for null case); however, we had nothing to say about accusative case assignment. If UG principles determine that all structural case assignment involves assignment of case to a goal by a φ-complete matching probe, we can hypothesise that accusative case is likewise assigned to a goal by a φ-complete probe which matches the goal in respect of its person and number features. But what could be the probe responsible for assignment of accusative case to (say) the accusative complement *them* in a transitive sentence such as that below?

(91)   You have upset them

Chomsky in recent work has suggested an answer along the lines of (92) below:

(92)   A **transitive light verb** carrying person and number φ-features serves as a probe which assigns accusative case to a goal with matching person and number features and an active (unvalued) case feature

Let's further suppose that:

(93)   A light verb is **transitive** only if it has a theta-marked external argument

In the light of (92) and (93), consider how the derivation of (91) proceeds.

The verb *upset* is merged with its complement THEY to form the VP *upset* THEY (capital letters being used to denote an abstract lexical item whose precise phonetic spellout as *they/them/their* has not yet been determined): the pronoun carries interpretable third-person, plural-number features and an uninterpretable (and unvalued) case feature. The resulting VP is then merged with a null transitive light verb which (since case assignment requires probe and goal to match in φ-features) will carry unvalued and uninterpretable person/number features, so forming the v-bar below (with interpretable features shown in **bold** and uninterpretable features in *italics*):

(94)

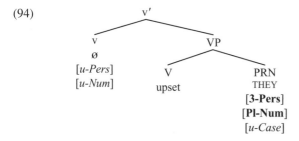

The null light verb probes and identifies THEY as the only active goal which carries an uninterpretable case feature. The goal THEY values (and, being φ-complete, deletes) the person/number φ-features of the light-verb probe (these will ultimately have a null spellout, like the light verb itself). Conversely, the transitive light verb values the unvalued case feature of THEY as accusative in accordance with (92) (so that THEY is ultimately spelled out as *them*) and (by virtue of being φ-complete) deletes it, so deriving:

(95)

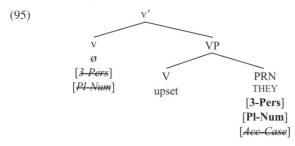

The null light verb is affixal, and so will trigger raising of the verb *upset* from V to v. Since the (causative) light verb in (95) is transitive, it projects an AGENT external argument. The relevant external argument is YOU in (91), and (if it refers to more than one individual) this enters the derivation with interpretable second-person and plural-number features, but an unvalued case-feature, so forming the vP (96) below:

(96)

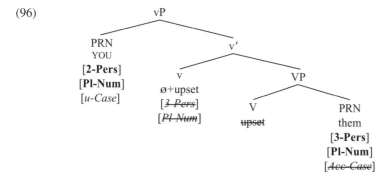

The vP thereby formed is merged with a null finite T containing the perfect auxiliary HAVE, which has an interpretable present-tense feature, uninterpretable (and unvalued) φ-features, and an uninterpretable [EPP] feature. Merging T with its vP complement derives:

(97)

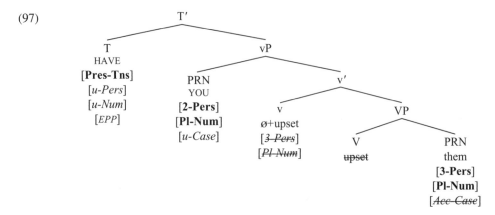

[T HAVE] then probes and locates the pronoun YOU as the only active goal with an unvalued case feature which it c-commands. This results in the pronoun valuing and deleting the person/number features of the auxiliary, and conversely in the auxiliary valuing the case feature of the pronoun as nominative, and deleting it: hence the items HAVE and YOU are spelled out as *have* and *you* at PF. The [EPP] feature of T triggers raising of the pronoun *you* from spec-vP to spec-TP (thereby deleting the [EPP] feature on T), deriving the structure (98) below:

(98)

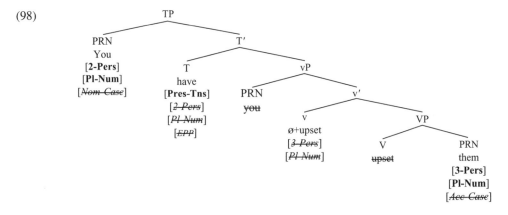

The resulting structure is then merged with a null declarative complementiser to derive the CP structure associated with (91) *You have upset them.* (On accusative case assignment in **double-object** structures like *give someone something*, see Goodall 1999.)

An interesting question arising from the assumption that the objects of transitive verbs are assigned accusative case by a light verb which projects an external argument is whether this analysis can be extended to the case-marking of (italicised) accusative subjects of the (bracketed) infinitival TPs in ECM/Exceptional Case-Marking structures like those below:

(99) (a)   They **proved** [*him* to have stolen the jewels]
   (b)   They **suspect** [*me* to be an agent for the FBA]
   (c)   I **believe** [*them* to be innocent]
   (d)   I have always **found** [*them* to be accommodating]

At first sight, the answer would appear to be straightforward. After all, if the italicised subject occupies spec-TP position within the bracketed TP complement, and if the bold-printed ECM verb originates as the head of a VP which is the complement of a transitive light verb and subsequently raises to adjoin to the light verb (in the manner shown by the dotted arrow below), (99a) will have the structure shown in (100) below at the end of the main-clause vP cycle (simplified by not showing the internal structure of T-bar):

(100)

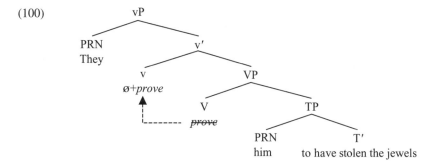

Since the light verb ø which occupies the head v position within vP is transitive (by virtue of having an external argument, namely *they*), and since it c-commands the infinitive subject *him*, it can assign accusative case to *him* with concomitant φ-feature matching (i.e. the light verb will contain unvalued person and number features which are valued by those of *him*; like the light verb itself, these will ultimately have a null phonetic spellout).

   However, an important question raised by the above analysis is how we account for the position of the italicised adverbial and prepositional expressions in ECM structures such as the following:

(101) (a)   The DA will **prove** [the witness *conclusively* to have lied] (adapted from Bowers 1993, p. 632)
   (b)   I **suspect** [him *strongly* to be a liar] (Authier 1991, p. 729)
   (c)   I've **believed** [Gary *for a long time now* to be a fool] (Kayne 1984b, p. 114)
   (d)   I have **found** [Bob *recently* to be morose] (Postal 1974, p. 146)

In sentences like (101), the italicised adverbial/prepositional expression is positioned inside the bracketed infinitive complement, and yet is construed as modifying the (bold-printed) transitive verb which lies outside the bracketed complement clause. How can we account for this seeming paradox? To make our discussion more concrete, let's consider how to derive (101a).

   If we assume that the adverb *conclusively* (by virtue of modifying the verb *prove*) originates as an adjunct to the V-bar headed by *prove*, the problem we face is accounting for how both the verb *prove* and the DP *the witness* end up in front of the adverb *conclusively*. Movement of the verb *prove* in front of *conclusively* is no problem if we suppose that verbs move from the head V position in VP to adjoin to a null light verb, and thereby come to occupy the head v position of vP. But how does the infinitival subject *the witness* come to be positioned above the adverb *conclusively*, but below the verb *prove*?

One possibility is that an ECM verb like *prove* (like infinitival *to* in raising structures) has an [EPP] feature and an unvalued person feature which together require the closest matching nominal expression which they c-command to be moved to the outer edge of VP. Given this assumption, the relevant part of the derivation of (101a) will proceed as follows. The verb *prove* merges with the infinitival TP *the witness to have lied* (whose structure we ignore here, in order to simplify exposition) to form the V-bar *prove the witness to have lied*, and the adverb *conclusively* merges with this V-bar to form the even larger V-bar *conclusively prove the witness to have lied*. Let's suppose that *the witness* has valued (third-)person and (singular-)number features, and an unvalued and uninterpretable case feature, so that at this stage we have formed the V-bar shown in simplified form below:

(102)

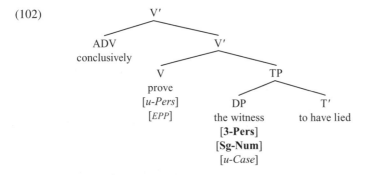

The uninterpretable person feature on the verb *prove* serves as a probe which picks out the closest active goal with a matching person feature, locating the DP *the witness*, which is active by virtue of its uninterpretable case feature: since the DP *the witness* is φ-complete, it values and deletes the person feature on the verb *prove*. The [EPP] feature of *prove* triggers movement of *the witness* to the outer edge of the relevant V-projection (and is thereafter deleted), so that *the witness* becomes the specifier of the V-bar in (102), forming the VP (103) below:

(103)

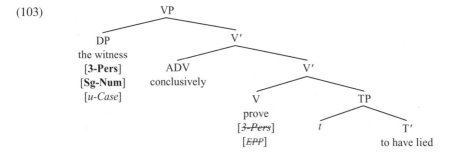

Because the verb *prove* is not φ-complete (by virtue of carrying only person and not number), it does not value or delete the case feature on the DP *the witness*, so that the latter remains active.

The VP in (103) is then merged as the complement of a null (affixal) light-verb. The light verb is transitive (since it has the external argument *the DA*), and transitive light verbs carry a complete set of unvalued φ-features, so that merging the relevant light verb with (103) above will form (104) below:

(104)

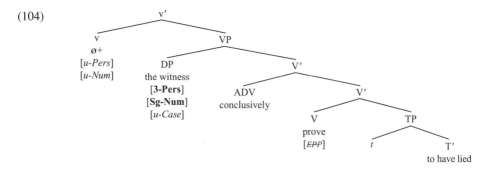

At this point, the light verb (active by virtue of its uninterpretable φ-features) serves as a probe and searches for an active matching nominal goal which it c-commands, locating *the witness* (which is active by virtue of its uninterpretable case feature). The light verb values the unvalued case feature of *the witness* as accusative in accordance with (92), and deletes it. The DP *the witness* in turn values and deletes the unvalued person and number features of the light verb. Since the light verb is affixal in nature (indicated by the + sign in ø+), it triggers raising of the verb *prove* to adjoin to the light verb. Since the light verb is transitive, it also projects an external argument (in this case, *the DA*) in spec-vP. Thus, at the end of the vP cycle, we have the structure shown in (105) below (simplified by showing only features of the light verb *ø* and the DP *the witness*, and by omitting a number of traces and other empty categories):

(105)

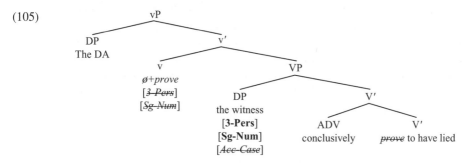

Subsequently, the resulting vP is merged as the complement of [T *will*], which serves as a probe valuing (as nominative) and deleting the uninterpretable case feature on *the DA* (not shown here); the [EPP] feature and unvalued person/number features of *will* trigger movement of *the DA* to become the specifier of the TP headed by *will*. Merging the resulting TP with a null declarative complementiser derives the structure associated with (101a) *The DA will prove the witness conclusively to have lied*.

9.8 Evidence for a further projection in transitive verb phrases

The account of the syntax of ECM subjects given in the previous section provides a way of capturing the intuition (defended in Postal 1974 and Lasnik and Saito 1991) that the subject of an ECM infinitive raises to become the object of the ECM verb. The raised subject *the witness* in (102)–(105) becomes the highest constituent within the inner VP core in which the ECM verb *prove* originates (as in López 2001); and since direct objects are the highest internal arguments within VP, this amounts to claiming that the infinitive subject is raised up to become the direct object of the verb *prove*.

However, some of the assumptions underlying this analysis seem questionable. For example, the assumption that a lexical verb like *prove* can have an [EPP] feature which triggers raising of the subject of its infinitive complement to become an internal argument of *prove* seems problematic from three standpoints. Firstly, [EPP] is a feature canonically associated with functional categories like T and C, and not with substantive (lexical) categories like V. Secondly, an internal argument of a verb is theta-marked by the verb, and yet the raised nominal *the witness* in a structure like (105) is not theta-marked by the ECM verb *prove* (but rather is a thematic argument of the verb *lied*). Thirdly, the verb *prove* starts out as a predicate with a single internal argument (a clausal complement), but ends up with two internal arguments – an accusative object and a clausal complement. This violates the **Projection Principle** suggested in earlier work by Chomsky (1981, p. 29) – a principle which requires that the properties of lexical items (including the kinds of arguments they permit) should remain constant throughout the derivation.

A further questionable aspect of the ECM analysis outlined in the previous section is the assumption that adverbs adjoin to intermediate projections. This is problematic in two respects. Firstly, other grammatical operations like movement seem 'blind' to intermediate projections, so that no intermediate projection can be a goal for movement (in the sense that no intermediate projection can undergo movement) or a target for movement (in the sense that no movement operation adjoins a moved constituent to an intermediate projection): on the contrary, only a head or a maximal projection can be a goal or target for movement. If movement cannot involve intermediate projections, we might assume that adjunction cannot either. Moreover, the assumption that adverbs can adjoin to intermediate projections seems to conflict with a principle suggested by Chomsky (1998, p. 49) to the effect that the selectional properties of a head must be satisfied before any other constituent can be introduced into the projection containing the head. Since a head selects its arguments, this suggests that a head must merge with its arguments before any material can be adjoined to the relevant projection – or in simpler terms, it suggests that adverbs can adjoin only to maximal projections, and not (as we have assumed throughout so far in this chapter) to intermediate projections. But if this is so, an analysis of ECM structures like that in (105) is untenable, because it presupposes that an adverb like *conclusively* can be adjoined to an intermediate V-bar projection of the verb *prove*.

However, the dilemma we face is that if we suppose that adverbs like *conclusively* adjoin only to maximal projections like VP, it follows that *conclusively* must adjoin to the VP in (105), so that in place of (105) we will have the structure shown in simplified form in (106) below:

(106)

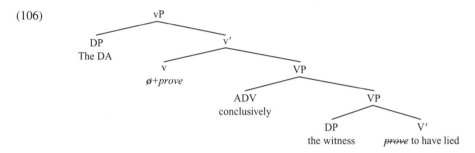

The twin problems posed by a structure like (106) are that on the one hand it wrongly predicts that (107a) below is grammatical, and that on the other it wrongly predicts that (107b) is ungrammatical:

(107) (a) *The DA will prove conclusively the witness to have lied
(b) The DA will prove the witness conclusively to have lied (= 101a)

How can we get round this problem without abandoning the claim that adverbs adjoin to maximal (and not intermediate) projections?

A solution advocated in Koizumi (1993, 1995) is to suppose that transitive verb phrases can be split into *three* projections rather than (as we have assumed so far) two, with an additional AgrOP (Object Agreement Projection) positioned between VP and vP. Work in the same era (dating back to Pollock 1989) similarly supposed that TP could be split into separate TP and AgrSP (Subject Agreement Projection) constituents: see Radford (1997a, §10.2–§10.9) for discussion of earlier work on Agr projections in English. However, after surveying the evidence for positing projections of abstract Agr(eement) heads, Chomsky (1995, p. 377) concludes that 'It seems reasonable to conjecture that Agr does not exist.' One objection which he voices to Agr heads is that they cannot be assigned any interpretation at the semantics interface, and hence will cause the derivation to crash.

Mindful of Chomsky's objections, Bowers (2002) proposes an alternative triple-projection account of the structure of transitive clauses in which located between vP and VP is a projection of a functional head which encodes an interpretable **Transitivity** property: he labels this head **Tr**, and assumes that it projects into a **TrP** 'Transitivity Phrase'. Bowers further supposes that Tr carries a set of (object-agreement) φ-features, and that it also has an [EPP] feature. On this view, (107b) will be derived as follows. The derivation proceeds in familiar ways until we reach the stage where the verb *prove* merges with its TP complement *the witness to have lied* to form the VP *prove the witness to have lied*. The adverb *conclusively* is then adjoined to this VP, expanding it into an even larger VP constituent. The resulting VP is then merged with a Tr(ansitivity) head which carries an interpretable transitivity feature (below shown crudely as [+**Trans**]), together with uninterpretable person/number/EPP features, so deriving (108) below:

(108)

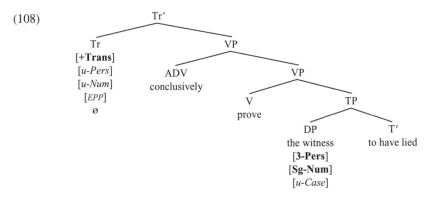

The Tr head is strong, and so triggers raising of the verb *prove* from V to Tr. Tr is also active for agreement and case-marking by virtue of its uninterpretable person/number features, and so probes and locates *the witness* as the only active goal within its domain. Agreement between the two leads to valuation of the person/number features of Tr and to valuation of the case feature of *the witness* as accusative; the uninterpretable features on probe and goal are also deleted once valued, since both probe and goal are φ-complete. (An interesting possibility which we will not explore further here is that accusative case is in fact an uninterpretable transitivity feature which is valued by the transitivity feature on Tr – in much the same way as nominative case may be an uninterpretable tense feature which is valued by the interpretable tense feature on T, as we saw in §6.6.) Since Tr has an [EPP] feature, it triggers raising of *the witness* to spec-TrP (thereby deleting its [EPP] feature), so deriving the structure shown in simplified form in (109) below:

(109)

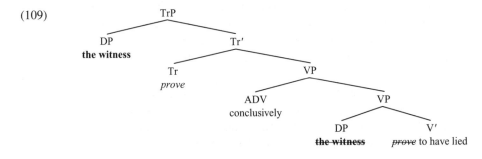

The resulting TrP is then merged with an agentive light verb (whose external argument is the AGENT *the DA*). The light verb is strong, so triggers raising of the verb *prove* from Tr to v, thereby forming the vP shown in simplified form below:

(110)

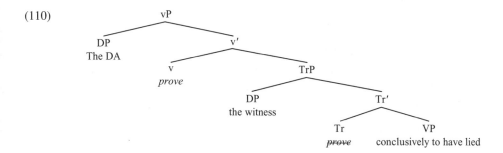

The derivation then continues in familiar ways, ultimately deriving (107b) *The DA will prove the witness conclusively to have lied*. This revised analysis of ECM structures is consistent with the twin assumptions that (i) adverbs adjoin only to maximal projections, and (ii) only functional heads (like Tr, T and C) can have an [EPP] feature.

However, these twin assumptions require us to rethink our earlier vP/VP analysis of simple transitive clauses. To see why, consider sentence (47a) above, repeated below:

(111)   Mary jumped the horse *perfectly* over the last fence

In the light of our revised assumptions, this will now be derived as follows. The verb *jumped* merges with its complement *over the last fence* and its specifier *the horse* to form the VP *the horse jumped over the last fence*. The VP-adverb *perfectly* adjoins to this VP, so forming the even larger VP *perfectly the horse jumped over the last fence*. The resulting VP is then merged with a Tr(ansitivity) head which carries an interpretable transitivity feature, uninterpretable person/number φ-features and an interpretable [EPP] feature, so forming the structure shown in simplified form below:

(112)

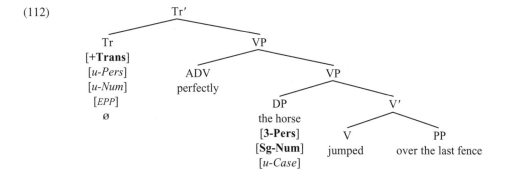

The Tr head is strong, and consequently triggers raising of the verb *jumped* from V to Tr. Agreement between the Tr head and the DP *the horse* values (and deletes) the person/number features of Tr and values (as accusative) and deletes the case feature of *the horse*. The [EPP] feature of Tr triggers movement of *the horse* to spec-TrP, so deriving the overt structure shown in skeletal form in (113) below:

(113)   [$_{TrP}$ the horse [$_{Tr}$ jumped] [$_{VP}$ perfectly over the last fence]]

The resulting TrP is then merged with an agentive light verb (whose external argument is the AGENT *Mary*). The light verb is strong, so triggers raising of the verb *jumped* from Tr to v, thereby forming the overt structure shown in highly simplified form below:

(114)   [$_{vP}$ Mary [$_v$ jumped] [$_{TrP}$ the horse [$_{VP}$ perfectly over the last fence]]]

The resulting vP will then be merged with a past-tense T constituent, with *Mary* raising to spec-TP. Merging the resulting TP with a null declarative complementiser will derive the syntactic structure associated with (111) *Mary jumped the horse perfectly over the last fence*.

If we follow Bowers (2002) in supposing that passive VPs also contain a TrP projection, we can offer an interesting account of the position of the italicised indefinite nominal in passives such as:

(115)   There were *several prizes* awarded

The (passive) verb *award(ed)* merges with its complement *several prizes* to form the VP *awarded several prizes*. This VP merges with a Tr head which (by virtue of being strong) triggers movement of the verb *awarded* from V to Tr and (by virtue of its [EPP] feature) triggers raising of the complement *several prizes* to become the specifier of the transitivity head Tr, so deriving the structure shown in skeletal form below:

(116)   [$_{TrP}$ several prizes [$_{Tr}$ awarded] [$_{VP}$ [$_v$ ~~awarded~~] ~~several prizes~~]]

This is then merged with a light verb containing the passive auxiliary *be*. Since *be* is a non-thematic verb which projects no external argument, expletive *there* can be merged in spec-vP, so deriving:

(117)   [$_{vP}$ there [$_v$ be] [$_{TrP}$ several prizes [$_{Tr}$ awarded] [$_{VP}$ [$_v$ ~~awarded~~] ~~several prizes~~]]]

The resulting vP is then merged with a finite T constituent which agrees with both *there* and *several prizes* (assigning nominative case to the latter), triggers raising of *be* from v to T, and also triggers raising of *there* from spec-vP to spec-TP, so ultimately deriving:

(118)   [$_{TP}$ There [$_T$ be] [$_{vP}$ ~~there~~ [$_v$ ~~be~~] [$_{TrP}$ several prizes [$_{Tr}$ awarded] [$_{VP}$ [$_v$ ~~awarded~~] ~~several prizes~~]]]]

The resulting TP is then merged with a null declarative complementiser, and BE is spelled out as *were* in the PF component. (See Chomsky 1999 for an alternative account of sentences like (115) in which the preverbal position of *several prizes* is claimed to be the result of a PF movement process.)

While passives like (115) allow the complement to be positioned preverbally, unaccusatives do not – as we see from the ungrammaticality of:

(119)   *There have *several guests* arrived

One way of accounting for this contrast is to suppose (following Bowers 2002) that passive verb phrases are vP+TrP+VP structures which contain a TrP projection which can house a preposed complement, whereas unaccusative verb phrases are simple vP+VP structures which (by virtue of lacking TrP) contain no landing site for a preposed complement.

9.9   Extending the shell analysis to nominals

In much work over the past three decades (dating back to Chomsky 1970), linguists have argued that there is cross-categorial symmetry between the structure of verb phrases and noun phrases. If this is so and if VPs have a complex shell structure comprising (at least) an inner VP core and an outer vP shell, we should expect to find that noun phrases too can be split into an outer nP shell headed by a light noun and an inner NP core headed by a lexical noun: the nP shell in turn would be embedded within higher-level nominal projections which house adjectives, possessors, determiners and other nominal modifiers (see Cinque 1994, Longobardi 1994, 1996, 2001 and Bernstein 2001 for discussion of nominal superstructure). In this section, we briefly explore the possibility of extending the shell analysis to noun phrases. Since comparatively little detailed research along these lines has been done, the remarks made in this section about nP shells are inevitably somewhat speculative.

To see how a shell analysis of nominals might work, consider the derivation of so-called **process nominals** (i.e. nominals describing a process) like that in (120) below:

(120)   Israel's withdrawal of troops from the occupied territories

Let's suppose that internal arguments of nouns are generally introduced by a preposition, the nature of which is determined by the theta-role carried by the relevant argument – e.g. the preposition *to* is typically used to introduce a GOAL argument, *by* an AGENT argument, *from* a SOURCE argument, *with* an INSTRUMENT argument and so on – and that a THEME argument of a noun can optionally be introduced by the preposition *of*. (It should be noted, however, that the counterpart of the English *of*-phrase may be a nominal morphologically inflected for genitive case in other languages, as is evident from Cornilescu's 2001 study of Romanian, and this raises the question of whether *of* in this type of use is a marker of inherent genitive case in English: we set this question aside here.) In (120), the DP *the occupied territories* is a SOURCE argument and so is introduced (and assigned accusative case) by the preposition *from*, and the expression *troops* (which is a QP headed by a null quantifier ø) is a THEME argument which can correspondingly be introduced (and assigned accusative case by) the preposition *of*. Merging the noun *withdrawal* with its SOURCE complement *from the occupied territories* forms the N-bar *withdrawal from the occupied territories*; this N-bar is in turn merged with the THEME complement *of ø troops* to form the NP shown below:

(121)

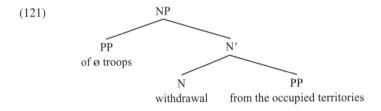

Let us suppose that the resulting NP is then merged with a null light noun, which is causative in sense and projects an AGENT external argument *Israel* (which is a DP headed by a null determiner), and (being affixal) triggers raising of the noun *withdrawal* to adjoin to the light noun, so deriving the nP structure (122) below:

(122)

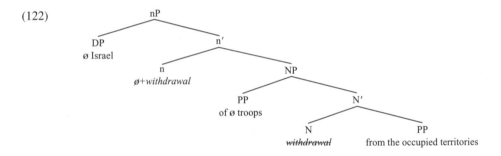

However, the derivation is not yet terminated – for two reasons. Firstly, under the DP hypothesis, nominal arguments are DPs headed by an (overt or null) determiner, so that the nP in (122) has to be merged with an appropriate kind of D constituent; and secondly, the DP *ø Israel* in (122) has an unvalued case feature which needs to be valued and deleted. Given that case is assigned to a goal by a c-commanding probe, an interesting possibility to explore at this juncture is that it is the head D of DP which assigns case to the nominal *ø Israel*. More specifically, let's suppose that the nP in (122) is merged with a null φ-complete determiner which has the property that it assigns structural genitive case to a goal with an unvalued case feature and matching φ-features, in accordance with (123) below:

(123)   **Genitive Case Assignment**
A null φ-complete determiner probe assigns genitive case to a matching case-unvalued goal

Let's also suppose that the genitive case assigned by D to a noun expression is spelled out in the PF component as the genitive suffix *'s*. If none of the constituents in (123) undergo any further movement operations, merger of the relevant null (genitive-case-assigning) determiner with the nP in (122) will derive the DP shown in simplified form in (124) below:

(124)

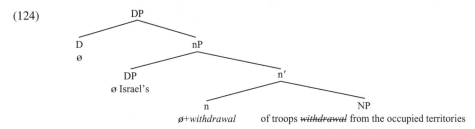

However, a potential problem for the analysis in (124) is posed by nominals such as:

(125)   Israel's *unexpected* withdrawal of troops from the occupied territories

If we suppose that an adjective like *unexpected* occupies some position above nP (perhaps serving as the specifier of a functional head F which has an adjectival specifier, as in Cinque 1994), we have to account for how the 'subject' of the nominal (the DP *Israel's*) comes to be positioned in front of the adjective *unexpected*. The answer suggested by Abney (1987) is that the subjects of nominals move into spec-DP. In terms of the framework adopted here, this means that D in (124) carries an [EPP] feature (in addition to a complete set of – initially unvalued – φ-features), and hence triggers movement of the genitive DP *Israel's* from spec-nP to spec-DP in the manner shown by the arrow in (126) below (with traces shown as **t**/*t*):

(126)

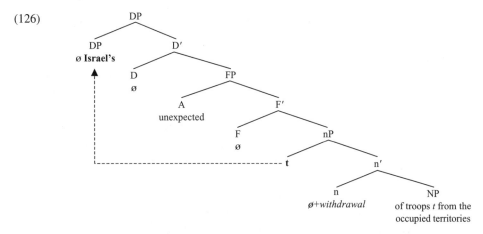

We can then account for the relevant word-order facts in a straightforward fashion. The claim that *unexpected* occupies the specifier (and not the head) position within FP is borne out by the possibility of substituting it by a phrasal constituent like

almost entirely unexpected – the significance of this being that phrases can only be specifiers, not heads. (Fu, Roeper and Borer 2001 present an alternative analysis of process nominals under which they contain an internal verb projection – hence VP rather than NP. Their evidence for positing a VP comes from the possibility of using a VP adverb like *suddenly* and the VP proform *do so* in nominals like *Israel's withdrawal of troops suddenly from the occupied territories before being asked to do so*. If adverbs adjoin to maximal projections and *suddenly* adjoins to VP, this raises the possibility that transitive nominals contain a nominal counterpart of the TrP/Transitivity Phrase projection which appears in transitive verb phrases, and that the head Tr constituent of TrP case-marks the complement *of troups* and attracts it to move to spec-TrP, with the noun *withdrawal* raising from the head V position of VP, through the head Tr position of TrP into the head v position of vP. However, we will not pursue this possibility any further here.)

The account of genitive case-marking outlined above can be extended to possessive constructions such as (127) below (intended to mean much the same as 'the picture of Mary which is in our possession'):

(127)   our picture of Mary

Let's suppose that the noun *picture* merges with its THEME complement *of ø Mary* (where *Mary* is a DP headed by a null determiner) to form the NP *picture of ø Mary*. Let's further suppose (following Carstens 2001) that the resulting NP merges with a null light noun which has the function of marking possession, and that this light noun projects as its external argument the pronoun WE to which it assigns the θ-role of POSSESSOR (its NP complement being in turn assigned the θ-role of POSSESSEE). Given the assumption that light nouns are affixal, the noun *picture* will raise from N to adjoin to the light noun, so deriving:

(128)

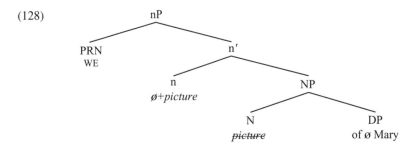

The resulting nP will then be merged with a null φ-complete determiner which assigns genitive case to the pronoun WE in accordance with (123), so that it will ultimately be spelled out as *our* at PF. If the relevant determiner also carries an [EPP] feature, it will trigger movement of the genitive possessor *our* from spec-nP to spec-DP, so deriving the structure shown in simplified form below:

(129)

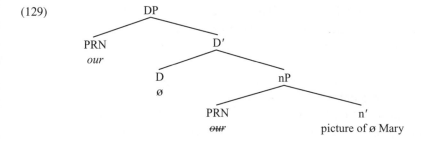

If adjectives occupy specifier position within a functional projection FP positioned between D and nP (as in (126) above), such an analysis will correctly predict that *our* precedes the adjective *latest* in *our latest picture of Mary*.

The analysis presented above follows Abney (1987) in positing that genitive nominals move to spec-DP in English. However, there is some evidence that (in some other languages, at least) the true landing-site of preposed possessives may be a position beneath DP. In this connection, consider the following possessive nominal in Italian:

(130)   la   loro bellissima casa
         the their beautiful   house
         'their beautiful house'

Here, the possessive pronoun *loro* 'their' occupies a position which is lower than that of the determiner *la* 'the' but higher than that of the attributive adjective *bellissima* 'beautiful'. So where is it positioned? We noted in §5.9 that work on the syntax of nominals has suggested that they contain a **NumP** 'Number Phrase' projection positioned immediately below DP. This being so, one possibility is to follow Valois (1991), Cinque (1994) and Carstens (2000, 2001) in positing that possessives in Italian (and perhaps genitive nominals in languages like English) move to spec-NumP. If so, and if we assume (as above) that adjectives occupy the specifier position within a functional projection FP, a nominal like *our latest picture of Mary* will have the structure shown in simplified form in (131) below:

(131)

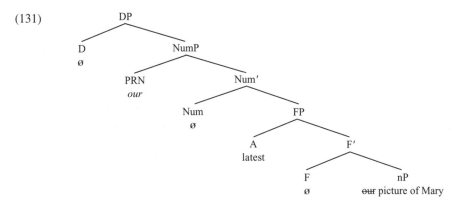

On the revised analysis in (131), it would be the head Num constituent of NumP which agrees with and assigns genitive case to the possessor WE and attracts it to move from the specifier position within nP to the specifier position within NumP.

The agreement-based analysis of structural genitive case assignment outlined here is not without posing problems, however. Not the least of these is that if the head Num constituent of NumP is the locus of the agreement properties of nominals, and if Num agrees with the possessor in possessive structures like (131), we should expect the overall DP to be plural (because the possessor *our* is plural) – and yet it is singular, as we see from the singular agreement required on the bold-printed verb in sentences like:

(132)   *Our latest picture of Mary* **is/*are** on the mantelpiece

Moreover, in Italian structures like (130), the determiner *la* 'the' and the adjective *bellissima* 'beautiful' are feminine singular and hence clearly agree with the feminine singular noun *casa* 'house' and not with the third-person-plural possessor *loro* 'their'. However, agreement facts are different in some other languages: for example, Dixon (2000) notes that the gender properties of a DP in certain types of possessive structure in Jarawara are determined by the possessor. We shall not delve into these issues here, but simply note the problems posed by an agreement-based analysis of genitive case-marking.

9.10   Summary

We began this chapter in §9.2 by outlining the claim made by Luigi Rizzi that in clauses which contain preposed focus/topic expressions, CP splits into a number of separate projections, viz. a Force Phrase/**ForceP**, a Topic Phrase/**TopP** and a Focus Phrase/**FocP** (with a Focus head being strong in finite clauses in English, but not a Topic or Force head). We pointed out that the **split CP** analysis of clauses raises interesting questions about the landing site of preposed wh-expressions; and we suggested that relative and exclamative wh-expressions move to the specifier position within the Force Phrase, but that interrogative wh-expressions move to the specifier position within the Focus Phrase in main-clause questions (though they move to the specifier position within the Force Phrase in complement-clause questions). In §9.3 we went on to examine Rizzi's claim that split CP structures also contain a Finiteness Phrase/**FinP**. We noted his suggestion that clauses containing both a topicalised and a focalised constituent are ForceP/TopP/FocP/FinP structures; clauses containing only a topicalised (but no focalised) constituent are ForceP/TopP/FinP structures; clauses containing a focalised (but no topicalised) constituent are ForceP/FocP/FinP structures; and clauses which contain neither a focalised nor a topicalised constituent are simple CPs (with the relevant force and finiteness features being **syncretised** on a single C head). In §9.4 we went on to outline work by Chomsky, Larson and Hale suggesting that VPs can be split into two distinct projections – an inner VP core headed by a lexical verb and an outer vP **shell** headed by an affixal **light verb**. In particular, we looked at the syntax of **ergative** verbs like *roll* which are used both intransitively in structures like *The ball rolled down the hill* and transitively in structures like *They rolled the ball down the hill*. We argued that the verb phrase in the transitive structures comprises an inner VP core contained within an outer vP shell headed by a causative light verb with an AGENT subject, and that the light verb triggers raising of the verb *roll* from V to v. We argued that data relating to the distribution of various types of adverb lend support to the shell analysis, and we extended the shell analysis to transitive prepositional structures such as *load the cart with hay*. In §9.5, we presented a VP shell analysis for **resultatives** like *turn the litmus-paper red*, and **double-object** structures like *get the teacher a present*. We went on to argue that **object-control** structures like *What decided you to take syntax?* can likewise be analysed in terms of a shell structure in which *you* originates as the subject of *decide* and *what* as the subject of a causative light verb; and we suggested that this analysis can be extended to other object-control predicates like *persuade*. In §9.6 we outlined Chomsky's vP shell analysis of simple transitive structures like *John read the book*, and showed how such an analysis could be extended to unergatives if these are analysed as transitive predicates which undergo object incorporation. We went on to outline a shell analysis of two-place unaccusative predicates, showing how this would account for the word order found in Belfast English imperatives such as *Go you to school!* We also saw how the shell analysis can handle raising structures such as *They seem to me to be fine*, if the EXPERIENCER *to me* is analysed as occupying spec-VP, and if the verb *seem* raises from V to v and so comes to be positioned in front of *to me*. We concluded that intransitive verb phrases (like their transitive counterparts) have a shell structure in which the verb raises from V to v, and we showed that this would enable us to provide an account of **locative inversion** structures like *Down the hill will roll the ball*. In §9.7 we outlined Chomsky's account of accusative case-marking, under which accusative case is assigned to a case-unvalued goal by a φ-complete transitive light-verb (i.e. one which has an external argument). We suggested a way of extending this analysis to ECM infinitive structures like *The DA will prove the witness conclusively to have lied*, arguing that the infinitive subject (*the witness*) raises to become the specifier of the VP headed by *prove*, and that the verb *prove* in turn raises to adjoin to a light verb which occupies the head v position of vP. We noted that this analysis amounts to claiming that the subject *the witness* of the infinitive complement raises up to become the object of the transitive verb *prove*. However, in §9.8 we argued that the analysis of ECM subjects proposed in §9.7 is problematic in certain respects: firstly, it assumes that the ECM subject is raised to become an internal argument of the verb *prove*, even though it is not theta-marked by *prove*; secondly, it assumes that the lexical verb *prove* can have an [EPP] feature, when this is canonically a property of functional categories like T and C; and thirdly, it assumes that adverbs like *conclusively* can adjoin to intermediate projections, even though other grammatical operations (like movement) cannot target intermediate projections. We presented Bowers's alternative analysis under which transitive verb phrases incorporate a TrP/Transitivity Phrase and thus have a tripartite vP+TrP+VP structure, with accusative objects (and ECM subjects) being case-marked via agreement with Tr and raising to spec-TrP, and the verb raising from V through Tr into v: we showed that such an analysis would allow us to suppose that adverbs only adjoin to maximal projections, and that only functional heads can have an [EPP] feature. We went on to show that if passive clauses also contain a TrP projection, we can provide a principled account of the preverbal position of passive complements in expletive structures like 'There were *several prizes* awarded.' In §9.9, we looked at ways in which the shell analysis could be extended to nominals, proposing an account of genitive case-marking in which a null φ-complete determiner assigns genitive case to a case-unvalued goal which it c-commands: however, we also noted that comparative evidence from Italian gives us reason to suppose that Num is the head which case-marks and attracts genitive expressions; and we highlighted empirical problems posed by the assumption that genitive case assignment involves agreement between a functional head (like D or Num) and a possessor.

Workbook section

Exercise 9.1

Assuming the grammaticality judgments given below (which are mine and which may be slightly different from those of some speakers), discuss how the relevant sentences could be analysed within the **split** CP framework. Where clauses are bracketed, concern yourself only with the structure of the bracketed material.

1	He admitted [that students only rarely enjoy syntax]
2	He admitted [that only rarely do students enjoy syntax]
3	*He admitted [that only rarely students enjoy syntax]
4	He admitted [that syntax, students only rarely enjoy]
5	*He admitted [syntax, students only rarely enjoy]
6	*He admitted [that syntax do students only rarely enjoy]
7	He admitted [that syntax, only rarely do students enjoy]
8	*He admitted [that syntax do only rarely students enjoy]
9	*He admitted [that only rarely do syntax, students enjoy]
10	*He admitted [that only rarely, syntax do students enjoy]

11   *He admitted [that only rarely, syntax, students enjoy]
12   What kind of courses do students only rarely enjoy?
13   *What kind of courses do only rarely students enjoy?
14   Syntax is something [which only rarely do students enjoy]
15   What's the reason [why syntax, students only rarely enjoy?]
16   I don't understand [why only rarely do students enjoy syntax]

Consider the implications for your analysis of assuming that Fin can be syncretised with any head immediately above it (whether a Force head, a Focus head or a Topic head) if at least one of them is null, if both Fin and the other head have the same strength (e.g. both are weak, or both are strong), and if Fin projects no specifier of its own.

Helpful hints

To simplify discussion, concern yourself only with the structure of the left periphery of the relevant clauses – i.e. the Force/Topic/Focus/Finiteness projections above the TP layer. Assume that you have reached a stage of derivation at which a TP has been formed whose head is a null third-person-plural present-tense affix (*Tns*), which merges with the verbal projection *enjoy syntax* to form the T-bar *Tns enjoy syntax*, and that the adverbial adjunct *only rarely* is then adjoined to this T-bar to expand it into the larger T-bar *only rarely Tns enjoy syntax*, which is then merged with its subject *students* to form the TP *students only rarely Tns enjoy syntax*. In accordance with the DP hypothesis, assume that both *syntax* and *students* are DPs headed by a null determiner. In relation to 15–16, assume that *why* originates in the position where it ends up.

Model answer for sentence 1

Rizzi posits that CP splits into multiple projections in clauses which contain a preposed topic or focus constituent. Although *only rarely* seems to function as a preposed focused expression and *syntax* as a preposed topic in the relevant examples above, neither the main *admitted* clause nor the complement *enjoy* clause contains a preposed topic/focus constituent in 1; hence, neither contains a FocP or TopP projection. Since Rizzi posits that **force** and **finiteness** features are syncretised on a single head (traditionally labelled C) in clauses which do not involve focalisation/topicalisation, both clauses in 1 will be CPs, the main clause headed by a null complementiser, and the complement clause headed by *that*. However, since our concern here is with the structure of the bracketed *that* clause which serves as the complement of the verb *admitted*, we concentrate on how this is derived.

Assume (as in the *helpful hints*) that we have reached a stage of derivation where we have formed the TP *ø students only rarely Tns enjoy ø syntax* (where *ø* is a null determiner, and *Tns* is a third-person-plural present-tense affix). Because there is no intervening topic or focus projection, the relevant force and finiteness features are here syncretised onto a single C/complementiser head (which is therefore marked as being both declarative and finite), so forming the structure shown in highly simplified form in (i) below:

(i)   [CP [C that_DEC, FIN] [TP ø students only rarely [T *Tns*] enjoy syntax]]

The (third-person-plural present-tense) *Tns* affix will subsequently be lowered onto the adjacent verb ENJOY in the PF component, with the result that this is ultimately spelled out as the third-person-plural present-tense form *enjoy*. The complementiser introducing the clause in (i) can be spelled out either as *that* by virtue of carrying a declarative-force feature (in accordance with (26i) in the main text), or can be given a null spellout as *ø* by virtue of carrying a finiteness feature (in accordance with (26ii) in the main text). We therefore correctly predict that alongside sentence 1, we can also have a sentence like (ii) below, in which the bracketed complement clause contains a null complementiser:

(ii)   He admitted [ø students only rarely enjoy syntax]

Exercise 9.2

Discuss how the syntax of the following sentences could be analysed within the VP shell framework, giving arguments in support of your analysis:

1   They will increase *the price* to 30 dollars
2   Shall we sit *him* in the chair?
3   Will you climb *me* up there? (Child English)
4   This might make *him* angry
5   He will explain *the problem* fully to me
6   You must show *her* that she can trust *you*
7   Tourists may smuggle *drugs* illegally into the country
8   She will remind *him* to close the windows
9   *The horse* was jumped perfectly over the fence
10   You could ask *him* politely to keep quiet
11   *The prosecution* must prove to the jury beyond reasonable doubt that the defendant is guilty
12   *Some evidence* does appear to have emerged of corruption
13   *The police* were reported by the press to have arrested a suspect
14   There are said to be *several people* suspected of corruption
15   *Several politicians* are widely thought to be suspected of corruption
16   There are said to have been *several people* detained
17   There are *several people* said to have been detained
18   There does seem to me to remain *some unrest* in Utopia
19   I believe there sincerely to remain *some unrest* in Utopia
20   Can you prove *him* to us to have defrauded the company?

Comment in particular on the syntax of the italicised constituents, saying what position each one occupies, what case it receives and how. In addition, discuss how the *shell* analysis of nominals briefly sketched in §9.9 could handle the syntax of the following nominals:

21   the return of the president from Ohio
22   the president's return from Ohio
23   the unwillingness of the chairman to admit responsibility

24   the chairman's unwillingness to admit responsibility
25   the decision by the chairman to admit responsibility
26   the enemy's surrender of the city to the allies
27   the surrender of the city to the allies by the enemy
28   the city's surrender to the allies by the enemy
29   the judge's instruction to the jury to acquit the defendant
30   the withdrawal of troops from the occupied territories by the Israelis

In relation to the merger of verbs and nouns with their internal arguments, assume that internal arguments are canonically projected within VP/NP in the hierarchical order given by the Thematic Hierarchy below:

(i)   THEME > other internal arguments > AGENT *by*-phrase argument > clausal argument

where > = 'is projected higher up in the VP/NP structure than'. This means that the first internal argument to be merged with a verb (as its complement) will be the lowest one on the hierarchy, and the second to be merged (as its specifier) will be the second lowest – and so on.

Helpful hints

In 11, take *beyond reasonable doubt* to be a PP which functions as an adjunct, and don't concern yourself with its internal structure. (In relation to this sentence and others, you might want to consider the issue of whether the relevant structures provide us with evidence about whether adjuncts adjoin to intermediate or maximal projections.) In 11 and 12, take the *that*-clause to be a CP but don't concern yourself with its internal structure. In 21 and 24, assume that a THEME argument (like *the president* in 21 and 22) and an EXPERIENCER argument (like *the chairman* in 23 and 24) can be projected into the syntax either as a PP introduced (and assigned accusative case) by the transitive preposition *of*, or as a DP containing an unvalued case feature. In 23, 24, 25 and 29, take the infinitival clause *to admit responsibility/to acquit the defendant* to be a CP with a null complementiser and a null PRO subject, but don't concern yourself with the internal structure of the relevant CP. In structures like 27, 28 and 30, assume that where a noun has three internal arguments, *two* of them serve as specifiers to the same head (the one which is higher on the thematic hierarchy being positioned above the other), so that heads may have **multiple specifiers** (as suggested by Chomsky 1995).

Model answer for sentence 1

The verb *increase* can be used not only as a transitive verb in sentences such as 1 above, but also as an intransitive verb in sentences such as:

(ii)   The price will increase to 30 dollars

Accordingly, we can take *increase* to be an ergative predicate which has much the same syntax as the verb *roll* discussed in the main text. This would mean that 1 is derived as follows. The verb *increase* merges with its PP complement *to 30 dollars* to form the V-bar *increase to 30 dollars*; this V-bar in turn merges with the DP *the price* to form the VP (iii) below:

(iii)

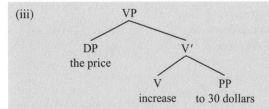

In accordance with the Thematic Hierarchy in (i), the THEME argument *the price* in (iii) occupies a higher position within the structure than the GOAL argument *to 30 dollars*. On Chomsky's account of ergative structures, the VP in (iii) subsequently merges with a causative light verb ø with an external AGENT argument (= *they*). The light verb is φ-complete and hence serves as a probe, identifying *the price* as an active goal (by virtue of its unvalued case feature), and assigning it accusative case in accordance with (92) in the main text. Because the light verb is affixal, the verb *increase* adjoins to it, so that at the end of the vP cycle we have the structure shown below:

(iv)

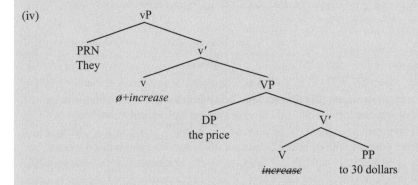

The vP in (iv) is then merged with a T constituent containing *will*, and this assigns nominative case to the subject *they* (since the two match in respect of their φ-features, albeit those of *will* are invisible). Since T has an [EPP] feature, it triggers raising of the subject *they* to spec-TP. Merging the resulting TP with a null declarative C forms the CP shown in simplified form below:

(v)   [CP [C ø] [TP **they** [T will] [vP ~~they~~ [v ø + *increase*] [VP the price [V ~~increase~~] to 30 dollars]]]]

An interesting question which is posed by the analysis sketched here is how we account for the position of the adverb *gradually* in a sentence such as:

(vi)   They will increase the price *gradually* to 30 dollars

An analysis along the lines of (iv) requires us to suppose that *gradually* is a V-bar adjunct which extends the V-bar *increase to 30 dollars* to the even larger V-bar *gradually increase to 30 dollars*. However, if we suppose that adjunction (like movement) cannot target intermediate projections and that adverbs canonically adjoin to maximal projections, we will then require a more complex analysis (like that proposed in Bowers 2002) on which transitive clauses have a tripartite vP+TrP+VP structure. On this alternative view, the VP in (iii) will merge with a Tr(ansitivity) head which is strong and so triggers movement of the verb *increase* from V to Tr. The Tr head agrees with and assigns accusative case to the DP *the price*, and its [EPP] feature triggers raising of *the price* to spec-TrP, so deriving the structure shown in simplified form below:

(vii)

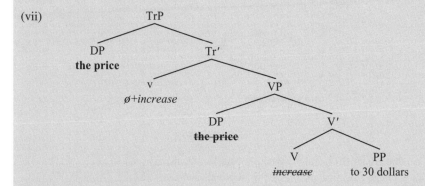

The resulting TrP is then merged with an agentive light verb whose subject is *they* and which (by virtue of being strong) triggers raising of the verb *increase* from Tr to v, so deriving the structure shown in skeletal form below:

(viii)   [vP they [v increase] [TrP the price [Tr ~~increase~~] [vP ~~the price~~ [v ~~increase~~] to 30 dollars]]]

The derivation will then proceed along the lines sketched earlier. Under the alternative TrP analysis sketched here, we could then say that the adverb *gradually* in (vi) is a VP-adjunct, and hence is adjoined to the VP in (vii) above.

Model answer for nominal 21

Return is an unaccusative noun with two arguments. In accordance with the Thematic Hierarchy (i), the SOURCE argument *from Ohio* (being lower on the hierarchy than the THEME argument *the president*) is the first argument to merge with the noun *return*, forming the N-bar *return from Ohio*. The resulting N-bar is then merged with the THEME argument *the president*. In the text and the helpful hints, we suggested that a THEME argument of a noun can (optionally) be introduced by the preposition *of*. If this happens here, the THEME argument will be projected into the syntax as the PP *of the president*, the case feature of *the president* being valued as accusative by the transitive preposition *of*. Merging *of the president* with the N-bar *from Ohio* will derive the NP shown in simplified form below:

(ix)

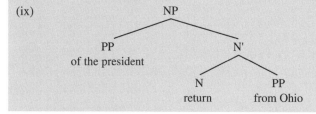

The resulting NP is then merged as the complement of a strong null light noun which triggers raising of the noun *return* from N to n. Merging the resulting nP with the determiner *the* will form the DP shown below:

(x)

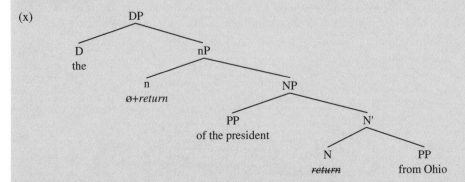

On the assumption that adjectives occupy a position between D and nP, such an analysis correctly predicts the position of the adjective *unexpected* in nominals such as:

(xi)   the *unexpected* return of the president from Ohio

10 Phases

10.1 Overview

In this chapter, we look at recent work by Chomsky suggesting that syntactic structure is built up in **phases** (with phases including CP and transitive vP). At the end of each phase, part of the syntactic structure already formed undergoes **transfer** to the phonological and semantic components, with the result that the relevant part of the structure is inaccessible to further syntactic operations from that point on. (An important point of detail to note is that since we are outlining Chomsky's ideas on phases here, we shall follow his assumptions about the structure of verb phrases and expletive structures.)

10.2 Phases

In §8.5, we outlined Chomsky's claim in recent work that all syntactic operations involve a relation between a **probe** P and a **local goal** G which is sufficiently 'close' to the probe (or, in the case of **multiple agreement**, a relation between a probe and more than one local goal). We noted Chomsky's (2001, p. 13) remark that 'the P, G relation must be local' in order 'to minimise search', because the Language Faculty can only hold a limited amount of structure in its 'active memory' (Chomsky 1999, p. 9). Accordingly, syntactic structures are built up one **phase** at a time. Chomsky suggests (1999, p. 9) that phases are 'propositional' in nature, and include CP and transitive vP (more specifically, vP with an external argument, which he denotes as v*P). His rationale for taking CP and v*P as phases is that CP represents a complete clausal complex (including a specification of force), and v*P represents a complete thematic (argument structure) complex (including an external argument).

Once all the operations which apply within a given phase have been completed, the **domain** of the phase (i.e. the complement of its head) becomes **impenetrable** to further syntactic operations. As we have already seen, Chomsky refers to this condition as the **Phase Impenetrability Condition/PIC** – and we can state it informally as follows (cf. Chomsky 2001, p. 5, ex. 6)

(1)   **Phase Impenetrability Condition/PIC**
The c-command domain of a phase head is impenetrable to an external probe (i.e. a goal which is c-commanded by the head of a phase is impenetrable to any probe c-commanding the phase)

The reason why the domain of the phase head is impenetrable to an external probe (according to Chomsky 2001, p. 5) is that once a complete phase has been formed, the domain of the phase undergoes a **transfer** operation by which the relevant (domain) structure is simultaneously sent to the phonological component to be assigned an appropriate phonetic representation, and to the semantic component to be assigned an appropriate semantic representation – and from that point on, the relevant domain is no longer accessible to the syntax. So, for example, once a complete CP phase has been formed, the TP which is the domain (i.e. complement) of the phase head C will be sent to the phonological and semantic components for processing. As a result, TP is no longer visible in the syntax, and hence neither TP itself nor any constituent of TP can subsequently serve as a goal for a higher probe of any kind: i.e. no probe c-commanding CP can enter into a relation with TP or any constituent of TP.

In order to make our discussion more concrete, consider the derivation of the following sentence:

(2)   Will Ruritania withdraw troops from Utopia?

Given Chomsky's vP+VP analysis of transitive verb phrases (which we shall adopt throughout here, setting aside Bowers's vP+TrP+VP analysis outlined in §9.8), (2) will be derived as follows. The verb *withdraw* merges with its complement *from Utopia* (with *Utopia* being a DP headed by a null determiner, given the DP hypothesis) and its specifier *troops* (which is a QP headed by a null partitive quantifier *ø*) to form the VP *ø troops withdraw from ø Utopia*. This is then merged with a causative light verb whose external AGENT argument is *Ruritania* (another DP headed by a null determiner): since the light verb is affixal, it triggers movement of the verb *withdraw* from its original (italicised) position in V to v, so deriving (3) below:

(3)

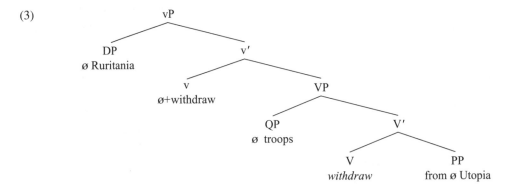

The light verb will agree with (and assign accusative case to) the QP ø troops. Since a transitive vP (i.e. a vP with an external argument) is a phase, and since the vP in (3) is transitive and has the external argument ø *Ruritania*, the VP constituent (by virtue of being the domain/complement of the light verb which is the head of the phase) will undergo **transfer** to the phonological and semantic components at this point, and thereafter cease to be accessible to further syntactic operations. Let's suppose that as part of the transfer operation, traces are marked as having a null spellout in the phonological component (this being indicated by ~~strikethrough~~), and that uninterpretable features which have been deleted by operation of agreement are removed from the structure handed over to the semantic component, but not from the structure handed over to the phonological component. Consequently, the phonological component will not spell out the trace of the verb *withdraw* in V, and only the constituents ø *troops* and *from Utopia* will be given an overt phonetic spellout.

The **syntactic computation** then proceeds once more, with [T *will*] being merged with the vP in (3) to form the T-bar shown below (*outline* font being used to indicate those parts of the structure which received an overt or null spellout in the phonological component after the VP underwent transfer at the end of the vP phase, and ~~strikethrough~~ marking traces receiving a null spellout):

(4)

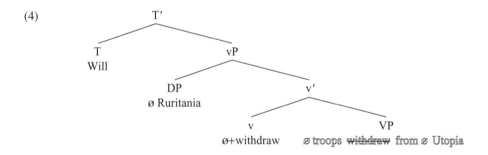

Since [T *will*] has uninterpretable (and unvalued) person/number features, it is an active probe which searches for a local goal to value and delete its unvalued features. Neither ø *troops* nor ø *Utopia* are accessible to the probe *will* (since both are contained within a VP which has already been transferred to the phonological and semantic components); however, the DP ø *Ruritania* is accessible to *will* and is syntactically active by virtue of its uninterpretable case feature. Hence, *will* agrees (invisibly) with and assigns (invisible) nominative case to the DP ø *Ruritania*. The auxiliary [T *will*] also has an [EPP] feature requiring movement of the closest matching goal to spec-TP; accordingly, the DP ø *Ruritania* is moved from its original (italicised) position in spec-vP to become the specifier of *will*, so deriving the structure:

(5)

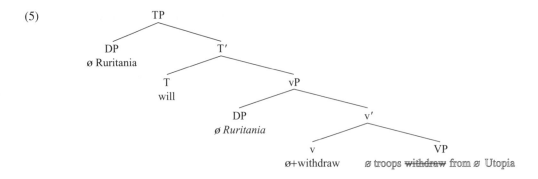

The resulting TP is merged with a null interrogative C. Let's suppose (as we did in §6.8) that yes–no questions contain a null yes–no question operator in spec-CP (e.g. a null counterpart of the adverb *whether*), and that C is strong/affixal and attracts *will* to move from its original (italicised) position in T to adjoin to the null C heading CP. If so, at the end of the CP cycle we will have the structure (6) below:

(6)

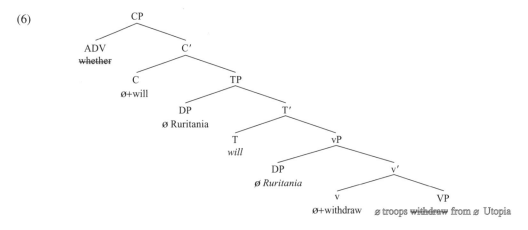

Since CP is a phase and the domain of the head of a phase is spelled out at the end of a phase, TP undergoes **transfer** to the phonological and semantic components at this point. The transfer operation results in the italicised traces of *will* and *ø Ruritania* receiving a null spellout in the phonological component.

   However, we are now left with something of a problem. We have come to the end of the derivation, but so far neither C nor the null yes–no question operator which serves as its specifier have been 'handed over' to the phonological and semantic components for further processing. In order to ensure that this happens, let's make the additional assumption in (7ii) below about transfer:

(7)   **Transfer**
   (i) At the end of each phase, the domain (i.e. complement of the phase head) undergoes *transfer*
   (ii) At the end of the overall derivation, all remaining constituents undergo transfer

In the case of (6), the two remaining constituents which have not yet undergone **transfer** are those at the **edge** of CP (the **edge** of a projection comprising its head and any specifiers/adjuncts it has) – i.e. the C-constituent containing *will* and the null yes–no question operator in spec-CP. Accordingly, these undergo transfer to the phonological/semantic components at the end of the overall derivation.

10.3   Intransitive and defective clauses

Our illustrative account of **phases** in the previous section involved a structure containing a transitive vP phase and a CP phase. However, since neither intransitive clauses (i.e. those containing a vP with no external argument) nor defective clauses (i.e. clauses which are TPs lacking a CP projection) are phases, things work differently in such structures – as we can illustrate in relation to the derivation of:

(8)   There are thought by some to remain numerous problems in Utopia

The unaccusative verb *remain* merges with its LOCATIVE complement *in ø Utopia* (*Utopia* being a DP headed by a null determiner) to form the V-bar *remain in ø Utopia*, and this V-bar is in turn merged with its THEME argument (the quantifier phrase *numerous problems*) to form the VP *numerous problems remain in ø Utopia*. This VP in turn is merged with a null light verb which, being affixal, triggers movement of the verb *remain* from its italicised position in V to adjoin to the light verb, so deriving:

(9)

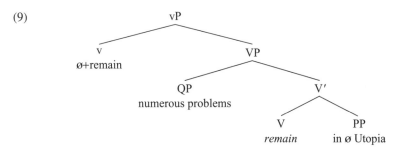

Although a transitive vP is a phase (and requires its domain to be spelled out), the vP in (9) is intransitive because it has no external argument (i.e. vP has no specifier). Hence, its VP complement does not undergo transfer at this point, and the syntactic derivation proceeds by merging the resulting vP with infinitival *to*. If (as Chomsky 2001, fn. 56 argues) infinitival *to* has an [EPP] feature and a person feature in defective clauses, it follows that *to* must project a specifier with person properties. In keeping with Chomsky's own assumptions about expletive *there* being directly generated in spec-TP and preference of Merge over Move, let's suppose that this requirement is satisfied by merging expletive *there* in spec-TP, so deriving:

(10)

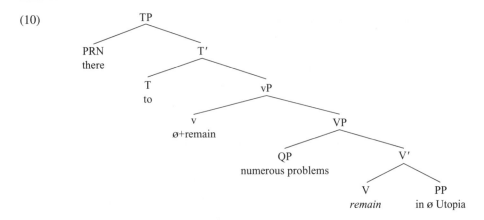

The TP in (10) is then merged as the complement of the passive participle *thought*, forming a V-bar constituent which is in turn merged with the AGENT *by*-phrase *by some* to form a VP. Given our assumption in the previous chapter that all verb phrases have a complex shell structure, the resulting VP will in turn be merged as the complement of a light verb (arguably one which is participial in nature, so accounting for why the verb is eventually spelled out in the passive-participle form *thought*, and why Chomsky 1999 uses the label PRT to denote the relevant participial head): since light verbs are affixal in nature, this means that the verb *thought* will raise to adjoin to the light verb. Merging the resulting vP with the passive auxiliary BE will derive the T-bar constituent shown below:

(11)

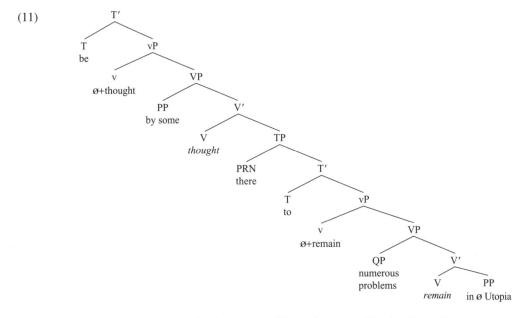

At this point, BE is an active probe by virtue of its uninterpretable (and unvalued) φ-features, and so it searches for an accessible active goal to value its person/number features. There are two such goals within the structure in (11), namely the third-person-expletive pronoun *there* (active by virtue of its uninterpretable person feature) and the third-person-plural QP *numerous problems* (active by virtue of its uninterpretable and unvalued case feature). Both *there* and *numerous problems* are accessible goals for BE since neither is contained within a structure which has undergone transfer. Chomsky (2001) suggests that a probe P locates every active matching goal G within its search space (i.e. within that part of the syntactic structure which is accessible to the probe by virtue of not yet having undergone transfer), and that where there is more than one such goal, the probe simultaneously agrees with all the relevant goals at the same time: cf. his (2001, p.13) remark that 'P can find any matching goal in the phase PH that it heads, simultaneously deleting uninterpretable features.' (We can assume that the pronoun *some* is not active at this point, because it falls within the domain of a closer probe *by* which will already have valued its case feature as accusative.) What this means is that since BE has uninterpretable person and number features, it will locate every active goal within its search space which has a person and/or number feature. Since *there* has a third-person feature which is uninterpretable (making it active), *there* is one such goal; likewise, *numerous problems* is another active goal, since it has third-person and plural-number features and is active by virtue of its uninterpretable case feature. Accordingly, BE simultaneously agrees in person with *there* and *numerous problems*, and in number with *numerous problems*, so that BE is assigned the values [third-person, plural-number]. Since *numerous problems* is φ-complete, it can delete the uninterpretable person/number features of BE. Conversely, BE (by virtue of being finite) can value the unvalued case feature of *numerous problems* as nominative, and (because BE is also φ-complete) can delete the relevant case feature (and also the person feature of *there*). The [EPP] feature of T is deleted by moving the closest active goal (i.e. *there*) from its original position as the specifier of *to* (italicised below) to become the specifier of BE. Merging the resulting TP with a null declarative complementiser derives the CP structure shown in simplified form in (12) below:

(12)

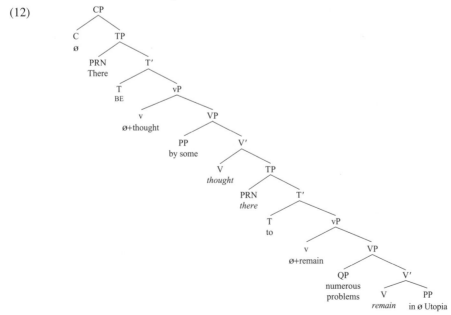

Since CP is a phase, the TP headed by [T BE] which constitutes its domain will undergo transfer at this point, in accordance with (7i). The italicised traces of moved constituents will be given a null spellout, and the auxiliary BE in T will be spelled out as *are* in the phonological component (since it has been valued as third person plural in the course of the derivation). The null C heading CP subsequently undergoes transfer by (7ii), and is assigned a null spellout in the phonological component, and interpreted in the semantic component as marking the relevant sentence as declarative in force.

In the context of our discussion of phases here, the key point which emerges is that neither an intransitive vP nor a defective TP clause constitutes a phase – e.g. in the case of (12), not the intransitive vP containing *remain*, or the vP containing the passive participle *thought*, or the defective TP complement of *thought*. In consequence, the relevant vP and TP constituents are still accessible in the syntax at the point where BE is introduced into the derivation, so allowing BE to agree with *numerous problems*.

10.4   Wh-movement through spec-CP

The phase-based theory of syntax outlined above has far-reaching consequences for the operation of A-bar movement operations like wh-movement – as we can illustrate in relation to the following sentence:

(13)   Where is it thought that he will go?

The derivation of (13) proceeds as follows. The unaccusative verb *go* is merged with its GOAL argument (the locative adverbial pronoun *where*) to form the V-bar *go where*, which in turn is merged with its THEME argument *he* to form the VP *he go where*. This in turn is merged with a null affixal light verb which triggers raising of the verb *go* to v from its original (italicised) position in V, so forming:

(14)

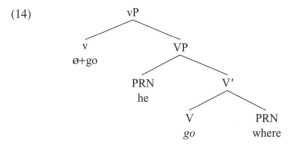

Since vP is intransitive (by virtue of the fact that the light verb has no external argument), vP is not a phase, and Transfer cannot apply at this point. The syntactic computation therefore continues, with [T *will*] merging with the vP in (14). *Will* agrees with (and assigns nominative case to) *he*, and the [EPP] feature of *will* triggers raising of *he* from its original position (italicised below) in spec-VP to spec-TP. Merging the complementiser *that* with the resulting TP forms the CP shown in (15) below:

(15)

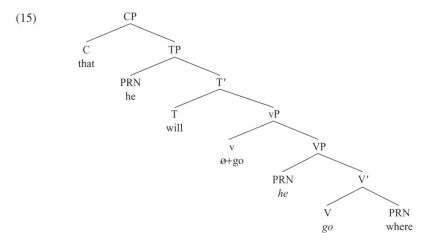

Since CP is a phase, its domain (i.e. its TP complement) will undergo transfer at this point. This means that neither TP nor any of the constituents of TP will subsequently be accessible to further syntactic operations – i.e. in effect, TP and its constituents are **frozen** in place once TP undergoes transfer.

However, this causes an obvious problem, since if all constituents of TP are frozen in place at this point, the wh-word *where* will be unable to move from the (sentence-final) VP-complement position it occupies in (15) to the (sentence-initial) main-clause CP-specifier position which it clearly needs to occupy in (13) *Where is it thought that he will go?* One way to overcome this problem is to assume that (as suggested in §8.9) wh-movement applies in a **successive-cyclic** fashion, and that the complementiser *that* in structures like (15) has an [EPP] feature and a [WH] feature which together trigger movement of the closest wh-expression (= *where*) to become the specifier of the complement-clause CP headed by *that* before *where* subsequently moves on to become the specifier of the main clause C constituent containing the inverted auxiliary *is*. If this is so, at the stage of derivation represented in (15) above, *where* will move from the italicised position shown in (16) below to become the specifier of *that*:

(16)

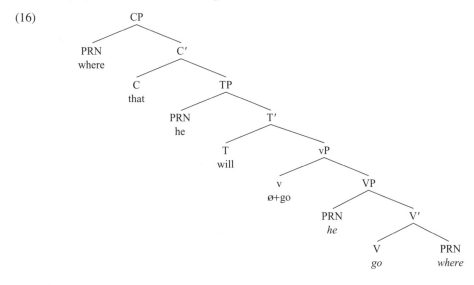

At this point (once all the operations which apply on the CP-cycle have applied) the domain of C (i.e. its TP complement) will undergo transfer in accordance with (7i), because CP is a phase: one consequence of this is that the italicised traces will be marked as receiving a null spellout in the phonological component.

After transfer of TP is completed, the syntactic computation continues. The CP in (16) is merged as the complement of the verb THINK, and the resulting VP is in turn merged as the complement of a participial light verb (ensuring that THINK is eventually spelled out as the passive participle *thought*), with the verb THINK (below shown as *thought*) raising to adjoin to the light verb. The resulting vP is in turn merged as the complement of [T BE], which has an [EPP] feature that is deleted by merger of expletive *it* in spec-TP (*it* in turn serving as a probe valuing the agreement features of BE). Merging the resulting TP with a null affixal C will trigger raising of BE from its original (italicised) position in T to C; since C also has a wh-attracting [EPP] feature, it will trigger movement of *where* from the italicised spec-CP position in the complement clause into spec-CP position in the main clause, so deriving the CP shown in simplified form in (17) below:

(17)

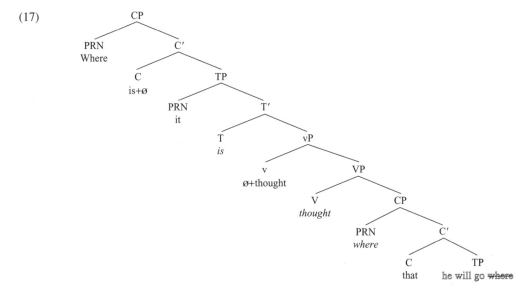

Since CP is a phase, its domain (= the main-clause TP) will undergo transfer by (7i) at this point, so that the italicised traces of *is, thought* and *where* will receive a null spellout in the phonological component. Subsequently, the constituents *where* and *is+ø* on the edge of the root CP undergo transfer by (7ii).

What our discussion here tells us is that just as A-movement applies in a successive-cyclic fashion (each time moving the relevant nominal into the next highest spec-TP position in the structure), so too (within a phase-based theory of syntax) A-bar movement operations like wh-movement must apply in a successive-cyclic fashion: this means that each time a new phase head is introduced into the structure, it will serve as a probe which attracts the closest wh-goal to move into its specifier position.

10.5　Wh-movement through spec-vP in transitive clauses

　　　　Our discussion in the previous section showed that the assumption that CPs are phases means that long-distance wh-movement requires successive-cyclic movement of a moved wh-expression through intermediate spec-CP positions. However, since transitive vPs are also phases, it follows that in structures containing one or more *transitive* vPs, wh-movement will have to pass through intermediate spec-vP positions as well (since transitive vPs are phases). We can illustrate how this works in terms of the following example:

(18)　　　What have they done?

(18) will be derived as follows. The verb DO (shown here in its spellout form *done*) merges with its thematic complement *what* to form the VP *done what*. This is merged with a transitive light verb whose external argument is *they* and which (by virtue of being affixal) triggers raising of *done* from V to v; the light verb (by virtue of being transitive) also values the case feature of *what* as accusative and (by virtue of being φ-complete) deletes it. Let's suppose that just as C can have an [EPP] feature attracting movement of a wh-expression, so too a transitive light-verb (perhaps by virtue of being a phase head, like C) can likewise have a wh-attracting [EPP] feature. This being so, *what* will be moved to become a second specifier for vP, forming the structure below:

(19)

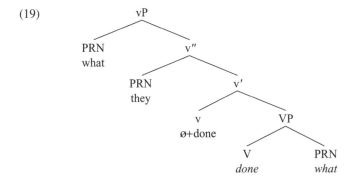

The notational convention assumed in (19) is that first merge of a head H with its complement forms an H-bar/H′ projection; second merge of H with a specifier forms an H-double-bar/H″ projection; third merge of H with another specifier forms an H-treble-bar/H‴ projection . . . and so on. However, by tradition, the maximal projection of H is denoted as HP: hence, the node labelled vP in (19) is a v-treble-bar projection, but is labelled vP because it is the maximal projection of the relevant light verb.

The double-specifier analysis in (19) is in accordance with Chomsky's (1998, p.16) assumption that a head can have **multiple specifiers** – in the case of (19), an inner specifier *they* representing the external argument of the light verb, and an outer specifier *what* which deletes the [EPP] feature of the light verb. In accordance with (7i), the VP in (19) will undergo transfer at the end of the vP phase, and the two italicised traces will thereby be given a null spellout. Of course, if *what* had not moved to spec-vP at this point, it would have been spelled out **in situ** and hence frozen in place, and thereby wrongly be predicted to be unable to undergo wh-movement. (Although we adopt Chomsky's multiple-specifier analysis here, it should be noted that one way of avoiding multiple specifiers would be to assume that light verbs are A-heads like T and hence only allow an argument as their specifier, and that *what* doesn't move to become a second specifier of vP, but rather moves to become the specifier of a separate A-bar head above vP – perhaps becoming the specifier of a **Focus** head. Note that in the terminology of Roberts 1994, a head like T which allows only an argument as its specifier is an **A-head**, and a head like C which allows either an argument or an adjunct as its specifier is an **A-bar head**.)

Since a transitive vP is a phase, the VP domain *done what* in (19) will undergo transfer at the end of the vP cycle, and the trace copies of the moved constituents *done* and *what* will each receive a null spellout. The derivation then proceeds by merging [T *have*] with the vP in (19), forming the T-bar (20) below:

(20)

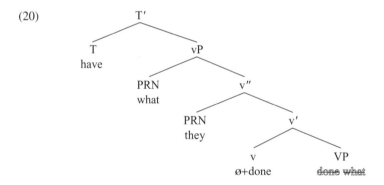

The probe *have* now searches for an appropriate goal. It needs to 'skip over' *what* and instead identify *they* as the expression that it agrees with, assigns nominative case to and attracts to move to spec-TP. Clearly we cannot say that *what* is inactive as a goal since it needs to be an active goal in order to be able to undergo subsequent wh-movement. However, it seems reasonable to suppose that *what* is active only for agreement with an A-bar head, not for agreement with an A-head. More specifically, we can suppose that a noun or pronoun expression which carries interpretable person/number/gender features is only active for agreement with an A-head if it has an unvalued and undeleted case feature: this would mean that *what* is ineligible for A-agreement because its case feature was valued as accusative and deleted by the transitive light verb at the earlier stage of derivation shown in (19) above. By contrast, since *they* in (20) has an unvalued case feature, it is active for A-agreement and A-movement (but not for A-bar movement). Accordingly, *have* agrees with, assigns nominative case to and triggers movement of the subject *they*, so deriving:

(21)

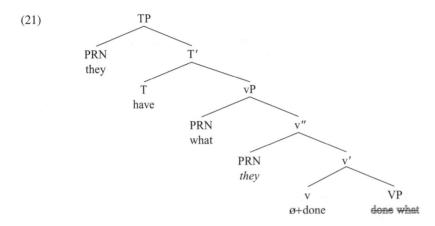

This TP is then merged with a null complementiser with a strong tense feature (triggering movement of *have* from T to C) and an [EPP] feature which triggers movement of *what* to spec-CP, so deriving:

(22)

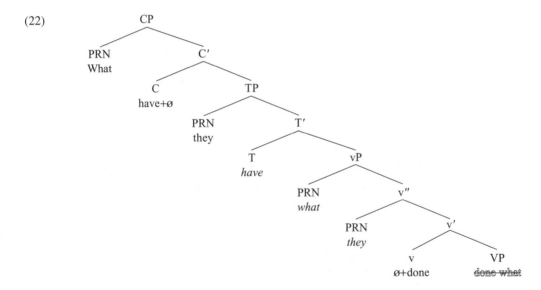

At the end of the CP phase, TP undergoes transfer in accordance with (7i) and the italicised traces are given a null spellout in the phonological component. Subsequently, the constituents at the edge of CP (i.e. its specifier *what* and its head *have+ø*) undergo transfer in accordance with (7ii).

Our discussion of the derivation of (18) *What have they done?* shows us that in transitive clauses A-bar movement will involve movement through spec-vP into spec-CP. An obvious implication of this is that wh-sentences like (23) below which contain two transitive clauses:

(23)   What might she think that they will do?

will correspondingly involve successive-cyclic wh-movement through two spec-vP positions (and likewise through two spec-CP positions) – as shown in skeletal form below:

(24)   [$_{CP}$ **What** [$_C$ might] she [$_{vP}$ ~~what~~ think [$_{CP}$ ~~what~~ [$_C$ that] they will [$_{vP}$ ~~what~~ do ~~what~~]]]]

More generally, a sentence containing *n* transitive verbs and *m* CPs intervening between the initial position of a wh-expression and its ultimate landing site will involve movement through *n* spec-vP positions and *m* spec-CP positions.

10.6   Evidence for successive-cyclic wh-movement through spec-CP

The discussion in the previous section shows how (in a phase-based theory of syntax in which CPs and transitive vPs are phases) theoretical considerations force successive-cyclic wh-movement through spec-CP and spec-vP. However, an interesting question which arises is whether there is any empirical evidence in support of the successive-cyclic analysis. As we shall see, there is in fact considerable evidence in support of such an analysis. In this section, we look at evidence in support of successive-cyclic movement through spec-CP; and in the next section, we examine evidence of successive-cyclic movement through spec-vP.

Let's begin by looking at evidence from English. Part of the evidence comes from the interpretation of reflexive anaphors like *himself*. As we saw in exercise 3.2, these are subject to Principle A of Binding Theory which requires an anaphor to be locally bound and hence to have an antecedent within the TP most immediately containing it. This requirement can be illustrated by the contrast in (25) below:

(25) (a)   *Jim was surprised that [$_{TP}$ Peter wasn't sure [$_{CP}$ that [**$_{TP}$** Mary liked this picture of himself best]]]

    (b)   Jim was surprised that [$_{TP}$ Peter wasn't sure [$_{CP}$ which picture of himself [**$_{TP}$** Mary liked best]]]

In (25a), the TP most immediately containing the reflexive anaphor *himself* is the bold-printed TP whose subject is *Mary*, and since there is no suitable (third-person-masculine-singular) antecedent for *himself* within this TP, the resulting sentence violates Binding Principle A and so is ill-formed. However, in (25b) the wh-phrase *which picture of himself* has been moved to the specifier position within the bracketed CP, and the TP most immediately containing the reflexive anaphor is the italicised TP whose subject is *Peter*. Since this italicised TP does indeed contain a c-commanding antecedent for *himself* (namely its subject *Peter*), there is no violation of Principle A if *himself* is construed as bound by *Peter* – though Principle A prevents *Jim* from being the antecedent of *himself*.

In the light of this restriction, consider the following sentence:

(26)   Which picture of himself wasn't he sure that Mary liked best?

In (26), the antecedent of *himself* is *he* – and yet *himself* is clearly not c-commanded by *he*, as we see from (27) below (simplified, and showing only overt constituents):

(27)

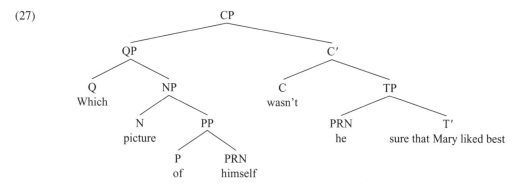

In fact, the only elements c-commanded by the pronoun *he* in (27) are T-bar and its constituents. But if *he* does not c-command *himself* in (27), how come *he* is interpreted as the antecedent of *himself* when we would have expected such a structure to violate Principle A of Binding Theory and hence to be ill-formed?

We can provide a principled answer to this question if we suppose that wh-movement operates in a successive-cyclic fashion, and involves an intermediate stage of derivation represented in (28) below (simplified by showing overt constituents only):

(28)   [*TP* He wasn't sure [*CP* which picture of himself that [*TP* Mary liked best]]]

(Note that (28) is an intermediate stage of derivation, not a complete sentence structure; if it were a sentence, in relevant varieties it would violate the **Multiply Filled Comp Filter** discussed in §6.11.) In (28), the anaphor *himself* has a c-commanding antecedent within the italicised TP most immediately containing it – namely the pronoun *he*. If we follow Belletti and Rizzi (1988), Uriagereka (1988) and Lebeaux (1991) in supposing that the requirements of Principle A can be satisfied at any stage of derivation, it follows that positing that a sentence like (26) involves an intermediate stage of derivation like (28) enables us to account for why *himself* is construed as bound by *he*. More generally, sentences like (26) provide us with evidence that long-distance wh-movement involves successive cyclic movement through intermediate spec-CP positions – and hence with evidence that CP is a phase. (See Fox 2000 and Barss 2001 for more detailed discussion of related structures.) At a subsequent stage of derivation, the wh-QP *which picture of himself* moves into spec-CP in the main clause, so deriving the structure (27) associated with (26) *Which picture of himself wasn't he sure that Mary liked best?*

A further argument for successive-cyclic wh-movement through spec-CP (and consequently for the phasehood of CP) is offered by McCloskey (2000), based on observations about **quantifier stranding/floating** in West Ulster English. As we saw in §7.6, in this variety, a wh-word can be modified by the universal quantifier *all*, giving rise to questions such as:

(29)   *What all* did you get for Christmas? (= 'What are all the things which you got for Christmas?')

McCloskey argues that in such sentences, the quantifier and the wh-word originate as a single constituent. He further maintains that under wh-movement, the wh-word *what* can either pied-pipe the quantifier *all* along with it as in (29) above, or can move on its own leaving the quantifier *all* stranded. In this connection, consider the sentences in (30) below:

(30) (a)   *What all* do you think that he'll say that we should buy?
     (b)   *What* do you think *all* that he'll say that we should buy?
     (c)   *What* do you think that he'll say *all* that we should buy?
     (d)   *What* do you think that he'll say that we should buy *all*?

McCloskey claims (2000, p. 63) that '*All* in wh-quantifier float constructions appears in positions for which there is considerable independent evidence that they are either positions in which wh-movement originates or positions through which wh-movement passes. We have in these observations a new kind of argument for the successive-cyclic character of long wh-movement.'

McCloskey argues that the derivation of (30a–d) proceeds along the following lines (simplified in a number of ways). The quantifier *all* merges with its complement *what* to form the structure [*all what*]. The wh-word *what* then raises to become the specifier of *all*, forming the overt QP [*what all*]. (An incidental detail to note here is that this part of McCloskey's analysis violates the **Remerger Constraint** which we posited in §6.5 to the effect that 'No constituent can be merged more than once with the same head.' One way of getting round this is to suppose that *what* moves to a spec-DP position above QP, rather than to spec-QP. However, we shall ignore this detail in what follows.) The resulting QP [*what all*] is merged as the object of *buy*, forming [*buy what all*]. If *what* undergoes wh-movement on its own in subsequent stages of derivation, we derive (30d) '*What* do you think that he'll say that we should buy *all*?' But suppose that the quantifier *all* is pied-piped along with *what* under wh-movement until we reach the stage shown in skeletal form below:

(31)   [CP *what all* [C that] we should buy]

If wh-movement then extracts *what* on its own, the quantifier *all* will be stranded in the most deeply embedded spec-CP position, so deriving (30c) '*What* do you think that he'll say *all* that we should buy?' By contrast, if *all* is pied-piped along with *what* until the end of the intermediate CP cycle, we derive:

(32)   [cp *what all* [c that] he'll say that we should buy]

If wh-movement then extracts *what* on its own, the quantifier *all* will be stranded in the intermediate spec-CP position and we will ultimately derive (30b) '*What* do you think *all* that he'll say that we should buy?' But if *all* continues to be pied-piped along with *what* throughout the remaining stages of derivation, we ultimately derive (30a) '*What all* do you think that he'll say that we should buy?'

There is also considerable empirical evidence in support of successive-cyclic movement through spec-CP from a number of other languages. One such piece of evidence comes from preposition **pied-piping** in Afrikaans. Du Plessis (1977, p. 724) notes that in structures containing a wh-pronoun used as the complement of a preposition in Afrikaans, a moved wh-pronoun can either **pied-pipe** (i.e. carry along with it) or **strand** (i.e. leave behind) the preposition – as the following sentences illustrate:

(33) (a)   *Waarvoor* dink julle [werk ons]?
            What-for think you   work we?
            'What do you think we are working for?'

    (b)   *Waar* dink julle [werk ons *voor*]?
            What think you   work we for? (same interpretation as 33a)

    (c)   *Waar* dink julle [*voor* werk ons]?
            What think you   for   work we? (same interpretation as 33a)

Du Plessis argues that sentences such as (33c) involve movement of the PP *waarvoor* 'what-for' to spec-CP position within the bracketed complement clause, followed by movement of *waar* 'what' on its own into the main-clause spec-CP position, thereby stranding the preposition in the intermediate spec-CP position. On this view, sentences like (33c) provide empirical evidence that long-distance wh-movement involves movement through intermediate spec-CP positions.

A rather different kind of argument for successive-cyclic wh-movement comes from the phenomenon of **wh-copying**. A number of languages exhibit a form of long-distance wh-movement which involves leaving an overt copy of a moved wh-pronoun in intermediate spec-CP positions – as illustrated by the following structures cited in Felser (2001):

(34) (a)   *Wêr*   tinke jo *wêr*'t   Jan wennet
            Where think you where'that Jan lives?
            'Where do you think that John lives?'   (FRISIAN, Hiemstra 1986, p. 99)

    (b)   *Waarvoor* dink julle *waarvoor* werk ons?
            What-for think you what-for work we?
            'What do you think we are working for?'
                                                (AFRIKAANS, du Plessis 1977, p. 725)

(c)   *Kas*   o Demiri mislenola *kas* i   Arìfa dikhla?
       Whom   Demir think   whom Arifa saw?
       'Whom does Demir think Arifa saw?'

       (ROMANI, adapted from McDaniel 1989, p. 569, fn.5)

(d)   *Wer* glaubst du, *wer* dass du   bist?
       Who think   you who that you are?
       'Who do you think that you are?'

       (GERMAN, Fanselow and Mahajan 2000, p. 220)

In cases of long-distance wh-movement out of more than one complement clause, a copy of a moved wh-pronoun appears at the beginning of each clause – as illustrated by (35) below:

(35)   *Wen* glaubst du, *wen* Peter meint, *wen* Susi heiratet?
           Who believe you who Peter thinks who Susi marries?
           'Who do you believe Peter thinks that Susi is marrying?'

           (GERMAN, Felser 2001, p. 13)

The wh-copies left behind at intermediate landing sites in sentences such as (34) and (35) suggest that long-distance wh-movement involves movement of the wh-expression through intermediate spec-CP positions – precisely as a phase-based theory of syntax would lead us to expect. (See Nunes 2001 for further discussion.)

A parallel wh-copying phenomenon is reported in an intriguing study of the acquisition of wh-questions by Ros Thornton (1995). She reports children producing long-distance wh-copy questions such as the following (1995, p. 147):

(36) (a)   **What** do you think [*what* Cookie Monster eats]?
     (b)   **Who** do you think [*who* the cat chased]?
     (c)   **How** do you think [*how* Superman fixed the car]?

In such cases, the bold-printed wh-word moves to the front of the overall sentence, but leaves an italicised copy at the front of the bracketed complement clause. What this suggests is that wh-movement involves an intermediate step by which the wh-expression moves to spec-CP position within the bracketed complement clause before moving into its final landing site in the main-clause spec-CP position. The error made by the children lies in not deleting the italicised medial trace of the wh-word. Of course, this raises the question of *why* the children don't delete the intermediate wh-word. One answer may be that the null complementiser heading the bracketed complement clause is treated by the children as being a clitic which attaches to the end of its specifier (just as *have* cliticises to its specifier in *Who've they arrested?*). Leaving an overt wh-copy of the pronoun behind provides a host for the clitic wh-complementiser to attach to. Such an analysis seems by no means implausible in the light of the observation made by Guasti, Thornton and Wexler (1995) that young children produce **auxiliary-copying** negative questions such as the following (the names of the children and their ages in years;months being shown in parentheses):

(37) (a)   What *did* he *did***n't** wanna bring to school? (Darrell 4;1)

    (b)   Why *could* Snoopy *could***n't** fit in the boat? (Kathy 4;0)

If we assume that contracted negative *n't* is treated by the children as a PF enclitic (i.e. a clitic which attaches to the end of an immediately preceding auxiliary host in the PF component), we can conclude that the children spell out the trace of the inverted auxiliary *did* in order to provide a host for the enclitic negative *n't*. More generally, data like (37) suggest that children may overtly spell out traces as a way of providing a host for a clitic.

A related phenomenon is reported by Alison Henry in her (1995) study of Belfast English. She notes that in main-clause wh-questions in Belfast English, not only the main-clause C but also intermediate C constituents show T-to-C movement (i.e. auxiliary inversion), as illustrated below:

(38)   What *did* Mary claim [*did* they steal]? (Henry 1995, p.108)

We can account for auxiliary inversion in structures like (38) in a straightforward fashion if we suppose that (in main and complement clauses alike in Belfast English) a C which attracts an interrogative wh-expression also carries an affixal [TNS] feature triggering auxiliary inversion. In order to explain auxiliary inversion in the bracketed complement clause in (38), we would then have to suppose that the head C of CP carries [WH, EPP] features which trigger movement of the interrogative pronoun *what* through spec-CP, given our assumption that C has an affixal [TNS] feature triggering auxiliary inversion in clauses in which C attracts an interrogative wh-expression. On this view, the fact that the complement clause shows auxiliary inversion provides evidence that the preposed wh-word *what* moves through the spec-CP position in the bracketed complement clause before subsequently moving into the main-clause spec-CP position.

Returning now to wh-questions produced by young children, it is interesting to note that a further type of structure which Ros Thornton (1995) reports one of the children in her study (= AJ) producing are wh-questions like (39) below:

(39) (a)   Which mouse *what* the cat didn't see?

    (b)   Which drink do you think [*what* the ghost drank]?

Here, the italicised C positions are filled by *what* – raising the question of why this should be. Thornton notes that a number of the children in her study also produced questions like:

(40)   Which juice *that* the ghost could drink?

This suggests that *what* in structures such as (39) is a wh-marked variant of *that*. More specifically, it suggests that (for children like AJ) the complementiser *that* is spelled out as *what* when it carries [WH, EPP] features and attracts a wh-marked goal to move to spec-CP.

In the light of this assumption, let's now look at how wh-movement applies in the derivation of (39b). Since the bracketed complement clause is transitive in

(39b) and a transitive vP is a phase, the wh-phrase *which drink* will move to spec-vP on the embedded clause vP cycle. Thus, at the stage when the complementiser *that* enters the derivation, we will have the overt structure below (a structure which is simplified by omitting all null constituents, including traces):

(41)   [c that$_{WH, EPP}$] the ghost [vP *which drink* drank]

The complementiser *that* has [WH, EPP] features and consequently attracts *which drink* to move to spec-CP, so deriving the overt structure shown in simplified form below:

(42)   [cP *which drink* [c that$_{WH, EPP}$] the ghost [vP drank]]

On the assumption that children like AJ spell out *that* as *what* when it carries the features [WH, EPP], the complementiser *that* will ultimately be spelled out as *what*. (By contrast, in standard varieties of adult English, the complementiser is always spelled out as *that*, irrespective of whether it is wh-marked or not.)

The next stage in the movement of the wh-phrase takes place on the main-clause vP phase, when *which drink* moves to spec-vP. At the point where the null complementiser heading the main clause is introduced into the derivation, we will have the following skeletal structure (with AFF denoting a tense affix, and the structure simplified by not showing trace copies or empty categories other than the main-clause C and T):

(43)   [c ø] you [T AFF] [vP *which drink* think [cP [c what] the ghost [vP drank]]]

The null main-clause complementiser has a strong [TNS] feature which triggers raising of the tense affix to C. It also has [WH, EPP] features which trigger movement of *which drink* to spec-CP, so deriving (44) below (with DO-support providing a host for the tense affix in the PF component):

(44)   [cP Which drink [c do+AFF+ø] you [vP think [cP [c what] the ghost [vP drank]]]]

On this view, the fact that the complementiser *that* is spelled out as *what* in (39b) provides evidence that wh-movement passes through the intermediate spec-CP position.

A more general conclusion which can be drawn from our discussion of (39) is that wh-marking of a complementiser provides us with evidence that the relevant complementiser triggers wh-movement (and indeed it may be that *what* in non-standard comparatives like *Yours is bigger than what mine is* has the status of a complementiser which triggers wh-movement of a null wh-operator). In this connection, it is interesting to note that McCloskey (2001) argues that long-distance wh-movement in Irish triggers wh-marking of intermediate complementisers. The complementiser which normally introduces finite clauses in Irish is *go* 'that', but in (relative and interrogative) clauses involving wh-movement we find the wh-marked complementiser *aL* (below glossed as *what*) – as the following long-distance wh-question shows:

(45)   Cén   t-úrscéal *aL*   mheas   mé *aL*   dúirt sé *aL*   thuig   sé?
        Which novel   *what* thought I   *what* said he *what* understood he?
        'Which novel did I think that he said that he understood?'

(Note that the word order in (45) is wh-word+complementiser+verb+ subject+complement.) McCloskey argues that the wh-marking of each of the italicised complementisers in (45) provides evidence that wh-movement applies in a successive-cyclic fashion, with each successive C which is introduced into the derivation having [WH, EPP] features which trigger wh-marking of C and wh-movement of the relevant wh-expression. Chung (1994) provides parallel evidence from wh-marking of intermediate heads in Chamorro. The work of McCloskey and Chung provides further evidence that a complementiser is only wh-marked if it carries both a [WH] feature and an [EPP] feature.

Overall, then, we see that there is a considerable body of empirical evidence which supports the hypothesis that long-distance wh-movement is successive-cyclic in nature and involves movement through intermediate spec-CP positions. Additional syntactic evidence comes from partial wh-movement in a variety of languages (see e.g. Cole 1982, Saddy 1991 and Cole and Hermon 2000), and from exceptional accusative case-marking by a higher transitive verb of the wh-subject of a lower finite clause (reported for English by Kayne 1984a, p. 5 and for Hungarian by Bejar and Massam 1999, p. 66).

10.7 Evidence for wh-movement through spec-vP in transitive clauses

In the previous section, we noted that theoretical considerations lead us to conclude that, if transitive vPs are phases, wh-movement must involve movement through intermediate spec-vP positions in transitive clauses. An important question to ask, therefore, is whether there is any empirical evidence of wh-movement through spec-vP. We shall see that there is.

One such piece of evidence comes from observations about *have*-cliticisation. In varieties of English such as my own, *have* when used as a main verb marking possession can contract onto an immediately adjacent pronoun ending in a vowel or diphthong, e.g. in sentences such as (46) below:

(46) (a)   They have little faith in the government
     (b)   They've little faith in the government

However, cliticisation is blocked when the object of *have* undergoes wh-movement, as we see from sentences like those below:

(47) (a)   How little faith *they have* in the government!
     (b)   *How little faith *they've* in the government

To see why this should be, let's take a closer look at the derivation of (47).

The verb *have* merges with the prepositional phrase *in the government* to form the V-bar *have in the government*. This is then merged with the QP *how little faith* to form the VP *how little faith have in the government*. The resulting VP is merged with a null light verb forming a v-bar which is in turn merged with its subject *they*, and the verb *have* raises to adjoin to the light verb. Being transitive, the light verb assigns accusative case to *how little faith*. Since a transitive light verb is a phase head, the light verb will carry [WH, EPP] features which trigger movement of the wh-marked QP *how little faith* to spec-vP. The resulting vP is merged with a T constituent which agrees with, case-marks and triggers movement to spec-TP of the subject *they*, so that on the TP cycle we have the structure shown in simplified form in (48) below:

(48)

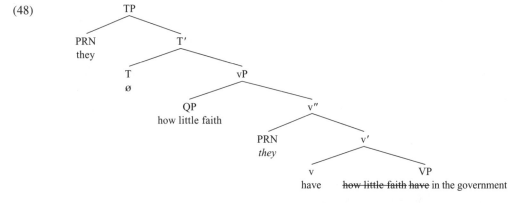

Since a finite T is generally able to attract possessive *have* to move from V to T, we might expect *have* to move from v to T at this point. But if *have* moves to T, it will then be adjacent to the subject *they*, leading us to expect *have* to be able to cliticise onto *they* in the PF component, so wrongly predicting that (47b) is grammatical. How can we prevent *have* cliticisation in such structures? One answer is to suppose that movement of *have* from v to T is blocked in structures like (48) by the intervening raised object *how little faith* in the outer spec-vP position. This would mean that the verb *have* remains in the head v position of vP rather than moving into T; and if *have* cannot move into T, it will not be adjacent to (and so cannot cliticise onto) the subject *they* in spec-TP. As should be obvious, this kind of account is crucially dependent on the assumption that the preposed wh-phrase *how little faith* moves through spec-vP before moving into spec-CP.

Interestingly, it would seem that an intervening non-object constituent does not block movement of *have* from v to T, as we see from the fact that *have*-cliticisation is possible in sentences such as:

(49)   This is a government [*which* they've very little faith in]

If transitive vPs are phases and trigger wh-movement to spec-vP, at the stage of derivation corresponding to that in (48) above, the bracketed relative clause in (49) will have the structure shown in simplified form in (50) below:

(50)   [TP they [T ∅] [vP *which* they [v **have**] [VP very little faith [V ~~have~~] in ~~which~~]]]

However, since *which* is not the object of *have* in (50) but rather is the object of the preposition *in*, it does not prevent *have* raising from v to T, and thereafter cliticising onto the subject *they* in spec-TP. So it would seem that (for reasons which are not clear) *have* is prevented from raising to T across its own object, but not across other intervening constituents.

A very different kind of evidence in support of wh-movement through spec-vP in transitive clauses comes from wh-marking of verbs (in languages with a richer verb morphology than English). We saw in §10.6 that a complementiser is wh-marked (in languages like Irish and Chamorro) if it has [EPP, WH] features and attracts a wh-marked goal. Chung (1994, 1998) presents evidence that wh-movement out of a transitive verb phrase likewise triggers wh-marking of the verb in Chamorro. We can illustrate this phenomenon of wh-marking of transitive verbs in terms of the following example (from Chung 1998, p. 242):

(51)   Hafa si Maria *s-**in**-angane-nña* as Joaquin?
         What PN Maria **wh**-say.to-AGR OBL Joaquin
         'What did Maria say to Joaquin?'

(PN denotes a person/number marker, AGR an agreement marker, and OBL an oblique case marker.) The crucial aspect of the example in (51) is that the direct object *hafa* 'what' has been moved out of the transitive verb phrase in which it originates, and that this movement triggers wh-marking of the italicised verb, which therefore ends up carrying the wh-infix *in*. This suggests that a transitive light verb carrying [EPP, WH] features attracts a wh-marked goal and undergoes agreement with the goal, resulting in the verb which is adjoined to the light verb being overtly wh-marked (though see Dukes 2000 for an alternative perspective on the relevant affixes in Chamorro). For further examples of wh-marking of intermediate verbs in long-distance wh-movement structures, see Branigan and MacKenzie (2002) on Innu-aimûn, and den Dikken (2001) on Kilega.

A related piece of evidence comes from participle agreement in French in transitive clauses such as (52b) below (discussed in Kayne 1989, Branigan 1992, Ura 1993, 2001, Bošković 1997, Richards 1997 and Sportiche 1998):

(52) (a) Il a *commis*   quelle bêtise?
          He has committed what blunder
          'What blunder did he make?'
     (b) Quelle bêtise il a *commise*?
          What   blunder he has committed
          'What blunder did he make?'

The participle *commis* 'committed' is in the default (masculine-singular) form in (52a), and does not agree with the feminine-singular in-situ wh-object *quelle bêtise* 'what blunder' (the final *-e* in these words can be taken to be an orthographic marker of a feminine-singular form). However, the participle *commise* in (52b) contains the feminine-singular marker *-e* and agrees with its preposed feminine-singular object *quelle bêtise* 'what blunder' and consequently rhymes with *bêtise*. What's going on here?

Let's look first at the derivation of (52a). The QP *quelle bêtise* 'what blunder' in (52a) is merged as the complement of the verb *commis* 'committed' forming the VP *commis quelle bêtise* 'committed what blunder'. The resulting VP is then merged with a null transitive light verb whose external AGENT argument is the pronoun *il* 'he'; since the light verb is affixal, it triggers movement of the verb *commis* 'committed' to adjoin to the light verb, so that at the end of the vP phase we have the structure (53) below:

(53)

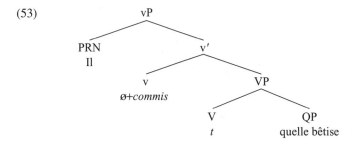

The light verb agrees in person/number φ-features with the object *quelle bêtise* 'what blunder' and assigns it accusative case. By hypothesis, the light verb has no [EPP] feature in wh-in-situ questions, so there is no movement of the wh-phrase *quelle bêtise* 'what blunder' to spec-vP. Subsequently the vP (53) is merged as the complement of the auxiliary *a* 'has' which agrees in person/number φ-features with (and triggers movement to spec-TP of) the subject *il* 'he'. Merging the resulting TP with a null complementiser which likewise has no [EPP] feature derives the structure associated with (52a) *Il a commis quelle bêtise?* (literally 'He has committed what blunder?').

Now consider the derivation of (52b). This is similar in a number of respects to that of (52a), so that (as before) the light verb agrees in person and number with (and assigns accusative case to) its object *quelle bêtise* 'what blunder'. But in addition, the light verb has [WH, EPP] features, and these attract the wh-marked object *quelle bêtise* 'what blunder' to move to become an additional (outer) specifier for the vP, so deriving the structure shown in (54) below:

(54)

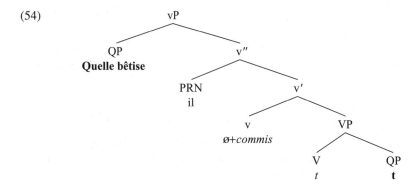

The resulting vP (54) is then merged as the complement of the auxiliary *a* 'has' which agrees in φ-features with (and triggers movement to spec-TP of) the subject *il* 'he'. Merging the resulting TP with a null interrogative complementiser which has [EPP, WH] features triggers movement of the wh-phrase to spec-CP, so deriving the structure associated with (52b) *Quelle bêtise il a commise?* (literally 'What blunder he has committed?')

In the light of the assumptions made above, consider why the participle surfaces in the agreeing (feminine-singular) form *commise* 'committed' in (52b), but in the non-agreeing (default) form *commis* in (52a). Bearing in mind our earlier observation that (in languages like Irish) a complementiser only shows overt wh-marking if it has an [EPP] feature as well as a [WH] feature, a plausible suggestion to make is that French participles only overtly inflect for gender/number agreement with their object if they have an [EPP] feature which forces movement of the object through spec-vP. However, any such assumption requires us to suppose that wh-movement proceeds through spec-vP in transitive clauses, and hence lends further support for Chomsky's claim that transitive vPs are phases. (The discussion here is simplified in a number of respects for expository purposes, e.g. by ignoring the specificity effect discussed by Richards 1997 pp. 158–60, and additional complications discussed by Ura 2001.)

Further evidence in support of successive-cyclic wh-movement through spec-vP in transitive clauses comes from observations about mutation in Welsh made in Tallerman (1993). Tallerman claims that *wh*-traces trigger so-called **soft mutation** of the initial consonant of a following word. In this connection, consider the sentence in (55) below (where PROG denotes a progressive aspect marker):

(55)   Beth wyt ti 'n   *feddwyl* oedd gen I?
          What are you PROG thinking was   with me
          'What do you think I had?'

What is particularly interesting here is that the italicised verb has undergone soft mutation, so that in place of the radical form *meddwyl* 'thinking', we find the mutated form *feddwyl*. Given independent evidence that Tallerman produces in support of claiming that wh-traces induce mutation, an obvious way of accounting for the use of the mutated verb-form *feddwyl* 'thinking' in (55) is to suppose that the wh-pronoun *beth* 'what' moves through spec-vP on its way to the front of the overall sentence, in much the same way as *what* moves in front of *think* in (24) above. We can then suppose that a wh-trace on the edge of vP triggers soft mutation on the lexical verb adjoined to the light verb heading the vP. (See Willis 2000 for a slightly different account of Welsh mutation.)

A further argument in support of wh-movement through spec-vP in transitive clauses comes from Spanish multiple-wh questions such as (56) below (discussed by Bošković 1997):

(56)   Qué dirá   quién?
          What will.say who?
          'What will who say?'

Adapting Bošković's account of this contrast to the framework presented here, let's suppose that (56) is derived as follows. The verb (which ultimately surfaces in the form) *dirá* 'will.say' (glossed simply as *say* in the numbered structures below, in order to save space) is merged with its complement *qué* 'what' to form the VP *dirá qué* 'will.say what'. This in turn is merged with a transitive light verb which assigns accusative case to *qué* 'what', triggers raising of the verb *dirá* 'will.say' from V to v, and merges with its AGENT argument *quién* 'who'. On the assumption that transitive vPs are phases, and that a wh-object which moves to spec-CP moves through spec-vP, the light verb will also have [EPP, WH] features which trigger raising of the closest wh-expression c-commanded by the light verb (namely the wh-object *qué* 'what') to become a second (outer) specifier for vP, forming the structure shown in skeletal form below (with ~~strikethrough~~ used to indicate constituents which ultimately receive a null spellout after transfer):

(57)   [$_{vP}$ qué$_{what}$ [$_{v''}$ quién$_{who}$ [$_{v'}$ [$_v$ dirá$_{say}$] [$_{VP}$ [$_v$ ~~dirá$_{say}$~~] ~~qué$_{what}$~~]]]]

The resulting vP in (57) is then merged with an abstract T constituent, to form a TP. Given that Suñer (1994) argues that postverbal subjects in Spanish remain in situ within the verb phrase but that verbs move to T in finite clauses, we can assume that the verb *dirá* 'will.say' moves from v to T, but the subject *quién* 'who' remains in situ in spec-vP, so that at the end of the TP cycle we have formed the skeletal structure:

(58)   [$_{TP}$ [$_T$ dirá$_{say}$] [$_{vP}$ qué$_{what}$ [$_{v''}$ quién$_{who}$ [$_{v'}$ [$_v$ ~~dirá$_{say}$~~] [$_{VP}$ [$_v$ ~~dirá$_{say}$~~] ~~qué$_{what}$~~]]]]]

The resulting TP is then merged with a null interrogative complementiser, to form the structure below:

(59)

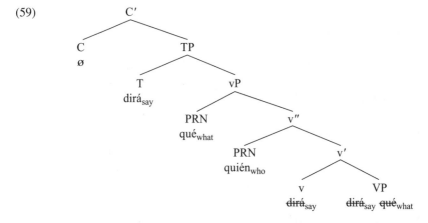

As in main-clause questions in English, C has [TNS, WH, EPP] features. The affixal [TNS] feature of C triggers raising of the verb *dirá* 'will.say' from T to C. The **Attract Closest Principle** requires the [EPP, WH] features of C to attract the closest wh-expression to move to spec-CP. Suppose that (following Chomsky 1995,

p. 358) we define closeness in terms of c-command, along the lines outlined below:

(60)   A probe X which c-commands two goals Y and Z is closer to Y than to Z if Y c-commands Z

(Note, incidentally, that this is a different definition of closeness from that given in §6.4, raising obvious questions about precisely how closeness should be defined – but we'll set this issue aside here.) It will then follow that (by virtue of having moved to the outer specifier position within vP) the wh-object *qué* 'what' is closer to C than the wh-subject *quién* 'who'. Accordingly, it is the former which moves to spec-CP, deriving the structure (61) below:

(61)   [$_{CP}$ Qué$_{what}$ [$_{C'}$ [$_C$ ø] [$_{TP}$ [$_T$ dirá$_{say}$] [$_{vP}$ ~~qué~~$_{what}$ [$_{v''}$ quién$_{who}$ [$_{v'}$ [$_v$ ~~dirá~~$_{say}$]
          [$_{VP}$ [$_v$ ~~dirá~~$_{say}$] ~~qué~~$_{what}$]]]]]]]

And (61) is the structure of (56) *Qué dirá quién?* 'What will who say?' Note that a crucial plank in the argumentation is the assumption that a wh-object in a transitive clause like (56) moves to spec-CP through spec-vP. (However, see Fitzpatrick 2002, pp. 457–8 for discussion of a potential problem.)

10.8 The role of phases in lexical selection

Hitherto, we have assumed that the main motivation for phases is to reduce the complexity of the computational operations which the syntax has to perform by ensuring that probes only have a limited search space within which to locate matching goals – and hence that all syntactic operations are local. However, Chomsky (1998) suggests that phases also have an important role to play in respect of lexical selection. We can illustrate this second role in relation to the following sentence (adapted from Chomsky 1998, p. 17, ex. (7ii)):

(62)   There must be a possibility that proofs will be discovered

Suppose that we have reached the stage of derivation represented informally below:

(63)   [$_T$ will] be discovered [proofs]

Since the **lexical array** for sentence (62) – i.e. the set of items we take out of the lexicon in order to form the sentence – includes expletive *there*, preference of Merge over Move will mean that we must select *there* at this point in order to satisfy the [EPP] requirement of [$_T$ *will*], so deriving:

(64)   there [$_T$ will] be discovered proofs

But this in turn means that we have no way of deriving (62), since (62) requires the nominal *proofs* to become the subject of *will* at the stage of derivation represented in (63). What are we to do at this point?

Chomsky (1998, pp. 19–20) suggests that the problem can be overcome in the following way. Suppose (as we have done throughout) that the first step in deriving a given expression is to take a set of items out of the lexicon, and that these constitute the **lexical array** out of which the expression will be composed. But suppose, in addition, that only a specific **subarray** of the items taken out of the lexicon can be accessed at any **phase** of derivation: in particular, suppose that the subarray out of which a given phase is built can comprise only a single occurrence of a phase head (e.g. C or a transitive light verb, v*) – cf. Chomsky's (1999, p. 9) claim that 'a subarray contains exactly one C or v*'. The subarray chosen is then 'placed in active memory (the "work space")' (Chomsky 1998, p. 19). Once a given lexical subarray is exhausted (i.e. all the items it contains have been merged in the relevant structure) and the derivation of the corresponding phase has been completed, the computation then selects another lexical subarray to build the next phase with . . . and so on. Returning now to (62) *There must be a possibility that proofs will be discovered*, let's suppose that our initial subarray of items comprises the set in (65) below:

(65)   {that, will, be discovered, proofs}

Suppose furthermore that we have reached the stage of derivation in (63) above. [$_T$ *will*] has an [EPP] feature requiring it to project a specifier. Preference of Merge over Move will mean that if the lexical subarray contains an expletive, this will be merged in spec-TP. But the subarray in (65) contains no expletive. Hence, the only way of deleting the [EPP] feature of [$_T$ *will*] in (63) is by movement of *proofs* to spec-TP, deriving:

(66)   [$_{TP}$ proofs [$_T$ will] be discovered *proofs*]

Merger of the complementiser *that* with the TP in (66) will in turn derive the CP (67) below:

(67)   [$_{CP}$ [$_C$ that] [$_{TP}$ proofs will be discovered *proofs*]]

The bracketed TP will undergo transfer at this point, and the italicised trace of *proofs* will be deleted from the structure transferred to the phonological component. Since we have now exhausted the lexical subarray in (65) and completed the derivation of the CP phase, the syntactic computation can now access a further subarray. Let's suppose that this comprises the set below (where ø is a null declarative complementiser):

(68)   {ø, there, must, be, a, possibility}

Successive merger operations introducing *possibility*, *a*, *be*, *must*, *there* and ø into the derivation will generate the structure (69) below:

(69)   [$_{CP1}$ ø [$_{TP1}$ there must be a possibility [$_{CP2}$ that [$_{TP2}$ proofs will be discovered]]]]

At this point, TP$_1$ will undergo transfer in accordance with (7i), and subsequently CP$_1$ will undergo transfer in accordance with (7ii) – so eventually deriving the structure associated with (62) *There must be a possibility that proofs will be discovered*.

10.9   Questions about phases

Having presented an account of phases in §§10.2–10.8 which is broadly consistent with Chomsky's recent work, we turn in this section to reflect on the nature of phases. One issue which arises out of our discussion in this chapter concerns the relation between EPP-hood and phasehood. In the system outlined in §§10.2–10.8, the relation seems relatively clear (at least for heads which trigger A-bar movement operations like wh-movement): complementisers and transitive light verbs are phase heads and can have an [EPP] feature triggering A-bar movement, whereas intransitive light-verbs which have no external argument are not phase heads and cannot have an [EPP] feature triggering A-bar movement. Note, however, that this leads to a potential asymmetry: both transitive and intransitive complementisers alike have an [EPP] feature, but only transitive (not intransitive) light verbs have an [EPP] feature. Below, I present a piece of evidence calling into question the assumption that intransitive vPs cannot have an [EPP] feature: the evidence suggests that just as a wh-expression extracted out of transitive vP moves through spec-vP, so too a wh-expression extracted out of an intransitive vP also moves through spec-vP.

The relevant evidence comes from intransitive multiple wh-questions such as the following in Spanish (kindly provided by Cris Lozano, who trialled them on native speakers of both Peninsular Spanish and Mexican Spanish, and obtained unanimous, clearcut grammaticality judgments):

(70) (a)   Adónde fue   quién?
           Where   went   who?
    (b)   *Quién   fue   adónde?
           Who   went   where?

(Imagine a scenario for such sentences in which a friend says to you 'President Phat Khat went to New York yesterday', and you say 'Sorry, I didn't hear you' and then go on to produce (70).) Unlike what happens in English, Spanish requires *adónde* (literally 'to.where', but here glossed simply as 'where') to be preposed, not *quién* 'who'. Why should this be?

Let's suppose that sentence (70a) is derived as follows. The unaccusative verb (which is ultimately spelled out as) *fue* 'went' is merged with its GOAL argument *adónde* 'where' to form the V-bar *fue adónde* 'went where' and the resulting V-bar is then merged with its THEME argument *quién* 'who' to form the VP *quién fue adónde* 'who went where'. This VP is in turn merged with an intransitive light verb, forming the structure shown below:

(71)

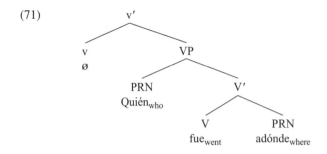

The light verb has a strong (affixal) V-feature, and so attracts the verb *fue* 'went' to move from V to v. If we suppose that the light verb also has [WH, EPP] features, it would be expected to attract the closest wh-expression to move to spec-vP. In terms of the c-command definition of closeness given in (60) above, *quién* 'who' is closer to the light verb than *adónde* 'where', and hence we'd expect *quién* 'who' to move to spec-vP. But the contrast in (70) suggests that the light verb is unable to attract *quién* 'who' and instead attracts *adónde* 'where'. This suggests that *quién* 'who' must be inactive for A-bar movement for some reason. But why?

The answer we shall suggest here is that:

(72)   An expression is only active for A-bar movement if it has an active A-bar feature (e.g. a wh-feature) but no active A-feature (e.g. no unvalued case feature)

The pronoun *quién* 'who' carries a case feature which is as yet unvalued at the stage of derivation shown in (71) above, and hence – given (72) – is inactive for an A-bar movement operation like wh-movement. If we suppose that the light verb attracts the closest wh-expression which is active for A-bar movement, it follows that the light verb will attract the locative pronoun *adónde* 'where' to move to spec-vP, so deriving the structure shown in simplified form in (73) below (strikethrough being used to indicate constituents which will ultimately receive a null spellout):

(73)   [$_{vP}$adónde$_{where}$ [$_{v'}$ [$_{v}$ fue$_{went}$] [$_{VP}$ quién$_{who}$ [$_{v'}$ [$_{v}$ ~~fue$_{went}$~~] ~~adónde$_{where}$~~]]]]

The resulting vP is then merged with a strong T constituent which triggers raising of verb *fue* 'went' to T, and which agrees with and assigns nominative case to the subject *quién* 'who', so deriving:

(74)   [$_{TP}$ [$_{T}$ fue$_{went}$] [$_{vP}$ adónde$_{where}$ [$_{v'}$ [$_{v}$ ~~fue$_{went}$~~] [$_{VP}$ quién$_{who}$ [$_{v'}$ [$_{v}$ ~~fue$_{went}$~~] ~~adónde$_{where}$~~]]]]]

The TP thereby formed is then merged with a strong interrogative C constituent which carries [TNS, WH, EPP] features. The affixal [TNS] feature of C triggers raising of the verb *fue* 'went' from T to C, and its [WH, EPP] features trigger movement of the closest active wh-expression to spec-CP. Since *adónde* 'where' is closer to C than *quién* 'who' in (73), it is the former which moves to spec-CP, so deriving the overt structure shown in highly simplified form below:

(75) $[_{CP}$ Adónde$_{where}$ $[_{C'}$ $[_C$ fue$_{went}]$ $[_{TP}$ ...$[_{vP}$ ...$[_{VP}$ quién$_{who}$ ...$]]]]]$

And (75) is the structure of (70a) *Adónde fue quién?* 'Where did who go?'

There are several points of interest which arise from the derivation sketched above. The first is that in order to derive (70a) we need to assume that *adónde* 'where' moves to spec-vP at the stage of derivation shown in (73) above: if this did not happen, both *quién* 'who' and *adónde* 'where' would remain in situ until C is introduced into the derivation, and since *quién* 'who' would then be the closest wh-expression to C, we would wrongly predict that (70b) **Quién fue adónde?* 'Who went where?' is the eventual outcome. More generally, the derivation outlined above leads us to suppose that intransitive vPs as well as their transitive counterparts can have an [EPP] feature which triggers successive-cyclic wh-movement through spec-vP.

We might therefore follow Legate (2002) in concluding that not only transitive vPs but also intransitive vPs are phases. However, such a conclusion is incompatible with the derivation for sentences like (70a) outlined here. The key point to note is that at the stage of derivation represented in (74) above, T must be able to agree with and assign nominative case to the subject *quién* 'who' in spec-VP; but if an intransitive vP is a phase, the Phase Impenetrability Condition (1) will block *quién* 'who' from serving as a goal for an external T probe, thereby leaving the uninterpretable case feature on *quién* 'who' and the uninterpretable person/number features on *fue* 'went' unvalued and undeleted, and causing the derivation to crash. In other words, the conclusion our discussion of sentences like (70) leads us to is that both intransitive and transitive light verbs can have [WH, EPP] features, but that only transitive vPs are phases. This leads to dissociation between the [EPP] property and phasehood. However, such a dissociation is found elsewhere (e.g. T in English has an [EPP] feature but is not a phase head).

Having looked at the relation between EPP-hood and phasehood, let's now turn to explore the question of whether (in addition to CPs and transitive vPs) other types of constituent may also be phases. Our discussion throughout this chapter so far has looked at the role of phases in the derivation of clausal structures, raising the question of whether there are also phases within the nominal domain. Reflecting on this question, Chomsky (1999, p. 11) writes: 'Considerations of semantic-phonetic integrity, and the systematic consequences of phase identification, suggest that the general typology should include among phases nominal categories.' Since phases do not allow any element to be extracted out of their domain, one way of accounting for contrasts like that in (76) below would be to suppose that definite DPs are phases:

(76) (a)   Who were you reading [a book about]?
   (b)   *Who were you reading [the/this/that/his book about?]

We could then say that extraction of *who* out of the bracketed indefinite DP in (76a) is permitted because indefinite DPs are not phases, whereas extraction of *who* out of the definite DP in (76b) is not permitted because definite DPs are phases, and the Phase Impenetrability Condition (1) prevents *who* from being extracted out of the NP *book about who* which is the complement of the head D of the bracketed definite DP. (It should be noted that Chomsky 1999, p. 36, fn. 28 envisages the possibility that 'phases include DPs'.)

The assumption that definite DPs are phases would offer us a new perspective on the following contrasts which we first looked at in §3.6:

(77) (a)   Nobody had expected that the FBA would assassinate the king of Ruritania
    (b)   [$_{CP}$ *That the FBA would assassinate the king of Ruritania*], nobody had expected
    (c)   *[$_{TP}$ *The FBA would assassinate the king of Ruritania*], nobody had expected that (NB *that* = ðət)
    (d)   [$_{DP}$ *The king of Ruritania*], nobody had expected that the FBA would assassinate
    (e)   *[$_{nP}$ *king of Ruritania*], nobody had expected that the FBA would assassinate the

In (77b–e) a variety of constituents have been preposed to highlight them. In (77b) the fronted expression is a CP which functions as the complement of a non-phasal head (namely the verb *expected*) and can be preposed under appropriate discourse conditions. In (77c) the fronted constituent is a TP which is the complement of a phasal head (namely the complementiser *that*), and preposing the relevant TP violates the Phase Impenetrability Condition (1). In (77d), the fronted expression is a DP which is the complement of a non-phasal head (namely the verb *assassinate*), and hence there is no prohibition on extraction. But in (77e), extraction of an nP complement of the determiner *the* results in ungrammaticality: we can account for this if we suppose that definite DPs are phases, since the Phase Impenetrability Condition will prevent extraction of the nP *king of Ruritania* because this is the complement of the phase head *the*. The reason why the head of a phase does not allow extraction of its complement (or of any element contained within its complement) is that at the end of a phase, the complement of a phase head undergoes transfer in accordance with (7i) and thereafter becomes syntactically inactive.

The hypothesis that definite DPs are phases also offers us an interesting account of why (in languages like English) possessives cannot be extracted out of their containing DPs – as we see from the contrast between the echo question in (78a) below and its wh-movement counterpart in (78b):

(78) (a)   You have framed [whose picture of Mary]?
    (b)   *Whose have you framed [~~whose~~ picture of Mary]?

Suppose that (in keeping with the analysis outlined at the end of §9.9) the bracketed DP in (78a) has the structure shown in (79) below, with *whose* superficially positioned in the specifier position within a NumP/Number Phrase projection:

(79)

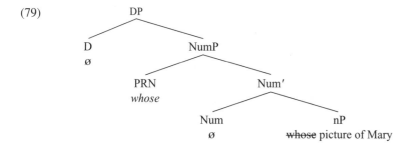

We can then account for why *whose* cannot be extracted out of the overall DP in (79) by supposing that a definite DP is a phase, and that at the end of the DP cycle, the NumP complement of DP undergoes transfer, with the result that *whose* cannot be extracted out of its containing NumP projection.

However, such an analysis is not entirely without posing problems. One such is how we account for the fact that the whole DP containing *whose* can undergo wh-movement:

(80)   *Whose picture of Mary* have you framed?

The head v of vP and the head C of CP in (80) contain [WH, EPP] features which attract the wh-pronoun *whose* (along with the pied-piped material *picture of Mary*) to move through spec-vP into spec-CP. But if a definite DP is a phase, the problem we face is that at the end of the DP cycle, the NumP constituent containing *whose* will undergo transfer to the PF and semantic components, and so the [WH] feature on *whose* will not be visible to either v or C. One apparent way of seemingly resolving this problem (without abandoning the assumption that a definite DP is a phase) would be to suppose that D has an [EPP] feature triggering movement of *whose* into spec-DP: but this would leave us with no phase-based account of why *whose* cannot subsequently be extracted from its containing DP in sentences like (78b). An alternative possibility (which would again allow us to continue to maintain that definite DPs are phases) would be to suppose that *whose* remains in spec-NumP but the wh-feature on *whose* percolates onto the head D of DP, perhaps via some form of agreement parallel to agreement between a complementiser and a subject in a number of languages. In this connection, it is interesting to note Haegeman's (1992, p. 47) claim that in West Flemish 'the complementiser of the finite clause agrees in person and number with the grammatical subject of the sentence it introduces'. Haegeman (1994, p. 131) provides the following illustrative data:

(81) (a)   ...*da* **den inspekteur** da   boek gelezen eet
             ...that the inspector   that book read   has
             '...that the inspector has read that book'

     (b)   ...*dan* **d'inspekteurs** da   boek gelezen een
             ...that the inspectors   that book read   have
             '...that the inspectors have read that book'

The italicised complementiser has the form *da* when the bold-printed subject is third person singular, but *dan* when it is third person plural. If the head C of CP can agree in person and number with the specifier of its TP complement in structures like (81), it seems no less plausible to suppose that the head D of DP can agree in *wh*-ness with the specifier of its NumP complement in structures like (79). This would mean that the overall DP would have a wh-marked head and hence could undergo wh-movement.

Some evidence which is consistent with the view that definite DPs are phases comes from observations about the pied-piping of possessive phrases in Tzotzil made by Aissen (1996). She notes that although (italicised) possessors are generally positioned postnominally in Tzotzil as in (82a) below, when the possessor is an interrogative pronoun, it is moved to the front of the DP containing it, and the whole containing DP is then moved to the front of the interrogative clause, as in (82b):

(82) (a)   Icham [xch'amal *li   Xune*]
            Died [child   the Xun]
            'Xun's child died'

     (b)   [*Buch'u* xch'amal] icham?
            [Who   child]   died
            'Whose child died?'

The interrogative possessor in (82b) appears to move to spec-DP, and this movement is consistent with the view that DP is a phase, since if the possessor remained in situ within the NP complement of D, PIC would prevent C from attracting the wh-pronoun (since NP and its constituents would be impenetrable to C). Movement of the interrogative pronoun to the edge of DP makes it accessible to C.

However, there are a number of problems which arise if we assume that definite DPs are phases. For example, Ross (1967) noted that corresponding to a sentence like (83a) below, we find a range of types of relative clause including like those bracketed in (83b–e):

(83) (a)   The government prescribes the height of the lettering on the covers of the
            reports
     (b)   Reports [*which* the government prescribes the height of the lettering on the
            covers of] are invariably boring
     (c)   Reports [*the covers of which* the government prescribes the height of the
            lettering on] almost always put me to sleep
     (d)   Reports [*the lettering on the covers of which* the government prescribes the
            height of] are a shocking waste of public funds
     (e)   Reports [*the height of the lettering on the covers of which* the government
            prescribes] should be abolished

Prior to wh-movement, the nominal containing the wh-pronoun *which* has the structure shown in skeletal form below:

(84)   [DP the height of [DP the lettering on [DP the covers of which]]]

This means that the italicised wh-moved expression in (83) has been moved out of three containing definite DPs in (83b), out of two in (83c), and out of one in (83d) – and all of these movements would be predicted to be impossible if definite DPs were phases.

One way round this problem (consistent with maintaining that definite DPs are indeed phases) would be to posit that (like other phase heads such as C and transitive v), the head D constituent of DP can have an [EPP] feature which allows it to attract a DP to move to its specifier position. This would mean that *which* in (83b) moves first to become the specifier of the DP *the covers of which*, then to become the specifier of the DP *the lettering on the covers of which*, then to become the specifier of the DP *the height of the lettering on the covers of which*, from there moving into spec-vP and thence into the spec-CP position which it occupies in (83b). An interesting question raised by the assumption that D can have an [EPP] feature triggering movement to its specifier position is why the NP *king of Ruritania* in (76e) cannot move to become the specifier of the DP *the king of Ruritania*, and from there go on to move to the front of the overall clause. The answer is that the **Remerger Constraint** prevents the NP *king of Ruritania* from moving to spec-DP, since this constraint tells us that a constituent which is merged as the complement of a given head cannot subsequently be remerged as its specifier. If DP is a phase, movement of the NP directly out of its containing DP will be blocked by the **Phase Impenetrability Condition** – as we saw earlier. (For an insightful discussion of extraction out of DPs, see Davies and Dubinsky 2003.)

However, the assumption that definite DPs are phases poses problems for case-marking. In languages with a richer case morphology than English, in a transitive sentence such as:

(85)   Mary chose *the red dress*

the accusative case which the transitive (light verb associated with the) verb *chose* assigns to its complement is carried not only by the (counterpart of the) determiner *the* but also by the (counterparts of the) adjective *red* and the noun *dress*. But if DP is a phase, its complement *red dress* will have been sent for transfer at the end of the DP cycle, leaving only the head D of DP visible for case-marking by the transitive (light) verb. Such an analysis would mean that we have to posit a PF operation which Schütze (2001) terms **case-spreading** to ensure that the case assigned to the determiner *the* in the syntax **spreads** to the adjective *red* and the noun *dress* in the morphology. What this means is that we end up with an asymmetric account of case-marking under which determiners are assigned case via agreement in the syntax, but adjectives and nouns are assigned case via a separate PF operation of case-spreading (which might be the analogue of the traditional notion of **concord**). Moreover, if the adjective *red* and the noun *dress* each have an unvalued and undeleted case feature at the end of the derivation, the derivation will crash at the semantics interface (since the undeleted case feature cannot be assigned any semantic interpretation). So, for an analysis along the lines sketched out here to be workable, we would have to abandon the claim that uninterpretable features must be deleted in the syntax and instead suppose that uninterpretable features are intrinsically uninterpretable and so (like phonological features) are not handed over to the semantic component at the end of the relevant part of the syntactic derivation. On this alternative view, the only requirement for an unvalued, uninterpretable feature would be that it should be assigned a value (in the syntax or morphology) in order to be spelled out at PF. As should be apparent from our brief discussion here, the potential repercussions of taking DPs to be phases are considerable.

A further possibility to be explored if there are parallels between phases in the clausal and nominal domains is that just as CPs introduced by the prepositional complementiser *for* are phases, so too prepositional phrases may also be phases. This would provide one way of accounting for the fact that (as noted in §9.6) the auxiliary probe *do* cannot pick out *me* as its goal in structures such as (86) below:

(86)

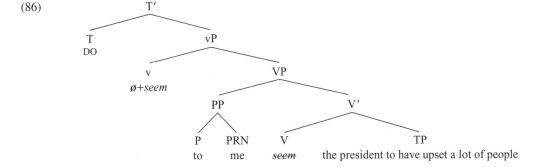

If PP is a phase, the Phase Impenetrability Condition (1) will mean that the pronoun *me* is impenetrable to any head outside the PP *to me*. Consequently, *me* cannot serve as a goal for *do*, and the probe *do* therefore locates the alternative goal *the president*, agreeing with it, assigning it nominative case and moving it to spec-TP. Merging the resulting TP with a null declarative complementiser derives the structure associated with:

(87)   The president does seem to me to have upset a lot of people

For, further details, see the discussion in §9.6.

However, one apparent problem posed by the assumption that PPs are phases is how we account for the fact that prepositional complements can be passivised in sentences such as:

(88) (a)   *Nothing* was agreed **on**
     (b)   *The information* was asked **for** by the Dean
     (c)   *Jim* can be depended **on** for sound advice
     (d)   *The president* was shouted **at** by his wife

In each of the sentences in (88), the italicised nominal seems to originate as the complement of the bold-printed preposition. If prepositional phrases are phases, we would expect the complement of a preposition to be impenetrable to an external head and hence not to be passivisable. To see why, suppose that we arrive at a point in the derivation of (88a) where we have generated the structure shown in simplified form below:

(89)   [$_T$ BE] [$_{vP}$ [$_v$ ~~agreed~~] [$_{VP}$ [$_V$ agreed] [$_{PP}$ [$_P$ on] nothing]]]

If PP is a phase, the domain of the PP phase (i.e. the *nothing* complement of the preposition *on*) will be impenetrable to the external T probe BE, so preventing BE from agreeing with, assigning nominative case to and triggering passivisation of *nothing*. An analysis along the lines of (89) would therefore wrongly predict that sentences like (88) are ungrammatical. Does the fact that sentences like (88) are grammatical therefore provide us with evidence that PPs are not phases?

Not necessarily. Radford (1988, pp. 427–32) argues that in prepositional passives like those in (88) above the preposition is adjoined to the verb (forming what pedagogical grammars of English sometimes call a **phrasal verb**). Part of the evidence in support of such an analysis is that it correctly predicts that no other (bold-printed) constituent can be positioned between the (italicised) verb and preposition in prepositional passives like (90) below:

(90) (a)   *The resolution was *agreed* **unanimously** *on* by the committee
     (b)   *His integrity can be *depended* **entirely** *on*
     (c)   *The information was *asked* **politely** *for* by the Dean
     (d)   *The president was *shouted* **angrily** *at* by his wife

If prepositional passives do indeed involve a structure in which the preposition is adjoined to the verb, (88a) will have a structure along the lines shown in simplified form in (91) below at the point at which the T probe BE is introduced into the derivation:

(91)   [$_T$ BE] [$_{vP}$ [$_v$ agreed+on] [$_{VP}$ [$_V$ ~~agreed+on~~] nothing]]

The probe [$_T$ BE] will then agree with, assign nominative case to and trigger passivisation of the pronoun *nothing*, thereby correctly predicting the grammaticality of (88a). If such an analysis can be maintained, sentences like (88) pose no problem for the hypothesis that PPs are phases.

A further empirical challenge to the phasal status of PPs comes from the fact that (in informal styles of English) the complement of a preposition can undergo wh-movement, so stranding the preposition in sentences like:

(92)   **Where** are you going *to*?

Suppose we follow Chomsky in assuming that intransitive light verbs do not have an [EPP] feature triggering wh-movement, and suppose that we have reached the stage of derivation shown in simplified form in (93) below:

(93)   [$_C$ ø] [$_{TP}$ you [$_T$ are] [$_{vP}$ [$_v$ going] [$_{VP}$ [$_V$ ~~going~~] [$_{PP}$ [$_P$ to] where]]]]

The affixal [TNS] feature of C will attract *are* to move from T to C. The [WH, EPP] features of C need to attract *where* to move to spec-CP in order to derive (92).

But if PP is a phase, *where* will have undergone **transfer** at the end of the PP phase and so be impenetrable to C (and indeed to any head outside PP). It would therefore seem that we wrongly predict that sentences like (92) are ungrammatical (as indeed their counterparts are in many other languages). Does this provide us with evidence that PPs are not phases?

Once again, not necessarily. After all, a phase head like C can have an [EPP] feature permitting a wh-expression to move into spec-CP, and then be attracted by a higher head. Suppose, therefore, that in colloquial English, a preposition can carry an [EPP] feature. If this is so, the wh-word *where* can move to spec-PP in (93), so that at the stage when C is introduced into the derivation, we will have the structure (94) below (if we follow Chomsky in assuming that intransitive verb phrases are not phases):

(94) $[_C$ ø$]$ $[_{TP}$ you $[_T$ are$]$ $[_{vP}$ $[_v$ going$]$ $[_{VP}$ $[_V$ ~~going~~$]$ $[_{PP}$ where $[_P$ to$]$ ~~where~~$]]]]$

Since the edge of a phase (i.e. its specifier and head) are accessible to a c-commanding probe, and since *where* is on the edge of PP in (94) by virtue of being its specifier, nothing prevents the C probe from picking out *where* as its goal, so triggering movement of *where* to spec-CP. Concomitant movement of the auxiliary *are* from T to C will derive the structure associated with (92) *Where are you going to?* If we suppose that the **Convergence Principle** (discussed in §6.7) requires preposing of the smallest accessible wh-constituent in structures like (94) it follows that we correctly predict that only *where* will be preposed, not the PP *where to* – so accounting for the ungrammaticality of:

(95)   *Where to are you going?

However, in sentence fragments like that produced by speaker B below, we do indeed find structures of the form wh-word+preposition:

(96)   SPEAKER A: We're going off on holiday next week
         SPEAKER B: Where to?

Structures like *where to?* may provide us with some evidence in support of supposing that prepositions can have an [EPP] feature triggering movement of a wh-expression to spec-PP (though it should be noted that structures like (96B) are subject to strong constraints on the choice of wh-word and preposition: see Radford 1993 for some discussion). A final point to note about prepositions with wh-complements is that if we assume that P does not have an [EPP] feature in those languages and language varieties which do not allow preposition stranding (e.g. formal styles of English), we can account for why sentences like (92) are not grammatical in the relevant languages/varieties.

Our discussion in this section has been exploratory in nature, considering the possibility that both transitive and intransitive light verbs may have an [EPP] feature which triggers A-bar movement, and that the CP and (transitive) vP phases found in the clausal domain may have analogues in the nominal domain, with DP and/or PP perhaps being phases. As is clear from our discussion in this section, any such claim is far from straightforward, and requires us to make additional assumptions if it is to be workable – e.g. about D having an [EPP] feature in sentences like (83), and P having an [EPP] feature in sentences like (92). Clearly, more research is needed in order to determine whether DPs and/or PPs are indeed phases.

10.10   The nature of A-bar movement

Throughout this chapter, we have made a number of informal assumptions about how A-bar movement operations like wh-movement work without looking at the precise mechanism which drives this movement. Chomsky (1998) suggests that we should expect A-bar movement to operate in a fashion parallel to A-movement. More specifically, he draws the following parallel:

> Take wh-movement. This would be point-by-point analogous to A-movement if the wh-phrase has an uninterpretable feature [wh-] and an interpretable feature [Q], which matches the uninterpretable probe Q of a complementiser in the final stage.   (Chomsky 1988, p. 44)

In footnote 92, he makes the following additional observation (where T_{DEF} denotes a defective T of the kind found in bare infinitival complements of raising and passive predicates):

> To complete the analogy, C (and v with its φ-set deleted) may have a non-specific P-feature analogous to [person] for T_{DEF}, perhaps contingent on the assignment of an [EPP] feature to a phase.

Let's try and tease out what this means for wh-movement.

To make our discussion more concrete, consider the derivation of a sentence such as:

(97)   Where might they think that he will go?

Assume that the derivation proceeds as discussed in relation to (13) *Where is it thought that he will go?* until we reach the stage of derivation when the complementiser *that* merges with its CP complement to form *that he will go where* (whose structure is shown in (15) above). Let's suppose that a wh-word contains an interpretable operator feature marking whether it is a question operator, a relative operator, or an exclamative operator, so that interrogative wh-words have the interpretable feature [**Q-Op**] 'question operator'. Let's further suppose (again following Chomsky) that wh-words also have an uninterpretable *wh*-feature which makes them active: since this is a P-feature (i.e. a peripheral feature associated with movement to the periphery of a phase) in Chomsky's terms, let's denote the relevant feature as [*wh-P*]. In addition, we can take the complementiser *that* in (97) to have an [EPP] feature and contingent on this (to use Chomsky's phrase) a 'non-specific P-feature'. Let's take the relevant P-feature to be an uninterpretable

P-feature, and let's assume that Chomsky's remark that it is 'non-specific' means that it enters the derivation unvalued – i.e. it enters the derivation as an uninterpretable and unvalued peripheral feature [*u-P*]. Finally, let's assume that the complementiser *that* (by virtue of being the head of a **declarative** clause) does not carry a Q-feature (i.e. does not carry a feature indicating that the clause is a question). Given these assumptions, at the point where the complementiser *that* is merged with its TP complement, we will have the structure shown in skeletal form below (where only features of immediate concern to us are shown):

(98)   [that] he will go [where]
         [*u-P*]   [*wh-P*]
         [*EPP*]   **[Q-Op]**

Recall that in §8.4 we noted (in relation to our discussion of T-agreement and nominative case-marking) that when a probe P which is an A-head (like T) locates a matching goal G, uninterpretable (person/number/case) features on one can only be deleted by the other if the deleter is **complete** (i.e. if it carries a complete set of person/number φ-features). Let's therefore assume that in much the same way, when a probe P is an A-bar head which locates a matching goal G, the one can only delete any uninterpretable A-bar features carried by the other if the deleter is complete (i.e. if it carries both a P-feature/peripheral feature and an O-feature/operator feature). Given this assumption, the derivation will proceed as follows. The uninterpretable [*u-P*] feature of *that* in (98) makes it an active A-bar probe which searches for a goal that can value its unvalued [*u-P*] feature, and locates *where*: accordingly, *where* values the [*u-P*] feature of *that* as [*wh-P*] – or, in simpler terms, wh-agreement takes place between *that* and *where*. Since *where* is complete (by virtue of having both a P-feature and an O-feature), it can also delete the uninterpretable [*wh-P*] feature of *that*. Conversely, however, *that* cannot delete the uninterpretable wh-feature on *where* because *that* is not complete (since it has a P-feature but no O-feature). The [*EPP*] feature of *that* is deleted by moving *where* to spec-CP, so that at the end of the relevant phase we have the overt structure shown in skeletal form below (as throughout, the term **overt structure** being used informally to indicate that, in order to reduce visual clutter, we have not shown constituents which have a null spellout – e.g. traces):

(99)

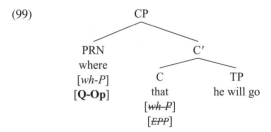

The TP complement of *that* undergoes transfer at this point in accordance with (7i) above. Note that the wh-feature carried by *where* has not yet been deleted and so remains active.

Assume that the derivation proceeds until the vP phase containing the transitive light verb associated with *think* is formed. Suppose that the transitive light verb also has an [EPP] feature and an unvalued, uninterpretable P-feature, but that the light verb has no O-feature (since only the head C of an interrogative clause has an operator feature). Much the same will happen on the vP cycle as happened on the CP cycle: that is, the unvalued [*u-P*] feature of the light verb will be valued as [*wh-P*] by wh-agreement with *where*, and thereafter deleted by complete *where*. The [EPP] feature of the light verb will trigger movement of *where* to a second specifier position above the external argument specifier *they*, so that at the end of the vP phase, we have the overt structure shown in (100) below:

(100)

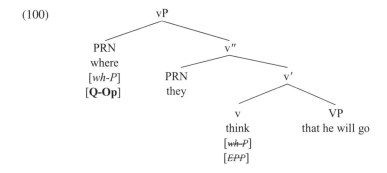

Once again, note that the wh-feature of *where* has not yet been deleted and so remains active. In accordance with (7i), the VP *that he will go* will undergo transfer at this point (since a transitive vP is a phase, so that its complement undergoes transfer at the end of the vP cycle).

The vP in (100) is then merged with [T *might*] and the subject *they* raises to spec-TP, deriving the TP *they might where think that he will go*. The resulting TP is subsequently merged with a null affixal complementiser *ø+* which has not only an uninterpretable [EPP] feature and an uninterpretable [*u-P*] feature, but also (because the clause which it heads is interrogative) an uninterpretable unvalued operator feature [*u-Op*]. Merger of the null complementiser with its TP complement derives the structure shown below (in which traces have been omitted to simplify exposition):

(101)

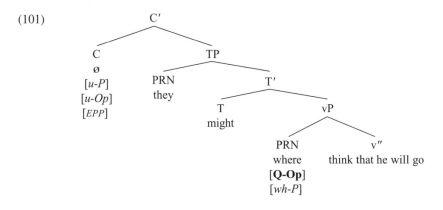

C is an active probe by virtue of its uninterpretable (and unvalued) peripheral and operator features, and locates *where* (which is active by virtue of its uninterpretable wh-feature) as a matching active goal. *Where* values the unvalued peripheral and operator features of C as [*wh-P*] and [*Q-Op*] respectively, and simultaneously deletes them (because *where* is complete by virtue of having both a P-feature and an O-feature). Since C is also complete, C can delete the wh-P feature of *where* (making it ineligible to serve as a goal for any other probe). The [EPP] feature of C is deleted by moving *where* into spec-CP. Since the null complementiser *ø* carries an affixal tense feature (not shown above), it triggers raising of the auxiliary *might* from T to C, so deriving the overt structure shown in highly simplified form in (102) below:

(102)

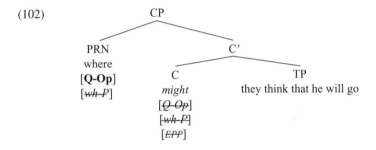

In the semantic component, a CP containing an interrogative operator in spec-CP will be interpreted as interrogative, and so (102) will receive an interpretation which can be loosely paraphrased as 'What is the place such that they might think that he will go there?', with *where* interpreted as an operator which binds a theta-marked trace in VP-complement position (the trace not being shown in (102) above).

There are two particular features of the analysis outlined here which merit further comment. One is that the analysis assumes that a wh-expression will remain an active goal until it encounters a C with an operator feature: only at that point will the wh-feature on the wh-expression be inactivated, making it ineligible to serve as a goal for another probe – hence making it ineligible to undergo further movement. We can illustrate this in terms of the following contrast:

(103) (a)   Has she asked [*where* he is going]?
      (b)   ***Where** has she asked [he is going]?

In (103), both the main clause and the bracketed complement clause are interrogative in nature and hence contain a C with (initially unvalued) O- and P-features. Accordingly, movement of *where* to become the specifier of the bracketed complement clause in (103a) will result in the wh-feature of *where* being inactivated by the null C heading the bracketed complement clause, since the complement clause C is complete by virtue of carrying O- and P-features. Hence, once *where* moves to the italicised spec-CP position within the bracketed clause in (103a) its [*wh-P*] feature is deleted, making it inactive and hence unable to subsequently move into the bold-printed spec-CP position in the main clause in (103b).

The second feature of the analysis to note is that Chomsky's assumption that an interrogative C contains an **uninterpretable** operator feature has important implications for the syntax of yes–no questions. What this in effect means (if yes–no questions contain the same kind of C constituent as wh-questions) is that yes–no questions must contain a null question operator in spec-CP. One reason for this is that the semantic component needs some means of identifying the relevant sentence as a question, and since Chomsky's Q-feature on C is an uninterpretable feature, it clearly cannot be this feature which identifies the structure as a yes–no question since the relevant feature will be deleted in the course of the derivation and thereby become invisible to the semantic component. A second reason is that (by hypothesis) C in questions contains unvalued and uninterpretable O- and P-features, and these need to be valued and deleted by an appropriate constituent. Let's therefore suppose that yes–no questions contain a null wh-operator – an invisible counterpart of the wh-adverb *whether* which could be used to introduce main-clause yes–no questions in Early Modern English sentences such as:

(104)   *Whether* dost thou profess thyself a knave or a fool? (Lafeu, *All's Well That Ends Well*, IV.v)

Let's further suppose that in sentences like (104), *whether* is directly merged in spec-CP, and contains an uninterpretable [*wh-P*] P-feature and an interpretable [**Q-Op**] O-feature, and that the head C of CP contains unvalued and uninterpretable O- and P-features. This being so, the CP in (104) will have the structure (105) below at the point when *whether* is merged in spec-CP (assuming that merger of *whether* in spec-TP deletes the uninterpretable [EPP] feature of C):

(105)

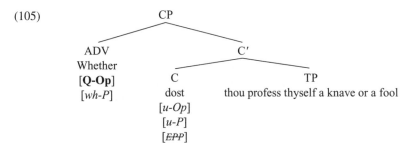

The operator *whether* (which is active by virtue of its uninterpretable wh-feature) serves as a probe which can value and (by virtue of being complete – i.e. having both an O-feature and a P-feature) delete the two unvalued and uninterpretable O- and P-features of C. Conversely, C (being complete) can delete the wh-feature of *whether*. Hence, agreement in O- and P-features between *whether* and C will result in the following structure at the end of the relevant phase:

(106)

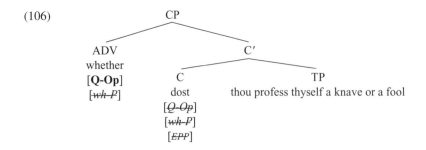

As desired, the only undeleted P-feature which survives at the end of the CP phase is the interpretable operator feature of *whether*. It may be that *whether* gets interpreted as a yes–no question operator because (unlike other wh-operators) it does not bind a trace (i.e. variable) – or its yes–no question interpretation may simply be part of the meaning of *whether*. We can suppose that yes–no questions in present-day English have a similar derivation, save that *whether* receives a null spellout in main clauses, in keeping with Rizzi's (2000) hypothesis that root specifiers in certain types of structure have a null spellout under appropriate conditions. (Note that the analysis of yes–no questions outlined above assumes that C in yes–no questions has the same feature composition as in wh-questions and hence has uninterpretable [Q-Op] and [wh-P] features. However, an alternative possibility is that C in yes–no questions may contain an **interpretable** operator feature, but no [wh-P] feature: such an analysis would obviate the need for positing a null variant of *whether* in spec-CP in main-clause yes–no questions in English.)

In this section, I have developed an analysis of wh-movement which attempts to implement the suggestion made by Chomsky (in the quotations given at the beginning of this section) about possible parallels between A-movement and A-bar movement. The parallels should be obvious: for example, just as a (complete) T probe carries unvalued person/number features and an [EPP] feature which triggers movement of a goal to spec-TP, so too a (complete) C probe carries unvalued peripheral/operator features and an [EPP] feature which triggers movement of a goal to spec-CP; and just as intermediate T constituents (like raising *to*) are incomplete, so too intermediate C constituents are incomplete. Likewise, just as the goal in A-movement carries interpretable person/number features and an uninterpretable case feature which makes it active, so too the goal in A-bar movement carries an interpretable operator feature and an uninterpretable peripheral feature [wh-P] which makes it active. The parallels are not exact, however: for example, one difference is that (under the analysis presented here) the uninterpretable [wh-P] feature carried by the moved wh-expression enters the derivation already valued (so that it can wh-mark an intermediate complementiser), whereas the uninterpretable case feature carried by a nominal enters the derivation unvalued.

There are also empirical problems posed by our attempt to implement Chomsky's analysis. To see why, let's return to consider the structure of Belfast English questions like (38) above, repeated as (107) below:

(107)   What did Mary claim [*did* they steal]? (Henry 1995, p.108)

Under the analysis of wh-movement sketched in this section, the intermediate C in the bracketed complement clause will enter the derivation carrying an unvalued P-feature [*u-P*] which will be assigned the value [*wh-P*] via agreement with the wh-pronoun *what*. This predicts that the head C of the complement clause CP will be *wh*-marked in precisely the same way as it would be if the wh-pronoun were relative or exclamative. But in fact that head C of the bracketed complement-clause CP seems to be marked as specifically *interrogative* in (107), and for this reason requires auxiliary inversion – unlike what happens in a relative clause structure like:

(108)   something **which** Mary claimed [*that* they stole/**did they steal]

where the italicised C constituent heading the bracketed complement clause can be spelled out as *that* but not as an inverted auxiliary like *did*. This suggests that the italicised intermediate C is marked as interrogative in a structure like (107), and as relative in a structure like (108). What this might suggest is that C must carry a clause-type feature of some kind, valued as relative if the clause contains a relative pronoun, and interrogative if it contains an interrogative pronoun. If what marks a pronoun as interrogative or relative is an interrogative operator feature [Q-Op] or a relative operator feature [R-Op], then it would seem as if intermediate C constituents do indeed carry an unvalued operator feature [*u-Op*] which is valued as relative/interrogative via agreement with the wh-pronoun. If this is so, then the topmost C constituent in a wh-structure must carry some additional feature which makes it complete – perhaps a **focus/topic** feature (bearing in mind that it is sometimes claimed that interrogative pronouns behave like focused constituents, and relative pronouns behave like topics), or alternatively a **scope** feature. Details need to be worked out, but I will not attempt to do this here.

Clearly, this and other alternative analyses of A-bar movement operations need to be evaluated in future research – and obvious questions posed by multiple wh-questions answered (one such question being how we ensure that only the 'highest' wh-expression in a multiple wh-question in English carries whatever feature makes such expressions active for wh-movement, and how the wh-expressions which remain in situ can be bound by C (as Pesetsky 1987 argues they must be) if C contains no interpretable interrogative feature. As noted in the Preface to the book, the **Minimalist Program** is precisely that – a programme to guide research: consequently, in relation to many (indeed, most) aspects of syntax we have more questions than answers at present.

10.11   Summary

In this chapter, we have taken a look at Chomsky's phase-based theory of syntax. In §10.2, we noted Chomsky's suggestion that the computational component of the Language Faculty can only hold limited amounts of syntactic structure in its working memory at any one time, and that clause structure is built up in **phases** (with phases including CP and transitive vP). At the end of each phase, the **domain** (i.e. complement of the phase head) undergoes transfer to the phonological and semantic components, with the result that neither the domain nor any constituent it contains are accessible to further syntactic operations from that point on. In §10.3 we saw that intransitive vPs and defective clauses (i.e. clauses which are TPs lacking an extended projection into CP) are not phases, and hence allow A-movement out of their complement, as in structures such as *Numerous problems are thought to remain in Utopia*. In §10.4 we saw that a phase-based theory of syntax requires us to assume that long-distance A-bar movement (e.g. of wh-expressions) involves movement through intermediate spec-CP positions, since CP is a phase and only constituents at the **edge** of a phase can undergo subsequent syntactic operations. In §10.5 it was argued that A-bar movement in transitive clauses involves movement through intermediate spec-vP positions. In §10.6 a range of arguments were presented in support of successive-cyclic A-bar movement through intermediate spec-CP positions, from structures including preposition stranding in Afrikaans, quantifier-stranding in West Ulster English, wh-copying in adult and child grammars, and wh-marking of complementisers in adult and child grammars. In §10.7 we looked at evidence from *have*-cliticisation in English, wh-marking of verbs in Chamorro, past-participle agreement in French, mutation in Welsh and multiple wh-questions in Spanish in support of claiming that wh-movement in transitive clauses involves movement through spec-vP. In §10.8 we looked at the role of phases in relation to lexical selection, noting that only a subarray of the items in the lexical array can be accessed on any given phase. In §10.9, we raised a number of questions about phases. We began by exploring the relation between EPP-hood and phasehood; we presented evidence (from multiple wh-questions in Spanish) that intransitive light verbs may have a wh-attracting [EPP] feature, and yet not be phases. We went on to explore the possibility that DP and/or PP may also be phases, noting that any such claim requires us to make a number of ancillary assumptions (e.g. about feature percolation and [EPP] features). In §10.10 we took a closer look at what drives wh-movement, exploring a way of implementing Chomsky's idea that an interrogative wh-word has an interpretable Q-feature and an uninterpretable wh-feature which makes it active, and conversely that an interrogative C has uninterpretable (and unvalued) Q- and P-features (with a non-interrogative C able to bear a P-feature but not a Q-feature). We noted that such an analysis would require us to suppose that yes–no questions contain an interrogative operator (e.g. a null counterpart of *whether*) in spec-CP. However, we also observed that the analysis proposed in the text left in its wake a number of unanswered questions for future research.

Workbook section

Exercise 10.1

Discuss the role played by phases in the derivation of the following sentences:

1   What is expected to happen to him?
2   What is it expected will happen to him?
3   What are you expecting will happen to him?
4   What is he expected to say to her?
5   What is it expected that he will say to her?
6   What are you expecting that he will say to her?
7   How many prizes are there expected to be awarded?
8   How many prizes are you expecting there to be awarded?
9   How many prizes are you expecting to be awarded?
10   How many questions have you found the answer to?
11   Who has done what?
12   Who has gone where?

Helpful hints

In 7–10, take *how many prizes/how many questions* to be QPs, with *many* as the head, *prizes/questions* as the complement and *how* as the specifier. In relation to 11 and 12, consider how the raising of *who* to spec-TP in English may help account for word-order differences with the corresponding Spanish examples discussed in the main text.

Model answer for sentence 1

The unaccusative verb *happen* is merged with its PP complement *to him*, forming the V-bar *happen to him*. This V-bar is then merged with the pronoun *what* to form the VP *what happen to him*. This VP is in turn merged with an intransitive light verb, which (being affixal) triggers raising of the verb *happen* from V to v. Since the relevant vP has no external argument, it is intransitive. If we follow Chomsky's assumption that intransitive vPs are not phases and their heads have no [EPP] feature, no wh-movement takes place at this point. The resulting vP merges with infinitival *to*, forming the T-bar in (i) below:

(i)

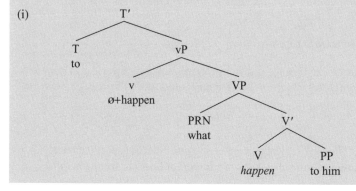

Since a (seemingly subjectless) infinitival complement of a passive participle is a defective clause (hence a TP headed by a defective T), infinitival *to* is defective here and so has person and [EPP] features, but no number feature. Infinitival *to* probes at this point, searching for an active goal with a person feature and an active A-feature, locating *what* (which has a person feature and is active by virtue of its unvalued case feature) and moving *what* to become the specifier of *to*, with the person feature of *to* being valued and deleted in the process, and the [EPP] feature of *to* likewise being deleted. The resulting TP is merged with the verb *expect* to form the VP *expect what to happen to him*. This VP will in turn be merged as the complement of an intransitive participial light verb (which Chomsky 1999 labels as *PRT* but which we label here as *v*) and thereby project into an intransitive participial vP: assuming that the head v of vP is affixal in nature, it will trigger raising of the verb *expect* to v (with *expect* being spelled out as the passive participle *expected* in the phonology). The resulting vP will in turn be merged as the complement of a finite T constituent [T BE], deriving the overt structure shown in simplified form below:

(ii)

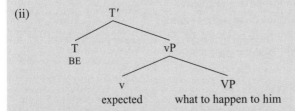

The probe BE identifies *what* as its goal (since *what* is active for agreement with an A-head by virtue of its unvalued case feature), agrees in person and number with *what* and (by virtue of its [EPP] feature) triggers movement of *what* to become the subject of BE. The resulting TP is merged with a null C constituent with carries [TNS, WH, EPP] features which trigger movement of *what* to spec-CP (but do not trigger T-to-C movement, if we adopt Pesetsky and Torrego's 2001 analysis of wh-subject questions, under which a wh-subject in a finite clause is tensed). Since CP is a phase, its TP domain will be spelled out at the end of the CP phase by (7i) in the main text, and the edge (= specifier and head) of CP will in turn be spelled out at the end of the overall derivation (which coincides with the end of the CP phase) by (7ii), so deriving the structure shown in skeletal form below (simplified by omitting all traces):

(iii)

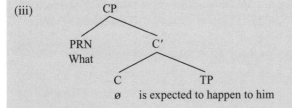

There is no movement of *is* from T to C, since C does not trigger auxiliary inversion in questions in which the preposed wh-word is the subject of the TP complement of C. The only phase in the structure is CP.

Exercise 10.2

Discuss the derivation of the following sentences, commenting on points of special interest. (Note that 3b and 6a,b are examples from non-standard varieties of English: see the **helpful hints**.)

1a	He is someone who/whom I believe has left
b	He is someone who/*whom it is believed has left
2a	He is someone [whom they claim to have died]
b	*They claim him to have died
3a	These are the people [who Clark thinks are telling the truth]
b	%These are the people [who Clark think are telling the truth]
4a	*Who were you asking what happened to?
b	*What were you asking happened to him?
5a	Who was expected to present the prizes?
b	*Who was decided to present the prizes? (= 'Who was it decided should present the prizes?')
6a	Who d'ya reckon what/*that seen'im? (= Who d'you think saw him?')
b	Who d'ya reckon that/*what 'e seen? (= Who d'you think that he saw?)
7a	How little honesty there is in the world!
b	*How little honesty there's in the world!
8a	%What is thought has happened to him? (sentence produced by interviewer, BBC Radio 5 Live)
b	There look like there have been some problems

Say why 8a is ungrammatical in standard varieties of English, and why sentences like 8b are identified by Chomsky (1998, p. 46, fn.94) as potentially problematic for a phase-based theory of syntax which assumes that all finite clauses are CPs and hence phases.

In addition, discuss the derivation of the following child wh-questions reported in Thornton (1995). (Sentences 11 and 12 are adapted slightly for the purposes of this exercise.)

9	Which dinosaur that Grover didn't ride on?
10	Which mouse what the cat didn't see?
11	Which animal do you think what was chasing the cat?
12	Which Smurf do you think who was chasing the cat?

Helpful hints

In sentences 2a and 3a,b, concern yourself only with the derivation of the bracketed relative clause structures. In relation to 2, consider the possibility that (in active uses) verbs like *claim* select a CP complement headed by a null infinitival complementiser which lacks the ability to assign case. Sentence 3b is a type of structure found in some (=%) varieties of Northeastern American English (according to Kimball and Aissen 1971) and in such clauses the verb is reported to agree with the relative pronoun. In 4a, take *who* to originate as the complement of *to*. Sentences 6a,b are types of structure found in a non-standard variety of colloquial British English. In relation to 8a, consider how you might rule out movement of *who* through spec-CP in the complement clause into spec-TP in the main clause, and say whether it is necessary to follow Ura (2001) in attributing the ungrammaticality of such examples to violation of an **Improper Movement Constraint** which prevents movement from an A-bar to an A position (or, equivalently, prevents an A-head like T from attracting a constituent in an A-bar position) – or whether the case-marking properties of the head C constituent of the complement clause CP provide us with an alternative account. In relation to 9 and 10, make the simplifying assumption that *didn't* is an inherently negative auxiliary which originates in T. In relation to 12, consider the possibility that an intermediate C with an [EPP] feature agrees in person, number *and* (animate or inanimate) *gender* with the subject of its clause.

Model answer for sentence 1a

What is puzzling about 1a is why the wh-pronoun can surface in the overtly accusative form *whom* when (prior to wh-movement) it was the subject of *has left* and so would have been expected to agree with (and be assigned nominative case by) *has*, and hence to be spelled out as nominative *who*. In order to try and find out what's going on here, let's take a look at the derivation of the relevant sentence.

The verb LEAVE is unaccusative, and so the relative pronoun *who* originates as its internal argument. Merging *leave* with *who* derives the VP *leave who*. This VP is then merged with a strong light verb which triggers raising of *leave* to adjoin to the light verb. Merging the resulting vP with the auxiliary *have* (which requires the verb *leave* to be spelled out in the perfect participle form *left* at PF) derives the structure (i) below (with italics marking a copy of a moved constituent):

(i)

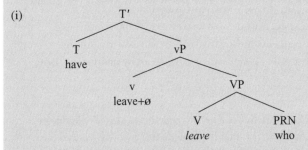

The unvalued person/number features of T serve as a probe, identifying *who* as a goal which is active by virtue of its unvalued case feature. Accordingly, *have* agrees with *who* and is ultimately spelled out at PF as *has*. We'd also expect the unvalued case feature of *who* to be valued as nominative via agreement with the finite T *have* at this point, but let's suppose that this doesn't happen. Instead, the EPP feature of T attracts *who* to move to spec-TP, so deriving the structure shown in skeletal form in (ii) below (trace copies left behind by movement being shown in italics):

(ii)   [$_{TP}$ who [$_T$ has] [$_{vP}$ [$_v$ leave] [$_{VP}$ [$_v$ *leave*] *who*]]]

The resulting TP is then merged with a C carrying [WH, EPP] features which attract *who* to move into spec-CP, and (since CP is a phase) the TP complement of C then undergoes transfer, so deriving the structure shown in (iii) below (with items being shown in their PF form, *outline* font indicating constituents which have undergone spellout, and ~~strikethrough~~ showing constituents which are given a null spellout in the PF component):

(iii)   [$_{CP}$ who [$_C$ ø] [$_{TP}$ ~~who~~ [$_T$ has] [$_{vP}$ [$_v$ left] [$_{VP}$ [$_v$ ~~left~~] ~~who~~]]]]

The CP in (iii) is then embedded as the complement of the verb *believe*, deriving the structure shown in skeletal form in (iv) below (simplified, inter alia, by showing only those constituents of TP which have been overtly spelled out):

(iv)   [$_{VP}$ [$_v$ believe] [$_{CP}$ who [$_C$ ø] [$_{TP}$ has left]]]

The VP in (iv) is then merged with a transitive light verb whose external argument is the pronoun (which is ultimately spelled out as) *I*, and the verb *believe* raises to adjoin to the light verb (leaving an italicised trace copy behind), forming the structure shown in simplified form in (v) below:

(v)

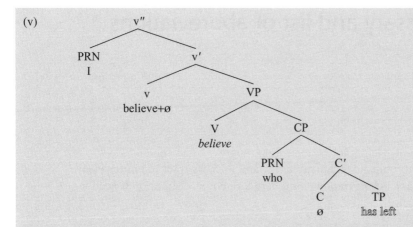

The light verb is transitive (by virtue of having an external argument) and so carries unvalued person/number features, allowing it to agree with and assign (exceptional) accusative case to the wh-pronoun *who* (which remains active at this point by virtue of its case feature not having yet been valued): accordingly, the accusative relative pronoun is spelled out as *whom* in formal styles, and as *who* in other styles. On the assumption that the light verb also carries [WH, EPP] features, it will trigger movement of *who* to become a second (outer) specifier for vP. The derivation will thereafter continue in a familiar fashion, with *I* agreeing with, being assigned nominative case by and moving to become the specifier of the relative clause T constituent, and *who* moving from spec-vP to become the specifier of the null C constituent heading the relative clause. Note, however, that a crucial feature of this analysis is the assumption that a transitive vP is a phase, and triggers successive-cyclic movement of an extracted wh-expression through spec-vP.

While the force of the argument presented above is somewhat weakened by the problematic status of *whom* in present-day English (discussed in Lasnik and Sobin 2000), it is interesting to note that Bejar and Massam (1999, p. 66) report a similar phenomenon (of exceptional case-marking of the subject of a finite clause by a higher transitive verb) in Hungarian sentences such as:

(vi)   Kiket   mondtad hogy szeretnél   ha eljönnék?
         Whom you.said that   you.would.like if came
         'Who did you say you would like it if they came?'

Bejar and Massam suppose that different links in a movement chain can be assigned different cases, with PF determining which of the various cases is actually spelled out. Their analysis overcomes an apparent violation of the Earliness Principle in the derivation outlined above, since we would have expected *who* to be assigned nominative case at the stage of derivation represented in (i) above. However, their proposal poses an apparent challenge to the claim that the different links in movement chains are identical copies, since this will clearly not be so if different chain links carry different cases.

Glossary and list of abbreviations

Bold print is used to indicate technical terms, and to cross-refer to entries elsewhere in the glossary. Abbreviations used here are: ch. = chapter; § = section number; ex. = exercise.

A: see **adjective, A-head, A-position, Binding**.

AAE: African American English.

A-bar: an A-bar position is a position which can be occupied by arguments or adjuncts alike. For example, the specifier position within CP is said to be an A-bar position because it can contain not only an argument like the italicised wh-phrase in '*Which car* did he fix?' but also an adjunct like the italicised adverbial phrase in '*How* did he fix the car?' **A-bar movement** is a movement operation (like **wh-movement**) which moves an argument or adjunct expression to an A-bar position. On **A-bar head**, see **A-head**.

Acc(usative): see **case**.

ACP: see **Attract Closest Principle**.

acquisition: the process by which people acquire their first language (= L1 acquisition) or a second language which is not their mother tongue (= L2 acquisition).

active: a contrast is traditionally drawn between sentence pairs such as (i) and (ii) below:

(i)   The thieves stole the jewels   (ii) The jewels were stolen by the thieves

(i) is said to be an **active** clause (or sentence), and (ii) to be its **passive** counterpart; similarly, the verb *stole* is said to be an active verb (or a verb in the active **voice**) in (i), whereas the verb *stolen* is said to be a passive verb (or a verb in the passive voice – more specifically, a passive **participle**) in (ii); likewise, the auxiliary *were* in (ii) is said to be a passive **auxiliary**. In a different use, a **probe** or **goal** is said to be **active** for movement/agreement if it carries an uninterpretable feature. See §8.4.

adequacy, criteria of: these are the criteria which an adequate grammar or linguistic theory must meet. See §1.3.

adjacency condition: a condition requiring that two expressions must be immediately adjacent (i.e. there must be no constituent intervening between the two) in order for some operation to apply. For example, *have* must be immediately adjacent to *they* in order to **cliticise** onto it in structures such as *They've gone home*.

adjective: this is a category of word (abbreviated to A) which often denotes states (e.g. *happy, sad*), which typically has an adverb counterpart in *-ly* (e.g. *sad/sadly*), which typically has comparative/superlative forms in *-er/-est* (e.g. *sadder/saddest*), which can often take the prefix *un-* (e.g. *unhappy*), and which can often form a noun by the addition of the suffix *-ness* (e.g. *sadness*), etc. See §2.2 and §2.3.

adjoin: see **adjunction**.

adjunct: One way in which this term is used is to denote an optional constituent typically used to specify e.g. the time, place or manner in which an event takes place. Another way in which it is used is to denote a constituent which has been attached to another to form a larger constituent of the same type. (See **adjunction**.)

adjunction: this is a process by which one constituent is adjoined (= attached) to another to form a larger constituent of the same type. For example, we could say that in a sentence like 'He should not go', the negative particle *not* (in the guise of its contracted form *n't*) can be adjoined to the auxiliary *should* to form the negative auxiliary *shouldn't*. In a sentence such as *He gently rolled the ball down the hill*, the adverb *gently* can be taken to be an adverb which adjoins to a verbal projection, extending it into a larger projection of the same kind. See §9.4.

adposition: a cover term subsuming **preposition** and **postposition**. For example, the English word *in* is a preposition since it is positioned before its complement (e.g. *in Tokyo*), whereas its Japanese counterpart is a postposition because it is positioned after its complement *Tokyo*. Both words are **adpositions**.

ADV/adverb: this is a category of word which typically indicates manner (e.g. 'wait *patiently*') or degree (e.g. '*exceedingly* patient'). In English, most (but not all) adverbs end in *-ly* (e.g. *quickly* – but also *almost*). See §2.2 and 2.3.

AFF: see **affix**

affective: an affective constituent is an (e.g. negative, interrogative or conditional) expression which can have a **polarity expression** like (partitive) *any* in its scope. So, for example, interrogative *if* is an affective constituent as we see from the fact that an interrogative *if*-clause can contain partitive *any* in a sentence such as 'I wonder *if* he has *any* news about Jim.'

affix/affixal: the term **affix** is typically used to describe a grammatical morpheme which cannot stand on its own as an independent word, but which must be attached to a host word of an appropriate kind. An affix which attaches to the beginning of a word (e.g. *un-* in *unhappy*) is called a **prefix:** an affix which attaches to the end of a word (e.g. *-s* in *chases*) is called a **suffix**. An **affixal** head is one which behaves like an affix in needing to attach to a particular kind of host word. See also **clitic**. **Affix Hopping** is an operation by which an unattached affix in T is lowered onto a verb: see §4.4. **Affix Attachment** is an operation whereby an unattached tense affix lowers onto a verb where possible, but is otherwise supported by use of the dummy auxiliary *do:* see §5.8.

AGENT: this is a term used to describe the semantic (= thematic) role which a particular type of argument plays in a given sentence. It typically denotes a person who deliberately causes some state of affairs to come about – hence e.g. *John* plays the thematic role of AGENT in a sentence such as '*John* smashed the bottle.' See §7.5.

agreement: an operation by which (e.g. in a sentence like *They are lying*) the person/number features of the T-constituent *are* get assigned the same values as those of its subject *they*, so that the present-tense auxiliary *are* is third person plural because it agrees in **person** and **number** with its third-person-plural subject *they*. See ch. 8.

A-head: an A-head is the kind of head (like T) which allows as its specifier an argument expression but not an adjunct expression. An A-bar head is the kind of head (like C) which allows as its specifier either an argument or an adjunct expression.

allomorphs: variant phonetic forms of a single morpheme. For example, the noun plural morpheme {s} in English has the three allomorphs /s/ (e.g. in *cats*) /z/ (e.g. in *dogs*) and /ɪz/ (e.g. in *horses*).

A-movement: movement from one **A-position** to another (typically, from a subject or complement position into another subject position). See ch. 7.

A-position: a position which can be occupied by an **argument**, but not by a non-argument expression (e.g. not by an adjunct). In practice, the term denotes a subject position, or a lexical complement position (i.e. a position occupied by a constituent which is the complement of a **lexical/substantive** head).

anaphor: this is an expression (like *himself*) which cannot have independent reference, but which must take its reference from an appropriate **antecedent** (i.e. expression which it refers to) within the same phrase or sentence. Hence, while we can say 'John is deluding himself' (where *himself* refers back to *John*), we cannot say *'Himself is waiting', since the anaphor *himself* here has no antecedent. A traditional distinction is drawn between **reflexive anaphors** (i.e. *self* forms like *myself/ourselves/yourself/yourselves/himself/herself/itself/themselves*) and the **reciprocal anaphors** *each other/one another* (e.g. 'They help each other/one another'). See §3.7 and ex.3.2.

animate: the term animate is used to denote (the gender of) an expression which denotes a living being (e.g. a human being or animal), while the term **inanimate** is used in relation to an expression which denotes lifeless entities. For example, the **relative pronoun** *who* could be said to be animate in gender and the relative pronoun *which* inanimate – hence we say *someone who upsets people* and *something which upsets people*.

antecedent: an expression which is referred to by a pronoun or anaphor of some kind. For example, in 'John cut himself shaving', *John* is the antecedent of the anaphor *himself*, since *himself* refers back to *John*. In a sentence such as 'He is someone who we respect', the antecedent of the relative pronoun *who* is *someone*.

AP: adjectival phrase – i.e. a phrase headed by an adjective, such as *fond of chocolate, keen on sport, good at syntax* etc.

appositive relative clause: a relative clause which is used as a parenthetical comment, as with the parenthesised relative clause in 'John (*who you met last week*) is a good friend of mine.' See **relative**.

arbitrary: when we say that an expression has 'arbitrary reference', we mean that it can denote an unspecified set of individuals, and hence have much the same meaning as English *one/people* or French *on*. In a sentence such as 'It is difficult [PRO to learn Japanese]', the bracketed clause is said to have an abstract pronoun subject PRO which can have arbitrary reference, in which case the sentence is paraphraseable as 'It's difficult for *people* to learn Japanese.' See §4.2.

argument: this is a term borrowed by linguists from philosophy (more specifically, from predicate calculus) to describe the role played by particular types of expression in the semantic structure of sentences. In a sentence such as 'John hit Fred', the overall sentence is said to be a **proposition** (a term used to describe the semantic content of a clause), and to consist of the predicate *hit* and its two arguments *John* and *Fred*. The two arguments represent the two participants in the act of hitting, and the predicate is the expression (in this case the verb *hit*) which describes the activity in which they are engaged. By extension, in a sentence such as 'John says he hates syntax' the predicate in the main clause is the verb *says*, and its two arguments are *John* and the clause *he hates syntax*; the argument *he hates syntax* is in turn a proposition whose predicate is *hates*, and whose two arguments are *he* and *syntax*. Since the complement of a verb is positioned internally within V-bar whereas the subject of a verb is positioned outside V-bar, complements are also referred to as **internal arguments**, and subjects as **external arguments**. Expressions which do not function as arguments are **non-arguments**. The **argument structure** of a predicate provides a description of the set of **arguments** associated with the **predicate**, and the **thematic role** which each fulfils in relation to the predicate. See §7.4 and §7.5.

array: the **lexical array** for a given expression denotes the set of lexical items out of which the expression is formed. The term **lexical subarray** denotes the particular subset of items from the lexical array out of which a particular **phase** is formed. See §10.8.

article: a term used in traditional grammar to describe a particular subclass of determiners: the determiner *the* is traditionally called the **definite article**, and the determiner *a* the **indefinite article**.

Asp/AspP: Aspect/Aspect Phrase. See §7.3.

aspect: a term typically used to denote the duration of the activity described by a verb (e.g. whether the activity is ongoing or completed). In sentences such as:

(i)   He has taken the medicine   (ii) He is taking the medicine

the auxiliary *has* is said to be an auxiliary which marks **perfect aspect**, in that it marks the perfection (in the sense of 'completion' or 'termination') of the activity of taking the medicine; for analogous reasons, **taken** is said to be a **perfect-participle** verb form in (i) (though it is referred to in traditional grammars as a 'past participle'). Similarly, *is* functions as an auxiliary which marks **progressive aspect** in (ii), because it relates to an activity which is ongoing or in progress (for this reason, *is* in (ii) is also referred to as a **progressive auxiliary**); in the same way, the verb *taking* in (ii) is said to be the **progressive-participle** form of the verb (though it is sometimes known in traditional grammars as a 'present participle').

aspectual auxiliaries: auxiliaries which mark **aspect** – e.g. perfect *have* and progressive *be*. See **aspect**.

associate: an expression which represents the thematic argument in an expletive *there* construction, and which is associated with the expletive subject *there:* e.g. *several prizes* in *There were awarded several prizes*.

asymmetric c-command: see **c-command**.

attract: to say that a head H *attracts* a constituent C is to say that H triggers movement of C to some position on the **edge** of HP (so that C may move to adjoin to H, or to become the specifier of H).

Attract Closest Principle: a principle of grammar requiring that a head H which **attracts** a particular type of constituent attracts the closest constituent of the relevant type which it c-commands.

attribute: see **value**.

attributive adjectives: these are adjectives which are used to modify a following noun expression – e.g. *red* in 'John has a *red* Ferrari', where *red* attributes the property of being red to the noun *Ferrari*. Attributive adjectives contrast with **predicative adjectives**, which are adjectives used in structures such as 'The house was *red*' or 'They painted the house *red*', (where the property of being red is said to be **predicated** of the expression *the house*).

AUX/auxiliary: a term used to **categorise** items such as *will/would/ can/could/shall/should/may/might/must/ought* and some uses of *have/be/do/ need/dare*. Such items have a number of idiosyncratic properties, including the fact that they can undergo **inversion** (e.g. in questions like '*Can* you speak French?'). By contrast, **main verbs** (i.e. verbs which are not auxiliaries) cannot undergo inversion – as we see from the ungrammaticality **'Speak* you French?' See §2.7.

AUXP: auxiliary projection/auxiliary phrase – i.e. a phrase headed by an auxiliary which does not occupy the head T position of TP. See §5.6.

auxiliary copying: a phenomenon whereby a moved auxiliary leaves behind an overt copy of itself when it moves – as with *can* in a Child English question like *What can I can have for dinner?*

auxiliary inversion: see **inversion**.

auxiliary selection: this term relates to the type of expression which a given auxiliary selects as its complement: e.g. in many languages (the counterpart of) BE when used as a perfect auxiliary selects only a complement headed by a verb with no **external argument**, whereas (the counterpart of) HAVE selects a complement headed by a verb with an external argument.

B: on **Principle B** of Binding Theory, see ex. 3.2.

bar: when used as a suffix attached to a category label such as N, V, P, T etc. (as in N-bar, V-bar, P-bar, T-bar etc.), it denotes an **intermediate projection** which is larger than a word but smaller than a phrase. Hence, in a phrase such as *university policy on drugs*, we might say that the string *policy on drugs* is an N-bar, since it is a projection of the head noun *policy*, but is an intermediate projection in that it has a larger projection into the NP *university policy on drugs*. The term **bar notation** refers to a system of representing projection levels which posits that (first) merge of a head H with its complement forms an H-bar constituent, (second) merge of a head with a specifier forms an H-double-bar constituent, (third) merge of a head with a further specifier forms an H-treble-bar constituent, and so on (with the **maximal projection** of H being labelled HP). On **A-bar position**, see **A-position**.

bare: a **bare infinitive** structure is one which contains a verb in the infinitive form, but does not contain the infinitive particle *to* (e.g. the italicised clause in 'He won't let *you help him*'). A **bare noun** is a noun used without any determiner to modify it (e.g. *fish* in '*Fish* is expensive'). A **bare clause** is one not introduced by an overt complementiser (e.g. *he was tired* in 'John said *he was tired*'). A theory of **bare phrase structure** is one in which there are no category labels or projection levels associated with constituents: see §3.8.

base form: the base form of a verb is the simplest, uninflected form of the verb (the form under which the relevant verb would be listed in an English dictionary) – hence forms like *go/be/have/see/want/love* are the base forms of the relevant verbs.

The base form can typically function either as an **infinitive** (e.g. 'Try to *stay*'), an imperative (e.g. '*Stay* with me tonight!'), a present-tense **indicative** form (e.g. 'They sometimes *stay* with me'), or a **subjunctive** form (e.g. 'I demand that he *stay* with me').

Binarity Principle: a principle of Universal Grammar specifying that all non-terminal nodes in syntactic structures (i.e. tree diagrams) are **binary-branching**. See §3.2.

binary: a term relating to a two-way contrast. For example, **number** is a binary property in English, in that we have a two-way contrast between **singular** forms like *cat* and **plural** forms like *cats*. It is widely assumed that **parameters** have binary settings, that features have binary values, and that all branching in syntactic structure is binary.

binary-branching: a tree diagram in which every non-terminal node has two daughters is binary-branching; a category/node which has two daughters is also binary-branching. See §3.2.

bind/binder/binding: to say that one constituent X binds (or serves as the binder for) another constituent Y (and conversely that Y is bound by X) is to say that X determines properties (usually, referential properties) of Y. For example, in a sentence such as 'John blamed himself', the reflexive anaphor *himself* is bound by *John* in the sense that the referential properties of *himself* are determined by *John* (so that the two refer to the same individual). The **C-command condition on binding** says that a bound form must be c-commanded by its antecedent. On principles A, B and C of **Binding Theory**, see ex. 3.2.

bottom-up: to say that a syntactic structure is derived in a **bottom-up** fashion is to say that the structure is built up from bottom to top, with lower parts of the structure being formed before higher parts.

bound: in a traditional use of this term, a bound form is one which cannot stand alone and be used as an independent word, but rather must be attached to some other morpheme (e.g. negative *n't*, which has to attach to some auxiliary such as *could*). In a completely different use of the term, a bound constituent is one which has a binder (i.e. antecedent) within the structure containing it (see **bind**).

bracketing: a technique for representing the categorial status of an expression, whereby the expression is enclosed in square brackets, and the lefthand bracket is labelled with an appropriate category symbol – e.g. [D the]. See §2.10.

branch: a term used to represent a solid line linking a pair of nodes in a tree diagram, marking a mother/daughter (i.e. containment) relation between them.

C: see complementiser.

canonical: a term used to mean 'usual', 'typical' or 'normal', as in 'The canonical word order in English is specifier+head+complement.' The term **canonical**

clause denotes a (non-defective) clause which is a full CP/complementiser phrase: see §4.6 and §4.7.

case: the different case forms of a pronoun are the different forms which the pronoun has in different sentence positions. It is traditionally said that English has three cases – **nominative** (sometimes abbreviated to **Nom**), **accusative** (= **Acc**, sometimes referred to as **objective**), and **genitive** (= **Gen**). Personal pronouns typically inflect overtly for all three cases, whereas noun expressions inflect only for genitive case. The different case forms of typical pronouns and noun expressions are given below:

nominative	I	we	you	he	she	it	they	who	the king
accusative	me	us	you	him	her	it	them	who(m)	the king
genitive	my	our	your	his	her	its	their	whose	the king's
	mine	ours	yours		hers		theirs		

As is apparent, some pronouns have two distinct genitive forms: a **weak** (shorter) form used when they are immediately followed by a noun (as in 'This is *my car*'), and a **strong** (longer) form used when they are not immediately followed by a noun (as in 'This car is *mine*'). In Chomsky and Lasnik (1995), it is suggested that the null subject PRO found in **control** constructions carries null case. In languages like English where certain types of expression are assigned case by virtue of the structural position they occupy in a given clause (e.g. accusative if c-commanded by a transitive head, nominative if c-commanded by finite intransitive head), the relevant expressions are said to receive **structural case**. Where a constituent is assigned case by virtue of its semantic function (e.g. a GOAL complement of certain types of verb is assigned dative case in German), it is said to receive **inherent case**. In languages like Icelandic where subjects can be assigned a variety of cases (e.g. some are accusative and others dative, depending on the choice of verb and its semantic properties), subjects are said to have **quirky case**. In the Italian counterpart of a structure like 'She gave him them' the **direct object** corresponding to English 'them' is assigned accusative case, and the indirect object corresponding to English 'him' is assigned a distinct case, traditionally called **dative case**. (On direct and indirect objects, see **object**.) On **nominative case assignment**, see §4.9 and §8.3; on **accusative case assignment**, see §4.9, §9.7 and §9.8; on **null case assignment**, see §4.9 and §8.8; and on **genitive case assignment**, see §6.7 and §9.9.

case particle: some linguists take *of* in structures like *destruction of the city* or *fond of pasta* to be a **genitive** case particle in the sense that the *of*-phrase (e.g. *of the city*) is taken to have genitive case, and *of* is said to be the morpheme which marks genitive case.

categorial: categorial information is information about the grammatical category that an item belongs to. A categorial property is one associated with members of a particular grammatical category.

categorise/categorisation: assign(ing) an expression to a (grammatical) **category**.

category: a term used to denote a set of expressions which share a common set of linguistic properties. In syntax, the term is used for expressions which share a common set of grammatical properties. For example, *boy* and *girl* belong to the (grammatical) category **noun** because they both inflect for plural number (e.g. *boys/girls*), and can both be used to end a sentence such as 'The police haven't yet found the missing –.' In traditional grammar, the term **parts of speech** was used in place of **categories**.

causative verb: a verb which has much the same sense as 'cause'. For example, the verb *have* in sentences such as 'He had them expelled' or 'He had them review the case' might be said to be causative in sense (hence to be a causative verb).

C-command: a structural relation between two constituents. To say that one constituent X c-commands another constituent Y is (informally) to say that X is no lower than Y in the structure (i.e. either X is higher up in the structure than Y, or the two are at the same height). More formally, a constituent X c-commands its sister constituent Y and any constituent Z that is contained within Y. A constituent X **asymmetrically c-commands** another constituent Y if X c-commands Y but Y does not c-command X. See §3.7.

C-command condition on binding: a condition to the effect that a bound constituent (e.g. a **reflexive anaphor** like *himself* or the trace of a moved constituent) must be **c-commanded** by its **antecedent** (i.e. by the expression which binds it). See §3.7 and ex. 3.2.

CED: See **Condition on Extraction Domains.**

chain: a set of constituents comprising an expression and any trace copies associated with it. Where a constituent does not undergo movement, it forms a single-membered chain.

citation: the **citation form** of a word is the form under which the word is listed in traditional dictionaries.

clause: a clause is defined in traditional grammar as an expression which contains (at least) a **subject** and a **predicate**, and which may contain other types of expression as well (e.g. one or more **complements** and/or **adjuncts**). In most cases, the predicate in a clause is a lexical (= main) verb, so that there will be as many different clauses in a sentence as there are different lexical verbs. For example, in a sentence such as 'She may think that you are cheating on her', there are two lexical verbs (*think* and *cheating*), and hence two clauses. The *cheating* clause is *that you are cheating on her*, and the *think* clause is *She may think that you are cheating on her*, so that the *cheating* clause is one of the constituents of the *think* clause. More specifically, the *cheating* clause is the **complement** of the *think* clause, and so is said to function as a **complement clause** in this type of sentence. Clauses whose predicate is not a verb (i.e. verbless clauses) are known as **small clauses:** hence, in 'John considers [Mary intelligent]', the bracketed expression is sometimes referred to as a **small clause**.

cleft sentence: a structure such as 'It was *syntax* that he hated most', where *syntax* is said to occupy **focus position** within the cleft sentence.

clitic(isation): the term **clitic** denotes an item which is (generally) a reduced form of another word, and which has the property that (in its reduced form) it must cliticise (i.e. attach itself to) an appropriate kind of **host** (i.e. to another word or phrase). For example, we could say that the contracted negative particle *n't* is a clitic form of the negative particle *not* which attaches itself to a finite auxiliary verb, so giving rise to forms like *isn't, shouldn't, mightn't* etc. Likewise, we could say that *'ve* is a clitic which attaches itself to a pronoun ending in a vowel, so giving rise to forms like *we've, you've, they've* etc. When a clitic attaches to the end of another word, it is said to be an **enclitic** (and hence to **encliticise**) onto the relevant word. Clitics differ from **affixes** in a number of ways. For example, a clitic is often a reduced form of a full word, and has a corresponding full form (so that *'ll* is the clitic form of *will*, for example), whereas an affix (like noun plural *-s* in *cats*) has no full-word counterpart. Moreover, clitics can attach to phrases (e.g. *'s* can attach to *the president* in *The president's lying*), whereas an affix typically attaches to a word stem (e.g. the past-tense *-ed* affix attaches to the verb stem *snow* in *snowed*).

close/closer/closest: in structures in which a head X attracts a particular kind of constituent Y to move to the **edge** of XP, X is said to attract the *closest* constituent of type Y, in accordance with the **Attract Closest Principle**. On one view of closeness, if X **c-commands** Y and Z, X is closer to Y than to Z if Y c-commands Z. See also **local**.

cognition/cognitive: (relating to) the study of human knowledge.

common noun: see **noun**.

COMP: see **complementiser**.

comparative: the comparative form of an adjective or adverb is the form (typically ending in *-er*) used when comparing two individuals or properties: e.g. 'John is *taller* than Mary', where *taller* is the comparative form of the adjective *tall*.

competence: a term used to represent native speakers' knowledge of the grammar of their native language(s).

complement: this is a term used to denote a specific grammatical function (in the same way that the term **subject** denotes a specific grammatical function). A complement is an expression which is directly **merged** with (and hence is the **sister** of) a head word, thereby projecting the head into a larger structure of essentially the same kind. In 'Close the door', *the door* is the complement of the verb *close*; in 'after dinner', *dinner* is the complement of the preposition *after*; in 'good at physics', *at physics* is the complement of the adjective *good*; in 'loss of face', *of face* is the complement of the noun *loss*. As these examples illustrate, complements typically follow their heads in English. The choice of complement (and the morphological form of the complement) is determined by properties of the head: for example, an auxiliary such as *will* requires as its complement an expression headed by a verb in the infinitive form (cf. 'He will *go/*going/*gone*'). Moreover, complements bear a close semantic relation to their heads (e.g. in 'Kill him', *him* is the complement of the verb *kill* and plays the semantic role of THEME argument of the verb *kill*). Thus, a complement has a close morphological, syntactic and semantic relation to its head. A **complement clause** is a clause which is used as the complement of some other word (typically as the complement of a verb, adjective or noun). Thus, in a sentence such as 'He never expected that she would come', the clause *that she would come* serves as the complement of the verb *expected*, and so is a complement clause. On **complement selection**, see **selection**.

complementiser: this term is used in two ways. On the one hand, it denotes a particular category of clause-introducing word such as *that/if/for*, as used in sentences such as 'I think *that* you should apologise', 'I doubt *if* she realises', 'They're keen *for* you to show up'. On the other hand, it is used to denote the pre-subject position in clauses ('the complementiser position') which is typically occupied by a complementiser like *that/if/for*, but which can also be occupied by an inverted auxiliary in sentences such as '*Can* you help?', where *can* is said to occupy the complementiser position in the clause. A **complementiser phrase** (**CP**) is a phrase/clause/expression headed by a complementiser (or by an auxiliary or verb occupying the complementiser position).

complex sentence: one which contains more than one **clause**.

component: a grammar is said to have three main components: a **syntactic/computational component** which generates syntactic structures, a **semantic component** which assigns each such syntactic structure an appropriate **semantic interpretation**, and a **PF component** which assigns each syntactic structure generated by the computational component an appropriate **phonetic form**. See §1.3.

compound word: a word which is built up out of two (or more) other words – e.g. *man-eater*.

computational component: see **component**.

concord: a traditional term to describe an operation whereby a noun and any adjectives or determiners modifying it are assigned the same values for features such as number, gender and case.

conditional: a term used to represent a type of clause (typically introduced by *if* or *unless*) which lays down conditions – e.g. 'If you don't behave, I'll bar you', or 'Unless you behave, I'll bar you'. In these examples, the clauses *If you don't behave* and *Unless you behave* are **conditional clauses**.

Condition on Extraction Domains: a constraint to the effect that only complements allow constituents to be extracted out of them, not specifiers or adjuncts.

configurational: positional – i.e. relating to the position occupied by one or more constituents in a tree diagram. For example, a configurational definition of a structural subject (for English) would be 'an argument which occupies the specifier position in TP'. This definition is configurational in the sense that it tells you what position within TP the subject occupies.

CONJ: see **conjunction**.

conjoin: to join together two or more expressions, usually by a **coordinating conjunction** such as *and/or/but*. For example, in 'Naughty but nice', *naughty* has been conjoined with *nice* (and conversely *nice* has been conjoined with *naughty*).

conjunct: one of a set of expressions which have been **conjoined**. For example, in 'Rather tired but otherwise alright', the two conjuncts (i.e. expressions which have been conjoined) are *rather tired* and *otherwise alright*.

conjunction/CONJ: a word which is used to join two or more expressions together. For example, in a sentence such as 'John was tired but happy', the word *but* serves the function of being a **coordinating conjunction** because it coordinates (i.e. joins together) the adjectives *tired* and *happy*. In 'John felt angry and Mary felt bitter', the conjunction *and* is used to coordinate the two clauses *John felt angry* and *Mary felt bitter*. In traditional grammar, **complementisers** like *that/for/if* are categorised as (one particular type of) subordinating conjunction.

constituent: a term denoting a structural unit – i.e. an expression which is one of the components out of which a phrase or sentence is built up. For example, the various constituents of a **prepositional phrase** (= PP) such as 'Straight into touch' (e.g. as a reply to 'Where did the ball go?') would be the preposition *into*, the noun *touch*, the adverb *straight* and the **intermediate projection** (P-bar) *into touch*. To say that X is an **immediate constituent** of Y is to say that X **immediately contains** Y (see **contain**), or equivalently that X is the mother of Y: see §3.7.

constituent structure: the constituent structure (or **phrase structure**, or **syntactic structure**) of an expression is (a representation of) the set of constituents which the expression contains. Syntactic structure is usually represented in terms of a **labelled bracketing** or a **tree diagram**. The **Constituent Structure Constraint** is a grammatical principle which specifies that only a head can occupy a head position, and that only a maximal projection can occupy a complement or specifier position.

constrained: see **restrictive**.

constraint: a structural restriction which blocks the application of some process in a particular type of structure. The term tends to be used with the rather more specific meaning of 'a principle of Universal Grammar which prevents certain types of grammatical operation from applying to certain types of structure'.

contain: to say that one constituent X **contains** another constituent Y is to say that Y is one of the constituents out of which X is formed by a merger operation of some kind. In terms of tree diagrams, we can say that X contains Y if X occurs higher up in the tree than Y, and X is connected to Y by a continuous (unbroken) set of downward branches (the branches being represented by the solid lines connecting pairs of nodes in a tree diagram). If we think of tree diagrams as a network of train stations, we can say that X **contains** Y if it is possible to get from X to Y by travelling one or more stations south. To say that one constituent X **immediately contains** another constituent Y is to say that Y occurs immediately below X in a tree and is connected to X via a branch (or, that X contains Y and there is no intervening constituent Z which contains Y and which is contained by X). See §3.7.

content: this term is generally used to refer to the semantic content (i.e. meaning) of an expression (typically, of a word). However, it can also be used in a more general way to refer to the linguistic properties of an expression: e.g. the expression **phonetic content** is sometimes used to refer to the phonetic form of (e.g.) a word: hence, we might say that PRO is a pronoun which has no phonetic content (meaning that it is a 'silent' pronoun with no audible form).

contentives/content words: words which have intrinsic descriptive content (as opposed to **functors**, i.e. words which serve essentially to mark particular grammatical functions). Nouns, verbs, adjectives and (most) prepositions are traditionally classified as contentives, while pronouns, auxiliaries, determiners, complementisers and particles of various kinds (e.g. infinitival *to*, genitive *of*) are classified as functors. See §2.4.

contraction: a process by which two different words are combined into a single word, with either or both words being reduced in form. For example, by contraction, *want to* can be reduced to *wanna, going to* to *gonna, he is* to *he's, they have* to *they've, did not* to *didn't* etc. See also **cliticisation**.

contrastive: in a sentence like '*Syntax*, I hate but *phonology* I enjoy', the expressions *syntax* and *phonology* are contrasted, and each is said to be **contrastive** in use.

control(ler)/control predicate: in non-finite clauses with a PRO subject which has an antecedent, the antecedent is said to be the **controller** of PRO (or to **control** PRO), and conversely PRO is said to be controlled by its antecedent; and the relevant kind of structure is called a **control structure**. So, in a structure like 'John decided PRO to quit', *John* is the controller of PRO, and conversely PRO is controlled by *John*. The term **control predicate** denotes a word like *try* which takes an infinitive complement with a (controlled) PRO subject. Verbs like *try* which take a complement containing a PRO subject controlled by the subject of *try* are called **subject-control predicates** (see §4.2); verbs like *persuade* in sentences like *I persuaded him to take syntax* which take an infinitive complement whose PRO subject is controlled by the object of the main verb (here, the *him* object of *persuade*) are called **object-control predicates** (see §9.5).

converge(nce): a **derivation** converges (and hence results in a well-formed sentence) if the resulting **PF-representation** contains only phonetic features, and the associated **semantic representation** contains only (semantically) interpretable features. The **Convergence Principle** is a UG principle requiring that when a probe attracts a goal carrying some feature [F], it triggers movement of the smallest constituent containing [F] which will lead to a convergent (hence well-formed) derivation: see §6.7.

coordinate/coordination: a **coordinate structure** is a structure containing two or more expressions joined together by a **coordinating conjunction** such as *and/but/or/nor* (e.g. 'John and Mary' is a coordinate structure). **Coordination** is the operation by which two or more expressions are joined together by a coordinating conjunction.

copula/copular verb: a 'linking verb', used to link a subject with a non-verbal predicate. The main copular verb in English is *be* (though verbs like *become, remain, stay* etc. also have much the same linking function). In sentences such as 'They are lazy', 'They are fools' and 'They are outside', the verb *are* is said to be a **copula** in that it links the subject *they* to the adjectival predicate *lazy*, or the nominal predicate *fools*, or the prepositional predicate *outside*.

copy/copying: the **Copy Theory of Movement** is a theory developed by Chomsky which maintains that a moved constituent leaves behind a (**trace**) copy of itself when it moves, with the copy generally having its phonetic features deleted and so being **null**: see §5.3, §6.3 and §7.2. **Feature Copying** is an operation by which the value of a feature on one constituent is copied onto another (e.g. the values of the person/number features of a subject are copied onto an auxiliary): see §8.3.

coreferential: two expressions are coreferential if they refer to the same entity. For example, in 'John cut himself while shaving', *himself* and *John* are coreferential in the sense that they refer to the same individual.

count/countability: a **count(able) noun** is a noun which can be counted. Hence, a noun such as *chair* is a count noun since we can say 'One chair, two chairs, three chairs etc.'; but a noun such as *furniture* is a **non-count/uncountable/mass noun** since we cannot say '*one furniture, *two furnitures, *three furnitures etc.'

The **countability** properties of a noun determine whether the relevant item is a **count noun** or not.

counterexample: an example which falsifies a particular hypothesis. For example, an auxiliary like *ought* would be a counterexample to any claim that auxiliaries in English never take an infinitive complement introduced by *to* (e.g. 'You ought to tell them').

CP: complementiser phrase: see **complementiser**.

crash: a derivation is said to **crash** (i.e. 'fail') if one or more features carried by one or more constituents is **illegible** at either or both of the **interface levels** (the phonetics interface and the semantics interface). For example, if the person or number features of HAVE remain unvalued in a sentence such as 'He HAVE left', the resulting structure will crash at the phonetics interface, since the PF component will be unable to determine whether HAVE should be spelled out as *have* or *has*.

cross-categorial properties: properties which extend across categories, i.e. which are associated with more than one different category. See §2.11.

cycle/cyclic: syntactic operations (like agreement and movement) are said to apply in a **cyclic** fashion, such that each time a head H is merged with one or more other constituents, a new **cycle** of operations begins (in the sense that any operation affecting H and one or more other constituents which it c-commands applies at this point). See §5.7.

D: see **determiner**.

Dat: an informal abbreviate for **dative case**. See **case**.

daughter: a node X is the daughter of another node Y if Y is the next highest node up in the tree from X, and the two are connected by a **branch** (solid line).

declarative: a term used as a classification of the **force** (i.e. semantic function) of a clause which is used to make a statement (as opposed to an **interrogative, exclamative** or **imperative** clause).

default: a default value or property is one which obtains if all else fails (i.e. if other conditions are not satisfied). For example, if we say that *-ø* is the default verbal inflection for regular verbs in English, we mean that regular verbs carry the inflection *-s* in third-person-singular present-tense forms, *-d* in past, perfect or passive forms, *-ing* if progressive or gerund forms, and *-ø* otherwise (by default).

defective: a defective item is one which lacks certain properties. For example, if we suppose that T constituents generally carry person and number features, then infinitival *to* in all infinitive structures except **control** infinitives is a defective T constituent in that (under Chomsky's analysis) it carries person but not number. Any clause containing a defective T constituent is a **defective clause**.

definite: expressions containing determiners like *the, this, that* etc. are said to have **definite reference** in that they refer to an entity which is assumed to be known to the addressee(s): e.g. in a sentence such as 'I hated the course', the DP *the course* refers to a specific (e.g. Minimalist Syntax) course whose identity is assumed to be known to the hearer/reader. In much the same way, personal pronouns like *he/she/it/they* etc. are said to have definite reference. By contrast, expressions containing a determiner like *a* are **indefinite**, in that (e.g.) if you say 'I'm taking a course', you don't assume that the hearer/reader knows which course you are taking.

DEG: a degree word like *so/too/how*.

demonstrative: this is a term used to refer to words like *this/that, these/those* and *here/there* which indicate a location relatively nearer to or further from the speaker (e.g. *this book* means 'the book relatively close to me', and *that book* means 'the book somewhat further away from me').

derivation: the derivation of a phrase or clause is the set of syntactic (e.g. merger and movement) operations used to form the relevant structure. The derivation of a word is the set of morphological operations used to form the word.

derivational morphology/suffix: derivational morphology is the component of a grammar which deals with the ways in which one type of word can be formed from another: for example, by adding the suffix *-ness* to the adjective *sad* we can form the noun *sadness*, so that *-ness* is a **derivational suffix**. See §2.2.

derivative: to say that the noun *happiness* is a derivative of the adjective *happy* is to say that *happiness* is formed from *happy* by the addition of an appropriate derivational morpheme (in this case, the suffix *-ness*).

derive: to **derive** a structure it to say how it is formed (i.e. specify the operations by which it is formed).

derived structure: a structure which is produced by the application of one or more syntactic (e.g. merger, movement or agreement) operations.

descriptive adequacy: a grammar of a particular language attains descriptive adequacy if it correctly specifies which strings of words do (and don't) form grammatical phrases and sentences in the language, and correctly describes the structure and interpretation of the relevant phrases and sentences. See §1.3.

DET/determiner: a word like *the/this/that* which is typically used to modify a noun, but which has no descriptive content of its own. Most determiners can be used either prenominally (i.e. in front of a noun that they modify) or pronominally (i.e. used on their own without a following noun) – cf. 'I don't like *that idea*/I don't like *that*'). See §2.5.

determiner phrase: a phrase like *the king (of Utopia)* which comprises a determiner *the*, and a noun complement like *king* or a noun phrase complement like *king of Utopia.* In work before the mid 1980s, a structure like *the king of Utopia* would have been analysed as a noun phrase (= NP), comprising the head noun *king*, its complement *of Utopia* and its specifier *the.* Since Abney (1987), such expressions have been taken to have the status of DP/determiner phrase.

direct object: see **object**.

direct theta-marking: see **theta-mark**.

discontinuous spellout: a phenomenon whereby part of a moved phrase is spelled out in the position in which it originates, and the remainder in the position in which it ends up – as in '*How much* do you believe *of what he tells you?*', where the wh-phrase *how much of what he tells you* moves to the front of the sentence, with *how much* being spelled out in the position it moves to, and *of what he tells you* being spelled out in the position in which it originates. See §6.3.

discourse: discourse factors are factors relating to the extrasentential setting in which an expression occurs (where extrasentential means 'outside the immediate sentence containing the relevant expression'). For example, to say that the reference of PRO is discourse-determined in a sentence such as 'It would be wise PRO to prepare yourself for the worst' means that PRO has no antecedent within the sentence immediately containing it, but rather refers to some individual(s) outside the sentence (in this case, the person being spoken to).

distribution/distributional: the distribution of an expression is the set of positions which it can occupy within an appropriate kind of phrase or sentence. Hence, a **distributional** property is in effect a word-order property.

domain: the **domain** (or, more fully, **c-command domain**) of a head H is the set of constituents c-commanded by H – namely its sister and all the constituents contained within its sister. For example, the domain of C includes its TP complement and any constituent of the relevant TP.

DO-support: this refers to the requirement for the 'dummy' (i.e. meaningless) auxiliary DO to be used to form questions, negatives or tags in sentences which would otherwise contain no auxiliary. Hence, because a non-auxiliary verb like *want* requires DO-support in questions/negatives/ tags, we have sentences such as '*Does* he want some?', 'He *doesn't* want any' and 'He wants some, *does* he?' See §5.8.

double-object construction: see **object**.

DP: see **determiner phrase**.

DP hypothesis: the hypothesis that all nominal arguments have the status of DPs – not just nominals like *the president* which contain an overt determiner, but also 'bare' nominal arguments like *politicians* and *promises* (in sentences like '*Politicians* break *promises*').

D-pronoun: a pronoun like *that* in 'I don't like *that*' which seems to be a pronominal determiner.

Earliness Principle: a principle which says that linguistic operations must apply as early in a derivation as possible.

Early Modern English/EME: the type of English found in the early seventeenth century (i.e. at around the time Shakespeare wrote most of his plays, between 1590 and 1620), also known as Elizabethan English.

echo question: a type of sentence used to question something which someone else has just said (often with an air of incredulity), repeating all or most of what they have just said. For example, if I say 'I've just met Nim Chimpsky' and you don't believe me (or don't know who I'm talking about), you could reply with an echo question such as 'You've just met who?'

ECM: see **Exceptional Case-Marking.**

economy: economy considerations require that (all other things being equal) syntactic representations should contain as few constituents and syntactic derivations involve as few grammatical operations as possible.

edge: the edge of a given projection HP is that part of HP which excludes the complement of H (hence, that part of the structure which includes the head H and any specifier/s which it has).

Elizabethan English: the type of English found in the early seventeenth century, during the reign of Queen Elizabeth I (i.e. at around the time Shakespeare wrote most of his plays, between 1590 and 1620), also known as Early Modern English/EME.

ellipsis/elliptical: ellipsis is a process by which an expression is omitted (in the sense that its phonetic features are deleted and so unpronounced), e.g. in order to avoid repetition. For example, in a sentence such as 'I will do it if you will do it', we can ellipse (i.e. omit) the second occurrence of *do it* to avoid repetition, and hence say 'I will do it if you will'. An **elliptical** structure is one containing an 'understood' constituent which has undergone **ellipsis** (i.e. been omitted).

embedded clause: a clause which is positioned internally within another constituent. For example, in a sentence such as 'He may suspect that I hid them', the *hid*-clause (= *that I hid them*) is embedded within (and is the complement of) the verb phrase headed by the verb *suspect*. Likewise, in 'The fact that he didn't apologise is significant', the *that*-clause (*that he didn't apologise*) is an embedded clause in the sense that it is embedded within a noun phrase headed by the noun *fact*. A clause which is not embedded within any other expression is a **root clause** (see **root**).

EME: see **Early Modern English**.

empirical evidence: evidence based on observed linguistic phenomena. In syntax, the term 'empirical evidence' usually means 'evidence based on grammaticality judgments by native speakers'. For example, the fact that sentences like *'Himself likes you' are judged ungrammatical by native speakers of Standard English provides us with empirical evidence that anaphors like *himself* can't be used without an appropriate antecedent (i.e. an expression which they refer back to).

empty: a constituent is empty/null if it is 'silent' and hence has no overt phonetic form. Empty categories include null subject pronouns like PRO and *pro*, null relative pronouns (like the null counterpart of *who* in *someone ~~who~~ I know well*), null determiners (like that in '*ø John* is tired') and null trace copies of moved constituents. See ch. 4.

enclitic/encliticise: see **clitic**.

entry: a **lexical entry** is an entry for a particular word in a dictionary (and hence by extension refers to the set of information about the word given in the relevant dictionary entry).

EPP: this was originally an abbreviation for the **Extended Projection Principle**, which posited that every T constituent must be extended into a TP projection which has a **specifier**. In more recent work, the requirement for a T constituent like *will* to have a specifier is said to be a consequence of T carrying an [EPP] feature requiring it to project a specifier. The **EPP Generalisation** specifies the conditions under which the [EPP] feature carried by a head is deleted via use of an expletive or via movement: see §8.6.

ergative: this term originally applied to languages like Basque in which the complement of a transitive verb and the subject of an intransitive verb are assigned the same morphological case. However, by extension, it has come to be used to denote verbs like *break* which occur both in transitive structures like 'Someone broke the window' and in intransitive structures like 'The window broke', where *the window* seems to play the same semantic role in both types of sentences, in spite of being the complement of *broke* in one sentence and the subject of *broke* in the other. See §9.4.

Exceptional Case-Marking/ECM: accusative subjects of infinitive clauses (e.g. *him* in 'I believe *him to be innocent*') are said to carry exceptional accusative case (in that the case of the accusative subject is assigned by the main-clause verb *believe*, and it is exceptional for the case of the subject of one clause to be assigned by the verb in a higher clause). Verbs (like *believe*) which take an infinitive complement with an accusative subject are said to be **ECM verbs**. See §9.7 and §9.8.

exclamative: a type of structure used to exclaim surprise, delight, annoyance etc. In English syntax, the term is restricted largely to clauses beginning with wh-exclamative words like *What!* or *How!* – e.g. 'What a fool I was!' or 'How blind I was!' See §6.9 and §9.2.

existential: an existential sentence is one which is about the existence of some entity. For example, a sentence such as 'Is there any coffee left?' questions the existence of coffee. Consequently, the word *any* here is sometimes said to be an **existential quantifier** (as is *some* in a sentence like 'There is some coffee in the pot').

experience: children's experience is the speech input which they receive (or, more generally, the speech activity which they observe) in the course of acquiring their native language.

EXPERIENCER: a term used in the analysis of semantic/thematic roles to denote the entity which experiences some emotional or cognitive state – e.g. *John* in 'John felt unhappy', or 'John thought about his predicament'. See §7.5.

explanatory adequacy: a linguistic theory meets the criterion of explanatory adequacy if it explains why grammars have the properties that they do, and how children come to acquire grammars in such a short period of time. See §1.3.

expletive: a 'dummy' constituent with no inherent semantic content, such as the pronoun *there* in existential sentences like 'There is no truth in the rumour', or the pronoun *it* in sentences such as *It is unclear why he resigned.* See §8.5 and §8.6.

expression: this word is used in the text as an informal term meaning a string (i.e. continuous sequence) of one or more words which form a **constituent**.

Extended Projection Principle: see **EPP**.

external argument: see **argument**.

extract/extraction: extract(ion) is another term for **move(ment)**, and so denotes an operation by which one constituent is moved out of another. For example, in a structure such as 'Who do you think [he saw —]' the pronoun *who* has been extracted out of the bracketed clause (i.e. it has been moved out of the position marked —), and moved to the front of the overall sentence. The **extraction site** for a moved constituent is the position which it occupied before undergoing movement.

extrapose/extraposition: a term used to denote a movement operation by which an expression (usually one which is very long, or highlighted in some way) is moved to the end of a given structure. For example, in a sentence like 'He bequeathed *his priceless collection of Ming vases* to Mary' the italicised object can undergo **extraposition/be extraposed** and thereby moved to the end of the sentence in 'He bequeathed to Mary *his priceless collection of Ming vases*.'

F: this symbol is used as a convenient notational device to denote an abstract functional head (or an abstract feature) of some kind.

feature: a device used to describe a particular grammatical property. For example, the distinction between count and non-count nouns might be described in terms of a feature such as [±COUNT]. On **Feature-Copying**, see **copying**. **Feature-Deletion** is an operation by which uninterpretable features are deleted: see §8.4. The **Feature Visibility Convention** specifies that deleted features are invisible in the semantic component but remain visible in the syntactic and PF components: see §8.4. The **Feature Inactivation Hypothesis** posits that an uninterpretable feature becomes inactive in the syntax (and invisible to the semantic component) immediately it is deleted: see §8.6.

feminine: this term is used in discussion of grammatical gender to denote pronouns like *she/her/hers* which refer to female entities.

FHC: see **Functional Head Constraint**.

filled: to say that a given position in a structure must be filled is to say that it cannot remain empty but rather must be occupied (usually by an overt constituent of an appropriate kind).

Fin/finite/FinP: the term **finite verb/finite clause** denotes (a clause containing) an auxiliary or non-auxiliary verb which can have a nominative subject like *I/we/he/she/they*. For example, compare the two bracketed clauses in:

(i)   What if [people annoy her]?   (ii) Don't let [people annoy her]

The bracketed clause and the verb *annoy* in (i) are finite because in place of the subject *people* we can have a nominative pronoun like *they*; by contrast, the bracketed clause and the verb *annoy* are non-finite in (ii) because *people* cannot be replaced by a nominative pronoun like *they* (only by an accusative pronoun like *them*): cf.

(iii)   What if [*they* annoy her]?   (iv) Don't let [*them*/*they* annoy her]

By contrast, a verb or clause which has a subject with accusative or null case in English is non-finite; hence the bracketed clauses and italicised verbs are non-finite in the examples below:

(v)   Don't let [them *annoy* her]   (vi) You should try [PRO to *help*]

Non-finite forms include **infinitive** forms like *be*, and **participle** forms like *being/been*. In work by Luigi Rizzi on split CP projections (discussed in §9.3), infinitival complementisers like Italian *di* 'of' and English *for* are said to occupy the head **Fin** ('Finiteness') position within a **FinP** ('Finiteness Phrase') projection.

first person: see **person**.

floating quantifier: a quantifier which is separated from the expression which it quantifies. For example, in a sentence such as 'The students have *all* passed their exams', *all* quantifies (but is not positioned next to) *the students*, so that *all* is a floating quantifier here.

Foc/focus/focusing/FocP: focus position in a sentence is a position occupied by a constituent which is highlighted in some way (usually in order to mark it as containing 'new' or 'unfamiliar' information). For example, in a **cleft sentence** such as 'It's *syntax* that they hate most' or a **pseudo-cleft** sentence such as 'What they hate most is *syntax*', the expression *syntax* is said to occupy **focus position** within the relevant sentence. **Focusing** denotes a movement operation by which a constituent is moved into a focus position at the beginning of a clause in order to highlight it (e.g. to mark it as introducing new information). Thus, in a sentence like '*Nothing* could they do to save her', the expression *nothing* has been focused by being moved to the front of the overall sentence from its underlying position as the complement of the verb *do*. In work on split CP projections by Luigi Rizzi (discussed in §9.2), preposed focused expressions are said to occupy the specifier position within a **FocP** ('Focus Phrase') projection which is headed by an abstract **Foc** ('Focus') head.

foot: the foot of a (movement) chain is the constituent which occupies the lowest position in the chain.

force: the complementisers *that/if* in a sentence such as *I didn't know* [*that/if he was lying*] are said to indicate that the bracketed clauses are declarative/interrogative in force (in the sense that they have the force of a question/a statement). In work on split CP projections by Luigi Rizzi (discussed in §§9.2–9.3), complementisers are said to constitute a **Force** head which can project into a **Force Phrase**.

formal: in an expression such as **formal speech style**, the word **formal** denotes a very careful and stylised form of speech (as opposed to the kind of informal colloquial speech style used in a casual conversation in a bar): in an expression such as **formal features**, the word **formal** means 'grammatical' (i.e. features which play a role in morphology/syntax).

fragment: an utterance which is not a complete sentence (in the sense that it does not constitute a clause). So, a phrase such as 'A new dress' used in reply to a question such as 'What did you buy?' would be a sentence-fragment. (By contrast, a sentence such as 'I bought a new dress' would not be a sentence-fragment, since it contains a complete clause.)

free relative clause: a clause containing a relative pronoun which has no overt antecedent, like that italicised in '*What you say* is true.' See **relative**.

front/fronting: fronting is an informal term to denote a movement operation by which a given expression is **fronted** – i.e. moved to the front of some phrase or sentence.

function: expressions such as **subject, specifier, complement, object, head** and **adjunct** are said to denote the grammatical function which a particular expression fulfils in a particular structure (which in turn relates to the position which it occupies and certain of its grammatical properties – e.g. case and agreement properties).

functional category/Functional Head Constraint/function word/functor: a word which has no **descriptive/lexical content** and which serves an essentially grammatical function is said to be a **function word** or **functor** (by contrast, a word which has descriptive/lexical content is a **content word** or **contentive**). A **functional category** is a category whose members are function words: hence, categories such as complementiser, auxiliary, infinitive particle, case particle, or determiner are all functional categories – as well as the expressions they head (e.g. C-bar/CP, T-bar/TP, D-bar/DP etc.). See §2.4. The **Functional Head Constraint** is a grammatical principle which specifies that the complement of a certain type of functional head (including C and D) cannot be preposed on its own without moving the functional head along with it: see §3.6.

gapping: a form of **ellipsis** in which the head word is omitted from one (or more) of the conjuncts in a coordinate structure in order to avoid repetition. For example, the italicised second occurrence of *bought* can be gapped (i.e. omitted) in a sentence such as 'John bought an apple and Mary *bought* a pear', giving 'John bought an apple, and Mary a pear.'

Gen: in one use, an abbreviation for **genitive case**; in another, an abbreviation for **gender**.

gender: a grammatical property whereby words are divided into different grammatical classes which play a role in **agreement/concord** relationships. In French, for example, nouns are intrinsically masculine or feminine in gender (e.g. *pommier* 'apple tree' is masculine, but *pomme* 'apple' is feminine), and determiners inflect for gender (as well as number), so that *un* 'a' is the masculine form of the indefinite article, and *une* is its feminine form. Determiners in French have to agree in gender (and number) with the nouns they modify, hence we say *un pommier* 'an apple tree', but *une pomme* 'an apple'. In English, nouns no longer have inherent gender properties, and adjectives/determiners don't inflect for gender either. Only personal pronouns like *he/she/it* carry gender properties in modern English, and these are traditionally said to carry **masculine/feminine/neuter** gender respectively (though the term **inanimate** is sometimes used in place of **neuter**).

generate/generative: the syntactic component of a grammar is said to **generate** (i.e. specify how to form) a set of syntactic structures. A grammar which does so is said to be a **generative grammar**.

generic: to say that an expression like *eggs* in a sentence such as 'Eggs are fattening' has a generic interpretation is to say that it is interpreted as meaning 'eggs in general'.

genitive: see **case**.

gerund: when used in conjunction with the progressive aspect auxiliary *be*, verb forms ending in *-ing* are **progressive participles**; in other uses they generally function as **gerunds**. In particular, *-ing* verb forms are gerunds when they can be used as subjects, or as complements of verbs or prepositions, and when (in literary styles) they can have a genitive subject like *my*. Thus *writing* is a gerund (verb form) in a sentence such as 'She was annoyed at [my *writing* to her mother]', since the bracketed gerund structure is used as the complement of the preposition *at*, and has a genitive subject *my*.

GOAL/goal: the term GOAL is used in the analysis of semantic/thematic roles to denote the entity towards which something moves – e.g. *Mary* in 'John sent *Mary* a letter': see §7.5. In a different sense, the term **goal** represents a constituent which agrees with a higher head which serves as a **probe:** see §8.2.

gradable/ungradable: words are **gradable** if they denote a concept or property which can exist in varying degrees. For example, *tall* is gradable since we can say (e.g.) *fairly/very/extremely tall*; by contrast, *dead* is ungradable, since it denotes an absolute property (hence it's odd to say *!very dead*).

grammar: in traditional terms, grammar includes morphology and syntax. In a broader Chomskyan sense, grammar includes phonology and structural aspects of semantics: i.e. a grammar of a language is a computational system which derives the Phonetic Form and Semantic Representation of expressions.

grammatical: an expression is **grammatical** if it contains no morphological or syntactic error, and **ungrammatical** if it contains one or more morphological or syntactic errors. **Grammatical features** are (e.g. person, number, gender, case etc.) features which play a role in grammatical operations (e.g. in determining case or agreement properties).

have-**cliticisation:** an operation by which *have* (in the guise of its contracted clitic variant /v/) attaches to an immediately preceding word ending in a vowel or diphthong, resulting in forms such as *I've, we've, they've* etc.

head: this term has two main uses. The head (constituent) of a phrase is the key word which determines the properties of the phrase. So, in a phrase such as *fond of fast food*, the head of the phrase is the adjective *fond*, and consequently the phrase is an adjectival phrase (and hence can occupy typical positions associated with adjectival expressions – e.g. as the complement of *is* in 'He is *fond of fast food*'). In many cases, the term *head* is more or less equivalent to the term *word* (e.g. in sentences such as 'An accusative pronoun can be used as the complement of a transitive head'). In a different use of the same word, the head of a movement chain is the highest constituent in the chain.

headed/Headedness Principle: an expression is **headed** if it has a **head**. The **Headedness Principle** specifies that every constituent must be headed. So, for example, an expression like *fond of fast food* is headed by the adjective *fond* and so is an adjectival phrase. See **head**.

head-first/-last: a head-first structure is one in which the head of an expression is positioned before its complement(s); a head-last structure is one in which the head of an expression is positioned after its complement(s). See §1.6.

head movement: movement of a word from one head position to another (e.g. movement of an auxiliary from T to C, or of a verb from V to T, or of a noun from N to D). See ch. 5.

Head Movement Constraint/HMC: a principle of Universal Grammar which specifies that movement between one head position and another is only possible between the head of a given structure and the head of its complement. See §5.5.

Head-Position Parameter: the parameter which determines whether a language positions a given type of head before or after its complement. See §1.6.

Head-Strength Parameter: a parameter whose setting determines whether a given kind of head is **strong** and can trigger movement of a lower head to attach to it, or **weak** and so cannot attract a lower head to move to attach to it. See §5.5.

HMC: see **Head Movement Constraint**.

homophonous: two different expressions are homophonous if they have the same phonetic form (e.g. *we've* and *weave*).

host: an expression to which a **clitic** or **affix** attaches. For example, if *n't* cliticises onto *could* in expressions like *couldn't*, we can say that *could* is the host onto which *n't* cliticises.

I: see **INFL**.

identification/identify: in the relevant technical sense, we can say that the inflection *-st* **identifies** (or enables **identification** of) the null *pro* subject as second person singular in a Shakespearean sentence such as 'Hast *pro* any more of this?' (Trinculo, *The Tempest*, II.ii). This is because *-st* in Elizabethan English is a second-person-singular inflection, and since subjects agree with finite verbs in person and number, it follows that the null *pro* subject must also be second person singular. See §5.5.

idiom: a string of words which has an idiosyncratic meaning (e.g. *hit the roof* in the sense of 'get angry').

I-language: I-language is a linguistic system internalised (i.e. internally represented) within the brain. See §1.3.

illegible: see **legible**.

immediate constituent: see **constituent**.

immediately contain: see **contain**.

Imp: a symbol used to designate an (affixal) imperative morpheme which occupies the head C position of CP in imperatives: see ex. 5.2.

impenetrable: inaccessible. See **Phase Impenetrability Condition**.

imperative: a term employed to classify a type of sentence used to issue an order (e.g. 'Be quiet!', 'Don't say anything!'), and also to classify the type of verb form used in an imperative sentence (e.g. *be* is an imperative verb form in '*Be* quiet!').

impoverished: poor (see **rich**).

inanimate: see **animate**.

Inclusiveness Condition: a grammatical principle proposed by Chomsky (1999, p. 2) which 'bars introduction of new elements (features) in the course of a derivation'.

indefinite: see **definite**.

indicative: indicative (auxiliary and main) verb forms are finite forms which are used (inter alia) in declarative and interrogative clauses (i.e. statements and questions). Thus, the italicised items are said to be indicative in **mood** in the following sentences: 'He *is* teasing you', '*Can* he speak French?', 'He *had* been smoking', 'He *loves* chocolate', 'He *hated* syntax.' An **indicative clause** is a clause which contains an indicative (auxiliary or non-auxiliary) verb. See **mood**.

indirect theta-marking: see **theta-marking**.

infinitive: the infinitive form of a verb is the (uninflected) form which is used (inter alia) when the verb is the complement of a modal auxiliary like *can*, or of the infinitive particle *to*. Accordingly, the italicised verbs are infinitive forms in sentences like 'He can *speak* French', and 'He's trying to *learn* French.' An **infinitive clause** is a clause which contains a verb in the infinitive form. Hence, the bracketed clauses are infinitive clauses in: 'He is trying [to help her]', and 'Why not let [him help her]?' (In both examples, *help* is an infinitive verb form, and *to* when used with an infinitive complement is said to be an **infinitive particle**.) Since clauses are analysed as phrases within the framework used here, the term **infinitive phrase** can be used interchangeably with **infinitive clause**, to denote a TP projection headed by the infinitive particle *to* (or by a null counterpart of the infinitive particle *to*).

INFL: a category devised by Chomsky (1981) whose members include finite auxiliaries (which are INFLected for tense/agreement), and the INFinitivaL particle *to*. In more recent work, T is used in place of INFL. See §2.8.

inflection/inflectional: an inflection is an **affix** which marks grammatical properties such as number, person, tense, case. For example, a plural noun such as *dogs* in English comprises the stem form *dog* and the plural number inflection *-s*. **Inflectional morphology** is the grammar of **inflections**.

inherent case: see **case**.

initial grammar: the earliest grammar of their native language developed by infants.

innateness hypothesis: the hypothesis that children have a biologically endowed innate language faculty. See §1.4.

in situ: a constituent is said to remain **in situ** (i.e. 'in place') if it doesn't undergo a given kind of movement operation.

interface levels: levels at which the grammar interfaces (i.e. connects) with speech and thought systems which lie outside the domain of grammar. **Phonetic Form** is the level at which the grammar interfaces with articulatory-perceptual (speech) systems, and **Semantic Representation** is the level at which it interfaces with conceptual-intentional (thought) systems.

intermediate projection: see **project(ion)**.

internal argument: see **argument**.

internalised grammar: a grammar which is internally represented within the mind/brain.

interpretable: a feature is (semantically) interpretable if it has semantic content: so, for example, a feature such as [Plural-Number] on a pronoun like *they* is interpretable, but a phonetic feature like [+nasal] is uninterpretable, and so too are many grammatical/formal features (e.g. case features). See §8.4.

interpretation: to say that an expression has a particular (semantic) interpretation is to say that it expresses a particular meaning. So, for example, we might say that a sentence such as 'He loves you more than Sam' has two different interpretations – one on which Sam has a subject interpretation and is implicitly understood as the subject of *loves you*, and a second on which Sam has an object interpretation and is implicitly understood as the object of *he loves*. The first interpretation can be paraphrased as 'He loves you more than Sam loves you', and the second as 'He loves you more than he loves Sam.'

interrogative: an interrogative clause or sentence is one which asks a question. See **question**.

intervention constraint: a principle specifying that in a structure of the form [...X...[...Y...[...Z...]]], X cannot attract Z if there is a constituent Y of the same type as Z which intervenes between X and Z. See §6.4.

intransitive: see **transitive**.

intuitions: judgments given by native speakers about the grammaticality, interpretation and structure of expressions in their language.

inversion/inverted: a term used to denote a movement process by which the relative order of two expressions is reversed. It is most frequently used in relation to the more specific operation by which an auxiliary (and, in earlier stages of English, non-auxiliary) verb comes to be positioned before its subject, e.g. in questions such as '*Can* you speak Swahili?', where *can* is positioned in front of its subject *you*. See ch. 5. An **inverted auxiliary/verb** is one which is positioned in front of its subject (e.g. *will* in '*Will* I pass the syntax exam?').

irrealis: an infinitive complement like that italicised in 'They would prefer (*for*) *you to abstain*' is said to denote an *irrealis* (a Latin word meaning 'unreal') event in the sense that the act of abstention is a hypothetical event which has not yet happened and may never happen.

island: a structure out of which no subpart can be extracted. For example, coordinate structures like *William and Harry* are **islands** in this sense. Hence, in a sentence like 'I admire William and Harry', we can topicalise the whole coordinate structure *William and Harry* by moving it to the front of the overall sentence (as in '*William and Harry*, I admire'), but we cannot topicalise *Harry* alone (as we see from the ungrammaticality of **'Harry* I admire William and').

K: case particle. See **case**.

label: a notational device used to represent linguistic properties of constituents. For example, if we say that the word *man* belongs to the category N of noun, we are using N as a label to indicate the categorial properties of the word *man* (i.e. to tell us what grammatical category *man* belongs to).

labelled bracketing: see **bracketing**.

landing site: the landing site for a moved constituent is the position it ends up in after it has been moved (e.g. the specifier position within CP is the landing site for a moved wh-expression).

Language Faculty: Chomsky argues that humans beings have an innate Language Faculty which provides them with an algorithm (i.e. set of procedures or programme) for acquiring a grammar of their native language(s). See §1.4.

LBC: see **Left Branch Condition**.

learnability: a criterion of adequacy for linguistic theory. An adequate theory must explain how children come to learn the grammar of their native languages in such a short period of time, and hence must provide for grammars of languages which are easily learnable by children. See §1.3.

Left Branch Condition: a **constraint** which specifies that in languages like English, the leftmost constituent of a nominal, adjectival or adverbial expression cannot be moved out of the expression containing it.

legible: to say that syntactic structures must be **legible** at the semantics and phonetics interfaces is to say that the structures inputted to the **semantic component** of the grammar must contain only features which contribute to semantic interpretation, and that the structures inputted to the **PF component** must contain only features which contribute to determining the phonetic form of an expression. Any structure which is not legible at a given interface is said to be **illegible** to the relevant interface.

level: in the sense in which this term is used in this book, constituents like T, T-bar and TP represent different **projection levels** – i.e. successively larger types of category (T being a **minimal projection**, T-bar an **intermediate projection** and TP a **maximal projection**). See **projection**.

lexical/lexicon: the word **lexical** is used in a number of different ways. Since a **lexicon** is a dictionary (i.e. a list of all the words in a language and their idiosyncratic linguistic properties), the expression **lexical item** in effect means 'word', the expression **lexical entry** means 'the entry in the dictionary for a particular word', the term **lexical property** means 'property of some individual word', the term **lexical learning** means 'learning words and their idiosyncratic properties' and the term **lexical array** means 'the set of words out of which a given expression is formed'. However, the word lexical is also used in a second sense, in which it is contrasted with **functional** (and hence means 'non-functional'). In this second sense, a **lexical category** is a category whose members are **contentives** (i.e. items with idiosyncratic descriptive content): hence, categories such as noun, verb, adjective or preposition are lexical categories in this sense. So, for example, the term **lexical verb** means 'main verb' (i.e. a non-auxiliary verb like *go*, *find*, *hate*, *want* etc.).

LF(-representation): (a representation of the) Logical Form (of an expression). See **representation**. The **LF-component** of a grammar is the (semantic) component which converts the syntactic structures produced by merger and movement operations into LF-representations.

light verb: this term is traditionally used to denote verbs (e.g. like *take/make* in expressions like *make fun of* and *take heed of*) with relatively little semantic content. However, in recent work on **VP shells** discussed in §§9.4–9.9, this term is extended to denote an abstract affixal verb (often with a causative sense like that of *make*) to which a noun, adjective or verb adjoins. For example, it might be claimed that the suffix *-en* in a verb like *sadden* is an affixal light verb which combines with an adjective like *sad* to form the causative verb *sadden* (which has a meaning loosely paraphraseable as 'make sad', or 'cause to become sad'). This type of analysis can be extended to verbs like *roll* as they are used in sentences like 'He *rolled* the ball down the hill', if we assume that *roll* here is used causatively (and so has a meaning paraphraseable as 'make roll', or 'cause to roll'), and hence involves adjunction of the verb *roll* to an abstract light verb (which can be thought of as a null verbal counterpart of *-en*).

link: a constituent (or position) which is part of a **movement chain**.

local: one constituent X can enter into a grammatical relation (e.g. an agreement relation) with another constituent Y only if Y is in the **local c-command domain** of X – i.e. only if Y is c-commanded by X and if Y is sufficiently close to X. In recent work, Chomsky has defined relative closeness (for syntactic operations like agreement) in terms of the **Phase Impenetrability Condition**.

LOCATIVE: this is a term which denotes the semantic/thematic function of a constituent. A locative expression is one which denotes place. So, for example, *there/where* are locative pronouns in sentences such as 'Are you going *there*?' or '*Where* are you going?' See §7.5.

locus: to say that T is the **locus** of tense is to say that the tense property associated with a tensed clause, or tensed auxiliary, or main verb originates as a tense feature (or tense affix) carried by the head T constituent of TP.

long-distance movement: a long-distance movement operation is one which moves a constituent out of one clause (TP/CP) into another.

main clause: see **root clause**.

main verb: a non-auxiliary verb. See **auxiliary**.

masc(uline): This term is used in discussion of grammatical **gender** to denote pronouns like *he/him/his* which refer to male entities.

mass noun: see **count noun**.

match: two constituents **match** in respect of some feature [F] either if one is valued for [F] and the other unvalued for [F], or if both carry the same value for [F]. See ch. 8.

matrix: in a sentence such as 'I think *he lied*', the (italicised) *lied* clause is an **embedded/complement clause** (by virtue of being embedded as the complement of the verb *think*), and the *think* clause is the **matrix clause**, in the sense that it is the clause immediately containing the *lied* clause.

maximal projection: see **projection**.

merge(r): an operation by which two constituents are combined together to form a single larger constituent. See ch. 3.

MFCF: see **Multiply Filled COMP Filter**.

Minimalism/Minimalist program: a theory of grammar developed by Chomsky whose core assumption is that grammars are minimally complex, perfect systems of optimal design. See §1.3.

minimal projection: see **projection**.

MIT: The Massachusetts Institute of Technology (located in Cambridge, Massachusetts), where Chomsky has worked for the past five decades.

modal/modality: a modal auxiliary is an auxiliary which expresses **modality** (i.e. notions such as possibility, futurity or necessity). The set of modal auxiliaries found in English is usually assumed to include *will/would/can/could/shall/ should/may/might/must/ought*, and *need/dare* when followed by a 'bare'(*to*-less) infinitive complement.

modifier/modify: in an expression such as *tall men*, it is traditionally said that the adjective *tall* **modifies** (i.e. attributes some property to) or is a **modifier** of the noun *men*. Likewise, in a sentence such as 'Eat slowly!', the adverb *slowly* is said to **modify** the verb *eat* (in the sense that it describes the manner in which the hearer is being told to eat).

module: an individual component of a larger system. For example, a grammar might be said to contain a **case module** – i.e. a component which accounts for the case properties of relevant constituents.

mood: this is a term describing inflectional properties of finite verbs. (Auxiliary and non-auxiliary) verbs in English can be in the **indicative mood, subjunctive mood** or **imperative mood**. Examples of each type of mood are given by the italicised verb forms in the following: 'He *hates* [= indicative] spaghetti'; 'The court ordered that he *be* [= subjunctive] detained indefinitely'; '*Keep* [= imperative] quiet!' The mood of the verb determines aspects of the interpretation of the relevant clause, so that e.g. subjunctive verbs occur in **irrealis** clauses.

morpheme: the smallest unit of grammatical structure. Thus, a plural noun such as *cats* comprises two morphemes, namely the stem *cat* and the plural suffix -*s*.

morphology/morphological: morphology studies how **morphemes** are combined together to form words. **Morphological** properties are properties relating to the form of words (i.e. relating to the inflections or affixes they carry). For example, it is a morphological property of regular count nouns that they have a plural form ending in -*s*.

morphosyntactic: a morphosyntactic property is a 'grammatical' property, i.e. a property which affects (or is affected by) relevant aspects of morphology and syntax. For instance, **case** is a morphosyntactic property in that (e.g.) pronouns have different morphological forms and occupy different syntactic positions according to their case: e.g. the nominative form of the first-person-plural pronoun is *we* and its accusative form is *us*; the two occupy different syntactic positions in that the nominative form occurs as the subject of a finite verb, whereas the accusative form occurs as the complement of a transitive verb or preposition: cf. '*We* disagree', 'Join *us*.'

mother: a constituent X is the mother of another constituent Y if X is the next highest node up in the tree from Y, and the two are connected by a branch (solid line). See §3.7.

multiple agreement: agreement between a **probe** and more than one **goal**. See §8.6.

multiple specifiers: in his (1995) book and subsequent work, Chomsky suggests that certain types of head may allow more than one specifier (e.g. a light verb with an external argument/subject as its inner specifier may attract a wh-expression to become its outer specifier: see §10.5).

multiple wh-questions: questions containing more than one wh-word. See §6.4.

Multiply Filled COMP Filter: a **constraint** which specifies that (in present-day English) no overt complementiser (like *that/if/for*) can have an overt specifier.

N: see **noun**.

natural language: a language acquired in a natural setting by human beings (hence, excluding e.g. computer languages, animal communication systems etc.).

NEG: the head constituent of a NEGP (i.e. of a Negation Phrase constituent which contains *not* as its specifier). See §5.7.

negation: an operation or construction in which some proposition is said to be false. Negation involves the use of some negative item such as *not, n't, nobody, nothing, never* etc. – though most discussions of negation tend to be about the negative adverbs *not/n't*. See §5.7.

negative evidence: in the context of discussions about the nature of the evidence which children make use of in acquiring their native language(s), this term relates to evidence based on the non-occurrence of certain structures in the child's speech input, or on correction of children by others (e.g. adults). See §1.8.

negative particle: this term typically denotes the negative adverbs *not/n't*.

NEGP: see **NEG**.

neuter: see **gender**.

neutralise/neutralisation: when a grammatical contrast (e.g. that between a singular noun like *cat* and a plural noun like *cats*) is not marked in some expression (e.g. the singular/plural noun form *sheep*), the contrast is said to have been neutralised or **syncretised** (in the relevant expression).

N-movement: movement of a noun to a higher position within a nominal expression. See §5.9.

node: a term used to denote each point in a tree diagram which carries a category label. Each node represents a separate constituent in the relevant structure.

Nom: an abbreviation for **nominative**. See **case**.

nominal: this is the adjective associated with the word *noun*, so that in principle a **nominal** (**expression**) is an expression containing a noun. However, the term is sometimes extended to mean 'expression containing a noun *or pronoun*'.

nominalisation/nominalising: nominalisation is a process by which some other type of expression is converted into a nominal (i.e. noun expression). For example, *-ness* is a nominalising (i.e. noun-forming) suffix in that if we suffix *-ness* to an adjective like *sad*, we form the noun *sadness*.

nominative: see **case**.

non-argument: see **argument**.

non-auxiliary verb: a 'lexical verb' or 'main verb' (like *want, try, hate, smell, buy* etc.) which requires DO-support to form questions, negatives and tags.

non-constituent: a non-constituent string is a sequence of words which do not together form a constituent.

non-count noun: see **count noun**.

no-negative-evidence hypothesis: the hypothesis that children acquire their native language(s) on the basis of positive evidence alone, and do not make use of negative evidence. See §1.8.

non-finite: see **finite**.

non-terminal: see **terminal**.

noun: a category of word (whose members include items such as *boy/friend/thought/sadness/computer*) which typically denotes an entity of some kind. See §2.2 and §2.3. In traditional grammar, a distinction is drawn between **common nouns** and **proper nouns**. Proper nouns are names of individual people (e.g. *Chomsky*), places (e.g. *Colchester, Essex, England*), dates (e.g. *Tuesday, February, Easter*), magazines (e.g. *Cosmopolitan*) etc., whereas common nouns (e.g. *boy,* *table, syntax* etc.) are nouns denoting general (non-individual) entities. Proper nouns have the semantic property of having unique reference, and the syntactic property that (unless themselves modified) they generally can't be modified by a determiner (cf. **the London*).

noun phrase/NP: a phrase whose head is a noun. In work prior to the mid 1980s, a structure such as *the king of Utopia* was taken to be a noun phrase/NP comprising the head noun *king*, its complement *of Utopia* and its specifier *the*. In more recent work, such expressions are taken to be **determiner phrases/DPs** comprising the head determiner *the* and a noun phrase/NP complement *king of Utopia*, with the NP in turn comprising the head noun *king* and its complement *of Utopia*. See §3.4 and §4.10.

NP: see **noun phrase**.

N-pronoun: a pronoun like *one* in 'Mary bought a green one' which has the morphological and distributional properties of a (count) noun.

null: a null constituent is one which is 'silent' or 'unpronounced' and so has no overt phonetic form. See ch. 4.

null case: the case carried by PRO (see **case**).

null subject: a subject which has grammatical and semantic properties but no overt phonetic form. There are a variety of different types of null subject, including the null *pro* subject which can be used in any finite clause in a language like Italian, the null counterpart of *you* found in English imperative clauses like 'Shut the door!', the null PRO subject found in non-finite control clauses like that bracketed in 'The prisoners tried [PRO to escape]', and the null truncated subject found in sentences like 'Can't find my pen. Must be on my desk at home.' See §4.2.

null-subject language: this term is used to denote a language which allows any finite clause of any kind to have a null *pro* subject. For example, Italian is a null-subject language and so allows us to say 'Sei simpatica' (literally 'Are nice', meaning 'You are nice'); by contrast, English is a **non-null-subject language** in the sense that it doesn't allow the subject to be omitted in this type of structure (hence ***'Are nice' is ungrammatical in English).

null-subject parameter: a parameter whose setting determines whether a language is a **null-subject language** or not. See §1.6.

Num: an abbreviation for the feature **Number**. In a different (but related) use, a category label denoting a particular head which is claimed by some to be the **locus** of number properties in noun expressions. It may correspond to the position which a noun like *invasione* 'invasion' moves to in an Italian nominal such as *la grande invasione italiana dell'Albania* (literally 'The great invasion Italian of.the Albania', and more idiomatically 'the great Italian invasion of Albania').

A Phrase headed by a **Num** constituent is labelled **NumP** 'Number Phrase'. See §5.9 and §10.9.

number: a term used to denote the contrast between singular and plural forms. In English, we find number contrasts in nouns (cf. 'one *dog*', 'two *dogs*'), in some determiners (cf. '*this* book', '*these* books'), in pronouns (cf. *it/they*), and in finite (auxiliary or main) verbs (cf. 'It *smells*', 'They *smell*').

object: the complement of a transitive item (e.g. in 'Help *me*', *me* is the object of the transitive verb *help*; and in 'for *me*', *me* is the object of the transitive preposition *for*). The term **object** is generally restricted to complements which carry accusative case – i.e. to nominal or pronominal complements: hence, *nothing* would be the object (and complement) of *said* in 'He said *nothing*', but the *that*-clause would be the **complement** (but not the object) of *said* in 'He said [that he was tired]' – though some traditional grammars extend the term object to cover clausal complements as well as (pro)nominal complements. In sentences such as 'She gave him them', the verb *give* is traditionally said to have two objects, namely *him* and *them:* the first object (representing the recipient) is termed the **indirect object**, and the second object (representing the gift) is termed the **direct object**; the relevant construction is known as the **double-object construction**. Where a verb has a single object (e.g. *nothing* in 'He said nothing'), this is the direct object of the relevant verb.

object-control predicate: see **control**.

objective: another term for **accusative**. See **case**.

one-place predicate: a predicate which has only one argument. See **argument**.

operator: this term is used in syntax to denote (e.g.) interrogative and negative expressions which have the syntactic properties that they trigger auxiliary inversion (cf. 'What *have you* done?', 'Nothing *have I* done') and allow a polarity item like partitive/existential *any* to occur in their scope (cf. 'What can *anyone* do?' 'Nothing can *anyone* do').

orphaned: see **stranded**.

overt: an expression is overt if it has a non-null phonetic form, but **null** if it has no phonetic content. Thus, *him* is an overt pronoun, but **PRO** is a null pronoun. The term **overt structure** is used in this book (though not more generally) as an informal expository term to refer to a simplified representation of the structure of a given expression which shows only the overt constituents which it contains (and hence excludes trace copies and other null constituents).

P: see **preposition**.

parameters: dimensions of grammatical variation within and across languages (e.g. the **Null-Subject Parameter, Head-Position Parameter, Wh-Parameter**). See §1.6.

parameter-setting: the process by which children determine which setting of a parameter is appropriate for the native language they are acquiring. See §1.7.

paraphrase: a paraphrase is an expression which has roughly the same meaning as the expression which it is being used to paraphrase, but which brings out the relevant meaning more clearly. For example, we can bring out the ambiguity of a sentence like *He loves you more than me* by saying that it has two different **interpretations**, one of which can be paraphrased as 'He loves you more than he loves me', and the other of which can be paraphrased as 'He loves you more than I love you.'

partial: a **labelled bracketing** is **partial** if it shows only part of the structure of a given sentence or expression (other parts being omitted to simplify exposition).

participle: a non-finite verb form which encodes **aspect** or **voice**. In European languages, participles have no person properties but (in languages like Latin or Icelandic which have a richer morphology than English) they may have number/gender/case properties. English has three types of participle: **progressive participles** (ending in *-ing*) used in conjunction with the progressive-aspect auxiliary *be* in sentences like 'It is *raining*'; **perfect participles** (generally ending in *-d* or *-n*) used in conjunction with the perfect-aspect auxiliary *have* in sentences like 'He has *gone* home'; and **passive participles** (also generally ending in *-d* or *-n*) used in conjunction with the passive-voice auxiliary *be* in sentences like 'He was *arrested* by Percy Plodd.'

particle: this is an informal term used to describe a range of (typically monosyllabic) items which are invariable in form, and which don't fit easily into traditional systems of grammatical categories. For example, infinitival *to* (e.g. 'Try to be nice') is said to be an **infinitive particle**; *of* as used in expressions like 'loss *of* face' is sometimes said to be a **genitive case particle**; *not* and *n't* are said to be **negative particles**. The term is sometimes extended to include prepositions used without a complement (e.g. *down* in 'He fell *down*').

partitive: a partitive quantifier is a word like *some/any* which quantifies over part of the members of a given set (as in '*Some* students enjoy syntax').

part of speech: see **category**.

passive: see **active**; see also **passivisation**.

passive participle: see **active, participle**.

passivisation: a movement operation whereby an expression which is the thematic complement of a verb becomes the subject of the same clause (as in '*The jewels were stolen*') or the subject of another clause (as in 'The minister was said to have lied to Parliament'). See §§7.7–7.8.

past tense: see **tense**.

PATIENT: a particular type of **theta-role**, denoting an entity which suffers the consequences of some action. For example, in a sentence such as 'John killed *Harry*', *Harry* is the PATIENT argument of the verb *kill*. The more recent term THEME is used in this book in place of the traditional term PATIENT. See §7.5.

percolation: an operation by which a feature which is attached to one category comes to be attached to another category higher up in the structure. See §6.7.

PERF: perfect-aspect auxiliary (e.g. *have* in 'He may *have* left'). See **aspect**.

perfect: in one sense of the word, in a sentence like 'He has gone home', *has* is an auxiliary marking **perfect aspect**, and *gone* is a **perfect participle**: see **aspect, participle**. In a different sense, by claiming that language is a perfect system, Chomsky means that grammars produce structures which are 'perfect' in that they are precisely of the form required to interface with speech and thought systems.

performance: a term which denotes observed language behaviour – e.g. the kind of things people actually say when they speak a language, and what meanings they assign to sentences produced by themselves or other people. Performance can be impaired by factors such as tiredness or drunkenness, giving rise to **performance errors**. Performance is contrasted with **competence** (which denotes fluent native speakers' knowledge of the grammar of their native language). See §1.3.

PERFP: phrase headed by a perfect-aspect auxiliary like *have*.

periphery: the periphery of a clause is that part of the clause structure which is positioned above TP – in other words the **edge** of CP (or its counterpart in a **split CP** system like that discussed in §§9.2–9.3).

Pers: an abbreviation of **person**.

person: in traditional grammar, English is said to have three grammatical persons. A first-person expression (e.g. *I/we*) is one whose reference includes the speaker(s); a second-person expression (e.g. *you*) is one which excludes the speaker(s) but includes the addressee(s) (i.e. the person or people being spoken to); a third-person expression (e.g. *he/she/it/they*) is one whose reference excludes both the speaker(s) and the addressee(s) – i.e. an expression which refers to someone or something other than the speaker(s) or addressee(s).

personal pronouns: these are pronouns which carry inherent **person** properties – i.e. first-person pronouns such as *I/we*, second-person pronouns such as *you*, and third-person pronouns such as *he/she/it/they*. See **person**.

PF(-representation): (a representation of the) **Phonetic Form** (of an expression). See **representation**. The **PF-component** of a grammar is the component which converts the syntactic structures generated by the computational component of the grammar into PF-representations, via a series of morphological and phonological operations. A **PF-clitic** is a **clitic** which attaches to another item in the

PF-component (not in the syntax), so that the two form a single phonetic word, but are not a single word in the syntax.

P-feature: a feature (e.g. a topic-, focus- or wh-feature) which attracts a constituent to move to the **periphery** of a clause.

phase: in work outlined in ch. 10, Chomsky argues that syntactic structures are built up in phases (phases including complementiser phrases and transitive verb phrases), and that once a phase has been produced, the domain/complement of the head of the phase undergoes **transfer** to the PF component and the semantic component, and thereby becomes impenetrable to further operations in the syntax.

Phase Impenetrability Condition: a **constraint** on grammatical operations which specifies that the domain/complement of a phase head is impenetrable/inaccessible to an external probe (i.e. to a probe which lies outside the relevant **phase**). See §8.5 and §10.2.

phi-features/φ-features: person and number features (and, in languages which have grammatical gender, gender features as well).

phonetic representation: see **representation**.

phonological features: features used to describe sound properties. For example, the difference between nasal and oral sounds might be described in terms of the feature [±NASAL].

phrase: the term **phrase** is used to denote an expression larger than a word which is a **maximal projection: see projection**. In traditional grammar, the term refers strictly to non-clausal expressions (hence, 'reading a book' is a phrase, but 'He is reading a book' is a clause, not a phrase). However, in more recent work, **clauses** are analysed as types of phrases: e.g. 'He will resign' is a tense phrase (TP), and 'That he will resign' is a complementiser phrase (CP). See §3.3 and §3.4.

phrase-marker: a tree diagram used to represent the syntactic structure of a phrase or sentence. See §3.7.

phrase structure: see **constituent structure**.

PIC: see **Phase Impenetrability Condition**.

pied-piping: a process by which a moved constituent drags one or more other constituents along with it when it moves. For example, if we compare a sentence like 'Who were you talking to?' with 'To whom were you talking?', we might say that in both cases the pronoun *who* is moved to the front of the sentence, but that in the second sentence the preposition *to* is **pied-piped** along with the pronoun *whom*. See §6.7.

PL: see **plural**.

plural: a plural expression is one which denotes more than one entity (e.g. *these cars* is a plural expression, whereas *this car* is a **singular** expression).

P-marker: see **phrase-marker**.

polarity expression: a word or phrase (e.g. a word like *ever* or a phrase like *at all* or *care a damn*) which has an inherent **affective** polarity, and hence is restricted to occurring within the scope of an affective (e.g. negative, interrogative or conditional) constituent. See **affective**.

positive evidence: In discussions of child language acquisition, this expression denotes evidence based on the actual occurrence of certain types of structure in the child's speech input. For example, hearing an adult say *Open it* gives a child **positive evidence** that verbs are canonically positioned before their complements in English. See §1.8.

possessive: a possessive structure is one which indicates possession: the term is most commonly used in relation to expressions like '*John's* book' or '*his* book' (where the italicised expressions denote the person who possesses the book). The italicised possessor in each structure is said to be **genitive** in **case**.

postposition: a type of word which is the counterpart of a **preposition** in languages which position prepositions after their complements. See **adposition**.

postulate: a postulate is a theoretical assumption or hypothesis; to postulate is to hypothesise.

PP: see **prepositional phrase**.

PPT: see **Principles-and-Parameters Theory**.

pragmatics: the study of how non-linguistic knowledge is integrated with linguistic knowledge in our use of language.

Pr: an abbreviation for the feature [present-tense]. See **tense**.

precede(nce): to say that one constituent **precedes** another is to say that it is positioned to its left (on the printed page) and that neither constituent contains the other. **Precedence** is left-to-right linear ordering.

preclausal: a preclausal expression is one which is positioned in front of a clause.

predicate: see **argument, predicative**.

Predicate-Internal Argument Hypothesis: the hypothesis that all the arguments of a predicate originate within a projection of the predicate. See §7.4.

predication: the process by which a **predicate** is combined with a **subject** in order to form a **proposition**. For example, in a sentence such as 'Boris likes vodka', the property of liking vodka is said to be predicated of *Boris*.

predicative: in structures such as 'John is *in Paris/very silly/a liar*', the italicised expressions are said to be predicative in that they predicate the property of being in Paris/being very silly/being a liar of John (i.e. they attribute the relevant property to John). A nominal like *a liar* when used predicatively is also referred to as a **predicate nominal**.

prefix: see **affix**.

prenominal: a prenominal expression is one which is positioned in front of a noun expression. For example, both *a* and *red* are prenominal in an expression such as *a red car*.

preposing: an informal term to indicate a movement operation by which a constituent is moved further to the left within a phrase or sentence.

preposition: a preposition is a word generally used to express location, manner etc. – e.g. *at/in/on/under/by/with/from/against/down* etc. In English, it is a characteristic property of prepositions that they are invariable, and that they can generally be modified by *straight/right*. Where a preposition has a nominal or pronominal complement, it is said to be **transitive**; where it has no complement, it is said to be **intransitive**. Hence *down* is a transitive preposition in 'He fell *down* the stairs', but an intransitive preposition in 'He fell *down*.'

prepositional phrase: a phrase whose head is a preposition – e.g. *in town, on Sunday, to the market, for someone else* etc.

preposition stranding: see **stranding**.

Pres/present tense: see **tense**.

principles: **principles of Universal Grammar/UG principles** describe potentially universal properties of natural language grammars: the terms **condition** and **constraint** are also used with much the same meaning as the term **principle**. Potential principles of Universal Grammar include the **Headedness Principle, Binary Principle, Attract Closest Principle** and **Phase Impenetrability Condition**.

Principles-and-Parameters Theory: this theory, developed in Chomsky (1981) and much subsequent work, claims that natural language grammars incorporate not only a set of innate universal **principles** which account for those aspects of grammar which are common to all languages, but also a set of **parameters** which account for those aspects of grammar which vary from one language to another. See **Principles** and **Parameters**.

PRN: see **pronoun**.

PRO: a null-case pronoun (known informally as 'big PRO', because it is written in capital letters) which represents the understood subject of an infinitive complement of a **control predicate**, e.g. in a structure such as 'John decided PRO to leave.' See §4.2.

pro: a null nominative-case pronoun (known informally as 'little pro', because it is written in lower-case letters) which represents the understood null subject of a finite clause in a **null-subject language**. A Shakespearean sentence such as 'Wilt come?' (= 'Will you come?', Stephano, *The Tempest*, III.ii) could be argued to have a null *pro* subject, and hence to have the structure 'Wilt *pro* come?', with *pro* having essentially the same interpretation as the second-person-singular pronoun *thou.* See §4.2.

probe: when a **head** is merged with its complement, it serves as a **probe** which searches for a matching goal within its complement (i.e. an expression which it can agree with). See §8.2.

proform: a proform is an expression (typically a word) which has no specific content of its own, but which derives its content from its **antecedent**. For example, in a sentence such as 'Mary may have been tired, but she didn't seem *so*', the antecedent of the word *so* is the adjective *tired:* hence *so* (in the use illustrated here) can be said to be an adjectival proform.

PROG: progressive-aspect auxiliary (e.g. *be* in 'He may *be* waiting for you'). See **aspect**.

PROGP: progressive phrase – i.e. a phrase headed by a PROG/progressive auxiliary constituent – e.g. *be waiting for you* in 'He may *be waiting for you.*'

progressive: see **aspect**.

project(ion): a **projection** is a constituent containing a head word. For example, a noun phrase such as *students of linguistics* is a **projection** of its head noun *students* (equivalently, we can say that the noun *students* here **projects** into the noun phrase *students of linguistics*). A **minimal projection** is a constituent which is not a projection of some other constituent: hence, heads (e.g. words) are minimal projections. An **intermediate projection** is a constituent which is larger than a word, but smaller than a phrase (e.g. *is working* in 'He is working'). A **maximal projection** is a constituent which is not contained within any larger constituent with the same head. So, for example, in a sentence like 'I've heard several *accounts of what happened*', the italicised noun phrase expression *accounts of what happened* is a maximal projection, since it is a projection of the noun *accounts* but is not contained within any larger projection of the noun *accounts* (if we assume that *several accounts of what happened* is a quantifier phrase headed by the quantifier *several*). By contrast, in a sentence such as 'I've heard several *accounts*', the italicised noun *accounts* is both a minimal projection (by virtue of the fact that it is not a projection of some other head) and a maximal projection (by virtue of the fact that it is not contained within any larger structure which has the same head noun). The **Projection Principle** is a UG principle suggested in earlier work by

Chomsky (1981, p. 29) which requires that the properties of lexical items should remain constant throughout the derivation: a related principle is the **Inclusiveness Condition**.

pronominal: a pronominal (expression) is a non-anaphoric pronoun like *him* which obeys **Principle B** of **Binding Theory** (and hence must not refer to any higher expression within the closest TP most immediately containing it). See ex. 3.2.

pronoun: the word *pronoun* is composed of two morphemes – namely *pro* (meaning 'on behalf of') and *noun:* hence, a pronoun is traditionally said to be a word used in place of a noun expression. Pronouns differ from nouns in that they have no intrinsic descriptive content, and so are functors. There are a range of different types of pronoun found in English, including the pronominal noun *one(s)* used in sentences like 'I'll take the red *one(s)*', pronominal quantifiers like *any* in 'I couldn't find *any*' and pronominal determiners like *this* in '*This* is hard'. The term **pronoun** is most frequently used to indicate a class of items (like *he/him/his*) traditionally referred to as **personal pronouns** (though analysed in much recent work as pronominal determiners). See §2.6.

proper noun: see **noun**.

proposition: this is a term used to describe the semantic content (i.e. meaning) of a sentence. For example, we might say that the sentence 'Does John smoke?' questions the truth of the proposition that 'John smokes.'

pseudocleft sentence: a sentence such as 'What he hated most was *syntax*', where *syntax* is said to occupy **focus position** within the overall sentence.

Q: in one use, an abbreviation for **quantifier**; in another use, an abbreviation for **question particle**.

quantifier: a quantifier is a special type of determiner used to denote quantity. Typical quantifiers include the **universal quantifiers** *all/both*, the **distributive quantifiers** *each/every*, the **existential/partitive quantifiers** *some/any* etc.

quantifier floating: see **floating quantifier**.

QP/quantifier phrase: a phrase whose head is a quantifier – e.g. an expression such as *many people*, or *few of the students*.

Q-pronoun: a pronoun like *many* in 'I don't eat *many*' which seems to be a pronominal quantifier.

question: this refers to a type of sentence which is used to ask whether something is true, or to ask about the identity of some entity. See **yes–no question** and **wh-question**.

question operator: the analysis of yes–no questions presented in §6.8 suggests that they contain a null interrogative operator (i.e. a null counterpart of *whether*).

quirky case: see **case**.

raising (**predicate**): the term **raising** is used in two senses. In its most general sense, it denotes any movement operation which involves moving some constituent from a 'lower' to a 'higher' position in a structure. However, it also has a more specific sense, indicating a particular kind of **A-movement** operation by which an expression is moved from being the subject of one clause to becoming the subject of another. The term **raising predicate** denotes a word like *seem* whose subject is raised out of subject position in a complement clause to become subject of the *seem* clause. See §7.9 and §7.10.

reciprocal: see **anaphor**.

reduced: a reduced form is a form of a word which has lost one or more of its segments (i.e. vowel/consonants), and/or which contains a vowel which loses its defining characteristics and is realised as a neutral vowel like schwa /ə/. For example, the auxiliary *have* has the full (unreduced) form /hæv/ when stressed, but has the various reduced forms /həv/, /əv/ and /v/ when unstressed.

reference/referential/referring: the reference of an expression is the entity (e.g. object, concept, state of affairs) in the external world to which it refers. A **referential/referring expression** is one which refers to such an entity; conversely, a **non-referential expression** is one which does not refer to any such entity. For example the second *there* in a sentence such as '*There* was nobody *there*' is referential (it can be paraphrased as 'in that place'), whereas the first *there* is non-referential and so cannot have its reference questioned by *where*? (cf. **'Where was nobody there?*).

reflexive: see **anaphor**.

relative: in a sentence such as 'He's someone [*who* you can trust]', the bracketed clause is said to be a **relative clause** because it 'relates to' (i.e. modifies, or restricts the reference of) the pronoun *someone*. The pronoun *who* which introduces the clause is said to be a **relative pronoun**, since it 'relates to' the expression *someone* (in the sense that *someone* is the **antecedent** of *who*). The **Relative Pronoun Spellout Condition/RPSC** specifies that a relative pronoun is given a null spellout if it occupies the specifier position within CP (optionally in a finite clause, obligatorily in a non-finite clause). See §6.10 and §6.11 for a general discussion of relative clauses. On the distinction between **appositive/free/restrictive relative clauses**, see the discussion of examples (127)–(131) in §6.11.

Remerger Constraint: a grammatical principle which specifies that no head can be remerged with a constituent with which it has already been merged.

representation: a **syntactic representation** (or **structural representation**) is a notation/device (typically, a tree diagram or labelled bracketing) used to represent the syntactic structure of an expression: a **semantic representation** is a representation of linguistic aspects of the meaning of an expression; a **PF-representation** is a representation of the phonetic form of an expression.

restrictive: a restrictive theory is one which imposes strong constraints on the types of structures and operations found in natural language grammars. See §1.3. In a different use of the word, the italicised clause in a sentence like 'I saw the man *who they arrested* on TV' is a **restrictive relative clause** in the sense that it restricts the class of men being referred to in the sentence to the one they arrested.

resultative: a verb such as *paint* in a sentence such as 'John *painted* his house pink' is said to be a resultative verb in that the result of the action of painting is that the house becomes pink. See §9.5.

R-expression: a referring expression containing a noun, like *John* or *the man next door*. See ex. 3.2.

rich: to say that a language has a **rich** system of agreement inflections is to say that it has a large number of inflectional affixes which attach to verbs and distinctively mark first/second/third-person forms and singular/plural forms, with little **syncretism**; to say that a language has an **impoverished/poor** system of agreement inflections is to say that it has only a small number of such inflections, and that these do not clearly and consistently differentiate first/second/third-person forms and singular/plural forms.

root: the root of a tree diagram is the topmost node in the tree. Hence, a **root clause** is a free-standing clause, i.e. a clause which is not contained within any other expression. In traditional grammar, a root clause is termed a **principal clause, independent clause** or **main clause**. By contrast, an **embedded clause** is a clause which is contained within some larger expression; and a **complement clause** is an (embedded) clause which is used as the complement of some item. So, in a sentence such as 'I think he loves you', the *think* clause (i.e. the expression *I think he loves you*) is a root clause, whereas the *loves* clause (i.e. the expression *he loves you*) is an embedded clause. Moreover, the *loves* clause is also a complement clause, since it serves as the complement of the verb *think*.

RPSC: Relative Pronoun Spellout Condition. See **relative**.

S/S′/S-bar: category label used in work in the 1960s and 1970s to designate a **sentence** or **clause**. See §3.3.

scope: the scope of an expression is the set of constituents which it modifies or which fall within (what we might call informally) its 'sphere of influence'. For example, a sentence like *He cannot be telling the truth* has a meaning paraphraseable as 'It is not possible that he is telling the truth', and in such a sentence the negative *not* is said to have scope over the modal auxiliary *can* (and conversely *can* is said to fall within the scope of *not*, or to have **narrow scope** with respect to *not*). By contrast, a sentence such as *You mustn't tell lies* has a meaning paraphraseable as 'It is necessary that you not tell lies', and in such a sentence, the auxiliary *must* is said to have scope over (or to have **wide scope** with respect to) the negative particle *n't*.

SCP: see **Strict Cyclicity Principle**.

SE: Standard English.

second person: see **person**.

select(ion)/selectional: when a word has a particular type of complement, it is said to **select** (i.e. 'take' or 'allow') the relevant type of complement (and the relevant phenomenon is referred to as **complement-selection**). For example, we can say that the word *expect* has the **selectional property** that it can select an infinitive complement (e.g. in structures like 'They expect *to* win').

semantics/semantic component: Semantics is the study of linguistic aspects of meaning. The **semantic component** of the grammar is the component which maps syntactic structures into semantic representations. See **representation**.

sentence: this term is usually used to denote a **root clause** – i.e. a free-standing clause which is not contained within some larger expression. See **root**.

sentence fragment: see **fragment**.

SG: an abbreviation for **singular**.

Shakespeare: Shakespeare's plays were written between (around) 1590 and 1620, and are examples of **Early Modern English/Elizabethan English** (though some have suggested that Shakespeare's English is rather conservative, and hence is more representative of a slightly earlier stage of English).

shell: this term is used in connection with the idea (discussed in §§9.4–9.8) that verb phrases comprise two different projections, an outer vP shell headed by a **light verb**, and an inner VP core headed by a **lexical verb**.

silent: see **null**.

simple sentence: one which contains a single **clause**.

singular: a singular expression is one which denotes a single entity (e.g. *this car* is a **singular** expression, whereas *these cars* is a **plural** expression).

sister: two nodes are sisters if they have the same mother (i.e. if they are directly merged with each other at some stage of derivation). See §3.7.

small clause: see **clause**.

SOURCE: a term used in the analysis of semantic/thematic roles to denote the entity from which something moves – e.g. the italicised expression in 'John returned *from Paris*.' See §7.5.

spec: see **specifier**. Terms like **spec-CP/spec-TP/spec-VP** (etc.) denote the specifier position within CP/TP/VP (etc.).

specification: the specification of an item is the set of features used to describe its properties.

specifier: the grammatical function fulfilled by certain types of constituent which precede the head of their containing phrase. For example, in a sentence such as 'John is working', *John* is superficially the specifier (and subject) of *is working*. In a sentence such as 'What did John do?' *what* is superficially the specifier of the CP headed by a C constituent containing the inverted auxiliary *did*. In a phrase such as 'straight through the window', *straight* is the specifier of the PP headed by the preposition *through*.

specifier-first: a specifier-first structure is one which has its specifier positioned in front of its head.

spellout: the point in a derivation at which part of a syntactic structure is sent to the PF component to be mapped into a PF-representation (i.e. a representation of its phonetic form). To say that an item has a **null spellout** is to say that it is 'silent' and so has a null phonetic form.

split CP/split NP/split VP: work by Luigi Rizzi discussed in §§9.2–9.3 has suggested that **CP** can be split into a number of distinct projections, including a **Force Phrase, Focus Phrase, Topic Phrase** and **Finiteness Phrase**. Similarly, work by Larson, Hale and Chomsky outlined in §§9.4–9.8 has suggested that verb phrases can be split into two different projections, an outer vP shell headed by a **light verb**, and an inner VP core headed by a **lexical verb**. In §9.9, a parallel split projection analysis of noun phrases is outlined. On **split spellout**, see **discontinuous spellout**.

stack(ing): to say (e.g.) that prenominal adjectives can be stacked in front of a noun is to say that we can have an indefinitely large number of adjectives positioned in front of a noun (e.g. 'a *big, red, juicy, ripe* apple').

star: an asterisk (*) used in front of an expression to indicate that the expression is ungrammatical.

stem: the stem of a word is the form to which inflectional affixes are added. So, a verb form like *going* comprises the stem *go* and the inflectional suffix *-ing*.

strand/stranded/stranding: a stranded (or **orphaned**) preposition is one which has been separated from its complement (by movement of the complement). For example, in an echo question like 'You're waiting for who?', the preposition *for* has not been stranded, since it is immediately followed by its complement *who*. But in '*Who* are you waiting *for?*' the preposition *for* has been **stranded** or **orphaned**, in that it has been separated from its complement *who:* the relevant phenomenon is termed **preposition stranding**. The **Stranding Constraint**

specifies that in formal styles of English, a preposition cannot be separated from its complement and thereby be stranded.

Strict Cyclicity Principle: a UG principle which specifies that a **cyclic** operation can only affect the overall head H of a structure and some other constituent within the structure headed by H. See §5.7.

string: a continuous sequence of words contained within the same phrase or sentence. For example, in the sentence 'They hate syntax', the sequences *They hate, hate syntax* and *They hate syntax* are all strings – but *They syntax* is not. Note that a string need not be a **constituent**.

strong: a **strong head** is one which can attract (i.e. trigger movement of) another head; a **weak head** is one which cannot trigger movement. For example, C in an interrogative main clause is strong in present-day English, and so attracts an auxiliary to move from T to C – e.g. in sentences like *Can you speak French?* On an entirely different use of these terms in the expressions **weak/strong genitive pronoun**, see **case**.

structural: see **case, representation**.

structure: see **constituent structure**.

stylistic variation: variation correlated with stylistic factors. For example, *whom* is used in formal styles and *who* in other styles in sentences like 'He is someone *whom/who* I admire greatly.'

subarray: see **array**.

subject: the (superficial structural) subject of a clause is a noun or pronoun expression which is normally positioned between a complementiser and an (auxiliary or non-auxiliary) verb. Syntactic characteristics of subjects include the fact that they can trigger agreement with auxiliaries (as in 'The president is lying', where the auxiliary *is* agrees with the subject *the president*), and they can be inverted with auxiliaries in main-clause questions (as in 'Is the president lying?', where the auxiliary *is* has been inverted with the subject *the president*).

subject control predicate: see **control**.

subjunctive: in a (formal-style) sentence such as 'The judge ordered that he *be* detained indefinitely', the passive auxiliary verb *be* is traditionally said to be in the **subjunctive mood**, since although it has exactly the same form as the infinitive form *be* (e.g. in infinitive structures such as 'To *be* or not to *be* – that is the question'), it has a nominative subject *he*, and hence is a **finite** verb form. In present-day spoken English, constructions containing subjunctive verbs are generally avoided, as they are felt to be archaic or excessively formal in style by many speakers. See **Mood**.

substantive: a **substantive category** is a category (like noun, verb, adjective, adverb, preposition) whose members are **contentives** (i.e. items with idiosyncratic descriptive content). See §2.4.

substitution: a technique used to determine the category which a given expression belongs to. An expression belongs to a given type of category if it can be substituted (i.e. replaced) in phrases or sentences like that in which it occurs by another expression which clearly belongs to the category in question. For example, we might say that *clearer* is an adverb in 'John speaks *clearer* than you' because it can be replaced by the adverbial expression *more clearly*. See §2.3.

successive-cyclic movement: movement in a succession of short steps. On the claim that head movement is successive-cyclic, see §5.5. On the claim that A-movement is successive-cyclic, see §8.9. On the claim that wh-movement is successive-cyclic, see ch. 10.

suffix: see **affix**.

superiority: wh-questions are said to show a **superiority effect** in the sense that in a question containing more than one wh-expression, it is the superior (i.e. highest) wh-expression which moves to the front of the interrogative clause. See §6.4.

superlative: the superlative is a form of an adjective/adverb (typically carrying the suffix -*est*) used to mark the highest value for a particular property in comparison with others. For example, *hardest* is the superlative form of *hard* in 'John is the *hardest* worker because he works *hardest*.'

syncretise/syncretism: in work on split CP projections discussed in §9.3, Rizzi has claimed that although **Force** and **Finiteness** are projected on separate heads when some (topicalised or focused) constituent intervenes between them, they are **syncretised** (i.e. collapsed/conflated) into a single head carrying both Force and Finiteness features when no constituent intervenes between them.

syntactic representation: see **representation**.

syntax: the component of a grammar which determines how words are combined together to form phrases and sentences.

T: a tense-marking constituent containing either a tensed auxiliary, or an abstract tense affix *Tns*, or a non-finite tense particle like infinitival *to*. **T-to-C movement** is movement of an auxiliary or non-auxiliary verb from the head T position of TP into the head C position of CP – as with the italicised inverted auxiliary in '*Is* it raining?'

tag: a string usually consisting of an auxiliary and a subject pronoun which is 'tagged' onto the end of a sentence. Thus, the italicised string is the tag in the following: 'The president isn't underestimating his opponents, *is he*?', and the overall sentence is known as a **tag question/tag sentence**.

taxonomy: a **taxonomy** is a classificatory system. A **taxonomic** theory of language is one which classifies constituents into different types. See §1.2.

tense: finite auxiliary and main verbs in English show a binary (two-way) tense contrast, traditionally said to be between **present-tense** forms and **past-tense** forms. Thus, in 'John *hates* syntax', *hates* is a present-tense verb form, whereas in 'John *hated* syntax', *hated* is a past-tense verb form. (An alternative classification which many linguists prefer is into [±PAST] verb forms, so that *hated* is [+PAST], and *hates* [−PAST].) This present/past-tense distinction correlates (to some extent) with time-reference, so that (e.g.) past-tense verbs typically describe an event taking place in the past, whereas present-tense verbs typically describe an event taking place in the present (or future). However, the correlation is an imperfect one, since e.g. in a sentence such as 'I *might* go there tomorrow', the auxiliary *might* carries the past-tense inflection -*t* (found on past-tense main verbs like *left*) but does not denote past time.

tensed: a tensed (auxiliary or non-auxiliary) verb form is one which carries (present/past) **tense** – e.g. *is, can, could, hates, went* etc. By extension, a tensed clause is one containing a tensed auxiliary or main verb. See **tense**.

terminal node: a node at the bottom of a tree.

ternary: three-way. For example, person properties might be described in terms of a ternary (three-valued) feature such as [1/2/3-Pers], with first-person pronouns like *we* being [1-Pers], second-person pronouns like *you* being [2-Pers] and third-person pronouns like *they* being [3-Pers]. A ternary-branching constituent is one which has three daughters.

thematic: on **thematic role**, see **theta-role**. On the **Thematic Hierarchy** which specifies where an argument carrying a given theta-role should be merged, see ex. 9.2. On the (different) **Thematic Hierarchy** which constrains how passivisation works, see §7.5.

THEME: the name of a specific theta-role (sometimes also termed PATIENT) representing the entity undergoing the effect of some action (e.g. *Harry* in 'William teased *Harry*').

theory of grammar: a theory which specifies the types of categories, relations, operations and principles found in natural language grammars. See §1.3.

theta-criterion/θ-criterion: a principle of Universal Grammar which specifies that each argument should bear one and only one theta-role to a single predicate, and that each theta-role associated with a given predicate should be assigned to one and only one argument. See §7.5.

theta-mark/θ-mark: to say that a predicate **theta-marks** its arguments is to say that it determines the theta-role played by its arguments. A predicate is said to **directly theta-mark** its complement(s), and to **indirectly theta-mark** its subject. See §7.5.

theta-role/θ-role: the semantic role played by an argument in relation to its predicate (e.g. AGENT, THEME, GOAL etc.). For example, in a sentence like *William teased Harry*, the verb *tease* assigns the θ-role AGENT to its subject *William* and the theta-role THEME to its complement *Harry*. See §7.5.

third person: see **person**.

three-place predicate: a predicate (typically a verb) which takes three arguments – e.g. the verb *give* in 'John gave Mary something' (where the three arguments of *give* are *John, Mary* and *something*). See **argument**.

Tns: an abstract affix which carries tense and agreement properties. See §4.4.

Top/Topic/Topicalisation/TopP: In a dialogue such as the following:

> SPEAKER A: I've been having problems with the Fantasy Syntax seminar
> SPEAKER B: *That kind of course*, very few students seem to be able to get their heads round

the italicised expression *that kind of course* can be said to be the **topic** of the sentence produced by speaker B, in the sense that it refers back to *the Fantasy Syntax seminar* mentioned by the previous speaker. An expression which represents 'old' or 'familiar' information in this way is said to be a **topic**. The movement operation by which the italicised expression moves from being the complement of the preposition *round* to the front of the overall sentence is traditionally termed **topicalisation**. In work by Luigi Rizzi on split CP projections discussed in §9.2, topic expressions which occur at the beginning of clauses are said to be contained within a **TopP** 'Topic Phrase' projection, headed by an abstract **Top** (= 'Topic') constituent.

TP: tense projection/tense phrase – i.e. phrase headed by a tense-marked auxiliary or an abstract tense morpheme *Tns*. See §§3.2–3.3.

trace (theory): a **trace** of a moved constituent is a null copy left behind (as a result of movement) in each position out of which a constituent moves. **Trace theory** is a theory which posits that moved constituents leave behind a trace **copy** in each position out of which they move. See §5.3, §6.3 and §7.2.

transfer: see **phase**.

transitive: a word is traditionally said to be transitive (in a given use) if it assigns accusative case to a noun or pronoun expression which it **c-commands**. So, *likes* in 'John *likes* him' is a transitive verb, since it assigns accusative case to its complement *him*. Likewise, infinitival *for* is a transitive complementiser, since it assigns accusative case to the subject of its infinitive complement (cf. 'I'm keen [for *him* to participate more actively]') An **intransitive** head etc. is one which has no complement, or which does not assign accusative case to (any expression contained within) its complement; hence e.g. *wait* is an intransitive verb in sentences like *I'll wait*, and likewise in *I'll wait for you*. See §4.9.

tree (diagram): A form of graph used to represent the syntactic structure of a phrase or sentence.

truncate/truncation: truncation is an operation by which a sentence is shortened by omitting one or more unstressed words at the beginning. For example, we can truncate a question like *Are you going anywhere nice on holiday?* by omitting *are* to form *You going anywhere nice on holiday?* and can further truncate the sentence by omitting *you* to give *Going anywhere nice on holiday?*

T-to-C movement: see **T**.

two-place predicate: a predicate which has two arguments – e.g. *tease* in 'William *teased* Harry' where the two arguments of the predicate *tease* are *William* and *Harry*. See **argument**.

UG: see **Universal Grammar**.

unaccusative: an unaccusative predicate is a word like *come* whose apparent 'subject' originates as its complement. See §7.6.

unary-branching: a unary-branching node is one which has a single daughter.

unbound: a constituent is unbound if it has no appropriate antecedent in an appropriate position within a given structure. For example, *himself* is unbound in a sentence such as *'She helped *himself*, since *she* is not an appropriate antecedent for *himself*, and there is no other appropriate antecedent for *himself* anywhere within the sentence.

unergative: an unergative predicate is a verb like *groan* in a sentence such as 'He was *groaning*' which has an AGENT subject but no overt object (though may have an incorporated object: see §9.6).

ungradable: see **gradable**.

ungrammatical: see **grammatical**.

Uniformity of Theta Assignment Hypothesis/UTAH: a hypothesis (developed by Baker 1988) which maintains that each theta-role assigned by a particular (kind of) predicate is canonically associated with a specific syntactic position: e.g. spec-vP is the canonical position associated with an AGENT argument.

uninterpretable: see **interpretable**.

Universal Grammar: those aspects of grammar which are universal, and which are assumed by Chomsky to be part of the innate knowledge which a child is born with.

universality: a criterion of adequacy for a theory of grammar, requiring that the theory be applicable to all natural languages. See §1.3.

unreduced: see **reduced**.

unspecified: to say that a constituent is **unspecified** for a given feature is to say that it lacks the relevant feature.

unvalued: see **value**.

UTAH: see **Uniformity of Theta Assignment Hypothesis**.

V: see **verb**.

v: see **light verb**.

value: in relation to a feature such as [SINGULAR-NUMBER], **number** is said to be an **attribute** (in the sense that it is the property being described) and **singular** its **value**. To **value** a feature is to assign it a value. For example, a finite auxiliary enters the derivation with its person and number features **unvalued** (i.e. not assigned any value), and these are then valued via agreement with the subject in the course of the derivation. See §8.3.

variety: a particular (e.g. geographical or social) form of a language.

verb: a category of word which has the morphological property that it can carry a specific range of inflections (e.g. the verb *show* can carry past-tense *-d*, third-person-singular present-tense *-s*, perfect *-n* and progressive *-ing*, giving rise to *shows/showed/shown/showing*), and the syntactic property that it can head the complement of infinitival *to* (e.g. 'Do you want to *show* me?') See §2.2 and §2.3. On **verb movement**, see **V-to-T movement**.

verb phrase: a phrase which is headed by a verb – e.g. the italicised phrase in 'They will *help you*.' See ch. 3.

V-to-T movement: movement of a verb out of the head V position in VP into the head T position in TP. See §5.4.

vocative: a vocative expression is one which is used to address one or more individuals, and which is set off in a separate tone-group at the beginning or end of the sentence (marked in the spelling by the use of a comma). So, for example, *Fred* is a vocative expression in 'Fred, can you give me a hand?' and similarly, *you two* is a vocative expression in 'Come here, you two!'

voice: see **active**.

VP/VPISH: on VP, see **verb phrase**. A **VP-adverb** is an adverb (like *perfectly*) which adjoins to a projection of a lexical verb (V). The **VP-Internal Subject Hypothesis/VPISH** is the hypothesis that subjects originate internally within VP/vP: see ch. 7.

vP: a phrase (maximal projection) headed by a light verb. A **vP-adverb** is an adverb which adjoins to a projection of a **light verb** (v).

weak: see **strong**.

wh: this is widely used as a feature carried by constituents which undergo wh-movement (hence e.g. the relative pronoun *who* in *someone who I think is lying* can be described as a wh-pronoun, as can the interrogative pronoun *who* in *Who are you waiting for?* and the exclamative quantifier *what* in *What fun we had!*).

wh-copying: a phenomenon whereby a moved wh-expression leaves behind an overt copy of itself when it moves – as with movement of *who* in a Child English question such as *Who do you think who chased the cat?*

wh-expression: an expression containing a wh-word (i.e. containing a word carrying a [wh] feature).

wh-island constraint: a constraint which specifies that wh-clauses (i.e. clauses beginning with a wh-expression) are **islands**, so that no constituent can be moved out of a wh-clause. See **island**.

wh-movement: a type of movement operation whereby a wh-expression is moved to the front of a particular type of structure (e.g. to the front of the overall sentence in '*Where* has he gone?'). See ch. 6.

wh-parameter: a parameter whose setting determines whether wh-expressions are (or are not) moved to the front of an appropriate type of clause (especially in relation to wh-questions). See §1.6.

wh-phrase: a phrase containing a **wh-word**.

wh-question: a question which contains a **wh-word**, e.g. 'What are you doing?'

wh-word: a word which begins with *wh* (e.g. *who/what/which/where/when/why*), or which has a similar syntax to *wh*-words (e.g. *how*).

word order: the linear sequencing (left-to-right ordering) of words within a phrase or sentence.

yes–no question: a question to which 'Yes' or 'No' would be an appropriate answer – e.g. 'Is it raining?'

References

Abney, S. P. (1987) 'The English Noun Phrase in Its Sentential Aspect', PhD diss., MIT.

Ackema, P. (2001) 'On the relation between V-to-I and the structure of the inflectional paradigm', *The Linguistic Review* 18: 233–63.

Acquaviva, P. (2002) 'The morphological dimension of polarity licensing', *Linguistics* 40: 925–59.

Adger, D. (2003) *Core Syntax: A Minimalist Approach*, Oxford University Press, Oxford.

Agbayani, B. (2000) 'Wh-subjects in English and the Vacuous Movement Hypothesis', *Linguistic Inquiry* 31: 703–13.

Aissen, J. (1996) 'Pied-piping, abstract agreement and functional projections in Tzotzil', *Natural Language and Linguistic Theory* 14: 447–91.

Akmajian, A. and Heny, F. (1975) *An Introduction to the Principles of Transformational Syntax*, MIT Press, Cambridge, Mass.

Alexiadou, A. and Anagnostopoulou, E. (2001) 'The subject-in-situ generalization and the role of case in driving computations', *Linguistic Inquiry* 32: 193–231.

Alexopoulou, T. and Kolliakou, D. (2002) 'On Linkhood, Topicalisation and Clitic Left Dislocation', *Journal of Linguistics* 38: 193–245.

Antony, L. and Hornstein, N. (2002) *Chomsky and His Critics*, Blackwell, Oxford.

Aronoff, M. (1976) *Word Formation in Generative Grammar*, MIT Press, Cambridge, Mass.

Aronoff, M. and Fuhrhop, N. (2002) 'Restricting suffix combinations in German and English: closing suffixes and the monosuffix constraint', *Natural Language and Linguistic Theory* 20: 451–90.

Atkinson, M. (2003) Unpublished course handouts, University of Essex.

Authier, J.-M. (1991) 'V-governed expletives, case theory and the projection principle', *Linguistic Inquiry* 22: 721–40.

Baker, C. L. (1970) 'Notes on the description of English questions: the role of an abstract question morpheme', *Foundations of Language* 6: 197–219.

Baker, M. (1988) *Incorporation*, University of Chicago Press, Chicago.

Baltin, M. (1995) 'Floating quantifiers, PRO and predication', *Linguistic Inquiry* 26: 199–248.

Baltin, M. (2002) 'Movement to the higher V is remnant movement', *Linguistic Inquiry* 33: 653–9.

Baltin, M. and Collins, C. (eds.) (2001) *The Handbook of Contemporary Syntactic Theory*, Blackwell, Oxford.

Barss, A. (2001) 'Syntactic reconstruction effects', in Baltin and Collins (eds.), pp. 670–96.

Basilico, D. (2003) 'The topic of small clauses', *Linguistic Inquiry* 34: 1–35.

Bejar, S. and Massam, D. (1999) 'Multiple case checking', *Syntax* 2: 65–79.

Belletti, A. (1988) 'The case of unaccusatives', *Linguistic Inquiry* 19: 1–34.

Belletti, A. and Rizzi, L. (1988) 'Psych-verbs and θ-theory', *Natural Language and Linguistic Theory*, 6: 291–352.

Bernstein, J. B. (2001) 'The DP hypothesis: identifying clausal properties in the nominal domain', in Baltin and Collins (eds.) pp. 536–61.

Bobaljik, J. (1995) 'Morphosyntax: the Syntax of Verbal Inflection', PhD diss., MIT.

Bobaljik, J. D. (2000) 'The rich agreement hypothesis in review', draft manuscript, McGill University (http://www.msgill.ca/Linguistics/faculty/bobaljik/).

Bobaljik, J. (2002) 'A-chains at the PF-interface: copies and "covert" movement', *Natural Language and Linguistic Theory* 20: 197–267.

Boeckx, C. (2000) 'A note on Contraction', *Linguistic Inquiry* 31: 357–66.

Boeckx, C. (2001) 'Scope reconstruction and A-movement', *Natural Language and Linguistic Theory* 19: 503–48.

Boeckx, C. and Stjepanović, S. (2001) 'Head-ing towards PF', *Linguistic Inquiry* 32: 345–55.

Borsley, R. (2002) 'Wh-phrases in Minimalism', unpublished paper, University of Essex.

Bošković, Ž. (1997) 'On certain violations of the superiority condition, AgrO and economy of derivation', *Journal of Linguistics* 33: 227–54.

Bošković, Ž. (2001) *On the Nature of the Syntax-Phonology Interface: Cliticization and Related Phenomena*, Elsevier, Amsterdam.

Bošković, Ž. (2002a) 'On multiple *wh*-fronting', *Linguistic Inquiry* 33: 351–83.

Bošković, Ž. (2002b) 'A-Movement and the EPP', *Syntax* 5: 167–218.

Bowerman, M. (1988) 'The "no negative evidence" problem: how do children avoid an overly general grammar?', in J. Hawkins (ed.), *Explaining Language Universals*, Blackwell, Oxford.

Bowers, J. (1993) 'The syntax of predication', *Linguistic Inquiry* 24: 591–656.

Bowers, J. (2002) 'Transitivity', *Linguistic Inquiry* 33: 183–224.

Braine, M. D. S. (1971) 'Three suggestions regarding grammatical analyses of children's language', in C. A. Ferguson and D. I. Slobin (eds.), *Studies of Child Language Development*, Holt Rinehart and Winston, New York, pp. 421–9.

Branigan, P. (1992) 'Subjects and Complementisers', PhD diss., MIT.

Branigan, P. and MacKenzie, M. (2002) 'Altruism, A-movement and object agreement in Innu-aimûn', *Linguistic Inquiry* 33: 385–407.

Brody, M. (1995) *A Radically Minimalist Theory*, MIT Press, Cambridge, Mass.

Brown, K. (1991) 'Double modals in Hawick Scots', in P. Trudgill and J. K. Chambers (eds.), *Dialects of English*, Longman, London, pp. 74–103.

Brown R., Cazden, C. and Bellugi, U. (1968) 'The child's grammar from I to III', in J. P. Hill (ed.), *Minnesota Symposium on Child Development*, vol. 2, pp. 28–73.

Brown, R. and Hanlon, C. (1970) 'Derivational complexity and order of acquisition in child speech', in J. R. Hayes (ed.), *Cognition and the Development of Language*, Wiley, New York, pp. 11–53.

Burton, S. and Grimshaw, J. (1992) 'Coordination and VP-internal subjects', *Linguistic Inquiry* 23: 305–13.

Burzio, L. (1986) *Italian Syntax*, Reidel, Dordrecht.

Carnie, A. (2000) 'On the definition of X^0 and XP', *Syntax* 3: 59–106.

Carrier, J. and Randall, J. H. (1992) 'The argument structure and syntactic structure of resultatives', *Linguistic Inquiry* 23: 173–234.

Carstens, V. (2000) 'Concord in Minimalist Theory', *Linguistic Inquiry* 31: 319–55.

Carstens, V. (2001) 'Multiple agreement and case deletion: against φ-(in)completeness', *Syntax* 4: 147–63.

Cheng, L. (1997) *On the Typology of Wh-Questions*, Garland, New York.

Cheng, L. and Rooryck, J. (2000) 'Licensing *Wh*-in-situ', *Syntax* 3: 1–19.

Chomsky, N. (1965) *Aspects of the Theory of Syntax*, MIT Press, Cambridge, Mass.

Chomsky, N. (1968) Interview with S. Hamshire in *The Listener*, May 1968.

Chomsky, N. (1970) 'Remarks on nominalisation', in R. A. Jacobs and P. S. Rosenbaum (eds.), *Readings in English Transformational Grammar*, Ginn, Waltham, Mass, pp. 184–221.

Chomsky, N. (1972) *Language and Mind* (enlarged edition), Harcourt Brace Jovanovich, New York.

Chomsky, N. (1981) *Lectures on Government and Binding*, Foris, Dordrecht.

Chomsky, N. (1982) *Some Concepts and Consequences of the Theory of Government and Binding*, MIT Press, Cambridge, Mass.

Chomsky, N. (1986a) *Knowledge of Language: its Nature, Origin and Use*, Praeger, New York.

Chomsky, N. (1986b) *Barriers*, MIT Press, Cambridge, Mass.

Chomsky, N. (1993) 'A minimalist program for linguistic theory', in Hale and Keyser (eds.), pp. 1–52 (reprinted as chapter 3 of Chomsky 1995).

Chomsky, N. (1995) *The Minimalist Program*, MIT Press, Cambridge, Mass.

Chomsky, N. (1998) *Minimalist Inquiries: the Framework*, MIT Occasional Papers in Linguistics, no. 15 (also published in R. Martin, D. Michaels and J. Uriagereka (eds.) (2000) *Step by Step: Essays on Minimalism in Honor of Howard Lasnik*, MIT Press, Cambridge, Mass., pp. 89–155).

Chomsky, N. (1999) *Derivation by Phase*, MIT Occasional Papers in Linguistics, no. 18 (also published in M. Kenstowicz (ed.) (2001) *Ken Hale: a Life in Language*, MIT Press, Cambridge, Mass., pp. 1–52).

Chomsky, N. (2001) 'Beyond Explanatory Adequacy', unpublished manuscript, MIT.

Chomsky, N. (2002) *On Nature and Language*, Cambridge University Press, Cambridge.

Chomsky, N. and Lasnik, H. (1977) 'Filters and Control', *Linguistic Inquiry* 8: 425–504.

Chomsky, N. and Lasnik, H. (1995) 'The theory of principles and parameters', in Chomsky 1995, pp. 13–127.

Chung, S. (1994) '*Wh*-agreement and "Referentiality" in Chamorro', *Linguistic Inquiry* 25: 1–45.

Chung, S. (1998) *The Design of Agreement: Evidence from Chamorro*, University of Chicago Press, Chicago.

Cinque, G. (1994) 'Evidence for partial N-movement in the Romance DP', in G. Cinque, J. Koster, J.-Y. Pollock, L. Rizzi and R. Zanuttini (eds.), *Towards Universal Grammar: Studies in Honor of Richard Kayne*, Georgetown University Press, Washington DC, pp. 85–110.

Cinque, G. (1999) *Adverbs and Functional Heads*, Oxford University Press, Oxford.

Citko, B. (2002) '(Anti)reconstruction effects in free relatives: a new argument against the Comp account', *Linguistic Inquiry* 33: 507–11.

Cole, P. (1982) *Imbabura Quechua*, North-Holland, The Hague.

Cole, P. and Hermon, G. (2000) 'Partial wh-movement: evidence from Malay', in Lutz, Müller and von Stechow (eds.), pp. 101–30.

Collins, C. (1997) *Local Economy*, MIT Press, Cambridge, Mass.

Collins, C. and Branigan, P. (1997) 'Quotative Inversion', *Natural Language and Linguistic Theory* 15: 1–41.

Contreras, H. (1986) 'Spanish bare NPs and the ECP', in I. Bordelois, H. Contreras and K. Zagona (eds.), *Generative Studies in Spanish Syntax*, Foris, Dordrecht, pp. 25–49.

Contreras, J. (1987) 'Small clauses in Spanish and English', *Natural Language and Linguistic Theory* 5: 225–44.

Cormack, A. and Smith, N. (1999) 'Where is a sign merged?', *Glot International* 4, 6: 21.

Cormack, A. and Smith, N. (2000a) 'Head Movement and negation in English', *Transactions of the Philological Society* 98: 49–85.

Cormack, A. and Smith, N. (2000b) 'Fronting: the Syntax and Pragmatics of "Focus" and "Topic"', *UCL Working Papers in Linguistics* 20: 387–417.

Cornilescu, A. (2001) 'Romanian nominalizations: case and aspectual structure', *Journal of Linguistics* 37: 467–501.

Costa, J. (2001) 'Postverbal subjects and agreement in unaccusative contexts in European Portuguese', *The Linguistic Review* 18: 1–17.

Crain, S. and Pietroski, P. (2002) 'Why language acquisition is a snap', *The Linguistic Review* 19: 163–83.

Culicover, P. (1991) 'Topicalization, inversion and complementiser in English', in D. Delfitto, M. Everaert, A. Evers and F. Stuurman (eds.), *OTS Working Papers: Going Romance and Beyond*, University of Utrecht, pp. 1–45.

Culicover, P. and Jackendoff, R. (2001) 'Control is not movement', *Linguistic Inquiry* 32: 493–512.

Culicover, P. and Levine, R. D. (2001) 'Stylistic Inversion in English: a reconsideration', *Natural Language and Linguisitc Theory* 19: 283–310.

Curtiss, S. (1977) *Genie: a Psycholinguistic Study of a Modern Day 'Wild Child'*, Academic Press, London.

Davies, W. and Dubinsky, S. (2003) 'On extraction from NPs', *Natural Language and Linguistic Theory* 21: 1–37.

Dayal, V. (2002) 'Single-pair versus multiple-pair answers: wh-in-situ and scope', *Linguistic Inquiry* 33: 512–20.

Déchaine, R.-M. and Wiltschko, M. (2002) 'Decomposing pronouns', *Linguistic Inquiry* 33: 409–42.

den Dikken, M. (2001) 'Pluringulars, pronouns and quirky agreement', *The Linguistic Review* 18: 19–41.

den Dikken, M. and Giannakidou, A. (2002) 'From *hell* to polarity: "Aggressively non-D-linked" wh-phrases as polarity items', *Linguistic Inquiry* 33: 31–61.

Denham, K. (2000) 'Optional *wh*-movement in Babine-Witsuwit'en', *Natural Language and Linguistic Theory* 18: 199–251.

Dixon, R. M. W. (2000) 'Categories of the Noun Phrase in Jarawara', *Journal of Linguistics* 36: 487–510.

Drubig, H. N. (2003) 'Toward a typology of focus and focus constructions', *Linguistics* 41: 1–50.

Dukes, M. (2000) 'Agreement in Chamorro', *Journal of Linguistics* 36: 575–88.

du Plessis, H. (1977) 'Wh-movement in Afrikaans', *Linguistic Inquiry* 8: 211–22.

Embick, D. and Noyer, R. (2001) 'Movement operations after Syntax', *Linguistic Inquiry* 32: 555–95.

Epstein, S. and Seeley, D. (1999) 'Specifying the GF "subject", eliminating A-chains and the EPP with a derivational model', ms. University of Michigan.

Ernst, T. (1991) 'On the scope principle', *Linguistic Inquiry* 22: 750–6.

Fabb, N. (1988) 'English suffixation is constrained only by selectional restrictions', *Natural Language and Linguistic Theory* 6: 527–39.

Fanselow, G. and Mahajan, A. (2000) 'Towards a minimalist theory of wh-expletives, wh-copying and successive cyclicity', in Lutz, Müller and von Stechow (eds.), pp. 195–230.

Fasold, R. (1980) 'The relation between black and white speech in the south', ms., School of Languages and Linguistics, Georgetown University, Washington DC.

Felser, C. (1999a) *Verbal Complement Clauses: a Minimalist Study of Direct Perception Constructions*, Benjamins, Amsterdam.

Felser, C. (1999b) 'Perception and control: A Minimalist analysis of English direct perception complements', *Journal of Linguistics* 34: 351–85.

Felser, C. (2001) 'Wh-copying, phases and successive cyclicity', draft ms, University of Essex.

Fillmore, C. J. (1968) 'The case for case', in E. Bach and R. T. Harms (eds.), *Universals in Linguistic Theory*, Holt Rinehart and Winston, New York, pp. 1–88.

Fillmore, C. J. (1972) 'Subjects, speakers and roles', in D. Davidson and G. Harman (eds.), *Semantics of Natural Language*, Reidel, Dordrecht.

Fitzpatrick, J. M. (2002) 'On Minimalist approaches to the locality of movement', *Linguistic Inquiry* 33: 443–63.

Fodor, J. D. and Crowther, C. (2002) 'Understanding stimulus poverty arguments', *The Linguistic Review* 19: 105–45.

Fox, D. (2000) *Economy and Semantic Interpretation*, MIT Press, Cambridge, Mass.

Frampton, J. and Gutmann, S. (1999) 'Cyclic computation, a computationally efficient minimalist syntax', *Syntax* 2: 1–27.

Frank, R. and Vijay-Shanker, K. (2001) 'Primitive c-command', *Syntax* 4: 164–204.

Freidin, R. and Vergnaud, J. R. (2001) 'Exquisite connections: some remarks on the evolution of linguistic theory', *Lingua* 111: 639–66.

Fu, J., Roeper, T. and Borer, H. (2001) 'The VP within process nominals: evidence from adverbs and the VP anaphor *do so*', *Natural Language and Linguistic Theory* 19: 549–82.

Goodall, G. (1999) 'Accusative case in passives', *Linguistics* 37: 1–12.

Green, L. (1998) 'Semantic and syntactic patterns in African American English', ms., University of Massachusetts.

Grewendorf, G. (2001) 'Multiple wh-fronting', *Linguistic Inquiry* 32: 87–122.

Grimshaw, J. (1993) 'Minimal Projection, Heads, and Optimality', draft ms., Rutgers University.

Groat, E. and O'Neil, J. (1996) 'Spell-out at the LF interface', in W. Abraham, S. D. Epstein, H. Thráinsson and C. J.-W. Zwart (eds.), *Minimal Ideas*, Benjamins, Amsterdam, pp. 113–39.

Gruber, J. S. (1965) 'Studies in Lexical Relations', PhD diss., MIT.

Gruber, J. S. (1976) *Lexical Structures in Syntax and Semantics*, North-Holland, Amsterdam.

Guasti, M. T. (2002) *Language Acquisition: the Growth of Grammar*, Bradford Books, MIT Press, Cambridge, Mass.

Guasti, M. T., Thornton, R. and Wexler, K. (1995) 'Negation in children's questions: the case of English', in B. MacLaughlin and S. McEwen (eds.), *Proceedings of the 19th Annual Boston University Conference on Language Development*, Cascadilla Press, Somerville, Mass, pp. 228–39.

Guilfoyle, E. (1983) 'Habitual aspect in Hiberno-English', *McGill Working Papers in Linguistics* 1: 22–32.

Guilfoyle, E., Hung, H. and Travis, L. (1992) 'Spec of IP and spec of VP: two subjects in Austronesian languages', *Natural Language and Linguistic Theory* 10: 375–414.

Haegeman, L. (1992) *Theory and Description in Generative Syntax: a Case Study of West Flemish*, Cambridge University Press, Cambridge.

Haegeman, L. (1994, 2nd edition) *Introduction to Government and Binding Theory*, Blackwell, Oxford.

Haegeman, L. (1995) *The Syntax of Negation*, Cambridge University Press, Cambridge.

Haegeman, L. (2000) 'Inversion, non-adjacent inversion and adjuncts in CP', *Transactions of the Philological Society* 98: 121–60.

Hagstrom, P. A. (1998) 'Decomposing Questions', PhD diss, MIT.

Hale, K. and Keyser, S. J. (1991) *On the Syntax of Argument Structure*, Lexicon Project Working Papers, MIT, Center for Cognitive Science, Cambridge, Mass.

Hale, K. and Keyser, S. J. (1993a) 'On argument structure and the lexical expression of semantic relations', in Hale and Keyser (eds.), pp. 53–109.

Hale, K. and Keyser, S. J. (1993b) (eds.) *The View from Building 20*, MIT Press, Cambridge, Mass.

Hale, K. and Keyser, S. J. (1994) 'Constraints on argument structure', in B. Lust, M. Suñer and J. Whitman (eds.), *Heads, Projections and Learnability*, Erlbaum, Hillsdale, NJ vol. 1, pp. 53–71.

Halle, M. and Marantz, A. (1993) 'Distributed morphology and the pieces of inflection', in Hale and Keyser (eds.), pp. 111–76.

Han, C.-H. (2001) 'Force, negation and imperatives', *The Linguistic Review*, 18: 289–325.

Harris, J. (1986) 'Expanding the superstrate: habitual aspect markers in Atlantic Englishes', *English World-Wide* 7: 171–99.

Hawkins, J. A. (2001) 'Why are categories adjacent?', *Journal of Linguistics* 37: 1–34.

Henry, A. (1995) *Belfast English and Standard English: Dialect Variation and Parameter-Setting*, Oxford University Press, Oxford.

Hiemstra, I. (1986) 'Some aspects of wh-questions in Frisian', *North-Western European Language Evolution (NOWELE)* 8: 97–110.

Holmberg, A. (2000) 'Am I unscientific? A reply to Lappin, Levine and Johnson', *Natural Language and Linguistic Theory* 18: 837–42.

Hornstein, N. (1995) *Logical Form: from GB to Minimalism*, Blackwell, Oxford.

Hornstein, N. (2000) 'On A-chains: a reply to Brody', *Syntax* 3: 129–43.

Hornstein, N. and Lightfoot, D. (eds.) (1994) *Verb Movement*, Cambridge University Press, Cambridge.

Huang, C.-T. J. (1982) 'Logical Relations in Chinese and the Theory of Grammar', PhD diss., MIT.

Huang, C.-T. J. (1993) 'Reconstruction and the structure of VP: some theoretical consequences', *Linguistic Inquiry* 24: 103–38.

Hurford, J. (1991) 'The evolution of the critical period for language acquisition', *Cognition* 40: 159–201.

Hyams, N. (1986) *Language Acquisition and the Theory of Parameters*, Reidel, Dordrecht.

Hyams, N. (1992) 'A reanalysis of null subjects in child language', in J. Weissenborn, H. Goodluck and T. Roeper (eds.), *Theoretical Issues in Language Acquisition*, Erlbaum, London, pp. 249–67.

Ingham, R. (2000) 'Negation and OV order in Late Middle English', *Journal of Linguistics* 36: 13–38.

Jackendoff, R. S. (1972) *Semantic Interpretation in Generative Grammar*, MIT Press, Cambridge, Mass.

Jaeggli, O. and Safir, K. (1989) *The Null Subject Parameter*, Kluwer, Dordrecht.

Johnson, K. (1991) 'Object positions', *Natural Language and Linguistic Theory* 9: 577–636.

Johnson, K. (2002) 'Restoring exotic co-ordinations to normalcy', *Linguistic Inquiry* 33: 97–156.

Jones, M. A. (1994) *Sardinian Syntax*, Routledge, London.

Julien, M. (2001) 'The syntax of complex tenses', *The Linguistic Review* 18: 125–67.

Kathol, A. (2001) 'Positional effects in a monostratal grammar of German', *Journal of Linguistics* 37: 35–66.

Kayne, R. S. (1984a) *Connectedness and Binary Branching*, Foris, Dordrecht.

Kayne, R. S. (1984b) 'Principles of particle constructions', in J. Guéron et al. (eds.) *Grammatical Representation*, Foris, Dordrecht, pp. 101–40.

Kayne, R. S. (1989) 'Facets of Romance past participle agreement', in P. Benincà (ed.), *Dialect Variation and the Theory of Grammar*, Foris, Dordrecht, pp. 85–103.

Kayne, R. S. (1994) *The Antisymmetry of Syntax*, MIT Press, Cambridge, Mass.

Kennedy, C. (2002) 'Comparative deletion and optimality in syntax', *Natural Language and Linguistic Theory* 20: 553–621.

Kennedy, C. and Merchant, J. (2000) 'Attributive comparative deletion', *Natural Language and Linguistic Theory* 18: 89–146.

Keyser, S. J. and Roeper, T. (1992) 'Re: the abstract clitic hypothesis', *Linguistic Inquiry* 23: 89–125.

Kimball, J. and Aissen, J. (1971) 'I think, you think, he think', *Linguistic Inquiry* 2: 241–6.

Kishimoto, H. (1992) 'LF pied piping: evidence from Sinhala', *Gengo Kenkyu* 102: 46–87.

Kishimoto, H. (2000) 'Indefinite pronouns and overt N-raising', *Linguistic Inquiry* 31: 557–66.

Kitagawa, Y. (1986) 'Subjects in English and Japanese', PhD diss., University of Massachusetts.

Klima, E. S. (1964) 'Negation in English', in J. A. Fodor and J. J. Katz (eds.), *The Structure of Language*, Prentice-Hall, Englewood Cliffs, NJ, pp. 246–323.

Koeneman, O. (2000) 'The Flexible Nature of Verb Movement', PhD diss., University of Utrecht.

Koizumi, M. (1993) 'Object agreement phrases and the split VP hypothesis', *MIT Working Papers in Linguistics* 18: 99–148.

Koizumi, M. (1995) 'Phrase Structure in Minimalist Syntax', PhD diss., MIT.

Koopman, H. and Sportiche, D. (1991) 'The position of subjects', *Lingua* 85: 211–58.

Kuroda, Y. (1988) 'Whether we agree or not', *Lingvisticae Investigationes* 12: 1–47.

Labov, W. (1969) 'Contraction, deletion and inherent variability of the English copula', *Language* 45: 715–62.

Landau, I. (1999) 'Elements of Control', PhD diss., MIT.

Landau, I. (2001) 'Control and Extraposition: the case of Super-Equi', *Natural Language and Linguistic Theory* 19: 109–52.

Landau, I. (2002) '(Un)interpretable Neg in Comp', *Linguistic Inquiry* 33: 465–92.

Lappin, S., Levine, R. D. and Johnson, D. E. (2000a) 'Topic . . . comment: the structure of unscientific revolutions', *Natural Language and Linguistic Theory* 18: 665–71.

Lappin, S., Levine, R. D. and Johnson, D. E. (2000b) 'The revolution confused: a response to our critics', *Natural Language and Linguistic Theory* 18: 873–90.

Lappin, S., Levine, R. D. and Johnson, D. E. (2001) 'The revolution maximally confused', *Natural Language and Linguistic Theory* 19: 901–19.

Larson, R. (1988) 'On the double object construction', *Linguistic Inquiry* 19: 335–91.

Larson, R. (1990) 'Double objects revisited: reply to Jackendoff', *Linguistic Inquiry* 21: 589–632.

Larson, R. (1991) '*Promise* and the theory of control', *Linguistic Inquiry* 2: 103–39.

Lasnik, H. (1995) 'Verbal Morphology: *Syntactic Structures* meets the Minimalist Program', in H. Campos and P. Kempchinsky (eds.), *Evolution and Revolution in Linguistic Theory*, Georgetown University Press, Georgetown, pp. 251–75.

Lasnik, H. (1998) 'Some reconstruction riddles', in *Penn Working Papers in Linguistics* 5: 83–98, Penn Linguistics Circle, University of Pennsylvania, Philadelphia.

Lasnik, H. (1999) 'Chains of arguments', in S. D. Epstein and N. Hornstein (eds.), *Working Minimalism*, MIT Press, Cambridge, Mass., pp. 189–215.

Lasnik, H. (2000) *Syntactic Structures Revisited: Contemporary Lectures on Classic Transformational Theory*, MIT Press, Cambridge, Mass. (with M. Depiante and A. Stepanov)

Lasnik, H. (2001) 'A note on the EPP', *Linguistic Inquiry* 32: 356–61.

Lasnik, H. and Saito, M. (1991) 'On the subject of infinitives', *Proceedings of the Chicago Linguistic Society* 27: 324–43, University of Chicago.

Lasnik, H. and Sobin, N. (2000) 'The *Who/Whom* Puzzle: on the preservation of an archaic feature', *Natural Language and Linguistic Theory* 18: 343–71.

Lasnik, H. and Uriagereka, J. (2002) 'On the poverty of the challenge', *The Linguistic Review* 19: 147–50.

Lebeaux, D. (1991) 'Relative clauses, licensing and the nature of derivation', in S. Rothstein (ed.), *Syntax and Semantics 25: Perspectives on Phrase Structure*, Academic Press, New York, pp. 209–39.

Lebeaux, D. (1995) 'Where does Binding Theory apply?', *University of Maryland Working Papers in Linguistics* 3: 63–88.

Lechner, W. (2001) 'Reduced and phrasal comparatives', *Natural Language and Linguistic Theory* 19: 683–735.

Legate, J. A. (2002) 'Some interface properties of the phase', unpublished paper, MIT.

Legate, J. A. and Yang, C. D. (2002) 'Empirical re-assessment of stimulus poverty arguments', *The Linguistic Review* 19: 151–62.

Lenneberg, E. (1967) *Biological Foundations of Language*, Wiley, New York.

Levin, B. and Rappaport Hovav, M. (1995) *Unaccusativity at the Syntax-Lexical Semantic Interface*, MIT Press, Cambridge, Mass.

Longobardi, G. (1994) 'Reference and proper names', *Linguistic Inquiry* 25: 609–66.

Longobardi, G. (1996) 'The syntax of N-raising: a minimalist theory', OTS Working Papers no. 5, Research Institute for Language and Speech, Utrecht.

Longobardi, G. (2001) 'The structure of DPs: some principles, parameters and problems', in Baltin and Collins (eds.), pp. 562–603.

López, L. (2001) 'On the (non)complementarity of θ-Theory and Checking Theory', *Linguistic Inquiry* 32: 694–716.

Lutz, U., Müller, G. and von Stechow, A. (eds.) (2000) *Wh-Scope Marking*, Benjamins, Amsterdam.

Lyons, C. (1999) *Definiteness*, Cambridge University Press, Cambridge.

Martin, R. (2001) 'Null case and the distribution of PRO', *Linguistic Inquiry* 32: 141–66.

McCloskey, J. (2000) 'Quantifier Float and *Wh*-Movement in an Irish English', *Linguistic Inquiry* 31: 57–84.

McCloskey, J. (2001) 'The morphosyntax of WH-extraction in Irish', *Journal of Linguistics* 37: 67–100.

McDaniel, D. (1989) 'Partial and multiple wh-movement', *Natural Language and Linguistic Theory* 7: 565–604.

McNally, L. (1992) 'VP-coordination and the VP-internal subject hypothesis', *Linguistic Inquiry* 23: 336–41.

McNeill, D. (1966) 'Developmental Psycholinguistics', in F. Smith and G. A. Miller (eds.), *The Genesis of Language*, MIT Press, Cambridge, Mass., pp. 15–84.

Marantz, A. (1984) *On the Nature of Grammatical Relations*, MIT Press, Cambridge, Mass.

Marcus, G. F. (1993) 'Negative evidence in language acquisition', *Cognition* 46: 53–85.

Moore, J. and Perlmutter, D. M. (2000) 'What does it take to be a dative subject?', *Natural Language and Linguistic Theory* 18: 373–416.

Morgan, J. L. and Travis, L. (1989) 'Limits on negative information in language input', *Journal of Child Language* 16: 531–52.

Moro, A. (1997) *The Raising of Predicates: Predicative Noun Phrases and the Theory of Clause Structure*, Cambridge University Press, Cambridge.

Murasugi, K. and Saito, M. (1994) 'Adjunction and cyclicity', *Proceedings of the 13th West Coast Conference on Formal Linguistics*, pp. 302–17.

Nakajima, H. (2001) 'Verbs in locative constructions and the generative lexicon', *The Linguistic Review* 18: 43–67.

Namai, K. (2000) 'Gender features in English', *Linguistics* 38: 771–9.

Nasu, N. (2001) 'Associating EPP with ø-completeness', *Proceedings of the North Eastern Linguistic Society* 31: 351–67.

Nasu, N. (2002) 'Aspects of the Syntax of A-Movement: a Study of English Infinitival Contructions and Related Phenomena', PhD diss., University of Essex.

Nunes, J. (1999) 'Linearization of chains and phonetic realisation of chain links', in S. D. Epstein and N. Hornstein (eds.), *Working Minimalism*, MIT Press, Cambridge, Mass., pp. 217–49.

Nunes, J. (2001) 'Sideward movement', *Linguistic Inquiry* 32: 303–44.

Nunes, J. and Uriagereka, J. (2000) 'Cyclicity and extraction domains', *Syntax* 3: 20–43.

Ochi, M. (1999) 'Multiple spell-out and PF-adjacency', *Proceedings of the North-Eastern Linguistic Society* 29.

Oya, T. (2002) 'Reflexives and resultatives: some differences between English and German', *Linguistics* 40: 961–86.

Parker, S. (1999) 'On the behaviour of definite articles in Chamicuro', *Language* 75: 552–62.

Pesetsky, D. (1987) '*Wh*-in-situ: movement and unselective binding', in E. J. Reuland and A. G. B. ter Meulen (eds.), *The Representation of (In)definiteness*, MIT Press, Cambridge, Mass., pp. 98–129.

Pesetsky, D. (1995) *Zero Syntax: Experiencers and Cascades*, MIT Press, Cambridge, Mass.

Pesetsky, D. (1997) 'Optimality Theory and Syntax: Movement and Pronunciation', in D. Archangeli and D. T. Langendoen (eds.), *Optimality Theory: an Overview*, Blackwell, Oxford, pp. 134–70.

Pesetsky, D. (1998) 'Some optimality principles of sentence pronunciation', in P. Barbosa, D. Fox, P. Hagstrom, M. McGinnis and D. Pesetsky (eds.), *Is the Best Good Enough?* MIT Press, Cambridge, Mass., pp. 337–83.

Pesetsky, D. (2000) *Phrasal Movement and Its Kin*, MIT Press, Cambridge Mass.

Pesetsky, D. and Torrego, E. (2001) 'T-to-C movement: causes and consequences', in M. Kenstowicz (ed.), *Ken Hale: a Life in Language*, MIT Press, Cambridge, Mass., pp. 355–426.

Phillips, C. (2003) 'Linear order and constituency', *Linguistic Inquiry* 34: 37–90.

Piattelli-Palmarini, M. (2000) 'The metric of open-mindedness', *Natural Language and Linguistic Theory*, 18: 859–62.

Picallo, M. C. (1991) 'Nominals and nominalization in Catalan', *Probus* 3: 279–316.

Platzack, C. and Holmberg, A. (1989) 'The role of AGR and finiteness', *Working Papers in Scandinavian Syntax* 44: 101–17.

Polinsky, M. and Potsdam, E. (2001) 'Long-distance agreement and Topic in Tsez', *Natural Language and Linguistic Theory* 19: 583–646.

Pollock, J.-Y. (1989) 'Verb movement, Universal Grammar, and the structure of IP', *Linguistic Inquiry* 20: 365–424.

Postal, P. M. (1966) 'On so-called pronouns in English', in F. Dinneen (ed.), *Nineteenth Monograph on Language and Linguistics*, Georgetown University Press, Washington DC (reprinted in D. Reibel and S. Schane (eds.) (1969) *Modern Studies in English*, Prentice-Hall, Englewood Cliffs, NJ, pp. 201–24).

Postal, P. M. (1974) *On Raising*, MIT Press, Cambridge, Mass.

Potts, C. (2002) 'The syntax and semantics of *as*-parentheticals', *Natural Language and Linguistic Theory* 20: 623–89.

Pullum, G. K. and Scholz, B. C. (2002) 'Empirical assessment of stimulus poverty arguments', *The Linguistic Review* 19: 9–50.

Radford, A. (1981) *Transformational Syntax*, Cambridge University Press, Cambridge.

Radford, A. (1988) *Transformational Grammar*, Cambridge University Press, Cambridge.

Radford, A. (1993) 'Head-hunting: on the trail of the nominal Janus', in G. Corbett, N. M. Fraser and S. McGlashan (eds.), *Heads in Grammatical Theory*, Cambridge University Press, Cambridge, pp. 73–11.

Radford, A. (1994) 'The syntax of questions in child English', *Journal of Child Language* 21: 211–36.

Radford, A. (1997a) *Syntactic Theory and the Structure of English*, Cambridge University Press, Cambridge.

Radford, A. (1997b) *Syntax: a Minimalist Introduction*, Cambridge University Press, Cambridge.

Radford, A., Atkinson, M., Britain, D., Clahsen, H. and Spencer, A. (1999) *Linguistics: an Introduction*, Cambridge University Press, Cambridge.

Ramat, P. (1999) 'Linguistic categories and linguists' categorizations', *Linguistics* 37: 157–80.

Reintges, C. H, LeSourd, P. and Chung, S. (2002) 'Movement, wh-agreement and apparent wh-in-situ', paper presented to Workshop on Wh-Movement, University of Leiden, December 2002.

Reuland, E. (2000) 'Revolution, discovery and an elementary principle of logic', *Natural Language and Linguistic Theory* 18: 843–8.

Reuland, E. (2001a) 'Primitives of Binding', *Linguistic Inquiry* 32: 439–92.

Reuland, E. (2001b) 'Confusion compounded', *Natural Language and Linguistic Theory* 19: 879–85.

Reuland, E. and Everaert, M. (2001) 'Deconstructing Binding', in Baltin and Collins (eds.), pp. 634–70.

Richards, N. (1997) 'What moves where when in which language?' PhD diss., MIT.

Rickford, J. R. (1986) 'Social contact and linguistic diffusion: Hiberno-English and New World Black English', *Language* 62: 245–89.

Ritter, E. (1991) 'Two functional categories in noun phrases: evidence from Modern Hebrew', in S. Rothstein (ed.), *Perspectives on Phrase Structure: Heads and Licensing*, Academic Press, New York, pp. 37–62.

Rizzi, L. (1992) 'Early null subjects and root null subjects', *Geneva Generative Papers* vol. 0, pp. 102–14.

Rizzi, L. (1997) 'The fine structure of the left periphery', in L. Haegeman (ed.), *Elements of Grammar*, Kluwer, Dordrecht, pp. 281–337.

Rizzi, L. (2000) 'Remarks on early null subjects', in M.-A. Freidemann and L. Rizzi (eds.), *The Acquisition of Syntax*, London, Longman, pp. 269–92.

Rizzi, L. (2001a) 'Relativized minimality effects', in Baltin and Collins (eds.), pp. 89–110.

Rizzi, L. (2001b) 'On the position "Int(errogative)" in the left periphery of the clause', in G. Cinque and G. Salvi (eds.), *Current Issues in Italian Syntax*, Elsevier, Amsterdam, pp. 287–96.

Rizzi, L. (2003) 'Locality and Left Periphery', to appear in A. Belletti (ed.), *Structures and Beyond: the Cartography of Syntactic Structures*, vol. 2, Oxford University Press, Oxford.

Roberts, I. (1993) *Verbs and Diachronic Syntax*, Kluwer, Dordrecht.

Roberts, I. (1994) 'Two types of head movement in Romance', in Hornstein and Lightfoot (eds.), pp. 207–42.

Roberts, I. (1997) 'Restructuring, head movement and locality', *Linguistic Inquiry* 28: 423–60.

Roberts, I. (1998) '*Have/Be* Raising, Move F and Procrastinate', *Linguistic Inquiry* 29: 113–25.

Roberts, I. (2000) 'Caricaturing dissent', *Natural Language and Linguistic Theory* 18: 849–57.

Roberts, I. (2001a) 'Who has confused what? More on Lappin, Levine and Johnson', *Natural Language and Linguistic Theory* 19: 887–90.

Roberts, I. (2001b) 'Head Movement', in Baltin and Collins (eds.), pp. 113–47.

Roberts, I. (2002) Paper on Verb Movement presented at visiting speaker seminar, University of Essex.

Rohrbacher, B. (1999) *Morphology-Driven Syntax: a theory of V-to-I raising and pro-drop*, Benjamins, Amsterdam.

Romero, M. (1997) 'The correlation between scope reconstruction and connectivity effects', in E. Curtiss, J. Lyle and G. Webster (eds.), *Proceedings of the XVI West Coast Conference in Formal Linguistics*, CLSI, Stanford, pp. 351–65.

Rosen, S. T. (1990) *Argument Structure and Complex Predicates*, Garland, New York.

Ross, J. R. (1967) 'Constraints on Variables in Syntax', PhD diss., MIT (published as *Infinite Syntax!* by Ablex Publishing Corporation, Norwood, NJ, 1986).

Ross, J. R. (1970) 'On declarative sentences', in R. A. Jacobs and P. S. Rosenbaum (eds.), *Readings in English Transformational Grammar*, Ginn, Waltham, Mass. pp. 222–72.

Runner, J. (1998) *Noun Phrase Licensing and Interpretation*, Garland, New York.

Rymer, R. (1993) *Genie: a Scientific Tragedy*, Harper Perennial, New York.

Sabel, J. (2002) 'A minimalist analysis of syntactic islands', *The Linguistic Review* 19: 271–315.

Saddy, D. (1991) 'Wh scope mechanisms in Bahasa Indonesia', in L. Cheng and H. Demirdache (eds.), *MIT Working Papers in Linguistics* 15: 183–218.

Sadock, J. M. (1984) 'West Greenlandic', in W. S. Chisholm (ed.), *Interrogativity*, Benjamins, Amsterdam, pp. 189–214.

Safir, K. (1986) *Syntactic Chains*, Cambridge University Press, Cambridge.

Safir, K. (1993) 'Perception, selection and structural economy', *Natural Language Semantics* 2: 47–70.

Sag, I. (1997) 'English relative clause constructions', *Journal of Linguistics* 33: 431–83.

Sampson, G. (2002) 'Exploring the richness of the stimulus', *The Linguistic Review* 19: 73–104.

Sauerland, U. (1998) 'The Meaning of Chains', PhD diss., MIT.

Sauerland, U. and Elbourne, P. (2002) 'Total reconstruction, PF movement and derivational order', *Linguistic Inquiry* 33: 283–319.

Scholz, B. C. and Pullum, G. K. (2002) 'Searching for arguments to support linguistic nativism', *The Linguistic Review* 19: 185–223.

Schütze, C. (2001) 'On the nature of default case', *Syntax* 4: 205–38.

Seppänen, A. and Trotta, J. (2000) 'The *wh+that* pattern in present-day English', in J. M. Kirk (ed.), *Corpora Galore: Analyses and Techniques in Describing English*, Rodopi, Amsterdam, pp. 161–75.

Shima, E. (2000) 'A preference for Move over Merge', *Linguistic Inquiry* 31: 375–85.

Sigurðsson, H. Á. (1991) 'Icelandic case-marked PRO and the licensing of lexical arguments', *Natural Language and Linguistic Theory* 9: 327–63.

Sigurðsson, H. Á. (1996) 'Icelandic finite verb agreement', *Working Papers in Scandinavian Syntax* 57: 1–46.

Sigurðsson, H. Á. (2002) 'To be an oblique subject: Russian vs. Icelandic', *Natural Language and Linguistic Theory* 20: 691–724.

Smith, N. (1998) 'Jackdaws, sex and language acquisition', *Glot International* 3, 7: 7.

Smith, N. (1999) *Chomsky: Ideas and Ideals*, Cambridge University Press, Cambridge.

Smith, N. and Cormack, A. (2002) 'Indeterminacy, inference, iconicity and interpretation: aspects of the grammar-pragmatics interface', in M. Makri-Tsilipakou (ed.), *Selected Papers on Theoretical and Applied Linguistics*, Aristotle University of Thessaloniki, pp. 38–53.

Sobin, N. (2002) 'The Comp-trace effect, the adverb effect, and minimal CP', *Journal of Linguistics* 38: 527–60.

Sorace, A. (2000) 'Gradients in auxiliary selection with intransitive verbs', *Language* 76: 859–90.

Speas, P. (1986) 'Adjunction and Projections in Syntax', PhD diss., MIT, Cambridge, Mass.

Spencer, A. J. (1991) *Morphological Theory*, Blackwell, Oxford.

Sportiche, D. (1988) 'A theory of floating quantifiers and its corollaries for constituent structure', *Linguistic Inquiry* 19: 425–49.

Sportiche, D. (1998) 'Movement, agreement and case', in *Partitions and Atoms of Clause Structure*, Routledge, London, pp. 88–243.

Stepanov, A. (2001) 'Late adjunction and minimalist phrase structure', *Syntax* 4: 94–125.

Stockwell, R., Schachter, P. and Hall Partee, B. (1973) *The Major Syntactic Structures of English*, Holt Rinehart and Winston, New York.

Stowell, T. (1981) 'Origins of Phrase Structure', PhD dissertation, MIT.

Stowell, T. (1982) 'The tense of infinitives', *Linguistic Inquiry* 13: 561–70.

Stroik, T. (1990) 'Adverbs as V-Sisters', *Linguistic Inquiry* 21: 654–61.

Stroik, T. (2001) 'On the light verb hypothesis', *Linguistic Inquiry* 32: 362–9.

Suñer, M. (1994) 'V-movement and the licensing of argumental *wh*-phrases in Spanish', *Natural Language and Linguistic Theory* 12: 335–72.

Suñer, M. (2000) 'The syntax of direct quotes with special reference to Spanish and English', *Natural Language and Linguistic Theory* 18: 525–78.

Svenonius, P. (2002a) 'Case is uninterpretable aspect',
    http://www.hum.uit.no/a/svenonius/paperspage.html.

Svenonius, P. (2002b) 'Icelandic case and the structure of events',
    http://www.hum.uit.no/a/svenonius/paperspage.html.

Tallerman, M. O. (1993) 'Case assignment and the order of functional projections in Welsh',
    in A. Siewierska (ed.), *Eurotyp Working Papers*, Programme in Language Typology,
    European Science Foundation, pp. 1–41.

Taraldsen, T. (1990) 'D-projections and N-projections in Norwegian', in M. Nespor and
    J. Mascarò (eds.), *Grammar in Progress*, Foris, Dordrecht, pp. 419–31.

Ten Hacken, P. (2001) Review of Radford 1997a/b, *Natural Language Engineering* 7/1.

Thomas, M. (2002) 'Development of the concept of "the poverty of stimulus" ', *The Linguistic
    Review* 19: 51–71.

Thornton, R. (1995) 'Referentiality and *Wh*-Movement in Child English: juvenile *D-
    Link*uency', *Language Acquisition* 4: 139–75.

Tieken-Boon van Ostade, I. (1988) 'The origins and development of periphrastic auxiliary *do*:
    a case of destigmatisation', *Dutch Working Papers in English Language and Linguistics*
    3: 1–30.

Traugott, E. C. (1972) *A History of English Syntax*, Holt Rinehart and Winston, New York.

Travis, L. (1984) 'Parameters and Effects of Word Order Variation', PhD diss., MIT.

Ura, H. (1993) 'On feature-checking for *wh*-traces', *MIT Working Papers in Linguistics* 18:
    243–80.

Ura, H. (2001) 'Local economy and generalized pied-piping', *The Linguistic Review* 18: 169–
    91.

Uriagereka, J. (1988) 'On Government', PhD diss., University of Connecticut.

Uriagereka, J. (1998) *Rhyme and Reason*, MIT Press, Cambridge, Mass.

Uriagereka, J. (2000) 'On the emptiness of "design" polemics', *Natural Language and
    Linguistic Theory* 18: 863–71.

Uriagereka, J. (2001) 'Cutting derivational options', *Natural Language and Linguistic Theory*
    19: 891–900.

Vainikka, A. and Levy, Y. (1999) 'Empty subjects in Finnish and Hebrew', *Natural Language
    and Linguistic Theory* 17: 613–71.

Valois, D. (1991) 'The Syntax of DP', PhD diss., University of California, Los Angeles.

Vikner, S. (1995) *Verb Movement and Expletive Subjects in Germanic Languages*, Oxford
    University Press, Oxford.

Vikner, S. (1997) 'V^0-to-I^0 movement and inflection for person in all tenses', in L. Haegeman
    (ed.), *The New Comparative Syntax*, Longman, London, pp. 189–213.

Wakelin, M. F. (1977, 2nd edn.) *English Dialects: an Introduction*, Athlone, London.

Watanabe, A. (2001) '*Wh*-in-situ languages', in Baltin and Collins (eds.), pp. 203–25.

Wexler, K. (1994) 'Optional Infinitives, Head Movement and the Economy of Derivations', in
    Hornstein and Lightfoot (eds.), pp. 305–50.

Williams, E. (1994) *Thematic Structure in Syntax*, MIT Press, Cambridge, Mass.

Willis, D. (2000) 'On the distribution of resumptive pronouns and *wh*-trace in Welsh', *Journal
    of Linguistics* 36: 531–73.

Wiltschko, M. (2001) 'The syntax of pronouns: evidence from Halkomelem Salish', *Natural
    Language and Linguistic Theory* 20: 157–95.

Wolfram, W. (1971) 'Black-white speech differences revisited', in W. Wolfram and N. H. Clark
    (eds.), *Black-White Speech Relationships*, Center For Applied Linguistics, Washington
    DC, pp. 139–61.

Woolford, E. (1991) 'VP-internal subjects in VSO and nonconfigurational languages', *Linguis-
    tic Inquiry* 22: 503–40.

Xu, L. (2003) 'Choice between the overt and the covert', *Transactions of the Philological Society* 101: 81–107.

Yang, C. D. (1999) 'Unordered Merge and its linearization', *Syntax* 1: 38–64.

Zagona, K. (1987) *Verb Phrase Syntax*, Kluwer, Dordrecht.

Zwart, C. J-W. (2001) 'Syntactic and phonological verb movement', *Syntax* 4: 34–62.

Zwicky, A. (2002) 'I wonder what kind of construction that this kind of example illustrates', in D. Beaver, L. D. Casillas Martínez, B. Z. Clark and S. Kaufmann (eds.), *The Construction of Meaning*, CSLI Publications, pp. 219–48.

Index